D1039237

Ethiopia & Eritrea

Jean-Bernard Carillet
Stuart Butler, Dean Starnes

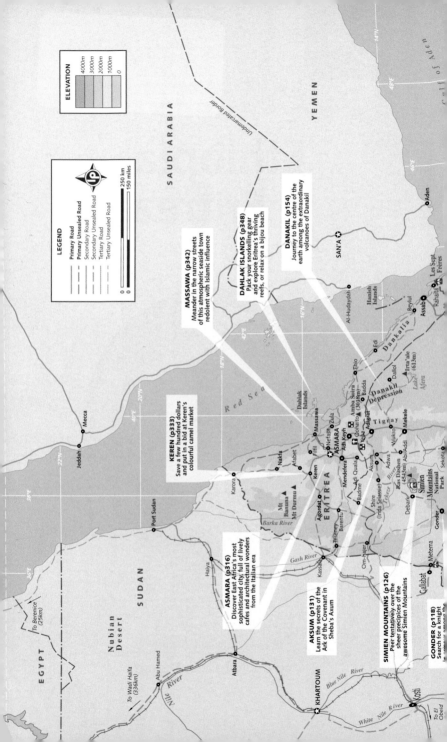

ELEVATION

4000m
3000m
2000m
1000m
0

LEGEND

Primary Road
Primary Unsealed Road
Secondary Road
Secondary Unsealed Road
Tertiary Road
Tertiary Unsealed Road

0 ——— 250 km
0 ——— 150 miles

MASSAWA (p342)
Meander in the narrow streets of this atmospheric seaside town redolent with Islamic influence

DAHLAK ISLANDS (p348)
Pack your snorkelling gear and explore Eritrea's thriving reefs, or relax on a bijou beach

DANAKIL (p154)
Journey to the centre of the earth among the extraordinary volcanoes of Danakil

KEREN (p333)
Save a few hundred dollars and put in a bid at Keren's colourful camel market

ASMARA (p316)
Discover East Africa's most sophisticated city, full of lively cafes and architectural wonders from the Italian era

AKSUM (p131)
Learn the secrets of the Ark of the Covenant in Sheba's Axum

SIMIEN MOUNTAINS (p126)
Peer tentatively over the sheer precipices of the awesome Simien Mountains

GONDER (p118)
Search for a knight

LAC ABBE (p292)
Soak up the solitude of awesome lunarscapes where *Planet of the Apes* was filmed

LAS GEEL (p278)
Follow the echoes of history amid this mysterious open-air gallery of prehistoric art

HARAR (p218)
Spend the day exploring the labyrinth of alleys and the night feeding drooling hyena

Though formally demarcated by the UN, the Ethiopia–Eritrea border is still disputed between the two countries.

The self-proclaimed Republic of Somaliland is currently an internationally unrecognised but de facto sovereign state.

BALE MOUNTAINS NATIONAL PARK (p179)
From wooded lowlands to breathtaking plateaus, search the park for rare and beautiful animals

LALIBELA (p156)
Witness Christianity in its most raw and powerful form in astonishing Lalibela

LOWER OMO VALLEY (p194)
Traditional villages, diverse cultures and Africa's last great bastion of tribal communities

NECHISAR NATIONAL PARK (p191)
Drift past the residents of the Crocodile Market, then search for zebra on the bleached grasslands of the savannah

On the Road

JEAN-BERNARD CARILLET Coordinating Author

In Djibouti I took the chance to leave the modern world behind and attempt the life of an Afar nomad by joining a caravan on Lac Assal (p291). After a few hours walking across what's considered one of the most desolate places on earth, I learnt a new respect for this extreme environment – and for its people.

STUART BUTLER This photo was taken in the Simien Mountains (p126). There were about a hundred baboons in this troop, some of which came within 2m of me. They were great fun and certainly a highlight of the mountains. Oh, just in case you're wondering, I'm the one in the background (although I often feel like the one in the foreground).

DEAN STARNES Watching me write is like watching paint dry, but it was still deemed interesting enough to attract the attention of these Banna tribesmen in Key Afar (p203). The little guy next to me even felt moved to write a few notes of his own. Another asked if I was from the CIA. We were both disappointed when I answered no.

For full author biographies see p385.

FESTIVALS & ACTIVITIES

The Horn is much more than a region characterised by political instability. Visitors are often overwhelmed by the sense of devotion that emanates from the incredibly colourful festivals that are held throughout the region. For outdoorsy types, a startling variety of adventure options beckons. Hiking, diving and snorkelling are all readily available, with the added appeal of fantastic settings that are a tonic to any city-weary soul. The region is also a nature-lover's dream, with a sensational variety of habitats and endemic species. You'd be hard pressed to find a better combination of nature and culture. The best part is, there'll be no crowds to hinder the experience.

Hiking

Few people in the Horn rate walking as a favourite pastime. From hauling firewood to trailing camels, the economic realities mean walking is simply a fact of life for locals. And with a landscape that covers all the geological highs and lows – from mist-shrouded Ethiopian mountains to the skin-searing Danakil Depression – you'll do well to join them.

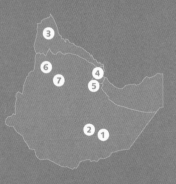

❶ Bale Mountains National Park
Ranging in altitude from 1500m to 4377m, a multiday trek in the Bale Mountains National Park (p179) offers a chance to spot a mountain nyala in a wooded valley one day, and an Ethiopian wolf atop a high plateau the next.

❷ Dodola Horse Trekking
Ideal for those without tents and camping equipment, a trek from Dodola (p178) in southern Ethiopia utilises sturdy little ponies, a string of simple mountain lodges and the lofty spine of the Bale Mountains. A memorable experience.

❸ Tsada Amba
The church of Tsada Amba (p336) is perched dramatically atop a narrow ridge. The 1000m ascent to get there is worth every bead of sweat. You'll be rewarded with sweeping views all around and treated to a foot massage by a monk.

❹ Goda Mountains
Waterfalls, forests, canyons, scenic vistas – what the little-known Goda Mountains (p293) lack in size is more than made up for in diversity, with walks of various lengths and difficulties. Your guides will be knowledgeable Afar nomads.

❺ Lac Assal
Africa's lowest point, Djibouti's Lac Assal (p291) offers an unforgiving yet eerie environment for hikers in search of a surreal buzz. Few experiences can compare with scrunching on white expanses of salt in the company of Afar nomads. Just don't forget your sunglasses.

❻ Simien Mountains
Staring over a precipice in the Simien Mountains (p126) and seeing, far, far below, on a tiny escarpment, a miniscule village completely isolated from the rest of the world, will make you grateful to be alive.

❼ Mesket Escarpment
Peering over the vertigo ledges of the Mesket Escarpment (p163) as you walk from village to village, then stopping for tea in an old farmer's house, is a real highlight of Ethiopia.

Diving & Snorkelling

Diving and snorkelling in the Horn are still largely unhyped, and that's why they're so attractive. No doubt you'll impress your friends when you get home with stories of close encounters with whale sharks in Djibouti, gorgeous reefs replete with tropical fish off the Eritrean coast, and literally untouched dive sites in Somaliland. Go diving and feel like a pioneer!

④

① Dahlak Islands

Absolutely no crowds and only one dive boat – yours – this is diving in the Dahlak Islands (p349). This pristine archipelago offers splendid dive sites and multihued fish life – not to mention a sense of the unknown. Snorkelling is equally amazing, with shallow and comfortably warm waters year-round.

② Berbera & Zeila

For a truly special experience, Somaliland is hard to beat. Where else in the world can you still dive uncharted territory? The diving business is still nascent, but diving is available along the sandy shores near Berbera (p280), while Zeila beckons pioneer divers.

③ Les Sept Frères Archipelago

Les Sept Frères Archipelago (p292) is one of the most charismatic dive areas in the southern Red Sea. With its high-voltage drift dives and dense concentration of pelagic species, this archipelago offers the full slate to seasoned divers.

④ Whale-Shark Spotting

Don't know what a *Rhincodon typus* is? It's time to get an education in the Bay of Ghoubbet (p292). Expect your flippers to be blown off by an interaction with one of Mother Nature's most impressive creatures – the whale shark.

Festivals

The people of the Horn are of many different religions, but they're all united by the
devotion shown during religious festivals.
Whether it's Christian pilgrims prostrating
themselves in prayer, villagers in Eritrea
or Somaliland breaking the Ramadan fast
or Hamer boys jumping bulls in southern
Ethiopia, it's all there to renew your own
faith in travel.

❶ Timkat

Join the thousands of white-robed faithful in Gonder as they sing and dance behind a solemn procession of regalia-draped priests during Ethiopia's most colourful festival, Timkat (p248), the feast of the Epiphany and the baptism of Christ.

❷ Meskel

In the 4th century, Queen Eleni dreamed the smoke of a great fire would lead her to the True Cross. Today her miraculous discovery is colourfully commemorated during Meskel (p249), with cross-topped bonfires, festivities and elaborately dressed clergy filling the streets of Aksum.

❸ Bull-Jumping Ceremony

Head to the Lower Omo Valley to witness a young man run across the backs of cattle to be initiated into the responsibilities of manhood, while, in a show of solidarity and stoic allegiance, women volunteer to be whipped with slender canes that leave lifelong scars (p203).

❹ Leddet (Christmas)

Being in Ethiopia for Leddet (Christmas; p248) is a dramatic throwback to a time when Christmas still had real meaning. Leddet isn't like Christmas at home; it's marked by an intense spiritual fervour, especially in Addis Ababa. There's no mad rush for last-minute presents and certainly no Santas in silly costumes.

❺ Fasika (Easter)

Stay up on the night of Easter Saturday mesmerised by the scenes surrounding you in Lalibela (p156). Hundreds of white robed pilgrims crowd the courtyards of the churches and pray under the moonlight. It's the most exotic thing you'll ever see.

Nature & Wildlife

The Horn of Africa may well be famous for its wealth of colourful festivals and historical sights, but it's also brimming with natural and ecological wonders – from powerfully majestic landscapes to pristine archipelagos. Don't forget the incredible abundance and variety of wildlife – with 862 species of birds and rare mammals, the Horn could be dubbed the 'Costa Rica of Africa'.

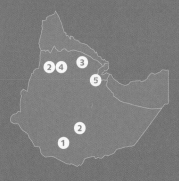

❶ Birdwatching

For sheer diversity Ethiopia is one of the best places in the world to see incredible exotic and endemic birds. Look for everything from the never-seen-alive Nechisar nightjar around Nechisar National Park (p191), to the wonderfully photogenic blue-breasted bee-eater near Mendefera in Eritrea.

❷ Ethiopian Wolf

Amongst the world's beautiful creatures, few are as easily spotted as the Ethiopian wolf – the world's rarest canid. To come nose to snout with one of the remaining 550 wolves, head to the Simien Mountains (p126) or Bale Mountains National Park (p179).

❸ Irta'ale & Danakil

The Danakil (p154) offers experiences fit for an adventurer. Load up your camels and scrunch across sheets of salt, shield your nose from the incredible sulphurous stink as you scramble up Irta'ale Volcano (p155) or just stare straight ahead into the desert voids.

❹ Gelada Baboons

Head to the Simien Mountains (p126) and get up close and very personal with a gelada baboon *(Theropithecus gelada)*, one of Ethiopia's most fascinating endemic mammals. It's the only primate that feeds on grass.

❺ Lac Abbé

Lac Abbé (p292) is famous for its extraordinary lunar landscape which is populated by large, spike-like calcareous chimneys. Hot springs dot the landscape, and fumaroles can also be found. This is what probably what hell looks like.

Contents

Regional Map Contents

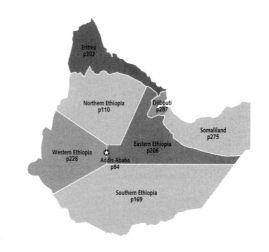

Eritrea p302

Northern Ethiopia p110

Djibouti p287

Somaliland p275

Eastern Ethiopia p206

Western Ethiopia p228

Addis Ababa p84

Southern Ethiopia p169

Destination Ethiopia & Eritrea

Sitting at one of Africa's great crossroads, in a reputedly unstable region, Ethiopia, Eritrea, Djibouti and Somaliland occupy a huge chunk of the Horn of Africa. They comprise an incredible variety of cultures and landscapes, from the Abyssinian highlands and the lofty peaks of the Simiens to scorching lowlands and the lowest point in Africa – the Danakil Depression and Lac Assal.

These four countries each have a very strong temperament. At times, these tough characters don't really gel together. Like four brothers living under the same roof, they often quarrel. Currently, the most intense wrangle involves Ethiopia and Eritrea. You'll quickly realise how bitter is the feud between these two countries. The case in point? A border squabble. There have been no military clashes since 2000, but the continued failure to officially demarcate (and recognise) the border means tensions are still high. The UN mission observing the no-man's-land between the two nations finally pulled out in 2008, arguing that it couldn't really fulfil its mission because of supply restrictions imposed by Eritrea. Despite the borderland in question being barren and holding no economic, religious or historical value (look up on Google Earth the town of Badme, and you'll see what we mean), many Ethiopians are passionate about getting back the land awarded to Eritrea by the 2002 border agreement. Much of the anti-Eritrea sentiment is fuelled by the economic hardship faced by Ethiopia since the 1998–2000 war.

For the tenacious Eritrean leaders, the enforcement of the UN Boundary Commission is a very important issue, and they have made it known that they will not compromise. They want the decision of the UN to be acknowledged by the Ethiopians, hence the stalemate. The situation is totally frozen and, at the time of writing, there was no hope of getting out of this quagmire. Eritrea now gets the worst reports from international agencies, such as Human Rights Watch and the Committee for the Protection of Journalists, and is considered by these organisations as one of the most closed countries in the world, playing in the same league as North Korea, Myanmar and Turkmenistan. Ask (discreetly) young Eritreans in Asmara how they envisage their future. Chances are they'll say they want to flee their country, which they are not allowed to do) because they have no future in what they perceive is a giant jail, according to research conducted by Human Rights Watch.

The problem is that the situation is worsening and is now disseminating into the whole of the Horn of Africa. The Ethiopia–Eritrea conflict has become a focal point on which everything revolves in East Africa. In this respect, Eritrea looks like the maverick. It's accused by the US government and the African Union of helping the Islamic Courts Union (who are suspected, according to US diplomatic sources, of supporting al-Qaeda) in Somalia, not so much out of sheer empathy with the organisation, but to weaken the Ethiopians. As if this wasn't enough, in 2008 Eritrea started a quarrel with its oh-so-gentle neighbour to the south, Djibouti, for reasons that are still not clear, and the border between the two countries is closed.

Fortunately, amid this seemingly chronic instability, there are two success stories. First of all, Djibouti. This may be one of the tiniest, youngest and least-known nations in Africa, but it could also be the most talented, the most adroit and the most opportunistic. While its larger, more power-

FAST FACTS: ETHIOPIA

Area: 1,098,000 sq km

Population: 85 million

Life expectancy: 48.83 years

GDP per capita: US$800

Biggest annual exports: coffee (US$500 million) and chat (US$100 million)

Average size of first lip plate worn by a Mursi girl: 4cm

Average size of lip plate for a Mursi adult woman: 11 cm

Highest Point: Ras Dashen (4543m)

Lowest Point Danakil Depression (-120m)

Number of train derailments between Dire Dawa and Djibouti: one per week

ful neighbours are embroiled in a never-ending border dispute, Djibouti stands out as a haven of stability and neutrality, despite the current tension with Eritrea. The French and American military presence certainly helps, as does the support of Dubai, which funds the development of the port – now one of the biggest in East Africa. The geographical position of the country, and its strategic value as a port and military base, is as important as ever. Djibouti plays the French and American cards simultaneously, while maintaining good relations with Ethiopia and Somaliland. Small in size, big in ambitions. Djibouti clearly aims at becoming the Dubai of East Africa, and it could well succeed.

Another success story is Somaliland. This separatist territory has nothing to do with the rest of Somalia. Thanks mainly to the predominance of a single clan (the Isaq), it has remained largely peaceful and stable since 1991, despite the odd terrorist attack. It has great oil and gas potential and voted for complete independence in 1997 before holding free presidential elections in 2003 and 2009. It has all the attributes of a 'normal' state: a parliament, free press, a currency, a flag…but nobody knows (or probably cares). Somaliland is still treated as a pariah by the international community and is not recognised as a separate state in the outside world, except by a few countries, including Ethiopia, which has a Liaison Office in Hargeisa. The main reason why the rest of the world is reluctant to accept Somaliland's independence is that the UN still hopes for an agreement covering all of Somalia, which they believe would avoid a potential 'Balkanisation' of the Horn. To Somalilanders, this sounds profoundly unfair. Unlike the rest of Somalia, they have managed to establish law and order in their country – no mean feat in the dispute-torn Horn!

At least Ethiopia and Somaliland are currently BFF (best friends forever). The Ethiopians see the port of Berbera as a convenient plan B, in case the situation with Djibouti deteriorates, and the Somalilanders are happy to see that Ethiopian diplomats support their efforts to gain international recognition.

From a travelling perspective, all these border issues are definitely a pain in the neck, and they bring lots of negative media coverage. It's a shame, because these four countries do need more tourists to foster internal growth. And for travellers, the situation in these four countries was perfectly safe at the time of writing.

Getting Started

There's no denying it: travelling in Ethiopia is not easy. The roads, though improving, still batter your bottom for hours on end and hotels (both budget and midrange) have been known to host a flea or two. Taking internal flights can add years to your posterior's life, but they can't save you from everything.

Surprisingly to some, Eritrea is an easier country to get around because the roads are in better shape and the distances between major sights and towns are much shorter than in Ethiopia. Neither country is perfect, though. Eritrea has its fair share of bureaucratic hurdles for travellers, including mandatory travel permits to get around outside the capital, and a currency declaration form.

Even more surprisingly, Somaliland is not *that* synonymous with tough travel. Sure, you'll have to hire an armed soldier to get around, but this quirky country doesn't pose many problems to seasoned travellers. And Djibouti? After having crisscrossed this tiny country – the most developed of the lot – all we can say is that it's a breeze to navigate but it'll blow your budget.

Wherever you choose to go, it'll be a memorable odyssey. Guaranteed.

WHEN TO GO
Ethiopia

There's some truth in the Ethiopian Tourism Commission slogan '13 Months of Sunshine'. Although the famed historical circuit and the rest of the highlands receive rain between mid-March and September, most days during this period still see their fair share of sunshine. The far east region and the

---

DON'T LEAVE HOME WITHOUT...

- A small torch (headlamps are best) for finding your shoes during power failures. Oh, and it's helpful for exploring amazing rock-hewn churches too!
- Batteries (torch and camera)
- Reading the medical checklist (p368) and updating your vaccinations (see p368)
- Sunblock, sunglasses and a hat
- Walking shoes if you plan to hike
- A folding umbrella for the sun (like most Ethiopians use) or for occasional downpours
- Flip-flops for those toe-curling bathrooms
- A warm sweater for chilly highland evenings
- Mosquito repellent
- Flea powder for cheap hotel beds and for socks when visiting remote churches
- Women's hygiene items
- High-energy bars (for vegetarians or travellers who don't take to local food)
- A water bottle and water-purification materials, needed for trekking and useful in reducing plastic waste while travelling
- Binoculars to spot that walia ibex dancing on a distant Simien slope
- Earplugs in case you don't agree with the bus driver's music selection
- A sink plug – water is very precious
- Checking visa requirements (p256, p361, p295 & p282).

northern highlands see even more sun, with significant rain only falling in July and August.

Early October, just after the rains, is a particularly good time to visit. The country is wonderfully green, the wildflowers are stunning and there are fewer visitors. Trekking during this time is especially sublime, though it's pretty amazing throughout the entire dry season (October to mid-March).

If you're planning a trip to visit the people of the Lower Omo Valley, you should avoid travelling in April, May or October, when rain makes most roads impassable.

Finally, you'd do well to plan your trip to coincide with one of Ethiopia's very colourful festivals (p248), particularly Timkat or Meskel. Be aware, however, that domestic flights and hotels often fill up far in advance of Ethiopian festivals and European Christmas.

See the Ethiopia (p245) and Eritrea (p356) climate charts for more information.

Eritrea

Although it is possible to visit Eritrea at any time of year, the ideal time climatewise is September to October and January to April. If you are able to, avoid travelling in Eritrea between June and August, when it's the rainy season in the highlands and western lowlands, and hot and torrid in the eastern lowlands.

With many Ethiopian Orthodox Christians in Eritrea, it's worth planning your trip to coincide with their religious festivals (see p358). Like in Ethiopia, Timkat and Meskel are particularly special.

Djibouti & Somaliland

The ideal time to visit Djibouti and Somaliland is in the cooler season, which runs from mid-October to mid-April. During this period, temperatures average 25°C.

COSTS & MONEY
Ethiopia

For most day-to-day expenses, Ethiopia is very cheap. Travellers who are willing to battle fleas in their nether regions and eat nothing but simple Ethiopian food can easily survive and get around on US$10 to US$15 per day (particularly outside the capital). The cheapest hotels are around US$4 and the most inexpensive meals cost around US$1.

Travellers keen on cleanliness, but still on a budget, can get by on US$15 to US$20 per day.

On top of this are guides' fees and admissions at the national parks and historic sites, as well as one-off transportation costs such as boat trips. Even with these extra costs, budget travellers who share some expenses and ride public transport shouldn't need more than US$20 to US$25 per day in Ethiopia.

Those staying in midrange hotels and eating at hotel restaurants can expect to pay around US$50 per day. This should cover admissions, guides and similar costs, but not internal flights or private transportation.

The cost of internal flights has seriously increased over recent years, but it's not beyond most budgets (from US$110 to US$200 one-way) and it's fairly good value considering some flights save a few days of bus travel! For 4WD rental, you'll have to cough up from US$120 to US $180 per day – ouch!

HOW MUCH?

Steaming *macchiato* US$0.20

100km by bus US$1.50-3

Minibus across town US$0.20

Internet per hr US$1-2

Tip for helpful priest US$0.75-1

See also Lonely Planet Index (inside front cover)

Eritrea

Travel in Eritrea is affordable, at least by Western standards. At the budget level, plan on US$20 to US$25 per day in the capital for a decent room, meals

TOP 10

• Addis Ababa

ETHIOPIA

ORTHODOX CHURCHES

Ethiopian Orthodox churches are everywhere, rising from Addis Ababa's skyline and dotting desolate and dramatic cliffs. Here's some you'll never forget.

1 Bet Giyorgis (p161)

2 Old St Mary of Zion (p135)

3 Debre Berhan Selassie (p122)

4 Yemrehanna Kristos (p164)

5 Abuna Aregawi (p145)

6 Abuna Yemata Guh (p149)

7 Bet Medhane Alem (p158)

8 Narga Selassie (p116)

9 Bet Amanuel (p160)

10 Holy Trinity Cathedral (p92)

FAVOURITE FESTIVALS

Ethiopia and Eritrea have a phenomenal mix of vibrant festivals, both Orthodox Christian and Islamic. For additional information, see p248.

1 Leddet, 6-7 January

2 Timkat, 19 January

3 Mawlid an-Nabi, March

4 Good Friday, March/April

5 Fasika, March/April

6 Kiddus Yohannes, 11 September

7 Meskel, 27 September

8 Eid al-Fitr, September/October

9 Festival of Maryam Zion, 30 November

10 Kulubi Gabriel, 28 December

ECOFRIENDLY HIDEAWAYS

Though the concept of ecotourism is still not widely recognised, there's a growing number of ecolodges and ecofriendly ventures in the Horn, especially in Ethiopia. Rejuvenate mind and body in one of those lovely places to stay.

1 Gheralta Lodge (p151)

2 Wenney Eco-Lodge (p172)

3 Dinsho Lodge (p183)

4 Mekonen Lodge (p194)

5 Strawberry Fields Eco Lodge (p196)

6 Salayish Lodge & Park (p208)

7 Bilen Lodge (p213)

8 Campement Touristique de la Forêt du Day (p293)

9 Campement Touristique de Bankoualé (p293)

10 Campement Touristique d'Asbole (p293)

in restaurants and public transport. Outside Asmara, you can get by on US$15 per day. Midrange travellers seeking some mod cons should plan on US$35 to US$50 in the capital, depending on the type of room you want.

The cost of renting a 4WD, which you might need to go to a number of places of interest, is around US$130 per day. If you're solo, this will blow your budget. Your best bet is to join a group or other travellers and share costs.

Djibouti & Somaliland

Djibouti easily wins the award of 'most expensive destination in the Horn', with prices that will make you feel you're closer to the Champs-Elysées than the Red Sea. Lodgings and transport are particularly expensive.

Good news if you're heading to Somaliland: it's relatively cheap. One downside: there's a number of mandatory add-ons (an armed soldier, a rental car) which, at the end of the day, make the trip not so cheap.

TRAVELLING RESPONSIBLY

We encourage you to consider the impact your visit will have on both the global environment and the local economies, cultures and ecosystems.

In the four countries covered in this guidebook, most tourist development so far is refreshingly small-scale and owned by locals. If you stay in guesthouses or medium-sized hotels, your cash will be going directly to the owners (and their families). Most of the food you'll eat in the Horn is locally grown.

Tourism in these countries is such a fledgling industry that the concept of ecotourism hasn't really taken off, except in Ethiopia at a pinch (see opposite for a selection of ecofriendly accommodation options). But most of the travel companies have a vested interest in carrying out their business sustainably; they all employ local guides who'll be happy to help you get a cultural immersion, such as in Southern Ethiopia or in Djibouti. See also the GreenDex of sustainable tourism listings on p403.

Bear in mind that people in this region are conservative in dress, and often religion, and it's appreciated if visitors follow suit, especially when visiting churches (churches in Ethiopia and Eritrea are very hallowed places) and mosques. Traditionally women never expose their shoulders, knees, cleavage or waist in public, and couples shouldn't display affection in public. Always remove your shoes before entering a church or a mosque. Never take a photo if permission is declined.

If you're invited to a house or a monastery it's thoughtful to give a gift in return. A contribution to the upkeep of the church is greatly appreciated after a visit.

You can support local businesses and skills by shopping at local markets and giving money or goods to local charities. Don't give directly to begging children.

Resist the temptation to buy any genuinely old artefacts such as manuscripts and scrolls sold in shops around Ethiopia. The country has already lost a vast amount of its heritage (see p253).

See also p244 for tips on how to minimise your impact on the environment.

A word about plastic bottles: don't crush them – they're a valuable commodity for children.

BORDER-CROSSING INFORMATION

To/From	From/To	Border Crossing Notes
Eritrea	Djibouti	The border is currently closed between Eritrea and Djibouti (see p296 and p363); use San'a (Yemen) as a transit hub
Eritrea	Ethiopia	All borders are currently closed between Eritrea and Ethiopia; use Cairo (Egypt), San'a (Yemen) or Nairobi (Kenya) as transit hubs
Ethiopia	Djibouti	There are two border crossings: Gelille and Galafi (see p262 and p296)
Ethiopia	Somaliland	The border crossing is at Wajaale (see p263 and p283)
Somaliland	Djibouti	The border crossing is at Loyaada (see p283 and p297)

Note that no visas are obtainable at borders. See country Directories in the respective country chapters for visa information.

TRAVEL LITERATURE

Michela Wrong's *I Didn't Do it for You* is a compelling and at times comedic account of Eritrea's contemporary history; it helps to understand the national psyche and the failure of democracy.

In *Eating the Flowers of Paradise,* Kevin Rushby travels the old trade route from Ethiopia's highlands to Yemen. By chewing *chat* (a mildly intoxicating leaf that's consumed primarily in eastern Ethiopia; it's illegal in Eritrea) at every invitation, Kevin gives a dangerously funny look into this unique drug's culture.

Part personal crusade, part celebration of all that is Ethiopia, *The Chains of Heaven* chronicles Philip Marsden's return to Ethiopia, a land that changed his life when he first visited in the early 1980s.

In *The Prester Quest,* Nicholas Jubber entertainingly voyages from Venice to Ethiopia on his quest to deliver – albeit 824 years late – Pope Alexander III's famed letter to Prester John, the mythical Christian king of the East.

Sheba: Through the Desert in Search of the Legendary Queen by Nicholas Clapp successfully blends personal travel accounts with thorough academic research to shed light on one of history's most famous and least understood characters.

By following the footsteps of 19th-century French literary legend Arthur Rimbaud through Egypt, Ethiopia, Djibouti and elsewhere, Charles Nicholl's *Somebody Else* isn't only an award-winning biography, but an interesting piece of travel literature too.

Wilfred Thesiger's classic *Life of My Choice* includes reminiscences of the author's childhood and early adult years in Ethiopia, including the coronation of Haile Selassie and Thesiger's renowned six-month journey through the Danakil in 1933.

INTERNET RESOURCES

Abyssinia Gateway (www.abyssiniacybergateway.net) Provides an exhaustive list of helpful and historical links for Ethiopia, Eritrea, Djibouti, Somaliland and Somalia.

All Africa (www.allafrica.com) This site collates daily news and helpfully sorts it into country profiles.

Asmera (www.asmera.nl) A comprehensive site on Eritrea with lots of tourist information, compiled by an individual.

CyberEthiopia (www.cyberethiopia.com) Like an Ethiopian Yahoo!, CyberEthiopia has quite useful information categorised into different sections.

Eriview (www.eriview.com) A good introduction to Eritrea's culture and history, as well as useful travel information.

Lonely Planet (www.lonelyplanet.com) Includes summarised information on travelling to Ethiopia, Eritrea and Djibouti, the Thorn Tree bulletin board, travel news and helpful web links.

Somaliland Government (www.somalilandgov.com) Official site of the Somaliland government, with useful external links.

Visit Somaliland (www.visitsomaliland.org) Has useful general info about travelling in Somaliland.

Itineraries
CLASSIC ROUTES

ETHIOPIA'S HISTORICAL CIRCUIT

Three to Five Weeks by Road (10 to 20 Days by Plane) / Addis Ababa to Addis Ababa

After a few days revelling in the chaos of **Addis Ababa** (p82), head north to bustling palm-fringed **Bahir Dar** (p111) for a day. Spend the next day at **Lake Tana** (p114) exploring some of the lake's centuries-old island monasteries.

Next, wander the extensive ruins of crenulated 17th-century castles in **Gonder** (p118). Looming 100km to the north, the **Simien Mountains** (p126) are home to easily visible wildlife, and days of East Africa's best trekking.

Take the long road north to **Aksum** (p131), where pre-Christian tombs underlie splendid 1800-year-old stelae (obelisks). After two days, wrangle up a 4WD and venture to the 3000-year-old ruins of Ethiopia's first capital, **Yeha** (p144), and to the cliff-top monastery of **Debre Damo** (p145).

If you didn't get your fill of heights at Debre Damo, head south and search out Tigray's precarious and stunning **rock-hewn churches** (p147).

After a short stop south in **Mekele** (p152) to view its moving museums, visit **Lalibela** (p156). Its 11 astounding rock-hewn churches and myriad of tunnels have poignantly frozen 12th- and 13th-century Ethiopia in stone. After three or so days here, it's back to Addis Ababa.

The historical sights along this loop north of Addis Ababa are monumental in both scale and detail. The journey, although spectacularly scenic, is monumental in itself, covering at least 2500km.

FROM HIGH TO LOW: ESSENTIAL ERITREA

**Ten Days to Two Weeks /
Asmara to Massawa**

A great trip for any first-time visitor to Eritrea, taking in the country's (accessible) star attractions. It's a busy but satisfying 800km journey that combines various landscapes, atmospheres and climates.

Start by spending two full days in fascinating **Asmara** (p316), visiting its mind-blowing collection of colonial-era architectural wonders and tantalising pastry shops. Beeline for the **National Museum** (p323) in preparation for Eritrea's archaeological sites and take a day trip to the **Debre Bizen Monastery** (p332), which offers breathtaking views, or enjoy the hush and greenery near **Filfil** (p332).

Next, push onto **Keren** (p333), whose attractive architecture, active markets and cheerful ambience deserves a day or two. Keren is the obvious launching pad for the fantastic ascent to the church of **Tsada Amba** (p336), which is dramatically perched on a narrow ledge. Back to Asmara, and it's time to head south. You might make a half-day stop in **Dekemhare** (p337) to recharge the batteries before spending the night in **Adi Keyh** (p337). The next day, explore the poignant ruins of **Qohaito** (p337) and expand your knowledge of Eritrea's mysterious past.

From Qohaito it's a short hop to **Senafe** (p339), where you can immerse yourself in the nearby ancient ruins of **Metera** (p340), one of Eritrea's most significant archaeological sites.

Having sampled the highlands' delights, head north to Asmara before proceeding east. Take the big plunge to **Massawa** (p342), on the coast, and mosey around Zanzibar-esque **Massawa Island** (p345).

Fancy a dip? Massawa is a jumping-off point for the pristine **Dahlak Islands** (p348), which are blessed with good diving and snorkelling opportunities. When you've run out of sunscreen, it's time to return to the highlands!

ROADS LESS TRAVELLED

LAKES, MOUNTAINS & MURSI: SOUTHERN ETHIOPIA

Two and a Half to Five Weeks / Addis Ababa to Omo Valley

Do what few others do in Ethiopia and point the compass south. En route from Addis Ababa to **Lake Ziway** (p171), and its hippos, birdlife and island monasteries, stop at **Tiya** (p170), a World Heritage Site and one of southern Ethiopia's most important stelae fields. More impressive birdlife is found just south at **Lake Langano** (p172) and **Lake Abiata-Shala National Park** (p172).

Next it's a night lakeside at **Awasa** (p176) or up in the lush hills at **Wondo Genet** (p175), before travelling east to **Dodola** (p178) for some multiday mountain horse treks, or further east to the bounty of **Bale Mountains National Park** (p179). Treks here offer unparalleled viewing of the endangered Ethiopian wolf and mountain nyala, and countless rare bird species.

Backtrack west through Shashemene before looping south to the southern Rift Valley lakes and **Arba Minch** (p189), where gargantuan crocodiles, zebras and the odd Abyssinian lion roam nearby **Nechisar National Park** (p191).

Slip south and visit intriguing **Konso villages** (p196) around **Konso** (p195), at the gateway to the cultural riches of the **Lower Omo Valley** (p194).

Cruise on the back of a truck into Hamer-and-bull-jumping territory at **Turmi** (p199) and into Galeb territory at **Omorate** (p202), which sits on the banks of the mighty Omo River itself. It's north from here for a respite from remoteness in **Jinka** (p197). Those with 4WDs can also descend into **Mago National Park** (p198), the home of the famed Mursi lip-stretchers.

This journey south from Addis Ababa offers some of Africa's most interesting peoples and Ethiopia's best wildlife. This 1500km foray is a tough slog, and takes almost twice as long using public transport.

This is an uncon-
ventional trip
you'll never forget,
offering plenty of
different experi-
ences, from walk-
ing through one
of most desolate
areas on earth and
swimming along-
side whale sharks
to marvelling at
rock paintings in
the desert and
attending a hyena
show.

BREAK THE MOULD   Ten Days / Harar to Djibouti via Somaliland

This itinerary will appeal to hardcore overlanders who are after something really different. Warm up in **Harar** (p218), famous for its nose-to-
snout encounters with hyena and its magical jumble of old alleyways.
Then bus it to **Jijiga** (p225), where you can already feel the flavour of
neighbouring Somaliland. The next morning, take the rickety old bus
that plies the route from Jijiga to **Wajaale** (p262), at the border with
Somaliland. Cross one of the weirdest borders in the world and take a
taxi to **Hargeisa** (p275), where it's highly possible you'll enjoy the smug
feeling of being the only foreigner wandering the streets. Pay a visit to
the camel market (and put in a bid if you dare). Need some cultural
sustenance? Speculate on Somalia's mysterious past at the fantastic
archaeological site of **Las Geel** (p278), replete with exceptionally well-
preserved rock paintings. Beach lovers should journey on to the port
town of **Berbera** (p280), with its unparalleled white beach. Work on your
suntan, scoff on grilled fish and recharge the batteries – you'll need it
for the strenuous ride from Hargeisa to **Djibouti City** (p287). Too taxing
for you? You can also fly from Hargeisa to Djibouti (about 40 minutes).
Allow at least two days to soak up Djibouti City's atmosphere, treat
yourself to a comfy room, enjoy the mischievous nightlife and make
the most of its gastronomic potential – you've earned it. Then spend
the day on a powder-soft beach on **Moucha Island** (p291). Too gentle for
you? Strap on your snorkelling gear and get up close and *very* personal
with whale sharks in the **Bay of Ghoubbet** (p292). If you're an incorrigible
landlubber, explore the apocalyptic wasteland of **Lac Assal** (p291) or **Lac
Abbé** (p292).

TAILORED TRIPS

MONASTERY FRENZY

Ethiopian Orthodox monasteries hold some of the region's greatest treasures, including brilliant illuminated manuscripts, precious crosses and vibrant murals. In most cases the monks are happy to show them off.

Unfortunately women are forbidden to visit several monasteries.

Surrounded by cliffs, atop an *amba* (flat-topped mountain), is the celebrated **Debre Damo** (p145). If you like heights, getting here is half the fun.

The **monasteries of Lake Tana** (p115) are some of the most historic in Ethiopia. Of them, Kebran Gabriel, Ura Kidane Meret, Dega Estefanos and Narga Selassie are the most atmospheric. Although there's little to see now, Lake Tana's Tana Cherkos monastery was rumoured to house the Ark of the Covenant for over 800 years.

Debre Tsion (p171), an island monastery on Lake Ziway, is also thought to have housed the Ark in the 9th century.

Other monasteries of note in Ethiopia are **Abba Pentalewon** (p139) and **Abba Liqanos** (p139) near Aksum, **Abba Garima** (p144) near Adwa, **Ashetan Maryam** (p164) near Lalibela and **Mt Zuqualla Maryam** (p209) near Debre Zeyit.

In Eritrea, **Debre Bizen** (p332) is renowned for containing over 1000 manuscripts and other church relics. **Debre Libanos** (p340), which sits in a rather stunning location, houses Eritrea's oldest church; inquire in Asmara if it's still off-limits to travellers.

BIRDWATCHING BONANZA

If you're a passionate twitcher then this circuit might take your fancy.

Spend a couple of days touring the northern Rift Valley lakes. Explore the shores of **Lake Ziway** (p171) for marsh species, then go to **Lake Langano** (p172), the home of over 300 species. Nearby is **Lake Abiata-Shala National Park** (p172), which hosts abundant acacia-related bird species and water birds. Stop at **Wondo Genet** (p175) to check out the forests, which host several endemics.

Then head east to the **Bale Mountains** (p179), where 16 of Ethiopia's 21 endemics are found. Next, forge east to the **Sof Omar Caves** (p184) and search for Salvadori's seedeater or serin. Then descend to the hot southern lowlands. Between Dollo-Mena and **Negele Borena** (p185), look out for the Degodi lark, Prince Ruspoli's turaco and the Sidamo long-clawed lark.

At the **Yabelo Wildlife Sanctuary** (p187), take in two of the world's most range-restricted species, the Stresemann's bush crow and white-tailed swallow.

If you want to live on in history as the first person to see a Nechisar nightjar alive, visit the **Nechisar National Park** (p191). Then take the long road back north towards Addis Ababa and complete your birdwatching bonanza at **Awash National Park** (p210), where six endemics live, including the white-winged cliff chat and the goldenbacked or Abyssinian woodpecker.

Ethiopia

JANE SWEENEY

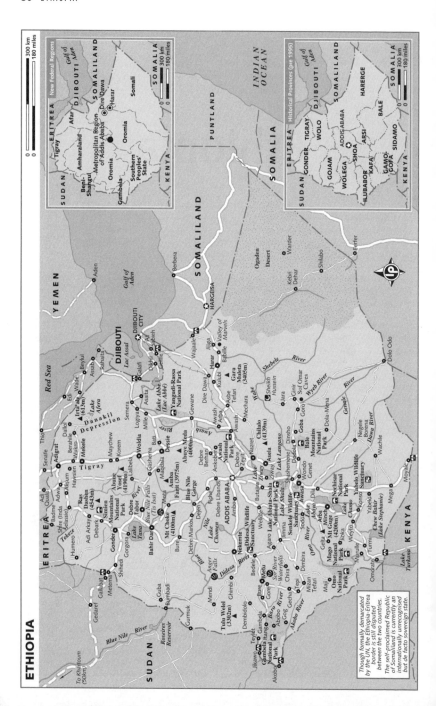

ETHIOPIA

Though formally demarcated by the UN, the Ethiopia-Eritrea border is still disputed between the two countries. The self-proclaimed Republic of Somaliland is currently an internationally unrecognised but de facto sovereign state.

History

From the ancient Aksumite civilisation's obelisks and the fascinating architectural wonders of medieval Lalibela to the castles of Gonder and the communist monuments of the Derg, Ethiopia wears its history on its sleeve. And what a history it is.

CRADLE OF HUMANITY?

In palaeoanthropology, where years are measured in tenths of millions, 40 years is less than a blink of an eye. However, 40 years worth of palaeoanthropological study can rock the very foundations of human history.

After Richard Leakey's discovery of skull 1470 near Kenya's Lake Turkana in 1972, which proved *Homo habilis* (the direct ancestor of *Homo sapiens*) had lived alongside *Australopithecus africanus* and therefore couldn't have evolved from them, the search was on for a new species that had branched into the genera *Homo* and *Australopithecus*, a species that would likely be Darwin's 'missing link'.

On 30 November 1974 Lucy was discovered in a dried-up lake near Hadar in Ethiopia's northeast. She was a new species, *A. afarensis*, and she miraculously walked on two legs 3.2 million years ago. Lucy's bipedal (upright walking) anatomy also shattered previous theories that hypothesised our ancestors only started walking upright after evolving larger brains. Lucy, the oldest and most complete hominid ever found, was famous and Ethiopia was tipped to claim the prize as the cradle of humanity.

After further finds in Ethiopia, like the 1992 discovery of the 4.4-million-year-old *A. ramidus*, whose foot bones hinted at bipedism, the ink on Ethiopia's claim was almost dry. However recent CT scans on a six-million-year-old hominid skeleton *(Orrorin tugenensis)* found in Kenya in 2001, and computer

Lucy was named after the Beatles' song *Lucy in the Sky with Diamonds*. It was playing in the archaeologists' camp when she was discovered.

WHICH HISTORY?

The following chapter contains the factual 'real' history that historians like to use, but it's important to remember that for the majority of Ethiopians this isn't the history they believe in. In Ethiopia, like in much of Africa, legends concerning magical deeds, ghostly creatures and possibly nonexistent folk heroes are not just legends, but are taken as solid fact and who cares if the historians say the dates and places don't add up! History is what you make of it and how you translate it, so just because there is no historical evidence saying that the Queen of Sheba existed, because the people believe she did and recount it as their history, then in Ethiopia that makes her real. It is important to keep this in mind when travelling through Ethiopia. You will find this 'people's history' recounted throughout this book.

TIMELINE

c 3.2 million BC	3500–2000 BC	2000–1500 BC
Lucy collapses and awaits discovery and fame 3.2 million years down the line. Ethiopia uses her as its basis for being the birthplace of mankind.	The Ancient Egyptians trade with the Land of Punt, which many people consider to be somewhere on the Eritrean or Somalian coast. Natural resources and slaves are reaped from Ethiopia's interior and shipped abroad.	Ge'ez, the precursor to the Amharic and Arabic languages, is developed somewhere in the vicinity of northern Ethiopia. Amazingly it is still spoken by priests in Ethiopia and Eritrea today.

aided reconstruction of a six- to seven-million-year-old skull *(Sahelanthropus tchadensis)* in Chad seem to suggest that Lucy and *A. ramidus* may not be part of the direct line of human evolution, but rather a lateral branch of it. This is undoubtedly highly controversial – visit Lucy in Addis Ababa's National Museum (p91) and show her some support!

Regardless of what still lies beneath the soil of Ethiopia, Kenya or Chad, it's clear to the palaeoanthropologists of today that human life as we know it started in this region of Africa. Although, 40 more years of palaeoanthropology may turn things upside down, again. All it takes is the blink of an eye.

LAND OF PUNT

Though this period is shrouded in darkness, Ethiopia and Eritrea are believed to have formed part of the ancient Land of Punt, an area that attracted the trading ships of the Egyptian Pharaohs for millennia.

Many valuable commodities such as gold, myrrh, ivory and slaves issued from the interior of the region and were exported from the coast.

It's thought the northern coastal region saw much migration from surrounding areas, and by 2000 BC it had established strong contacts with the inhabitants of southern Arabia.

> According to the Greek poet Homer (800 BC), the Greek gods, including Zeus himself, visited Ethiopia. Homer refers to the people as 'blameless Ethiopians'.

PRE-AKSUMITE CIVILISATION

The cultural significance of the southern Arabian and the East African cultures mixing was enormous. One consequence was the emergence of a number of Afro-Asiatic languages, including Ge'ez which laid the foundation for modern Amharic (much like Latin did for Italian). Amazingly, Ge'ez script is still read by many Christian priests in Ethiopia and Eritrea.

Most significant was the rise of a remarkable civilisation in Africa's Horn in 1500 BC. The fact that the influence of southern Arabia was so clear (the Sabaean script and in the worship of Sabaean gods), that the civilisation appeared to mushroom overnight and was very localised, and that it benefited from specialist crafts, skills and technologies previously unknown in the area, led many scholars throughout history to believe that the civilisation was actually spawned by Arabian settlers, and not Africans.

> Ethiopia was named by the Greeks, who saw the country as a far-off realm, populated by remarkable people and extraordinary animals. It means 'Land of the Burnt Faces'.

However, scholars of late argue with great conviction that this civilisation was indeed African and while undoubtedly influenced by Sabaean ideas, it developed from within from local effort and initiative. If proved correct, histories of the Horn will have to be completely rewritten.

Whatever the origin, the civilisation was a very important one. The most famous relic of the times is the extraordinary stone 'temple' of Yeha (p144).

1500–400 BC	400 BC–AD 200	200–500
An Arabian-influenced civilisation rises in northern Ethiopia; the country's first capital, Yeha, is founded, but by who? Historians remain uncertain whether Yeha and Africa ruled Arabia or Arabia ruled Yeha.	The great Aksumite kingdom is formed and thrives on Red Sea trade and rich natural resources. It is first mentioned in the 1st Century AD book *Periplus of the Erythraean Sea*.	The Aksumite kingdom reaches its apogee, and many magnificent monuments rise. At its height the kingdom controls lands from the Nile to Arabia and is counted among the most powerful Kingdoms of the ancient world.

KINGDOM OF AKSUM

The Aksumite kingdom, which grew to rank among the most powerful kingdoms of the ancient world, was the next civilisation to rise in present-day Ethiopia. The first written evidence of its existence (*Periplus of the Erythraean Sea*, written by a Greek-speaking Egyptian sailor) was from the 1st century AD, but by this point its realm of influence was wide, suggesting it rose to prominence much earlier. New archaeological evidence hints it may have emerged as early as 400 BC.

Aksum, its capital, is thought to have owed its importance to its position, situated at an important commercial crossroads. To the northwest lay Egypt, and to the west, near the present-day Sudanese border, were the rich, gold-producing lowlands. To the northeast, in present-day Eritrea, was the Aksumite port of Adulis, positioned at the crux of an extensive trading route. Exports included frankincense, grain, animal skins, rhino horn, apes and particularly ivory (tens of thousands of elephants were reported to roam the region). Imports of dyed cloaks, cheap unlined coats, glassware, and iron for making spears, swords and axes flowed in from Egypt, Arabia and India. Syrian and Italian wine and olive oil were also imported, as was much gold and silver plate for the king. The flourishing trade allowed the Aksumite kingdom to thrive.

Aksum also benefited from its well-watered agricultural lands, which were further exploited by the use of well-designed dams, wells and reservoirs.

During its heyday between the 3rd and 6th centuries, the Aksumite kingdom stretched into large parts of southern Arabia, and west into the Sudanese Nile Valley. Aksumite society was rich, well organised, and technically and artistically advanced. During this era, an unparalleled coinage in bronze, silver

> Those intrigued by the ancient civilisation of Aksum should pick up Professor David W Phillipson's *Ancient Ethiopia*. It's excellent and is an easy read.

> The first program in Michael Wood's sumptuously filmed and highly entertaining BBC documentary series *In Search of Myths and Heros* seeks out the truth behind the Sheba legend. It's available on DVD from the BBC (www.bbcshop .com).

THE DAYS BEFORE SHEBA

Historians might like to insist that little is known about the founding of the Aksumite Kingdom, but ask the average Ethiopian and they'll tell you something very different. Aksum, they will say, was founded by none other than the Great-Grandson of Noah, Aksumawi. His new kingdom flourished for a while, but one day Wainaba, a giant snake, 170 cubits long, attacked the city, killed the king and then ruled for 400 dark years. The snake was a foul tempered and dangerous creature and in order to placate him the people of Aksum fed him a diet of milk and virgins. Eventually salvation came in the form of a man named Angabo who, crossing the Red Sea from the land of the Sabeans, offered to kill the serpent in exchange for the throne. The people of Aksum agreed, but rather than fighting the serpent as the Aksumites expected, Angabo proved himself wise and fed the serpent a goat laced in poison.

The kingdom quickly recovered, Angabo married and was borne a daughter. That daughter was named Makeda and on her father's death she became the woman we today know as the Queen of Sheba.

300–325	400–500	615
Aksum's Great Stele collapses; the catastrophic event signals the end of paganism and the birth of Christianity in Ethiopia.	The famous Nine Saints, a group of Greek-speaking missionaries, arrive in northern Ethiopia. In addition to solidifying Christianity as the main religion of the region, they construct a series of monasteries, including Debre Damo.	Prophet Mohammed's daughter and successor flee persecution in Arabia and introduce Islam to Ethiopia. Some believe that the Christian king let them stay because he thought they were persecuted Christians, not followers of a new faith.

and gold was produced and extraordinary monuments were built, all of which are visible in Aksum today (see p131). The kingdom also exerted the greatest influence of all on the future of Ethiopia: it introduced Christianity.

THE COMING OF CHRISTIANITY

The Ethiopian church claims that Christianity first reached Aksum at the time of the apostles. According to the Byzantine ecclesiastical historian Rufinus, it arrived on Ethiopian shores by accident rather than by design, when a Christian merchant from Syria, returning from a long voyage to India with his two young students, stopped for water on Africa's coast. However, Ethiopian tradition records a different version of events saying that Christianity reached the country through Abba Salama, a wandering Saint.

Whoever you believe, what's certain is that Christianity didn't become the state religion until around the beginning of the 4th century. King Ezana's stone inscription (p138) makes reference to Christ, and his famous coins bear the Christian Cross – the world's first to do so.

The end of the 5th century AD brought the famous Nine Saints, a group of Greek-speaking missionaries who established well-known monasteries in the north of the country, including Debre Damo (p145). At this time, the Bible was first translated from Greek into Ge'ez.

Christianity shaped not just Ethiopia's spiritual and intellectual life, but also its cultural and social life, including its art and literature. Today almost half of Ethiopia's population is Orthodox Christian.

THE COMING OF ISLAM & THE DEMISE OF AKSUM

According to Muslim tradition, the Prophet Mohammed was nursed by an Ethiopian woman. Later, the Muslim Hadith (collection of traditions about Mohammed's life) recounts that Mohammed sent some of his followers to Negash in AD 615, to avoid persecution in Arabia.

When things calmed in Arabia, most refugees returned home. However, Negash continues to be a crucial pilgrimage point for Ethiopia's Muslims (see p147).

Good relations between the two religions continued until at least King Armah's death. Thereafter, as the Arabs and Islam rose to prominence on

Mahfuz timed his annual raids to take advantage of Christian Ethiopia's weakened state during their 55-day fast before Fasika (Orthodox Easter).

Check out J Spencer Trimingham's *Islam in Ethiopia* for an insight into Ethiopia's 2nd-most popular religion.

A MAN OF MORALS

Considered the father of modern Ethiopia, Amda Seyon (also known as Gebre Meskel) ruled from 1314 to 1344. Known as a military mastermind he vastly expanded the size of the Christian Empire through the use of force and his rule is considered something of a golden age for Ethiopia. Military mastermind he may have been, he was accused of sleeping with at least one of his sisters and marrying his father's concubine!

640–750	1137–1270	1270
The Aksumites lose their hold on Red Sea trade and the kingdom collapses. Ethiopia enters a long 'dark age' about which almost nothing at all is known.	The Zagwe dynasty rises from Ethiopia's 'dark ages' and produces, with a little helping hand from a gang of angels, the astounding rock-hewn churches of Lalibela.	Yekuno Amlak establishes the 'Solomonic dynasty' and Ethiopia enters its well-documented Middle Ages. It was also at this time that the *Kebra Negast* was written. It further enhances the emperors' claim to Solomonic decent.

the opposite side of the Red Sea, trade slowly shifted away from Christian Aksum and it eventually became isolated. The economy slumped, coins ceased to be minted and hard times set in. Aksum's commercial domination of the region was over (see the boxed text, p134).

After Aksum's decline around AD 700, Ethiopia endured what is commonly known as its 'dark age'.

THE ZAGWE DYNASTY

The 12th century witnessed a new capital (Adafa) rise in the mountains of Lasta, not far from present day Lalibela. It was established under a new power: the Zagwe dynasty.

Although the Zagwe dynasty reigned from around AD 1137 to 1270, and left the astonishing rock-hewn churches of Lalibela (see p156), this period is still shrouded in mystery. Seemingly, no stones were inscribed, no chronicles written, no coins minted, and no accounts of the dynasty by foreign travellers have survived.

It's not certain what brought the Zagwe dynasty to an end; it was likely a combination of infighting within the ruling dynasty and local opposition from the clergy. In 1270 the dynasty was overthrown by Yekuno Amlak; political power shifted south to the historical province of Shoa.

THE ETHIOPIAN MIDDLE AGES

Yekuno Amlak, claiming to be a descendant of King Solomon and Queen Sheba, established the 'Solomonic dynasty' (p50) that would reign for the next 500 years. His rule would also ring in the start of what's known as the Ethiopian Middle Ages, a period more documented than any other in the nation's past.

With its all-powerful monarchy and influential clergy, the Middle Ages were a continuation of the past. However, unlike the past, the kingdom's capitals were itinerant and were little more than vast, moving military camps. There was no longer minted money and trade was conducted by barter with pieces of iron, cloth or salt.

Culturally, the period was important for the significant output of Ge'ez literature, including the nation's epic, the *Kebra Negast* (p62). It was also at this time that contacts with European Christendom began to increase. With the rising threat of well-equipped Muslim armies in the East, Europe was seen as a Christian superpower.

Europe, for its part, dreamed of winning back Jerusalem from the 'Saracens', and realised the important strategic position occupied by Ethiopia. At the time, it was almost the only Christian kingdom outside Europe. Ethiopia even became a candidate for the location of legendary Prester John, an immensely wealthy and powerful Christian monarch believed to reign in a far-off land in the East (p122).

It's hard to find but if Prester John's your man then sci-fi writer Robert Silverberg turns his hand to historical detective in the excellent book *The Realm of Prester John*.

1400	1400–1600	1490–1529
French aristocrat Duc de Berry sends the first European ambassador to Ethiopia. In turn, Ethiopians journey to Europe where many join churches, particularly in Rome.	Rumours about Prester John, a powerful Christian king based in Ethiopia, spread throughout Europe. Excitement mounts that he will help Christian Europe gain control of the Holy Lands.	Mahfuz declares jihad on Christian Ethiopia and starts the bloody Muslim–Christian wars, the most costly in the country's history. His successor, Ahmed Gragn the Left-Handed, eventually defeats the emperor himself in 1529.

ITINERANT COURTS

During the Ethiopian Middle Ages, the business of most monarchs consisted of waging wars, collecting taxes and inspecting the royal domains.

Obliged to travel continuously throughout their far-flung empire, the kings led a perpetually nomadic existence. And with the rulers went their armies, courtiers and servants; the judges, prison officers and priests; the merchants, prostitutes and a whole entourage of artisans: butchers and bakers, chefs, tailors and blacksmiths. The camps could spread over 20km; for transportation up to 100,000 mules were required.

The retinue was so vast that it rapidly exhausted the resources of the location. Four months was usually the maximum possible length of stay, and 10 years had to pass before the spot could be revisited.

The peasantry were said to dread the royal visits as they dreaded the swarms of locusts. In both cases, everything that lay in the path of the intruders was consumed.

In the early 15th century, the first European embassy arrived in Ethiopia, sent by the famous French aristocrat Duc de Berry. Ethiopians in their turn began to travel to Europe, particularly to Rome, where many joined churches already established there.

THE MUSLIM-CHRISTIAN WARS

The first decades of the 16th century were plagued by some of the most costly, bloody and wasteful fighting in Ethiopian history, in which the entire empire and its culture came close to being wiped out.

From the 13th century, relations with the Muslim Ethiopian emirates of Ifat and Adal were showing signs of strain. With the increasing competition for control of the valuable trade routes connecting the Ethiopian highlands with the Red Sea, tension was growing.

In the 1490s animosities came to a head. After establishing himself at the port of Zeila in present-day Somalia, a skilled and charismatic Muslim named Mahfuz declared a jihad against Christian Ethiopia and made 25 annual raids into the highlands of Shoa. Emperor Lebna Dengel finally halted Mahfuz's incursions, but not before he had carried off huge numbers of Ethiopian slaves and cattle.

An even more legendary figure was Ahmed Ibn Ibrahim al Ghazi, nicknamed 'Ahmed Gragn the Left-Handed'. After overthrowing Sultan Abu Bakr of Harar, Ahmed declared his intention to continue the jihad of Mahfuz. Carrying out several raids into Ethiopian territory, he managed in March 1529 to defeat Emperor Lebna Dengel himself.

Ahmed then embarked on the conquest of all of Christian Ethiopia. Well supplied with firearms from Ottoman Zeila and southern Arabia (which he

1529–1535	1543–59	1550
Ahmed Gragn the Left-Handed expands his kingdom and by 1532 has taken most of eastern and southern Ethiopia. In 1535 he defeats a Portuguese/Ethiopian army near Lake Tana.	Emperor Galawdewos, with help from Portugal, finally defeats and kills Muslim raider Ahmed Gragn. Intermittent fighting continues for many years until Galawdewos finds his head detached from his body after attacking Harar.	The Oromo people move north from Kenya and plunge the country into 200 more years of intermittent armed conflict. It's during this period, and in response to Oromo attacks that the famous walls of Harar are built.

pragmatically exchanged for captured Christian slaves), the Muslim leader had, by 1532, overrun almost all of eastern and southern Ethiopia.

In 1535 the Emperor Lebna Dengel appealed in desperation to the Portuguese, who were already active in the region. In 1541 an army of 400 well-armed musketeers arrived in Massawa (in present-day Eritrea), led by Dom Christovão da Gama, son of the famous mariner Vasco da Gama. They met Ahmed near Lake Tana, where he quickly routed them before lopping off the young and foolhardy head of Dom Christovão.

In 1543 the new Ethiopian emperor, Galawdewos , and his amassed army joined ranks with the surviving Portuguese force and met Ahmed at Wayna Daga in the west. This time, the Christians' huge numbers proved too powerful and Ahmed was killed, and his followers fled. However, Muslim raids led by Ahmed's wife and nephew continued in the years following. In infuriation, and without the back-up of his main army, Galawdewos attacked the rich trading Muslim city of Harar in 1559. He met the same fate as Dom Christovão, and his head was paraded around Harar on a stick.

The Muslim-Christian wars were terribly costly. The Christian monarchy was nearly wiped out, and the once mighty Muslim state of Adal lay in ruins. Many of the most beautiful churches and monasteries in Ethiopia, along with their precious manuscripts, church relics and regalia, lay in ashes.

OROMO MIGRATIONS & THE JESUITS

A new threat to the Ethiopian empire arose in the mid-16th century, filling the power vacuum left behind by the weakened Muslims. The nomadic pastoralists and warrior horsemen of the Oromos (known to the Amharas as Gallas, a pejorative term) began a great migration northwards from what's now Kenya.

For the next 200 years intermittent armed conflict raged between the empire and the Oromos. For the empire, the Oromo expansion meant loss of territory and vital tax revenue. The Oromos also challenged the old Muslim state; the old city walls seen in Harar today (see p218) were built in response to Oromo conflicts.

Early in the 17th century the Oromo threat led several Ethiopian emperors to seek an alliance with the Portuguese-backed Jesuits. Two emperors, Za-Dengel and Susenyos, even went as far as conversion to Catholicism. However, imposing Catholicism on their population provoked widespread rebellion. Za-Dengel was overthrown and, in 1629, Susenyos' draconian measures to convert his people incited civil war.

As many as 32,000 peasants are thought to have lost their lives in the bloodshed that followed, most at the hands of Susenyos' army. Eventually Susenyos backed down and the Orthodox faith was re-established.

Susenyos' son and successor, Fasiladas, expelled the meddling Jesuits and forbade all foreigners to set foot in his empire. For nearly 130 years

Donald N Levine's imaginative *Wax & Gold* provides outstanding insight into Amharic culture, though chapter six is rather far-fetched!

1629	1636	1706–1721
Emperor Susenyos converts to Catholicism and tries to force his people to do likewise. His subjects are not happy and in the civil war that follows an estimated 32,000 die. Susenyos eventually decides Catholicism wasn't such a good idea.	Emperor Fasiladas founds Gonder, the first permanent capital since Lalibela; he also expels all foreigners from the empire. The new capital flourishes and Ethiopia enters another golden age.	The court in Gonder is thrown into turmoil as coups, assassination and court rumour become a virtual hobby for the people of the royal city. Three monarchs hold power in just 15 years.

only one European, a French doctor Charles Poncet, was allowed to enter Ethiopia. He famously wrote about Emperor Iyasu's grandeur in *A Voyage to Ethiopia* (translation).

Though the Jesuits' interference had caused great suffering and bloodshed in Ethiopia, they left behind one useful legacy: books. Pero Pais wrote the first serious history of the country. Other writings included detailed accounts of Ethiopia's cultural, economic and social life.

With the rising Ottoman hold in the east, and the Oromo entrenchment in the south, the political authority of Shoa had become increasingly circumscribed. It was time to relocate the centre of power – again.

THE RISE & FALL OF GONDER

In 1636, following the old tradition of his forefathers, Emperor Fasiladas decided to found a new capital. However, Gonder was different from its predecessors: it was to be the first permanent capital since Lalibela. Fasiladas' plan worked and Gonder flourished for well over a century.

By the 17th century's close, Gonder boasted magnificent palaces, beautiful gardens and extensive plantations. It was also the site of sumptuous feasts and extravagant court pageantry, attracting visitors from around the world. Its thriving market even drew rich Muslim merchants from across the country.

Under the ample patronage of church and state, the arts and crafts flourished. Impressive churches were built, among them the famous Debre Berhan Selassie, which can be seen to this day (see p122). Outside Gonder, building projects included some remarkable churches at Lake Tana's historic monasteries (p114).

But not all was sweet in Gonder's court, and between 1706 and 1721 everyone from royal bodyguards, the clergy and nobles to ordinary citizens tried their hand at conspiracy. Assassination, plotting and intrigue became the order of the day, and the ensuing chaos reads like something out of Shakespeare's *Macbeth*. No less than three monarchs held power during this turbulent period, at least one meeting a sticky, poisonous end. Emperor Bakaffa's reign (1721–30) briefly restored stability, during which time new palaces and churches were built, and literature and the arts once again thrived.

However, by the time of Iyasu II's death in 1755, the Gonder kingdom was back in turmoil. The provinces started to rebel. Ethnic rivalries surfaced and came to head in a power struggle between the Oromo people, who'd become increasingly absorbed into the court, and the Tigrayan ruler, Ras Mikael Sehul. Assassination and murder again followed and central government fell apart.

Between 1784 and 1855 the emperors were little more than puppets in the hands of rival feudal lords and their powerful provincial armies. The country

Despite a slightly condescending view of the 'primitive negroes' Alan Moorehead's *The Blue Nile*, which depicts the history of the river, land and those who sought its source, remains a classic of the genre.

The ultimate guide to the historical treasures of the north is Stuart Munro-Hay's *Ethiopia: The Unknown Land: A Cultural and Historical Guide*.

1755–1855	**1855**	**1855–1872**
Emperor Iyasu II dies and the central government in Gonder quickly collapses; Ethiopia slips back into the dark ages and a century of endless civil war and skirmishes between rival war lords follows.	Kassa Haylu outsteals, outwits and outmanoeuvres his rivals to become Emperor Tewodros; he unites a feuding Ethiopia and embarks on ambitious modernisation programs.	Tewodros builds numerous roads, establishes an army and promotes Amharic over Ge'ez as the language of everyday use. He also makes the mistake of imprisoning a group of Britons attending his court.

disintegrated and civil war became the norm. After Gonder's renaissance, Ethiopia had stepped right back into the dark ages. Thankfully, much of Gonder's architectural grandeur survived and remains intact (see p118).

Ethiopian historians later referred to the time after Iyasu II's death as the period of the *masafent* (judges), after the reference in the Book of Judges 21:25 when 'every man did that which was right in his own eyes'.

EMPEROR TEWODROS

After the fallout of Gonder, Ethiopia existed only as a cluster of separate and feuding fiefdoms. That was until the mid-19th century, when a unique man dreamt of unity.

Kassa Haylu, raised in a monastery and the son of a western chief, had first been a *shifta* (bandit) after his claim to his deceased father's fief was denied. However, he eventually became a Robin Hood figure, looting the rich to give to the poor. This gained him large numbers of followers and he began to defeat the rival princes, one after another, until in 1855 he had himself crowned Emperor Tewodros.

The new monarch soon began to show himself not just as a capable leader and strong ruler but as a unifier, innovator and reformer as well. He chose Maqdala, a natural fortress south of Lalibela, as his base and there he began to formulate mighty plans. He established a national army, an arms factory and a great road network, as well as implementing a major program of land reform, promoting Amharic (the vernacular) in place of the classical written language, Ge'ez, and even attempting to abolish the slave trade.

But these reforms met with deep resentment and opposition from the land-holding clergy, the rival lords and even the common faithful. Tewodros' response, however, was ruthless and sometimes brutal. Like a tragic Shakespearean hero, the emperor suffered from an intense pride, a fanatical belief in his cause and an inflated sense of destiny. This would eventually be his downfall.

Frustrated by failed attempts to enlist European, and particularly British, support for his modernising programs, Tewodros impetuously imprisoned some Britons attending his court. Initially successful in extracting concessions, Tewodros overplayed his hand, and it badly miscarried. In 1868 large, heavily armed British forces, backed by rival Ethiopian lords, inflicted appalling casualties on Tewodros' men, many of them armed with little more than shields and spears.

Refusing to surrender, Tewodros played the tragic hero to the last and penned a final dramatic and bitter avowal before biting down on a pistol and pulling the trigger.

Tewodros' defeat gravely weakened Ethiopia. This did not escape the watchful eyes of colonial powers, now hungry for expansion.

'He eventually became a Robin Hood figure, looting the rich to give to the poor.'

1872–76	1875–76	1889
After helping the British dispose of Tewodros, Kassa Mercha wins the battle of succession and rises as Emperor Yohannes.	Egyptian forces attempt to invade the country, but Emperor Yohannes puts up a good fight and ends their ambitions.	Yohannes' successor, Emperor Menelik, signs a friendship treaty with Italy and grants the region that is now Eritrea to Italy. Italy takes this to mean that all of Ethiopia is now its protectorate. Addis Ababa becomes the new capital.

EMPEROR YOHANNES

In the aftermath of Tewodros' death, there arose another battle for succession. Using his weaponry gained from the British in exchange for his support of their Maqdala expedition, Kassa Mercha of Tigray rose to the fore. In 1871, at the battle of Assam, he defeated the newly crowned Emperor Tekla Giorgis.

After proclaiming himself Emperor Yohannes the following year, Kassa reigned for the next 17 years. In contrast to Tewodros, Yohannes staunchly supported the church and recognised the independence of local lords. With the latter, he struck a bargain: in exchange for keeping their kingdoms, they were obliged to recognise the emperor's overall power, and to pay taxes to his state. In this way, Yohannes secured the religious, political and financial backing of his subjects.

Yohannes also proved himself a skilful soldier. In 1875, after the Egyptians had advanced into Ethiopia from the coastal area, Yohannes drew them into battle and resoundingly routed them at Gundat and then again at Gura in 1876. His victories not only ended any Egyptian designs on the territory, but brought much captured weaponry, turning his army into the first well-equipped force in Ethiopian history.

But soon another power threatened: the Italians. The opening of the Suez Canal in 1869 greatly increased the strategic value of the Red Sea, which again became a passageway to the East and beyond.

In 1885 the Italians arrived in Massawa (in present-day Eritrea), and soon blockaded arms to Yohannes. The failure of the British to impede the arrival of the Italians made Yohannes furious. He accused them of contravening the 1884 Hewett Treaty. Though protesting otherwise, Britain privately welcomed the Italians, both to counter French influence on the Somali coast (in present-day Djibouti), and to deter any Turkish ambitions.

Meanwhile, the Mahadists (or Dervishes) were raising their heads in the west. Dislodging the Egyptians and British, they overran Sudan before arriving in Ethiopia and eventually sacking Gonder in 1888.

Yohannes rushed to meet the Dervishes at Qallabat in 1889 but, at the close of yet another victory, he fell, mortally wounded by a sniper's bullet.

EMPEROR MENELIK

Menelik, King of Shoa since 1865, had long aspired to the imperial throne. Confined at Maqdala for 10 years by Tewodros, he was yet reportedly much influenced by his captor, and also dreamt of Ethiopia's unification and modernisation.

After his escape from Maqdala and his ascendancy in Shoa, Menelik concentrated on consolidating his own power, and embarked on an aggressive, ruthless and sometimes brutal campaign of expansion. He occupied territories across the south, forcing various ethnic groups under his empire's yoke.

Philip Marsden tells the ultimately tragic tale of Emperor Tewodros II in his beautifully executed book on Ethiopia, *The Barefoot Emperor*.

1896	**1913–1916**	**1915**
Tired of Italy's expanding ways, Emperor Menelik stuns the world by thrashing the Italian army in the Battle of Adwa. The 1889 friendship treaty is annulled and Italy recognises Ethiopian independence but hangs onto Eritrea.	Emperor Menelik dies and Lij Iyasu takes over the reins of power for just three years before being deposed and succeeded by Menelik's daughter, Zawditu, who rules through a regent, Ras Tafari Makonnen.	Thanks to the shoe-making skills of two engineers the Djibouti–Addis Ababa rail line is completed, expanding Ethiopian trade and ushering in the rapid development of Addis Ababa.

Relations with the Italians were at first good; Menelik had been seen as a potential ally against Yohannes. On Yohannes' death, the Italians recognised Menelik's claim to the throne and, in 1889, the Treaty of Wechale was signed. In exchange for granting Italy the region that was later to become Eritrea, the Italians recognised Menelik's sovereignty and gave him the right to import arms freely through Ethiopian ports.

However, a dispute over a discrepancy in the purportedly identical Amharic and Italian texts – the famous Article 17 – led to disagreement. According to the Italian version, Ethiopia was obliged to approach other foreign powers through Italy, which essentially reduced Ethiopia to a lowly Italian protectorate. Relations rapidly began to sour.

In the meantime, the Italians continued their expansion in their newly created colony of Eritrea. Soon, they were spilling into territory well beyond the confines agreed to in both treaties.

Despite the Italians' attempts to court Tigray's local chiefs, the latter chose to assist Menelik. Nevertheless, the Italians managed to defeat Ras Mangasha and his Tigrayan forces and occupied Mekele in 1895.

Provoked at last into marching north with his forces, Menelik shocked the international world by resoundingly defeating the Italians at Adwa (see the boxed text, p144). It was one of the biggest and most significant battles in African history – numbering among the very few occasions when a colonial power was defeated by a native force. To the rest of Africa, Ethiopia became a beacon of independence in a continent almost entirely enslaved by colonialism.

Menelik then set his sights on modernisation. He abandoned the Shoan capital of Ankober and soon founded the new capital, Addis Ababa. During his reign, electricity (see p92) and telephones were introduced, bridges, roads, schools and hospitals built, and banks and industrial enterprises established.

The greatest technological achievement of the time was undoubtedly the construction of Ethiopia's railway, which eventually linked Addis Ababa to Djibouti in 1915 (see the boxed texts, p215 and p270).

IYASU

Menelik died a natural death in 1913. Iyasu, his raffish young grandson and nominated heir, proved to be very much a product of the 20th century. Continuing with Menelik's reforms, he also showed a 'modern' secularist, non-sectarian attitude.

The young prince built mosques as well as churches, took several Muslim as well as Christian wives, and supported the empire's peripheral populations, which had for years suffered at the oppressive hands of Amharic settlers and governors.

'Ethiopia became a beacon of independence in a continent almost entirely enslaved by colonialism.'

1930–31	1935–36	1936
After the death of Zawditu and years of careful posturing, Ras Tafari is crowned as Emperor Haile Selassie and dubbed the Chosen One of God. A year later Ethiopia gets its first written constitution which grants the emperor almost total power.	Italy invades Ethiopia; illegal use of mustard gas and bombing of civilian targets kills 275,000 Ethiopians; Italy loses 4350 men. In 1936 the Italians capture Addis and Selassie flees the country. The King of Italy is made Emperor of Ethiopia.	In June 1936 Haile Selassie makes a plea to the League of Nations asking for help. The League responds by lifting sanctions against Italy.

Iyasu and his councillors pushed through a few reforms, including improving the system of land tenure and taxation, but they faced ever-deepening opposition from the church and nobility.

Finally, after also upsetting the allied powers with his dealings with the Weimar Republic (Germany), Austria and the Ottoman Empire, a pretext for his removal was found. Accused by the nobles of 'abjuring the Christian faith', the prince was deposed in 1921. Zewditu, Menelik's daughter, was proclaimed empress, and Ras Tafari (the son of Ras Makonnen, Menelik's cousin) was proclaimed the prince regent.

RAS TAFARI

The 2nd edition of Bahru Zewde's widely acclaimed *A History of Modern Ethiopia 1855–1991* contains two particularly readable sections: Harold G Marcus' *Ethiopia* and Richard Pankhurst's *The Ethiopians*.

Prince Ras Tafari boasted more experience and greater maturity than Iyasu, particularly in the field of foreign affairs. In an attempt to improve the country's international image, he succeeded in abolishing the Ethiopian slave trade.

In 1923 Tafari pulled off a major diplomatic coup by securing Ethiopia entry into the League of Nations. Membership firmly placed Ethiopia on the international political map, and also gave it some recourse against the grasping designs of its European, colonial neighbours.

Continuing the tradition begun by Menelik, Tafari was an advocate of reform. A modern printing press was established as well as several secondary schools and an air force. In the meantime, Tafari was steadily outmanoeuvring his rivals. In 1930 the last rebellious noble was defeated and killed in battle. A few days later the sick empress also died. Ras Tafari assumed the throne.

EMPEROR HAILE SELASSIE

On 2 November 1930 Tafari was crowned Emperor Haile Selassie. The extravagant spectacle was attended by representatives from across the globe and proved a terrific public relations exercise. It even led indirectly to the establishment of a new faith (see p173).

The Emperor by Ryszard Kapuscinski offers bizarre insights into Haile Selassie's imperial court through interviews with servants and close associates of the emperor. Some historians question its authenticity though.

The following year, Ethiopia's first written constitution was introduced. It granted the emperor virtually absolute power, his body was even declared sacred. The two-house parliament consisted of a senate, which was nominated by the emperor from among his nobles; and a chamber of deputies, which was elected from the landholders. It was thus little more than a chamber for self-interested debate.

Ever since the day of his regency, the emperor had been bringing the country under centralised rule. For the first time, the Ethiopian state was unambiguously unified.

ITALIAN OCCUPATION

By the early 20th century Ethiopia was the only state in Africa to have survived Europe's colonial scramble. However, Ethiopia's position between the

1940–1950	1941–42	1960
Ethiopia establishes its first national bank, a new national currency, its first university and its first (and only) airline – Ethiopian Airlines.	British, Commonwealth and Ethiopian forces liberate Ethiopia from Italian occupation, Haile Selassie reclaims his throne and Ethiopia its independence. In the following years the country modernises fast.	In response to growing discontent over the emperor's autocratic rule, the imperial bodyguard stage a coup d'etat, which is defeated by the army and air force.

two Italian colonies of Eritrea and Somalia made her an enticing morsel. Any Italian attempt to link its two colonies would require expansion into Ethiopia. When Mussolini seized power, the inevitable happened.

From 1933, in an effort to undermine the Ethiopian state, Italian agents, well heeled with funds, were dispatched to subvert the local chiefs, as well as to stir up ethnic tensions. Britain and France, nervous of pushing Mussolini further into Hitler's camp, refrained from protests and turned a blind eye.

In 1934 a minor skirmish known as the Wal Wal incident took place between Italian and Ethiopian forces. Italy had found its pretext. Though the export of arms was banned to both countries, in Italy's case (itself a major arms manufacturer), the embargo was meaningless.

Italian Invasion

On 3 October 1935 the invasion began. Italians, overwhelmingly superior in both ground and air forces, invaded Ethiopia from Eritrea. First the northern town of Aksum fell, then Mekele.

The League of Nations issued sanctions against Italy, but they proved to be little more than a slap on the wrist. If the Suez Canal had been closed to the Italians, or an oil embargo put in place, the Italian advance – as Mussolini was later to admit – might have been halted within weeks.

Campaigning

Terrified that the international community would impose more serious embargoes, and keen to keep Italian morale high, Il Duce pressed for a swift campaign.

Impatient with progress made, he soon replaced De Bono, his first general. Pietro Badoglio, his replacement, was authorised 'to use all means of war – I say all – both from the air and from the ground'. Implicit in the instructions was the use of mustard gas, which contravened the 1926 Geneva Convention. Also in contravention was Italy's repeated bombing of civilian targets, including Red Cross hospitals.

Despite overwhelming odds, the Ethiopians succeeded in launching a major counterattack, known as the Christmas Offensive, at the Italian position at Mekele at the end of 1935.

However, the Italians were soon on the offensive again. Backed by hundreds of planes, cannons and weapons of every type, the Italian armies swept across the country. In May 1936 Mussolini triumphantly declared: 'Ethiopia is Italian'.

Meanwhile, Emperor Haile Selassie had fled Ethiopia (some Ethiopians never forgave him for it) to present Ethiopia's cause to the world. On 30 June 1936 he made his famous speech to the League of Nations in Geneva. The league staggeringly responded by lifting the sanctions against Italy

It wasn't until 1996 that the Italian Ministry of Defence finally admitted to the use of mustard gas in this war.

1962	**1972–74**	**1974**
Addis Ababa is made the headquarters of the Organization of African Unity. To prove just how united Africa is, Haile Selassie unilaterally annexes Eritrea; separatist Eritreans launch a bitter guerrilla war.	A dreadful famine strikes and around 200,000 people die. This further increases resentment toward the emperor, and students start protesting.	After years of growing discontent and increasing street protests Haile Selassie is unceremoniously deposed as emperor on 12 September; the Derg declare a socialist state on 20 December.

later that year. Only the USSR, USA, Haiti, Mexico and New Zealand refused to recognise Italy's conquest.

Occupation & Resistance

Soon Ethiopia, Eritrea and Somalia were merged to become the colonial territory of 'Africa Orientale Italiana' (Italian East Africa).

Hoping to create an important economic base, Italy invested heavily in its new colony. From 1936 as many as 60,000 Italian workers poured in to work on Ethiopia's infrastructure.

Ethiopia kept up a spirited resistance to Italian rule throughout its brief duration. Italy's response was famously brutal. Mussolini personally ordered all rebels to be shot, and insurgencies were put down using large-scale bombing, poison gas and machine-gunning from the air.

Ethiopian resistance reached a peak in February 1937 with an assassination attempt on the much-hated Italian viceroy, Graziani. In reprisal, the Italians spent three days shooting, beheading or disembowelling several thousand people in the capital.

The 'patriot's movement' (the resistance fighters) was mainly based in the historical provinces of Shoa, Gonder and Gojam, but drew support from all parts of the country; many fighters were women.

Graziani's response was simple: 'Eliminate them, eliminate them, eliminate them'. But Ethiopian resolve stiffened and resistance grew. Although in control of major towns, Italy never succeeded in conquering the entire country.

The outbreak of WWII, particularly Italy's declaration of war against Britain in 1940, dramatically changed the course of events. Britain at last reversed its policy of tacit support of Italy's East African expansion and initially offered Ethiopia assistance on the Sudan–Ethiopia border. Later, in early 1941, Britain launched three major attacks.

Though not then widely recognised, the Ethiopian patriots played a major role before, during and after the liberation campaign, which ended on 5 May 1941 when the emperor and his men entered Addis Ababa.

POSTLIBERATION ETHIOPIA & THE DERG

The British, who'd entered Ethiopia as liberators, initially seemed to have simply replaced Italy as occupiers. However, Anglo-Ethiopian treaties in 1942 and 1944 eventually marked Ethiopia's resumption of independence.

The 1940s and '50s saw much postwar reconstruction, including (with US assistance) the establishment of a new government bank, a national currency, and the country's first national airline, Ethiopian Airlines.

New schools were developed and, in 1950, the country's first institution of higher education was established: the University College of Addis Ababa (now Addis Ababa University).

> 'Graziani's response was simple: "Eliminate them, eliminate them, eliminate them".'

1977–78	1977–79	1984
Somalia invades the Ogaden region of Ethiopia. Somali forces are eventually defeated in 1978, but only with massive help from Cuban and Soviet forces.	Colonel Mengistu Haile Mariam emerges as leader of the Derg. Thousands of government opponents die in the Red Terror campaign.	Israel launches 'Operation Moses', a six-week operation to secretly airlift 8000 Ethiopian Jews to Israel.

In 1955 the Revised Ethiopian Constitution was introduced. Although for the first time the legislature included an elected chamber of deputies, the government remained autocratic and the emperor continued to hold all power.

In 1962 Addis Ababa became the headquarters of the Organisation of African Unity (OAU) and, in 1958, of the UN Economic Commission for Africa (ECA).

Discontent

Despite modernisation, the pace of development was slow and dissatisfaction with it, and with the emperor's autocratic rule, began to grow. Finally, taking advantage of a state visit to Brazil in December 1960, the emperor's imperial bodyguard staged a coup d'etat. Though put down by the army and air force, it signalled the beginning of the end of imperial rule in Ethiopia.

Discontent simmered among the students too, who protested in particular against land tenure, corruption and the appalling famine of 1972–74 in which an estimated 200,000 died.

Meanwhile, international relations had also been deteriorating. In 1962 Ethiopia abrogated the UN-sponsored federation with Eritrea and unilaterally annexed the Eritrean state.

Then war broke out in 1964 with Somalia over joint claims to Ethiopia's Somali-inhabited region of the Ogaden Desert.

The 1974 Revolution & the Emperor's Fall

By 1973 an increasingly powerful and radical military group had emerged. Known as the Derg (Committee), they used the media with consummate skill to undermine the authority of the emperor himself. They famously flashed striking footage of starvation from Jonathan Dimbleby's well-known BBC TV report on the Wolo famine in between clips of sumptuous palace banquets.

The result was an unprecedented wave of teacher, student and taxi strikes in Addis Ababa. Even army mutinies began to be reported. At crisis point, the prime minister and his cabinet resigned and a new one was appointed with the mandate to carry out far-reaching constitutional reforms. But it was too late.

On 12 September 1974 Emperor Haile Selassie was deposed, unceremoniously bundled into the back of a Volkswagen, and driven away to prison. Ministers, nobles and close confidants of the emperor were also arrested by the Derg. The absolute power of the emperor and the divine right of rule of the century-old imperial dynasty were finished – forever?

The Derg soon dissolved parliament and established the Provisional Military Administrative Council (PMAC) to rule the country.

Emerging as the leader of the Derg was Colonel Mengistu Haile Mariam who rode the wave of popular opposition to Selassie's regime, as well as the Marxist-Leninist ideology of left-wing students.

'The Derg used the media with consummate skill to undermine the authority of the emperor.'

1984–85	**1991–93**	**1995**
Famine haunts much of highland Ethiopia and up to a million people die. The reasons for the famine are climatic and political. A huge relief operation spearheaded by Bob Geldof and a not very good song is launched in the West.	The Derg are defeated by the rebel EPRDF, Ethiopia's experiment with communism ends, Mengistu scuttles off to Megace's Zimbabwe where he remains to this day. Following a referendum Eritrea becomes independent.	The Federal Democratic Republic of Ethiopia is proclaimed and the first fair elections are held. Former guerrilla leader Meles Zenawi is proclaimed prime minister.

And what happened to the emperor? It's thought he was murdered by Mengistu himself in August 1975. Evidence for the crime? The ring of Solomon, rumoured to have been plucked from the murdered emperor's hand, was spotted on Mengistu's middle finger.

The Socialist Experiment

On 20 December 1974 a socialist state was declared. Under the adage *Ityopya Tikdem* or 'Ethiopia First', banks, businesses and factories were nationalised as was the rural and urban land. Raising the status of Ethiopian peasants, the campaign was initially much praised internationally, particularly by Unesco.

In the meantime, the external threats posed by Somalia and secessionist Eritrea were increasing. In July 1977 Somalia invaded Ethiopia. Thanks to the intervention of the Soviet Union, which flooded socialist Ethiopia with Soviet state-of-the-art weaponry, Somalia was beaten back. In Eritrea, however, the secessionists continued to thwart Ethiopian offensives.

Internal political debate also degenerated into violence. In 1977 the Red Terror campaign was launched to suppress all political opponents. At a conservative estimate, 100,000 people were killed and several thousand more fled abroad.

The Demise of the Derg

Red Terror only cemented the stance of those opposing the Derg. Numerous armed liberation movements arose, including those of the Afar, Oromo, Somali and particularly Tigrayan peoples. For years, with limited weaponry, they fought the military might of the Soviet-backed Derg.

In 1984–85 another appalling famine followed a drought, in which up to a million people died. Failed government resettlement campaigns, communal farms and 'villageisation' programmes aggravated the disaster in many areas, while Mengistu's disinclination to help the province of Tigray – the worst affected region and home to the powerful Tigrayan People's Liberation Front (TPLF) – caused thousands more to die.

When the EPRDF rolled into Addis Ababa it was navigating with photocopies of the Addis Ababa map found in Lonely Planet's *Africa on a Shoestring*.

The various opposition groups eventually united to form the Ethiopian People's Revolutionary Democratic Front (EPRDF), which in 1989 began its historic military campaign towards Addis Ababa.

Doubly confronted by the EPRDF in Ethiopia and the Eritrean People's Liberation Front (EPLF) in Eritrea; with the fall of his allies in Eastern Europe; and with his state in financial ruin as well as his own military authority in doubt, Mengistu's time was up and he fled the country on 21 May 1991. Seven days later, the EPRDF entered Addis Ababa and the Derg were done.

Mengistu received asylum in Zimbabwe, where he remains to this day, despite being tried in absentia in Ethiopia and sentenced to death.

1997	1998–2000	2000–2001
Eritrea drops the birr as its national currency and introduces the nakfa. This leads to a souring of the relationship between the two neighbours.	Likened to two bald men fighting over a comb, Ethiopia and Eritrea's leaders go to war over a sliver of barren wasteland. By the close of hostilities 70,000 are thought to have died and tens of thousands internally displaced.	A formal peace agreement is signed by Ethiopia and Eritrea and a demilitarised zone is established along the border under the supervision of the UNMEE.

THE ROAD TO DEMOCRACY (1991–95)

After the war of liberation, Ethiopia and Eritrea's leaders showed a similar determination and zeal to rebuild their countries.

In July 1991 a transitional charter was endorsed, which gave the EPRDF-dominated legislature a four-year, interim rule under the executive of the TPLF leader, Meles Zenawi. First and foremost, Mengistu's failed socialist policies were abandoned, and de facto independence was granted to Eritrea.

In August 1995 the Federal Democratic Republic of Ethiopia was proclaimed, a series of elections followed, and the constitution of the second republic was inaugurated. Meles Zenawi formed a new government.

In 1992 the body of Haile Selassie was finally discovered. It had been unceremoniously buried beneath Mengistu's old presidential office toilet.

THE ETHIOPIA-ERITREA WAR

Despite being friends and having fought against the Derg side by side for more than a decade, Meles Zenawi and Eritrea's president, Isaias, soon clashed. Amazingly, all it took for the relationship to sour was Eritrea's introduction of the nakfa currency to replace the Ethiopian birr in November 1997.

In May 1998 Eritrea upped the stakes by occupying the border town of Badme, followed, a month later, by the bombing of a school in Mekele, killing 55 people, many of whom who were children. Ethiopia followed suit by bombing military installations outside Asmara, only to have Eritrea cluster-bomb civilians in Adigrat.

In February 1999 a full-scale military conflict broke out that left tens of thousands dead on both sides before it finally ceased for good in mid-2000. During this time there were mass exportations of Eritreans from Ethiopia and Ethiopians from Eritrea.

Although Ethiopia had agreed to peace earlier, it wasn't until Ethiopia recaptured all territory and went on to occupy parts of central and western Eritrea that Eritrea finally agreed to a ceasefire.

In December 2000 a formal peace settlement was signed in Algiers. In April 2001 a 25km-wide demilitarised strip, which ran the length of the internationally recognised border on the Eritrean side, was set up under supervision of the UN Mission in Ethiopia and Eritrea (UNMEE).

In July 2008 the mandate of UNMEE came to an end after, according to the UN, 'crippling restrictions imposed by Eritrea'. This event led to widespread fears of a new war, but so far these fears remain unfounded; although the two armies do continue to eye each other suspiciously over the desert, and tensions remain high.

Although only published locally, *Eritrea's War* by Paul Henze delves into the 1998–2000 Ethiopia-Eritrea War.

Aidan Hartley's *The Zanzibar Chest* recalls his days as a foreign correspondent throughout Africa and includes chapters on the last days of the Derg. It's one of the most powerful and wonderfully crafted books you could hope to read.

ETHIOPIA TODAY

The 15 May 2005 elections returned the EPRDF and Zenawi to power, but while the election run-up and the voting polls were witness to few irregularities, there were numerous reports by EU observers about questionable

2005	2006–09	2006–09
After controversial 15 May elections, mass protests turn deadly when government troops fire on unarmed demonstrators. Thousands of people, including opposition politicians, journalists and newspaper editors are detained by the police.	Ethiopia invades Somalia in order to dislodge the Islamic Courts Union. It becomes embroiled in a guerrilla war and finally pulls out in early 2009.	Tensions between Ethiopia and Eritrea come close to boiling over and both sides begin massive troop build-ups in the border region. Fortunately tensions subside and war is averted.

vote counting at the constituency level and the announcing of the results by state-run media.

Despite EPRDF losing 209 of the 536 seats they had held since the 2000 election, including all 23 in Addis Ababa, these results (and news of election irregularities) were not well taken, especially in the capital.

The initial government-released results in June led to mass protests in Addis Ababa, where government troops arrested thousands of opposition party members and killed 22 unarmed civilians. Similar protests and mass strikes occurred in early November, which resulted in troops killing 46 civilians and arresting thousands more. Leaders of political party the Coalition for Unity and Democracy, as well as owners of private newspapers, were also arrested and charged with inciting the riots. The government's actions were condemned by the EU and many Western governments.

If internal political turmoil wasn't enough, relations with Eritrea also heated up in late 2005 and troops once again amassed along the border, but fortunately the tension soon subsided again.

However, Ethiopia's army has kept itself busy in other spheres. In 2006 Ethiopia launched an invasion of Somalia in order to dislodge the Islamic Courts Union (who are widely thought to support al-Qaeda) who had gained control of much of the country (and ironically brought the first semblance of peace Somalia had seen in years). By the end of the year Ethiopian troops had pushed the ICU back to the far south of Somalia, but they soon found themselves tangled up in a messy guerrilla war with the ICU slowly beginning to win back lost ground. Many observers suspected that Eritrea was secretly arming and aiding the ICU in its war with Ethiopia; something ICU leader Hassan Dahir Aweys finally admitted was true (though in what form he didn't say). Unwilling to get bogged down in a long and bloody battle in Somalia Ethiopia called for an African Union force to take its place and the Ethiopians began to withdraw. By early 2009 all their troops were back in Ethiopia.

In many ways Ethiopia is better off today than it has been in hundreds of years, but in other ways the country continues to walk on a knife-edge. Relations with Eritrea remain very bleak. Tensions are high (but currently stable) over the Ethiopia–Eritrea border demarcation and many observers believe that Somalia is being used as a battleground for a proxy war between the two nations. In addition, a low intensity war against separatist groups is taking place in the Ogaden region, the economy is wobbling, the number of urban jobless rising fast and an exploding population is putting massive strains on already tired soils to produce enough food to feed everybody. If Ethiopia is to flourish it will have to play all its cards right.

Recounting events over the past half a century across Africa, Martin Meredith's *The State of Africa* includes a couple of chapters on Ethiopia and is by far the best history of modern Africa currently available.

2007	2008	2009
In September Ethiopia celebrates the new millennium, and catches up with the rest of us.	THE UNMEE mandate expires after 'crippling restrictions' from Eritrea and UN troops withdraw from the border region, leaving the two nations eyeing each other nervously.	In mid-2009 Ethiopia admits that some of its forces have returned to Somalia and are engaged in battling Islamic extremists once again.

The Culture

Encompassed on all sides by the enemies of their religion, the Aethiopians slept near a thousand years, forgetful of the world, by whom they were forgotten.

Edward Gibbon, The History of the Decline
and Fall of the Roman Empire, 1776–88

THE NATIONAL PSYCHE

The Ethiopians are nothing if not proud, and for good reason. To them, Ethiopia has stood out from all African nations and proved itself to be a unique world of its own – home to its own culture, language, script, calendar and history. Ethiopian Orthodox Christians and Muslims alike revel in the fact that Ethiopia was the only nation on the continent to successfully fight off colonisation.

But with their pride comes other traits. The Ethiopians can be a stubborn, violent and xenophobic people; but on the flipside they can be incredibly gregarious, warm, welcoming and kind and will often go miles out of their way to help a stranger. Proud though they are, there are times when Ethiopians seem desperate to be somebody else. Many of the younger generations, brought up on hand-outs by aid agencies, can be anything but proud of Ethiopia and sometimes it can seem as if every other young Ethiopian you meet, at least in urban areas, wants to run away to America.

The highlands have been dominated by a distinctive form of Christianity since the 4th century. Although undeniably devout and keen to dispense centuries worth of Orthodox legends and tales dating back to Aksum and the Ark of the Covenant, Christians, like all Ethiopians, nonetheless still cling to a surprising amount of magic and superstition.

Belief in *zar* (spirits or genies) and *buda* (the evil eye with the power to turn people into mischievous hyenas by night) is rife and as such even Christians adorn their children, from baptism, with charms or talismans around their necks to deter such spirits and terrible diseases.

Yet this apparent religious contradiction is quite natural to Ethiopians. In a historically isolated area where rhetoric and reasoning have become highly valued and practised, where eloquent communication and sophisticated wordplay are considered an art form and where the ability to argue a case in point while effectively sitting on the fence is now aspired to, ambiguity and complexity are as much a part of the Ethiopian psyche as it is a part of their religion.

> In the past, the causes of famine have had less to do with environmental factors – Ethiopia has abundant natural resources – and more to do with economic mismanagement and inequitable and oppressive government.

LIFESTYLE

Other than religion, which undoubtedly plays a huge role in almost all Ethiopians' daily life, it's agriculture and pastoralism that fill the days of well over 80% of the country's population. Everyone is involved, right down to stick-and-stone-wielding four-year-old children who are handed the incredible responsibility to tend and herd the family's livestock.

With almost everyone toiling out in the fields, it's not surprising that only 42.7% (CIA figures) of the population is literate. Since young children are needed to help with the family plots and animals, only 66% (UNICEF figures) of children attend primary school. Older children are in even more demand in the workforce, which means secondary schools see only 31% of kids. If all children under 16 were forced to attend school, Ethiopia's workforce would be ravaged and almost half of the country's entire population would be attending classes.

Ethiopian families are incredibly close and most people live with their parents until marriage. After marriage, the couple usually join the household of the husband's family. After a couple of years, they will request a plot of land from the village, on which to build their own house.

Divorce is relatively easy in Ethiopia and marriage can be dissolved at the request of either party (adultery is usually given as justification). In theory, each partner retains the property he or she brought into the marriage, though sometimes allowances are made for the 'wronged' partner.

WHO DOES SHE THINK SHE IS?

The most beautiful and alluring woman ever to live had hairy legs and the cloven foot of the devil. Her fame has lasted three thousand years, yet nobody remembers her name. She's a player in the ancient legends of Judaism, Christianity and Islam, yet no one knows where she lived. She's the mother of the throne of Ethiopia, the most famous daughter of Yemen and the original Jerusalem pilgrim. Even today she remains a household name, and any girl seen to be getting above herself can expect to be compared with her. She is, of course, the Queen of Sheba, but she may never even have existed.

Though she appears in the writings of all three monotheistic religions, it's the Ethiopian story (in which she is known as *Makeda*) of her life that is most famous in the West, while for Christian Ethiopians the story is virtually the very cornerstone of their culture, history and lifestyle. According to the Kebra Negast (Ethiopia's national epic), the Queen of Sheba's first public appearance was when she paid a visit to the court of King Solomon in 10th century BC Jerusalem. The reasons and results of her visit vary and though many people say that King Solomon was the wisest person in the world and that the queen travelled to Jerusalem in order to test his wisdom with 'difficult questions and riddles', it seems more likely that trade was the real reason for the meeting. The Ethiopian legend reveals how after her arrival Solomon became enraptured with her beauty and devised a plan to have his wicked way with her. He agreed to let her stay in his palace only on the condition that she touched nothing of his. Shocked that Solomon should consider her capable of such a thing, she agreed. That evening Solomon laid on a feast of spicy and salty foods. After the meal, Sheba and Solomon retired to separate beds in his sleeping quarters. During the night Sheba awoke, thirsty from all the salty food she had consumed, and reached across for a glass of water. The moment she put the glass to her lips Solomon awoke and triumphantly claimed that she had broken her vow. 'But it's only water', she cried, to which Solomon replied, 'And nothing on earth is more precious than water'.

Ethiopian tradition holds that the child that resulted from the deceitful night of passion that followed was to become Menelik I, from whom the entire royal line of Ethiopia claims direct descent (in truth the line, if it ever existed, has been broken a number of times).

But there's more to this tale than just the birth of the Ethiopian Royal Line. This is also the story of the arrival of the Ark of the Covenant in Ethiopia and the conversion of its people to Judaism. It's said that the centrepiece of Solomon's famous temple was the Ark of the Covenant, and that as long as the Jews had the Ark nothing bad could come of them. However, when Menelik travelled to Jerusalem to meet his father, his luggage was a little heavier on his return trip. Secreted away among his dirty laundry was the Ark of the Covenant.

Finding out whether Sheba existed and where her capital was located has not proved easy. The strongest claims have come from both Ethiopia, which claims that Aksum was her capital, and Yemen, which says it was Ma'rib. Both cities were important trade and cultural centres and it's quite likely that both were, if not ruled by the same monarch, then certainly closely tied through trade. However, so far neither has yielded any evidence to suggest that the Queen of Sheba ever existed. Whatever the truth, the legend persists, and every Ethiopian will swear to you that Aksum was the home of the most beautiful cloven-footed woman to ever live.

Although women continue to lag behind men economically, they are highly respected in Ethiopian society. The same can't be said for gays and lesbians. Homosexuality is severely condemned – traditionally, religiously and legally – and remains a topic of absolute taboo.

Social Graces

Mixed in with religion and survival, numerous social graces also play a large part in people's daily lives. For example, a nod or head bow accompanying greetings shows special respect, thanks or appreciation. Deference is also shown by supporting the right arm (near the elbow) with the left hand during shaking. When Ethiopians enter a room they try and shake hands with everyone (including children). If hands are dirty or wet, limp wrists are offered. They also believe it's polite to kiss babies or young children, even if you've just met them.

Kissing on the cheek is also very common among friends and relatives of either sex.

Names are also important in Ethiopia, and the exchange of first names (surnames are rarely used) is the first important stage in forming a friendship. To address someone formally, they add the following prefixes to first names: *Ato* for men, *Weizero* for married women and *Weizerit* for unmarried women.

When receiving a gift, Ethiopians extend both hands as using only one is seen as showing reluctance or ingratitude.

> A staggering 13% of Ethiopian children are missing one or both parents. Nearly a quarter of these parents have been lost through AIDS.

GOVERNMENT

Government consists of a federation of regional states that are governed by two assemblies: the 548-member Council of Peoples' Representatives (CPR), which is the legislative arm of the federation, and the smaller 108-member Federal Council (FC), which serves as the senate, with a merely supervisory role. The president has a mainly ceremonial role. The prime minister, Meles Zenawi, is the head of state and appoints the 18-member cabinet. Zenawi has served as prime minister since 1995. For a long time he was regarded as one of the new wave of African leaders, ready to lead an open and democratic government. Sadly, disputed elections, summary disappearance of opposition supporters and a crackdown on the media have disappointed those who had high hopes for his leadership.

Under the new republic's principle of 'ethnic federalism', the old provinces were divided into 11 new regions, including the city-state of Harar and the metropolitan regions of Addis Ababa and Dire Dawa. Each has its own autonomous council and holds its own elections. The regions are demarked largely along linguistic lines, and five of Ethiopia's largest ethnic groups (the Oromo, Amhara, Tigrayan, Somali and Afar) now have their own regional states. See p30 for a map of the regions.

> Thanks to the Orthodox calendar, Ethiopia is a full seven to eight years (depending on the exact date) behind the Western calendar. There are also thirteen months in a year.

POPULATION

Ethiopia's population has squeezed past the 85-million mark, an astounding figure considering the population was just 15 million in 1935. In the previous edition of this book, we stated that Ethiopia's population growth rate was 2.5% and that if it continued at that level then Ethiopia would be bursting at the seams with almost 120 million people in 2025. Well, the population growth rate hasn't stayed at that rate – it has risen to a staggering 3.2%, giving Ethiopia one of the fastest-growing populations in the world. Though AIDS, which affects 2.1% of the population, will inevitably slow future growth, this population explosion is the biggest problem facing Ethiopia today.

ETHIOPIAN HAIRSTYLES

Hairstyles in all societies form an important part of tribal identification. Reflecting the large number of ethnic groups, Ethiopian hairstyles are particularly diverse and colourful. Hair is cut, shaved, trimmed, plaited, braided, sculpted with clay, rubbed with mud, put in buns and tied in countless different fashions. In the Omo Valley, hairstyles are sometimes so elaborate and valued that special wooden headrests are used as pillows to preserve them.

In rural areas, the heads of children are often shaved to discourage lice. Sometimes a single topknot or tail plait is left so that 'God should have a handle with which to lift them unto Heaven', should he decide to call them!

Though a trend of urbanisation is starting to emerge, 83% of the people still live in rural areas.

Although 84 languages and 200 dialects are spoken in Ethiopia, the population can be broken down into eight broad groups, which are detailed in the following pages. For details about the Lower Omo Valley's unique peoples, see p200.

The Oromo

Although traditionally most of the Oromo were nomadic pastoralists, it was the skilled Oromo warrior horsemen that put fear into Ethiopians when they migrated north from present-day Kenya in the mid-16th century. It was the Oromo who inspired Harar's leaders to build a wall around the city and even led Ethiopian emperors to (briefly and much to the disgust of the general population) accept Catholicism in order to gain Portugal's military support.

Every Ethiopian emperor (bar one) since Yekuno Amlak established the Solomonic dynasty in 1270 has been Amhara. Yohannes (r 1872–89), who was Tigrayan, is the only exception.

Today, most Oromo are sedentary, making a living as farmers or cattle breeders. They are Muslim, Christian and animist in religion, and are known for their egalitarian society, which is based on the *gada* (age-group system). A man's life is divided into age-sets of eight years. In the fourth set (between the ages of 24 and 32), men assume the right to govern their people.

They are the largest ethnic group in the country, making up 32% of its population. Over 85% of the massive 350,000-sq-km Oromia region's population are Oromo. Many Oromo resent the Tigray-led national government and the Oromo Liberation Front (OLF) continues to lobby for separation from Ethiopia.

The Amharas

As great warriors, skilful governors and astute administrators, the Amhara have dominated the country's history, politics and society since 1270, and have imposed their own language and culture on the country. In the past this was much resented by other tribal groups, who saw it as little more than a kind of colonialism.

Amhara tend to be devoutly Christian, although there are some Muslim Amhara. They're also fanatical about their land and 90% of them are traditional tillers of the soil: they produce some of the nation's best *tef* (endemic cereal grain used for *the* national staple, injera).

Making up 30% of Ethiopia's population, they're the second-largest ethnic group. Over 90% of the Amharaland region's people are Amhara.

The Tigrayans

Much like the Amharas, the Tigrayans are fiercely independent and zealously attached to their land. They disdain all manual labour with the single exception of agriculture.

Most live in the Tigray region, where both Christianity and Islam were introduced to Ethiopia. Ninety-five per cent of Tigrayans are Orthodox Christian, and most devoutly so. Tigrayans are Ethiopia's third-largest ethnic group, comprising around 6% of the population.

As a result of the Tigrayan People's Liberation Front (TPLF) playing the major role in the bringing down of the Derg (see p46), many Tigrayans feature in Ethiopia's government, including Prime Minister Meles Zenawi. This has caused resentment among other groups.

The Somali

The arid lowlands of the southeast dictate a nomadic or seminomadic existence for the Somali. Somali society is 99% Muslim, strongly hierarchical, tightly knit and based on the clan system, which requires intense loyalty from its members. In the harsh environment in which they live, ferocious competition for the scant resources leads to frequent and sometimes violent disputes (thanks to an abundant supply of AK-47s) over grazing grounds and sources of water.

The Somali make up 95% of the Somali region's people, and 6% of Ethiopia's population.

The Afar

The Afar, formerly also known as the Danakils, inhabit the famous region of Dankalia, which stretches across Ethiopia's east, Djibouti's west and into Eritrea's southeast. It's considered one of earth's most inhospitable environments. Rightly or wrongly, they've proudly latched onto early-20th-century adventurer Wilfred Thesiger's portrayal of them as famously belligerent and proud. Thesiger wrote of the Afar winning social prestige in the past for murdering and castrating members of an opposing tribe.

The Afar comprise 4% of Ethiopia's population.

The Sidama

The Sidama, a heterogeneous people, originate from the southwest and can be divided into five different groups: the Sidama proper, the Derasa, Hadiya, Kambata and Alaba. Most Sidama are farmers who cultivate cereals, tobacco, *enset* (false-banana tree found in much of southern Ethiopia) and coffee. The majority are animists and many ancient beliefs persist, including a belief in the reverence of spirits. Pythons are believed to be reincarnations of ancestors and are sometimes kept as house pets. The Sidama social organisation, like the Oromo's *gada* system, is based on an age-group system.

The Sidama comprise about 3.5% of Ethiopia's population and most live in the Southern Nations, Nationalities and People's region.

The Gurage

Semitic in origin, the Gurage practise herding or farming, and the *enset* plant is their favoured crop. They are known as great workers, clever improvisers

AIDS IN ETHIOPIA

There's no denying that AIDS is a serious problem in Ethiopia, though infection rates have thankfully slowed fractionally (though are still rising) in urban areas over the past few years. Addis Ababa has the country's highest rate of AIDS, with 7.5% of its population infected. In rural areas the rate is a much lower 2.1%, but sadly this is increasing as well.

AIDS is now the single greatest threat to economic development in Ethiopia. Nearly half the deaths recorded in Addis Ababa in 2007 were HIV-AIDS related. The government continues to use hard-hitting warnings on TV and radio, as well as the ubiquitous posters around the country.

and skilled craftspeople. Many work as seasonal labourers for the highlanders. Their faith is Christian, Muslim or animist, depending on the area from which they originate.

They comprise only 2% of Ethiopia's population, but make up more than 10% of the population in the Southern Nations, Nationalities and People's region.

The Harari

Also Semitic in origin are the Harari people (sometimes known as Adare), who have long inhabited the walled Muslim city of Harar. The people are particularly known for their distinct two-storey houses, known as *gegar* (see the boxed text, p222), and for the very colourful traditional costumes still worn by many Harari women today. In the past, the Harari were known as great craftspeople for their weavings, baskets and bookbinding. They're also renowned Islamic scholars.

SPORT
Running

The popularity of running in Ethiopia took off in the 1960s when the marathon runner Abebe Bikila won gold medals at the Tokyo and Rome Olympics (famously running barefoot at the latter). Things were taken to another level by Haile Gebreselassie, one of the world's greatest distance runners of all time. Since 1992 he's managed to win two Olympic golds, nine World Championships and has set dozens of world records over distances between 3000m and 25km. In the last few years he's concentrated on marathons and has proved just as dominating in this field. Gebreselassie's most recent victories were at the 2008 Berlin Marathon and 2009 Dubai Marathon. Much to the disappointment of his countrymen, he pulled out of the 2008 Beijing Olympics marathon citing poor air quality.

The annual 10km Great Ethiopian Run (p96) attracts over 20,000 participants and is the largest mass-participation run in Africa.

Football

Ethiopians love their football (soccer). Throughout the country you'll see children chasing footballs – constructed of everything from plastic bags to rubber bands – through clouds of dust to the cheers of all.

Adults and kids alike have a passion for the English Premier League, with urban crowds piling around TVs to watch their two favourites, Manchester United and Arsenal.

There are seven Ethiopian Premier League teams in Addis Ababa alone and another nine across the country.

Other Sports

Ethiopia also boasts its own indigenous sports. *Genna* is a type of hockey without boundaries, traditionally played during the festival of Leddet. *Gugs* – a physical (and sometimes fairly violent) game of tag on horseback – is also most commonly seen at festivals, including Ethiopian new year and Meskel. In the past, the games prepared young warriors for war. Addis Ababa's Jan Meda Sports Ground is the best place to catch both *genna* and *gugs*.

Although entirely un-Ethiopian, table tennis and table football enjoy fanatical support. Even in the most obscure towns, tables line the dusty streets and are always in use. Don't step in unless you're pretty good and don't mind losing some money!

Carambula, which is a cueless version of pool (introduced by Italians), is also very popular.

Want to woo the locals and have some serious fun streetside? Hone your table-tennis and table-football skills before arriving!

MULTICULTURALISM

Ethiopia's mix of cultures has been pretty stable over the past few centuries, with only the expulsion of Eritrean citizens after the recent Ethiopia–Eritrea War, and influxes of Sudanese refugees into the western lowlands shifting the status quo.

Despite the nation's regions being divided along ethnic lines in 1995, there's still some resentment, particularly among the Oromo, that has led to violence over the fact that the minority Tigrayan and Amhara people maintain control of the national government.

Many travellers also notice that some Ethiopian highlanders, regardless of their ethnic background, seem to show a slight disdain for Ethiopians from the lowlands.

'Faith is an extremely important part of an Ethiopian's life.'

MEDIA

Ethiopian TV, Radio Ethiopia and the country's most widely circulated newspapers, the *Addis Zemen* and the *Ethiopian Herald,* are state controlled. You'll even notice that the Ministry of Information shares a building with Ethiopian TV!

After the May 2005 elections, the EU had harsh criticism of the state-owned media for regularly releasing unofficial results that highlighted the government's victories and virtually ignoring the victories of opposition parties. They blasted Radio Ethiopia and Ethiopian TV for 'completely ignoring' the press conferences and important statements given by opposition parties, information that CNN and the BBC thought newsworthy.

According to the BBC, when government forces opened fire on unarmed protesters in June and November 2005, state-owned media also severely under-reported civilian casualties.

Government censorship of private media is still present. Since 1992, when the 'Press Law' came into effect, numerous journalists have been arrested without trial for publishing critical articles of the government. The editor of *Agere* died untried in prison in 1998. Several owners of private media were arrested and their newspapers shut down during the postelectoral violence in 2005. Things have loosened up a little since then, though the government still holds two Eritrean and one Oromo journalist in prison.

RELIGION

Faith is an extremely important part of an Ethiopian's life. Orthodox Christians bring religion into everyday conversation just as much as their Muslim counterparts. Although Orthodox only slightly outnumber Muslims (50% to 32%), Christianity has traditionally dominated the country's past. The vast majority of highlanders are Orthodox and the religion continues to heavily influence the highlands' political, social and cultural scene. Most Muslims inhabit the eastern, southern and western lowlands, but there are also significant populations in the country's predominantly Christian towns, including Addis Ababa.

Ethiopian Orthodox Christianity

As the official religion of the imperial court right up until Emperor Haile Selassie was deposed in 1974, the Orthodox church continues to carry great clout among the Ethiopian people and is regarded as the great guardian and repository of ancient Ethiopian traditions, directly inherited from Aksum (p33).

Ethiopia was the second country (after Armenia) to adopt Christianity as its state religion and it's been a truly unifying factor over the centuries.

By the same measure, it's also legitimised the oppression of the people by its rulers.

Ethiopian Orthodox Christianity is thought to have its roots in Judaism – some even say that this is the home of the Lost Tribes of Israel. This Jewish connection explains the food restrictions, including the way animals are slaughtered. Even the traditional round church layout is considered Hebrew in origin. Ancient Semitic and pagan elements also persist.

Circumcision is generally practised on boys, marriage is celebrated in the presence of a priest, and confession is usually only made during a grave illness.

Islam

Ethiopia's connection with Islam is as distinguished as its connection with Christianity. Though bloody religious wars were fought in Ethiopia in the past, Ethiopia's Christian and Muslim inhabitants generally coexist in harmony. Fundamentalism is rare in Ethiopia, and it's uncommon to see women wearing the *hijab* (veil), though the majority wear either headscarves or *shalmas* (a gauze-thin length of fabric draped around the head, shoulders and torso).

'Traditional African beliefs are still practised by an estimated 11% of Ethiopia's population.'

Negash, in Tigray, where Islam was introduced in 615 AD and the shrine of Sheikh Hussein in the Bale region are both greatly venerated and attract national and international pilgrims.

The famous walled city of Harar is also an important Islamic centre in its own right and is home to an astonishing number of shrines and mosques. In the past, it was renowned as a centre of learning.

Traditional African Beliefs

Traditional African beliefs are still practised by an estimated 11% of Ethiopia's population, particularly in the lowland areas of the west and south. These range from the Konso's totemism (see the boxed text, p196) to animism (associated with trees, springs, mountains and stones), in which animals are ritually slaughtered and then consumed by the people. Elements of ancestor worship are still found among the Afar people. The Oromo traditionally believe in a supreme celestial deity known as Wak, whose eye is the sun.

The Falashas

Falashas (Ethiopian Jews) have inhabited Ethiopia since pre-Christian times. Despite actively engaging in wars over the years to defend their independence and freedom, few now remain: war, some persecution (though much less than seen elsewhere) and emigration in the latter part of the 20th century have greatly reduced their numbers.

In 1984 around 8000 Falashas fled Ethiopia and walked on foot to Sudan, where the Israeli and US secret services secretly airlifted them to Israel. A further operation took place in 1991, when 34 Israeli aircraft secretly transported some 14,325 Jews to Israel over a 36-hour period (by the time the planes had landed, there were actually two extra passengers as two women gave birth during their flights!).

Tiny populations of Falashas remain north of Lake Tana in the northwest of Ethiopia; their beliefs combine a fascinating mixture of Judaism, indigenous beliefs and Christianity.

WOMEN IN ETHIOPIA

Legally, women in Ethiopia enjoy a relatively equitable position compared with some African countries. They can own property, vote and are represented in government, though there are still some cases in which women's rights are impeded.

KNOW YOUR ETHIOPIAN SAINTS

In Ethiopia the air seems to be saturated with the stories of saints, magic, ghosts and monsters. For the majority of Ethiopians these tales are not wild legends, but solid fact. Don't be surprised if, on asking about the history of a church, you end up listening, spellbound, to a story so unlikely that you assume it's nothing but an ancient legend, only for the storyteller to turn around and announce that the events recounted happened just a year or so ago. As a traveller, it's important that you don't dismiss these stories out of hand. Ethiopians, like many Africans, live a life very different from those in the West. It's a life lived close to the rhythm of nature, in which the dead are never far away. Every Ethiopian has their favourite saint, and there's hardly an Ethiopian church not adorned with colourful, vibrant murals. In most cases the paintings follow a set pattern, depicting the important personalities of Ethiopia's peculiar pantheon of saints. Here's a quick key:

Abuna Aregawi One day while wandering at the foot of a cliff, Abuna Aregawi spotted a plateau high above him. Deciding it was the ideal spot for a nice, quiet hermit's life, he prayed to God for assistance. Immediately, a large python stretched down from above and lifted him onto the plateau. The famous monastery of Debre Damo was then founded. The saint is usually depicted riding up the snake.

Abuna Samuel He lived near the Takezze River, where he preached and performed many miracles, accompanied by a devoted lion. He is usually depicted astride his lion.

Belai the Cannibal Although not a saint, he's a favourite theme in religious art. Devouring anyone who approached him, including his own family, Belai yet took pity one day on a leper begging for water in the Virgin's name. After Belai died – some 72 human meals later – Satan claimed his soul. St Mikael, the judge, balanced Belai's victims on one side, the water on the other. However, the Virgin cast her shadow on the side of the scales containing the water, and caused them to tip. Belai's soul was saved.

Equestrian Saints They are usually depicted on the north wall of the Holy of Holies and may include Fasiladas, Claudius, Mercurius, Menas, Theodorus and George.

Mary Little known outside Ethiopia are the charming legends and miracles concerning Mary and the childhood of Jesus and the flight to Egypt. A tree is often depicted hiding the holy family – and the donkey – from Herod's soldiers during the flight to Egypt; the soldiers are confused by the sound of the donkey braying. Sometimes a furious Mary is shown scolding Jesus, who's managed to break a clay water jug.

St Eostateos Also known as St Thaddeus, he's said to have arrived in Ethiopia borne up the Nile from Egypt on three large stones. Apparently water continued to obey him: whenever the saint chose to cross a river or a lake, the waters parted conveniently before him.

St Gabriel God's messenger is usually represented cooling the flames of a fiery furnace or cauldron containing three youths condemned by Nebuchadnezzar: Meshach, Shadrach and Abednego.

St Gebre Kristos This Ethiopian prince sacrificed all his belongings to lead a life of chastity, and ended up a leprous beggar. He's usually depicted outside his palace, where only his dogs now recognise him.

St Gebre Manfus Kiddus While preaching peace to the animals in the desert, this saint came across a bird dying of thirst. Lifting it, he allowed the bird to drink the water from his eye. He's usually depicted clad in furs and girded with a hempen rope and surrounded by animals.

St George The patron saint of Ethiopia features in almost every church. He's depicted either as the king of saints, with St Bula – who at first refused to recognise his kingship – looking on petulantly in the background, or as the great dragon slayer on his horse.

St Mikael The judge of souls and the leader of the celestial army, St Mikael evicted Lucifer from heaven. In most churches, the portals to the Holy of Holies are guarded by a glowering Mikael, accompanied by Gabriel and Raphael.

St Raphael He rescued an Egyptian church from the tail of a thrashing beached whale and is usually depicted killing the whale with his spear.

St Tekla Haimanot The saint prayed for seven years standing on just one leg, until the other finally withered and fell off! Throughout, a bird brought him just one seed a year for sustenance. For his devotion, God awarded him no fewer than three sets of wings. The saint is normally depicted in his bishop's attire, surrounded by bells.

St Yared Ethiopia's patron saint of music is sometimes shown standing before his king with an orchestra of monks along with their *sistra* (sophisticated rattles), drums and prayer sticks. In the background, little birds in trees learn the magic of music.

Life for many women is extremely hard; to make ends meet many have to resort to extreme actions. Many foreigners are shocked to see just how many prostitutes there are in Ethiopia and just how openly it's practised. Put simply, prostitution doesn't have the same social stigma as it does in the West. Often prostitutes are just students trying to get by. Others are widows, divorcees or refugees, all with little or no hope of finding other

---

THE TABOT & THE ARK OF THE COVENANT

'Mounted on his stead and dressed in robes of mysterious colour and wearing vestments that his forefather King David had worn when he led the Ark of Zion into Jerusalem, King Iyasu rode past the priests and deacons who had lined the road to greet him and entered the sanctuary of the Ark. Here he requested that the Priests bring forth the Ark of Zion. When it's carried to him the Ark is locked in a chest with seven seals, each of which has its own key and own technique for opening. The first six seals are opened but when the priests get to the seventh seal it will not open. But then, when the King himself stands before the Ark, the seventh seal miraculously springs open and the King speaks to the Ark and it replies and advises him on how to rule wisely.'

From the Royal Chronicles of King Iyasu, *1691.*

Few other objects in history match the enduring legend of the Ark of the Covenant. But what is this Ark and is it really sitting quietly inside a tacky Aksum chapel? The Old Testament says that the Ark was constructed on Mt Sinai by Moses, and that it houses the two stone tablets on which are inscribed the Ten Commandments. It is also said to contain the Rod of Aaron and a jar of mannah. Other more recent descriptions of its contents include that of 17th-century Ethiopian Emperor Susenyos, who, when asked by a Portuguese Jesuit to describe the contents of the Ark, said that it contained the 'figure of a woman with very large breasts'. Such a figure was common in ancient fertility beliefs.

In Old Testament days the Ark was housed in King Solomon's Great Temple in Jerusalem and was used by the Israelites as an oracle. It was also carried into battle. After the sacking of the Great Temple in 587 BC, the Bible falls silent as to the Ark's whereabouts – some say it was buried in a secret chamber under the Temple Mount in Jerusalem, and others say it was destroyed. But according to Ethiopian tradition, the Ark of the Covenant was carried off from Jerusalem and brought to Ethiopia in the 1st millennium BC by Menelik, the son of Solomon and Sheba. It's now believed to sit in Aksum's St Mary of Zion church compound (see p135).

Today, every other Ethiopian church has a replica of the Ark (or more precisely the Tablets of Law that are housed in the Ark) known as the *tabot*. Kept safe in the *maqdas* (Holy of Holies or inner sanctuary), it's the church's single most important element, and gives the building its sanctity (rather as the tabernacle does in the Roman Catholic Church).

During important religious festivals, the *tabot* is carried in solemn processions, accompanied by singing, dancing, the beating of staffs or prayer sticks, the rattling of the sistrum (a sophisticated rattle, thought to be directly descended from an ancient Egyptian instrument used to worship Isis) and the beating of drums. It's a scene that could have come straight out of the Old Testament:

'They carried the Ark of God on a new cart…David and all the house of Israel were dancing before the Lord with all their might, with songs and lyres and harps and tambourines and castanets and cymbals.'

2 Sam. v. 3–5

That the chapel at Aksum contains something of great spiritual significance is undoubted, but is it the real Ark of the Covenant? The simple answer is that nobody actually knows. The biggest problem with Ethiopia's claim for the Ark is that if it was brought to the country by Menelik I, then why is its presence not widely mentioned in written documents until the 17th century? At the end of the day though, does it really matter what exactly is inside that Aksum chapel? The very fact that many people believe that this chapel contains the word of God should be enough to make it real.

forms of employment. With no social security system, it's often their only means of survival. Though not exactly a respected profession, prostitution is considered a perfectly viable means of making a living. HIV-AIDS levels among prostitutes is thought to be close to 50% in Addis Ababa. Outside the city, men should be warned that almost all women in bars are prostitutes.

Many Ethiopian women also have to endure the practice of female genital mutilation, (genital cutting). The UN has stated that 74% of Ethiopian women between the ages of 15 and 49 have undergone some form of female genital mutilation; in the Somali regions of Ethiopia this figure rises to 97%.

Reasons given in the Horn for genital mutilation vary from hygiene and aesthetics to superstitions that uncut women can't conceive. Others believe that the strict following of traditional beliefs is crucial to maintaining social cohesion, much like male circumcision is to Jews. Some also say that it prevents female promiscuity.

No matter what the reason, there's no doubt that female genital mutilation brings enormous physical pain and suffering. An estimated 15% of girls die postoperatively and those who survive suffer countless ongoing complications and pain, as well as untold psychological suffering.

For information about travelling in Ethiopia as a woman, see p257.

The 1984 evacuation of Ethiopian Jews to Israel was captured in an Israeli–French film, *Live and Become* (2005).

ARTS

The church, traditionally enjoying almost as much authority as the state, is responsible for both inspiring Ethiopia's art forms and stifling them with its great conservatism and rigorous adherence to convention.

Long neglected and ignored, the cultural contributions of Ethiopia's other ethnic groups are only now receiving due credit and attention.

Music

Whether it's the solemn sounds of drums resonating from a church, the hilarious ad-libbing of an *azmari* (see the boxed text, p60) or Ethiopian pop blaring in a bus, Ethiopian music is as interesting as it's unavoidable.

Ethiopian music CDs are available throughout the country. Music stalls are everywhere – keep an ear out. Older cassette versions are usually only found in Addis Ababa.

CHURCH MUSIC

Yared the Deacon is traditionally credited with inventing church music, with the introduction in the 6th century of a system of musical notation.

Aquaquam (church music) uses resonating drums – the *kabaro* and the *tsinatseil* (sistrum; a sophisticated rattle, thought to be directly descended from an ancient Egyptian instrument used to worship Isis). Percussion instruments are primarily used since their function is to mark the beat for chanting and dancing. The *maquamia* (prayer stick) also plays an essential role in church ceremonies and, with hand-clapping, is used to mark time. Very occasionally a *meleket* (trumpet) is used, such as to lead processions.

You'll get plenty of opportunities to hear church music in Ethiopia. In the solemn and sacred atmosphere of the old churches, with the colour of the priestly robes and the heady perfume of incense, it can be quite mesmerising.

SECULAR MUSIC

Strongly influenced by church music, secular music usually combines song and dance, emphasises rhythm, and often blends both African and Asian

---

MINSTRELS & MASENKOS

An ancient entertainment that continues to this day is that provided by the singing *azmari* (wandering minstrel) and his *masenko* (single-stringed fiddle). In the past, the *azmari* accompanied caravans of highland traders to make the journey more amusing.

At court, resident *azmaris*, like European jesters, were permitted great freedom of expression as long as their verses were witty, eloquent and clever.

Today, *azmaris* can be found at weddings and special occasions furnishing eulogies or poetic ballads in honour of their hosts.

In certain *azmari beats* (azmari bars) in the larger towns, some *azmaris* have become celebrities in their own right. They prance around grass-covered floors and sing about everything from history to sex, to your funny haircut. Although you won't understand a word (it's all in Amharic), you'll end up laughing; the locals' laughter is simply that contagious. And remember these two things: it's all done in good fun, and really your haircut isn't that bad!

---

elements. The Amharas' and Tigrayans' highland music, as well as that of the peoples living near the Sudanese border, is much influenced by Arab music, and is very strident and emotive.

Wind and percussion instruments are used. The *begenna* is a type of harp similar to that played by the ancient Greeks and Romans. The most popular instrument in Ethiopia is the *krar,* a five- or six-stringed lyre, which is often heard at weddings or used to attract customers to traditional pubs or bars.

In the highlands, particularly the Simien and Bale Mountains, shepherd boys can be found with reed flutes. The *washint* is about 50cm long, with four holes, and makes a bubbling sound that is said to imitate running water. It's supposed to keep the herds close by and calm the animals.

Modern composers and performers include Tesfaye Lemma, Mulatu Astatike and Tefera Abunewold.

SONG

Traditionally passed down from generation to generation, every ethnic group has their own repertoire of songs, from *musho* (household songs) and *lekso* (laments for the dead) to war songs, hunting songs and lullabies for the cradle and caravan.

Ethiopian male singing in the highlands is often in falsetto. The most characteristic element of female singing is the high-pitched trilling. The tremulous and vibrating ululations can be heard on solemn, religious occasions.

Modern, traditional singers to look out for include Habtemikael Demissie, Yirga Dubale, Tadesse Alemu and the female singer Maritu Legeese.

MODERN MUSIC

Ethiopian modern music is diverse and affected by outside influences, and ranges from classical Amharic to jazz and pop. Modern classical singers and musicians include the late Assefa Abate, Kassa Tessema and the female vocalist Asnakech Worku. The latter two are known for their singing and *krar* playing. Girma Achanmyeleh, who studied in England, is known for his piano playing. The composer Mulatu Astatike is well known for his jazz.

Amharic popular music boasts a great following with the young. Unlike many other African countries, it's generally much preferred to Western music, and can be heard in all the larger towns' bars and discos. For most Westerners, Ethiopian music is a little like Ethiopian food – an acquired taste!

The most famous Ethiopian pop singers have huge followings, both in Ethiopia and among the expat populations abroad. Many either record and live or spend time in America. Among the best known (and those to listen out for) is Tewodros Kassahun ('Teddy Afro') whose political album *Yaasteseryal,* which was released in 2005 during a time of heightened political tension following disputed elections, got him on the wrong side of the government, but sent his popularity sky-rocketing. Four songs from the album were eventually banned by the government. In 2008 he was jailed after being involved in a hit-and-run accident; though many believe the jail sentence was also politically motivated. Other names to watch out for are Ephrem Tamiru, Tsehaye Yohannes, Berhane Haile and Ali Bira.

Female artists more than hold their own. Gonder-born, American-based Aster Aweke has produced 20 albums since the late 1970s. She's popularly known as Africa's Aretha Franklin. Her early works are only found in cassette form in Addis Ababa. Hot on Aster's tail for international fame is Ejigaheyehu Shibabaw (known as 'Gigi'), who rose to prominence after her 1997 album *Tsehay.* Her singing was heard in the Hollywood movie *Beyond Borders.* A relative newcomer to the scene is Zeritu Kebede (also known as 'Baby').

Francis Falceto, an Ethiopian music expert, compiles popular Ethiopian contemporary music into great CDs known as 'Ethiopiques'. Twenty-three volumes have been produced to date; pick them up from www.budamusique.com or download tracks at www.emusic.com.

Dance

Dance forms an extremely important part of the lives of most Ethiopians, and almost every ethnic group has its own distinct variety. Although the *iskista* – in which the shoulders are juddered up and down and backwards and forwards, in a careful rhythm, while the hips and legs stay motionless – is the best known, there are myriad others.

Dance traditionally serves a variety of important social purposes: from celebrating religious festivities (such as the *shibsheba,* a priestly dance), to celebrating social occasions such as weddings and funerals and, in the past, to motivating warriors before departing for battle.

Still found in rural areas are dances in praise of nature, such as after a good harvest or when new sources of water are discovered, and dances that allow the young 'warriors' to show off their agility and athleticism. Look out for the *fukara* (boasting dance), which is often performed at public festivals. A leftover from less peaceful times, it involves a man holding a spear, stick or rifle horizontally above his shoulders at the same time as moving his head from side to side and shouting defiantly at the 'enemy'.

Among the tribes of the Omo Valley in the south, many dances incorporate jumping and leaping up and down, a little like the dances of Kenya's Maasai. All dancing is in essence a social, communal activity, and you'll often be expected to join in. If you do give it a go, you'll win a lot of friends! Declining to dance can infer a slight.

OUR TOP FIVE MODERN ETHIOPIAN MUSIC CD PICKS

- *Yasstesseriyal* by Tewodros Kassahun
- *Gigi* by Ejigaheyehu Shibabaw
- *Ebo* by Aster Aweke
- *Zeritu* by Zeritu Kebede
- *Zion Roots* by Abyssinia Infinite

Literature

Literature has a long and illustrious history in Ethiopia. Inscriptions in Ge'ez, a South Semitic language, have been found to date as far back as 2500 years; though it wasn't until Aksumite times that it became widely used as a language of literature. It was during this early period that the Bible was translated from Greek into Ge'ez.

Even though Ge'ez had long since died as a spoken language, the 13th and 14th centuries are considered to mark the golden age of Ge'ez literature, in which many works were translated from Arabic, as well as much original writing produced. It's thought that in the early 14th century the Kebra Negast (below) was written.

During the 16th-century Muslim–Christian wars, book production ground to a halt and copious amounts of literature were destroyed. By the 17th century, Ge'ez was in decline as a literary language, but that didn't mean the value of books had been lost. It's around this time that rumours spread of a vast library hidden on the mysterious flat-topped mountain of Amba Gishen. Inside the library's endless halls could be found every kind of book, including the works of Job and Abraham and the lost Book of Enoch. What makes this tale so extraordinary is that in 1773 a Ge'ez version of the lost Book of Enoch was discovered in Ethiopia (to this day it remains the only complete copy ever found).

Amharic, now Ethiopia's official language, was the Amharas' language. It was Emperor Tewodros who encouraged the local language in an attempt to promote national unity. In a continuation of the trend begun in the 14th century, Tewodros and other emperors right up to Haile Selassie funded writers whose compositions and poetic laudatory songs were written to praise the ruler's qualities and munificence.

Under the Derg (p44), both writing and writers were suppressed. Be'alu Girma is a well-known example of one of the many artists who disappeared during their reign.

For a full translation of the Kebra Negast, check out www.sacred-texts .com/chr/kn/.

POETRY

Written in Amharic as well as other Ethiopian languages, poetry, along with dance and music, is used on many religious and social occasions, such as weddings or funerals. Rhymed verse is almost always chanted or sung in consonance with the rhythm of music.

Poetry places great stress on meaning, metaphor and allusion. In Ge'ez poetry, the religious allusions demand an in-depth knowledge of Ethiopian religious legends and the Bible.

FOLK LITERATURE

Perhaps the source of the greatest originality and creativity is the vast folk literature of Ethiopia, most of it in oral form and existing in all languages

---

KEBRA NEGAST

Written during the 14th century by an unknown author(s), the Kebra Negast (Glory of Kings) is considered Ethiopia's great national epic. Like the Quran to Muslims or the Old Testament to Jews, it's a repository of Ethiopian national, religious and cultural sentiment.

It's notoriously shrouded in mystery, perhaps deliberately so. Some controversially suggest it may even represent a massive propaganda stunt to legitimise the rule of the so-called 'Solomonic kings', who came to power in the 13th century and who, the book claims, were direct descendants of the kings of Israel.

Its most important legend is that of Solomon and Sheba (see the boxed text, p50).

and dialects. It encompasses everything from proverbs, tales and riddles to magic spells and prophetic statements. For a country in which most of the population have always (and continue) to be illiterate, folk literature has been the method by which the nation's history has been passed down from one generation to the next. As a local expression goes, 'Every time an old person passes away, it's as if a whole library were lost'.

Architecture

Ethiopia boasts some remarkable historical architecture. Though some monuments, such as the castles of Gonder, show foreign influence, earlier building styles, such as those developed during the Aksumite period, are believed to be wholly indigenous and are of a high technical standard.

ASKUMITE ARCHITECTURE

The 'Aksumite style' of stone masonry is Ethiopia's most famous building style. Walls were constructed with field stones set in mortar, along with sometimes finely dressed corner stones. In between came alternating layers of stone and timber, and protruding ends of round timber beams, known as 'monkey heads'. The latter are even symbolically carved into Aksum's great obelisks (see p134), which may just be the nation's greatest architectural achievements. The Aksumites were undoubtedly master masons.

The best examples of Aksumite buildings are seen at Debre Damo and the church of Yemrehanna Kristos (p164).

The Aksumite style is additionally seen in Lalibela's rock-hewn churches, as well as in modern design today. Keep an eye out for the ancient motifs in new hotel and restaurant designs.

ROCK-HEWN ARCHITECTURE

Ethiopia's rock-hewing tradition probably predates Christianity and has resulted in nearly 400 churches across the country. The art form reached its apogee in the 12th and 13th centuries in Lalibela, where the Zagwe dynasty produced 11 churches that continue to astound. They're considered among the world's finest early Christian architecture.

The churches are unique in that many stand completely free from the rock, unlike similar structures in Jordan and Egypt. The buildings show extraordinary technical skill in the use of line, proportion and decoration, and in the remarkable variety of styles.

The rock-hewn churches of the Tigray region, though less famous and spectacular, are no less remarkable.

GONDER ARCHITECTURE

The town of Gonder and its imperial enclosure represent another peak in Ethiopian architectural achievement. Although Portuguese, Moorish and

---

ETHIOPIAN HOUSES

Ethiopian houses are famously diverse; each ethnic group has developed its own design according to its own lifestyle and resources.

In general, the round *tukul* (hut) forms the basis of most designs. Circular structures and conical thatched roofs better resist the wind and heavy rain. Windows and chimneys are usually absent. The smoke, which escapes through the thatch, fumigates the building, protecting it against insect infestations such as termites.

Sometimes the huts are shared: the right side for the family, the left for the animals. Livestock are not only protected from predators, but in some regions they also provide central heating!

Indian influences are all evident, the castles are nevertheless a peculiarly Ethiopian synthesis. Some have windows decorated with red volcanic tuff, and barrel- or egg-shaped domes.

Painting

Traditionally, Ethiopian painting is largely limited to religious subjects, particularly the life of Christ and the saints. Every church in Ethiopia is decorated with abundant and colourful murals, frescos or paintings.

Much Ethiopian painting is characterised by a naive realism. Everything is expressed with vigour and directness using bold colour, strong line and stylised proportions and perspective. Like the stained-glass windows in European Gothic churches, the paintings served a very important purpose: to instruct, inspire and instil awe in the illiterate and uneducated.

Though some modern artists (particularly painters of religious and some secular work) continue in the old tradition (or incorporate ancient motifs such as that of the Aksumite stelae), many artists have developed their own style. Borrowing freely from the past, but no longer constrained by it, modern Ethiopian painting shows greater originality of expression and is now a flourishing medium.

Among the young painters to look out for are Behailu Bezabeh, an acute observer of everyday life in the capital; Daniel Taye, who is known for his darker, more disturbing images; Geta Makonnen, whose artwork addresses social issues; the sculptor Bekele Makonnen, with his thought-provoking installations revolving around moral and social values; and Tigist Hailegabreal, a versatile young woman artist who's concerned with women's issues such as prostitution and violence against women.

The vast stained-glass window in Addis Ababa's Africa Hall (p94) is the work of one of Africa's best-known painters, Afewerk Tekle (see the boxed text, p93).

Arts & Crafts

Ethiopia boasts a particularly rich tradition of arts and crafts. This is partly due to the wide range of raw materials available, from gold to good hardwood and fine highland wool. Additionally, the number and diversity of the country's ethnic groups (64 according to some reckon-

ILLUMINATED MANUSCRIPTS

Without doubt, illuminated manuscripts represent one of Ethiopia's greatest artistic achievements. The best-quality manuscripts were created by monks and priests in the 14th and 15th centuries. The kings, the court and the largest and wealthiest churches and monasteries were the main patrons. The manuscripts were characterised by beautifully shaped letters, attention to minute detail and elaborate ornamentation. Pictures included in the text brought it to life and made it more comprehensible for the uneducated or illiterate.

Bindings consisted of thick wooden boards often covered with tooled leather. The volume was then placed into a case with straps made of rough hides so that it could be slung over a shoulder.

On the blank pages at the beginning or at the end of the volume, look out for the formulae *fatina bere* (literally 'trial of the pen') or *bere' sanay* (literally 'a fine pen'), as the scribes tried out their reeds. Some are also dated and contain a short blessing for the owner, as well as the scribe.

Sadly, due to the Muslim and the Dervish raids of the early 16th and late 19th centuries respectively, few manuscripts date prior to the 14th century. Modern times have seen huge numbers being pillaged by soldiers, travellers and explorers.

ings), and the differing needs arising from the different environments, have ensured this.

Traditional arts and crafts include basketware (Harar is considered the centre), paintings, musical instruments, pottery, hornwork, leatherwork and woodcarving. The best woodwork traditionally comes from Jimma in western Ethiopia, where forests of tropical and temperate hardwoods once flourished. The Gurage and Sidamo also work wood.

Other crafts include metalwork (materials range from gold and silver to brass, copper and iron, and products include the famous and diverse Ethiopian crosses), as well as weaving. The Konso are known for their woollen products; the Gurage and Dorze for their cotton products, which include the famous *kemis* (traditional women's dresses) and *shamma* (togas) of the highlander men. Special skills are particularly required for making the ornate and beautifully coloured *tibeb* (borders) of the women's *natala* (shawls). Debre Berhan is considered the capital of rug making.

Remember that if you're buying authentic crafts, ensure that they aren't made from indigenous woods or wildlife products.

Theatre

Ethiopia boasts one of Africa's most ancient, prolific and flourishing theatrical traditions. Because theatre is written mainly in Amharic, however, it's practically unknown outside the country. Having largely resisted European influence, it's also preserved its own very local flavour and outlook.

Ethiopian theatrical conventions include minimal drama, sparse characterisation (with actors often serving as symbols) and plenty of extended speeches. Verse form is still often used and rhetoric remains a very important element of Ethiopian plays. Audiences tend to be participatory. Modern playwrights include Ayalneh Mulatu.

There are usually a few productions put on each week in Addis Ababa (see p104 for venues).

Cinema

Ethiopia, which was never colonised, missed out on the 'benefit' of colonial support for setting up a film industry enjoyed by other African countries in the 1950s and '60s.

Solomon Bekele was one of the pioneers of Ethiopian cinema and is best known for his Amharic feature film *Aster*. Easily Ethiopia's most famous English-speaking film-maker is Haile Gerima, whose latest film *Teza* (released in early 2008), which focuses on life under the Derg, has been a massive hit in Ethiopia and was awarded the main prize at the 2009 Fespaco (the most prestigious African film festival) event in Burkina Faso. At the time of writing *Teza* was not yet available for general release on DVD, though when it does its success means it will probably be fairly easy to come across outside of Ethiopia. Gerima's other big success was his 2000 film *Adwa*.

'Ethiopia boasts one of Africa's most ancient, prolific and flourishing theatrical traditions.'

Food & Drink

The image of Ethiopia abroad is of a country still haunted by famine and yes, it's true, Ethiopian Airlines really does get people asking if they'll be fed on-board. So, it might come as a surprise to learn that Ethiopian food, and the myriad ways in which it's prepared, is some of the most diverse on the continent.

Not just is this food diverse, it's also unique and it would be safe to say that Ethiopia's food is much like Ethiopia itself, completely different from anything you may have experienced anywhere else. Plates, bowls and even utensils are replaced by injera, a one of its kind pancake of countrywide proportions. Atop its rubbery confines can sit anything from spicy meat stews to colourful dollops of boiled veg and cubes of raw beef.

Whether it's the spices joyfully bringing a tear to your eye or the slightly sour taste of the clammy injera sending your tongue into convulsions, one thing's for sure, Ethiopian fare provokes a strong reaction in all and though you might not always enjoy it, you'll never forget it.

STAPLES & SPECIALITIES

If you want to save yourself some embarrassment (unlike us), never inhale as you're placing injera laden with *berbere* into your mouth.

Popular breakfast dishes include *enkulal tibs* (scrambled eggs made with a combination of green and red peppers, tomatoes and sometimes onions, served with bread), *ful* (chickpea and butter purée) and *injera fir fir* (torn-up injera mixed with butter and *berbere*, a red powder containing as many as 16 spices or more).

At lunch and dinner the much heralded Ethiopian staples of *wat, kitfo* and *tere sega* come out to play with the ever-present injera.

Injera

Just like your first kiss, your first taste of injera is an experience you'll never forget.

It's the national staple and the base of almost every meal. It is spread out like a large, thin pancake, and food is simply heaped on top of it. An American tourist is said to have once mistaken it for the tablecloth. Occasionally, injera is served rolled up beside the food or on a separate plate, looking much like a hot towel on an aeroplane.

Just like your first kiss, most first impressions of injera are not too positive! The overwhelmingly sour taste can be enough to make some people retch (though we hope you didn't do that on your first kiss!), but give it another few mouthfuls and it'll start to grow on you. The sour taste contrasts beautifully with the fiery sauces it's normally served with. Like bread, it's filling; like a pancake, it's good for wrapping around small pieces of food and mopping up juices. It's also much easier to manipulate on the plate than rice and it doesn't fall apart like bread – all up injera is quite a clever invention, really.

Although injera may look like old grey kitchen flannel, grades and nuances do exist. With a bit of time and perseverance, you may even become a connoisseur.

Low-quality injera is traditionally dark, coarse and sometimes very thick, and is made from millet or even sorghum. Good-quality injera is pale (the paler the better), regular in thickness, smooth (free of husks) and *always* made with the indigenous Ethiopian cereal *tef*. Because *tef* grows only in the highlands, the best injera is traditionally found there, and highlanders tend to be rather snooty about lesser lowland versions.

Wat

The ubiquitous companion of injera, *wat* is Ethiopia's version of curry and can be very spicy – fortunately the injera helps to temper the heat.

In the highlands, *bege* (lamb) is the most common constituent of *wat*. *Bure* (beef) is encountered in the large towns, and *figel* (goat) most often in the arid lowlands. Chicken is the king of the *wat* and *doro wat* is practically the national dish. Ethiopian Christians as well as Muslims avoid pork. On fasting days, and throughout Lent, meat dishes are avoided and various vegetarian versions of *wat* are available.

Kai wat is a stew of meat boiled in a spicy (thanks to oodles of *berbere*) red sauce. *Kai* sauce is also used for *minchet abesh,* which is a thick minced-meat stew topped with a hard-boiled egg – it's one of our favourites, particularly with *aib* (like dry cottage cheese).

Most Ethiopians seem to be under the impression that all foreigners are terrified of spicy food and so, unless you specifically ask for *kai wat,* you'll often be served the yellow coloured *alicha wat,* a much milder, and really rather dull tasting *wat.*

> If you become a massive fan of *kitfo* or *tere sega,* best get tested for tape worms (see p373) when you get home. Hopefully there'll be no pain to go with your tasty gain.

Kitfo

Kitfo is a big treat for the ordinary Ethiopian. The leanest meat is reserved for this dish, which is then minced and warmed in a pan with a little butter, *berbere* and sometimes *tosin* (thyme). It can be bland and disgusting, or tasty and divine. If you're ravenous after a hard day's travelling, it's just the ticket, as it's very filling. A tip? Ask for a heap of *berbere* on the side.

Traditionally, it's served just *leb leb* (warmed not cooked), though you can ask for it to be *betam leb leb* (literally 'very warmed', ie cooked!). A *kitfo* special is served with *aib* and *gomen* (minced spinach).

In the Gurage region (where it's something of a speciality) it's often served with *enset* (*kotcho;* false-banana 'bread'). *Kitfo beats* (restaurants specialising in *kitfo*) are found in the larger towns.

Another favourite meat dish of ours is *siga tibs,* which consists of small strips of fried meat served with onions, garlic and spices.

Tere Sega

Considered something of a luxury in Ethiopia, *tere sega* (raw meat) is traditionally served by the wealthy at weddings and other special occasions.

TASTY TRAVEL

With raw meat being a staple in Ethiopia, what dishes could possibly constitute a radical departure for those wishing to truly travel their tastebuds?

High on the exotic factor would have to be *trippa wat* (tripe stew), which still curls our toes and shakes our stomachs. And if unleavened bread that's been buried in an underground pit and allowed to ferment for at least a month suits your fancy, order some *enset* with your *kitfo*. Enset is made from the false banana plant and closely resembles a fibrous carpet liner.

Fermentation of an entirely different sort can lead you down a very different path. If you're not catching an early bus the next morning, try the local *araki,* a grain spirit that will make you positively gasp (some travellers liken it to a stronger version of Greek ouzo). The Ethiopians believe it's good for high blood pressure! *Dagem araki* is twice-filtered and is finer. It's usually found in local hole-in-the-wall bars.

For something a little stronger, how about knocking back a shot of the holy water used at the Debre Libanos Monastery to wash the 1500-year-old leg of Saint Tekla Haimanot? See the boxed text on p111 for more.

Some restaurants also specialise in it. Not unlike butcher shops in appearance, these places feature carcasses hanging near the entrance and men in bloodied overalls brandishing carving knives. The restaurants aren't as gruesome as they sound: the carcass is to demonstrate that the meat is fresh, and the men in overalls to guarantee you get the piece you fancy – two assurances you don't always get in the West.

A plate and a sharp knife serve as utensils, and *awazi* (a kind of mustard and chilli sauce) and *berbere* as accompaniments. Served with some local red wine, and enjoyed with Ethiopian friends, it's a ritual not to be missed – at least not for red-blooded meat eaters. It's sometimes called *gored gored.*

DRINKS

Ethiopia has a well-founded claim to be the original home of coffee (see the boxed text, p234), and coffee continues to be ubiquitous across the country. As a result of Italian influence, *macchiato* (espresso with a dash of milk), cappuccino and a kind of cafe latte known as a *buna bewetet* (coffee with milk) are also available in many of the towns. Sometimes the herb rue (known locally as *t'ena adam,* or health of Adam) is served with coffee, as is butter. In the western highlands, a layered drink of coffee and tea is also popular. If you want milk with coffee, ask for *betinnish wetet* (with a little milk).

In lowland Muslim areas, *shai* (tea) is preferred to coffee, and is offered black, sometimes spiced with cloves or ginger.

Most cafes also dabble in fresh juice, though it's usually dosed with sugar. If you don't want sugar in your juice or in your tea or coffee, make it clear when you order. Ask for the drink *yale sukkar* (without sugar). Bottled water is always available, as is the local favourite Ambo, a natural sparkling mineral water from western Ethiopia.

One drink not to be missed is *tej,* a delicious – and sometimes pretty powerful – local 'wine' or mead made from honey, and fermented using a local shrub known as *gesho. Tej* used to be reserved only for Ethiopian kings and their court and comes in many varieties. It's served in little flasks known as *birille.*

There are several breweries in Ethiopia that pump out decent beers like Harar, Bati, Meta, Bedele, Dashen and Castel. Everyone has a different favourite, so explore at will.

Though no cause for huge celebration, local wine isn't at all bad, particularly the red Gouder. Of the whites, the dry Awash Crystal is about the best bet. Unless you're an aficionado of sweet red, avoid Axumite. Outside Addis Ababa, wine is usually only served in the restaurants of midrange hotels.

It doesn't seem to matter how remote you are, all the standard international soft drinks are available everywhere, all of the time.

Finally, in the Somali regions in the east, camel milk is a speciality. Locals claim that it gives most foreigners the shits, but we can happily report that our stomachs are stronger than that!

Contrary to the myth started by 18th-century Scottish explorer James Bruce, Ethiopians don't carve meat from living animals. Whether it occurred in ancient times, remains uncertain.

If looking for quality *tej,* ask a local. They'll know who makes it with pure honey and who cheats by adding sugar.

REACHING THE PARTS OTHERS CAN'T

Did we say that soft drinks (sodas) were always available everywhere you go? Well not in March 2009 they weren't. The global credit crisis hit Ethiopia as well and while stock markets may not have crashed in Addis the country did run out of bottle tops. All of which meant that even in Addis Ababa a bottle of Coca-Cola was as rare as a Buddhist temple in Lalibela!

THE COFFEE CEREMONY

The coffee ceremony typifies Ethiopian hospitality. An invitation to attend a ceremony is a mark of friendship or respect, though it's not an event for those in a hurry.

When you're replete after a meal, the ceremony begins. Freshly cut grass is scattered on the ground 'to bring in the freshness and fragrance of nature'. Nearby, there's an incense burner smoking with *etan* (gum). The 'host' sits on a stool before a tiny charcoal stove.

First of all coffee beans are roasted in a pan. As the smoke rises, it's considered polite to draw it towards you, inhale it deeply and express great pleasure at the delicious aroma by saying *betam tiru no* (lovely!). Next the beans are ground up with a pestle and mortar before being brewed up.

When it's finally ready, the coffee is served in tiny china cups with at least three spoonfuls of sugar. At least three cups must be accepted. The third in particular is considered to bestow a blessing – it's the *berekha* (blessing) cup. Sometimes popcorn is passed around. It should be accepted with two hands extended and cupped together.

Enjoy!

CELEBRATIONS

Food plays a major role in religious festivals of both Muslims and Ethiopian Orthodox Christians. During the month of Ramadan, Muslims fast between sunrise and sunset, while Ethiopian Orthodox abstain from eating any animal products in the 55 days leading up to Ethiopian Easter.

Orthodox Ethiopians also abstain from animal products each Wednesday and Friday. There are a very large number of Orthodox feast days, of which 33 honour the Virgin Mary alone.

While it has no religious connotations, Ethiopians have even taken to celebrating the serving of coffee (see the boxed text above).

WHERE TO EAT & DRINK

Outside Addis Ababa and major towns, there isn't a plethora of eating options. You're usually constrained to small local restaurants that serve one pasta dish and a limited selection of Ethiopian food. If there's no menu, use the 'Eat Your Words' section (p70) to inquire what's available. In larger towns, local restaurants and hotels both offer numerous Ethiopian meals. The hotels' menus also throw some, normally very forgettable, Western meals into the mix.

Kitfo beats are specialist restaurants in larger towns that primarily serve *kitfo*. Similarly *tej beats* are bars that focus on serving *tej*.

Unlike Addis Ababa, where restaurant hours vary widely, most restaurants elsewhere are open daily from around 7.30am to 10pm. *Tej beats* tend to open later (around 10am), but also close about 10pm.

Quick Eats

What have the Romans done for us? Fancy fluffy cakes are the last thing you'd associate with Ethiopia, but like Monty Python's Romans, the Italians did do something right. Cafes and pastry/cake shops *(keak beats)* are common in all big towns and their sweet treats and steaming caffeine top-ups will tempt you off the street time and again. Fresh juices are usually available at each.

Outside town, roadside snacks such as *kolo* (roasted barley), *bekolo* (popcorn) and fresh fruit make great between-meal fillers.

VEGETARIAN & VEGANS

On Wednesday, Friday and throughout the build up to Fasika (Lent), vegetarians breathe easy as these are the traditional fasting days, when no animal

---

ETHIOPIA'S TOP FIVE RESTAURANTS

■ **Serenade** (p101) Although up a dark alley, it is a vibrant and flavourful place that'll make your tastebuds scream for joy. Heaven for vegetarians.

■ **Habesha Restaurant** (p101) Serving is an art form at this quality Ethiopian eatery.

■ **Shangri-la Restaurant** (p102) Sit by the fire and cosy up to your *tere sega* (raw meat).

■ **Ristorante Castelli** (p102) In a country where almost every restaurant serves spaghetti, Castelli's is the first prince of pasta.

■ **Gheralta Lodge** (p151) The Italian boss of this superb up-country lodge is a member of the Slow Food Association and his devotion to the art of eating shows. People beg to eat his Italian and Ethiopian meals.

---

products should be eaten. Ethiopian fasting food most commonly includes *messer* (lentil curry), *gomen* (collard greens) and *kai iser* (beetroot).

Apart from fasting days, Ethiopians are rapacious carnivores and vegetables are often conspicuous by their complete absence. If you're vegetarian or vegan, the best plan is to order alternative dishes in advance. If not, some dishes such as *shiro* (chickpea purée) are quite quickly prepared. Note that fancier hotels tend to offer fasting food seven days a week.

If you're really concerned about available vegetarian food then the best bet is to come during the 55 days proceeding Fasika (p249). It's also a good idea to keep a small stack of vegetarian snacks on hand.

HABITS & CUSTOMS

Eating from individual plates strikes most Ethiopians as hilarious, as well as rather bizarre and wasteful. In Ethiopia, food is always shared from a single plate without the use of cutlery.

In many cases, with a simple *Enebla!* (Please join us!), people invite those around them (even strangers) to join them at their restaurant table. For those invited, it's polite to accept a morsel of the food to show appreciation.

In households and many restaurants, a jug of water and basin are brought out to wash the guests' outstretched hands before the meal. Guests remain seated throughout (though it's polite to make a gesture of getting up if the person serving is older).

When eating with locals, try not to guzzle. Greed is considered rather uncivilised. The tastiest morsels will often be laid in front of you; it's polite to accept them or, equally, to divide them among your fellow diners. The meat dishes such as *doro wat* are usually the last thing locals eat off the injera, so don't hone in on it immediately!

When attracting someone's attention, such as a waiter or porter, it's polite to call *yikerta* (excuse me) or to simply clap your hands. Whistling or snapping your fingers, by contrast, is considered rude. Don't be offended if waiters snatch away your plates the moment you've finished; it's considered impolite to leave dirty dishes in front of customers.

EAT YOUR WORDS

Want to get your fill of *ful*? Do yourself a favour and learn a little of the local lingo. For pronunciation guidelines see p376.

Useful Phrases

breakfast	*kurs*
lunch	*mësa*
dinner	*ërat*

Is there a cheap (restaurant) near here?	*ëzzih akababi, rëkash (mëgëb bet) alleu?*
I want to eat…food.	*yeu…mëgëb ëfeullëfallō*
Ethiopian	*itèyopiya*
Arab	*arab*
Italian	*talyan*
Western	*faranji*
I'm vegetarian/I don't eat meat.	*sëga albeullam*
Can I have it mild?	*alëcha yimëtallëny?*
Do you have…	*…alle?*
bread/bread rolls	*dabbo*
round bread	*ambasha*
chips	*yeu dënëch tëbs*
salad	*seulata*
sandwich	*sandwich* (usually spicy meat between plain bread)
soup	*meureuk* (usually a spicy lamb or beef broth)
yogurt	*ërgo*
water	*wuha*
water (boiled)	*yeu feula wuha*
water (sterilised)	*yeu teutara wuha*
sparkling mineral water	*ambo wuha*
bottled 'flat' water	*highland wuha*
soda/soft drink	*leuslassa*
juice	*chëmaki*
milk	*weuteut*
tea	*shai*

Kevin Rushby's brilliant book *Eating the Flowers of Paradise* is an entertaining and adventurous story of his journey through the Ethiopia, Djibouti and Yemen in search of the perfect chat session.

If you already know your *kekel* from your *kai wat* and want to learn more Amharic, pick up Lonely Planet's *Amharic Phrasebook*.

DO'S & DON'TS

Do

■ Bring a small gift if you've been invited to someone's home for a meal. Pastries or flowers are good choices in urban areas, while sugar, coffee and fruit are perfect in rural areas.

■ Use just your right hand for eating. The left (as in Muslim countries) is reserved for personal hygiene only. Keep it firmly tucked under the table.

■ Take from your side of the tray only; reaching is considered impolite.

■ Leave some leftovers on the plate after a meal. Failing to do so is sometimes seen as inviting famine.

■ Feel free to pick your teeth after a meal. Toothpicks are usually supplied in restaurants.

Don't

■ Be embarrassed or alarmed at the tradition of *gursha,* when someone (usually the host) picks the tastiest morsel and feeds it directly into your mouth. The trick is to take it without letting your mouth come into contact with the person's fingers, or allowing the food to fall. It's a mark of great friendship or affection, and is usually given at least twice (once is considered unlucky). Refusing to take *gursha* is a terrible slight to the person offering it!

■ Put food back onto the food plate – even by the side. It's better to discard it onto the table or floor, or keep it in your napkin.

■ Touch your mouth or lick your fingers.

■ Fill your mouth too full. It's considered impolite.

coffee	*buna*
strong/weak	*weufram/keuchën*
with/without	*beu/yaleu*
honey	*mar*
sugar	*sëkwar*
beer	*bira*

Food Glossary

Most of the following are served with injera.

NONVEGETARIAN

alicha wat	mild stew (meat and vegetarian options)
asa wat	freshwater fish served as a hot stew
bege	lamb
beyainatu	literally 'of every type' – a small portion of all dishes on the menu; also known by its Italian name *secondo misto*
bistecca ai ferri	grilled steak
bure	beef
derek tibs	meat (usually lamb) fried and served *derek* ('dry' – without sauce)
doro	chicken
doro wat	chicken drumstick or wing accompanied by a hard-boiled egg served in a hot sauce of butter, onion, chilli, cardamom and *berbere*

EATING THE FLOWERS OF PARADISE

Head to eastern Ethiopia and you don't have to be there long to notice the bulging cheeks of the chat chewer. Chat, *khat*, *qat* or *miraa* are the leaves of the shrub *Catha edulis*. Originating in the hills of eastern Ethiopia the chat plant has spread across parts of East Africa and into southern Arabia and for many of the inhabitants of this broad swathe of land the afternoon chat chewing session has become almost a pivotal point of life.

Classed by the WHO as a drug of abuse that can produce mild to moderate psychic dependence it has been banned in most Arab and Western countries, including Eritrea where possession is an offence, the USA and almost all European nations except for the UK where it's currently legal (though there is talk of this changing).

Traditionally, chewing chat is an important social activity in parts of Ethiopia (primarily the Somali regions), but its use is growing rapidly throughout the country despite government attempts to dissuade people from using it.

Environmentally the consequences of chat are bad news. It's a very thirsty plant and with the total amount of land given over to the plant growing fast (the profits to be made by farmers is far higher from chat than from other crops) it's likely to have a major impact on local water tables.

The effects of chat have long been debated – most users will insist that it gives an unbeatable high, makes you more talkative (at least until the come down when the chewer becomes withdrawn and quiet), suppresses hunger, prevents tiredness and increases sexual performance. Others will tell you that it gives no noticeable high, makes you lethargic, slightly depressed, constipated and reduces sex drive! Most Western visitors who try it report no major effects aside from a possible light buzz and an unpleasant after taste.

If you're going to chew chat then you need to make sure the setting is perfect in order to enjoy the experience. Ask for the sweetest chat you can get (most Ethiopians regard this as poor quality chat, but first time chewers find even this very bitter) and get a good group of people together to chew with, because chat is, above all else, a social drug. Take yourself off to a quiet and comfortable room – ideally one with a view, sit back, relax and enjoy the conversation whilst popping leaves individually into your mouth where you literally just store them in one cheek gently chewing them. All going well you'll be a chat 'addict' by the end of the day.

dulet	minced tripe, liver and lean beef fried in butter, onions, chilli, cardamom and pepper (often eaten for breakfast)
fatira	savoury pastries
figel	goat
kai wat	lamb, goat or beef cooked in a hot *berbere* sauce
kekel	boiled meat
kitfo	minced beef or lamb like the French steak tartare, usually served warmed (but not cooked) in butter, *berbere* and sometimes thyme
kwalima	sausage served on ceremonial occasions
kwanta fir fir	strips of beef rubbed in chilli, butter, salt and *berbere* then usually hung up and dried; served with torn-up injera
mahabaroui	a mixture of dishes including half a roast chicken
melasena senber tibs	beef tongue and tripe fried with *berbere* and onion
minchet abesh	minced beef or lamb in a hot *berbere* sauce
scaloppina	escalope
tere sega	raw meat served with a couple of spicy accompaniments (occasionally called *gored gored*)
tibs	sliced lamb, pan fried in butter, garlic, onion and sometimes tomato
tibs sheukla	*tibs* served sizzling in a clay pot above hot coals
trippa	tripe
wat	stew
zilzil tibs	strips of beef, fried and served slightly crunchy with *awazi* sauce

VEGETARIAN

aib	like dry cottage cheese
atkilt-b-dabbo	vegetables with bread
awazi	a kind of mustard and chilli sauce
bekolo	popcorn
berbere	as many as 16 spices or more go into making the famous red powder that is responsible for giving much Ethiopian food its kick; most women prepare their own special recipe, often passed down from mother to daughter over generations, and proudly adhered to
dabbo fir fir	torn up bits of bread mixed with butter and *berbere*
enkulal tibs	literally 'egg *tibs*', a kind of Ethiopian scrambled eggs made with a combination of green and red peppers, tomatoes and sometimes onions, served with *dabbo* (bread) – great for breakfast
enset	false-banana 'bread'; a staple food (also called *kotcho*)
ful	chickpea and butter purée eaten for breakfast
genfo	barley or wheat porridge served with butter and *berbere*
gomen	minced spinach
injera	large Ethiopian version of a pancake/plate
injera fir fir	torn-up bits of injera mixed with butter and *berbere*
kai iser	beetroot
kolo	roasted barley
messer	a kind of lentil curry made with onions, chillies and various spices
shiro	chickpea or bean purée lightly spiced, served on fasting days
sils	hot tomato and onion sauce eaten for breakfast
ye som megeb	a selection of different vegetable dishes, served on fasting days

Environment

The farmer who eats his chickens as well as all their eggs will have a bleak future.

Tigrayan proverb

THE LAND

With a land area of 1,098,000 sq km, Ethiopia is five times the size of Britain and twice the size of Texas. Its topography is remarkably diverse, ranging from 20 peaks higher than 4000m to one of the lowest points on the Earth's surface: the infamous Danakil Depression, which lies almost 120m below sea level and sprawls into neighbouring Eritrea and Djibouti.

Two principal geographical zones can be found in the country: cool highlands and their surrounding hot lowlands.

Ethiopia's main topographical feature is the vast central plateau (the Ethiopian highlands) with an average elevation between 1800m and 2400m. It's here that the country's major peaks are found, including Ras Dashen at 4620m, Ethiopia's highest mountain and Africa's 10th highest. Highland areas continue northward into western Eritrea where the highest peak, Emba Soira, reaches 3018m.

The mountains are also the source of four major river systems, the most famous of which is the Blue Nile. Starting from Lake Tana and joined later by the White Nile in Sudan, it nurtures the Egypt's fertile Nile Valley. The other principal rivers are the Awash, the Omo and the Wabe Shebele.

Southern Ethiopia is bisected diagonally by the Rift Valley. Averaging around 50km wide, it runs all the way south to Mozambique. The valley floor is home to many of Ethiopia's most important lakes, including a well-known chain south of Addis Ababa.

The northern end of the Rift Valley opens into the Danakil Depression, a low-lying area that extends through northern Ethiopia to the coast (where the ever-widening Rift Valley will be flooded by sea water sometime in the next couple of million years as East Africa gradually splits off from the rest of Africa).

WILDLIFE

Ethiopia's ecosystems are diverse, from high Afro-alpine vegetation to desert and semidesert scrubland. Rounding out the roster of habitats are six more unique ecosystems: dry evergreen montane forests and grassland; small-leaved deciduous forests; broad-leaved deciduous forests; moist evergreen forests; lowland semi-evergreen forests; and wetlands.

The massive Ethiopian central plateau is home to several of these ecosystems, as well as a distinctive assemblage of plants and animals. Isolated for millions of years within this 'fortress environment', and unable to cross the inhospitable terrain surrounding the plateau, many highland plants and animals evolved their own unique adaptations.

FUNNY FROGS

During a scientific expedition to the Harenna Forest in the Bale Mountains a few years ago, biologists discovered four entirely new frog species in the space of just three weeks. Many of the frogs appear to have made peculiar adaptations to their environment. One species swallows snails whole, another has forgotten how to hop and a third has lost its ears.

Animals

Simply because it lacks large crowds of cavorting elephants, giraffes and rhinos, Ethiopia is mistakenly written off by many Westerners as simply a historical destination. What they don't know is that Ethiopia currently hosts 277 mammal species, 200 reptile species, 148 fish species and 63 amphibian species. And that doesn't even include the birds!

To date, more than 860 species of birds have been recorded (compared with just 250 in the UK). Of Africa's 10 endemic mainland bird families, eight are represented in Ethiopia; only rockfowls and sugarbirds are absent. Families that are particularly well represented are falcons, francolins, bustards and larks.

More noteworthy is the fact that of all the species in Ethiopia, 31 mammals, 21 birds, nine reptiles, four fish and 24 amphibians are endemic (found only in Ethiopia). The biggest thrill of all is the realisation that you have a pretty good chance of spotting some of the rarest species, including the Ethiopian wolf, which is the planet's rarest canid (dog family member).

The Afro-alpine habitat, within the Bale and Simien Mountains National Parks, boasts the largest number of endemic mammals and hosts mountain nyalas, walia ibexes, Ethiopian wolves, gelada baboons, Menelik's bushbuck and giant molerats. In addition, 16 of Ethiopia's endemic birds are also found in these lofty confines (see the boxed text, p76, for the lowdown on Ethiopia's endemic birdlife and birding itineraries).

At the opposite end of the elevation spectrum, the sprawling deserts and semidesert scrublands of Ethiopia, Eritrea and Djibouti host the endangered African wild asses and Grevy's zebras, as well as the Soemmering's gazelles and beisa oryx. Birds include ostriches, secretary birds, Arabian, Kori and Heuglin's bustards, Abyssinian rollers, red-cheeked cordon bleus and crested francolins.

Widespread but discontinuous deciduous forests are home to greater and lesser kudus, hartebeest, gazelles, De Brazza's monkeys and small populations of elands, buffaloes and elephants. Limited numbers of Grevy's zebras and

The Nechisar nightjar (Caprimulgus solala) is known from a single wing found squashed on the road near Nechisar National Park in 1990. No one has ever seen a living specimen of this enigmatic bird. 'Solala' in its scientific name means 'single winged'.

Birdwatchers will be thrilled by the newest guide to this region's unique birdlife, Birds of the Horn of Africa: Ethiopia, Eritrea, Djibouti, Somalia, and Socotra by Nigel Redman, Terry Stevenson and John Fanshawe.

THE BLEEDING HEART BABOON

The gelada baboon *(Theropithecus gelada)* is one of Ethiopia's most fascinating endemic mammals. In fact not a baboon at all, it makes up its own genus of monkey.

Of all the nonhuman primates, it's by far the most dexterous. It also lives in the largest social groups (up to 800 have been recorded), and is the only primate that feeds on grass and has its 'mating skin' on its chest and not on its bottom – a convenient adaptation, given that it spends most of its time sitting!

The gelada also has the most complex system of communication of any nonhuman primate and the most sophisticated social system: the females decide who's boss, the young males form bachelor groups, and the older males perform a kind of grandfather role looking after the young.

Although the males sport magnificent leonine manes, their most striking physical feature is the bare patch of skin on their chest. This has given rise to their other popular name: the 'bleeding heart baboon'. The colour of the patch indicates the sexual condition of not just the male (his virility), but also his female harem (their fertility).

Although its population is shrinking, the gelada population is the healthiest of Ethiopia's endemic mammals. Its current population is thought to number between 40,000 and 50,000.

Resented for its alleged damage to crops and pasture, it has become the scapegoat for more sinister goings-on, too. According to local police reports, gelada baboons are responsible for local thefts, burglaries, rapes and even murders – in one case bursting into a house to drag an adult man 1.5km before shoving him off a cliff face! If in doubt, blame the gelada!

Unless you want to test locals' theories, don't chase or try to feed the gelada.

beisa oryx also inhabit these areas. Birdlife includes the white-bellied go-away bird, superb starling, red-billed quelea, helmeted guinea fowl, secretary bird, Ruppell's long-tailed starling, gambaga flycatcher, red-cheeked cordon bleu, bush petronia and black-faced firefinch.

Wandering the evergreen forests in the southwestern and western parts of the country are bushpigs, forest hogs, Menelik's bushbucks and more De Brazza's monkeys. Around Gambela, in the lowland semi-evergreen forest, are rare populations of elephants, giraffes, lions and the hard-to-spot white-eared kob, a beautiful golden antelope found in larger numbers in southern Sudan. The colourful birdlife includes Abyssinian black-headed orioles, Abyssinian hill babblers, white-cheeked turacos, scaly-throated honeyguides, scaly francolins, emerald cuckoos and yellow-billed coucals.

Hippos and crocodiles are also found around Gambela in the wetlands along the Baro River. They also populate some of the Rift Valley lakes in

---

ETHIOPIA'S ENDEMIC BIRDS

There's no denying that the diversity and beauty of Ethiopia's astounding 862 recorded bird species could convert even the most die-hard nonbirder into a habitual and excited twitcher. It's the endemic bird species that really set Ethiopia apart.

An amazing 21 species are found nowhere else in the world. Thirteen more are semi-endemic, shared only with Eritrea.

The best time to visit Ethiopia for birding is between November and February, when some 200 species of Palaearctic migrants from Europe and Asia join the already abundant African resident and intra-African migrant populations. The most likely time to spot birds is from dawn to 11am and from 5pm to dusk, although birds can be seen throughout the day.

Endemics of Ethiopia

- Abyssinian catbird *(Parophasma galinieri)* – juniper forests within the Bale Mountains (p179).
- Abyssinian longclaw *(Macronyx flavicollis)* – Afro-alpine grassland in the Bale Mountains (p179).
- Abyssinian slaty flycatcher *(Dioptrornis chocolatinus)* – highland woodlands bracketing the southern Rift Valley.
- Ankober seedeater or serin *(Serinus ankoberensis)* – around Ankober (p167) and in the Simien Mountains (p126).
- Black-headed siskin *(Serinus nigriceps)* – Afro-alpine grassland and heather forests in the Bale Mountains (p179).
- Blue-winged goose *(Cyanochen cyanopterus)* – Gefersa Reservoir (p228) and Sanetti Plateau in the Bale Mountains (p179).
- Degodi lark *(Mirafra degodiensis)* – around Negele Borena (p185).
- Erlanger's Lark *(Calandrella erlangeri)* – common in the highlands.
- Ethiopian cliff swallow *(Hirundo)* – Lake Langano (p172).
- Harwood's francolin *(Francolinus hardwoodi)* – in the Jemma Valley, northeast of Debre Libanos (p109).
- Nechisar nightjar *(Caprimulgus nechisarensis)* – Nechisar National Park (p191).
- Prince Ruspoli's turaco *(Tauraco ruspolii)* – around Negele Borena (p185).
- Salvadori's seedeater or serin *(Serinus xantholaema)* – Sof Omar (p184) and around Negele Borena (p185).
- Sidamo long-clawed lark *(Heteromirafra sidamoensis)* – near Negele Borena (p185).

the south – Lake Chamo is famous for its massive crocodiles. Rouget's rails and white-winged flufftails are found in the wetland swamps, while Senegal thick-knees and red-throated bee-eaters live in riverbank habitats.

The odd leopard, gazelle, jackal and hyena still roam the dry evergreen montane forest and grassland found in Ethiopia's north, northwest, central and southern highlands. Birds of note include black-winged lovebirds, half-collared kingfishers and several endemic species (for more information, see opposite).

ENDANGERED SPECIES

The International Union for the Conservation of Nature and Natural Resources (IUCN) lists seven species in Ethiopia as critically endangered; one is Ethiopia's endemic walia ibex. Amazingly, you have a pretty good chance of spotting this rare animal in the Simien Mountains National Park.

- Spot-breasted plover *(Vanellus melanocephalus)* – found near rivers and streams in the Bale Mountains (p179).
- Stresemann's or Abyssinian bush crow *(Zavattariornis stresemanni)* – Yabelo Wildlife Sanctuary (p187).
- White-cheeked turaco *(Tauraco leucolophus)* – common in the highlands.
- White-tailed swallow *(Hirundo megaensis)* – Yabelo Wildlife Sanctuary (p187).
- White-throated seedeater *(Serinus xanthopygius)* – around Ankober (p167) and the Blue Nile Falls (p110).
- Yellow-fronted parrot *(Poicephalus flavifrons)* – Wondo Genet (p175), Menagesha Forest (p229) and the Bale Mountains (p179).
- Yellow-throated seedeater or serin *(Serinus flavigula)* – Awash National Park (p210) and near Ankober (p167).

Semi-endemics of Ethiopia & Eritrea

- Abyssinian woodpecker *(Dendropicus abyssinicus)* – Awash National Park (p210); rare but widespread.
- Banded barbet *(Lybius undatus)* – Awash National Park (p210) and in the southern Rift Valley.
- Black-winged lovebird *(Agapornis swinderiana)* – common in the highland woodlands.
- Brown sawwing *(Psalidoprocne oleagina)* – Yabelo Wildlife Sanctuary (p187).
- Ethiopian cisticola *(Cistocola lugubris)* – common in montane grasslands.
- Rouget's rail *(Rougetius rougetii)* – associated with marshes and river systems in the highlands. Common in the Bale Mountains (p179).
- Rüpell's black chat *(Myrmecocichla melaena)* – common in the rock highlands of Tigray (p147).
- Thick-billed raven *(Corvus crassirostris)* – common in the highlands.
- Wattled Ibis *(Bostrychia carunculata)* – common in the highlands.
- White-backed black tit *(Parus leuconotus)* – Wondo Genet (p175) and the Bale Mountains (p179). Also in Addis Ababa (p82).
- White-billed starling *(Onychognathus albirostris)* – in and around Lalibela (p156).
- White-collared pigeon *(Columba albitorques)* – common in the highlands, including Addis Ababa (p82).
- White-winged cliff chat *(Myrmecocichla semirufa)* – common in the rock highlands of Tigray (p147) and Awash National Park (p210).

A further 19 species in Ethiopia are listed as endangered by IUCN. These include the endemic mountain nyala and Ethiopian wolf, both easily viewed in Bale Mountains National Park. Nechisar National Park formerly hosted the endangered African hunting dog and what is likely Ethiopia's rarest endemic bird, the Nechisar nightjar. Vulnerable bird species are Prince Ruspoli's turaco (see opposite), Salvadori's serin, Stresemann's bush crow, the Sidamo long-clawed lark, the Degodi lark, the Ankober serin and the white-tailed swallow.

Plants

Ethiopia's flora is no less exceptional for the same reason. Ethiopia was classed as one of the world's 12 most important hotspots for crop plant diversity by the famous Russian geneticist Nikolai Vavilov, and is thought to possess extremely valuable pools of crop plant genes. Between 600 and 1400 plants species are thought to be endemic; a whooping 10% to 20% of its flora.

The small-leaved deciduous forests can be found all over the country apart from the western regions, at an altitude of between 900m and 1900m. Vegetation consists of drought-tolerant shrubs and trees with either leathery persistent leaves or small, deciduous ones. Trees include various types of acacia. Herbs include *Acalypha* and *Aerva*.

The western and northwestern areas of Ethiopia host broad-leaved deciduous forests, while tall and medium-sized trees and understorey shrubs of the moist evergreen forests also occupy the west, as well as the nation's southwest. Even further west are the lowland semi-evergreen forests around Gambela. Vegetation there consists of semi-evergreen trees and shrub species, as well as grasses.

Covering much of the highlands, and the north, northwest, central and southern parts of the country, is the dry evergreen montane forest and grassland. This habitat is home to a large number of endemic plants. Tree species include various types of acacia, olive and euphorbia. Africa's only rose, the *Rosa abyssinica,* is here.

Within the Afro-alpine vegetation habitat, you'll see the endemic giant lobelia *(Lobelia rhynchopetalum),* an endemic species of globe thistle, as well as the so-called 'soft thistle'. On the high plateaus at around 4000m are many varieties of gentian.

Look out for fig and tamarind trees along the Baro River in the west, as well as along river banks or *wadis* (seasonal rivers) in the highlands and the northwest.

SPOT THE ENDEMIC FLORA

Ethiopia has more unique species of flora than any other country in Africa. This fact is becoming abundantly clear thanks to the ongoing Flora of Somalia project, which has documented more than 400 new species of flowering plants in Ethiopia, including a newly discovered Acacia tree that grows by the millions over 8000 sq km.

In September and October, look out particularly for the famous yellow daisy known as the Meskel flower, which carpets the highlands; it belongs to the sunflower family, six members of which are endemic.

In towns and villages, the endemic yellow-flowered *Solanecio gigas* is commonly employed as a hedge. Around Addis Ababa, the tall endemic *Erythrina brucei* tree can be seen. In the highlands, such as in the Bale Mountain and Simien Mountain National Parks, the indigenous Abyssinian rose is quite commonly found. Also in the Bale Mountains, look out for the endemic species of globe thistle *(Echinops longisetus).*

THE STRANGE CASE OF THE VANISHING TURACO

In a remote patch in the deep south of Ethiopia lives one of the country's rarest, most beautiful and most enigmatic birds – the Prince Ruspoli's turaco, first introduced to the world in the early 1890s. It was 'collected' by an Italian prince (who gave his name to the bird) as he explored the dense juniper forests of southern Ethiopia.

Unfortunately, the intrepid prince failed to make a record of his find, and when he was killed shortly afterwards near Lake Abaya following 'an encounter with an elephant', all hope of locating the species seemed to die with him.

The turaco finally reappeared in the 1940s. Just three specimens were obtained, then the turaco disappeared again. It wasn't until the early 1970s that the bird was rediscovered.

Today, recent sightings in the Arero forest, east of Yabelo, around the Genale River off the Dola-Mena-Negele Borena Road, suggest that the bird may not, after all, be as elusive as it would have us believe. You may find your own turaco in acacia or conifer woodlands in the southwestern corner of Ethiopia.

The Dankalia region, Omo delta and Ogaden Desert contain drought-resistant plants such as small trees, shrubs and grasses, including acacia. Succulent species include euphorbia and aloe. The region is classified as desert and semidesert scrubland.

NATIONAL PARKS & WILDLIFE SANCTUARIES

There are 15 national parks and three wildlife sanctuaries in Ethiopia. They range from the unvisited Kuni-Muktar Wildlife Sanctuary to the famed Simien Mountains National Park, a Unesco World Heritage Site.

Most parks were delineated in the 1960s and 1970s during the time of Emperor Haile Selassie to protect endangered or endemic animals. In the process, land was forcefully taken from the peasants, a measure much resented by locals.

Park borders continue to overlap with local communities, and conflicts over conservation continue, despite wildlife authorities trying to encourage locals' participation in the conservation of wildlife (for more information, see p193). For instance, trees in Lake Abiata-Shala National Park continue to fall victim to the needs of its growing human population.

For several years Nechisar and Omo National Parks were run by the non-profit **African Parks Foundation** (www.africanparks-conservation.com), which tried very hard to balance the complicated issues raised by local communities settling within park boundaries and taking a huge toll on already stressed habitats and wildlife populations. In the face of growing anger over their attempts to safeguard wildlife, the foundation pulled out in October 2008 and it remains to be seen what steps Ethiopia takes to solve these issues.

ENVIRONMENTAL ISSUES

Despite civil wars taking their toll on the environment, Ethiopia's demographic pressures have been the main culprit. About 95% of its original forest is believed to have been lost to agriculture and human settlement.

Ethiopia's population has almost quintupled in the last 70 years and continues to grow at 2.5%; the pressures for living space, firewood, building materials, agricultural land, livestock grazing and food will only further reduce natural resources and wipe out larger areas of wildlife habitat.

The deforestation has resulted in soil erosion, an extremely serious threat in Ethiopia because it exacerbates the risk of famine. Although hunting and poaching over the centuries has decimated the country's once large herds of elephants and rhinos, deforestation has also played a role.

Endemic Mammals of Ethiopia, by Jill Last and published by the defunct Ethiopian Tourism Commission, gives decent descriptions of the appearance and behaviour of Ethiopia's mammals. It's usually available in Addis Ababa.

Wildlife and forests were both victims of the most recent civil war, where whole forests were torched by the Derg to smoke out rebel forces. Additionally, large armies, hungry and with inadequate provisions, turned their sights on the land's natural resources and much wildlife was wiped out.

Up until recently, armed conflict between tribes in the Omo and Mago National Parks continued to impede wildlife conservation efforts.

Today, things are more under control. Hunting is managed by the government and may even provide the most realistic and pragmatic means of ensuring the future survival of Ethiopia's large mammals. Poaching, however, continues to pose a serious threat to some animals.

TOP PARKS & SANCTUARIES

Park	Features	Activities	Best time to visit
Southern Ethiopia			
Bale Mountains National Park (p179)	steep ridges, alpine plateaus; Ethiopian wolves, mountain nyala and 16 endemic birds	trekking, birdwatching	Oct-Jan
Lake Abiata-Shala National Park (p172)	crater lakes, hot springs; red-billed hornbills, Didric's cuckoos, Abyssinian rollers, superb starlings	birdwatching, walking	Nov-Dec
Mago National Park (p198)	savannah, open woodland; elephants, hartebeest, buffaloes, many birds	visiting Mursi tribes, wildlife drives	Jun-Sep & Jan-Feb
Nechisar National Park (p191)	savannah, acacia woodland; Burchell's zebras, Swayne's hartebeest, crocodiles, greater kudu, 320 bird species	wildlife drives, boat trips	Nov-Feb
Omo National Park (p204)	savannah, open woodland; elephants, buffaloes, lions	visiting Mursi, Dizi and Surma tribes	Jun-Sep & Jan-Feb
Senkele Wildlife Sanctuary (p175)	open acacia woodland; Swayne's hartebeest, Bohor reedbucks, spotted hyenas, greater spotted eagles	wildlife drives	Nov-Feb
Yabelo Wildlife Sanctuary (p187)	acacia woodland, savannah grasses; Stresemann's bush crows, white-tailed swallows, Swayne's hartebeest, gerenuks	wildlife drive, birdwatching	year-round
Northern Ethiopia			
Simien Mountains National Park (p126)	dramatic volcanic escarpments and plateaus; walia ibexes, gelada baboons, Simien wolves, lammergeyers	trekking, birdwatching, wildlife viewing	Oct-Jan
Eastern Ethiopia			
Awash National Park (p210)	semiarid woodland; beisa oryxes, Soemmering's gazelles, kudu, six endemic bird species	birdwatching, wildlife viewing	Oct-Feb
Western Ethiopia			
Gambela National Park (p240)	semiarid woodland, deciduous forests; savannah Nile lechwe, white-eared kobs, elephants	rugged wildlife drives/treks	Dec-Mar

RESPONSIBLE TRAVEL: ENVIRONMENT

Although there are a few sustainable ecotourism projects popping up across Ethiopia, the concept is still not widely known. Some effort on your part is a good step in the right direction.

▪ Water is a precious and scarce resource in some parts of Ethiopia (including Gonder, Aksum and Lalibela). Try not to waste it by letting taps and showers run unnecessarily.

▪ If you're buying authentic crafts, ensure that they aren't made from indigenous woods or wildlife products.

▪ Be sensitive to wildlife.

▪ If a campfire is necessary, ensure the wood used is eucalyptus and be sensitive to the fire's location as it can disturb wildlife.

▪ Never litter.

▪ Avoid driving off-road as it can harm or disturb animals and nesting birds.

For tips on responsible trekking, see p244.

An excellent organisation in the UK that can provide more information for concerned travellers is London-based **Tourism Concern** (www.tourismconcern.org.uk).

In late 2005 a new conservation action plan and a new wildlife proclamation were accepted by the government and sent to parliament for approval. Besides crafting stricter environmental regulations, these new programs were designed to unite previously scattered wildlife and environmental activities under the umbrella of a radically restructured Ethiopian Wildlife Conservation Authority, thus bringing new hope and energy to the cause of protecting Ethiopia's tattered ecosystems.

For more on wildlife conservation, contact the **Ethiopian Wildlife Conservation Authority** (Map pp86-7; ☎ 0115 504389; PO Box 386, Addis Ababa).

Addis Ababa
አዲስ አበባ

Since its establishment in the 19th century, Addis Ababa has always seemed like a magical portal and a gateway to another world. For the rural masses of Ethiopia it was, and is, a city whose streets are paved in gold. If you open enough doors the portal will lead you to another life; a richer and easier life where anything is possible.

If you're a foreign visitor then the portal of Addis Ababa stands on the verge of an ancient and mystical world. A world of swashbuckling adventure where great wisdom is hidden in far away mountain monasteries; a world where, ironically, life can seem both richer and easier than the one you've just left behind.

For both these groups Addis – Africa's fourth-largest city and its diplomatic capital – is a place to traverse as quickly as possible. Yet by doing so you skip the key that links these two worlds. Put simply, if you bypass the contrasts and contradictions of Addis – the shepherd from the countryside bringing his flock to a city market, the city priest with the business investments, the glossy nightclubs with the country girl prostitutes – then you risk failing to understand Ethiopia altogether.

And there are other incentives to lingering awhile in the capital. Food is probably most people's number-one priority. For tourists Addis might mean never facing a plate of injera again; for a villager from the backblocks of Ethiopia, Addis might mean never facing drought or worse again.

Whichever way you view it, Addis is an essential part of any Ethiopian story, and you'd be wise to linger in the portal for awhile.

HIGHLIGHTS

- Delve into the Aladdin's treasure trove that is the astounding **Ethnological Museum** (p90)

- Meet your long-lost Auntie Lucy, our pint-sized ancient ancestor, at the **National Museum** (p91)

- Tickle your tongue with your first injera and *wat* experience and satisfy your rumbling tummy in Ethiopia's best **restaurants** (p99)

- Throw back a *tej* or sip on a cool cocktail as you kick-start a night on the tiles Addis style (p103)

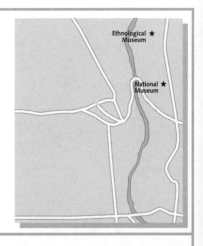

Ethnological ★
Museum

National ★
Museum

- POPULATION: 2.8 MILLION

HISTORY

Unlike Addis Ababa's numerous predecessors as capitals, the locations of which were chosen according to the political, economic and strategic demands of the days' rulers, Addis Ababa was chosen for its beauty, hot springs and agreeable climate. Why the drastic (and pleasant) change of convention in the late 19th century? Perhaps it was because it was the first time a woman had any say in the matter! Yes, it was the actions of Taitu, the consort of Menelik II, which led to the birth of Addis Ababa.

Menelik's previous capital, Entoto, was in the mountains just north of present-day Addis Ababa and held strategic importance as it was easily defended. However, it was unattractive and sterile, leading Taitu to request a house be built for her in the beautiful foothills below in an area she named Addis Ababa (New Flower). In the following decade, after Menelik's power increased and his need for defence waned, he moved his court down to Taitu and Addis Ababa.

A lack of firewood for the rapidly growing population threatened the future of Addis Ababa in 1896 and Menelik even started construction of a new capital, Addis Alem (New World), 50km to the west. In the end, it was the suggestion of a foreigner (thought to be French) to introduce the rapidly growing eucalyptus tree that saved the new capital.

Since 1958 Addis Ababa has been the headquarters of the UN Economic Commission for Africa (ECA) and, since 1963, the secretariat of the Organisation of African Unity (OAU). Many regard the city as 'Africa's diplomatic capital'.

ORIENTATION

Addis Ababa is massive and incoherent. It could be likened to a sprawling 250-sq-km injera adorned with sporadic piles of *tibs,* spaghetti, *mahabaroui* (a mixture of dishes, including half a roast chicken) and Sichuan noodles! To navigate the city, it's best to break it down into these distinct dishes/districts.

The mound of smoking *tibs,* representing the central (or meaty) part of the city, is at the end of Churchill Ave, the southern section of which is named Gambia St. Here you'll find many government and commercial buildings.

The steaming heap of spaghetti would symbolise Piazza, a district whose legacy and architecture is owed to the Italian occupation. Piazza is found atop the hill at Churchill Ave's north end and houses budget hotels, as well as many cafes and bars.

To the east of Piazza is Addis Ababa University, several museums and the landmark roundabouts of Arat Kilo and Siddist Kilo. South from there is Menelik II Ave, which boasts the National Palace, Africa Hall,

---

ADDIS ABABA IN...

Two Days

Start in Piazza with a steaming *macchiato* (espresso with a dash of milk) at **Tomoca** (p102), before visiting **St George Cathedral & Museum** (p93). Next, get ready to say hello to Auntie Lucy, your long-lost ancestor, in the **National Museum** (p91). From there, stroll north and absorb the magnitude of the **Yekatit 12 Monument** (p93).

After lunch explore the massive **Merkato** (p93) and, after checking you still have all your belongings, finish the day dining and drinking *tej* (honey wine) at a **traditional Ethiopian restaurant** (p99), while enjoying a show of song and dance.

Day two, and the morning kicks off with more culture when you marvel at the brilliant **Ethnological Museum** (p90). In the afternoon pay your respects to Haile Selassie at the Holy Trinity Cathedral (p92) and then pray to a different kind of God. The God of shopping! The strip of shops along Churchill Ave should do nicely; don't miss **Hope Enterprises** (see the boxed text, p89). Finish your day off at the wonderful **Serenade Restaurant** (p101).

Four Days

With four days, you could complete the two-day itinerary at a slower pace (more *macchiatos!*), squeezing in extra sights like the **Beta Maryam Mausoleum** (p94) and **Natural History Museum** (p94). Art-lovers should visit **Asni Gallery** (p94) and **Afewerk Tekle's home and studio** (p94), or head out of town to the extraordinary **Wusha Mikael Church** (p107).

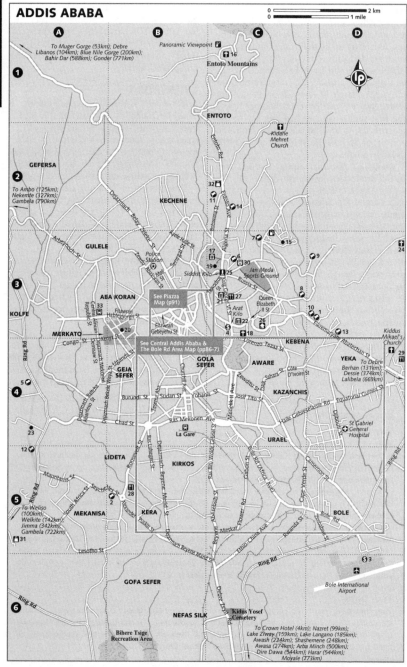

ADDIS ABABA

0   2 km
0   1 mile

To Muger Gorge (53km); Debre Libanos (104km); Blue Nile Gorge (200km); Bahir Dar (588km); Gonder (771km)

Panoramic Viewpoint

Entoto Mountains

ENTOTO

Kidane Mehret Church

GEFERSA

To Ambo (125km); Nekemte (327km); Gambela (790km)

KECHENE

Arbegnoch St

GULELE

Police Station

Siddist Kilo

Jan Meda Sports Ground

Queen Elizabeth II St

ABA KORAN

See Piazza Map (p91)

Filwaran Habtegiyorgis St

Filwaran Gebeyehu St

Arat Kilo

KOLFE

MERKATO

Ring Rd

GEJA SEFER

Congo St

Kenya St

See Central Addis Ababa & The Bole Rd Area Map (pp86-7)

GOLA SEFER

AWARE

KEBENA

YEKA

Kiddus Mikael's Church

To Debre Berhan (131km); Dessie (374km); Lalibela (669km)

Burundi St

Sudan St

Yohanis St

KAZANCHIS

Côte D'Ivoire St

St Gabriel General Hospital

Chad St

Ras Mekonen Ave

La Gare

URAEL

LIDETA

KIRKOS

Mauritania St

To Weliso (100km); Welkite (142km); Jimma (342km); Gambela (722km)

MEKANISA

South Africa St

Lesotho St

KERA

BOLE

Ring Rd

GOFA SEFER

Kidus Yosef Cemetery

NEFAS SILK

Bole International Airport

Bihere Tsige Recreation Area

To Crown Hotel (4km); Nazret (99km); Lake Zeway (159km); Lake Langano (185km); Awash (224km); Shashemene (248km); Awasa (274km); Arba Minch (500km); Dire Dawa (544km); Harar (544km); Moyale (773km)

a series of new urban parks and at its southern end, the huge and ugly Meskal Sq. This melange of attributes must be likened to a meal of this, that and everything *(mahabaroui)*.

Thanks to the new ring road built by the Chinese, the southeast of the city, on and around Bole Rd between Meskal Sq and the airport, is thriving with exciting development that contrasts sharply with the rest of the city. You guessed it – the Sichuan noodles!

Maps

Various hotels and tour companies sell the reasonable InfoSolution map that uses all the new street names. It costs Birr100. If names aren't important, the most accurate map of Addis Ababa's convoluted street layout is the *City Map of Addis Ababa* (2003, scale 1:25,000) produced by the **Ethiopian Mapping Authority** (Map pp86-7; ☎ 0115 518445; Menelik II Ave; ☺ 8.30am-12.30pm & 1.30-5.30pm Mon-Thu, 8.30-11.30am & 1.30-4.30pm Fri). The EMA charge a paltry Birr23.

INFORMATION
Bookshops

The big hotels such as the Ghion, Hilton and Sheraton all sell a good, but pretty pricey selection of books, magazines and newspapers.

Africans Bookshop (Map p91; Hailesilase St; ☺ 9am-1pm & 2.30-7pm Mon-Sat) The best place for secondhand books on Ethiopia, particularly those out of print. Selection is very limited.

Bookworld Friendship City Center (Map pp86-7; Bole Rd; ☺ 9am-9pm Mon-Sat, 11am-8pm Sun); Haile Gebreselassie Rd (Map pp86-7; Haile Gebreselassie Rd; ☺ 8am-9pm); Lime Tree Restaurant (Map pp86-7; Bole Rd; ☺ 7am-11pm); Piazza (Map p91; Wavel St; ☺ 8am-8pm Mon-Sat) The best place for books in English (as well as

some in French). There's also a small section on Ethiopia and some foreign magazines. Prices are more than you'd pay at home, but much cheaper than the hotels.

Emergency

Emergency 24-hour numbers:
Fire brigade (☎ 912)
Police (☎ 991)
Red Cross Ambulance service (☎ 917)

Internet Access

Although internet is everywhere, fast connections are still as rare as a cheetah on Bole Rd. Some convenient outlets are listed here.

TAD Business Centre (Map pp86-7; off Haile Gebreselassie Rd; per hr Birr12; ☺ 9am-9pm) Half a dozen new computers that do actually connect you to the wider world.

Compunet (Map pp86-7; Bole Rd; per hr Birr15; ☺ 8.30am-9pm) It's an ADSL broadband connection, though not as fast as you'd wish.

Fiber Computer Engineering (Map p91; Dejazmach Jote St; per hr Birr15) There are connections – most of the time.

Maam Internet Café (Map pp86-7; Bole Rd; per hr Birr15; ☺ 7.30am-9pm) Looks impressive but isn't quite as broadband as it claims.

Nina Internet Service (Map p91; Mundy St; per hr Birr15; ☺ 8am-10pm) Of the several Internet cafes around here, Nina is the most comfortable and images can be burnt to CD with USB connections.

Internet Resources

Addis All Around (www.addisallaround.com) This excellent website previews forthcoming cultural events and lists general city information.

Laundry

Every hotel does laundry and their service is inevitably cheaper and quicker than the laundries that line Bole Rd.

CENTRAL ADDIS ABABA & THE BOLE RD AREA

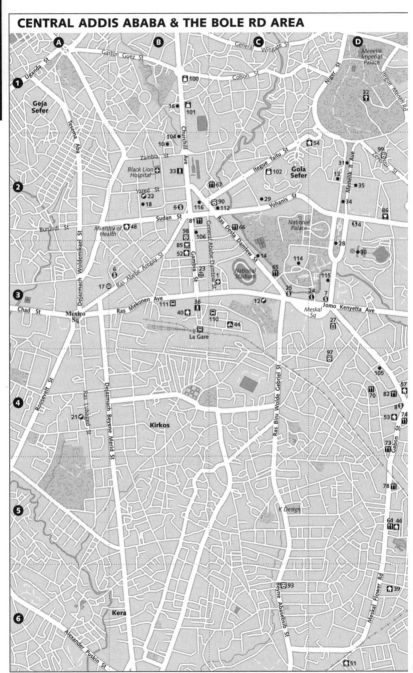

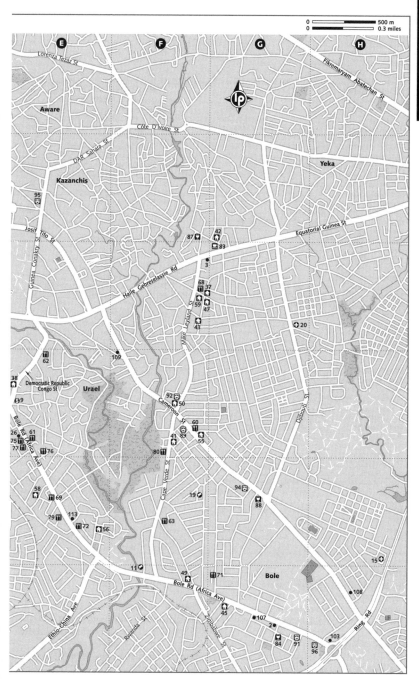

ADDIS ABABA

Libraries
Institute of Ethiopian Studies (Map p84; ☎ 0111
239740; www.ies-ethiopia.org; Addis Ababa University,
Algeria St) This institute boasts the world's best collection
of books in English on Ethiopia. It's free for a half-day's
casual use.
National Archives & Library of Ethiopia (Map pp86-
7; ☎ 0115 530058; ☻ closed morning Mon) Shelves
groan under the weight of 20,000 books on Ethiopia. The

English-language section is quite good. It is located off
Sudan St.

Medical Services
Bethzatha Hospital (Map pp86-7; ☎ 0115 514470;
☻ 24hr) This quality private hospital, off Ras Mekonen
Ave, is recommended by most embassies.
Ghion Pharmacy (Map pp86-7; ☎ 0115 518606; Ras
Desta Damtew St).

Hayat Hospital (Map pp86-7; ☎ 0116 624488; Ring Rd; ☺ 24hr) A reliable option near the airport.
St Gabriel Hospital (Map pp86-7; ☎ 0116 613622; Djibouti St; ☺ 24hr) This private hospital has good X-ray, dental, surgery and laboratory facilities.
Zogdom Pharmacy (Map pp86-7; Bole Rd).

Money

You will have no trouble at all finding a bank to change cash or travellers cheques, and most larger Dashen Bank branches have ATMs that accept foreign Visa cards (not MasterCard, Plus or Cirrus). We've denoted those with nonstandard hours (see p245 for standard hours).

Commercial Bank Arat Kilo (Map p84; Adwa St; ☺ open through lunch); Bole International Airport (Map p84; Bole Rd; ☺ 24hr); Bole Rd (Map pp86-7; Bole Rd); Churchill Ave (Map pp86-7; Churchill Ave); Josif Tito St (Map pp86-7; Josif Tito St); Lower Piazza (Map p91; General Wingate St; ☺ open through lunch); Meskal Sq (Map pp86-7; cnr Menelik II Ave & Meskal Sq); Mexico (Map pp86-7; Ras Abebe Aregay St); Upper Piazza (Map p91; Hailesilase St; ☺ open through lunch) All these branches change travellers cheques and cash (US dollars and euros).

Dashen Bank Bole Rd (Map pp86-7); Sheraton Hotel (Map pp86-7; Itegue Taitu St; ☺ 7-11am, noon-7pm & 8-11pm) Offers Visa and MasterCard cash advances. Also changes travellers cheques and cash. The Bole Rd branch is just off Bole Rd and has an ATM. There is also an ATM in the lobby of the Ras Hotel (p97).

United Bank (Map pp86-7; Hilton Hotel, Menelik II Ave; ☺ 6am-10.30pm) Convenient hours and changes travellers cheques and cash.

Wegagen Bank Bole Rd (Map pp86-7; Bole Rd); Meskal Sq (Map pp86-7; Meskal Sq) This private bank changes travellers cheques (slightly higher commissions) and cash.

HOPE SPRINGS ETERNAL

Wanting to help Addis Ababa's many street children is natural. However, giving them money or food (which in most cases is quickly exchanged for money) isn't recommended as it invariably leads to more problems for them and their community. To solve this dilemma, **Hope Enterprises** (Map pp86-7; ☎ 0111 560345; Churchill Ave; ☺ 8am-12pm & 1-5pm Mon-Sat) was created. It sells meal tickets (eight for Birr4) that you can distribute to needy children. Each day several hundred children redeem the tickets for a 'simple but nourishing meal' at the centre.

Post

Junior post offices Meskal Sq (Map pp86-7; cnr Menelik II Ave & Meskal Sq); Mexico (Map pp86-7; Ras Abebe Aregay St); Piazza (Map p91; Cunningham St) Offers postal services for postcards and letters only.
Main post office (Map pp86-7; Ras Desta Damtew St) The only post office to offer poste restante and international parcel services (see p252 for shipping rates).

Telephone & Fax

Trying to use the public phones on the street will result in nothing but a few new additions to your growing collection of grey hairs.
Telecommunications office (Map pp86-7; ☎ 0115 514977; Gambia St) International calls at standard rates (see p254).

Tourist Information

The highly useful, monthly magazine *What's Up!* lists restaurants, shopping venues,

---

SIREN SCAM

One scam that still seems to be snagging tourists is the 'siren scam'. It takes various forms, including offering you a 'cultural show' or a traditional coffee ceremony.

The venue is usually somebody's living room, where a hostess will promptly dish out copious quantities of *tej* (honey wine) and, perhaps, traditional dancers and musicians will perform.

Suddenly the 'entertainment' comes to an end and an amount upwards of Birr1000 is demanded. Approaches are made to couples or groups, as well as to single males. Most commonly, the person approaching you is a young, well-dressed Ethiopian male, often claiming to be a student.

If you end up in a situation like this, offer to pay for anything you've consumed (a litre of quality *tej* shouldn't be more than Birr25), and if it's not accepted, threaten to call the police. The area around the hotels in the Piazza and Churchill Ave seem to be prime hunting grounds for potential victims.

nightclubs and events. It's available (haphazardly) at large hotels, smart restaurants and art galleries.

Tourist Information Centre (Map pp86-7; ☎ 0115 512310; Meskal Sq; ⏲ 8.30am-12.30pm & 1.30-5.30pm Mon-Thu, 8.30-11.30am & 1.30-5.30pm Fri) This helpful office does its best to provide information about the city and itineraries elsewhere. It also has some informative brochures about the rest of Ethiopia.

Travel Agencies

For information on travel agencies in Addis Ababa, see p270.

DANGERS & ANNOYANCES

Violent crime in Addis Ababa is fortunately rare, particularly where visitors are concerned. However, petty theft and confidence tricks are problematic.

The Merkato has the worst reputation as pickpockets abound – targeting not just *faranjis* (foreigners, especially Western ones) but Ethiopians as well. An old ploy is for someone to step blindly into you, while another gently lifts your belongings in the subsequent confusion. A less subtle tactic now being used involves someone diving at your feet and holding your legs while another pilfers your pockets. You are advised to leave hand luggage and jewellery in your hotel if you plan on visiting the Merkato.

Other spots where you should be vigilant include the Piazza, where many foreigners get pickpocketed or mugged, Meskal Sq, minibus stands, outside larger hotels and Churchill Ave, where adult gangs have been known to hang around the National Theatre. Common

gang ploys are to feign a fight or argument and, when one man appeals to you for help, the other helps himself to your pockets. Don't let any of this scare you, though – Addis is very safe compared with many other African capitals. On a personal note, we never felt even remotely threatened at any time during our most recent trip to the city when researching this book.

SIGHTS

Most sights are scattered throughout the city centre and Piazza, though there is a concentration of major museums and other sights in the vicinity of Arat Kilo and Siddist Kilo, which sit east of Piazza and north of the city centre.

Ethnological Museum

Set within Haile Selassie's former palace and surrounded by the beautiful gardens and fountains of Addis Ababa University's main campus is the enthralling **Ethnological Museum** (Map p84; Algeria St; adult/student Birr20/10; ⏲ 8am-5pm Mon-Fri, 9am-5pm Sat & Sun). Even if you're not normally a museum fan, this one is worth a bit of your time – it's easily one of the finest museums in Africa.

The show starts before you even get inside: look for the intriguing set of stairs spiralling precariously skyward near the palace's main entrance. Each step was placed by the Italians as a symbol of Fascist domination, one for every year Mussolini held power (starting from his march to Rome in 1922). A small Lion of Judah (the symbol of Ethiopian monarchy) sits victoriously atop the final step, like a jubilant punctuation mark at the end of a painfully long sentence.

STRANGE STREET SPELLINGS

Prior to 2005, finding a street sign in Addis was truly an art form. Today, finding a street sign is easy…it's finding one spelled correctly that's an art form!

Rumour has it that the shiny new signs were bequeathed by the Chinese contractors after they finished the ring road. Who's responsible for the misspellings is anyone's guess. Some of the many gaffes include Haile Selassie becoming Hailesilase, Joseph Tito becoming Josif Tito, Ras Makonnen becoming Ras Mekonen and Meskel Sq becoming Meskal Sq.

The new naming concept involved the removal of many colonial names and the introduction of many correctly spelt African ones, including each member state of the Organisation of African Unity (OAU). This has further added to the confusion as virtually none of the locals know these new names, and most people continue to refer to the pre-2005 names.

To stay consistent and limit confusion, we're using the creative new spellings on the actual street signs for our maps and text. Now all we need do is wait for the taxi drivers to catch up with us!

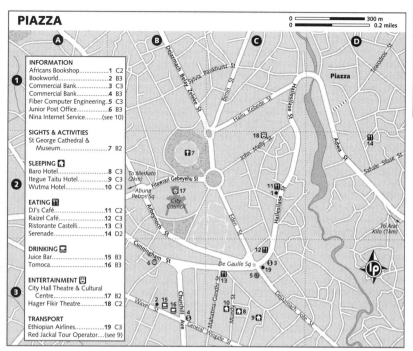

PIAZZA

INFORMATION
Africans Bookshop.................1 C2
Bookworld...........................2 B3
Commercial Bank..................3 C3
Commercial Bank..................4 B3
Fiber Computer Engineering..5 C3
Junior Post Office.................6 B3
Nina Internet Service.........(see 10)

SIGHTS & ACTIVITIES
St George Cathedral &
   Museum.........................7 B2

SLEEPING
Baro Hotel...........................8 C3
Itegue Taitu Hotel................9 C3
Wutma Hotel.......................10 C3

EATING
DJ's Café............................11 C2
Raizel Café.........................12 C3
Ristorante Castelli................13 C3
Serenade............................14 D2

DRINKING
Juice Bar............................15 B3
Tomoca..............................16 B3

ENTERTAINMENT
City Hall Theatre & Cultural
   Centre.............................17 B2
Hager Fikir Theatre.............18 C2

TRANSPORT
Ethiopian Airlines................19 C3
Red Jackal Tour Operator....(see 9)

Within the entrance hall you'll find a small exhibition dedicated to the history of the palace, and the doorway to the Institute of Language Studies library (p96).

This contemporary museum truly comes into its own on the 1st floor, where superb artefacts and handicrafts from Ethiopia's peoples are distinctively displayed. Instead of following the typical static and geographical layout that most museums fall into, these displays are based upon the life cycle. First comes Childhood, with birth, games, rites of passage and traditional tales. We particularly enjoyed the 'Yem Tale', a story of selfishness, dead leopards and sore tails! Adulthood probes into beliefs, nomadism, traditional medicine, war, pilgrimages, hunting, body culture and handicrafts. The last topic is Death and Beyond, with burial structures, stelae and tombs. The exhibition gives a great insight into Ethiopia's many rich cultures.

Other rooms on this floor show the preserved bedroom, bathroom and exorbitant changing room of Emperor Haile Selassie, complete with a bullet hole in his mirror courtesy of the 1960 coup d'état.

The 2nd floor plays home to two drastically different, but equally delightful displays. The vibrant hall focuses on religious art, with an exceptional series of diptychs, triptychs, icons, crosses and magic scrolls. Magic scrolls, like the Roman lead scrolls, were used to cast curses on people or to appeal to the gods for divine assistance. The collection of icons is the largest and most representative in the world. Senses of another sort are indulged in the small cavelike corridor that sits next to the hall. Inside, traditional music gently fills the air and the black surrounds leave you nothing to look at besides the instruments – brilliant.

It's well worth coming to this museum twice; once at the start of your journey through Ethiopia and once at the end when you'll be able to put everything into context.

National Museum ብሔራዊ መ-ዚየም
Although slightly less visually stimulating than the Ethnological Museum, the **National Museum** (Map p84; ☎ 0111 117150; King George VI St; admission Birr10; ☒ 8.30am-5pm) is no less thought-provoking. Its collection is ranked among the

most important in sub-Saharan Africa, but sadly most of its exhibits are poorly labelled, lit and displayed.

The palaeontology exhibit on the basement level contains fossilised evidence of some amazing extinct creatures, like the massive sabre-toothed feline *Homotherium* and the gargantuan savannah pig *Notochoerus*. However, the stars of the exhibit are two remarkable casts of **Lucy** (see p31), a fossilised hominid discovered in 1974. One lays prone, while the other stands much like she did some 3.2 million years ago, truly hitting home how small our ancient ancestors were. The real bones are preserved in the archives of the museum.

The periphery of the ground floor focuses on the pre-Aksumite, Aksumite, Solomonic and Gonder periods, with a wide array of artefacts, including an elaborate pre-1st-century-AD bronze oil lamp showing a dog chasing an ibex, a fascinating 4th-century-BC rock-hewn chair emblazoned with mythical ibexes, and ancient Sabaean inscriptions. The middle of the room hosts a collection of lavish royal paraphernalia, including Emperor Haile Selassie's enormous and rather hideous carved wooden throne.

On the 1st floor, there's a vivid display of Ethiopian art ranging from early (possibly 14th-century) parchment, to 20th-century canvas oil paintings by leading modern artists. Afewerk Tekle's massive *African Heritage* and Abebe Zelelew's *Genital Mutilation* are some of the most moving pieces.

The 2nd floor contains a collection of secular arts and crafts, including traditional weapons, jewellery, utensils, clothing and musical instruments.

English-speaking guides are available for free (they should be tipped afterwards) and help to bring things alive a little.

Holy Trinity Cathedral
ቅዱስ ስላሴ ቤተ ክርስቲያን

Off Niger St, this massive and ornate **cathedral** (Map p84; ☎ 0111 564619; admission Birr30; ⏰ 7am-6pm Mon-Fri, 9am-6pm Sat & Sun) is believed to be the second-most important place of worship in Ethiopia, ranking behind only the Old Church of St Mary of Zion in Aksum. It's also the celebrated final resting place of Emperor Haile Selassie and his wife Empress Menen Asfaw. Their massive Aksumite-style granite tombs sit inside and are a sight indeed.

The exterior, with its large copper dome, spindly pinnacles, numerous statues and flamboyant mixture of international styles, provides an interesting and sometimes poignant glimpse into many historical episodes of Ethiopia's history.

Inside, there are some grand murals, the most notable being Afewerk Tekle's depiction of the Holy Trinity, with Matthew (man), Mark (lion), Luke (cow) and John (dove) peering through the clouds. There are also some brilliant stained-glass windows and two beautifully carved imperial thrones, each made of white ebony, ivory and marble.

To the south of the cathedral is the memorial and graves of the ministers killed by the Derg (see p44) in 1974. Due to the prime minister's compound being behind this memorial, photographs are strictly forbidden.

The churchyard also hosts the graves of many patriots who died fighting the Italian occupation, including the great Resistance fighter Ras Imru. West of the cathedral is the tomb of the famous British suffragette Sylvia Pankhurst. Sylvia was one of the very few people outside Ethiopia who protested Italy's occupation; she moved to Addis Ababa in 1956.

Purchase tickets at the administration office 20m west of the main gate. Self-appointed guides charge Birr10 to Birr15 per person.

MENELIK BUYS A NEW CHAIR

If Emperor Menelik II, the founder of Addis Ababa, was alive today he'd have been the first in the queue for the latest mobile phone or other technological gadget. If it was new and flashy he just had to have one. So when he first heard about a new invention in America called the electric chair he decided that Ethiopia just had to have a couple of these ingenious death machines. After months of waiting the new contraptions arrived in Addis. When he first saw them the emperor was delighted with the craftsmanship that had gone into them and asked for a demonstration. It was only then, and no doubt to the great relief of the chosen 'demonstrator', that Menelik's technicians suddenly realised that electricity hadn't yet been turned on in Ethiopia…

AFEWERK TEKLE

Born in 1932, Afewerk Tekle is one of Ethiopia's most distinguished and colourful artistic figures. Educated at the Slade School of Art in London, he later toured and studied in continental Europe before returning to work under the patronage of Emperor Haile Selassie. A painter as well as a sculptor and designer, he's also a master fencer, dancer and toastmaster.

Proud to have 'survived three regimes' (when friends and peers did not), his life has hardly been without incident. In almost cinematic style, a 'friendly' fencing match turned into an attempt on his life, and a tussle over a woman led to his challenging his rival to a duel at dawn. In the royal court of the emperor, he once only just survived an assassination attempt by poisoned cocktail.

The artist famously makes his own terms and conditions: if he doesn't like the purchaser he won't sell, and his best-known paintings must be returned to Ethiopia within a lifetime. He's even turned down over US$12 million for the work considered his masterpiece, *The Meskel Flower*.

St George Cathedral & Museum
ቅዱስ ጊዮርጊስ ቤተ ክርስቲያንና መ-ዘ/ም

Commissioned by Emperor Menelik to commemorate his stunning 1896 defeat of the Italians in Adwa, and dedicated to St George (Ethiopia's patron saint), whose icon was carried into the battle, this Piazza **cathedral** (Map p91; Fitawrari Gebeyehu St) was completed in 1911 with the help of Greek, Armenian and Indian artists. The Empress Zewditu (in 1916) and Emperor Haile Selassie (in 1930) were both crowned here.

Thanks to its traditional octagonal form and severe neoclassical style, the grey stone exterior is easily outdone by the interior's flashes of colour and art. Sections of ceiling glow sky-blue and boast gilded golden stars, while the outer walls of the Holy of Holies are covered in paintings and mosaics by artists such as the renowned Afewerk Tekle.

In the grounds just north of the cathedral is the **museum** (admission Birr20; ⏰ 9am-noon & 2-5pm Tue-Sun). It's well presented and contains probably the best collection of ecclesiastical paraphernalia in the country outside St Mary of Zion in Aksum. Items include beautiful crowns, hand crosses, prayer sticks, holy scrolls, ceremonial umbrellas and the coronation garb of Zewditu and Haile Selassie. The free tour, which includes the cathedral, is interesting and helpful in demystifying the peculiarities of the Orthodox church.

Yekatit 12 Monument
የካቲት 12 መታሰቢያ ሐውልት

Rising dramatically from Siddist Kilo is this moving **monument** (Map p84; Siddist Kilo) to the thousands of innocent Ethiopians killed by the Italians as retribution for the attempt on Viceroy Graziani's life on 19 February 1937.

Derg Monument
የድል ሐው-ልት (ድላችን)

Nothing in the capital is as poignant a reminder of the country's painful communist rule as the towering **Derg Monument** (Map p86-7; Churchill Ave). Topped by a massive red star and emblazoned with a golden hammer and sickle, the cement obelisklike structure climbs skyward in front of Black Lion Hospital.

Merkato መርካቶ

Wading into the market chaos just west of the centre known as **Merkato** (Map p84; ⏰ 6am-7pm Mon-Sat) can as rewarding as it can be exasperating. You may find the most eloquent aroma wafting from precious incense. You may also find that your wallet has been stolen and that you've got stinky shit on your shoe.

Some people say it's the largest market in Africa, but as its exact boundaries are as shady as some of its characters, this is a little hard to verify. What should be noted, however, is that this isn't one of those nicely photogenic markets with goods laid out on the ground or on little stalls. Most vendors now have permanent tin shacks in which to house their wares, so in some eyes this changes the market from a scene of exotica to just a slum.

The mass of stalls, produce and people may seem impenetrable, but on closer inspection the market reveals a careful organisation with different sections for different products. If you search long enough, you can find everything from Kalashnikovs to camels for sale. Not interested in leaving Merkato on the back of your own humped, frothy-mouthed beast while firing live rounds into the air? Well, you can spend your birr on pungent spices, silver jewellery or anything else that takes your fancy. There's even a 'recycling market', where sandals (made out of old tyres), coffee pots (old Italian olive tins) and other interesting paraphernalia can be found.

We could tell you that bargaining is the order of the day and that you should be vigilant with your valuables, but you're seasoned travellers and you already know that!

Merkato is at its liveliest on Saturday, when people from all over the country flock in, but once again, do be warned that if you're going to be robbed anywhere in Ethiopia it will be here!

Natural History Museum
የተፈጥሮ ታሪክ ሙዚየም

Go eye to eye with a bloated leopard in this **zoological museum** (Map p84; ☎ 0111 571677; Queen Elizabeth II St; admission Birr10; ☺ 9am-5pm Tue-Sun). Yes, sometimes the stuffers just don't know when to stop stuffing! Don't let the poor leopard scare you off; most animal specimens here are rather remarkable and there's no better way to spot nature's amazing intricacies. Besides magically iridescent butterflies, you'll see an impressive walia ibex, numerous antelopes and an astounding bird collection comprising 450 species common to Ethiopia.

Addis Ababa Museum
አዲስ አበባ ሙዚየም

Despite only being founded on the centenary of the city in 1986, the **Addis Ababa Museum** (Map pp86-7; ☎ 0115 153180; Bole Rd; admission Birr15; ☺ 9am-5.30pm Tue-Sun) is the town's scruffiest museum. That said, perusing candid portraits of the redoubtable Empress Taitu, rakish Lej Iyassu and the very beautiful Empress Zewditu, along with pictures of the capital in its infancy, is still worth an hour or so. It's unbelievable that the raucous city outside was nothing more than tents on a hill just over a century ago.

There's also a 'first-in-Ethiopia room' with a picture of the first telephone in Ethiopia and another of Menelik with Bede Bentley in Addis Ababa's first motor car (1907).

And we'd be remiss if we didn't mention the chummy (and over-inflated) lion and leopard near the entrance. Will somebody let the Natural History Museum know they've escaped?!

Africa Hall አፍሪካ አዳራሽ

Built in 1961 by Emperor Haile Selassie, **Africa Hall** (Map pp86-7; ☎ 0115 445098; Menelik II Ave), near Meskal Sq, is the seat of the UN's ECA. The Italian-designed building isn't very interesting, apart from the friezelike motifs that represent traditional Ethiopian *shamma* (shawl) borders.

Far more interesting is *Africa: Past, Present and Future,* a monumental stained-glass window inside by the artist Afewerk Tekle. Measuring 150 sq metres, it fills one entire wall and is one of the biggest stained-glass windows in the world. During some hours of the day, the white marble floor of the foyer is flooded with colour. It's well worth a visit (by appointment only).

Beta Maryam Mausoleum
ቤተ ማርያም መቃብር

Also known as Menelik's Mausoleum, the **Beta Maryam Mausoleum** (Map pp86-7; Itegue Menen Rd; ☺ 8am-5pm) is located just south of Menelik's palace and offers an enchantingly eerie experience for travellers. After the priest has rolled up the carpet and pried open the large metal door in the floor, you will descend into the thick air of the creepy crypt. There you will find the four elaborate marble tombs of Empress Taitu, Emperor Menelik, Empress Zewditu and Princess Tsehai Haile Selassie.

A self-appointed guide should set you back about Birr10 to Birr15 per person.

Asni Gallery
አስኒ ጋሊሪ (የሸሸል አዳራሽ)

Housed in the 1912 villa of Lej Iyasu's minister of justice, the **Asni Gallery** (Map p84; ☎ 0111 238796; admission free; ☺ 10am-5.30pm Tue-Sat, closed Jul & Aug) annually hosts six or seven splendid contemporary art exhibitions of emerging and established Ethiopian artists. Other events include workshops and lectures; look for announcements in the *Addis Tribune* or *What's Up!*

The turn-off is about 4km northeast of town centre, just north of the French embassy. Take a minibus from Arat Kilo heading to 'Francey' and get off at the Total petrol station. It's a short walk from there.

Afewerk Tekle's Home & Studio
የአፈወርቅ ተክሌ ቤት ና ስቲዲዮ

A member of several international academies and with a drawer full of international decorations – about 100 at last count, including the British Order of Merit – Afewerk Tekle is considered among Africa's greatest artists.

A 90-minute tour of **Villa Alpha** (Map p84; ☎ 0113 715941; www.maitreafewerktekle.com; admission per person US$30; ☒ closed 1 Jul-15 Sep), Afewerk's home and studio, is offered by the artist himself (by appointment only). Besides gazing at his most famous paintings, *The Meskel Flower, Mother Ethiopia* and *The Simien Mountains,* you'll also see striking works like *The Chalice and Cross* and hear stories about his life and Villa Alpha itself – all quite fascinating.

If you're thinking of souvenirs, signed and numbered reproductions on canvas are a snip at US$200 to US$400, while vivid tapestries climb into the thousands.

The house and studio is west of the centre in a side street off the Ring Rd, 200m from the Ghanaian embassy.

The artist did tell us that he is considering emigrating and if he does decide to move abroad (he didn't tell us where), then you'll probably struggle to find a taxi in Addis that can take you to him…

For more information on Afewerk Tekle see the boxed text, p93.

Lion of Judah Monument
ጥቁር አንበሳ ሐው-ልት

Long the symbol of Ethiopia's monarchy, the Lion of Judah is ubiquitous throughout the country. Although images of the almighty animal abound in Addis Ababa, it's the storied history of the **Lion of Judah Monument** (Map pp86-7; Gambia St) that makes this statue significant.

After being erected on the eve of Haile Selassie's coronation in 1930, it was looted by Italians in 1935 and placed in Rome next to the massive Vittorio Emanuelle Monument. In 1938, during anniversary celebrations of the proclamation of the Italian Empire, Zerai Deress, a young Eritrean, spotted the statue and defiantly interrupted proceedings to kneel and pray before it. After police verbally and physically attempted to stop his prayers, he rose and attacked the armed Italians with his sword while screaming 'the Lion of Judah is avenged!' He seriously injured several officers (some reports say he killed five) before he was shot. Although he died seven years later in an Italian prison, his legend lives on in Ethiopia and Eritrea.

The Lion of Judah Monument was eventually returned to Addis Ababa in the 1960s.

Addis Ababa, Ethiopia & Africa Parks

Straddled by Menelik II Ave and climbing sequentially northwards from Africa Hall, these three new **urban parks** (Map pp86-7; Menelik II Ave) opened in early 2006. Lovely landscaping, with winding walkways, churning channels of cascading water, tidy trees and green grass, unite the three parks and make a pleasant respite in the city centre.

ACTIVITIES

Thanks to hosting the UN's ECA, activities are more catered to businesspeople than backpackers. Though, after returning from a tough slog out on the Ethiopian roads, many travellers indulge in a heavenly massage, steam bath or sauna. Cooling swims are also justifiably popular.

Massage, Steam Bath & Sauna

The **Boston Day Spa** (Map pp86-7; ☎ 0116 636557; Bole Rd; ☒ 8.30am-8.30pm) has a great reputation. Massages start at Birr200. A session in the sauna, steam bath and jacuzzi is Birr200 and includes a free foot massage. They also provide a waxing service and have a hairdresser.

A sublime massage at the **Sheraton Hotel** (Map pp86-7; ☎ 0115 171717; Itegue Taitu St; ☒ 9am-9pm) starts at Birr165. Use of the sauna and jacuzzi is Birr240.

While certainly not as sophisticated as the previous three options, the **Addisu Filwoha Hotel & Hot Springs** (Map pp86-7; ☎ 0115 517317; ☒ 24hr) complex is powered by Addis Ababa's original raison d'être: its natural hot springs. A public bath in the steaming mineral water is only Birr8 to Birr12, while a sauna is Birr28. You don't have to be in Ethiopia long to realise that sexual attitudes are fairly free and easy and this place is no exception (for heterosexual couples, anyway). In fact, if you go as a couple it's expected that you will have sex in the bath. Make sure you follow the rules, which say that you must use a condom, which you then have to leave neatly in the corner! The complex is off Yohanis St.

Running

If you want to run with the best of the best, come to **Meskal Square** before dawn (5am is a good time) where you'll find household-name runners going through their paces as they jog up and down the square. If you complete the entire circuit, running up and down each aisle, you'll have sweated through 42km. Note that the standard is high and weekend-warrior runners will be considered an obstacle – if you fall into this category then it's best to just watch!

Horse Riding

Equus Ethiopia (☎ 0911 102609; www.equus-ethiopia .com; Birr2000) organise two-day horse-riding trips through the Menagesha Forest not far from Addis. Food, accommodation and your steed are included in the price. They also organise much longer multiday horse-trekking trips throughout central Ethiopia.

Swimming

Beat the heat with some underwater action. The sweetest swims in town are to be had at the **Sheraton Hotel** (Map pp86-7; Itegue Taitu St; nonguest admission weekday/weekend Birr120/185) and **Hilton Hotel** (Map pp86-7; Menelik II Ave; nonguest admission weekday/weekend Birr100/150).

COURSES

Institute of Language Studies (Map p84; ☎ 0111 239702; Addis Ababa University, Algeria St) teaches three Ethiopian languages (Amharic, Tigrinya and Orominya). Classes start in early December and early April, lasting three to four months (48 hours of lectures).

Head immediately left after entering the main university gates. The office is on the 2nd floor, room 210.

TOURS

There are no scheduled tours of Addis Ababa itself; however, if you contact one of Addis Ababa's many travel agencies (see p270), most can usually arrange something.

FESTIVALS & EVENTS

Although Addis doesn't boast any major festivals of its own, it's a great place to catch some of the national festivals. For Leddet and Timkat, head to Jan Meda Sports Ground where the most exuberant celebrations take place. During Leddet the festivities also include a traditional game of *genna* (hockey without boundaries). When the festival of Meskel is underway, Meskal Sq is one of the best places to be in the country. For more details on these festivals, see p248.

Inaugurated in 2001, the 10km **Great Ethiopian Run** (www.ethiopiarun.org) is now the biggest mass participation race on the continent. It takes over the city on the last Sunday of November and attracts over 20,000 runners. Whether running or watching, it's a fun time and it's a great chance to see some of East Africa's elite athletes in action.

For minor festivals and upcoming cultural events, check out www.addisallaround.com.

SLEEPING

Accommodation runs the gamut in Addis – brandish your flip-flop and do battle with almighty insects, or sink into your sumptuous suite at the Sheraton. It's all up to you, your budget and the strength of your flip-flops.

But the one thing that unites all hotels in Addis is value for money. Put simply, the vast majority are not.

For many years, budget travellers have congregated around the Piazza; however, with the hotels there starting to look a bit creaky and a handful of newer options springing up in and around the more salubrious surrounds of Bole and Haile Gebreselassie Rds, it could be time for a change of scene.

Hotel owners in Addis quote their rates in a mixture of birr or US dollars, though all accept payment in birr. We have quoted prices using the currency the hotel uses. All hotels listed here have parking facilities unless mentioned otherwise.

Centre
BUDGET

Holland House (Map pp86-7; ☎ 0115 155279; wims_hollan house@ethionet.et; camping Birr70, jeep Birr70, truck/bus Birr100, r Birr70; 🖳) Hidden in the maze of lanes to the east of the train station this campsite, the sole overlanders' party in the city, is a cramped area normally overflowing with hardened road warriors talking about oil filters. For campers without a truck to kip in, privacy can be very hard to come by and the rooms are very basic (bring your own mattress). There's a busy bar, frequent party nights, a kitchen for guest use and even an in-house mechanic.

Lido Hotel (Map pp86-7; ☎ 0115 514488; Sudan St; d from Birr178) Set behind some doum palms and cactus plants off Sudan St, the rooms at this clean hotel will bring a sparkle to the eye (rooms 8 and 9 are the brightest of the bunch) and the attached restaurant, with delights like vegetable lasagne (Birr35), will bring a smile to the lips.

Buffet de la Gare (Map pp86-7; ☎ 0911 411241; s/d Birr140/180) Once upon a time the chuff-chuffing of passing steam trains would have soothed you to sleep here. With the trains no longer functioning, peace and quiet prevails, but the atmosphere harks back to the age of rail travel – the attached bar even looks like a train carriage. The handful of rooms, set around a garden, are old but clean and come with some character.

MIDRANGE
Ras Hotel (Map pp86-7; ☎ 0115 517060; fax 0115 517327; Gambia St; s/d incl breakfast from Birr151.80/202.40) Set squarely in the town centre, this government-run hotel might be fading a little and feel a bit like a sanatorium, but it's a real institution and has a constant buzz of people coming and going. The large rooms are a fair deal and some have views over the slums – so that's nice. Aside from the location the best asset are the numerous facilities, including a decent bar and restaurant, internet cafe and travel agent.

TOP END
Sheraton Hotel (Map pp86-7; ☎ 0115 171717; www.luxury collection.com/addis; Itegue Taitu St; s/d from US$552.50/630, villa US$12,500; ✖ ▢ ▨) One of Africa's most elite hotels, the Sheraton is astounding and, in a country like Ethiopia, almost obscene. Actually even in a country like the USA, spending US$12,500 a night on a room would still be considered obscene! Needless to say it's only really presidents and top diplomats spending your taxes who stay here.

Bole Rd Area
BUDGET
Wanza Hotel (Map pp86-7; ☎ 0115 504893; Democratic Republic Congo St; s/d Birr80/120) Despite sporadic flowing hot water and the odd creepy-crawly to cuddle up with, this place, with cosy rooms, comfortable beds and helpful owner, is one of Addis Ababa's better bare-bones options.

Almaz Pension/Almaz Tadesse Guest House (Map pp86-7; Democratic Republic Congo St; d/tw without bathroom Birr130/180, s/d with bathroom Birr180/200; ▢) The cheaper rooms here are several floors up in a tower block (no lift), which at least lets you burn off the cake you ate earlier. The ground floor rooms are darker but spacious and comfy. There's no sign – look for the pizzeria sign and it's 10m down the side alley and on the left through the double white doors. The

internet here is devastatingly fast for Addis. Good value.

MIDRANGE
Tina Pension and Guest House (Map pp86-7; ☎ 0115 549090; tinapension@yahoo.com; d incl breakfast Birr300, ste Birr600; ▢) On a dusty back lane off Bole Rd and surrounded by flowering trees, this clean and secure guesthouse offers decent rooms with frilly bedspreads and hot-water showers. It feels far removed from the hustle of the city centre.

Weygoss Guest House (Map pp86-7; ☎ 0115 512205; s/d incl breakfast US$45/55) Lacking a sign and hidden up an alley just north of Ethio Supermarket, this five-storey guesthouse is well looked-after and friendly. It's very popular with foreigners looking to adopt a local child and some might find the resultant atmosphere a little strange.

Meridian Hotel (Map pp86-7; ☎ 0116 615050; meridian-hotel@ethionet.et; Zimbabwe St; d/tw incl breakfast US$58/68; ▢) It's a little dated, but as one of the few midrange hotels not to have raised their prices out of all proportion to inflation over the past couple of years, it now represents good value for this category. Discounts are also easy to come by.

Selam Pension (Map pp86-7; ☎ 0115 533171; selam pension2@yahoo.com; Gabon St; d/tw incl breakfast Birr230/450) Without doubt this shining white palace offers one of the better deals in Addis. It's brand new so still very clean, though the bathrooms are a little cramped. It's also well run and far enough from the road to mean honking horns won't interrupt your sleep – too much! The sign is in Amharic only, so ask someone to point it out.

TOP END
Kuriftu Guest House/Boston Guest House (Map pp86-7; ☎ 0116 623809; thekuriftuguesthouse@yahoo.com; 6th fl Boston Partners Bldg, Bole Rd; r incl breakfast US$125; ▢) It's not cheap, but if you're after class with a homely tint then this intimate hotel has a lot of character. The colours are sunburst Mediterranean and the furnishings a stylised orange and white, the beds are enormous and the showers are like waterfalls. Other perks include free massages, sauna and wi-fi internet throughout.

Piazza & North
BUDGET
At all of the following budget hotels, keep your eyes peeled for dodgy individuals. We've

received reports of theft from both the Itegue Taitu and Wutma (though in none of the cases did the victims suspect the staff), and at all three hotels, touts, sleezers and no-hopers congregate outside.

Itegue Taitu Hotel (Map p91; ☎ 0111 560787; www .taituhotel.com; r without bathroom Birr66-191, r with bathroom Birr154-299) Appear in the dream of an empress! Built at the whim of Empress Taitu in 1907, this is the oldest hotel in Addis, and the main building is virtually a museum piece full of beautiful old furniture. However, it could be so much more if someone gave it just a bit of care. The newer block contains a wide range of rooms, including some very jolly doubles. There are plenty of facilities, a lovely garden in which breakfast is served and lots of other travellers to hang out with. All up it offers a cash-strapped overlander a classy experience for very little coin.

Baro Hotel (Map p91; ☎ 0111 551447; barohotel @ethionet.et; Mundy St; d inside main bldg Birr70, s/d/tw in courtyard rooms Birr95/130/130) Vying with the Wutma Hotel over the road for the title of Backpacker King, the rooms at the Baro, which are decidedly skanky, come out in 2nd place, but its garden, which is a fantastic place to meet other travellers, wins it big points.

Wutma Hotel (Map p91; ☎ 0111 562878; wutma @yahoo.com; Mundy St; s/d Birr100/150) No, it doesn't have Baro's garden atmosphere or cosy nook to watch satellite TV, but its smallish grey-walled rooms outshine all but a few of Baro's, and it's certainly much better maintained. The downstairs restaurant is as popular with travellers as the Baro's garden. There are no parking facilities.

MIDRANGE

Ras Amba Hotel (Map p84; ☎ 0115 530098; Queen Elizabeth II St; s/d/tr US$53/69/91; 🖳) Tucked quietly away east of Piazza and affording superb views over much of the city is this charming choice. There's a gorgeous rooftop terrace, rooms are relatively modern and comfortable and the carpets not too stained. Most have balconies and all have satellite TVs. It's sadly overpriced though.

SouthWest
BUDGET

Amel Pension (Map pp86-7; ☎ 0114 674058; off Meskal Flower St; d Birr150) We hope you're an early-morning person because the next-door mosque's pre-dawn prayer call is like the alarm clock from Hell. If you do like early mornings, then you'll find that this is a decent option with rooms that feels worth the price. The rooms are giant pink cubes with erratic electricity supplies.

Palm Pension (Map pp86-7; ☎ 0114 162606; off Meskal Flower St; d Birr200) If this wasn't so far out it would be a great deal – it's very peaceful, has a pocket-sized garden, safe parking for exhausted jeeps and large, tidy rooms kept polished and smart. To get there cross the railway tracks at the end of Meskal Flower St and walk down the dirt road for 100m.

MIDRANGE

our pick **La Source Guest House** (Map p84; ☎ 0114 665510; Meskal Flower Rd; s/d incl breakfast Bir220/288) Finally, Addis has produced a guesthouse that truly feels like it offers value for money. It's sparkling clean with constant hot water and it even has that rare thing – character, in abundance. All the rooms have loud and lovely African art and masks adorning the walls, rainbow-tainted bedspreads and furnishings made of bendy, twisted tree branches. There are a couple of lovely communal areas with big-screen satellite TVs and an open-to-all afternoon coffee ceremony. There's a generator to see you through the blackouts and it's on a quiet and safe side street.

TOP END

Adot-Tina Hotel (Map pp86-7; ☎ 0114 673939; www.adot tina.com; Meskal Flower Rd; s/d incl breakfast from US$87-100; 🖳) The small and plush rooms of this intimate business-class hotel, which come with either a deep relaxing bath or a space-age shower that was far too complicated for us to work out, are really good value. However, the seal on the deal might be the free sauna and gym (OK, maybe the gym isn't so appealing to some) and the best internet we found anywhere in Ethiopia.

East
BUDGET

Around Mike Leyland St and Haile Gebreselassie Rd are some of the best budget and midrange hotels in Addis. In addition you'll find plenty of restaurants and bars and none of the touts or hustlers of the Piazza. Currently few travellers stay here but expect that to start changing fast as word spreads.

Yahoo Pension (Map pp86-7; ☎ 0913 103562; off Mike Leyland St; r from Birr70) Basic but well-kept and clean, which is all that really matters. Unusually for this price all rooms have attached bathrooms (cold water only). The staff are ever smiling and it's on a tranquil side street. For the price it's hard to find fault.

Lana Pension (Map pp86-7; ☎ 0116 552125; off Mike Leyland St; r Birr100) With oversized rooms, not a speck of muck in sight, hot-water showers and a pleasant, and safe, location this might well be the best budget digs in all of Addis. The only drawback might be that the owner only speaks Amharic.

Addis Pension (Map pp86-7; ☎ 0116 184495; off Mike Leyland St; r Birr150) The rooms at this modern pension are small and space is at a premium, but they've made the most of what they have and crammed in all the luxuries you really need – bed, table and a bathroom with a hot shower. Compared with what's on offer downtown, this is a bargain.

Mr Martins Cozy Place (Map pp86-7; ☎ 0911 423972; Mike Leyland St; s/d/apt Birr100/120/180; ⌨) This colourful little German-run backpackers is fast gaining a name for itself as one of the better-value cheapies in the city. All the rooms are impeccably clean, though a little poky, and there's a pleasant courtyard restaurant to hang out in. All rooms share clean common bathrooms.

Henok Guest House (Map pp86-7; ☎ 0116 624234; off Mike Leyland St; r from Birr200) The rooms here, which are set around a sun-baked courtyard, are clean and as well-cared for as you can hope to find in this price range. It's tucked away up a maze of dusty tracks, so it stays nice and quiet. Electricity isn't a strong point.

MIDRANGE

ourpick **Dream Palace Guest House** (Map pp86-7; ☎ 0111 6635972; wubguesthouse@ethionet.et; off Haile Gebreselassie Rd; r Birr150-500; ⌨) This superb option has something for all purse strings. Around the back of the house are a handful of simple and spotless cubical rooms with hot-water showers. Next up, and in the main building, come the spacious, well-planned midrange rooms (Birr300). Finally you get the magnificent royalty-wannabe rooms, which have massive arched windows and two-person jacuzzis, among other creature comforts. It's in a quiet location behind the run-down Axum Hotel, and has safe parking.

TOP END

Desalegn Hotel (Map pp86-7; ☎ 0116 624524; desalegne hotel@ethionet.et; Cape Verde St; s/d/tw incl breakfast US$76/76/91; ⌨) Despite being at the low end of the top-end spectrum, service here is first class. The bathrooms are more modern than most and rooms are spotless and large, though they're stretched at the seams with furniture, satellite TVs and fridges. The downside is that you get stung if travelling solo or with someone who really is 'just a friend'. There's a terrace bar with panoramic views, a free gym and reasonably priced steam baths and massages.

TDS Hotel (Map pp86-7; ☎ 0116 635816; Cameroon St; d/ste US$59/75; ⌨) This impressive new hotel has a manic cleaner who stalks the corridors hunting down every speck of dirt and wiping it out, dark wood furniture that's been polished until it shines like a mirror, super-comfortable beds and possibly the best showers in the country. On top of all that there's a decent restaurant and friendly service.

EATING

You lucky, lucky souls…you've either just stepped off a plane (Welcome to Ethiopia! Lucky you!) and can indulge in a feast of gastronomic pleasures for a fraction of what it would cost at home, or you've just arrived from several weeks in Ethiopia's wilds (How amazing was that?! Lucky you!) and now have what looks like Manhattan's menu on your doorstep. Middle Eastern or Mexican? French or Ethiopian? Due to Il Duce's imperial ambitions and many an Italian immigrant, Addis Ababa also boasts some extraordinary Italian cuisine. The Bole Rd area is king (or should we say maharajah) when it comes to Indian. Eat what you choose and enjoy.

Many restaurants, particularly the smarter ones, add a 15% tax and 10% service charge to their bills; check before you order.

Many Ethiopian restaurants offer a 'traditional experience': traditional food (called 'national food') in traditional surroundings with traditional music in the evening. You sit in short traditional Ethiopian chairs, eating from a communal plate on a *mesob* (Ethiopian table).

If you feel more adventurous, try the *kitfo beats* (pronounced 'kitfo bet'), which are typically ignored by tourists. These restaurants usually serve little other than *kitfo* (minced beef or lamb like the French steak tartare, usually served warmed – but not cooked – in butter, *berbere* and sometimes thyme).

If meat isn't your thing, you'll love Wednesday and Friday because fasting food (a variety of vegetarian dishes) is served by all Ethiopian restaurants.

Check out Food & Drink (p66) for more information about Ethiopian cuisine and eating etiquette.

Cafes and pastry shops are omnipresent in Addis, and you'll find them perfect for an afternoon or early morning pick-me-up. Places that stand out for their drinks are found on p102, while those that make the grade in the edible end of the spectrum are found here.

Centre

Dashen Traditional Restaurant (Map pp86-7; ☎ 0115 529746; mains Birr15-40; ⏱ 10am-10pm) From the outside, this Ethiopian eatery doesn't look promising. However, if you venture in past the courtyard, you'll find a lovely low-key dining area, with stone walls, local art and bamboo furniture. The soft lighting and intimate surrounds are perfect for your first awkward attempts at injera. Its fasting food is particularly good (it's also available with fish). The restaurant is off Itegue Taitu St.

China Bar & Restaurant (Map pp86-7; Ras Desta Damtew St; mains Birr18-60; ⏱ 11.30am-10.30pm) If you're craving something sweet or sour, this central Chinese is the most convenient place – though not everybody rates the food. We thought it passed the test.

Yeshi Buna (Map pp86-7; Ras Desta Damtew St; meals Birr20-30) One of a chain of local coffee shops with brain-bending strength caffeine fixes served in the traditional style, and a good range of Ethiopian meals.

Shaheen (Map pp86-7; ☎ 0115 171717; Sheraton Hotel, Itegue Taitu St; mains Birr50-160; ⏱ noon-3pm & 7-11pm) Set within the Sheraton's confines, Shaheen is Addis Ababa's most sophisticated Indian restaurant. The decor in the restaurant is grand and the melange of Indian curries and tandooris is vast.

Cottage Restaurant & Pub (Map pp86-7; ☎ 0115 516359; Ras Desta Damtew St; mains Birr60; ⏱ noon-2pm & 6-10pm) This cosy wooden cottage is an expat favourite for a smart lunch. While the menu is varied, ranging from Madras chicken curry and pizza to veal medallions in a *morille* (mushroom) sauce, its speciality is the beef fondue (Birr195 for two). Few leave disappointed.

Stagion (Map pp86-7; ☎ 0115 171717; Sheraton Hotel, Itegue Taitu St; mains Birr65-280; ⏱ noon-3pm & 7-11pm) If *risotto alle vongole e verdurine fresche dell'orto* (rice simmered with clams and garden vegetables) or *cartuccio di pesce persico del Nilo con patate e pinoli* (fillet of Nile perch with pine seeds and potatoes) makes your stomach quiver with excitement, slide into this great Italian restaurant.

Bole Rd Area

La Parisienne (Map pp86-7; Gabon St; pastries Birr2-5; ⏱ 6am-8pm) If you're staying in this part of town (in fact even if you're not), then there's only one place for breakfast and that's this mega-popular terrace cafe with superb *macchiato*, croissants and freshly squeezed orange juices. If the waitresses could only develop more of a Gallic 'I can't be bothered to serve you' shrug then you'd think you were on the Champs-Élysées.

Pasticceria Gelateria – Roby's Pastry (Map pp86-7; Bole Rd; desserts Birr4-7; ⏱ 7am-8pm) Doles out refreshing homemade ice cream and mouthwatering cakes.

Sunshine Chicken House (Map pp86-7; Bole Rd; mains Birr7-20) If chicken is your thing, this solid old cafe-cum-fast-food-joint serves them up in thirty different ways, from classic spit-roasted to stir-fried.

New York, New York (Map pp86-7; Bole Rd; mains Birr15-20; ⏱ 8am-10pm) Missing the Big Macs of the Big Apple? Then fill yourself with Big Boy burgers at this evergreen expat fuel stop.

Addis Sport & le Petit Café (Map pp86-7; Bole Rd; mains Birr15-30; ⏱ 6am-10pm) Although it's a jack-of-all-trades restaurant, this place is renowned for its superb *ful* (chickpea and butter purée). Despite the name there isn't a giant TV screen showing the football over and over again; neither do its patrons look very sporty.

Lime Tree (Map pp86-7; Bole Rd; mains Birr17-34; ⏱ 7am-11pm) The evergreen, ever-lime Lime Tree remains one of the hippest places in Addis to have a light lunch. The menu includes such delights as pita stuffed with tabouli or felafel, and chicken coconut curry. The decor is bright and bold and there's an in-house bookshop, gallery and noticeboard.

Rico's Restaurant, Pizzeria & Bar (Map pp86-7; ☎ 0115 539462; Bole Rd; mains Birr20-35; ⏱ noon-10pm) A stylish, brightly lit place serving everything from Moroccan kebabs to blackened Cajun fish and buffalo wings dripping with Texan BBQ sauce.

Sangam Restaurant (Map pp86-7; Bole Rd; mains Birr20-50; ⏱ 11.30am-3pm & 6.30-10pm) If you've developed a craving for a cracking curry, try this atmospheric eatery. Here you can wrap your lips around *mughali biryani* (fragrant rice), tandoori dishes or butter chicken masala – absolutely delicious! There are also great lunchtime *thalis* (mixed meals) available every day but Sunday.

Almendi Restaurant (Map pp86–7; mains Birr25-75; 7-10pm) You'll leave this excellent Arabian-style eatery as full as an egg. We ordered a simple shish kebab and it arrived with flat bread, soup, salad and various meats in sauces – all tasty and very filling! The *mendi* (sheep) is also great and the *fetira* (bread with honey) makes a perfect accompaniment. It's 100m down a dirt lane leading off Democratic Republic Congo St.

Antica Restaurant (Map pp86–7; ☎ 0116 634841; mains Birr30-40; noon-2.30pm & 6-10pm) Watch chefs manoeuvre airborne dough while you wait for your delectable thin-crust pizza at this upscale Italian option. There are two-dozen pizzas on the menu – toppings range from anchovies and capers to prosciutto and sausage. There's also a cafe-bar downstairs that comes alive in the evening. It's off Cape Verde St.

Fasika Restaurant (Map pp86–7; mains Birr35-45; 11.30am-3pm & 6pm-midnight Mon-Sat) Although less sophisticated than Habesha, Fasika also has a great atmosphere, with an exotic interior and live music most nights from 8pm. Its kitchen is equally apt and produces fine Ethiopian fare. It's located 150m up a dirt lane off Bole Rd's north end.

Gati Thai (Map pp86–7; ☎ 0912 156396; mains Birr40-70; 11.30am-11pm Mon-Sat, 5.30-11pm Sun) Addis's lonely Thai restaurant is a much-appreciated respite from injera or pasta.

Makush Art Gallery & Restaurant (Map pp86–7; ☎ 0115 526848; Bole Rd; mains Birr45-70; noon-2pm & 6-10pm) Surrounded by vivid paintings, wood-carvings, candlelit tables, attentive waiters and elevator music (hey, nothing's perfect!), the ambience of this restaurant definitely outdoes the food, which can only be described as passable Italian. It's in an office tower above Ethio Supermarket.

our pick **Jewel of India** (Map pp86–7; ☎ 0115 513154; Gabon St; mains Birr50-60; 6.30pm-11pm) This authentic Indian-run restaurant specialises in tandoori dishes, but whatever you opt for is certain to tickle your taste buds in just the right way. And what a treat it is to taste spicy food with texture and form rather than just heat!

Sana'a Restaurant (Map pp86–7; Gabon St; mains Birr50-80; 11am-3pm & 6-9pm) For both the local Muslim and Christian communities this busy place is a lunchtime institution – queues can form for a table out the door! The reason they all flock here? Good honest Yemeni fare, including spicy hot *salta* (a highland stew/soup) and the house special, Yemeni-style chicken and rice. All meals come with a healthy dose of Yemeni fun and conversation.

Habesha Restaurant (Map pp86–7; Bole Rd; mains Birr60-80; noon-3pm & 6pm-2am) For an Ethiopian meal that looks as good as it tastes, come to this Bole eatery where serving seems to be an art form. After a flurry of handwork, our injera was beautifully laden with everything from *gored gored* (raw beef cubes with *awazi*, which is a kind of mustard and chilli sauce) to vegetarian fasting food. There's also live music and traditional dancing every night at 8pm. This is the perfect place for your first taste of Ethiopia.

Piazza and North

DJ's Café (Map p91; Hailesilase St; pastries Birr5; 6.30am-8.30pm) Pictures of jazz and blues legends line the walls of this fashionable Western-style cafe, and superb cakes and coffees line happy tummies.

Raizel Café (Map p91; Hailesilase St; mains Birr9-18; 7am-9.30pm) This slick modern cafe speedily serves tasty cheeseburgers, tuna melts, French fries and breakfast omelettes to a fashionable, young crowd. So young is the crowd that halfway through his burger, this 34- (coming on 26-) year-old author looked around and realised he qualified for the creepy-old-man award!

Lucy Gazebo and Restaurant (Map p84; King George VI St; mains Birr24-50; 8.30am-8pm) Next to the National Museum and a favourite haunt of expats, this bright and airy restaurant with al-fresco dining in the garden serves flavourful pastas (some vegetarian options), calzones and heavenly salads.

our pick **Serenade** (Map p91; ☎ 0911 200072; mains Birr60-80; 7pm-midnight Wed-Sat, 10am-3pm Sun) Just east of Piazza, off Tewodros St, and tucked up a dark cobblestone alley is this magnificent Mediterranean eatery. It's a vibrant place, with lush walls, hardwood floors, great service and food that will leave you and your stomach in a heavenly daze. Peruse the creative menu of Beirut-meets-Milan dishes and choose from such succulent treats as braised lamb with caramelised onions, lentils, lemon and *raison orange* couscous or Tuscan Skillet (zucchini, onion, celery, bell pepper, tomato, mozzarella and spinach cooked with olive oil, fresh oregano and thyme). Then there's dessert – cardamom and saffron ice cream – enough said. Even the toilets here are divine, so much so that they actually make a more appealing bedroom than most upcountry hotels! Reserve a table (or the toilet) in advance.

Ristorante Castelli (Map p91; ☎ 0111 571757; Mahatma-Gandhi St; mains Birr60-90; ◷ noon-2.30pm & 7-10.30pm Mon-Sat) Hung behind the imposing and friendly Italian owner are the mugs of Swedish royalty, Bob Geldof, Brad Pitt, Angelina Jolie and ex-US presidents, some of the more famous people who've come here for Addis' best Italian food. The pasta is homemade and all the ingredients are as fresh and natural as an olive in a Sicilian garden. The result is little short of excellent. We devoured the divine *fettuccine al tartufo* (fettuccine in truffle sauce). Reservations are wise.

South West

Backyard (Map pp86-7; ☎ 0114 673501; Meskal Flower Rd; mains Birr20-40; ◷ 11am-midnight Mon-Fri, 9am-midnight Sat & Sun) Freshly transported from the Mediterranean, this pastel-cool restaurant has a tasty range of light pastas and salads, but it's the drool-inducing steaks that it's most renowned for – heaven indeed during the fasting period. Given the quality of the food, this restaurant is shockingly cheap.

East

17 17 (Map pp86-7; Cameroon St; mains Birr10-15; ◷ noon-midnight) Come dinner and lunch, this local option is alive with action. Tables spill from the restaurant's interior out to a large courtyard topped by flowering vegetation. The food isn't the best, but it's filling and cheap and the atmosphere is enjoyable. There's no sign by the gate, so look for a string of lights in a tree next to a well-lit butcher.

Elsa Restaurant (Map pp86-7; Mike Leyland St; mains Birr25-35; ◷ noon-10pm) This simple outdoor restaurant has received high marks from expats for its quality fare. The *yetsom beyaynetu* (variety of fasting foods) is perfect for vegetarians, while *yedoro arosto* (roasted chicken) and *gored gored* assuage carnivorous cravings. Half the neighbourhood like to come here for an afternoon drink. There's also an attached

cafe with a fair selection of cakes and better coffee and an internet cafe with deadly slow connections (Birr6 per hour). Weekends are barbecue nights.

Shangri-la Restaurant (Map pp86-7; ☎ 0116 632424; Cape Verde St; mains Birr30-60; ◷ noon-6pm & 6pm-midnight) Shangri-la has earned a well-deserved reputation as an atmospheric place for great Ethiopian food, especially *tere sega* (raw meat), which is available on Thursday, Saturday and Sunday. Fasting food is available on Wednesday and Friday. There's an outdoor dining area with an open fire, and a cosy bar serving quality *tej*.

Restaurante O'Portugues (Map p84; ☎ 0912 610554; mains Birr80-150) With the ingredients brought from far-away Portugal, you really can eat salty Atlantic *bacalhau* or Alentejo pork washed down with Portuguese wines and an extraordinary view over the whole of Addis. It's also known as Face of Addis.

Self-Catering

Novis Supermarket (Bole Rd area Map pp86-7; Bole Rd; ◷ 8am-10pm Mon-Sat, 9am-9pm Sun; southwest Map p84; Roosevelt St; ◷ 8am-9pm Mon-Sat, 9am-8pm Sun) Boasting the likes of brie, taleggio, gorgonzola and gouda, this supermarket is heaven for cheese-lovers. There's also a great selection of Italian prosciutto, wine and chocolate.

Shi Solomon Hailu Supermarket (Map pp86-7; Gambia St; ◷ 8am-8pm) Well stocked with Western faves, ranging from cereals and biscuits to mineral water and tomato sauce.

Ethio Supermarket (Map pp86-7; Bole Rd; ◷ 24hr) It never closes and is well stocked – enough said.

DRINKING

You won't go thirsty in Addis Ababa. Sip some of the world's best (and cheapest) coffee, down a healthy juice or simply sway home after swallowing your share of *tej*.

Cafes

There are hundreds of cafes serving great coffee in Addis; the following are a few that caught our attention.

our pick Tomoca (Map p91; Wavel St; coffees Birr3) Coffee is serious business at this great old Italian cafe in Piazza. The beans are roasted on site (you can literally smell them roasting from a block away) and Tomoca serves what's likely the capital's best coffee. If that isn't enough, it's also dripping in 1920's atmosphere. Beans are also sold by the half-kilo (Birr41).

National Café (Map pp86-7; Gambia St; coffees Birr2-4) An ever-popular institution that's little more than a dark hole in the wall. For those not afraid of daylight, there's also a few sun-grabbing tables out on the pavement.

Ras Hotel (Map pp86-7; Gambia St; coffees Birr4-5) This central hotel's terrace is a perfect place for a late-afternoon coffee.

Juice Bars

Most of Addis Ababa's cafes also serve freshly squeezed juices or slushy blends of everything from strawberries to avocado.

Lime Tree (Map pp86-7; Bole Rd; juices Birr6-10; 7am-11pm) With luscious lassis and creative juices, Lime Tree is the premier place to indulge in liquid treats of the chilly variety. We downed a lime juice with mint, and it refreshingly pummelled our thirst.

Juice Bar (Map p91; Wavel St; juices Birr6; 7am-9pm) This no-name juice bar, three doors up from Tomoca, is easy to spot thanks to the great piles of fruit outside. It might look like any other juice bar producing any old juice, but it's not and it doesn't. Trust us.

Juice Corner (Map pp86-7; off Haile Gebreselassie Rd; juices Birr8-12) Bored of avocado and mango juices? Then you'll think this place, with such exotics as Energiser (banana, strawberry and yogurt), rocks. We'd even go so far as to say it has the best juice in town.

Pubs & Bars

Addis Ababa's bar scene is becoming ever more cosmopolitan and diverse, though remember this is still no Nairobi when it comes to the quantity and quality of bars – many are hole-in-the-wall dives where all but the most thick-skinned would feel uneasy. However, a growing middle class and increasing numbers of expats have led to some swanky joints, the majority of which are found in and around Bole Rd.

Small local drinking holes charge Birr4 for a bottle of beer, while established bars can charge up to Birr15. Most places are open until 2am during the week, and 5am on the weekend.

Virgo Lounge (Map pp86-7; Cameroon St; closed Mon) This bright and hip drinking den sits above Kaldi's Coffee in southeastern Addis Ababa. With colourful contemporary furniture, modern lighting and mellow music, this is an ideal place to kick back and chill out.

Black Rose (Map pp86-7; Bole Rd; closed Mon) Hiding in a modern building above the Boston Day Spa, this plush bar possesses a cool vibe and a refined clientele – we felt well out of place! Music ranges from Ethiopian to Western and Indian.

Mask Bar (Map pp86-7) This tiny bar is as gaudy as it is cool. Above the glowing green beer bottles that comprise the bar hang masks of all sorts: some historical, some available in any tourist-tat shop. The crowd ranges from expats to well-heeled locals. It's well signposted off Bole Rd.

Old Milk House (Map pp86-7; Josif Tito St) Moving house has done nothing to dampen the crowds at this popular Dutch-owned bar, which sits just east of Menelik II Ave and on the 10th storey of a residential block. You can also fill up on western fast-food staples for around Birr40, as well as fill your walls with some of the art on sale.

Tej Beats

If authentic experiences are what you're after, there's no better place than a *tej beat* (pronounced 'tedj bet') to down the famed golden elixir (honey wine). Most are open from 10am to around 10pm, but are busiest in the evening. They're the traditional haunt of men, so women should try and keep a low profile. They never have signs, so you'll have to ask locals to point them out.

Topia Tej Beat (Map pp86-7) Off Haile Gebreselassie Rd, tucked up an alley behind the Axum Hotel, this is Addis' top *tej beat* and the only one to serve pure honey *tej*. A small flask (Birr7) on an empty stomach had our head spinning. Half-litre (Birr13) and litre (Birr23) bottles are also available. It's a congenial place with tables surrounding a tiny garden.

ENTERTAINMENT

We could blow hot air up your tailpipe, like some guides do, and tell you Addis Ababa's entertainment scene is astounding and the options are endless, but we won't. What we will tell you is that there's enough going on to keep you entertained and a few things that will leave you smiling.

The publication *What's Up!* and the website Addis All Around (www.addisallaround .com) highlight upcoming events on Addis Ababa's entertainment scene.

Jazz Clubs

All but one of these clubs don't have a cover charge, but they all ask a hefty Birr12 to Birr15 for a beer.

Coffee House (Map p84; Madagascar St) Located northeast of Siddist Kilo, opposite the Egyptian embassy, is this fancy club. Every Thursday great live jazz performances start at 10pm.

our pick **Club Àlize** (Map pp86-7; off Bole Rd; entry Birr25) Thursday is Ethio-jazz night extraordinaire at this ubercool new bar-club where a mixed expat and local crowd knock back cocktails and beers to the unique tunes.

Harlem Jazz (Map pp86-7; Bole Rd) This large and mellow venue just north of the airport hosts live jazz Sunday, Tuesday and Friday from 10pm.

La Gazelle Piano Bar (Map pp86-7; Bole Rd) Head down into this dark and moody bar for live jazz every night.

Nightclubs

Nightlife in Addis Ababa is slowly starting to mature with some modern clubs joining the circuit and, in the places listed below, music is almost gaining prominence over prostitution. While most nightclubs open at 11pm, there's no point in arriving before midnight. Those open during the week close around 2am; things wrap up nearer to 5am on weekends. Cover charges vary between Birr25 and Birr50 at most venues, depending on the day (but are sometimes free). Expect to drop a minimum of Birr15 for a beer and Birr20 for a cocktail.

Divine (Map pp86-7; 2nd fl, Sheger Bldg, Cameroon St) Slip into a sleek leather lounger, sip a cocktail and groove to heavy hip-hop and rap in this sleek nightclub.

Club Illusion (Map pp86-7; cnr Ras Desta Damtew & Itegue Taitu St; ☾ Thu-Sat) This is Addis Ababa's most raucous club. It's in the basement of the Ambassador Cinema. There's occasional live music.

D-Cave Club (Map pp86-7; Beyene Abasebsib St; ☾ Thu-Sat) This nightclub, which lurks beneath the Global Hotel in southwest Addis Ababa, hosts well-known DJs most weekends. Music ranges from Ethiopian to hip-hop and drum and bass.

Club Platinum & Lounge (Map pp86-7; Mike Leyland St; ☾ Thu-Sat) Currently the flavour of the month and packed every weekend with teenagers and twentysomethings.

Memo Club (Map pp86-7) About 200m west of Bole Rd, this is another of Addis Ababa's hot spots. Cosy seats, red lights and the odd full-length mirror surround the circular dance floor, which usually reverberates with African and Western tunes. Sadly, it's also popular with expats shopping for prostitutes.

Addis Live (Map pp86-7; Cape Verde St) Attracts a younger crowd (mainly Ethiopian) and plays a good mix of hip-hop and reggae. It's pretty quiet during the week.

Azmari Beats

What in the world is an *azmari beat*? Check out the boxed text, p60.

Yewedale (Map pp86-7; Zewditu St) Thanks to some of the city's best *azmaris* performing here, it's resoundingly popular and you may have trouble finding a seat.

Fendika Azmari Beat (Map pp86-7; Zewditu St) This *azmari beat* rivals Yewedale and is only a few minutes' walk down the street. It's littered with Ethiopian cultural items and is always home to a good time.

Traditional Music, Dance & Theatre

Amharic theatre is hard to come by these days, with venues only hosting shows once or twice a week. Traditional music and dance are much more accessible, with many restaurants putting on traditional shows in the evenings. *Azmari beats* (see above) are also atmospheric places to catch both. For general information on Ethiopian theatre, music and dance see p65.

National Theatre (Map pp86-7; ☎ 0115 514577; Gambia St; tickets Birr10) This impressive building, with its massive marble and bronze entrance hall (and odd pigeon), hosts theatre most weekends at 5pm.

City Hall Theatre & Cultural Centre (Map p91; ☎ 0111 1550520; Fitawrari Gebeyehu St; tickets Birr15-20) A plush 1000-seat place in the Piazza, which shows productions on Tuesdays and Fridays. Sometimes there's traditional Ethiopian music on public holidays.

Hager Fikir Theatre (Map p91; ☎ 0111 119820; John Melly St; tickets Birr15) Hager Fikir occasionally stages theatre, musicals and dancing.

Cinema

Cinema is more popular than ever – even pushing theatre out of most theatres. Most films are in English or have English subtitles (some have both!).

Ambassador Cinema (Map pp86-7; Ras Desta Damtew St; admission Birr7) An institution, this central cinema puts on the usual diet of action-packed and slightly passé Hollywood movies. Films are shown daily in three sessions.

National Theatre (Map pp86-7; ☎ 0115 514577; Gambia St; tickets for Hollywood films Birr4, Amharic films Birr15) There is no more atmospheric place in which to catch a film than this imposing old building. Hollywood showings are normally fairly old.

SHOPPING

Spend some spare change or spend your kid's college fund; the spectrum of prices and quality of goods for sale in the capital is simply that vast. You'll find most of the cheap souvenir stalls along or around Churchill Ave and in Piazza – haggling is always the way of the day!

Haileselassie Alemayehu (Map pp86-7; Churchill Ave) Although known for its silver jewellery and mix-and-match bead counter, this shop sells a wide array of items, like paintings, baskets, icons, woodcarvings and traditional clothing. Thanks to fixed (and fair) prices, there's no hassle here. It's also a good place to get your bearings on what items should cost elsewhere.

Entoto Market (Map p84; Entoto Ave) If you're interested in blankets or traditional clothing like a *shamma* (toga-style dress worn by highlander men), head to this group of stalls lining Entoto Ave, a few hundred metres north of Botswana St and the Spanish embassy. Unlike Churchill Ave or Piazza, this is where locals do their shopping.

Gallery 21 (Map pp86-7; Churchill Ave) Of all the shops/stalls north of Haileselassie Alemayehu on Churchill Ave, this has the biggest selection (if you ask to see the back room) and the best-quality pieces, though the prices are higher than most.

St George Interior Decoration & Art Gallery (Map pp86-7; Itegue Taitu St) This is located near the Sheraton for one obvious reason: nobody staying elsewhere can afford to shop here! However, the artwork and traditionally inspired modern furniture are exquisite and it's worth a wander.

Makush Art Gallery & Restaurant (Map pp86-7; Bole Rd) Has an excellent, carefully selected collection of high-quality furniture and paintings from various Ethiopian artists.

Alert handicraft shop (Map p84; ☎ 0113 211518; ⏰ 8am-noon & 1-5pm Mon-Fri, 8am-noon Sat) Here, the Berhan Taye Leprosy Disabled Persons Work Group produces and sells beautiful handbags, pillow covers and wall hangings, each emblazoned with vibrant embroidery. The items are so Ethiopian, yet they wouldn't feel out of place in a Kathmandu or Bangkok market. The shop is off Ring Rd, southwest of the city centre in the Alert Hospital compound; follow the signs to the canteen.

GETTING THERE & AWAY
Air
DOMESTIC FLIGHTS

All domestic flights are operated by **Ethiopian Airlines** (www.flyethiopian.com; Bole Rd Map pp86-7; ☎ 0116 633163; Bole Rd; Gambia St Map pp86-7; ☎ 0115 517000; off Gambia St; Hilton Hotel Map pp86-7; ☎ 0115 511540; Menelik II Ave; ⏰ 7am-8.30pm Mon-Sat, 8am-noon Sun; Piazza Map p91; ☎ 0111 569247; Hailesilase St). These offices are open daily from 8.30am to 5pm, unless stated otherwise. There are several more offices scattered across the city. The useful 24-hour reservation number is ☎ 0116 656666.

Schedules change quite frequently and flight durations vary depending on which stopovers the plane is making en route.

Flights leaving from Addis Ababa are listed in the following table.

Destination	Fare (US$)	Duration (hr)	Frequency
Aksum	200	2	daily
Bahir Dar	133	1	2-3 daily
Dire Dawa	137	1	daily
Gambela	177	2	Wed, Fri, Sat, Sun, Mon
Gonder	153	1½	daily
Jimma	116	1	daily
Lalibela	136	2-2½	2 daily
Mekele	180	1	daily

INTERNATIONAL FLIGHTS

For information regarding international flights and international airlines serving Addis Ababa, see the Getting There & Away section on p259.

Bus

Buses to Awasa (Birr37, six hours), Debre Zeyit (Birr6, 45 minutes), Lake Langano (Birr31, 4½ hours), Nazret (Birr12, two hours), Shashemene (Birr31, five hours) and Ziway (Birr25, three hours) leave from the **short-distance bus station** (Map pp86-7; Ras Mekonen Ave). Awasa and Shashemene are also serviced from the long-distance bus station.

Long-distance buses depart from **Autobus Terra** (Map p84; Central African Republic St), northwest of Merkato. Buses for the following destinations leave officially at 6am, but you should be at the station by 4.30am if you've any hope for a ticket. Be very wary of pickpockets and bag snatchers here.

Destination	Fare (Birr)	Duration
Aksum	160	2 days
Arba Minch	64	12 hours
Awasa	37	6 hours
Bahir Dar via Dangala	71	1½ days
Bahir Dar via Mota	65	12 hours
Dessie	52	9 hours
Dire Dawa	68	11 hours
Gambela	105	2 days
Goba	65	13 hours
Gonder	92	2 days
Jijiga	105	2 days
Jimma	45	9 hours
Jinka	100	2 days
Lalibela	95	2 days
Mekele	100	2 days
Moyale	99	1½ days
Robe	62	12 hours
Shashemene	31	5 hours
Matama (Sudan border)	124	2 days

There are several services to Shashemene and Awasa after the first 6.30am departure, though they all leave before noon.

A couple of slick new 'luxury buses' now fly down the country's highways, and when we say luxury we really mean luxury. These puppies have reclining seats, air-con, on-board toilets and even free snacks and drinks! The best established is **Selam Buses**, whose station and ticket office (Map pp86-7; ☎ 0115 544831/0911 403978) is close to the railway station. They have daily services (all departing at 5.30am) to Bahir Dar (Birr130), Gonder (Birr170), Mekele (Birr200), Dessie (Birr102), Harar (Birr122), Dire Dawa (Birr120) and Jimma (Birr90). Possibly even slicker are **Sky Buses** (Map pp86-7; ☎ 0116 630574; room 404, 4th fl, Friendship Bldg, Bole Rd) who have buses to Bahir Dar (Birr182.05, 12 hours, 6am Wed), Gonder (Birr203.95, one day, 5.30am Wed & Fri) and Dire Dawa (Birr175.05, one day, 6am Sun).

Car & 4WD

Although it's possible to hire a self-drive car, you're usually restricted to the capital. Hiring a chauffeured 4WD, although ex-

pensive, removes most limits on where you can travel. Four-wheel drives are rented by almost all of Addis' travel agents (see p270). For more details on hiring see p264.

Minibus

With sealed roads now all but connecting Addis Ababa with Bahir Dar and Gonder, private minibus services are starting to crop up. They're very fast (not always a good thing!) and cut journey times down to six or seven hours for Bahir Dar and 10 hours for Gonder. There's no station per se, but commission agents tend to patrol for customers near the Wutma Hotel in Piazza.

GETTING AROUND

Though a sprawling city, Addis Ababa is fairly easy to get around.

To/From the Airport

Bole International Airport (Map p84) lies 5km southeast of the city centre; both international and domestic flights depart from here.

Minibuses from Piazza, Mexico Sq and Meskal Sq serve the airport daily from 6am to 8pm (Birr1.30). Some charge an additional Birr2 or Birr3 for excess luggage.

Blue city taxis to the airport should cost around Birr40 from anywhere south of Meskal Sq to around Birr50 to Birr60 if leaving from Piazza; add Birr15 at night or early in the morning. From the airport, prices should be similar, though you'll be asked for at least double or triple this (see p246). A taxi association has a booth at the airport's exit and charges a fixed rate US$10. Taxi drivers belonging to this association have yellow taxis.

Bus

Buses in Addis Ababa are considered poor man's transport. They're cheap but slow, run less regularly than the minibuses and are notoriously targeted by pickpockets. The minibuses are a much better bet.

Car

Parking isn't usually too much of a problem in Addis Ababa. Most of the larger hotels and restaurants have guarded parking spaces and don't usually mind you leaving your car there. In other places, it's worth paying for a guard. Anywhere you park on the street a 'parking warden' (we're not sure how genuine they are!) appears and leaves a little note on your windscreen noting the time of arrival and they then charge you based on that.

Minibus

Addis Ababa is served by an extensive network of little blue-and-white minibuses, which are fast, efficient, cheap and a great way of getting around.

Minibuses operate from 5.30am to around 9pm (till 8pm Sunday). Journeys cost roughly Birr1.30 (though exact prices depend on the distance).

Minibus stops can be found near almost every major intersection. Major ones include Arat Kilo, De Gaulle Sq in Piazza, Meskal Sq, Ras Mekonen Ave near La Gare and in front of the main post office on Churchill Ave.

To catch the right minibus, listen to the destinations screamed by the *woyala* (attendants) hanging out the windows. 'Bole!', 'Piazza!' and 'Arat Kilo!' are the most useful to travellers. If confused, ask and someone will point you in the right direction.

Taxi

Most taxis operate from 6am to 11pm. Short journeys (up to 3km) usually cost foreigners Birr30 to Birr40 (more at night). Medium/long journeys cost Birr40/50. If you share a taxi, the normal fare is split between each person.

If you want to visit a lot of places in Addis Ababa, negotiate with a driver for a half- or full-day fare (Birr300 for a full day is pretty reasonable). A 'city tour' lasting a couple of hours should cost around Birr150 to Birr200.

Taxis can be found outside larger hotels, as well as the National Theatre, national stadium and on De Gaulle Sq in the Piazza. At night, many line up outside the nightclubs.

AROUND ADDIS ABABA

The cacophonous sounds of traffic can chase the most ardent Addis Ababa adorer into the hills occasionally. Lucky for them, the hills contain some historic churches (one hewn from rock in the 12th century) and some remote wilderness.

As well as the places listed here, sights further afield outside Addis Ababa that can still make good day trips include the crater lakes of Debre Zeyit (p206), Menagesha National Forest (p229), Ambo (p229), Mt Wenchi (p230) and the stelae field at Tiya (p170).

ENTOTO MOUNTAINS
የእንጦጦ ተራሮች

North of town are the Entoto Mountains, the site of Menelik's former capital. There's a terrific but windy panoramic view of Addis Ababa below. Near the summit is the octagonal **Entoto Maryam Church** (Map p84; ☯ Sun), which hosted Menelik's coronation in 1882.

To get to Entoto, take a taxi or minibus to the terminus of Entoto Ave from Arat Kilo. From there another minibus will take you to Entoto Maryam Church.

WUSHA MIKAEL CHURCH
ሁሻ ሚካኤል ቤተ ክርስቲያን

The **Wusha Mikael Church** (Map p84; admission Birr30) is a few kilometres east of the town centre. Though local priests date it back to the 3rd century AD, it most probably dates back to the 12th century. If you're mad and not planning to visit the churches at Lalibela or Tigray in the north, it's definitely worth a peek as an example of this extraordinary building tradition. Unfortunately, from July to October it's usually flooded with rainwater.

The church is tricky to find, so ask locals en route (most know it as Tekle Haymanot).

Northern Ethiopia

NORTHERN ETHIOPIA

Once upon a time, in the mountain vastness, a drawbridge lowered and a white stallion galloped forth from a crystal castle. On his back was an emperor dressed in gold robes living on a mountain of fire. Northward the emperor rode, past craggy peaks and terrifying chasms haunted by baboons with bleeding hearts, until he arrived at a chapel containing the words of God carved onto stone tablets by Moses. Above the chapel leered giant obelisks erected in memory of a queen known only as Sheba who loved a faraway king named Solomon. After praying for advice to the oracle of the Ark of the Covenant, the emperor sped forward over mountains where Syrian monks climbed the tails of serpents to build treasure-filled monasteries. As he rode, the King of Kings turned his head to the left, and off in the far distance he saw the glitter of a desert made of gold. The riding became harder, the wrinkles of the earth more spectacular still, but the end of the pilgrimage was in sight. Ahead of the emperor lay the new Jerusalem; the holy city of Lalibela where St George demanded a team of angels build him a church fit for a slayer of dragons.

It might sound like a fanciful fairytale, but not so long ago, in the days when science was fantasy and fairytales werereality, this was how the wider world viewed northern Ethiopia. Today, of course, science is reality and fairytales are nothing but children's fantasy, which our ever-shrinking world has cast aside. But, if you ever feel that the hectic, modern world we're living in is getting too much, then just remember that there is one place in which dragon-slaying knights still live and where the ghosts of emperors still haunt the highlands. Its name is northern Ethiopia. It's the home of fairytales and it will be unlike anywhere else you know.

HIGHLIGHTS

- Immerse yourself in Christianity in its most raw and powerful form in the mind-blowing rock-hewn maze of churches in **Lalibela** (p156)

- Search for hidden treasure in the dank gloom of ancient Aksumite tombs and ponder the mysteries of the stelae of **Aksum** (p131)

- Lace up your boots and trek through the sublime **Simien Mountains** (p126), home to magnificent wildlife and unparalleled panoramas of endless Abyssinian abysses

- Sail your good ship past centuries-old monasteries to the source of the Blue Nile on magical **Lake Tana** (p114)

- Recreate a feast for 30,000 in the hallowed halls of the royal castles of **Gonder** (p118)

- Climb a snake's tail (p145), dodge a sword-welding ghost and make sure your club isn't turned into a lion while exploring the magnificent rock-hewn churches of **Tigray** (p147)

Climate

The central and northern highlands are fairly mild with average daytime temperatures of 18°C. The bulk of the rain falls between May and September, with July and August being the wettest. The region of Tigray and parts of northeastern Amharaland are drier, only receiving significant rain in July and August.

The Danakil Depression, whose floor scrapes to 116m below sea level in places, regularly surpasses 45°C.

National Parks

If northern Ethiopia was devoid of astounding historical finds, Simien Mountains National Park would truly still be on the world map. It's home to rare endemics, like the walia ibex and Ethiopian wolf, as well as large populations of the intriguing gelada baboon. It also offers Ethiopia's best trekking and some of Africa's most astounding panoramas from its 4000m plateaus and peaks.

Getting There & Away

Ethiopian Airlines (www.flyethiopian.com) connects Addis Ababa with Bahir Dar, Gonder, Lalibela, Aksum and Mekele.

Most people who enter northern Ethiopia overland are travelling by bus from Addis Ababa, which sits conveniently at the bottom of the historical circuit. Although possible, few people access the Addis Ababa–Bahir Dar road from the western highland town of Nekemte. The only other overland option is from Sudan at the Metema crossing (p263).

Getting Around

Ethiopian Airlines has flights interconnecting Bahir Dar, Gonder, Lalibela, Mekele and Aksum.

Road construction is booming and freshly sealed sections of road connect Addis Ababa with Bahir Dar and Gonder (though still expect a few older potholed sections!). In the east, new sections of sealed road now all but link Adigrat, Mekele and Woldia. The old sealed road connecting Addis Ababa to Woldia is also close to completion. While fresh roads have reduced the extensive bus network's travel times, journeys are still lengthy due to the massive distances being covered. Expect at least 10 solid days of bus journeys to complete the 2500km-long historical circuit.

The only area in which you'll have trouble finding regular public transport is around the rock-hewn churches of Tigray.

To visit the Danakil Depression, you'll have to travel by private or rented 4WD.

THE HISTORICAL CIRCUIT

The historical circuit stretches over the entire breadth of northern Ethiopia. It covers all the major historical sites and provides access to natural attractions, like the Simien Mountains and Danakil Depression.

Most visitors move in a clockwise direction, travelling through Bahir Dar, Gonder and Aksum, before looping back southwards. This leaves what's arguably the best for last – lovely Lalibela.

ADDIS ABABA TO THE BLUE NILE GORGE

The road north to the Blue Nile Gorge offers some historical and natural sights to break up the long journey to Bahir Dar.

Even if you don't plan on stopping, keep an eye out for the shepherds in their delightful reed 'raincoats', the Amhara women in their pleated highland skirts and the men carrying their indispensable *dula* (wooden staffs).

Muger River Gorge
የሙ-ገር ወንዝ ሸለቆ

The Muger River Gorge, some 50km north of Addis Ababa, is a good spot for a bit of rambling and wildlife-watching. The endemic gelada baboons are often seen here, as are cacophonous collections of colourful birds.

Access is from the village of Durba, which sits 17km west of Chancho and the Addis Ababa–Bahir Dar road. There is a couple of daily share-taxis linking Durba and Chancho (Birr7, 45 to 60 minutes), though more run on Saturday. To continue north or south from Chancho, you can hop on the buses running between Addis Ababa and Bahir Dar.

Debre Libanos ደብረ ሊባኖስ

Lying 104km north of Addis Ababa is one of Ethiopia's most holy sites. The monastery of **Debre Libanos** (admission Birr50, personal video cameras Birr50) was founded in the 13th century by a priest credited not only with the spread of Christianity throughout the highlands, but also with the restoration of the Solomonic

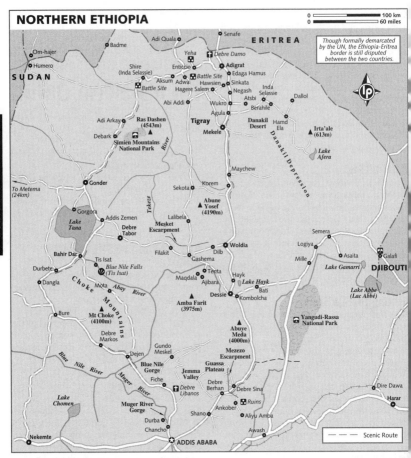

NORTHERN ETHIOPIA

Though formally demarcated by the UN, the Ethiopia-Eritrea border is still disputed between the two countries.

line of kings. The priest was Tekla Haimanot, today one of Ethiopia's most revered saints (see the boxed text, p57).

Although no trace of the ancient monastery remains (a casualty of the Muslim–Christian wars), the site is impressively set beneath a cliff on the edge of a gorge and is a peaceful place to wander.

Since the saint's time, Debre Libanos has served as the principal monastery of the old Shoa region, and remains one of Ethiopia's largest and most important. Today, five religious schools are found here.

Many Ethiopians continue to make pilgrimages and some still seek out the area's curative holy waters – said to be good for warding off evil spirits and for stomach disorders.

The present **church** was built in 1961 by Haile Selassie after a priest prophesied that a new church would ensure a long reign. It's built in the emperor's peculiar style: monumental and pretty hideous.

Five minutes up the hill from the monastery is Tekla Haimanot's **cave**, where the saint is said to have done all his praying. It's also the source of the monastery's holy water.

Two buses run daily from Addis Ababa to Debre Libanos (Birr15, two to 2½ hours).

Blue Nile Gorge አባይ ሽለቆ

North of Fiche, around 200km from Addis Ababa, begins one of Ethiopia's most dramatic stretches of road. It serpentines to the bottom of the Blue Nile Gorge, 1000m below.

Before the Italians built the bridge with their usual civil-engineering flair, the Blue Nile River separated the historical provinces of Shoa and Gojam. Although your eyes will undoubtedly be drawn downward to the bridge and gorge, don't forget to look up – lammergeier vultures regularly soar on the gorge's thermal currents.

NORTH TO BAHIR DAR

There are now two ways of reaching Bahir Dar from the Blue Nile Gorge: via Mota, along the shorter but bumpier unsealed road; or via Debre Markos, which is 100km longer, but along a lovely sealed road that helps to make this a much faster ride.

Nowadays most Addis Ababa buses travel through Debre Markos and the journey can be completed in one very long day. In a private vehicle you can, if all the stars are aligned in your favour, whip from Addis to Bahir Dar in just seven hours or so.

If you're driving and want to split the journey, Debre Markos' **Glory Hotel** (camping/s/d Birr60/60/80) has safe parking and the sort of frilly bed spreads your gran would just love. Take a good book with you into the bathroom as the door handles have a tendency to fall off, leaving you trapped inside!

If the bus isn't going to make it to Bahir Dar in one day, then you'll probably find yourself bedding down in one of Dangla's (78km south of Bahir Dar) dives. The Temnasera Pension is the best of the bunch.

BAHIR DAR ባሕር ዳር

pop 180,094 / elev 1880m

Ethiopians like to describe Bahir Dar as being their Riviera and, with its wide streets shaded by palm trees and sweeping views across shimmering blue waters, it's hard to argue.

It's a great place to spend a few days. Besides some sights around town, you're on the doorstep of Lake Tana's mystical monasteries.

In the 16th and 17th centuries, various temporary Ethiopian capitals were established in the vicinity of Lake Tana. It was here where Jesuits attempted – with disastrous consequences – to impose Catholicism on the Ethiopian people. One Jesuit building, which was built by the well-known Spanish missionary Pero Pais, can still be seen today in the compound of St George's Church.

In the 1960s Haile Selassie toyed with the idea of moving his capital here.

Information

INTERNET ACCESS

Click Internet (per hr Birr12) One of a couple of internet points in this block.

Global Computer (per hr Birr12; ☾ 8am-8pm) The connections are as slow as a decomposing tortoise, but that still makes them faster than most in town.

MEDICAL SERVICES

Gamby Higher Clinic & Pharmacy (☎ 0582 202017; ☾ 24hr) Town's best medical facility.

MONEY

Commercial Bank (☾ 8am-4pm Mon-Fri, to noon Sat) Of Bahir Dar's three Commercial Bank branches, this is the only one that changes travellers cheques and cash (US dollars and euros).

Dashen Bank (☾ 8am-noon & 1-4pm Mon-Fri, 8am-noon Sat) Has an ATM that accepts international Visa cards. It can also give cash advances on Visa.

Wegagen Bank (☾ 8am-5pm Mon-Fri, 8am-4pm Sat) Only changes US dollars and euros.

LEGLESS IN LIBANOS

Legless Tekla Haimanot, descendant of Zadok, the priest who anointed King Solomon, is one of the most revered saints in Ethiopia thanks both for his part in restoring the Solomonic dynasty to Ethiopia and for his miracle-working prowess. He started working his magic even before he was born – when his mother was molested by a pagan king, Tekla Haimanot called forth the Archangel Mikhael (hidden inside a thunderstorm) who promptly turned the king mad. While still in his teens he could perform that old biblical favourite of turning water into wine and by the time of his death, he'd performed every miracle in both the Old and New Testaments. But it's for his devotion to prayer that he's best remembered. For 20 years he stood stock still and prayed until eventually his right leg turned rotten and fell off. Unperturbed he carried on for a further seven years, balancing on his remaining left leg. Today his leg is kept hidden inside the Debre Libanos monastery. Once a year it's brought out and pilgrims drink the holy water used to clean the leg.

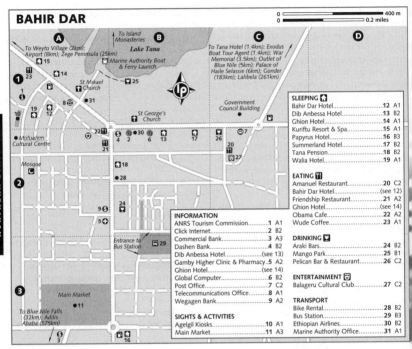

BAHIR DAR

INFORMATION
ANRS Tourism Commission	**1** A1
Click Internet	**2** B2
Commercial Bank	**3** A3
Dashen Bank	**4** B2
Dib Anbessa Hotel	(see 13)
Gamby Higher Clinic & Pharmacy	**5** A2
Ghion Hotel	(see 14)
Global Computer	**6** B2
Post Office	**7** C2
Telecommunications Office	**8** A1
Wegagen Bank	**9** A2

SIGHTS & ACTIVITIES
Agelgil Kiosks	**10** A1
Main Market	**11** A3

SLEEPING
Bahir Dar Hotel	**12** A1
Dib Anbessa Hotel	**13** B2
Ghion Hotel	**14** A1
Kuriftu Resort & Spa	**15** A1
Papyrus Hotel	**16** B3
Summerland Hotel	**17** B2
Tana Pension	**18** B2
Walia Hotel	**19** A1

EATING
Amanuel Restaurant	**20** C2
Bahir Dar Hotel	(see 12)
Friendship Restaurant	**21** A2
Ghion Hotel	(see 14)
Obama Cafe	**22** A2
Wude Coffee	**23** A1

DRINKING
Araki Bars	**24** B2
Mango Park	**25** B1
Pelican Bar & Restaurant	**26** C2

ENTERTAINMENT
Balageru Cultural Club	**27** C2

TRANSPORT
Bike Rental	**28** B2
Bus Station	**29** B3
Ethiopian Airlines	**30** B2
Marine Authority Office	**31** A1

POST
Bahir Dar is served by one post office.

TELEPHONE
Telecommunications office (🕒 8am-noon & 2-6pm Mon-Fri, 8am-noon Sat) International calls. Standard rates are outlined on p254.

TOURIST INFORMATION
ANRS Tourism Commission (☎ 0582 201686; 🕒 8.30am-12.30pm & 1.30-5.30pm Mon-Fri) Although staff are keen to help, it offers little more than brochures on the area (Birr3).

TRAVEL AGENCIES
The following agencies are noted for arranging boat trips onto Lake Tana.
Dib Anbessa Hotel (☎ 0582 201436) A bit pushy sales wise, but reliable enough.
Ghion Hotel (☎ 0582 200363) It's less polished, but probably best for budget travellers looking to share costs.

Dangers & Annoyances
Malaria is endemic, particularly in May and from mid-September to mid-October. Take adequate preventive measures (see p371 for more information).

Women, accompanied by male companions or not, should not walk along the waterfront path that runs from the Ghion Hotel into town. We have received a large number of complaints regarding serious hassle from men hanging out here.

Tourist hustlers can be a problem here, especially around the bus station. Most 'know' the best place to stay or the 'cheapest' boat operators – thankfully you know better.

Sights & Activities
Lounging lakeside and watching pelicans skirting the surface might be the most relaxing way to pass time. You may also glimpse the flimsy, yet unsinkable *tankwa* canoe. Made from woven papyrus, they can take huge loads, including oxen! They are exactly the same as the papyrus boats depicted on the walls of ancient temples in Egypt. If you'd like to see them being made, head west of town to the little village of **Weyto**.

If you are allergic to scenic lakesides and love dusty action, visit the large and lively

main market in the town's southwest. It's busiest on Saturday. Sure a guide would help you find things more quickly, but isn't getting lost half the fun?

Just to save you a day of unfruitful looking, we'll be kind enough to tell you the delightful *agelgil* (ingenious leather-bound lunch boxes used by local travellers) are no longer sold in the market. They're sold by streetside kiosks near the ANRS Tourism Commission. Bahir Dar's versions are funky and furry, thanks to being made from goatskin.

The famous **outlet of the Blue Nile** (Map p115) is located 5km outside the town, around 1km north from the Blue Nile bridge. Along the river, keep an eye out for hippos and crocodiles. For more information on the outlet of the Blue Nile, see p117.

Just south of the bridge is a massive new **war memorial** (Map p115) dedicated to those who died fighting the Derg (p44). It's quite the sight, its fountain cascading down to the Blue Nile.

Further south of the memorial is Bezawit Hill, the summit of which hosts the former **Palace of Haile Selassie** (Map p115) and offers panoramic views over the Blue Nile River. The palace isn't currently open to visitors.

For those Lake Tana monasteries you may have heard about, see p114. Information on the Blue Nile Falls is found on p117.

Sleeping

BUDGET

Walia Hotel (☎ 0582 200151; r Birr30) The tiny but immaculately presented rooms here get fresh coats of paint on a regular basis, which leaves them looking like the smartest boy at the party. Even the communal toilets don't smell too bad! For the price you can't really fault it.

Tana Pension (☎ 0918 081730; d without bathroom Birr40) It's as cheap as chips, and to be honest it shows. The rooms need to go on a date with a cloth and a broom and the common bathrooms leave something to be desired. However, the rooms are big and bright and at least the sheets get a regular spin in the washing machine.

Bahir Dar Hotel (☎ 0582 200788; s with/without bathroom Birr50/60, d with/without bathroom Birr60/70) Even with its pongy toilets this cheerful place, with simple rooms huddled around a popular courtyard restaurant (noise is a problem at times), is a good deal.

Ghion Hotel (☎ 0582 200363; ghionbd @telecom.net.et; camping Birr50, r Birr177.60; P Q) Although the rooms here are as tired and worn as your favourite pair of travel socks, there's no denying Ghion's beautiful lakeside setting. Rooms are supposedly identical, but in reality quality varies – although all have paper-thin partitions so that, intentionally or not, you can listen in on your neighbours' most intimate moments! The gardens, full of flowers and paradise flycatchers, are gorgeous. It's easily the most popular place for *faranjis* (foreigners) to get their heads down.

MIDRANGE & TOP END

Dib Anbessa Hotel (☎ 0582 201436; fax 0582 201818; d/tw Birr250/280) Overlook the frayed carpets and you'll find that the rooms here, with their soft beds and balconies with sweet views, offer fair value. The exposed wires in the showers could make for some electrifying moments if you're not careful.

Summerland Hotel (☎ 0582 206566; www .enjoybahirdar.com; s/d/tw Birr316.25/455.40/480.70) While the brown beds, brown curtains, brown furniture and fairly brown atmosphere may not remind you very much of carefree summer days, there's no denying that it's functional and comfortable.

Papyrus Hotel (☎ 0582 205100; s/d/tw Birr399/498/499; Q ☎) This huge resort-style hotel is a good deal. The carpets in the spacious rooms are refreshingly stain free and there are plenty of facilities on offer, including an enormous pool complete with fringing sunloungers – now we're really on holiday!

Kuriftu Resort & Spa (☎ 0582 2264868; www.kurift uresortspa.com; r from US$168; P Q ☎) At the time of research this flash new lodge was about to open for business. The huge, luxurious stone cottages peer out across the lake waters and a soon-to-be-completed pool and spa. The refined rooms are filled with furnishings made entirely of locally produced natural materials and the service is excellent.

Eating

Bahir Dar Hotel (mains Birr9-15) If you want local atmosphere and great Ethiopian fare, there's nowhere better than this hotel's courtyard. Sit under the stars, enjoy the music (and bonfires on weekends) and dine for pennies.

Wude Coffee (mains Birr12-20; ⏰ 6am-10pm) For high-class Ethiopian fare in a chic city-style cafe come to this popular new restaurant where you can munch away either inside or at an outdoor table.

Ghion Hotel (mains Birr12-20) Its lakefront terrace is a pleasant spot for a meal. The tilapia (a freshwater fish) is usually well prepared, but the pasta with white garlic sauce was totally inedible!

Friendship Restaurant (mains Birr12-29; ⏰ 8am-10pm) Make friends with a pizza or re-acquaint yourself with some even better injera and *wat* (stew) at this 1st-floor restaurant that opens later than most.

Amanuel Restaurant (mains Birr13) Excellent fish fresh from the lake in all its slippery forms can be found at this old lake dog's restaurant.

He was everyone's favourite poster boy at the time of research, but will Obama live up to the hype? If the name of **Obama Cafe** (mains Birr13) has changed by the time you get there, you'll know the answer! In the meantime this cafe, with its Ethiopian staples, is as popular as the president himself.

Drinking

Pelican Bar & Restaurant (beers Birr6) Drinking, not eating, is the name of the game at this streetside bar with outdoor tables.

Mango Park (beers Birr6-7) One of several lakeside places, this one is perfect for a chilledout afternoon drink. It's usually packed with local students, families and the odd pelican (watch out, the pelicans never pay for their round).

If you want something that will knock you off your feet, visit the hole-in-the-wall *araki* (grain spirit) bars near the bus station.

Entertainment

Balageru Cultural Club (admission free; beers Birr8) If you'd like an entertaining cultural experience and a good laugh, visit this place. Various *azmari* (see the boxed text, p60) do their thing to the rapturous joy of locals. If you're brave enough to dance and do your thing, you'll win lots of friends.

Getting There & Away
AIR
Ethiopian Airlines (☎ 0582 200020; ⏰ 8-11.45am & 2-5.45pm) has two or three flights daily to Addis Ababa (US$113, one hour), and one or two

to Gonder (US$74, 20 minutes), Lalibela (US$98, 1¼ hours) and Aksum (US$130, two to three hours).

BUS & MINIBUS
You have a variety of painfully long ways to reach Addis Ababa. One bus heads there via the Debre Markos route (Birr100, one day, 6am), while a simultaneous service departs via the Mota route (Birr80, two days). Minibuses take seven hours to Addis Ababa (Birr180) or you can cruise in style on the air-con Solomon Bus (Birr130, 10 hours, 6am). Tickets for these buses are bought at the bus station, though do note that touts will try to steer you onto a minibus. Regular buses travel to Gonder (Birr50, four hours, every two-hourly throughout the day) and Debre Tabor (Birr34, three hours). A couple of buses trundle to and from Tis Isat (Birr5, 45 minutes) for the Blue Nile Falls every morning up until 9am. There's also a daily 6am service to Lalibela (Birr90, 10 hours). All buses leave from the main station.

FERRY
A ferry sails every Sunday at 7am for Gorgora (Birr157.20, 1½ days), on the northern shore of Lake Tana. It typically overnights in Konzola (Map p115). Buy tickets the day before at the **Marine Authority office** (Map p112; ☎ 0582 200730; ⏰ 8am-noon & 1.30-5.30pm Mon-Fri, 8am-noon Sat).

There's no restaurant or cafe on board, though there are stops at restaurants en route.

Getting Around
Bikes are perfect for Bahir Dar; hire one just south of Tana Pension (Birr5 per hour).

If you're in a hurry, flag a passing taxi. They cost Birr10 to Birr15 for short hops. The 8km airport trip will set you back Birr60.

LAKE TANA & ITS MONASTERIES
ጣና ሃይቅና ገዳማት
At first sight, Lake Tana's beauty is obvious: its azure waters lapping on lush shores, islands dotting its distant horizon and squadrons of pelicans flirting with its surface. Explore a bit further and you'll discover there's also some artificial beauty in the form of centuries-old monasteries full of glorious treasures and paintings.

This lake is Ethiopia's largest, covering over 3500 sq km, and its waters are the source of

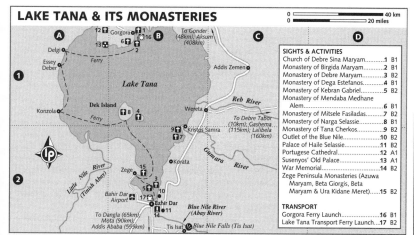

LAKE TANA & ITS MONASTERIES

SIGHTS & ACTIVITIES	
Church of Debre Sina Maryam..........**1** B1	
Monastery of Birgida Maryam..........**2** B1	
Monastery of Debre Maryam..........**3** B2	
Monastery of Dega Estefanos..........**4** B1	
Monastery of Kebran Gabriel..........**5** B2	
Monastery of Mendaba Medhane	
Alem..........**6** B1	
Monastery of Mitsele Fasiladas..........**7** B2	
Monastery of Narga Selassie..........**8** B1	
Monastery of Tana Cherkos..........**9** B2	
Outlet of the Blue Nile..........**10** B2	
Palace of Haile Selassie..........**11** B2	
Portugese Cathedral..........**12** A1	
Susenyos' Old Palace..........**13** A1	
War Memorial..........**14** B2	
Zege Peninsula Monasteries (Azuwa	
Maryam, Beta Giorgis, Beta	
Maryam & Ura Kidane Meret)......**15** B2	

TRANSPORT	
Gorgora Ferry Launch..........**16** B1	
Lake Tana Transport Ferry Launch...**17** B2	

NORTHERN ETHIOPIA

the Blue Nile, which flows 5223km north to the Mediterranean Sea.

Sights & Activities

A trip out onto the lake is as obligatory as it is enjoyable. Although the obvious highlights are the monasteries, the lake also offers some prime bird habitats.

MONASTERIES

While the boat engine's buzz is anything but a throwback to ancient times, your first meetings with the remarkable cross-wielding priests after stepping onto the islands just may be.

Many monasteries date from the late 16th or early 17th century, though most were founded much earlier and may even have been the site of pre-Christian shrines.

If you want help deciphering the murals adorning the monasteries' walls, check out Know Your Ethiopian Saints on p57.

Although it's possible to see all the monasteries over several long days, you'll likely to have had your fill after one full day. Yes, it is possible to have too much of a good thing. If you have a 40HP speedboat, 11 hours and priests who are quick with the keys, you could conceivably visit these gems: Kebran Gabriel, Narga Selassie, Daga Estefanos, Tana Cherkos and Ura Kidane Meret.

Note that women can only visit certain monasteries, although these number among the most interesting. Admission to each monastery is collected by the priests. Priests

rarely have change, so bring lots of Birr1 and Birr10 notes for tips and fees. All monasteries charge Birr30 and toting a small video camera costs an additional Birr50 per monastery (the exception is Tara Cherkos, which charges Birr50 and stiff fees for cameras). If visiting the monasteries on the Zege Peninsula, you will be required to take a local guide (Birr50 per group). Most of them are pretty clued up on the history of each church.

All the stated journey times are for a one-way trip from Bahir Dar in a 40HP speedboat (add about 30% more time for a 25HP boat). See Getting Around (p117) for boat-hire information.

One of the most beautiful and atmospheric monasteries, **Kebran Gabriel** (men only) dates from the 17th century. It features a 12-columned portico and good paintings on the maqdas (inner sanctuary). Spot the depiction of Iyasu before Christ. It's half an hour away by boat and a short walk from the landing stage.

The original 14th-century church at **Debre Maryam** was rebuilt by Tewodros in the 19th century. It contains beautiful old manuscripts and a collection of church treasures. It's 30 minutes by boat and a short walk through coffee, mango and fig trees.

Ura Kidane Meret is the Zege Peninsula's most famous monastery and its maqdas is very beautifully painted. A compendium of Ethiopian religious iconography, it holds an important collection of 16th- and 18th-century crosses and crowns. The peninsula

---

MARY & ZARA

The Virgin Mary is held in high esteem in Ethiopia – sometimes it can feel as if she's bigger than her son himself. No other saint has as many saint days as her and no other saint brings forth such genuine sentiments of devotion. It wasn't always like this though. It was the 15th-century King Zara Yaqob, a fanatical Christian, who elevated her to such heights. Zara Yaqob was a man of determination who rekindled the glory of Aksum, reunited the fractured kingdom and commissioned numerous works of religious literature. He was also a vicious tyrant who beat his own wife to death and had his son tortured and thrown in the slammer. But it was religion and the worship of the Virgin in particular that really got him excited. Paranoid that the world was full of fallen angels determined to bring evil to his court, he had a team of priests pace the corridors of his palace day and night reciting prayers and splashing holy water about. He ordered that both the Old and New Testaments be read in their entirety during church services (which can't have done anything for church attendance) and ordered all his subjects to affix a crucifix to their processions and have 'I renounce the accursed, I am the slave of Mary, mother of the Creator of the universe' tattooed on their left arm, 'I deny the devil' on their right and a crucifix on their foreheads (a practice that is still common today).

Despite his more eccentric traits Zara Yaqob is regarded as one of the most important Ethiopian emperors both for holding the nation together and for his elevation of Mary.

---

is 35 minutes by boat from Bahir Dar. As the most-visited monastery, it attracts the most souvenir sellers and hustlers – though it's all very low key.

Set in the middle of the lake on Dek Island, **Narga Selassie** is peaceful, atmospheric and little visited. Built in the mid-18th century, it resembles Gonder's castles. Effigies of Mentewab and James Bruce are engraved on the church's exterior, as are fine 18th-century paintings and crosses. It's 2½ hours by boat and a two-minute walk from the landing stage.

One of the lake's most sacred monasteries, **Dega Estefanos** (men only) was rebuilt in the mid-19th century and houses a 16th-century painting of the Madonna, and mummified remains in glass coffins of five former Ethiopian emperors (13th to 17th centuries), including the now somewhat manky body of Zara Yaqob – one of the most important Ethiopian emperors (see boxed text above). The founder of this monastery was a saint who sailed to the island in 1268 on a stone boat. The boat is still visible halfway along the trail to the monastery. The island is east of Dek Island.

It's said the Ark of the Covenant was hidden at mysterious and historic **Tana Cherkos** (admission Birr50, camera Birr100, video camera a whooping Birr500; men only) for 800 years. The present 19th-century church is rather modest. Tana Cherkos is 2½ hours from Bahir Dar by boat. From the landing it's a 45-minute walk uphill.

Though most of the treasures of **Mitsele Fasiladas** were stolen in the 1990s, it's still worth visiting if you're in the vicinity. The setting is attractive and the old church's foundations remain. It's on an island just south of Tana Cherkos and is a short walk from the landing.

Like Ura Kidane Meret, **Beta Giorgis** and **Beta Maryam** are found on the Zege Peninsula. There's an important collection of crowns in a little 'museum' (attributed to Yohannes IV) and interesting paintings in the monasteries, probably dating from the 19th century or later. Beta Giorgis has some fantastic paintings, but Beta Maryam's paintings recently suffered heavy damage due to a flood. Fortunately Ethiopian artistic talent isn't yet dead and the paintings are being resurrected right now. Both monasteries are a short walk from the landing stage through lemon trees and coffee plants.

Also on Zege Peninsula, **Azuwa Maryam** has interesting 19th- or 20th-century paintings and a small museum. It's five minutes' walk from the landing stage.

BIRDWATCHING
For fans of our feathered friends, Lake Tana's various habitats offer up numerous bird species. Besides the heralded white pelicans, you may glimpse the likes of lesser flamingos, lesser kestrels, wattled cranes, bush petronias, hornbills, paradise flycatchers, kingfishers and various parrots.

Spots to peruse include the areas around Mitsele Fasiladas (a popular breeding ground for wetland birds), Debre Maryam, the Blue Nile's outlet, Dek Island and Lake Tana's eastern shore.

OUTLET OF THE BLUE NILE

You don't visit the outlet of the Blue Nile to say hello to the river. You visit it to say goodbye to Lake Tana's water and wish it well on its 5223km journey to the Mediterranean. You may even see a hippo or two.

It's about 30 minutes from Bahir Dar by speedboat. For info about reaching the outlet by road, see above.

Getting Around

There's no shortage of boat operators in Bahir Dar, and shifty commission agents lurk everywhere.

People who've been happiest have booked boats through the travel agencies on p112.

Prices are always negotiable, but the standard half-day tour to the Zege Peninsula and other nearby monasteries costs Birr400 for a group of up to five people in a boat with a 40HP engine. A full-day trip visiting distant islands and monasteries costs a very negotiable Birr1300. Always ensure that a guide is included in the cost. Although last-minute

arrangements are possible, it's best to arrange things the day before.

Before leaving, ensure your boat has life jackets and spare fuel. It's wise to bring a raincoat or umbrella and something warm.

The adventurous can troll the shoreline and try to hire a *tankwa* to visit Debre Maryam.

BLUE NILE FALLS (TIS ISAT)
ጢስ እሳት

The Blue Nile looks like a sluggish beast as it meanders slowly out of Lake Tana, but you only have to travel as far as the quiet village of Tis Isat to see the Nile in a very different mood. The gentle river pours over the side of a sheer chasm and explodes into a melange of mists and rainbows before continuing on its tumultuous path to Khartoum where it finally gets to kiss the White Nile. Tis Isat (Water that Smokes) or Tis Abay (Nile that Smokes) is impressive enough today, but just think what it used to be like a few years ago before the hydroelectric project, just upstream, stole most of the falls' energy.

As well as the falls (most impressive during the rainy season), the countryside around here makes for a pretty picnic spot and

NORTHERN ETHIOPIA

JAMES BRUCE: IN SEARCH OF THE SOURCE

Half undressed as I was by the loss of my sash, and throwing my shoes off, I ran down the hill towards the little island of green sods, which was about two hundred yards distant.

…It is easier to guess than to describe the situation of my mind at that moment – standing in the spot which had baffled the genius, industry and enquiry of both ancients and moderns, for the course of near three thousand years.

James Bruce, Travels to Discover the Source of the Nile *(1790)*

One of the first European explorers in this part of Africa was a Scot, James Bruce, who was passionate about unknown lands.

After serving as consul general in Algiers, he set off in 1768 in search of the Nile's source – a puzzle that had preoccupied people since the time of the Egyptian pharaohs.

After landing in Massawa, Eritrea, he made his way to the powerful and splendid court of Gonder, where he became close friends with Empress Mentewab.

In 1770 he reached the source of the Abay, the main river that empties into Lake Tana. There he declared the mystery of the Nile's source solved. He dedicated his discovery to King George III and returned home to national acclaim.

In fact, Bruce had traced only the source of the *Blue* Nile River, the main tributary of the Nile. Not only that, but he'd been beaten to his 'discovery' – as he very well knew – over 150 years earlier by a Spanish Jesuit, Pero Pais.

Of greater interest was the account of his journey, *Travels to Discover the Source of the Nile,* published in 1790. It remains a very useful source of information on Ethiopia's history and customs. His contemporaries considered much of it as gross exaggeration, or even as pure fiction. Given his earlier claims, no wonder.

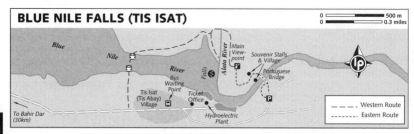

BLUE NILE FALLS (TIS ISAT)

NORTHERN ETHIOPIA

you may see parrots, bee-eaters, lovebirds, touracos, white-throated seedeaters and vervet monkeys.

The falls are located 32km southeast of Bahir Dar, just beyond Tis Isat village. The **ticket office** (admission Birr15, personal video cameras Birr100; 7am-5.30pm) can arrange official guides (Birr30), but they aren't really necessary.

The path to the falls starts 50m west of the ticket office. From there, walk east for about 1km until you see a tiny waterfall sign at a small junction. Go left (north) and after 400m you'll see a couple of rocky footpaths (on your left). They lead down the so-called eastern route, which crosses a 17th-century Portuguese bridge before turning west and climbing up past the little settlement towards the falls.

From the main viewpoint continue along a path that leads over the narrow Alata River before backtracking to the base of the falls.

From here you can complete the circuit by winding up along the path to the river above the falls and crossing its banks by motorboat (following the so-called western route). The entire walk shouldn't take more than 90 minutes. The **boat service** (one way/return Birr10/20) usually operates daily from 6.30am to 6pm. Trips in local *tankwas* are forbidden. If you're here early in the morning, watch for crocs.

Less energetic and mobile people may want to approach and return from the falls on the less steep western route.

Getting There & Away

Buses from Bahir Dar leave every few hours for Tis Isat village (Birr5, 45 bumpy minutes), which is also known as Tis Abay.

From Tis Isat, the last bus travelling back to Bahir Dar leaves between 3pm and 4pm. We've sadly heard of locals trying to make travellers miss the last bus and then charg-

ing them Birr100 for a ride. Another scam we discovered was men telling us upon arrival in Tis Isat that to ensure a seat on the bus back, we'd need to pay them to hold it for us.

It's usually pretty easy to hitch back to Bahir Dar (Birr10) if you've missed the last bus.

The **Ghion Hotel** (0582 200363) in Bahir Dar runs two daily tours (8am and 3pm) to the falls. It charges Birr100 per person for a group of at least four.

GONDER ጎንደር
pop 206,987 / elev 2210m

It's not what Gonder is, but what Gonder was that is so enthralling. The city lies in a bowl of hills where tall eucalyptus trees shelter tin-roofed houses, but rising above these, and standing proud through the centuries, are the walls of castles bathed in blood and painted in the pomp of royalty. Often called the Camelot of Africa, this description does the royal city a disservice: Camelot is legend, whereas Gonder is reality.

Surrounded by fertile land and lying at the crossroads of three major caravan routes it's easy to understand why Emperor Fasiladas (reigned 1632–67) made Gonder his capital in 1636. To the southwest lay rich sources of gold, civet, ivory and slaves, to the northeast lay Massawa and access to the Red Sea, and to the northwest lay Sudan and Egypt.

At the time of Fasiladas' death, Gonder's population already exceeded 65,000 and its wealth and splendour had become legendary. Drifting through the old palaces, banqueting halls and former gardens it's not difficult to imagine the courtly pageantry, ceremony and intrigue that went on here.

The city flourished as a capital for well over a century before infighting severely weakened the kingdom (see the boxed text, The Rise and Fall of Gonder on p38). In the 1880s what remained of Gonder was extensively looted by the Sudanese Dervishes. Despite this, and the damage sustained by British bombs during the liberation campaign of 1941, much of Gonder remains amazingly intact.

Today, Gonder is a great place to spend a few days and is a convenient base to make the leap into the Simien Mountains.

Orientation

Although Gonder is fairly spread out, it's still a great place to navigate on foot or by bicycle. The piazza marks the centre of town and is laden with the most shops and services. Just south of the piazza is the Royal Enclosure and all its treasures, while the road leading north is dotted with restaurants and hotels.

NORTHERN ETHIOPIA

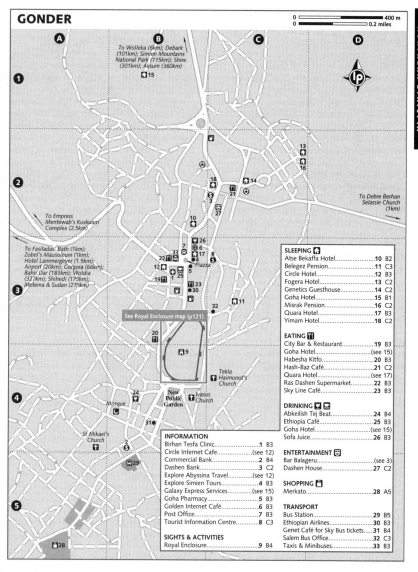

GONDER

0   400 m
0   0.2 miles

To Wolleka (6km); Debark (101km); Simien Mountains National Park (115km); Shire (301km); Aksum (360km)

To Empress Mentewab's Kuskuam Complex (2.5km)

To Fasiladas' Bath (1km); Zobel's Mausoleum (1km); Hotel Lammergeyer (1.5km); Airport (20km); Gorgora (66km); Bahir Dar (183km); Woldia (327km); Shihedi (175km); Metema & Sudan (215km)

To Debre Berhan Selassie Church (1km)

See Royal Enclosure map (p121)

Piazza

Tekla Haimonot's Church

New Public Garden

Iyasus Church

Mosque

St Mikael's Church

INFORMATION
Birhan Tesfa Clinic	1	B3
Circle Internet Cafe	(see 12)	
Commercial Bank	2	B4
Dashen Bank	3	C2
Explore Abyssina Travel	(see 12)	
Explore Simien Tours	4	B3
Galaxy Express Services	(see 15)	
Goha Pharmacy	5	B3
Golden Internet Café	6	B3
Post Office	7	B3
Tourist Information Centre	8	C3

SIGHTS & ACTIVITIES
Royal Enclosure	9	B4

SLEEPING
Atse Bekaffa Hotel	10	B2
Belegez Pension	11	C3
Circle Hotel	12	B3
Fogera Hotel	13	C2
Genetics Guesthouse	14	C2
Goha Hotel	15	B1
Misrak Pension	16	C2
Quara Hotel	17	B3
Yimam Hotel	18	C2

EATING
City Bar & Restaurant	19	B3
Goha Hotel	(see 15)	
Habesha Kitfo	20	B3
Hash-Baz Café	21	C2
Quara Hotel	(see 17)	
Ras Dashen Supermarket	22	B3
Sky Line Café	23	B3

DRINKING
Abkeilish Tej Beat	24	B4
Ethiopia Café	25	B3
Goha Hotel	(see 15)	
Sofa Juice	26	B3

ENTERTAINMENT
Bar Balageru	(see 3)	
Dashen House	27	C2

SHOPPING
Merkato	28	A5

TRANSPORT
Bus Station	29	B5
Ethiopian Airlines	30	B3
Genet Café for Sky Bus tickets	31	B4
Salem Bus Office	32	C3
Taxis & Minibuses	33	B3

Information

INTERNET ACCESS

Circle Internet Cafe (Circle Hotel; per hr Birr15) Some of the town's fastest connections.

Golden Internet Café (per hr Birr12) Possibly even faster connections.

MEDICAL SERVICES

Birhan Tesfa Clinic (☎ 0581 115943; ⊙ 24hr) Gonder's best medical facility.

Goha Pharmacy (⊙ 8am-9pm Mon-Sat) Helpful and well stocked.

MONEY

Commercial Bank (⊙ 8am-4pm Mon-Fri, 8am-noon Sat) Changes cash and travellers cheques.

Dashen Bank (⊙ 8am-4.30pm Mon-Fri, 8am-noon Sat) Has an ATM that accepts international Visa cards only.

POST

Post office (⊙ 8.30am-12.30pm & 2-5.30pm Mon-Fri)

TOURIST INFORMATION

Tourist information centre (☎ 0581 110022; amh tour@ethionet.et; ⊙ 8.30am-12.30pm & 1.30-5.30pm Mon-Fri, 8.30am-12.30pm Sat) Helpful information and licensed city guides (Birr150 per day). Can arrange out-of-city 4WD tours (Simien Mountains day trips etc).

TRAVEL AGENCIES

These reliable agencies can arrange everything from city tours to Simien Mountains treks. Prices range and negotiations are always in order.

Explore Abyssinia Travel (☎ 0581 118965; www .exploreabyssinia.com) As well as countrywide tours and car hire, it also has a book exchange.

Explore Simien Tours (☎ 0581 10040; fasilm_675 @yahoo.com; Quara Hotel)

Galaxy Express Services (☎ 0115 510355; Goha Hotel) All bookings must be made through this Addis Ababa phone number.

Dangers & Annoyances

Several travellers have complained about children hassling them for money with improbable sob stories. Other people have reported having beggars yelling 'fuck off' or other such welcomes at them.

Another annoyance, especially if you're left lathered at the time, is Gonder's lack of water – do your best to conserve.

Sights

ROYAL ENCLOSURE የፋሲለደስ ግቢ

A queen, who slew the brother of the King of Kings, was dangled by a rope from the branches of a tree outside the **Royal Enclosure** (Map p121; admission Birr50, personal video cameras Birr75, guides Birr50; ⊙ 8.30am-12.30pm & 1.30-6pm), her limp body hanging alongside those of common criminals and traitors. The flayed and stuffed bodies of rebels who had dared to challenge royal authority lay out in the open and were chewed on at night by dogs and hyenas. And on the other side of those mighty walls the Lions of Judah, descendants of Solomon and Sheba, wore crowns emblazed in emeralds and jewels and sat on cushions of gold while banqueting on raw flesh. The Gonder of yesteryear was a city of extreme brutality and immense wealth. Today the wealth and brutality are gone, but the memories linger and the trees continue to whisper stories of bodies swaying by a rope in the breeze.

The entire 70,000-sq-metre compound containing numerous castles and palaces has been almost completely restored with the aid of Unesco and was made a World Heritage Site in 1979. By far the most impressive, and also the oldest, building is **Fasiladas' Palace** (found in the compound's south). It stands 32m tall and has a crenulated parapet and four domed towers. Made of roughly hewn stones, it's reputedly the work of an Indian architect and shows

---

VOLUNTEERING GONDER STYLE

Yenege Tesfa (☎ 0918 774745; www.yenegetesfa.org) is a local NGO working with street kids in Gonder. It has an orphanage and provides educational programs for the town's children, as well as medical facilities. Following the success of Hope Enterprises in Addis Ababa, Yenege Tesfa also sells meal tickets that you can distribute to the town's street children. Tickets are available from most of the bigger hotels for Birr0.50 per ticket. It also actively encourages tourists to visit some of its project sites. Contact Yenege Tesfa in advance if you're interested in doing this.

Link Ethiopia (☎ 0911 748055; www.linkethiopia.org) is a UK-based education charity providing materials and volunteer teachers to schools in the Gonder region. Each volunteer is given pre-departure training.

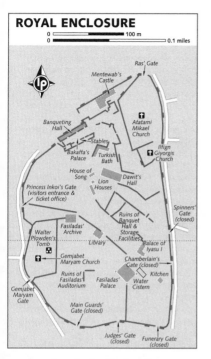

ROYAL ENCLOSURE

an unusual synthesis of Indian, Portuguese, Moorish and Aksumite influences.

The main floor was used as a dining hall and formal reception area; note the recessed Star of David above several doorways, which trumpet Fasiladas' link to the Solomonic dynasty. The small room in the northern corner boasts its original beam ceiling and some faint frescoes.

On the 1st floor, Fasiladas' prayer room has windows in four directions, each overlooking Gonder's important churches. On the roof, religious ceremonies were held, and it was from here that the emperor addressed his people. Above Fasiladas' 2nd-floor bedroom was the watchtower, from where it's (apparently) possible to see all the way to Lake Tana.

Behind the castle's eastern corner are various ruined buildings, including the remains of the **kitchen** (domed ceiling) and **water cistern** (thought by some to be a pool).

To the palace's northeast is the saddle-shaped **Palace of Iyasu I**. The son of Yohannes I, Iyasu I (reigned 1682–1706) is considered the greatest ruler of the Gonderine period. Iyasu's palace was unusual for its vaulted

ceiling. The palace used to be sumptuously decorated with gilded Venetian mirrors and chairs, with gold leaf, ivory and beautiful paintings adorning the walls. Visiting travellers described the palace as 'more beautiful than Solomon's house'. Although a 1704 earthquake and British bombing in the 1940s have done away with the interior and roof, its skeletal shell reeks of history.

North of Iyasu's palace are the relics of its **banquet hall** and **storage facilities**. To the west is the quadrangular **library** of Fasiladas' son, Yohannes I (reigned 1667–82), which has sadly been renovated and plastered over by the Italians. Once an impressive palace decorated with ivory, only the tower and walls of **Fasiladas' Archive** remain. It sits northwest of the library.

The compound's northern half holds vestiges of **Dawit's Hall** and **House of Song**, in which many religious and secular ceremonies and lavish entertainments took place. Emperor Dawit (reigned 1716–21) also built the first of two **Lion Houses** (the second was built by Selassie) where Abyssinian lions were kept until 1992.

When Dawit came to a sticky end (he was poisoned in 1721), Emperor Bakaffa (reigned 1721–30) took up the reins of power and built the huge **banqueting hall** and the impressive **stables**.

Between the stables and Dawit's Hall is the **Turkish bath** (*wesheba*), which apparently worked wonders for those suffering from syphilis! At the southern end you'll see the fire pit and the ceiling's steam vents.

Bakaffa's consort was responsible for the last castle, **Mentewab's Castle**, a two-storey structure that's now part of an Ethiopian cultural heritage project. Note the Gonder cross being used as a decorative motif.

FASILADAS' BATH ፋሲለ መዋኛ

Around 2km northwest of the town centre lies **Fasiladas' Bath** (admission incl in Royal Enclosure ticket; ☽ 8.30am-12.30pm & 1.30-5.30pm), which has been attributed to both Fasiladas and Iyasu I.

The large, rectangular sunken pool, which is reputedly larger than an Olympic pool, is overlooked by a small but charming building, thought by some to be Fasiladas' second residence. It's a beautiful and peaceful spot, where snakelike tree roots envelop, support and digest sections of the stone walls.

PRESTER JOHN OF THE INDIES

I, Prester John, who reign supreme, exceed in riches, virtue and power all creatures who dwell under Heaven...In our territories are found elephants, dromedaries and camels and almost every kind of beast. Honey flows in our land, and milk abounds...No poison can do harm here and no noisy frogs croak, no scorpions are there, and no serpents creep through the grass. No venomous reptiles can exist or use their deadly power.

Prester John

The letter the mysterious Christian ruler Prester John wrote to the Byzantine Emperor Manuel Comnenus I in 1165 went on to inform of how his kingdom contained 'Centaurs, Amazons and shrinking giants'. There was a river that flowed from Paradise 'and in it are found emeralds, sapphires and many other precious stones'.

His palace, so he said, was a 'palace of crystal with a roof of ebony and everyday thirty thousand people sit down to eat at tables of gold supported by columns of amethyst'. The great ruler himself wore robes spun from gold by salamanders that lived on a mountain of fire.

It was impressive stuff, but what really grabbed the attention of medieval Europe was Prester John's promise that he would ride forth from his kingdom with 10,000 cavalry and 100,000 foot soldiers and, alongside the armies of Western Europe, they would retake the Holy Lands from the Muslims.

The Christian Crusaders had lost much of the Holy Land and were on the verge of losing Jerusalem itself. News of Prester John's letter spread like wildfire throughout Christian Europe. It was partially in order to find Prester John's kingdom that the Portuguese launched the age of European exploration that changed the world forever.

Having first looked unsuccessfully in Asia, the focus turned to Ethiopia. When the Portuguese finally reached Gonder, they found a Christian kingdom that was a far cry from the glorious legend and certainly in no position to aid the reconquest of Jerusalem.

And of Prester John? It turned out that one of the most intriguing figures of medieval Europe was nothing more than collective imagination, and the letter that started it all was a fake created by a German monk.

Even so, Prester John, the most famous king of Ethiopia who wasn't, continues to symbolise the mystery of this corner of the world.

Although the complex was used for bathing (royalty used to don inflated goatskin lifejackets for their refreshing dips!), it was likely to have been constructed for religious celebrations, the likes of which still go on today. Once a year, Fasiladas' Bath is filled with water (the water comes from a river 500km away and it takes up to a month to fill) for the Timkat (p248) celebration. After being blessed by a priest, the pool becomes a riot of splashing water, shouts and laughter as a crowd of hundreds jumps in. The ceremony replicates Christ's baptism in the Jordan River, and is seen as an important renewal of faith.

Just east of the main compound is **Zobel's Mausoleum**. Local legend states it's named after Yohannes I's horse, which heroically brought Iyasu (Yohannie' son) back from Sudan after his father's death. Not only was the horse a good walker, but it was also pretty good at show jumping and is

said to have been able to clear 25m in one single leap.

If you don't want to walk, minibuses (Birr0.90) leaving from near the piazza pass here.

You must obtain your ticket at the Royal Enclosure before visiting Fasiladas' Bath.

DEBRE BERHAN SELASSIE CHURCH
ደብረ ብርሃን ስላሴ ቤተ ክርስቲያን

If it weren't for a swarm of bees, the beautiful church of **Debre Berhan Selassie** (admission Birr25; ✆ 6am-12.30pm & 1.30-6pm) would have probably been destroyed like most of Gonder's other churches by the marauding armies of the Sudanese Dervishes in the 1880s. When the Dervishes showed up outside the gates of the church, a giant swarm of bees surged out of the compound and chased the invaders away. This was a lucky intervention – Debre Berhan Selassie is one of the most stunning churches in the nation. It's the roof, with its rows and rows of winged cherubs, that draws most eyes. Exactly how many of these there are is surprisingly hard to pin down. We did a quick and not very scientific head count and came up with 135 – see what you get!

Full of all the colour, life, wit and humanity of Ethiopian art at its best, the walls provide a compendium of Ethiopian saints, martyrs and lore. Aside from the cherubs the highlights have to be the devilish Bosch-like depiction of hell and the Prophet Mohammed atop a camel being led by a devil. Although most paintings within the church are historically and happily attributed to the 17th-century artist Haile Meskel, this is highly unlikely to be the case because the remarkable rectangular church of today only dates back to the late 18th century. The original church, which was destroyed by fire, was circular (its foundations are still visible) and was created in the 1690s by Iyasu I.

A large stone wall with 12 rounded towers surrounds the compound and represents the 12 Apostles. The larger 13th tower (entrance gate) symbolises Christ and is shaped to resemble the Lion of Judah. If you have a keen eye, you'll be able to spot the lion's tail in the wall west of the church. Some historians hypothesise the symbolic architecture is evidence that the emperor planned to bring the Ark of the Covenant here from Aksum.

Flash photography inside the church is forbidden. Priests offer tours but a small contribution for the church should be left afterwards.

The church lies around 2km northeast of the Royal Enclosure.

EMPRESS MENTEWAB'S KUSKUAM COMPLEX ቀስቋም ደብር

It might not be as well preserved as the Royal Enclosure, but what this royal compound, known as **Kuskuam** (admission Birr25, personal video cameras Birr75; ☉ 8am-6.30pm), lacks in order it more than makes up for in melancholy. The complex was built in 1730 for the redoubtable Empress Mentewab, after the death of her husband (Emperor Bakaffa). It's said that she chose to move out here because she was a bit too keen on boys and living out here would keep her out of gossip's way. Gossip and the boys didn't stay away though: according to locals, when James Bruce stayed here with the empress

during his explorations of the highlands, he got to discover more than just the source of the Blue Nile…

Like the Royal Enclosure, it's made up of a series of buildings, including a long, castellated palace used for state receptions and to house the royal garrison. Its exterior is decorated with red volcanic tuff; spot the figures of crosses and Ethiopian characters and animals, such as St Samuel riding his lion.

The nearby smaller building is said to have been the empress's private residence. To the residence's west used to be a fine church. However, after damage from British bombing, it had to be rebuilt. For a tip the church guardian will open up a trap door and lead you down into the church's vaults where, under the faint light of a dying bulb, an old sheet will be whipped off a glass-fronted coffin and the skeletons of the empress, her son and her grandsons (Emperors Iyasu II and Iyo'as) will stare back at you.

Below the complex lies a series of tiny doll-sized mud-and-stick houses that religious students live in while training to become monks.

The complex lies in the hills 3.5km northwest of town. A taxi from the piazza, taking in here and Fasiladas' Bath, should cost about Birr80 return.

WOLLEKA (FALASHA VILLAGE) ወለቃ

Around 6km north of Gonder several 'Star of David' and 'Falasha Village' signs point the way to what would be better described as the former Falasha village of Wolleka. Once the home to a thriving population of Falashas or Ethiopian Jews, most were airlifted to Israel between 1985 and 1991 and today only a couple remain. Sadly, the pottery for which they were once famous has degenerated into clumsy, half-hearted art. Project Ploughshare Women's Crafts Training Center is helping disadvantaged women rekindle this craft.

After the adoption of Christianity as the state religion, Falashas had their land confiscated for refusing to convert. To survive, many became skilled craftsmen. Recent research suggests Falashas may have provided the labour for the castle's construction and decoration.

The highlight of a trip here is to grab a glimpse of highland village life rather than Jewish monuments or culture.

Tours

City tours, which take in all the major sites, are easily arranged at the tourist information centre. Guides cost Birr150 per full day, and you can either walk, ride bikes, hop on local minibuses or charter a taxi for the day (around Birr50 per hour).

For Simien Mountains tours and treks, see Planning (p127).

Festivals & Events

Particularly good times to visit Gonder are during the festivals of Leddet (Christmas) and Timkat. For more information on both of these festivals, see p248.

Sleeping

BUDGET

Yimam Hotel (☎ 0581 110470; r without bathroom Birr60) The rooms here, set around a large courtyard, are a toe-curling pink colour, cramped and not very inviting, but compared with the common toilets, which smell like two-week-old injera, they are heaven indeed.

Belegez Pension (☎ 0918 772997; d with/without bathroom Birr120/80) Once again retaining the crown of best-value cheapie in Gonder, the small and simple rooms here are spick and span and the showers gush forth steamy hot H_2O. The sunny courtyard provides safe parking and is a good place to make new friends. The staff are very traveller-aware. Reservations are wise.

Circle Hotel (☎ 0581 101991; d/tw Birr115/150) Spinning up the staircase to the top of this hotel is like being on a fairground ride. The bright, tiled rooms are spacious, but the bathrooms aren't too special and the toilet seats are ripped up and painful to hang-out on. The downstairs bar shows the big English Premiership games and match times are posted on the door outside.

Misrak Pension (☎ 0581 110069; d Birr150) Prices are entirely *faranji*-fied but the rooms are spotless, the mattresses comfortable and the tiny bathrooms 'oh so clean!' It's set around a pleasant garden.

Quara Hotel (☎ 0581 110040; cgfbg@yahoo.com; r with/without bathroom Birr200/150) A friendly hotel that acts as a home base for various local NGOs. The rooms are tidy, but you'd better have eaten all your carrots when you were young because the lighting is terrible.

MIDRANGE & TOP END

our pick Genetics Guesthouse (☎ 0918 049191; d/tw Birr150/250) This new guesthouse is a jewel in the mounds of dross. The rooms are huge, immaculate and the stylish bright red-and-white walls frame numerous pictures. The beds are divinely comfortable and guarantee a decent night's kip, the furnishings are good quality and there's piping hot water (most of the time!). It's easily the most exciting hotel in town.

Fogera Hotel (☎ 0581 110405; s/d US$20/25) While the rooms in this old Italian building are fading fast (though room 3 has retro-cool flowery wallpaper), the garden *tukuls* (conical thatched huts) have aged better and are a fair deal.

Atse Bekaffa Hotel (☎ 0581 117711; s/d US$25/30) A massive new venture with equally massive rooms. What really sets it apart are the little extras – ornate bed heads and colour coordination. Longer stays bring discounts.

Hotel Lammergeyer (☎ 0581 122993; s/d/tw US$25/35) Very close to Fasiladas' Bath this clean place, which has received lots of positive feedback, has a warm, family vibe, bright, sunny rooms with small bathrooms. There's a small cafe-restaurant.

Goha Hotel (☎ 0581 110634; ghion@ethionet.et; s/d US$38/51; 🖳) Perched on a high natural balcony providing a vantage point that would make a soaring vulture sick with envy, this is easily the best top-end hotel in town. The rooms have wool wall hangings, stone walls and embroidered bedding, but the water and electricity are as erratic as everywhere else in Gonder. You needn't pack your swimming costume for the pool – the tide is out!

Eating & Drinking

Hash-Baz Café (snacks Birr2) With great croissants, cakes and pastries, this is a fine spot for breakfast. It also whips up some cool juices to match the cool interior.

Sky Line Café (mains Birr12-15) With a raised terrace overlooking the bustling streets and a decent breakfast menu (though do make sure you pronounce juice very clearly, otherwise you'll end up with several portions of chips just like we did!), this is a fine place to kick off the day's events.

City Bar & Restaurant (mains Birr20) Many locals will tell you that this place, on the 1st floor of the Golden Gate Bridge (which isn't actually gold, or even a bridge), produces the finest injera and *wat* in Gonder. We won't argue. If injera isn't to your tummy's liking, the *faranji* food is OK too.

Habesha Kitfo (mains Birr20-35) Lovingly and traditionally decked out with a woven mat floor, cow-hide stools, leather chairs and the odd live duck, this place drips in character and is the ideal spot in which to indulge in great Ethiopian food. Vegetarian fasting food is available daily and there's a decent gift shop attached.

Quara Hotel (mains Birr28-32) When the residents of Gonder want to impress, it'll be to the restaurant of this central hotel that they take their guests. Most of the food is designed to suit the belly of *faranjis* and includes such items as steak and chips and pizza.

Ras Dashen Supermarket (🕗 8am-9pm) Load up on Simien Mountains supplies here.

Goha Hotel (beer Birr8) There's nowhere better in town for a sunset drink than the hotel's lofty garden terrace.

Ethiopia Café (drinks Birr2-4.50) This classic art-deco Italian cafe in the heart of the piazza is a true throwback to the days of yesteryear. The coffee is strong and the beer is cheap.

Abkeilish Tej Beat (bottles of tej Birr5-7) This well-known *tej beat* (purveyor of honey wine) is the best place to delve into some stiff *tej*.

Sofa Juice (juices Birr6) If your insides are calling for drinks of a healthy variety, get your vitamin and fruity fix at this juice haven.

Entertainment

Mimicking the success of Bahir Dar's Balageru Cultural Club, several traditional bars have opened in Gonder. *Azmaris* (see the boxed text, p60) sing along to their *masenkos* (single-stringed fiddle), women dance and everybody has a good time.

Bar Balageru (admission free) The most fun and most packed. A glass of *tej* is Birr6.

Dashen House (drinks Birr6-8) The large outdoor terrace here is indisputably the town's favourite beer haunt. Further up the road, towards the Genetics Guesthouse, is a whole series of truly grimy and hard-core bars and clubs, but be warned that almost all of the women at these hang out under red light bulbs.

Shopping

Merkato (🕗 sunrise-sunset) The obvious choice for shoppers. Within the market, and on surrounding streets, you'll find baskets, pottery and cloth stalls.

Getting There & Away

For information about reaching Sudan, see p263.

AIR

Ethiopian Airlines (☎ 0581 110129) flies once or twice daily to Addis Ababa (US$158, 1½ to two hours), Bahir Dar (US$74, 20 minutes), Lalibela (US$98, 30 minutes) and Aksum (US$110, 1¾ hours).

BUS

Buses leave for Addis Ababa (Birr94, two days, 6am), Bahir Dar (bus/minibus Birr23/35, four hours, three buses daily, many minibuses), Debark (Birr22, 3½ hours, several daily), Gorgora (Birr12, 1½ hours, two daily), Woldia (Birr84, two days, 5.30am) and Metema on the Ethiopia–Sudan border (Birr31, six to seven hours, 5.30am). For Aksum, go first to Shire (Birr57, 10 hours, 6am). For longer journeys, buy tickets a day in advance. Salem Buses (Birr170, 11 to 12 hours, 5am) and Sky Buses (Birr204, 11 hours, 5am Thursday & Saturday) run luxury air-con buses complete with reclining seats, TVs, toilets and, on Sky Buses, even snacks to Addis Ababa.

Getting Around

A taxi to or from the airport, which is 21km from town, costs between Birr50 and Birr60. Chartering a taxi to see Gonder's sights costs about Birr50 per hour, but you'll have to negotiate hard for this. Taxis and minibuses congregate near the piazza.

Minibuses charge between Birr0.60 and Birr1.75 for hops around town; *garis* (horse-drawn carts) cost around Birr1 to Birr5.

AROUND GONDER

Gorgora ጎርጎራ

pop 4783 / elev 1880m

The little lakeshore town of Gorgora, 67km south of Gonder, has a slow and green tropical vibe and feels like something from the *African Queen*. It makes a pleasant excursion, especially for travellers interested in birds (see p116).

SIGHTS & ACTIVITIES

The most interesting relic of Gorgora's former days as a temporary capital is the attractive **Church of Debre Sina** (Map p115; admission Birr30, video cameras Birr100). Built in 1608 by Emperor Susenyos' son on the site of a 14th-century monastery, it's decorated with fading 17th-century polychromatic frescoes. Ask to see the 'Egyptian St Mary'.

Emperor Susenyos (reigned 1607–32) built a **palace** (Map p115; admission free) on a peninsula 10km west of Gorgora, which can be reached in 30 minutes by road or boat. Compared with Gonder, it's a shambles but historical architecture buffs should make the trip. Also in the area is the **Portuguese Cathedral** (Map p115; admission free) built by Susenyos. The decrepit state is evidence of his failed attempt to force Catholicism on his people.

If the lake's waters are calling, you can visit Tana's northern monasteries. **Mendaba Medhane Alem** (Map p115; admission Birr20, men only) hosts ancient biblical manuscripts and some of Ethiopia's most dedicated priests, while **Birgida Maryam** (Map p115; admission Birr20, men only) is known for its 16th-century painting of Mary. Both are around 30 minutes from Gorgora by boat.

With the exception of Debre Sina, you'll need a local guide to find most of the sights. Guides can normally be found hanging around the Gorgora Port Hotel and they charge Birr50 per person. They can also organise birdwatching trips.

SLEEPING & EATING

Gorgora Port Hotel (☎ 0581 4670003; camping Birr50.50, s/d Birr150/187, 3-bedroom cottage Birr220) Set among a riot of flowers there's a wide range of rooms available here: from overpriced and grubby standard rooms to good-value cottages that come with room for six and beautiful lake views. Electricity runs (sometimes!) between 6pm and 10pm. The restaurant (mains Birr7 to Birr16) has limited food.

GETTING THERE & AROUND

Two daily buses run to Gonder (Birr13, 1½ hours) at 5am and 8am.

A ferry sails from Gorgora for Bahir Dar every Thursday at 6am (Birr157, 1½ days). The ferry typically overnights in Konzola, where there's food and a couple of cheap hotels. Buy tickets at the **Lake Tana Transport Enterprise office** (Map p115; ⏱ 8-11.30am & 2-5.30pm Mon-Fri, 8am-noon Sat). Boats for touring the monasteries out on the lake are available through either this same office for Birr150 per hour, or they can also be organised with the staff at the Gorgora Port Hotel from Birr133.

SIMIEN MOUNTAINS NATIONAL PARK
የሰሜን ተራሮች ብሔራዊ ፓርክ

No matter how you look at them, the Simien Mountains will leave you speechless. This massive 4000m-high table of rock, riven with gullies, offers easy but immensely rewarding trekking along the edge of a plateau that falls sheer to the plains far, far below. It's not just the scenery (and altitude) that will leave you speechless, but also the excitement of sitting among a group of 100 gelada baboons or watching magnificent walia ibex joust on the rock ledges.

Whether you come for a stroll or a two-week trek, the Simien Mountains make a great break from the historical circuit's constant monument-viewing. Besides the mythical baboons (see the boxed text, p75), the mountains are also home to a variety of other endemic mammals, birds and plants. Thanks to the wildlife the park is a World Heritage Site.

Although facilities for trekkers are few (the undeveloped state of the park is actually one of its attractions), the mountains are nevertheless easily accessible and treks can be quickly organised.

The Simien Mountains aren't to be missed – they undoubtedly rank among Africa's most beautiful ranges.

Geography & Geology

Comprising one of Africa's principal mountain massifs, the Simiens are made up of several plateaus, separated by broad river valleys. A number of peaks rise above 4000m, including Ras Dashen (4543m), which is highly touted – incorrectly so – by Ethiopian tourism officials as the fourth-highest mountain in Africa. They seem to have happily forgotten the Ruwenzori Range's Mt Speke (4890m), Mt Baker (4844m), Mt Emin (4792m), Mt Gessi (4717m) and Mt Luigi (4626m), as well as Tanzania's Mt Meru (4566m)!

The Simiens' landscape is incredibly dramatic. It was formed by countless eruptions, some 40 million years ago; layer upon layer of molten lava was poured until it reached a thickness of 4000m. The subsequent erosion produced the mountains' jagged and spectacular landscapes seen today.

The famous pinnacles that sharply and abruptly rise from the surrounding landscape are volcanic necks, the solidified plumbing of the eroded ancient volcanoes.

The 179-sq-km park lies within the 'Afro-alpine' zone, between 1900m and 4543m elevation.

Wildlife

The mountains are home to three of Ethiopia's larger endemic mammals: the walia ibex (numbers were estimated at around 600 and increasing at the last survey conducted in 2005), the gelada baboon (estimated to number around 6000) and the elusive Ethiopian wolf (71 were seen in and around the park in 2005). Other mammals sometimes seen are rock hyraxes, jackals, bushbucks and klipspringers.

Endemic birds include the often-seen thick-billed raven and the less common black-headed siskin, white-collared pigeon, white-billed starling, wattled ibis, spot-breasted plover, white-backed black tit and Ankober seedeater or serin. Though common, one of the most memorable sights (and sounds!) is the lammergeier soaring low.

Along the roadside on the approach to Sankaber, look out for the endemic ivory-coloured Abyssinian rose.

Planning

Although organising trekking yourself at park headquarters in Debark is straightforward, it still takes two hours to complete. It's best to arrive at headquarters the afternoon before you plan on starting your trek.

Organising treks through agencies in Gonder and Addis Ababa is easy, but you'll end up paying a lot more for the same trip.

WHEN TO GO

December to March is the driest time; after the rainy season in October, the scenery is greenest and the wildflowers are out.

During the main rainy season, between June and September, mist often obscures the views and trails can be slippery underfoot. However, you're still assured of several hours of clear, dry weather for walking; the rain tends to come in short, sharp downpours.

Daytime temperatures are consistently between 11.5°C and 18°C, while 3°C is typical at night. Between October and December, night-time temperatures can dip below freezing.

PARK FEES

Park entry fees include camping and are payable at the **park headquarters** (☎ 0581 113482/0581 170407; admission per 12 hours Birr90, 5-seat vehicle Birr20;

🕑 8.30am-12.30pm & 1.30-5.30pm Mon-Fri, 8.30am-noon & 2-5pm Sat & Sun).

Entrance fees won't be refunded once paid. However, if mules, cooks, guides and scouts aren't used (because of bad weather or acclimatisation difficulties), their fees can be refunded; make sure this is clear before setting off.

MAPS

The most useful trekking map is produced by the well-respected Institute of Geography, University of Berne, Switzerland: the *Simen* [sic] *Mountains Trekking Map* (2003; 1:100,000). The park rents a laminated version for Birr20 per day. If you want your own copy, it's best to get it before leaving home. It can also occasionally be found for between Birr200 and Birr250 in Gonder or in Debark's Simien Park Hotel (p130).

EQUIPMENT

Mattresses (Birr15 per day), sleeping bags (Birr15 per day), two-person tents (Birr30 per day) and cooking equipment and gas stoves (Birr40 per day) can be hired at park headquarters. Debark's petrol station sells kerosene (parrafin).

SUPPLIES

Outside Debark, there are no shops; though you can buy eggs, chickens and sheep from mountain villages. Your guide will negotiate prices. Mule handlers will gladly kill, skin and roast a sheep if they can tuck in too.

Gonder is a better place to stock up as Debark's food supplies are limited to a few tin cans, biscuits, pasta, tomato sauce and milk powder, plus some fresh fruit and vegetables. Stoves, lanterns and kerosene are also available in Gonder. Anything 'specialised', such as packet soups, should be bought in Addis Ababa.

Water is available during the trek but should be treated. Make sure the cook, if you have one, boils the water sufficiently.

Though eucalyptus wood (sold by villagers on the mountain) is permitted for fires, it's best to bring a stove. Burning wood from indigenous trees is strictly forbidden.

GUIDES, SCOUTS, COOKS & MULES

Cooks, scouts, mules and guides are all organised at park headquarters. Only the scouts are compulsory.

SIMIEN MOUNTAINS NATIONAL PARK

Official guides (Birr120 per day) are recommended and help translate while in villages. Although freelancers, they're trained by the national park on courses established by an Austrian team. Most are excellent; a few are less so. Guides work by rota, but you should not be afraid to ask for another if you're not happy with the one assigned to you.

Official guides work on a rota basis directly with the park, but many can also be hired privately. We have had very good reports regarding the services of **Dawoud Sulayman Mekonnon** (daw_sulay@yahoo.com).

Most people who've hired cheaper unofficial guides off the street end up regretting the decision. See p247 for more.

'Scouts' (armed park rangers) are compulsory (Birr40 per day). Few speak English, but what they lack in conversation they make up for in willingness to help.

Cooks can be hired for Birr75 per day (cooking for one to five people), a welcome and not-too-costly luxury for some.

Porters aren't available, but mules (Birr35 per day) with handlers (Birr35 per day) can be hired. The guide and scout will expect at least one mule for carrying their blankets and provisions. Check mules for tender feet (ask the owner to walk the mule up and down) and signs of saddle sores. If in doubt, ask for another.

Guides, scouts, cooks and mule handlers should bring their own food. In reality many bring token supplies or nothing at all and will then look to you for sustenance. This is

OK if you know about it in advance – sadly most people don't and the result is that everybody goes hungry. We have received dozens of complaints regarding this. Either check that they have enough or bring extra packets of rice etc.

If you plan on covering two days' worth of trekking in one, you'll have to pay your team double for the day.

See p252 for post-trek tipping advice.

ORGANISED TREKS

There are numerous tour operators or travel agencies in Addis Ababa (see p270) and several more in Gonder (p120) that can organise transport, guides, equipment rental and food. However, they charge you a lot more to hire exactly the same services from the park headquarters that you can easily arrange yourself.

There are also numerous freelance 'agents' in Gonder offering to organise treks for you, but most receive mixed reviews at best from travellers.

Trekking

The foot that is restless, will tread on a turd.

Ethiopian proverb

Most treks begin and end in Debark, but it's possible to use 4WDs to start or end your hike anywhere between Debark and Chenek. If you have time, strong legs and a hatred of doubling back, you could finish your trek at Adi Arkay, 75km north of Debark.

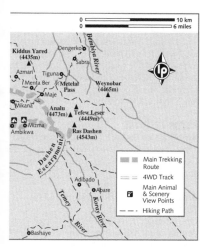

Once on the mountains you'll be following centuries-old paths that crisscross the slopes and connect villages with pasturelands. They make terrific trekking routes; the walking itself is generally not challenging and gradients aren't too steep.

Be sure to allow time for acclimatisation when planning your routes, particularly if you're aiming for Ras Dashen. Review the Safety Guidelines for Trekking (p243) and Responsible Trekking (p244) boxed texts.

CHOOSING A TREKKING ROUTE

For spectacular scenery, head for Geech. For walia ibex, Chenek is good (be sure to get here no later than 9am). Gelada baboons are best between Buyit Ras and Sankaber; Chenek and Geech aren't bad either. For pleasant walking, the stretch between Geech and Chenek is good. For lammergeiers, head to Chenek.

Ras Dashen, frankly, doesn't offer a great deal beyond the satisfaction of 'bagging it'. And thanks to an odd perspective from its summit, nearby peaks actually look higher. This has led disgruntled trekkers to drag their guides up peak after peak, repeatedly musing the 'one over there' is higher!

Most people trek for four or five days. In four you can trek to Geech and back; with an extra day you could get to Chenek, taking in Mt Bwahit. If time is of the essence then in two days you could walk from Debark to Sankaber and back. While for the dedicated with around 10 days to play with, you could bag Ras Dashen (these times include the re-

turn journey to Debark). If you're short on time and want to maximise your time in the mountains, using a vehicle to access Sankaber will save at least two days.

The following Debark to Chenek trek is the classic five-day route; the lower camps can be bypassed using a vehicle. Times vary from person to person, and also depend on whether exact routes are followed. The following routes and times have been devised in consultation with local guides.

DEBARK TO CHENEK TREK
Debark to Buyit Ras (10km, Three to Four Hours)

Sankaber can be reached in a single day, but many trekkers prefer to break at Buyit Ras, where there's an abundance of gelada baboons. There's also a camping spot with beautiful views, though you'll have to share the area with the Simien Park Lodge. If you push on to Sankaber, it's another 13km (around three to four hours).

Buyit Ras to Geech Camp via Sankaber (25km, Seven to Eight Hours)

The dirt road will take you straight to Sankaber, but the scenic route along the escarpment isn't to be missed. There are particularly good views between Michibi and Sankaber. Look out for gelada baboons.

From Sankaber to Geech it's between four and five hours' walk.

Geech Camp to Chenek via Imet Gogo (20km, Seven to Nine Hours)

Geech to Chenek takes about five to six hours, but you'd be crazy not to take in Imet Gogo, around 5km northeast of Geech. It takes 1½ to two hours one way.

The promontory, at 3926m, affords some of the most spectacular views of the Simien Mountains. To make a day of it, you could continue to the viewpoint known as Saha. From Saha, you can head for the viewpoint at Kadavit (2.5km, 30 to 40 minutes) and then return to camp.

You can also trek to Chenek via Imet Gogo using Saha as a starting point (eight to nine hours). Saha lies around 3km from Geech.

From Imet Gogo you have two choices: the first is to return to Geech by your outward route, then head directly south and back across the Jinbar River to where you'll eventually meet the dirt road that leads to Chenek.

NORTHERN ETHIOPIA

The alternative, which is harder but more scenic, is to follow the escarpment edge south all the way to Chenek.

Near Chenek is Korbete Metia, a stunning spot with a sinister side. It was here that some regional officials were executed. Korbete Metia loosely translates to 'the place where skin was thrown down'. Lammergeiers are often seen here.

Chenek is probably the best spot in the Simien Mountains for wildlife.

Chenek to Mt Bwahit & Return (6km, Two to Three Hours)

If you can spare a little more time, the ever-tempting summit of Mt Bwahit (4430m) lies to the southeast of Chenek camp.

Around 20 minutes from the camp towards Mt Bwahit, there's a spot that affords one of the best opportunities for glimpsing, at long range (around 300m to 400m), the walia ibex. This animal, a member of the wild goat family, lives on the crags of the steep escarpment above 3000m. Come very early in the morning or late in the afternoon (after 4pm) with binoculars.

RETURN ROUTES

For the return journey you can either retrace your footsteps (Sankaber is seven to eight hours away), or get to Sankaber by taking the scenic local trail up to Ambaras through the village of Argin. The trail affords good views of the escarpment and the foothills of Mt Bwahit.

ONWARD TO RAS DASHEN
Chenek to Ambikwa (22km, Eight to Nine Hours)

If the mountain vistas keep on calling, why not push on to the Big Daddy of them all, Ras Dashen? Heading on from Chenek, the first day takes you along a track leading eastward and then southeastward up towards a good viewpoint on the eastern escarpment, to the north of Mt Bwahit. To the east, across the vast valley of the Mesheba River, you can see the bulk of Ras Dashen.

Ambikwa to Ras Dashen & Return (17km, Eight to 10 Hours)

Most trekkers stay two nights at Ambikwa and go up to the summit of Ras Dashen on the day in between. It's a good idea to start at first light.

At Ras Dashen there are three distinct points, and much debate about which is the true summit. Whichever peak you go for, the total walk from Ambikwa to reach one summit is about five to six hours. If you want to knock off the others, add two to three hours for each one. Returning by the same route takes about three to four hours.

RETURN ROUTES
Ambikwa to Debark (77km, Three Days)

Most trekkers return from Ambikwa to Debark along the same route via Chenek and Sankaber.

Ambikwa to Adi Arkay (About 65km, Three to Five Days)

One alternative return route is to trek from Ambikwa to Arkwasiye, to the northeast of Chenek, taking in the nearby peaks of Beroch Wuha (4272m) and Silki (4420m).

From Arkwasiye to Adi Arkay will take another two to three days of strenuous walking, via Sona (three hours from Arkwasiye).

From Adi Arkay, which lies 75km north of Debark, you can continue northward to Aksum.

OTHER ROUTES

There are endless alternatives for keen trekkers, such as a return route from Ras Dashen back to Ambikwa and Chenek, via the east and north sides of the Mesheba River.

One slightly more challenging route that will give you a taste of the highlands as well as the lowlands, and bags some 4000m peaks on the way (and is much more interesting than climbing Ras Dashen), is from Debark to Adi Arkay via Sankaber, Geech, Chenek (climbing Mt Bwahit at 4430m), Arkwasiye (climbing Beroch Wuha at 4272m) and Sona (climbing Silki at 4420m). The route should take around nine to 10 days. Note that since it takes the guides, mules and other members of your trekking entourage two further days to return to Debark from Adi Arkay, you must pay two days' extra fee.

Sleeping & Eating
DEBARK

Simien Park Hotel (☎ 0581 17005; s with/without bathroom Birr120/50, d with/without bathroom Birr180/70) About 600m north of park headquarters, the older rooms with common bathrooms are as popular with flies as they are trekkers. Behind these rooms a newer block contains tiled en-suite rooms with occasional hot water and slightly fewer flies.

Giant Lobelia Hotel (☎ 0581 170566; globeliahotel @yahoo.com; s/d Birr110/200) The rooms at this sterile, giant pink flower of a hotel vary a lit-tle, so ask to see a few first, however, it's the best place to stay and the manager cannot do enough for you. The downstairs restau-rant gets lively at night and produces fair *faranji*-flavoured food.

ON THE MOUNTAINS

If you don't have camping equipment (and don't want to rent it), you can do as the guides do: stay with locals (you should con-tribute about Birr20 per night). Don't expect luxuries. A floor or wooden platform covered with a goatskin serves as your bedroom; any number and combination of animals, chil-dren, chickens and especially fleas will be your roommates. Note that most guides do their best to discourage this and you might have to push hard for them to admit that it's possible.

Camping (per 24hr Birr20) The obvious choice for trekkers. It's possible anywhere, but if you're in the vicinity of an the official camp (Sankaber, Geech and Chenek) it's more con-venient to drop your tent there. These camps have huts for your guides and scouts, as well as long-drop loos.

Sankaber Lodge (dm Birr40) This spartan lodge has a couple of nine-bed dorms. Don't expect more than a rickety bed, blanket, some old bed linen and possibly the odd flea.

Simien Park Lodge (☎ 0582 310741; www.simiens .com; dm US$31, r from US$135) At 3260m Africa's highest hotel offers a polished service and comfortable rooms in *tukul* huts that have underfloor heating and solar-powered hot showers. Unfortunately most rooms are per-fectly positioned to not quite take advantage of the stupendous views. The dorm consists of bare bones, two bunks per room and common showers. A portion of its profits (2.5%) go to local projects, which makes it about as close as north Ethiopia gets to an ecolodge.

Getting There & Around

Two morning buses run from Debark to Gonder (Birr21, 3½ hours). The only bus running north to Shire (for Aksum) is the Gonder service that passes through Debark between 9am and 10am, but is almost always

full. If you want to get a seat on it, the national park office will reserve you a place by getting somebody in Gonder to keep a seat warm for you by sitting in it between Gonder and Debark where you swap places! They charge Birr200 for this service and you need to ar-range it at least a day in advance. Failing this an uncomfortable seat in a goods truck can be all yours for around Birr150.

It's possible to arrange 4WDs through the park office to drop you off at Sankaber (one way/return Birr800/1600), but it's not a reli-able service and requires several days' notice. It's technically forbidden for tourists to ride the occasional supply trucks that take goods to villages in and around the park.

SHIRE ሺሬ
pop 43,967 / elev 595m

The sun-blinded and dusty university town of Shire, marked on some maps as Inda Selassie, is of interest to travellers only because it pro-vides a link with Aksum, 60km to the east.

If you get stuck in Shire (and you will if you arrive here after 4pm), you can choose between two hotels. The **Lalibela Hotel** (r without bathroom Birr50) has dirty and overpriced rooms. Those we saw had condoms scattered across the floor, which at least gave them some character! More salubrious is the **Gebar Shire Hotel** (☎ 0344 443427; gebshire@ethionet.et; s/d/tw Birr195.50/230/258.75), a flash new hotel at the northern edge of town; though its rooms are disappointingly contraceptive-free.

There are several buses (Birr15 to Birr20, 1½ hours) and minibuses to Aksum daily (Birr25, 1½ hours). And one daily bus to Gonder (Birr90, around 10 to 15 hours, 6am).

AKSUM አክሱም
pop 44,629 / elev 2130m

Aksum is a riddle waiting to be solved. Did the Queen of Sheba really call the town's dusty streets home? Does the very same Ark of the Covenant that Moses carried down from Mt Sinai reside in that small chapel? Are there ac-tually secret hordes of treasure hidden inside undiscovered tombs? And just what exactly do those famous stelae signify?

Aksum is more than just a collection of lifeless ruins though. The town, albeit rural at heart, has a vibrancy, life and continuing national importance very rarely found at an-cient sites. Pilgrims still journey here in their thousands to pay homage at its great churches and all Ethiopians believe passionately that the Ark of the Covenant resides here.

While no longer a wealthy metropolis, the town continues to flourish as a centre of local trade and life continues as it has for millennia. Around the crumbling palaces, farmers go on ploughing their land, women continue to wash their clothes in the Queen of Sheba's Bath, and market goers and their donkeys hurry past the towering stelae.

Dr Neville Chittick once described Aksum as 'the last of the great civilisations of Antiquity to be revealed to modern knowledge'. Yet even today Aksum still hasn't revealed all its secrets, and an exploration of its ruined tombs and palaces is sure to light a spark of excitement in all.

This Unesco World Heritage Site is undoubtedly one of the most important and spectacular ancient sites in sub-Saharan Africa. Don't miss it.

History

The early history of Aksum, like most Ethiopian history, is shrouded in such a fog of legend that the truth remains largely unknown. While debate rages about whether or not Aksum really was the Queen of Sheba's capital in the 10th century BC, what is certain is that a high civilisation started to rise here as early as 400 BC.

By the 1st century AD, Greek merchants knew Aksum as a great city and the powerful capital of an extensive empire. For close to 1000 years, Aksum dominated the vital sea-borne trade between Africa and Asia and the kingdom numbered among the ancient world's greatest states. But then, quite suddenly, the power of Aksum collapsed and the city turned into a forgotten backwater. Only now, a thousand years later, are archaeologists starting to take a serious interest in the city. What is certain is that the real secrets of ancient Aksum remain hidden under layers of dust and rock awaiting a real-life Indiana Jones. For more information see Kingdom of Aksum (p33) and the boxed text, p134.

Information

INTERNET ACCESS

Africa Hotel (Map p133; per hr Birr30) Town's fastest and most reliable internet option – yes, you really can read an email!

Internet Centre (Map p133; per hr Birr30) Slow but usually steady connections.

MEDICAL SERVICES

St Mary Hospital (Map p133; ☽ 24hr).

St Mary Pharmacy (Map p133; ☎ 0347 752646; ☽ 7.30am-9.30pm) Helpful and well stocked.

St Michael Clinic (Map p133; ☽ noon-2pm & 5-10pm Mon-Fri, 8am-10pm Sat & Sun) Helpful clinic and the doctor speaks decent English.

MONEY

Commercial Bank (Map p133; ☽ 8-11am & 1-3pm Mon-Fri, 8-11am Sat) Changes cash and travellers cheques. Aksum's Commercial Bank has the distinction of being the site of the first ever TPLF operation, in which a dozen members of the organisation robbed the bank and with the money were able to launch a guerrilla movement that was to change the map of the Horn. However, we do advise against trying such stunts yourself.

Wegagen Bank (Map p133; ☽ 8am-4pm Mon-Sat) Exchanges cash and travellers cheques.

POST

A small and pretty reliable post office (Map p133) is next to the Old Palace.

TELEPHONE

Telecommunications office (Map p133; ☽ 7am-10pm Mon-Sat) International calls. Standard rates (p254).

TOURIST INFORMATION

Tigrai Tourism Commission (Map p133; ☎ 0347 753924; ☽ 7am-6pm) One of the country's most friendly and helpful offices. Official tourist office guides cost Birr150 per group.

Sights

One admission ticket (adult/student Birr50/25) covers all sights within the immediate vicinity of Aksum, except the St Mary of Zion church compound and the monasteries of Abba Pentalewon and Abba Liqanos. The ticket is good for the duration of your stay, and you can purchase it from the Tigrai Tourism Commission. All sights are open between 8am and 5pm unless stated otherwise.

If you can get your hands on Stuart Munro-Hay's *Ethiopia: The Unknown land* you'll find an excellent compendium to Aksum's history, archaeology and major sites and monuments.

Although you can see the monuments on your own, an official guide is recommended. All are trained and many are history students, so you'll get much more out of your visit. Bring a torch for the tombs.

AKSUM

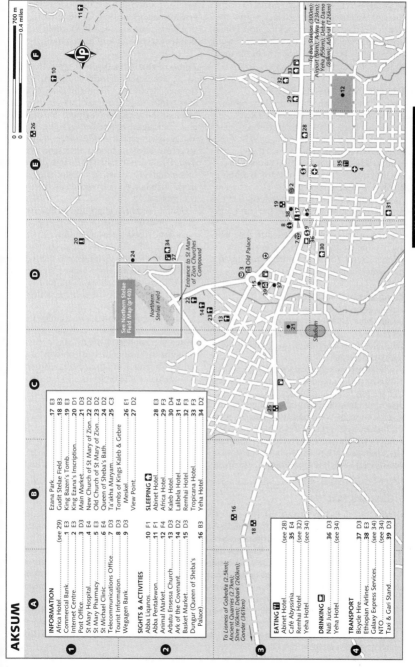

INFORMATION	
Africa Hotel	(see 29)
Commercial Bank	1 E3
Internet Centre	2 E3
Post Office	3 D3
St Mary Hospital	4 E4
St Mary Pharmacy	5 E3
St Michael Clinic	6 E4
Telecommunications Office	7 D3
Tourist Information	8 D3
Wegagen Bank	9 D3

SIGHTS & ACTIVITIES	
Abba Liqanos	10 F1
Abba Pentalewon	11 F1
Animal Market	12 F4
Arbatu Ensessa Church	13 D3
Ark of the Covenant	14 D2
Basket Market	15 D3
Dungur (Queen of Sheba's Palace)	16 B3
Ezana Park	17 E3
Gudit Stelae Field	18 B3
King Bazen's Tomb	19 E3
King Ezana's Inscription	20 D1
Main Market	21 D3
New Church of St Mary of Zion	22 D2
Old Church of St Mary of Zion	23 D2
Queen of Sheba's Bath	24 D2
Ta'akha Maryam	25 C3
Tombs of Kings Kaleb & Gebre Meskel	26 E1
View Point	27 D2

SLEEPING ⌂	
Abinet Hotel	28 E3
Africa Hotel	29 F3
Kaleb Hotel	30 D4
Lalibela Hotel	31 E4
Remhai Hotel	32 F3
Tropicana Hotel	33 F3
Yeha Hotel	34 D2

EATING ⌊	
Abinet Hotel	(see 28)
Café Abyssinia	35 E4
Remhai Hotel	(see 32)
Yeha Hotel	(see 34)

DRINKING ⌑	
Nati Juice	36 D3
Yeha Hotel	(see 34)

TRANSPORT	
Bicycle Hire	37 D3
Ethiopian Airlines	38 E3
Galaxy Express Services	(see 34)
NTO	(see 34)
Taxi & Gari Stand	39 D3

To Lioness of Gobedra (2.5km);
Ancient Quarries (2.7km);
Shire (60km); Debark (260km);
Gonder (361km)

To Bus Station (300m);
Airport (9km); Adwa (23km);
Yeha (55km); Debre Damo
(66km); Adigrat (126km)

See Northern Stelae
Field Map (p140)

Northern
Stelae Field

Entrance to St Mary
of Zion Churches
Compound

Old Palace

Stadium

NORTHERN ETHIOPIA

AKSUMITE STELAE የአክሱም ሐወ-ልቶች

Ancient Aksum obelisks (stelae) pepper the area, and whether you're looking down on a small specimen or staring up at a grand tower, you'll be duly bowled over. See the boxed text, p136, for the lowdown.

NORTHERN STELAE FIELD TOMBS

Despite the dizzying grandeur of the numerous rock needles reaching for the stars that are found here, it's what's under your feet that is most important. Amazingly, 98% of the treasures of Aksum remain buried under the ground and you may well find yourself hearing the sound of an unopened tomb echoing below your feet as you explore. This is part of Aksum's appeal – the thought that fascinating finds, secrets and maybe even treasures lurk in the depths.

Most of the tombs excavated to date had been pillaged by robbers, so very little is known about Aksumite burial customs or the identities of those buried.

Tomb of the Brick Arches

Dating from the end of the 3rd century, this tomb (Map p140) is remarkably well preserved and contains four rock-cut chambers, subdivided by a series of brick arches built with lime mortar.

The tomb was first excavated by archaeologists in 1974, and though tomb robbers had beaten them to it by centuries, they still discovered fragments of gold jewellery, beads, bronze objects, weapons and glass objects. Further excavations revealed a cast plaque, the holes of which matched rivets atop one stele (see the boxed text, p136). Nobody knows who was buried here, but archaeologists surmise

that the tomb contained the bodies of an elderly woman, a man and one other person and that the treasures found within would indicate that they were people of high standing.

Tomb of the False Door

In 1972 the unique Tomb of the False Door (known locally as the Tomb of King Ramhai; Map p140) was discovered. It lies in the western extremity of the Northern Stelae Field and is thought to date between the late 4th and early 5th centuries AD. More complex in structure, its stone blocks are also larger and more finely dressed than those found in some other tombs. Comprising an antechamber and inner chamber, it's surrounded on three sides by a passage.

Above the tomb, at ground level, a rectangular, probably flat-roofed building would once have stood (measuring some 12 sq metres by 2.8m high). Above the stairs descending into the tomb's chamber was a stone slab carved with a false door almost identical to those found on the stelae. Look for the iron clamps fixing blocks of stone together like giant staples.

All the tomb's contents were stolen in centuries past and, judging from the lengths to which the robbers went to gain access, it's thought to have contained objects of great value. The much-mutilated single stone sarcophagus can still be seen.

Tomb of Nefas Mawcha

The megalithic Tomb of Nefas Mawcha (Map p140) consists of a large rectangular central chamber surrounded on three sides by a passage. The tomb is unusual for its large size, the sophistication of the structure and the

---

AKSUM'S FALL

After Aksum lost its grip on the Red Sea trade due to the rise of Islamic Arabs' fortunes, the society quickly imploded and sent Ethiopia into the dark ages for five centuries. Why this happened when it was still rich in natural resources is the subject of many theories.

The environmental argument suggests that Aksum's ever-increasing population led to overcropping of the land, deforestation and eventually soil erosion. The climatic explanation claims that a slight 'global warming' took place, which finished Aksum's agriculture and eventually led to drought and famine. The military argument claims that Aksum was undermined by continual incursions from neighbouring tribes, such as the Beja from the northwest of the country.

According to tradition, Aksumite power was usurped around the 9th century by the dreaded warrior queen Gudit (or Judit), a pagan or Jew, who killed the ruling king, burnt down the city and sabotaged the stelae. Intriguingly, this legend seems to be born out by at least two documents written at about this time.

size of the stones used for its construction (the stone that roofs the central chamber measures 17.3m by 6.4m and weighs some 360 tonnes!). It's believed the force of the Giant Stele crashing into its roof caused the tomb's spectacular collapse. Locals believe that under this tomb is the 'magic machine', the original implement the Aksumites used to shape and carve the stelae and tombs – the same machine was apparently also used to create some of the rock-hewn churches of Tigray. Legend also relates how several secret passages lead off from this tomb. For years this was regarded as just legend, but then, just recently, it was discovered that passages do indeed lead away from this tomb and that one links up with a so far unexplored and unopened tomb just to the east.

Mausoleum

The so-called mausoleum (Map p140) was discovered in 1974 but not excavated until the mid-1990s. A monumental portal (hewn from a single slab of granite) marked the tomb's entrance and was also carved with the stelae's curious false door motifs. The portal leads into a passageway with 10 chambers. In total the tomb covers some 240 sq metres. Part of the tomb had been disfigured at some unknown date by robbers, who succeeded in digging through 1.5m of solid masonry.

ARCHAEOLOGICAL MUSEUM
አርኪዮሎጂ መ-ዝየም

The well-laid out and fascinating **Archaeological Museum** (Map p140; ⏱ 8am-noon & 2-6pm) contains fine and well-preserved Sabaean and early Ge'ez inscriptions, some dating back over 2500 years. There's also an interesting variety of objects found in tombs: ranging from ordinary household objects, such as drinking cups, lamps and incense burners, to quite sophisticated glassware, including perfume bottles.

There's a particularly nice collection of Aksumite coins dating from the 4th to 6th centuries AD, though those housed in the Ethnological Museum (p90) in Addis Ababa are finer. You'll also see beautiful lion gargoyles, and the charming pot shaped like a three-legged bird. Much of the pottery was produced in ancient Aksum and the tradition continues today. An ancient amphora from Turkey or Cyprus also provides evidence of ancient trading routes.

ST MARY OF ZION CHURCHES
የማርያም ጽዮን ቤተክርስቲያኖች

Though religions have come and gone Aksum has remained a holy city throughout and opposite the Northern Stelae Field, in a walled compound, lies the centre of the universe for Christian Ethiopians: the churches of St Mary of Zion (admission Birr120, personal video cameras Birr100; ⏱ 7.30am-12.30pm & 2.30-5.30pm Mon-Fri, 9am-noon & 2.30-5.30pm Sat & Sun).

A church of some form or other has stood at this spot since the very earliest days of Ethiopian Christianity and it was God himself who, descending from heaven, indicated that a church should be built here. Sadly the earliest churches are long gone, but two churches, a chapel and some ruins remain. The rectangular old church (Map p133), at the southern end of the complex, is a remarkable example of traditional architecture built by the Emperor Fasiladas, the founder of Gonder, in 1665. It's thought that the old podium on which it sits may well belong to Africa's first church, which was erected by King Ezana or King Kaleb in the 4th or 6th century.

Inside there are fine murals, including a painting of the Nine Saints (see The Coming of Christianity, p34), and a collection of ceremonial musical instruments.

Unfortunately, Ezana's original church (the remains of which can be seen between the chapel and the new church) was destroyed during the incursions of Ahmed Gragn the Left-Handed in 1535. It's said that this original church was covered head to toe in gold and that when it was destroyed and burnt the gold melted and ran like water in a river.

The huge **new church** of St Mary of Zion (Map p133) was built in the 1960s and displays Haile Selassie's usual unusual taste. OK, let's not beat around the bush. It's truly hideous. Still it does cut a dramatic silhouette on the skyline. Beside it, a disproportionately tall bell tower, shaped to resemble the biggest stele of all, sprouts heavenwards.

Nearby is a little **museum** containing a breathtaking haul of treasure, including an unsurpassed collection of former Ethiopian rulers' crowns and a dazzling display of gold and precious stones, which goes a long way to indicating the sheer wealth of the Church. This is certainly one Ethiopian museum you absolutely shouldn't miss. Technically women are not allowed inside, but the rule

NORTHERN ETHIOPIA

A QUICK GUIDE TO AKSUM'S STELAE

For as long as 5000 years, monoliths have been used in northeast Africa as tombstones and monuments to local rulers. In Aksum, this tradition reached its apogee. Like Egypt's pyramids, Aksum's stelae were like great billboards announcing to the world the authority, power and greatness of the ruling families. Aksum's astonishing stelae are striking for their huge size, their incredible, almost pristine, state of preservation, and their curiously modern look. Sculpted from single pieces of granite, some come complete with little windows, doors and even door handles and locks that make them look remarkably like tower blocks. In fact, anybody who knows the desert town of Shibam in Yemen is certain to notice that the mud tower blocks there look remarkably like these stelae.

Despite the stone being famously hard, Aksum's masons worked it superbly, often following an architectural design that mirrored the traditional style seen in Aksumite houses and palaces (for more details on Aksumite architecture, see p63).

Metal plates, perhaps in the form of a crescent moon and disc (pagan symbol of the sun), are thought to have been riveted to the top of the stelae both at the front and back. The crescent is also an ancient pagan symbol, originating from southern Arabia. In 1996 a broken plate that perfectly matched the rusty rivet holes atop a stelae was excavated. It bore the effigy of a face, perhaps that of the ruler to whom the plate's stelae was dedicated. Despite these discoveries many aspects of the stelae are still shrouded in mystery.

For one, Ethiopian traditions believe that the Ark of the Covenant's celestial powers were harnessed to transport (4km from the quarries) and raise the mighty monoliths; the largest weighed no less than 517 tonnes! While far from proven, archaeologists think that the earthly forces of elephants, rollers and winches were responsible.

Northern Stelae Field

The Northern Stelae Field is Ethiopia's biggest and most important stelae field. It contains over 120 stelae, though the original number was higher – some have been removed, others probably lie buried.

The stelae range from 1m to 33m in height and from simple slabs of stone (the majority) to finely dressed rectangular blocks, usually with flat sides and a rounded or conical apex. Though they were undoubtedly connected with the practice of human burial, it's not yet certain if every stele marks a tomb. The three largest and most famous stelae (Great Stele, King Ezana's Stele and Rome Stele) are found here and are described in this box.

In the courtyards of **Enda Iyesus** (Map p140), a stele decorated with a disc and a crescent moon can be seen. In 1997 another huge stele (18m) was discovered near the church.

Among the various other stelae is one that boasts a unique decoration. It lies on the ground around 200m to the north of King Ezana's Stele. Measuring around 9m in length, its upper section is carved like a pointed arch. Near the top, a small house-like object is carved in relief (on one side of the stone, supported by a pillar; Map p140), formed by a rectangle surmounted by a triangle. Some have claimed that this is early proof of Aksum's claim to house the Ark of the Covenant.

Laying prone between the Mausoleum and Tomb of the False Door is another important stele, albeit unassuming and unfinished (Map p140). The fact it's unfinished is strong evidence that the final carving of stelae was finished on site and not at the quarries.

King Ezana's Stele

Although standing slightly off kilter, this magnificent 24m-high stele (Map p140) has done something no other stele of similar stature has done – remained standing (albeit today it's with the aid of a crane!). Henry Salt, the British traveller and first foreigner to describe it in 1805, proclaimed it 'the most admirable and perfect monument of its kind'.

It's considered by many as the most important of Aksum's stelae because it holds important religious significance. The stone platform at its base is believed to have served as an altar. Within the platform are four foot-deep cavities, which probably held sacrificial offerings. And what's the grand significance of all those little cavities? It depends on how important you think *gabeta* (a traditional board game) is!

Despite its pagan background, this stele has been embraced by the Ethiopian Orthodox church and is a centrepiece during the celebrations of Maryam Zion.

The Great Stele

Lying like a broken soldier, this massive 33m stele (Map p140) is believed to be the largest single block of stone that humans have ever attempted to erect, and overshadows even the Egyptian obelisks in its conception and ambition.

Scholars theorise that it fell during its erection sometime early in the 4th century. Comparing the unworked 'root' with the sleek, carved base and the intricate walia ibex carvings near its top gives you a vivid idea of the precision, finesse and technical competence of Aksumite's stone workers.

As it toppled it collided with the massive 360-tonne stone sheltering the central chamber of **Nefas Mawcha's tomb** (Map p140). This shattered the upper portion of stele and – according to Unesco – collapsed the tomb's central chamber, scattering the massive roof supports like tooth-picks. Seeing that no other stele was ever raised here, it's obvious the collision sounded the death knell on the long tradition of obelisk erection in Aksum. Some scholars have even suggested that the disaster may have actually contributed to the people's conversion to Christianity, like an Ethiopian Tower of Babel. More controversially, some propose it may have been sabotaged deliberately to feign a sign of God. Whatever the origin of its downfall, the stele remains exactly where it fell 1600 years ago, a permanent reminder of the defeat of paganism by Christianity.

The Rome Stele

At 24.6m high, the Rome Stele (or Aksum Obelisk to those in Rome) is the second-largest stele ever produced at Aksum and the largest to have ever been successfully raised. Like the Great Stele, its ornate carvings of multistoreyed windows and doors adorn all four sides. Pillagers raiding the site are believed to have accidentally caused its collapse sometime between the 10th and 16th centuries.

In 1937, the stele's broken remains were shipped to Italy on Mussolini's personal orders. On arrival it was reassembled and raised once more, this time in Rome's Piazza di Porta Capena. It remained in Rome until 2005, when decades of negotiations were finally victorious over diplomatic feet-dragging.

After its return to Aksum in April 2005, Unesco planned to raise the stele in its original position. However, while doing a geophysical survey of the site they discovered numerous new tombs surrounding the field, some even under the parking lot. After much head-scratching by engineers the stele has finally been re-erected and stands proud, by far the most impressive of all the stelae.

Gudit Stelae Field

Though they're less immediately arresting than those found in the centre of town, the stelae in the Gudit Stelae Field (Map p133), on the south side of Dungur (Queen of Sheba's Palace), are still worth a visit.

Named after Queen Gudit (see Aksum's Fall, p134), most stelae in this field are small, undressed and lie on the ground. Locals suggest the largest stele marks the Queen of Sheba's grave.

Despite excavations in the 1970s and 1990s, little is known about the field. Though some mark graves, neither rock-hewn nor constructed tombs have been found. Finds here did include a set of fine 3rd-century glass goblets, which has led scholars to suggest the area was the burial site of Aksumite society's lesser nobles.

The walk to the complex is lovely at dusk, when you'll meet the farmers and their animals returning home before nightfall.

NORTHERN ETHIOPIA

didn't appear to be heavily enforced when we were last there.

Finally, in between the old and new church is the real reason for most people's devotion: a tiny, carefully guarded chapel inside of which is the legendary **Ark of the Covenant** (Map p133). For more on the Ark and the Ethiopian claim to it see p58 and p141. Don't think you can take a peek: just one specially chosen guardian has access to the Ark. In fact nobody is allowed remotely near the chapel and foreigners are not even allowed close to the railings guarding the chapel – we were told that this was because a couple of years ago two tourists had the insensitivity to try to climb over the railings and rush into the chapel! No matter what you think of the legend, there is no denying that to be in this church compound during a major service or festival, when thousands of pilgrims pour into the city, is an experience of pure devotion and faith that that will leave you spellbound.

TOMBS OF KINGS KALEB & GEBRE MESKEL
የንጉስ ቃሌብና የንጉስ ገብረ መስቀል መቃብር
Set on a small hill 1.8km northeast of the Northern Stele Field and offering views of the jagged mountains of Adwa are these two tombs (Map p133). According to local tradition, they're attributed to the 6th-century King Kaleb (p142) and his son, King Gebre Meskel.

Although the twin tombs' architecture resembles the Tomb of the False Door, they actually show more sophistication, using irregular-shaped self-locking stones that don't require iron clamps. The 19th-century British traveller Theodore Bent exclaimed magnanimously that the tombs were 'built with a regularity which if found in Greece would at once make one assign them to a good period'!

Of the two tombs, Gebre Meskel (to the south) is the most refined. The precision of the joints between its stones is at a level unseen anywhere else in Aksum. The tomb consists of one chamber and five rooms, with one boasting an exceptionally finely carved portal leading into it. Inside that room are three sarcophagi, one adorned with a cross similar to Christian crosses found on Aksumite coins. While this points towards an age around the 6th century, which, very interestingly, corresponds with local tradition, many believe that Meskel was actually buried at Debre Damo.

Like Meskel's tomb, King Kaleb's is accessed via a long straight stairway. Inside you'll notice the stones are larger, more angular and

less precisely joined. This is handy because it's said that if you lick the end of a blade of grass and slide it between certain gaps in the stone work when you remove it, you might be lucky enough to find a pearl attached to the end. Of those who attribute the making of the tomb to Kaleb, few accept that he was actually buried here. Common theory is that his body lies at Abba Pentalewon Monastery, where he lived after abdicating his throne. The tomb's unfinished state adds credence to that theory. If you feel like a long walk, bring several sets of batteries for your torch and, most importantly, have a knack for finding secret passages. Local rumour has it that there's a secret tunnel leading from here to Arabia! Scoff you may, but as so often happens around Aksum, the legend turned out to have a figment of truth to it. Recently a tunnel system has indeed been discovered – the entrance can be seen a few metres from Gebre Meskel's tomb. The tunnels lead off to the north, south, east and west, but so far nobody knows where they go. One theory suggests they may link up to a palace recently discovered in the vicinity (still awaiting excavation and currently closed to the public).

Above ground, a kind of raised courtyard combines the two tombs. Some scholars have suggested that two parallel churches with a basilica plan lay here, probably postdating the tombs.

Abraham, our driver, related another tale to us regarding these tombs. He told us he had seen a treasure map that leads to Kaleb's tomb and 'once here you must take three or four paces, but I don't remember which, into the tomb then turn left, or maybe it was right, and search for a secret door beyond which you'll find treasure'. Needless to say, with instructions like that Abraham hasn't yet retired to a life of luxury on a Caribbean yacht – maybe you'll have better luck…

Treasure or not, these two tombs with their bats roosting in the corners and ghosts hiding in the recesses are among the most fascinating and mystical sites in Aksum.

KING EZANA'S INSCRIPTION
የንጉስ ኢዛና ጽሑፍ
On the way up to the tombs of Kings Kaleb and Gebre Meskel, you'll pass a little shack containing a remarkable find stumbled upon by a farmer in 1981. Inside is an Ethiopian version of the Rosetta Stone, a pillar inscribed in Sabaean, Ge'ez and Greek.

It dates from between AD 330 and AD 350 and records King Ezana's Christian military campaigns in Ethiopia and southern Arabia, as well as his quest to return the Ark to Aksum from Lake Tana.

The inscription (Map p133) apparently contains a curse: 'the person who should dare to move the tablet will meet an untimely death'. Needless to say, the tablet remains exactly where it was found! You should tip the guardian Birr3 to Birr5 for opening the hut.

QUEEN OF SHEBA'S BATH
የንግስት ሳባ መዋኛ

Despite the colourful legends, this large reservoir (Map p133) almost certainly was not where Sheba played with her rubber duck. It was also more likely an important source of water rather than a swimming pool or gargantuan bath. Nobody is totally sure of its age, but it's certainly been used as a water source for millennia. Its large size is even more impressive considering it was originally hewn out of solid rock – no small feat in the world of ancient engineering. It's also known as Mai Shum, which translates to 'Water of Chief'.

Sadly, the outer portion of the bowl was coated with concrete in the 1960s, giving it the feel of a half-hearted attempt at a modern reservoir, instead of an impressive ancient relic.

Today, there are two legends regarding the place: one says that the waters are cursed (local boys occasionally drown here); the other says the waters are blessed and that anybody drinking from here will never get sick. Local women obviously believe the latter as queues of them form to wash clothes and gather drinking water.

ABBA PENTALEWON & ABBA LIQANOS MONASTERIES
የአባ ጴንጣሊዎንና የአባ ሊቃኖስ ገዳማት

Around 2km from the tombs of Kings Kaleb and Gebre Meskel, and thought to date from the 4th century, is the **Abba Pentalewon Monastery** (Map p133; admission Birr30, men only). Built by Abba Pentalewon, one of the Nine Saints (p57) and a man who is said to have prayed nonstop for 40 years, this is a beautiful little church filled with fine illuminated manuscripts, metal crosses, censers and sistra, which can usually be brought out by the priests. The site of the monastery was sacred to pagans and it's thought the monastery was built here to bolster Christianity and eradicate pagan beliefs.

From Abba Pentalewon, it's around 20 minutes by foot to the **Abba Liqanos Monastery** (Map p133; admission Birr30, men only), which again was built by one of the Nine Saints and also boasts excellent views and contains similar religious paraphernalia. Ask to see the crowns of King Kaleb and Gebre Meskel. The original church is said to have been very beautiful, but was destroyed by Mengistu when the surrounding area was occupied by rebels.

Neither church is a must-see, but the walk to them is pleasant and the priests are friendly.

KING BAZEN'S TOMB የንጉስ ባዜን መቃብር
Despite being the crudest of tombs, roughly hewn into solid rock instead of constructed with fine masonry, this place (Map p133) has a slightly magical feel about it. Stand in its dark depths and look up its rock-hewn stairs through its arched entranceway and you'll see why. It's even better if explored by candlelight.

According to local tradition, King Bazen is thought not just to have reigned at Christ's birth, but to have been one of the Three Wise Men and it was he who brought news of the birth of Christ to Ethiopia.

Near the tomb's entrance there's a rectangular pit containing a row of smaller burial chambers (including a few that appear to be unfinished). Judging from the number of tombs and stelae found nearby, the burial site may once have been quite large and important.

EZANA PARK ኢዛና መናፈሻ
Within a rather ugly tin-roofed *tukul* in this central park (Map p133) is another famous 4th-century AD stone of King Ezana. This inscription is also written in Sabaean, Ge'ez and Greek and records the honorary titles and military victories of the king over his 'enemies and rebels'. One section of script thanks the God of War, thus placing the stone's age before Ezana's conversion to Christianity.

It was moved to its present location from eastern Aksum by the Italians in the 1930s because, of all things, it stood in the way of their plan to widen the road.

TA'AKHA MARYAM ተኣኻ ማርያም
Early excavations revealed that Ta'akha Maryam (Map p133) was a magnificent palace, probably dating from the 4th or 5th century AD. Unfortunately, much of the stone was removed and what remained was obliterated when the Italians cut a road straight through it.

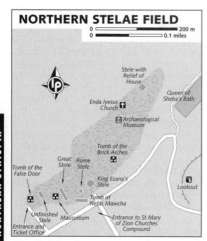

cessed at intervals and tapering with height, are typically Aksumite. The stairwells suggest the existence of at least one upper storey. The well-preserved flagstone floor is thought to have belonged to a throne room. The palace also contains a private bathing area and a kitchen, where two large brick ovens can still be seen.

Much like Queen of Sheba's Bath, nobody is quite sure of the age of the complex. Some say it dates to around the 6th or 7th century AD; others think it could vastly predate that.

Lioness of Gobedra ጎበድራ

It was here that the Archangel Mikael fought a tremendous battle with a fierce lioness. The fight ended when the saint mustered all his strength and hurled the lion into a massive boulder. The impact had such force that the outline of the beast is still visible today.

It's often overlooked by visitors but is worth the visit, especially since it's so close to the ancient quarries of Aksum. It's around 3km west of Aksum off the Shire road. It's quite a rough walk from the road over boulders and through scrub, and you'll need a guide or one of the all-too-willing local children to help you find it.

ANCIENT QUARRIES

Near the lioness, at a site on Gobedra Hill known as Wuchate Golo, are the ancient quarries of Aksum, the birthplace of the famous stelae. Mystery still surrounds the tools that were used by the master craftsmen of Aksum, but you can see clearly, in one area, the process by which they cut the hard stone from the rock. After the intended break was mapped out, a row of rectangular sockets was cut. Wooden wedges were next inserted

Today, little more than a few piles of rubble and a couple of dressed stone blocks remain, strewn on either side of the road.

Covering a vast area of some 120m by 80m and encircled by huge stone walls, Ta'akha Maryam would have been far larger than medieval European palaces of the time, and contained at least 50 rooms.

DUNGUR (QUEEN OF SHEBA'S PALACE)
ዱንጉር (የንግስት ሳባ ቤተ መንግስት)

The structure at Dungur, popularly known as the Queen of Sheba's Palace (Map p133), though far more likely to be the mansion of a nobleman, is similar to Ta'akha Maryam, but it is much better preserved (though smaller) and fully excavated (in places rather clumsily restored).

The architectural style, with small undressed stones set in a timber framework and walls re-

---

AKSUMITE COINS

Aksumite coinage provides a vital and fascinating source of information on the ancient kingdom. The coins bear the names, effigies and sometimes lineage of no fewer than 20 different kings, and probably served propagandist purposes.

Beautifully struck, the coins depict the royal crowns, clothing and jewellery of the kings – even the large earrings worn by some monarchs. A curiosity still unexplained by historians is the fact that almost all the coins are double-headed: on one side the king is depicted with his crown on the other, he dons a modest head cloth.

These coins are valuable not just for their beauty: they also provide a rare factual record of who ruled and when. The historians who studied them found something that would rock the foundations of traditional Ethiopian history. Many of the kings of the traditional history failed to appear on the coins while those on the coins failed to appear in the historical lists.

into the sockets and made to expand either by the use of water, by percussion or by hammering in metal wedges, which caused the rock to fracture. In another place, you'll see a stele almost completely freed from the rock, but strangely abandoned.

OTHER SIGHTS

Aksum has two sleepy markets that burst to life on Saturday. In the centre of town is the traditional **main market** (Map p133), with spices and the like, while to the east is the **animal market** (Map p133), ripe with

ABA WOLDSEMBENT, PRIEST   *Stuart Butler*

Aksum is full of wonders to gawp at, but if there is one thing that every visitor really wants to see it's the one thing they can't: the Ark of the Covenant.

Like all visitors I was fascinated by the thought that a great biblical relic could be just beyond my grasp, hidden in that chapel. Imagine if it could be scientifically proven to be there. Imagine how it could change everything we do and don't believe in. I wanted to know more and so I cornered Aba Woldsembent, an elderly priest, outside the famous chapel and talked him into sitting down with me and telling me what he knew. I had heard that the Ark can choose where it goes, so I was interested to know why it chose Aksum.

'The Ark came here because Ethiopia is a holy country and because Jesus and Mary came to Aksum and Jesus promised Mary that it would come here.'

This response confused me. 'But I thought Menelik brought the Ark here long before Jesus or Mary were born?'

'Yes, Menelik brought the Ark here, but before Menelik was born Jesus came here and promised Mary it would come to Aksum.'

Before I can ask any more about this obvious contradiction in dates, the interview was interrupted by a group of priests greeting Aba Woldsembent. There is much discussion between the group about the strange foreigner and his stranger questions, then, once everybody is satisfied, they all sit down to listen to the rest of the interview.

'How do they decide who will be the guardian of the Ark?' I ask.

'All the monks meet and they select the name of the next guardian. He must then remain in the chapel forever and never leave. He can choose to abdicate, but even then he can never leave the chapel grounds. If he dies his body is burnt in the chapel.'

'And who is the current guardian and how long has he been guardian?' I inquire.

'His name is Aba Gabriel Meskal. He has been guardian for 51 years. He is from Aksum. They are normally from Aksum.'

I decide to try a more daring question, 'Is the Ark an oracle? Can it speak?'

Without batting an eyelid Aba Woldsembent replies, 'The guardian gives the Ark incense and it will then speak to him.'

Excitedly I ask what it says.

'It's a secret.'

I try another tack and ask what is inside the Ark.

'It's a secret. You cannot ask this question. Only God knows. God and Moses.'

I had read that the Jews once carried the Ark into battle and its presence ensured victory. I asked if Ethiopian emperors had ever taken the Ark into battle.

'We still take it into battle now and we win with it. A few years ago, on 12 September, the Ark was taken around the compound of the chapel and because of that we beat Eritrea in the war. The Ark is better than a Kalashnikov.'

I was impressed, but surely that meant that other people had seen the Ark, so I asked if it was commonly seen by people other than the guardian.

'Many have seen it since its creation.'

'And what happens if you see it?'

'You catch fire.'

'And if the Ark ever leaves Aksum what would happen?'

'Then the world would be destroyed.' And with that cheery comment Aba Woldsembent lost interest in the interview, got up and wandered off.

camels, donkeys and fodder. A **basket market** (Map p133; ☙ Sat) takes place near the massive tree shading the taxi and *gari* stand.

It's worth taking a wander around the **old quarter** surrounding the church of St Mary of Zion complex. It's in these dusty streets that it really hits you that Aksum is more than just a collection of dead ruins; rather it is a living, breathing slice of the present, in which a strong continuity with the past persists. Camels and donkeys carting heavy loads trudge past street stalls selling religious tack, and pilgrims in white stream in from the countryside.

Festivals & Events

On 30 November, Aksum hosts one of Ethiopia's largest festivals, the **Festival of Maryam Zion**. In the days leading up to the event, thousands of pilgrims arrive and sleepy Aksum truly awakens. Celebrations start at King Ezana's Stele, where the monarchs of the Orthodox church line the steps and watch performers in the street below.

For an unforgettable experience make your way to the compound of the St Mary of Zion church between 1am and sunrise on the day of the festival and witness a sea of white-robed pilgrims curled up asleep. Standing among the slowly shifting sea are a few scattered priests reading by candlelight.

Sleeping

Aksum suffers from severe water shortages and whether you're roughing it or living it up, don't expect to be having a sing-song in the shower every morning.

Rooms become scarce and prices rise during major festivals, especially during Maryam Zion. Reservations are wise.

BUDGET

Lalibela Hotel (Map p133; ☎ 0347 753541; d without bathroom Birr30) This hotel doesn't feel the need

for fancy touches and what you see is what you get, which in this case is a small bed plonked in the middle of a bare room. The common bathrooms are tidy and there's a permanent coffee ceremony taking place in the attached bar.

Africa Hotel (Map p133; ☎ 0347 753700; africah @ethionet.et; d/tw Birr70/90; ☐) With an eager and omnipresent owner, this place offers a smooth stay and is easily the most popular budget guesthouse in town. The rooms are simple and bright and the bathrooms very clean. Unfortunately, when we passed by, several guests were complaining about having to share their beds with some friendly fleas. For an extra Birr10, you can nab one with satellite TV. There's also a cafe and restaurant with mediocre food. Call for a free airport transfer.

Tropicana Hotel (Map p133; ☎ 0911 420374; trop cana@yahoo.com; d without bathroom Birr60, d/tw Birr80/160) With bubbly staff and clean-as-a-pin rooms with superb hot showers (at least when the water and electricity are both running!), this new hotel is vying for the top spot with the nearby Africa Hotel. The attached restaurant serves decent Ethiopian fare (Birr12 to Birr15), the TV blurts out BBC World day and night and the prostitute-red bar next door is a fun place for a few wobbly pops.

Kaleb Hotel (Map p133; ☎ 0347 752222; d/tw Birr100/150) With quiet rooms set around a garden courtyard, Kaleb has probably the nicest budget setting. The rooms are large and quite pleasant, but it's mega overpriced.

Abinet Hotel (Map p133; ☎ 0347 753857; abneth @yahoo.com; s/d/tw Birr120/120/150) The cute rooms here come packed with chairs and tables, as well as teeny balconies with glorious views over a car park.

MIDRANGE & TOP END

Remhai Hotel (Map p133; ☎ 0347 752168; camping Birr150-200, s/d/ste Birr230/315/600; ☐ ☒) The rooms here are as tired as a sprinter running a mara

---

SWAPPING GOLD FOR GOD

King Kaleb was the richest and most powerful ruler the Aksumite empire ever saw. By AD 540 he controlled a vast swathe of land from the mountains of Ethiopia to the deserts of Arabia, and his power was rivalled only by Persia and Byzantium. When he appeared to his subjects, dripping in gold and precious stones, it was as if he himself were a jewel. But despite having everything money could buy and much that it couldn't, one day, after a vicious campaign in Arabia, he let it all go and, abdicating his throne and sending his crown to hang in the Church of the Holy Sepulchre in Jerusalem, he retired to the Abba Pentalewon Monastery (p139) where he lived out his life in prayer.

thon, but otherwise it's comfortable enough to ensure that it's often full. During our last visit the pool was as dry as the Sahara in August.

Yeha Hotel (Map p133; ☎ 0347 752377; ghion@ethio net.et; s/d/tw Birr480/480/550.57; 💻) Perched atop a bluff overlooking the stelae and the Mary of Zion churches, this hotel has the most enviable location. The rooms are identical to its state-owned brothers (Bahir Dar's Tana Hotel, Gonder's Goha Hotel and Lalibela's Roha Hotel), which means they're dated, but comfortable, cosy and contain satellite TVs.

Eating & Drinking

Restaurants tend to wrap things up early in Aksum, with most places being closed or out of food by 8pm.

Abinet Hotel (Map p133; mains Birr15-20) If you ask locals where the best place to eat is, they'll say Remhai. But if you ask them where they like to eat, they'll say Abinet. The spaghetti is unusually good. Some people complain about poor service but we had no problems.

Café Abyssinia (Map p133; mains Birr18-35) Right in front of the hospital, this place serves as cafe, bar and restaurant. The Ethiopian and *faranji* fare is reasonable, and though pizza is almost certainly off the menu they should be able to sizzle up a steak.

Remhai Hotel (Map p133; mains Birr30) How does beef stroganoff followed by crème caramel sound? This hotel's Western restaurant is easily the best place to eat in Aksum and for once, most of what is on the menu is actually in the kitchen as well.

Yeha Hotel (Map p133; set lunch menu Birr75, beers Birr8) The food is fair, the view is grand and the three-course lunch is good value. The menu is a mix of *faranji* and Ethiopian selections. The lofty terrace of this hotel is the perfect place for a cool beverage, especially during a scenic sunset when kites (a type of raptor) ride the fading thermals and soar low overhead.

Nati Juice (Map p133; juice Birr7) Pineapple, banana, avocado and mango meet lips.

Or for something entirely different, seek out a *tella beat* (local beer house) in the tiny streets around town; they're great places for Tigrayan dancing. The locals will help you find one.

Getting There & Away

Ethiopian Airlines (Map p133; ☎ 0347 752300) flies to Addis Ababa (US$200, two to 3½ hours, daily) via Lalibela (US$112, 40 minutes) and Gonder (US$110, two hours) or via Mekele (US$78, one hour, Saturday).

For buses to Gonder and Debark (Simien Mountains), go to Shire first. There are several buses/minibuses before 4pm (Birr15 to Birr20/25, 1½ hours). There are also many services to Adwa (Birr6, 45 minutes), but only one daily bus to Adigrat (Birr30, five hours) and two buses for Mekele (Birr35, 6am, seven hours).

Numerous freelance agents rent 4WD vehicles (with driver and guide) for trips to Yeha (Birr500), Debre Damo (Birr700) and even the rock churches of Tigray (per day Birr900 to Birr1200). These figures required lengthy negotiations. The tourism office can help arrange vehicles, or talk to staff at the Africa Hotel or either NTO or Galaxy Express at the Yeha Hotel.

Getting Around

A taxi to the new airport, 7km from town, costs Birr50 to Birr60, or Birr10 'shared'. From the airport, rates are set at Birr15 per person. Almost all the popular hotels will provide a free airport pickup if you call in advance (and many just have vans waiting to meet incoming flights anyway).

Contract taxis charge foreigners around Birr10 for short hops; longer journeys cost Birr12 to Birr20. Share-taxis cost Birr0.75 to Birr1 to cross town.

Garis cost Birr2 to Birr5 for short journeys, or Birr20 for Dungur and Birr30 for the Lioness of Gobedra. You'll need to negotiate hard. *Garis* and taxis linger near the giant tree at the basket market grounds. Just south from there, bicycles (Birr10 per hour) can be hired.

ADWA አድዋ

pop 45,823 / elev 1907m

Like Aksum, unassuming, urban Adwa belies its status. For Ethiopians, the town holds huge significance. It was in the dramatic mountains surrounding Adwa that the Emperor Menelik II inflicted the biggest defeat ever on a colonial army in Africa, thus Ethiopia was saved from colonisation (see the boxed text, p144).

Today you might wonder if Adwa has in fact just been involved in a war. A huge refurbishment of the town and the construction of many new roads have turned it, for at least the next couple of years, into a noisy, dusty and very unpleasant place. Needless to say, with

---

THE BATTLE OF ADWA

In September 1895, as the rains began to dwindle, Emperor Menelik II issued a decree: all the able-bodied men of his empire should gather for a march north, a march for all of Ethiopia. Behind the vast army trundled 40 cannons, hundreds of mules and 100,000 rifles. In the north, the Italians were ready.

Initial skirmishes followed and amazingly the Ethiopians and their sturdy mules captured the Italian strongholds at Amba Alage and Enda Iyesus. Serious shortages of food soon followed, leading both sides to sue for peace, but Italy's continued insistence on their protectorate claim meant an agreement couldn't be reached.

In February 1896 Crispi, Italy's prime minister, sent his famous telegram to General Baratieri. In it he declared the motherland was 'ready for any sacrifice to save the honour of the army and the prestige of the monarchy'.

In the early morning hours four days later, the Italians made their move. Stumbling in the darkness over difficult terrain, with inaccurate maps and with no communication between the three offensive brigades, the surprise attack was a disaster. Menelik, whose spies had long before informed him of the forthcoming attack, met the Italians with thundering artillery and fierce fighting on every front.

Nearly half the Italian fighting force was wiped out – over 6000 soldiers – and of the five Italian field commanders, three were killed, one was wounded and another was captured. Finally, laying down their arms, the Italians ran. Though the Ethiopians had lost almost equal numbers, the day was clearly theirs.

To this day the battle of Adwa is celebrated annually and, like the Battle of Hastings in Britain or the War of Independence in America, it's the one date every Ethiopian child can quote.

---

little to see and its proximity to Aksum, it's very missable.

About 6km due east of Adwa is the **monastery of Abba Garima** (admission Birr30, men only). Said to have been founded by one of the Nine Saints in the 6th century, it's known for its collection of religious artefacts, including what may be Ethiopia's oldest manuscript. Perhaps dating to the 8th century, it's kept under lock and key and only the lucky are given a glimpse. Head 7km south of Adwa before turning east for the final 3km. It's possible to drive or hike; bring plenty of water.

The best places to stay are either the **Abraham Hotel** (☎ 0910 324570; s/d Birr50/70) or the pricier, but no posher, **Soloda Hotel** (☎ 0347 711063; d/tw Birr77/110).

Numerous minibuses connect Adwa to Aksum (Birr6, 45 minutes). For Adigrat (Birr23, 3½ hours) three buses run daily. For Yeha (Birr8, 50 minutes) there are eight buses a day. Contract taxis cost around Birr250 to Birr350 to Yeha, and Birr450 to Birr600 to Debre Damo.

YEHA የሃ

Yeha, 58km north of Adwa, is considered the birthplace of Ethiopia's earliest civilisation

nearly three millennia ago. Heated debate continues among scholars as to whether it was founded by Sabaean settlers from Arabia or by Ethiopians influenced by Sabaean ideas. For a long time it was assumed to be the work of Arabian immigrants, but recently archaeologists have come to the conclusion that Yeha was created by a mix of the two groups. Even so, the so-called temple's immense, windowless, sandstone walls do indeed look like something straight out of Yemen.

Yeha's **ruins** (admission Birr50, personal video cameras Birr100) are impressive for their sheer age dating between the 5th and 8th century BC and for their stunning construction. Some of the temple's sandstone building blocks measure over 3m in length and are so perfectly dressed and fitted together – without a trace of mortar – that it's impossible to insert so much as a 5 cent coin between them. The whole temple is a grid of perfect lines and geometry.

Almost 200m to the northeast are the remains of **Grat Beal Gebri**, a monumental structure distinguished for its unusual square-sectioned, monolithic pillars (such features are also found in the Temple of the Moon in Ma'rib in Yemen). Important rock-hewn tombs have also been found in the vicinity. Amazingly, these finds and the temple are all that remain of Ethiopia's first capital.

Next to the temple is the new **Church of Abuna Aftse** (admission incl with ruins), which was built over the 6th-century-AD original. Incorporated into its walls are stones removed from the temple. In the west wall there's an exceptional relief of ibexes, stylised and with lowered horns. The ibex was a sacred animal of southern Arabia.

The small **museum** (admission incl with ruins), contains an outstanding collection of beautifully incised ancient Sabaean inscriptions, believed to originate from the temple, as well as some good (and unusually large) manuscripts and silver and gold crosses.

Getting There & Away

See Adwa (p143) and Aksum's Getting There & Away section (p143) for transport information.

DEBRE DAMO ደብረ ዳሞ

It was Abuna Aregawi, the leader of the Nine Saints (below), who established the monastery of **Debre Damo** (admission Birr100, men only) atop this sheer-sided *amba* (flat-topped mountain). Standing at the mountain base and straining your neck upwards, you might wonder how anybody managed to surmount this impossible peak and build a monastery on this island in the sky. Well you forget that Abuna Aregawi had God on his side and that God, knowing this was a fine place for a saint to find peace, made a giant snake lower its tail down the mountain and allow Aregawi to clamber up it to the summit.

Today the monastery remains just as inaccessible but, for those without God on their side, or for those scared of giant serpents, the monks will pull you up the cliff face using a slightly too-weathered looking leather rope (Birr20). Even so it takes some snerves and a good head for heights (unless, like us, you just close your eyes!). Women, some might say luckily for them, are not allowed up the rope to the monastery.

Debre Damo is one of the most important monasteries in Ethiopia and is thought to date back to Aksumite times and the 6th-century reign of King Gebre Meskel. It boasts what's likely the oldest standing church in the country (10th or 11th century AD) and possibly all of Africa. It's also a great example of an Aksumite-style building.

The monastery's formidable cliffs also allowed Aksumite monarchs to coop up excess male members of the royal family here, thus removing possible threats to their reign.

Today, the 500-sq-metre monastery hosts some 80 monks, who are entirely self-sufficient. They have their own livestock (if you could bring up a cow they'd be grateful) and water reservoirs hewn deep into the rock.

Sights

The remarkable **Abuna Aregawi church** is an almost prototypical example of Aksumite architecture. One window, with its wooden tracery, is virtually a replica of that depicted in stone on the largest of the Aksumite stelae. Look out for the famous Aksumite frieze: a row of false window openings constructed of wood. Also notable are the beams and ceiling, famously decorated with carved wooden panels depicting Ethiopian wild animals such as elephants, lions, gazelles, rhinos, giraffes and snakes. Various recent paintings can be seen too.

The monastery has long been used as a safeguard for religious treasures. It now has an outstanding collection of at least 50 **illuminated manuscripts**, among them some of Ethiopia's oldest surviving fragments, though they're rarely brought out to visitors.

THE NINE SAINTS

Though it was Abba Salama who first brought the Christian faith to Ethiopia in the year AD 330, he didn't make great inroads into converting the masses. Instead this task was left to a group of wandering holy men who were eventually to become known as the Nine Saints. In the 5th century they arrived in the mountains of Ethiopia after years of travel throughout the Middle East; each chose a mountaintop on which to construct a monastery and preach the new religion. The best known of these saints is Abuna Aregawi, founder of the vertigo-inspiring Debre Damo monastery.

Interestingly in 1940 a haul of Afghani gold coins dating between 100 BC and AD 100 was discovered up here – nobody is any the wiser how they got up this mountain.

Getting There & Away

There's no public transport to Debre Damo, although any transport on the Aksum–Adigrat road can drop you at the well-signposted junction (5km southeast of the village of Bizet). From there it's a toasty 11km walk (around three hours); bring water, food and sunscreen.

Catching rides to Adwa, Adigrat or Aksum from the junction is hit and miss, especially in the late afternoon. If there's a group of you, it's easiest to hire a 4WD in Aksum (p143) or Adigrat (opposite). Contract minibuses are cheaper, but they can only really get you within 4km or 5km of Debre Damo.

ADIGRAT አዲግራት

pop 88,342 / elev 2473m

Adigrat, Tigray's second-largest town, is situated on what was Ethiopia's most important junction with Eritrea prior to the 1998 con-flict. Today the border is still closed, though tensions have eased somewhat.

Adigrat makes a useful stop-off point to or from Aksum, otherwise it's a very humdrum kind of place.

Information

There are dozens of 'internet' cafes, though as far as we are aware none of them actually have the internet!

Commercial Bank (☼ 8.30am-12.30pm & 1-3.30pm Mon-Fri, 8.30-11.30am Sat) Changes cash and travellers cheques.

Sights

Nothing is screaming to be seen here, but if you're filling in time, a couple of Orthodox churches are worth a peek: the 19th-century **Adigrat Chirkos** south of the town centre, and the 20th-century fortress-like **Medhane Alem** in the north.

The large tiled dome on the skyline belongs to the **Holy Saviour Catholic Cathedral**.

The labyrinth of tin shacks that's now the **market** is found 500m east of Medhane Alem church.

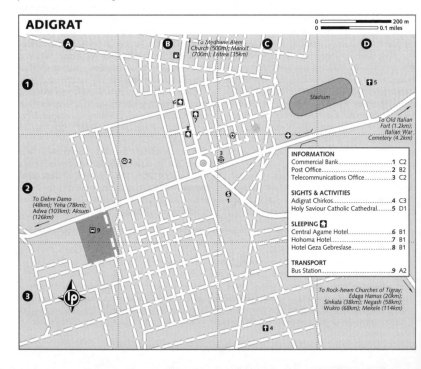

ADIGRAT

| 0   200 m |
| 0   0.1 miles |

To Medhane Alem Church (500m); Market (700m); Eritrea (35km)

Stadium

To Old Italian Fort (1.2km); Italian War Cemetery (4.2km)

To Debre Damo (48km); Yeha (78km); Adwa (103km); Aksum (126km)

INFORMATION
Commercial Bank	1 C2
Post Office	2 B2
Telecommunications Office	3 C2

SIGHTS & ACTIVITIES
Adigrat Chirkos	4 C3
Holy Saviour Catholic Cathedral	5 D1

SLEEPING
Central Agame Hotel	6 B1
Hohoma Hotel	7 B1
Hotel Geza Gebreslase	8 B1

TRANSPORT
Bus Station	9 A2

To Rock-hewn Churches of Tigray; Edaga Hamus (20km); Sinkata (38km); Negash (58km); Wukro (68km); Mekele (114km)

Sleeping & Eating

our pick **Hohoma Hotel** (☎ 0344 452469; d/ste Birr100/110) Its name, possibly inspired by Santa's brother, is just as fantastic as this hotel's value. The cosy rooms have oh-so-soft beds, bathrooms that glitter and water that's hot. The night will, we suspect, be a pleasing one!

Alternative, but dirtier, accommodation can be found at **Central Agame Hotel** (☎ 0344 452466; d with/without bathroom Birr80/50) or the smart **Hotel Geza Gebreslase** (☎ 0344 452500; s/d/tw Birr150/200/250).

As well as all the normal boring Ethiopian impressions of Western food, at **Hohoma Restaurant** (mains Birr12-40) it's also possible to dive into the local speciality, *ta'ilo*. All we'll tell you is that injera fans will rejoice with this one and, if you look on the underside of the middle table on the right-hand side, you may well find the remains of our *ta'ilo* that we stuck there when the waitress wasn't looking – sorry!

Getting There & Away

A sealed road now connects Adigrat to Mekele, with buses (Birr15, three hours, six daily) and minibuses (Birr23, 2½ hours, four daily) covering the route. Buses also serve Adwa (Birr24, 3½ hours, three daily), Aksum (Birr30, five hours, two daily) and Shire (Birr43, 6½ hours, one daily). For Wukro (Birr14, 1¾ hours) and Negash (Birr12, 1½ hours), take the Mekele bus.

Minibuses run to Sinkata (Birr8, one hour), Edaga Hamus (Birr4, 30 minutes) and Wukro (Birr14, 1½ hours).

NEGASH ነጋሽ

On a small hill, 56km south of Adigrat, is the tiny town of Negash, which, like Aksum and Adwa, belies its prestigious past.

Negash was the first site of Muslim settlement in Ethiopia. Fleeing persecution in Saudi Arabia in Mohammed's own lifetime, a community of Muslims, including Mohammed's daughter, took refuge here. It was in fact the Prophet Mohammed who suggested they flee to Ethiopia, where he assured them they would find a 'land of righteousness'. When the Aksumite king first asked the refugees to explain themselves and their new religion, the group's spokesman recited the 19th Surah of the Quran, which focuses on the Virgin Mary. On hearing this the king burst into tears of joy and, thinking the

refugees were just persecuted Christians, he granted them land. Islamic tradition says that the Aksumite king himself eventually converted to Islam and that after his death he was buried in Negash. Today a small mosque stands on the site of the 7th-century original, where the king was said to have been buried. An ancient cemetery, also believed to date from the 7th century, was recently excavated. In 2003 Ethiopia's richest man, billionaire Sheikh Mohammed Hussein Al-Amoudi (the Addis Ababa Sheraton is one of his properties) also built a mosque here.

To many Ethiopian Muslims, Negash is the most holy Islamic site after Mecca, and thousands make a pilgrimage here each year. Despite this, just 3% of Tigray is Muslim; the mosque sits amid a sea of Christian churches.

Minibuses and buses that ply the route between Adigrat and Mekele stop here.

ROCK-HEWN CHURCHES OF TIGRAY

The landscapes of northern Tigray are almost fairytale-like. The luminous light bathes a sandy, semidesert wasteland out of which climb a thousand needles of rock, rising high into the cloudless sky like the spines of a giant porcupine. As in every good fairytale, however, there is more to this porcupine than initially meets the eye. Atop these spires of rock, in the most impossible-to-reach locations, is a hidden gallery of wonder and a stash of religious jewels in the form of ancient monasteries boasting colourful histories of magic, monsters and holy wanderers.

Some of the 120-odd churches (plus a few invisible ones) may even predate those at Lalibela, and may possibly represent a crucial link between Aksum and Lalibela – chronologically, artistically and technically. The architectural features, though less perfect than at Lalibela, are just as remarkable and intriguing. For most people, however, it's not the monasteries themselves but the clamber, through stunning scenery and up sheer cliff faces that turn the hands sweaty with fright, that is the real highlight of this extraordinary region.

History

Until the mid-1960s, the churches were almost unknown outside Tigray itself. Even today very little is known about their origins, their history or their architects. Their remote and precarious positions have led scholars to think they were being hidden from raiding Muslims.

While local tradition attributes most of the churches to the 4th-century Aksumite kings, Abreha and Atsbeha, as well as to 6th-century rulers, most historians date them between the 9th and 15th centuries.

Orientation & Information

Most churches are located in groups or clusters. The Gheralta cluster, with the highest number of churches, located in the most mind-bending of settings, is considered the most important. The Takatisfi cluster, only 3km east of the Mekele–Adigrat road, is the most accessible. Other famous clusters are the Tembien and Atsbi.

Churches are supposed to charge Birr50 for admission. If you're asked for more, simply hand over Birr50, firmly but politely. For more on this see the box, The Trouble with Tigray, opposite.

Good walking shoes are essential. Bring a torch, lots of small notes (priests never have

change) and water. This is a semi-desert region, so it gets very hot clambering up a sheer cliff face in direct sunlight.

The helpful staff at the Tigray Tourism Commission offices in Aksum (p132), Mekele (p152) and **Wukro** (☎ 0344 430340; ⏰ 8am-5pm) advise on itineraries, sell maps and the informative *Tigrai: The Open-Air Museum* booklet (Birr5), and can usually wrangle up an official guide (per day Birr150).

If you're really keen, search for Ivy Pearce, David R Buxton or Ruth Plant's research on Tigray before leaving home.

Sights

Between Adigrat and Mekele there's a plethora of churches, 120 at last count. Many are pretty inaccessible, meaning visiting some churches involves steep climbs or scrambling up almost sheer rock faces using toeholds.

All this somehow adds to the churches' attraction. To come across an absolute jewel hidden for centuries in the mountains, after a long and arduous toil through Tigray's arid and rocky landscape, makes for a very rewarding excursion. Just remember that the

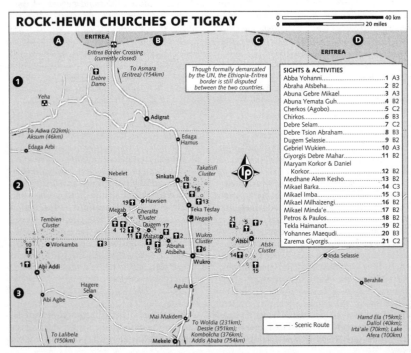

ROCK-HEWN CHURCHES OF TIGRAY

0 ———————— 40 km
0 ———————— 20 miles

Though formally demarcated by the UN, the Ethiopia-Eritrea border is still disputed between the two countries.

SIGHTS & ACTIVITIES

Abba Yohanni	**1** A3
Abraha Atsbeha	**2** B2
Abuna Gebre Mikael	**3** A3
Abuna Yemata Guh	**4** B2
Cherkos (Agobo)	**5** C2
Chirkos	**6** B3
Debre Selam	**7** C2
Debre Tsion Abraham	**8** B3
Dugem Selassie	**9** B2
Gebriel Wukien	**10** A3
Giyorgis Debre Mahar	**11** B2
Maryam Korkor & Daniel Korkor	**12** B2
Medhane Alem Kesho	**13** B2
Mikael Barka	**14** C3
Mikael Imba	**15** C3
Mikael Milhaizengi	**16** B2
Mikael Minda'e	**17** B2
Petros & Paulos	**18** B2
Tekla Haimanot	**19** B2
Yohannes Maequdi	**20** B3
Zarema Giyorgis	**21** C2

THE TROUBLE WITH TIGRAY

The rock-hewn churches of Tigray are spectacular, but visiting them comes with strings attached. The problem is that, to generalise, the priests aren't interested in having tourists visit their churches, but they are interested in the money we bring. During the course of this book's research we heard complaints from a number of people about harassment from priests after more money or, after the entry fee had been handed over, a point-blank refusal to allow entry into a church without giving a 'tip' for 'the key' or something similar. Once in a church, some of the priests are also highly reluctant to turn on the lights or point anything out unless more money is donated. This behaviour quickly becomes very trying and, for independent travellers, the whole experience can be highly frustrating. In fact, we were locked inside one church by a priest who refused to let us go until we handed over more money!

However, the regional tourist authority is aware that it has a problem and is trying to solve it. As we go to press, the latest news is that all churches will soon have a fixed entrance ticket of Birr50, and receipts will be provided. Apparently official government guides will also be provided 'in order to create a hustle-free tourist environment'. We can only hope that this improves matters enormously. In the meantime, the easiest way to visit the churches and truly enjoy the experience is to join an organised tour with a guide who can negotiate and deal with the priests on your behalf.

---

churches' remote locations haven't made restoration work feasible yet and several are in desperate need of repair.

Unlike many of the churches of Lalibela, which were monolithic (carved out of the ground and only left attached to the earth at the base), the Tigrayan churches are generally semimonolithic (only partially separated from the host rock) or built into pre-existing caves.

Patience is essential for your enjoyment as it can often take up to an hour to locate some priests. With a full day, a 4WD and quick-keyed priests, you can usually see three, possibly four, churches (depending on the hikes involved).

GHERALTA CLUSTER

The drive through the Gheralta cluster is fantastic, particularly between Dugem and Megab, with stratified mountains and sharp peaks rising like Aksumite stelae from the plains. Avoid visiting this cluster on Wednesday as the priests are usually at market. Minor churches of note in this cluster include Giyorgis Debre Mahar, Mikael Minda'e and Tekla Haimanot.

Abraha Atsbeha አብርሃ አጽብሃ

Architecturally speaking, this semimonolithic 10th-century church (although legend has it that it was built in the 3rd or 4th century) is one of Tigray's finest. It's large and cruciform in shape, with interesting architectural features such as cruciform pillars and step capitals. There's also well-preserved 17th- and 18th-century murals. The obtrusive portico was an attempt by Italians to win over locals by proving they weren't Muslims. Among its many treasures is a crucifix said to belong to Abba Salama, the first Christian in Ethiopia. However, the priest is highly unlikely to show you this or any of the other treasures. It's easily accessible and sits just off the road, 45km west of Wukro.

Abuna Yemata Guh አቡነ የማታ ጉህ

Although less impressive architecturally, this **church** (Birr60 plus various tips) is likely the most rewarding in Tigray. It's spectacularly located within a cliff face, halfway up a sheer rock pinnacle that towers like a lonely castle off the burnt plains 4km west of Megab. The first 45 minutes of the climb is mildly challenging, with a couple of tricky sheer sections requiring toehold action. The last two minutes require nerves of steel – our hands are sweating just thinking about it! Even if you can't make the final scramble and precarious ledge walk over a 200m drop, it's still worth getting that far as the views from the baptism chamber are astounding.

Inside are beautiful and well-preserved frescoes that adorn two cupolas, but never mind those. It's how this church was created that is so intriguing. It's said that when Abuna Yemata first turned up here, the local villagers were suspicious of him and tried to chase him away with clubs and spears. In retaliation Abuna Yemata turned their weapons into lions and leopards, which promptly ate the attackers. After that, to show he wasn't really the neighbour from hell, Abuna Yemata brought all his attackers back to life and baptised them. Ten of the resurrected decided to stay with Abuna Yemata on the mountaintop and devote their life to God. Yemata told them that in order to be successful at this they must never again see the face or hear the voice of a woman. Instead they must grow vegetables. But how did Yemata and his followers actually build their church up here? Well, they didn't. Instead, Jesus descended and told them that four giant rocks were currently battling it out to the north for the honour of being Yemata's church. The winner then magically appeared in this spot as the completely formed church.

Debre Tsion Abraham
ደብረ ጽዮን አብርሃም
Rectangular in shape, with six massive freestanding pillars, this church is known for its diverse architectural features, including decorated cupolas, bas-reliefs and carved crosses on the walls and ceiling. It also has beautiful, though faded and damaged, 16th-century murals and an unusual, large 15th-century ceremonial fan. It sits like a fortress on a hill about 500m south of Dugem and requires a steep 50-minute walk.

Maryam Korkor ማርያም ቆርቆር
Although an unsightly green from the outside, this impressive, cross-shaped church is known for its architectural features (cruciform pillars, arches and cupolas), fine 17th-century frescoes and church treasures. It's also one of the largest churches in the area. The church is around 500m south of Megab and involves a fairly steep 50-minute ascent. Just a couple of minutes' walk from Maryam Korkor is the church of **Daniel Korkor**. It sits atop a paralysing precipice and offers astounding views.

Dugem Selassie ዱግም ስላሴ
This tiny older church lies within a newer one. Its large, double-tomb chamber has three 'shelves'; look out for the beautifully carved ceiling above the maqdas. It was probably converted to a church later. It's on the southern edge of the village of Dugem, just off the road.

Yohannes Maequdi ዮሃንስ መኽዳይ
This rectangular chapel has six freestanding pillars that support a ceiling carved with geometrical designs. While it's best known for well-preserved murals covering the walls, it's the intense atmosphere that most visitors remember. From the village of Matari it's around a 40-minute walk (about 1km south of Dugem) via a steep footpath.

Abuna Gebre Mikael አቡ-ነ ገብረ ሚካኤል
Considered one of Gheralta's finest churches, this church's cruciform plan is hewn into a domelike rock. It features good frescoes and carefully carved columns, pillars, cupolas and arches. It's around 15km south of Abuna Yemata Guh and requires a steep climb, negotiating a few obstacles on the way.

TAKATISFI CLUSTER
Medhane Alem Kesho መድኃኔዓለም ከሾ
Also known as Adi Kesho, this church is one of Tigray's oldest and finest rockhewn churches. Its exterior and interior walls are roughly hewn, which only makes the elaborately carved coffered ceiling that much more special. Ask if you can watch them unlock the door from the inside – rather ingenious indeed! From the end of the 4WD track, it's a leisurely 10-minute climb up to the church.

Mikael Milhaizengi ሚካኤል ምልህዘንጊ
This tiny church, with its stooped doorway, is hewn into the top of a small bleached hill and is thought to date from the 8th century. It's known for its 3m-high carved dome ceiling that resembles an *himbasha* (a favourite round bread of Tigrayans). It's about 45 minutes' walk from Medhane Alem Kesho and a 15-minute walk from Petros and Paulos.

Petros & Paulos ፔጥሮስ ና ጳውሎስ
Only partly hewn, this wood, stone and mortar **church** (Birr50, although the area's friendliest monk only charged us Birr30) is built on a steep ledge and has delightful old murals that are very rapidly deteriorating. Behind the church the skulls of a couple of former monks are lying around enjoying the view. From Wukro, or Adigrat, take a minibus to Teka Tesfay and walk about 3km from the junction. It's a five-minute climb to the church up a rickety wooden ladder.

WUKRO CLUSTER ው-ትሮ
Chirkos ጨርቆስ
This crooked cruciform sandstone church is semimonolithic and boasts beautiful cruciform pillars (notice the swirling sandstone laminae), cubical capitals, an outstanding Aksumite frieze and a barrel-vaulted ceiling. Haile Selassie oddly and unfortunately ordered the angular roof squared with concrete for aesthetic reasons in 1958. It lies around 500m from Wukro and is the most easily accessible church.

TEMBIEN CLUSTER
Avoid visiting on a Saturday as most priests will be away at market.

Abba Yohanni አባ ዮሃኒ
Impressively located partially up a 300m-high sheer cliff face, this church is named after a baby who was raised by a monk and suckled by goats. It's said that when the child first saw a naked woman the Holy Ghost descended in the form of a dove and saved him from the awful sight! The church has a three-aisled and four-bayed interior, eight finely hewn cruciform pillars that support the ceiling and 10 vaults. It's also home to interesting church treasures and sits 15km from Abi Addi, including a 1km walk and a short climb with footholds. If the church has captured your imagination, you'll be pleased to know that a further 42 churches founded by Yohannes are in the vicinity. The only problem is that not only are they all invisible, some are also guarded by a sword-yielding Yohannes.

Gebriel Wukien ገብርኤል ው-ቄን
Architecturally interesting, this church has three aisles and four bays. It features interesting well-carved details, six massive, finely hewn freestanding pillars and three cupolas. It's 16km northwest of Abi Addi, and involves an easy 15-minute walk and then a 10-minute climb up a mountain.

ATSBI CLUSTER
As with the Tembien cluster, most priests (and their keys) are away at market on Saturday. Minor churches in the Atsbi cluster include Cherkos (Agobo) and Zarema Giyorgis.

Mikael Barka ሚካኤል ባርካ
Atop a small but panoramic hill and behind an ugly 1960s facade sits this small rock-hewn church. It's cruciform in shape and probably dates from the 13th century. It's 17km from Wukro, and reaching it involves a 10-minute climb.

Mikael Imba ሚካኤል እምባ
Of all Tigray's rock-hewn churches, Mikael Imba most resembles those seen at Lalibela. A three-quarter monolith, the interior is huge (16.6m wide and 9m deep) with 25 pillars (nine freestanding) holding up the 6m-high ceiling. The view from here is great. It's 9km south of Atsbi and has an easy 20-minute ascent, which is finished with a short ladder.

Debre Selam ደብረ ሰላም
This church or 'church within a church' has exceptional architecture, with an inner rock-hewn section and interior structures constructed according to ancient Aksumite architectural style (alternating layers of rock and wood). There's a beautiful carved arch leading into the maqdas. The setting is lovely and there are good views from the top. It's close to Atsbi and also involves a simple 20-minute ascent.

Sleeping & Eating
The accommodation situation around the churches has improved enormously in the last couple of years, so there are now superb options for all pockets with more top-end places on the way.

The sandy village of **Hawsien**, where the following are located, is probably the best base as it's close to the most interesting churches and fairly easy to get to.

Adulis Hotel Hawzen (☎ 0346 670385; d without bathroom Birr50) While we've seen better we've certainly seen much worse. The clean rooms with equally clean common bathrooms represent good value for money.

Tourist Hotel (☎ 0346 670238; s/d Birr80/100) This decent hotel has rooms set around a large courtyard that look and feel brand new, which they are. The rooms even come with rare luxuries, like hot-water showers and toilets with toilet seats.

our pick Gheralta Lodge (☎ 0346 670344, Addis office 0111 5545489; www.gheraltalodgetigrai.com; s/d/tr from Birr220/660/760) When we walked into this divine Italian lodge our jaws dropped to the floor. When we were told the price our jaws dropped through the floor. Unfortunately they were full and we couldn't stay; we cried, we screamed, we kicked, we begged, but in the end we had to leave. Put simply, this might be the best-value accommodation we have ever seen in Africa. Don't miss eating at the restaurant, which for Birr60 provides a set Italian or Ethiopian menu that will be some of the finest food you eat anywhere in Ethiopia. Book ahead. For the car-less they can also organise superb tours of the churches for a meagre Birr700 for four people. A percentage of the lodge's profits are are used in community-development projects. Back on the main Adigrat–Mekele road, the village of **Wukro** has a couple of decent hotels that make good bases for exploring the nearby churches.

Teklimillennium Pension (☎ 0344 43053; s/d without bathroom Birr15/20) With bright pink rooms set around a bright green garden and a price that even the most tightly sealed of wallets can't fault this place is hard to beat.

Dengolo Park Pension (☎ 0914 783608; r Birr70) This new establishment on the southern edge of town has clean rooms with hot showers and toilet seats that have already managed to do that mystical de-attaching themselves from their anchors on the toilet-bowl rim thing that Ethiopian toilets are so good at.

Getting There & Around
Many of the churches are in remote places, some 20km to 30km off the main road. A private 4WD is the easiest way of reaching them, but if you have camping equipment and lots of time, an exploration by bus and foot is both possible and very enjoyable.

The villages of Hawsien, Edaga Hamus, Wukro, Atsbi, Abi Addi and Sinkata are all served by minibuses. Some villages, such as Megab and Hawsien, are only well served on market days.

Quite good gravel roads now connect the villages with most churches. See Getting There & Away in Aksum (p143), Adigrat (p147) and Mekele (p154) for details on hiring 4WDs and locals buses.

MEKELE መቐለ
pop 215,546 / elev 2062m
The friendly and rapidly expanding university city of Mekele, Tigray's capital, owes its importance to the Emperor Yohannes IV, who made it his capital in the late 19th century. For the traveller, it's the home of two rewarding museums and provides a useful base for visits

to the nearby rock-hewn churches of Tigray and the baking Danakil Depression.

Information
There's no shortage of cheap internet cafes (Birr10 to Birr14 per hour) along the south end of Alula and Guna Sts. The town also has its requisite post office.

Comel Internet Café (per hr Birr10; ☯ 8am-9pm) Patience, patience, it'll get there eventually.

Commercial Bank (Alula St; ☯ 8am-noon & 1-3.30pm Mon-Fri, 8-11.30am Sat) Changes cash and travellers cheques. There's a second branch near Lucy Park.

Dashen Bank & Western Union (☯ 8am-noon & 1-4.30pm Mon-Fri, 8am-noon Sat) Has an ATM accepting international Visa cards.

Emmanuel Clinic & Dental Unit (☎ 0344 404692; ☯ 8.30am-noon & 2-5pm Mon-Fri, 8.30am-noon Sat) A reliable clinic with diagnostic laboratory. Just down the street is northern Ethiopia's best bet for dental action.

Telecommunications office (☎ 0344 410667) International calls. Standard rates (p254).

Tigrai Tourism Commission office (☎ 0344 409360; tigrai.tourism@ethionet.et; 3rd fl, Government of National State of Tigrai Trade, Industry & Transport Bldg; ☯ 8.30am-12.30pm & 1.30-5.30pm Mon-Fri) Helpful and can advise you on a rock-hewn-church itinerary. At the time of research, a new office was due to open at the airport.

Sights
YOHANNES IV MUSEUM
The Italian-designed stone palace built for Emperor Yohannes IV (reigned 1872–79) in 1873 is now an interesting **museum** (admission Birr24; ☯ 8am-5pm). Beneath the impressive vaulted juniper roof is a significant collection of Ethiopian manuscripts, crosses and icons. Many items had mysteriously formed part of a private collection in France, before being returned to Ethiopia in 2001. Upstairs, in the emperor's personal quarters, are some ornate gilded saddles and an audacious throne.

MARTYRS' MEMORIAL MONUMENT & MUSEUM
From a distance this **memorial** (admission Birr10; ☯ 8am-5pm) could be mistaken for the world's biggest golf ball and tee. From up close it's another story, with stirring statues flanking the towering monument and compellingly illustrating the true cost of war.

Just north is a **museum** (admission incl with memorial) that hauntingly and proudly exalts the successes and sacrifices made by TPLF during the 1970s and '80s.

NORTHERN ETHIOPIA

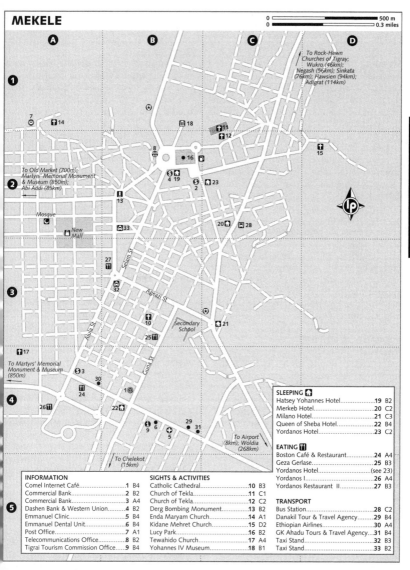

NORTHERN ETHIOPIA

SLEEPING		
Hatsey Yohannes Hotel	**19**	B2
Merkeb Hotel	**20**	C2
Milano Hotel	**21**	C3
Queen of Sheba Hotel	**22**	B4
Yordanos Hotel	**23**	C2

EATING		
Boston Café & Restaurant	**24**	A4
Geza Gerlase	**25**	B3
Yordanos Hotel	(see 23)	
Yordanos I	**26**	A4
Yordanos Restaurant II	**27**	B3

TRANSPORT		
Bus Station	**28**	C2
Danakil Tour & Travel Agency	**29**	B4
Ethiopian Airlines	**30**	A4
GK Ahadu Tours & Travel Agency	**31**	B4
Taxi Stand	**32**	B3
Taxi Stand	**33**	B2

INFORMATION		
Comel Internet Café	**1**	B4
Commercial Bank	**2**	B2
Commercial Bank	**3**	A4
Dashen Bank & Western Union	**4**	B2
Emmanuel Clinic	**5**	B4
Emmanuel Dental Unit	**6**	B4
Post Office	**7**	A1
Telecommunications Office	**8**	B2
Tigrai Tourism Commission Office	**9**	B4

SIGHTS & ACTIVITIES		
Catholic Cathedral	**10**	B3
Church of Tekla	**11**	C1
Church of Tekla	**12**	C2
Derg Bombing Monument	**13**	B2
Enda Maryam Church	**14**	A1
Kidane Mehret Church	**15**	D2
Lucy Park	**16**	B2
Tewahido Church	**17**	A4
Yohannes IV Museum	**18**	B1

OTHER SIGHTS

Thanks to this city's burgeoning economy and rapidly increasing population, the **old market** has been cast out of the town centre (in favour of a modern concrete mall) and now sits almost 1km to the west. If you're an extremely early riser you'll enjoy being there around 4am to witness the camel cara-vans arriving from the Danakil Depression loaded down with bars of salt (see the boxed text, p156).

About 200m southwest of the telecom-munications building, there's an intriguing statue rising in a roundabout: it's a monu-ment dedicated to 2500 people who were killed in Hawsien by a Derg bombing raid.

There are several churches, both old and new, dotting the city and their towers are visible throughout.

Sleeping
BUDGET

Queen of Sheba Hotel (☎ 0344 410718; Guna St; s/d without bathroom Birr30/60) This swimming-pool blue hotel has tiny rooms set around a courtyard. The staff speak Amharic only but are very friendly, and it's a good cheap option.

Merkeb Hotel (☎ 0344 410360; d/tw Birr70/100) If you can snag a room away from the cacophony emanating from the bus station, then this is a good bet. The spacious rooms gather lots of light, are comfortable and have hot-water showers and toilets with seats that are firmly attached.

Hatsey Yohannes Hotel (☎ 0344 406762; s/tw incl breakfast Birr95/125) This is a sweet choice; it's well run, clean and has carpeted rooms :ith fairly reliable hot-water showers and satellite TV with more static than TV. The frilly bedspreads are a highlight – if you like that kind of thing. There's a generator to cope with the frequent power cuts.

MIDRANGE & TOP END

Milano Hotel (☎ 0344 418724; hotelmilano@yahoo.com; tw/d Birr120/130) Despite pushy staff and terrifying wiring, this massive hotel complex offers good value and doesn't discriminate between locals and *faranjis* price wise. Apparently the doubles are 'special' and therefore more expensive than the twins, though we couldn't see any difference.

our pick **Yordanos Hotel** (☎ 0344 413722; s/d/tw/ste Birr180/220/320/520) You'll find unexpected style at this lovely new hotel. The rooms have desks, fridges, satellite TV and enormous beds that come complete with a romantic sprinkling of rose petals. The modern bathrooms have cool, dark tiles and the suites even have jacuzzis with room for two – get busy making bubbles!

Eating

our pick **Boston Café & Restaurant** (mains Birr15-25; 🕃) Not only is it named after a US city, but it also looks like it belongs in one; its sparkling-clean air-con bliss is the perfect place in which to hide from the rigours of the Ethiopian road for a while. While doing your hiding why not indulge in some of the superb cakes, juices, snacks and mains, including a good lasagne?

Its sophisticated bar is also a relaxed spot for a cocktail (seriously!) in the evening. It's down a little side alley next to the impressive new shopping centre.

Geza Gerlase (Guna St; mains Birr15-30) This cultural restaurant within a traditional *tukul* is the best place to enjoy excellent Ethiopian dishes Specialities include *zilzil tibs* (strips of beef fried and served slightly crunchy with *awazi* sauce) and *kitfo* (minced beef or lamb like the French steak tartare, usually served warmed – but not cooked – in butter, *berbere* and sometimes thyme). Vegetarians steer clear.

Yordanos Restaurant (mains Birr25-50) Part of the stylish hotel of the same name, this place is a wonderful spot in which to fill your tummy with Western dishes, including a good fried chicken, pastas and steaks all of which are several cuts above average. There are two other branches in town, one of which, Yordanos I, serves thin-base pizzas (Birr20 to Birr30).

Getting There & Away

Ethiopian Airlines (☎ 0344 400055) flies to Addis Ababa (US$180, 1½ hours, daily) and Aksum (US$78, 30 minutes, Thursday).

Numerous morning buses run to Adigrat (Birr14, three hours), while one runs on to Aksum (Birr34, 8½ hours, 6am). To Addis Ababa, you have the choice of a normal service (Birr100, two days, 5am) or three deluxe Selam Buses (Birr100, 1½ days, 6am). For Lalibela, take the normal Addis Ababa bus and get off in Woldia (Birr34, 5½ hours).

For the Tigray churches, minibuses leave from the bus station daily for Abi Addi (Birr17, three hours, several daily), Wukro (Birr6, one hour, 10 daily) and Hawsien (Birr21, 2½ hours, five daily). For Atsbi, go to Wukro first.

There is a number of tour companies operating trips to the rock-hewn churches and the daunting Danakil Depression. **GK Ahadu Tours & Travel Agency** (☎ 0344 406466; gkahadu@telecm .net.eto) and **Danakil Tour & Travel Agency** (☎ 0914 702648) are the two leading operators. Both offer quality, but very expensive, 4WD tours. The Danakil Tour & Travel Agency also gives you the chance to saddle up a camel and join one of the salt caravans.

DANAKIL DEPRESSION ደንካል በርሃ

It's better to die than live without killing.

Afar proverb

Bubbling volcanoes light up the night sky, sulphurous mounds of yellow contort into monstrous shapes and mirages of camels cross lakes of salt. Lying 100m below sea level the Danakil Depression is about the hottest and most inhospitable place on earth. In fact so surreal is the moonscape here that for all intents and purposes it's not actually a part of earth at all. If you want genuine, raw adventure, then few corners of the globe can match this overwhelming wilderness. But come prepared because, with temperatures frequently saying hello to 45°C, a quarter of the continent's active volcanoes, appalling 'roads' and ferocious tribes, visiting this region is no walk in the park.

The most amazing site has to be **Irta'ale Volcano** (613m), which has been in a state of continuous eruption since 1967. Its small southerly crater is one of the only permanent lava lakes on the planet. A night-time hike to its summit for sunrise is as captivating as it is exhausting. Taking camels is a viable option.

If you'd like to visit the lowest place on the continent and see great warts of twisted sulphur, head for **Dallol** (-116m), which is about 25km north of the village Hamd Ela (and officially the hottest place on earth with a year-round average temperature of 34.4°C). This is also where much of the salt is mined out of the ground by hand. More rewarding is a trip to **Lake Afera** (-102m), which is 30km (or five to nine hours by 4WD!) south of Irta'ale. Its waters are bright green and its salty shores have been harvested for centuries by the Afar people (p53), a nomadic ethnic group known in the past for their legendary ferocity.

An excursion into this harsh and astounding world isn't something everyone can handle; due to a number of tourist deaths, tour companies actually recommend that people with heart conditions do not visit. This is because the extreme conditions can inflame any heart problems. In addition, a group of tourists were kidnapped in this region in 2007 (subsequently released) and there was another attempted kidnapping in 2008. Despite these things a trip here is something nobody will ever forget, but whatever you do, do not attempt to visit during the summer.

Trips here can be organised through either tour operators in Addis Ababa (see p270) or those listed in Mekele (opposite). If you're travelling with a group of private 4WDs (taking only one 4WD is suicide), you must contact the **Afar Tourism Commission** (☎ 0336 660181; fax 0336 660448) regarding permission and to arrange picking up your mandatory Afar guide (Birr100 per day) at the Afar tourist office near Berahile. If you'd like a hand with the Afar formalities, stop in at the Tigrai Tourism Commission office in Mekele (p152). Besides helping with advice on permissions and pointing you in the right direction, staff can also help you plan your itinerary.

KOREM ቆረም
pop 29,340 / elev 2539m

Heading south from Mekele it takes only a couple of hours along a smooth paved road to reach the market town of Maychew where, without warning, the world becomes an explosion of spectacular mountain peaks, covered in lush rugs of green forests and terraced fields. An hour beyond Maychew and you pass the beautiful blue pool of Lake Ashenge, overflowing with grebes, ducks, ibises and others; it's fantastic birding territory. Just over the brow of the hill from the lake is Korem. In 1984 it was turned into probably the most infamous town in Ethiopia when BBC reporter Michael Burke opened his news report with the words, 'Dawn, and as the sun breaks through the piercing chill of night on the plains outside Korem…' With the harrowing report that followed the world became aware of the terrible famine that was to claim around a million lives and scar Ethiopia right up to the present day.

It's hard to reconcile yesterday's Korem with today's. Now it's a lush and fertile place, where water flows year-round and the fields are bursting with crops. The beauty of this region makes it a delightful place for some truly off-the-beaten-path hiking. The most obvious thing is to base yourself in Korem and make a day walk to and around the lake (take binoculars for the birds and expect to be the object of considerable and very friendly curiosity). For further adventures the hills are criss-crossed with trails linking remote villages. Explorers will have a field day creating wonderful memories around here.

For accommodation the **Girmay Minuts Hotel** (☎ 0345 510278; s/d Birr100/150) on the northern edge of town is the best place to stay.

Note that if you have your own set of wheels, you can take a dusty and bumpy dirt road from Korem straight to Lalibela which cuts a big chunk off the normal journey via Woldia.

SALT FOR GOLD

Since earliest times and right up to the present day, salt, a precious commodity for people and their animals, has been used as a kind of currency in Ethiopia. According to Kosmos, a 6th-century Egyptian writing in Greek, the kings of Aksum sent expeditions west to barter salt, among other things, for hunks of gold.

Mined in the Danakil Depression, the mineral was transported hundreds of kilometres west across the country to the Ethiopian court in Shoa. Later, the salt was cut into small, rectangular blocks, which came to be known as *amole*; their value grew with every kilometre that they travelled further from the mine.

To this day, Afar nomads and their camels continue to follow this ancient salt route. Cutting the bars by hand from the salt lakes in eastern Ethiopia, they spend weeks travelling by caravan to market, where the bars will be bartered.

Though nowadays the people of the Danakil Depression mine salt in order to earn gold in the highland markets, once upon a time it was the other way around. Long ago, so long that nobody really remembers, the salt of the Danakil was all gold – endless thousands of tonnes of pure gold. People say that Danakil had more gold than anywhere else on earth and its people lived like royalty. Wealth made them greedy, lazy and forgetful of God. In order to punish them, God turned all the gold to salt. But one day, so the locals say, when the people are no longer greedy, God will turn it all back into gold again and then the people of Danakil will once more be able to swap gold for salt.

WOLDIA ወልድያ
pop 24,533 / elev 2112m

The town of Woldia provides a springboard for visits to its famous neighbour, Lalibela, 120km to the northwest. Stock up on petrol, batteries and anything you might need from a pharmacy before leaving. Lalibela, despite its fame, is still the back of beyond.

Of the numerous cheap places to stay, **Arsama Hotel** (☎ 0333 313395; d with/without bathroom Birr50/30) is the best, but don't take that as a great recommendation.

The **Mechare Hotel** (☎ 0333 310233; d Birr100) has big, bright rooms, although this brightness just allows you to see the mounds of dirt and clouds of mosquitoes more easily.

The bus to Lalibela (Birr39, five to seven hours) is supposed to leave at 6am, but doesn't usually leave until 9am or 10am (when it's full).

There are also three daily buses to Dessie (Birr20, 2½ hours), Mekele (Birr42, 5½ hours) and Addis Ababa (bus/minibus Birr72/120, 1½ days, 6am).

LALIBELA ላሊበላ
pop 14,668 / elev 2630m

I am weary of writing more about these buildings, because it seems to me that I shall not be believed if I write more…but swear I by God in Whose power I am, that all that is written is the truth, and there is much more than what I have written, and I have left it that they may not tax me with its being falsehood.

Francisco Alvares (early 16th-century Portuguese writer) from Ho Preste Joam das Indias: Verdadera informa-cam das terras do Preste Joam (1540)

Nearly 1000 years ago a poisoned man was taken by angels to the first, second and third heavens. Here he was shown a fabulous city of rock-hewn churches. Then God himself commanded him to return to earth and, re-creating what he had seen, build a new Jerusalem.

At the start of the 21st century this vision of heaven still exists; its buildings frozen in stone, its soul alive with the rites and awe of Christianity at its most ancient and unbending. No matter what you've heard about Lalibela, no matter how many pictures you have seen of its breathtaking rock-hewn churches, its dimly lit passageways or its hidden crypts and grottoes, nothing on earth can prepare you for the reality of seeing the new Jerusalem for yourself. It is truly the wonder of Africa. A night vigil here, during one of the big religious festivals, when white-robed pilgrims in their hundreds crowd the courtyards of the churches and priests in royal robes wade through the crowds to worship

NORTHERN ETHIOPIA

in a church made by the hands of angels, is to witness Christianity in its most raw and powerful form.

History

Lalibela, initially known as Roha, was the Zagwe dynasty's capital in the 12th and 13th centuries. After the death of King Lalibela, the ruler credited with the construction of the churches, the town was named after him.

In a rare consensus, scholars and local tradition both claim that the churches date from around King Lalibela's reign in the 12th or 13th century. Legend states that Lalibela was poisoned by his half-brother and while in a coma he went on a journey to heaven (others say Jerusalem) where God instructed him to

return to Ethiopia and re-create the holy city of Jerusalem there.

Even the names of Lalibela's features echo those of Jerusalem: the River Jordan, Calvary and the Tomb of Adam. However, the buildings are so different from each other in style, craftsmanship and state of preservation that they may span a much longer period than Lalibela's reign.

The consensus between scholars and local tradition is thrown out the window when discussions about who built the churches arise. Some wizardly scholars with powerful calculators have estimated that it would have taken a workforce of 40,000 to construct the churches, while locals claim that, toiling all the hours of daylight, the earthly workforce was then

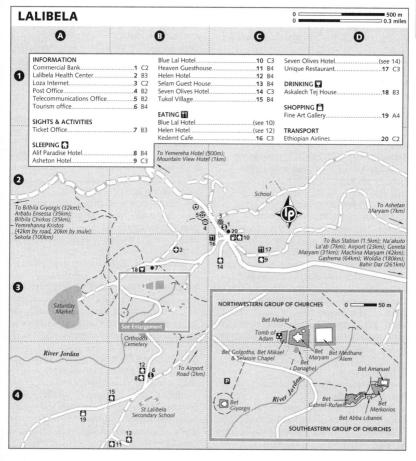

replaced by a celestial one, who toiled all the hours of darkness. In this way, the churches rose at a miraculous speed.

However, foreign intervention, whether celestial or mortal, can almost certainly be ruled out. Long a victim of the usual 'it can't be African' chauvinism, Lalibela in fact almost certainly represents the pinnacle of a very long-standing Ethiopian building tradition.

Exceptional masonry skills had long been in existence during the days of Aksum, and indeed most of the churches show clear characteristics of the ancient Aksumite style. If angels did build the churches, they were almost certainly Ethiopian angels.

Information

Commercial Bank (8-11am & 1-3pm Mon-Fri, 8-11am Sat) Changes cash and travellers cheques. A number of the top-end hotels can change US dollars and euros but rates are poor.

Lalibela Health Center (☎ 0333 360416; 8.30am-noon & 1.30-5.30pm)

Loza Internet (8am-9pm; per hr Birr60) Of the several internet cafes in town this is by far the best. For Ethiopia it offers shockingly fast connections.

Telecommunications office (8am-8pm) International calls. Standard rates (p254). It's next to the post office.

Tourism office (☎ 0333 360167; 8am-noon & 1.30-5.30pm Mon-Fri) This office offers some helpful advice and sells several small booklets on Lalibela.

Dangers & Annoyances

Thanks to a concerted effort from the local authorities, harassment from unlicensed 'guides' has dropped considerably in the past couple of years. Even so, there are still a few, including children, lurking about. Using children as guides encourages them to play truant at school, while using unlicensed guides encourages unhealthy migration to Lalibela (and more unemployed 'guides' harassing travellers). Hiring either also won't contribute to your visit as few children or unlicensed guides know much about the churches.

Sights

Lalibela's **rock-hewn churches** (admission Birr200, personal video cameras Birr100; 6am-6pm) are remarkable for three main reasons: many are not carved into the rock but freed entirely from it, the buildings are so refined and there are so many within such a small area.

Although time has treated the churches with remarkably gentle gloves, Unesco has built rather hideous scaffolding and roofing over most churches to protect frescoes from water seepage. Fortunately they won't detract from your enjoyment too much.

Although visiting without a guide is possible – getting lost in the warren of tunnels is quite memorable and usually not permanent – you'll miss out on many of the amazing subtleties each church has to offer. We'd recommend going once with a guide and once solo, in whichever order you choose. Local licensed guides can be arranged at the tourism office for a set fee of Birr150 per day (Birr200 for groups of five or more). However, during slow times licensed guides on the street (always ask to see their licence) will occasionally drop their fees.

The **ticket office** (8am-noon & 2-5pm) lies beside the path leading to the northern group of churches and Bet Medhane Alem. Tickets give access to all churches in town for the duration of your stay. There are rumours that these admission charges will increase to Birr300 during the lifetime of this book.

Note that camera flashes inside churches cause great damage to the murals and frescoes, so please resist using one. Many of the priests are more than happy to show off their church's treasures and pose obligingly beside them for photos. It is customary and polite to tip them something small afterwards (Birr5).

The self-appointed shoe bearers found at each church doorway seemed to have disappeared at the time of research, but should they return a tip of Birr1 per person per church is fair.

Lastly, don't forget to bring your torch.

NORTHWESTERN GROUP OF CHURCHES

This group contains six of Lalibela's 11 churches and sits immediately behind the ticket office. From a size perspective, this group is easily the most impressive.

Bet Medhane Alem ቤተ መድኃኔዓለም

Resembling a massive Greek temple more than a traditional Ethiopian church, Bet Medhane Alem (Saviour of the World) is impressive for its size and majesty. Said to be the largest rock-hewn church in the world, it measures 33.5m by 23.5m and is over 11.5m high.

Some scholars have suggested that the church may have been a copy in rock of the original St Mary of Zion church in Aksum.

The building is surrounded by 34 large, rectangular columns (many actually replicas of the originals). The three jointed at each corner are thought to represent the Holy Trinity. There are a further 38 columns inside that support the gabled roof.

The interior consists of a barrel-vaulted nave and four aisles. Look for the three empty graves in one corner, said to have been prepared symbolically for Abraham, Isaac and Jacob. Pierced stone 'panels' fill the windows, each decorated with different central crosses. You may be allowed to see the famous 7kg gold Lalibela cross. In 1997 it was stolen by an Ethiopian antique dealer and sold to a Belgian tourist for US$25,000. Thankfully, it was recovered.

Bet Maryam ቤተ ማርያም

Connected to Bet Medhane Alem by a tunnel is a large courtyard containing three churches. The first, Bet Maryam, is small yet designed and decorated to an exceptionally high standard. Dedicated to the Virgin, who's particularly venerated in Ethiopia, this is the most popular church among pilgrims. Some believe it may have been the first church built by Lalibela.

On its eastern wall you'll see two sets of three windows. According to scholars, the upper set is thought to represent the Holy Trinity, while the lower three, set below a small cross-shaped window, are believed to represent the crucifixion of Jesus and the two sinners. The lower right window has a small irregular-shaped opening above it, a signal that this sinner was accepted to heaven after repenting his sins and asking for Jesus' help. The lower left window, which represents the criminal who mocked Jesus and was sentenced to hell, has the small irregular-shaped opening below it.

Above the western porch and squeezed beneath the roof is a rare and beautifully carved bas-relief of St George fighting the dragon.

Inside, the ceilings and upper walls are painted with very early frescoes, and the columns, capital and arches are covered in beautifully carved details such as birds, animals and foliage, including a curious two-headed eagle and two fighting bulls, one white, one black (thought to represent good and evil).

At the nave's eastern end is a column that's kept permanently wrapped in cloth. Nobody knows what lies beneath, though rumours abound – ask your guide.

Bet Meskel ቤተ መስቀል

Carved into the courtyard's northern wall at Bet Maryam is the tiny semi-chapel of Bet Meskel. Four pillars divide the gallery into two aisles spanned by arcades.

Keep an eye out for the cross carved in relief beneath stylised foliage on one of the spandrels of the arches.

Bet Danaghel ቤተ ድንግል

To the south of the Bet Maryam courtyard is the chapel of Bet Danaghel, said to have been constructed in memory of the maiden nuns martyred on the orders of the 4th-century Roman emperor Julian in Edessa (modern-day Turkey). Many of its features – the cruciform pillars and bracket capitals – are typical architectural features of the churches.

Bet Golgotha, Bet Mikael & Selassie Chapel ቤተ ጎልጎታ፣ ቤተ ሚካኤልና ስላሴ የፀሎት ቤት

A tunnel at the southern end of the Bet Maryam courtyard connects it to the twin churches of Bet Golgotha and Bet Mikael (also known as Bet Debre Sina).

Bet Mikael serves as an anteroom to the Selassie Chapel, one of Lalibela's holiest sanctuaries. It contains three monolithic altars. One is decorated with a beautiful relief of four winged creatures with their hands held up in prayer; it's thought to represent the four evangelists. Unfortunately, the chapel is very rarely open to the public.

Bet Golgotha is known for containing some of the best early examples of Ethiopian Christian art. On the so-called Tomb of Christ (an arched recess in the northeast of the church), a recumbent figure is carved in high relief; above it, in low relief, hovers an angel. Almost as amazing are the life-size depictions of seven saints carved into the walls' niches.

Close to the Tomb of Christ is a movable slab of stone, which is said to cover the most secret place in the holy city: the tomb of King Lalibela himself. Such is the importance and sanctity of Golgotha that a visit is said to assure your place in heaven.

Bet Golgotha also boasts some of Lalibela's most important religious treasures. You may be shown a blackened metal cross (thought to symbolise the nails of crucifixion) and a large prayer stick (composed of wood, iron and horn), both supposed belongings of King Lalibela. Sadly women are not allowed into Bet Golgotha.

Standing in a deep trench in front of the western facade of Bet Golgotha is the so-called Tomb of Adam. It consists of a giant, hollowed-out block of stone.

SOUTHEASTERN GROUP OF CHURCHES

Although smaller in size than the northwestern group, the southeastern cluster offers not only one of Lalibela's most finely carved churches but also some intrigue, with various historians debating whether some churches had pasts as prisons and palaces.

Bet Gabriel-Rufael ቤተ ገብርኤል ሩፋኤል

Its entrance flanked to the west by a sloping sliver of hewn rock known as the 'Way to Heaven', this imposing twin-church marks the main entrance to the southeastern group.

Unlike most Lalibela churches its entrance is at the top and is accessed by a small walkway, high over the moat-like trench below. This, along with its curious, irregular floor plan, has led scholars to propose that Bet Gabriel-Rufael may have been a fortified palace for Aksumite royalty as early as the 7th and 8th centuries.

Although the section of Bet Rufael's roof that collapsed has been rebuilt, services only take place in Bet Gabriel. Once inside the complex you'll realise its monumental facade was its most interesting feature.

Bet Merkorios ቤተ መርቆሪዮስ

Reached via a long, narrow and pitch-black tunnel that starts from Bet Gabriel-Rufael, this current church may have started as something altogether different. The discovery of ankle shackles among other objects has led scholars to believe that the building may have served as the town's prison, or house of justice.

Due to a large section of roof collapsing, the interior is a fraction of its former size. Don't miss the beautiful fresco thought to represent the Three Wise Men. With their little flipper hands and eyes that look askance, they're delightfully depicted; it may date from the 15th century. The 12 Apostles are also represented in a less attractive fresco, probably of a later date.

The painting on cotton fabric is believed to date from the 16th century, though the priests will claim it's from the 14th century. Formerly, such paintings were plastered to the church walls with a mixture of straw, ox blood and mud.

Bet Amanuel ቤተ አማኑኤል

Freestanding and monolithic, the Bet Amanuel is widely considered as one of Lalibela's most finely carved churches. Some have suggested the church was the royal family's private chapel.

It perfectly replicates the style of Aksumite buildings, with its projecting and recessed walls mimicking alternating layers of wood and stone. To appreciate this fully, you should make a day trip to Yemrehanna Kristos (p164), which is one of Ethiopia's best-preserved Aksumite structures.

The most striking feature of the interior is the double Aksumite frieze in the nave. Although not accessible, there's even a spiral staircase connecting the four-pillared walls to an upper gallery. In the southern aisle, a hole in the floor (beneath the donation box) leads to a long, subterranean tunnel (one of three) that connects the church to Bet Merkorios and Bet Gabriel-Rufael.

Outside, you may see the odd 'sacred bee' flying about. Behind a high door in the courtyard's southern wall is their hive. Throughout Ethiopia, honey produced in churches is believed to possess special healing properties.

The chambers in the walls are the old graves of pilgrims who requested to be buried here.

Bet Abba Libanos ቤተ አባ ሊባኖስ

Bet Abba Libanos is hewn into a rock face and is unique among Lalibela's churches in that it's a hypogeous church. In English, that means only the roof and floor remain attached to the strata.

Like Bet Amanuel, many of its architectural features, such as the friezes, are Aksumite. Curiously, although it looks large from the outside, the interior is actually very small. The carved corners of its cubic capitals are unique; some guides say they may represent angel eyes.

The church is said to have been constructed in a single night by Lalibela's wife, Meskel Kebra, with a little help from angels. The church seems to grow from the rock

---

HOOFPRINTS & SAINTLY REMINDERS

Just as King Lalibela was finishing off his series of churches, he was suddenly paid an unexpected visit. Astride a white horse and decked out in full armour came Ethiopia's patron saint, George. However, the saint turned out to be severely piqued: not one of the churches had been dedicated to him.

Profusely apologetic, Lalibela promised to make amends immediately by building him the most beautiful church of all.

Today, the priests of Bet Giyorgis (meaning 'Place of George') point out the hoofprints left behind by the saint's horse, permanently imprinted in stone on the side of the trench.

---

and gives you a vivid idea of the work required to excavate these churches.

A tunnel leads off the church to the tiny chapel of Bet Lehem.

BET GIYORGIS ቤተ ጊዮርጊስ

Resting all on its own, south and west of the northwestern and southeastern groups, is Lalibela's masterpiece, Bet Giyorgis. Standing on the brow of its compound, you'll have little doubt that it's the most mesmerising object in all of Ethiopia.

Representing the apogee of the rock-hewn tradition, the Bet Giyorgis is the most visually perfect church of all, a 15m-high three-tiered plinth in the shape of a Greek cross. Due to its exceptional preservation, it also lacks the obtrusive scaffolding seen on the other churches.

Inside, light flows in from the windows and illuminates the ceiling's large crosses – beauty in simplicity. There are also two 800-year-old olive-wood boxes; one (with the opposing corkscrew keys) is rumoured to have been carved by King Lalibela himself. Inside this box is also a crucifix, which is rumoured to have been made with gold brought from King Solomon's temple in Jerusalem.

Be warned that some of the cavities in the walls surrounding the church hold unsettling mummified corpses.

See also the boxed text above.

Festivals & Events

The most exciting time to visit is during a major festival, when thousands of pilgrims crowd in for Timkat, Leddet and Fasika. Meskel and Kiddus Yohannes are also busy. See p248 for dates and details.

Outside these periods, try to attend at least one church's saint's day; inquire at your hotel.

Sleeping

Accommodation in Lalibela is expensive and vacancies are almost nonexistent during the festival period and European Christmas, so reservations up to six months in advance aren't unheard of. However, prices for reserved rooms during these times treble or more. If you arrive during a festival without reservations, you'll risk being forced into a dive. Conversely, if there's space, you'll end up paying a fraction of what you would have if you'd made those costly reservations.

Discounts are negotiable in most hotels from May through August.

Lalibela suffers from water shortages, particularly during dry season and high tourism season. Hotels may limit showering to early mornings and evenings or may give out buckets of warm water instead. Lengthy electrical cuts are still a problem.

BUDGET

Helen Hotel (☎ 0333 360053; s with/without bathroom Birr80/60, d with/without bathroom Birr120/70) The rooms here could do with being tidied up a bit but the price is good and chances are the gorgeous family who run it will quickly adopt you as one of their own.

Alif Paradise Hotel (☎ 0911 556211; alpara hotel@yahoo.com; old block s/tw Birr80/120, new block s/tw Birr150/200) The huge investment the owners of this place have recently put into it has paid off with the rooms in the new block being bright, tiled and clean with bathtubs and views. The older rooms, though tatty, are still decent value. A new restaurant should be completed by the time you read this.

Asheton Hotel (☎ 0333 360030; r Birr100) This classic budget-traveller haunt offers genuine bang for your buck with cosy whitewashed rooms, walls decorated with local art and embroidered bedding. The showers are hot, the service is pleasant and the garden courtyard a quiet spot to relax in.

Selam Guest House (☎ 0333 3600374; d/tw Birr100/200) This very friendly guesthouse still had that new out-of-the-wrapper look when we passed by. The rooms are plain and simple, and the bedspreads are made from traditional Ethiopian textiles.

Blue Lal Hotel (☎ 0333 360380; d & tw Birr120-150) Although extremely austere, these rooms are bright, clean and the showers spurt out hot water – some of the time. Land room 2, 3 or 4 and you'll have a balcony to play on.

Heaven Guesthouse (☎ 0333 360075; s/d without bathroom US$12/15) If this really is heaven then all we can say is that heaven is a lot cheaper than we imagined it to be. We can also tell you that heaven isn't always equal, so have a look at a few rooms first: some are a bit boring, but others have pretty bedspreads and open-plan bathrooms.

MIDRANGE & TOP END

Seven Olives Hotel (☎ 0333 360020; s/d/tw US$15/27/27; ▢) The oldest hotel in Lalibela continues to receive many positive recommendations. It has comfortable rooms that look across lovely gardens full of bird tables and hundreds of unfeasibly colourful birds. The only bad point we could come up with is that many of the bathrooms are a bit mouldy.

Yemereha Hotel (☎ 0333 360862; www.greenland ethiopia.com; s/d/tw US$35/45/45) Run by the long-established Greenland Tours, this is an excellent new addition to the Lalibela hotel scene. The spacious rooms are beautifully furnished with local art and crafts and at the end of a long day's church gazing, the baths fill to the brim with steaming H_2O. However, the 'eco' in the advertising is sadly just a word.

Tukol Village (☎ 0333 360564; s/d US$40/50) Despite the manager's attitude towards tourists, the clean and classy *tukuls* on offer at this Dutch-owned place remain very popular. Past guests have even included Bill Clinton (if you want to sleep in the same bed as Bill did, take room 11). Apparently Mr Clinton didn't tip; it might have been the manager that put him off.

Mountain View Hotel (☎ 0333 360804; www.mountains viewhotel.com; s/d US$43/55.50) Eagles get all dewy-eyed and jealous over the stupendous views over the distant plains from this impeccable new hotel. The rooms are standard business class in look and feel and therefore don't quite fit in with village life in Lalibela; however, if comfort is what you want, then comfort is what you'll get.

Eating

Unique Restaurant (mains Birr10-15) Opposite the Asheton Hotel, this dark and understated little restaurant, serving cheap and tasty Ethiopian dishes, receives regular positive reviews from happy punters.

Kedemt Cafe (mains Birr10-20) One of several identikit, and equally good, restaurants in town that locals flock to for a good injera stuffing.

Blue Lal Hotel (mains Birr12-20) This carefully groomed restaurant has a traditional grass-covered floor and big bright injera baskets on every table. The Ethiopian food is superb and the *faranji* dishes aren't far behind either. The highlight are the pizzas – some of the best in north Ethiopia.

Helen Hotel (mains Birr15) The restaurant at this friendly hotel needs a bit of notice to prepare pasta or injera-flavoured meals, but the results don't disappoint. The meals are a couple of courses long and the staff have an eye for detail in the presentation category.

Seven Olives Hotel (mains Birr15-35) Eat inside the modern *tukul* or dine alfresco on the leafy terrace. An Ethiopian chef with US experience has trained the staff to make more than the usual *faranji* fare. The result is the nicest eating experience for miles around.

Drinking

Besides having a cold sunset drink on the Seven Olives Hotel's terrace, there's one other drinking experience you shouldn't miss.

Askalech Tej House (flask of tej Birr5) Also known as 'torpedo', it serves *tej* (honey wine) of varying potency. There's usually traditional music after 7pm.

Shopping

Fine Art Gallery (☯ 7am-8pm) This is one shop that stands out from Lalibela's throng of souvenir shacks. Inside are beautiful watercolour and sepia paintings created by Tegegne Yirdaw, a local artist who can count Princess Anne as one of his work's admirers.

Getting There & Away

Ethiopian Airlines (☎ 0333 360046) flies at least once daily to Addis Ababa (US$136, 1½ to two hours), Gonder (US$98, 30 minutes) and Aksum (US$112, 40 minutes). It's not currently possible to fly from Lalibela to Bahir Dar (though you can do it in the opposite direction).

Overland, the best approach is currently from Woldia via Gashema. Gashema can also be reached from the west but transport is sporadic at best. With your own vehicle (or oodles of patience), it's a rewarding journey to arrive from the north via Adwa, Abi Addi and Sekota. On that note, fuel (out of the barrel) is now available in Lalibela.

Two buses depart daily at 6am for Woldia (Birr36, five to seven hours), with one continuing to Addis Ababa (Birr95, two days) after overnighting in Dessie (Birr58, 8½ to 10 hours). There's a daily bus to Bahir Dar (Birr65, 10 hours). The bus station is an inconvenient couple of kilometres out of town and with no transport it's a long, hot and very sweaty walk. Fortunately locals will point out the shortcut, which reduces the hike somewhat. If you call ahead most hotels will arrange a pickup for you.

Getting Around

Most midrange hotels offer a transfer service to the airport, which is 23km south of town.

Of the midrange hotels that arrange 4WD hire to visit the churches outside town (right), the Seven Olives has the best prices.

If you think Landrovers are crude brutes, you can hire a mule for longer or steeper treks; ask at your hotel. A full day should set you back Birr100 per mule and driver.

AROUND LALIBELA

Many other fascinating churches and monasteries lie within a day's striking distance of Lalibela, and a journey to them, whether by foot, mule or 4WD, is rewarding. Don't forget to look for the endemic white-billed starlings while on the go. The stunning countryside is also home to unique ecotourism treks.

Ecotreks on the Mesket Escarpment

Though it lacks the bragging status of the Simien Mountains, trekking on the Mesket Escarpment surrounding Lalibela is a wonderful experience that mixes astounding scenery, historical riches and a fascinating insight into the life of Ethiopian highlanders. Many people regard walking here as one of the highlights of their Ethiopian adventure. Treks are organised through the noteworthy local charity **Tourism in Ethiopia for Sustainable Future Alternatives** (TESFA; ☎ 0111 225024; www.community-tourism-ethiopia.com).

TESFA's goal is 'to work in partnership with local communities to enable them to generate sustainable improvements in their livelihood through the development of their own tourism-related enterprises, while also contributing to the protection of their physical and cultural environments'. Save the Children (UK) and the Royal Netherlands Embassy have helped fund the project.

Treks are typically three to five days long and take place along the top of the escarpment, which houses caves, rock-hewn churches, fascinating columnar basalt outcrops and little villages. Because you stay on the escarpment, gradients are quite low and you'll find the walking is fairly easy.

TESFA has three camps in local villages (with more on the way), each currently consisting of traditional yet comfortable *tukuls*. Wajela camp sits near an interesting cave complex, Mequat Maryam teeters near the escarpment edge and offers incredible vistas – even the view from the toilet is inspiring – and Yadukulay (50km south) is set on a twin-peaked hill.

Treks – including guides, packing mules and drivers, accommodation, meals (breakfast, lunch, dinner and the odd snack), tea and coffee – cost Birr450 per person per day (there are discounts for children).

Transportation to and from Lalibela must be arranged privately, though TESFA recommends the local 4WD operator **Habtamu** (b_h2007@yahoo .com) who charges Birr600 to Birr1000 for drop-offs at Meket.

Due to limited space, these treks must be booked well in advance. TESFA is also in the process of opening up new trekking regions, including in the mountains immediately behind Lalibela and up in Tigray. Both these routes were virtually ready to go at the time of research. Contact TESFA for more information.

Churches & Monasteries

The churches around Lalibela vary greatly in style, design and age; some are even thought to predate those in Lalibela. Tucked away and still absent from any modern maps, many of the churches require a guide to find them.

See Lalibela's Getting Around section (left) for transport details.

YEMREHANNA KRISTOS የmeasurement ክርስቶስ

Despite **Yemrehanna Kristos** (admission Birr75, video cameras Birr50) being one of Ethiopia's best-preserved late-Aksumite buildings, few people reward themselves with a visit. And a reward it is for this is a beautiful church with a friendly priest and, for the macabre, there's even a bunch of dead dudes hanging out here. The church is about 1½ hours (45km) away from Lalibela by 4WD.

The church is unusual because it's built rather than excavated. Seeing the stepped exterior facade, created from alternating wood and stone layers, you'll truly come to appreciate why so many of Lalibela's rock-hewn churches look like they do. And knowing that Yemrehanna Kristos may predate Lalibela's churches by up to 80 years, you have before you a virtual blueprint of greatness.

Incredibly, the whole church sits on a foundation of carefully laid olive-wood panels, which 'float' it perfectly above the marshy ground below. The carving and decoration are exceptional, especially the cruciform windows and the elaborate nave ceiling. Conceiving how the massive marble arches were placed so accurately in such surrounds is almost harder to grasp than the construction of Lalibela's churches.

Behind the church lies a pile of mummified bodies (the priests told us there were over 10,000 of them): some are those of pilgrims who've come here to die over the centuries, others are said to be those of the workmen who were brought in from far away Jerusalem to help Yemrehanna Kristos construct the church.

This entirely inspiring and slightly spooky complex sits within a cave roofed by basalt lava flows. The ugly brick wall at the front was built in 1985 to improve the church's security.

It's also possible to get here by foot or mule. Both options take about five hours to cover the shorter 20km distance.

ARBATU ENSESSA አርባቱ እንሰሳ

West of Yemrehanna Kristos, around 35km from Lalibela, is **Arbatu Ensessa** (admission Birr50). It's a three-quarter monolith church in a wild, overgrown but rather beautiful setting. It's thought to have been built by King Kaleb in AD 518. *Arbatu ensessa* means 'the four beasts' after the four Evangelists, Matthew, Mark, Luke and John.

BILBILA CHIRKOS ቢልቢላ ጨርቆስ

Close to Arbatu Ensessa is **Bilbila Chirkos** (admission Birr50). An interesting three-quarter monolith, it's known particularly for its ancient frescoes. Also attributed to King Kaleb, it's thought to date from AD 523. It's a three-minute walk from the road.

BILBILA GIYORGIS ቢልቢላ ጊዮርጊስ

Lying to the west of Arbatu Ensessa, around 32km from Lalibela, **Bilbila Giyorgis** (admission Birr50) is another attributed to King Kaleb. It resembles Bet Abba Libanos in design.

According to tradition, five swarms of bees took up residence shortly after the church was completed. They still reside here and their sacred honey is said to have curative properties, particularly for psychological disorders and skin problems. The priest will let you taste it. It's 20 to 30 minutes' walk up the hill to the church from the road.

ASHETAN MARYAM አሼታን ማርያም

Set at 3150m, atop a mountain that rises directly above Lalibela, is this **monastery** (admission Birr50). Understandably, there are commanding views in all directions. The local priests believe they're 'closer to heaven and God' here, and it's easy to see why.

The monastery's construction is believed to span Lalibela's and Na'akuto La'ab's reigns; some even claim King Na'akuto La'ab lies buried in the chapel. Church treasures include parchment and some icons.

Although the architecture here compares pretty poorly with Lalibela, it's the stunning mountain scenery you really come for.

The 1½-hour climb (one way) is quite steep. Many travellers take mules, though you'll still need to walk over the rockiest parts.

NA'AKUTO LA 'AB ናቁቶ ላአብ

Lying 7km from Lalibela, just off the airport road, is this **church** (admission Birr50) attributed to King Lalibela's successor. It's simple but attractive (apart from the outer security wall), and built under a natural cave. It was almost certainly the site of a much older shrine.

Empress Zewditu built the ugly inner red-brick building. Some very old stone receptacles collect the precious holy water as it drips from the cave roof.

The church boasts various treasures said to have belonged to its founder, including crosses, crowns, gold-painted drums and an illuminated Bible.

GENETA MARYAM ገነታ ማርያም

Near the source of the Tekeze River, 31km from Lalibela, lies **Geneta Maryam** (admission Birr50). It's thought to have been built around 1270 by Yekuno Amlak, who restored the Solomonic line. With its rectangular shape and 20 massive rectangular pillars that support it, Geneta Maryam resembles Lalibela's Bet Medhane Alem. It's also known for its remarkable 13th-century paintings.

On the western wall, there's a moon-shaped face of Christ; and on the southern side, very grumpy-looking elephants. Geneta Maryam is about four hours by foot from Lalibela, or 1½ hours by vehicle.

MACHINA MARYAM መቺና ማርያም

Two hours' walk from Geneta Maryam and six hours' walk from Lalibela is the remote church of **Machina Maryam** (Emachina Lideta Maryam; admission Birr50), said traditionally to have been constructed by three virgins during the reign of King Gebre Meskel in AD 537.

The church is constructed under an overhanging rock in a natural cave. It rather resembles Yemrehanna Kristos in design and many features are Aksumite, but its beautiful frescoes, some of hunting scenes with one-eyed lions, are the main attraction.

There are many bricked-up tombs in the church. Bodies buried under the rock are said to be preserved forever. The church is little visited, but is worth the long and steep ascent.

DESSIE ደሴ

pop 120,029 / elev 2470m

Unfortunate Dessie appears to have been occupied before the job of building it had been completed. The result is a dusty, noisy, chaotic and ugly strip of half-built, or maybe half-collapsed, buildings. One thing's for sure: this girl wouldn't win any beauty contests. However, you may end up spending a night here because it's a major transport hub for Lalibela, Hayk and Bati.

Information

There are several internet cafes (Birr15 per hour), pharmacies, a good health clinic and banks (change cash and travellers cheques) along the main drag. There are pickpockets aplenty around the bus station – be vigilant.

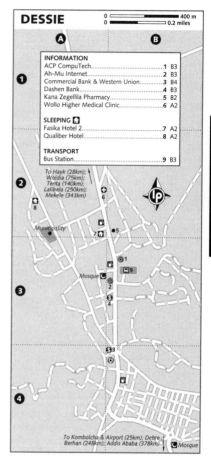

Sleeping

Rooms can be in short supply, especially on weekends, so call ahead.

Fasika Hotel 2 (☎ 0331 112932; d/tw Birr120/150) On a quieter side street the rooms here are kept ship-shape. Other pluses are the hot-water boilers. It's just a shame there is so little water to fill them.

Qualiber Hotel (☎ 0331 111548; d Birr130) It's not saying much but this place has the best rooms in town. What's the finest aspect of these tidy rooms? The fairly reliable water supply. Heck, sometimes it's even warm water.

Getting There & Away

Normal buses leave for Addis Ababa (Birr51, 10 hours, five daily) or you can treat your battered bottom to a posh Selam Bus seat (Birr102, 10 hours, 4am), Lalibela (Birr43, 8½ to 10 hours, one daily), Mekele (Birr54, nine hours, one daily) and Woldia (Birr15, 3½ hours, three daily). Buses and minibuses also run at least every half-hour to Kombolcha (Birr5, 30 minutes).

HAYK ሃይቅ
pop 14,319 / elev 2030m

Lying 28km north of Dessie on a peninsula is the little town of Hayk, known for its monastery and lake.

The **monastery** (admission Birr100) dates from the mid-13th century and was founded by Abba Iyasus Moa. Between the 13th and 15th centuries it was among Ethiopia's most important monasteries. Today it hosts the oldest-known manuscript to record its own date: the book of the four gospels produced for the monastery between 1280 and 1281. It's open to men only, but is really only worth a visit (and forking out that much money) if you have a serious interest in Ethiopian churches.

For most people the lovely lake is a far bigger draw, this is especially so if you've got an eye for the birds. There are a couple of cafes on the lake shore, which make for a good place for a lingering lunch. They also have basic and seriously overpriced rooms in traditional thatch huts for Birr200.

At least 15 minibuses or buses (Birr5, one hour) run daily to the village of Hayk.

KOMBOLCHA ኮንቦልቻ
pop 68,766 / elev 1850m

The dramatic and curvaceous descent from Dessie to Kombolcha outdoes anything the twin towns have to offer. Kombolcha is less of a transportation hub than Dessie, but it's slightly less dirty and noisy, which makes it a more pleasant option to break your journey between Addis Ababa and Lalibela.

The town's 'best' sleeping option, **Tekle Hotel** (☎ 0335 510056; d with/without bathroom Birr150/69) has dark, gloomy and overpriced rooms, though the bathrooms with their stone walls and oversized showers are, probably quite by chance, almost fashionable. There's also a decent restaurant.

The showers at the **Kombolcha Wine Hotel** (☎ 0335 512091; d Birr100) pump forth hot water on a fairly frequent basis and that's about the only positive we can come up with. If quenching tummy rumbles is more of a priority, you'll

be pleased to know that this is by far the finest place in town to eat; however, despite the name, don't expect much wine.

Frequent buses serve Dessie (Birr5, 30 minutes). One bus leaves daily for Addis Ababa (Birr48, 8½ hours).

BATI ባቲ
pop 24,257 / elev 1502m

The little town of Bati, 41km east of Kombolcha, is renowned for its large, colourful **Monday market** (9am-3pm), which attracts up to 10,000 Afar, Oromo and Amharas from all around.

A real meeting of the tribes, Bati, with its Somalian overtones, feels like another world from highland Ethiopia and is a fascinating place to get lost. The market is Ethiopia's largest after Addis Ababa's Merkato, but it certainly eclipses the capital's for interest and exotica. Highlights are the *chat* (p72) and livestock markets, both of which are found on the other side of town from the main market ground. Also keep an eye peeled for the old gallows (dating from the emperor's day).

If you want to get an early start on proceedings, the **Tourist Hotel** (☎ 0335 530548; d with/without bathroom Birr85/70) is the pick of the bunch.

At least one bus and 10 to 15 minibuses leave for, and arrive from, Kombolcha daily (Birr7 to Birr9, 1¼ hours).

DEBRE BERHAN ደብረ ብርሃን
pop 65,214 / elev 2840m

Small, yet somehow sprawling, the town of Debre Berhan sits 130km northeast of Addis Ababa. Despite being the 15th-century capital of Emperor Zara Yaqob and the site of Ahmed Gragn the Left-Handed's slaughter of the imperial army, Debre Berhan is most famous for its woollen blankets and rugs. Check them out at the cooperative near the telecommunications office.

The drive from here north to Debre Sina, which takes you off the **Guassa Plateau** and down the dramatic Mezezo Escarpment, is unforgettable. This plateau offers a number of bracing walking opportunities with breezy views to the plains far below. Hiking here is totally undeveloped and you'll need to be fully self-sufficient. The easiest, and most obvious, place to begin your ramble is from where the plateau drop-off runs just metres from the road, just before the tunnel on the main road that leads to Debre Sina. The are plenty of nervous gelada baboons around here and plenty of considerably less nervous salesmen hawking hats made of baboon fur. Unfortunately these guys refuse to take no for an answer and will follow you for miles over the mountains.

Rooms at the **Akalu Hotel** (☎ 0116 811115; d Birr100) , which are set around a courtyard, are classier than you'd expect. The beds even have fancy bedheads – how exciting.

The first thing you'll notice about the **Eva Hotel** (☎ 0116 813607; r Birr200), a pink palace at the southern end of town, is its lovingly crafted gardens. The love extends to the rooms as well, which are spotless and quiet. The town's best restaurant is also found here.

Numerous buses/minibuses serve Addis Ababa (Birr21, 2½ hours). One bus leaves daily at 6am for Kombolcha (Birr46, seven hours).

ANKOBER አንኮበር
pop 2228 / elev 2465m

The little town of Ankober lies 40km southeast of Debre Berhan. Right up until the late 19th century, when Addis Ababa was founded, it was the capital of the Shoan princes.

Set atop a hill 2km from town are the ruins of Menelik II's old palace. Though little more than a section of wall remains, the walk here is a good one and the area is renowned as a birders' haven. It's the official home of a very rare endemic bird, the Ankober serin. The white-throated seedeater and yellow-throated seedeater are often seen here too.

If you want to stay then the **Ankober Lodge** (☎ 0116 180907; d Birr772) offers positioning, peace and quiet, but not much else.

Two morning buses run between Debre Berhan and Ankober (Birr11, two hours).

NORTHERN ETHIOPIA

Southern Ethiopia

Southern Ethiopia is a canvas ripped in two. Its landscape has been torn apart by the Great Rift Valley, a process that has left a trail of lakes peppering the land like droplets of water on a waxed stone. Some of these, like Lake Chamo, are home to giant crocodiles while others, like Lake Awasa, support thriving communities of fishermen and farmers.

In the southeast the Bale Mountains offer rewarding treks across a plateau amid Afro-alpine plants and rare wildlife. It is here, hunting for giant molerats, that you'll likely encounter the world's rarest canid, the Ethiopian wolf.

Like the land, the tribes of the south, such as the Mursi lip-stretchers and body painting Karo, have also felt the touch of an artist's brush.

For better or worse, the frayed seam that holds our world of smart phones, Facebook friends and reality TV apart from theirs is being picked undone. Across this cultural chasm both sides now stare slack-jawed at the oddity we see in each other. To travel in the Lower Omo Valley fifteen years ago was unheard of. To travel here today is a privilege. Not that it always seems so.

When the incessant demands for money, the monotony of the food and frustratingly slow travel takes its toll, it's all too easy to forget what an extraordinary place you're in. But you won't forget for long. It's just possible that as a small and tentative hand slips into yours and you stroll with a child who speaks a language even your guide doesn't know, the trip down south may suddenly become the best of them all.

HIGHLIGHTS

- Wipe the sweat from your brow as you barter for an inscribed calabash at a tribal market in **Dimeka** (p203), **Key Afar** (p203) or **Turmi** (p199)

- Keep your voice steady as you return the cold, reptilian stare of a resident of Lake Chamo's **crocodile market** (p192)

- Make yourself small so that you don't frighten away a rare Ethiopian wolf in the **Bale Mountains National Park** (p179)

- Shake your booty until your hips hurt with the **Dorze** (p193) of the Guge Mountains

- Marvel at the strength of the men who work the black ooze in the **The House of Salt** (p187)

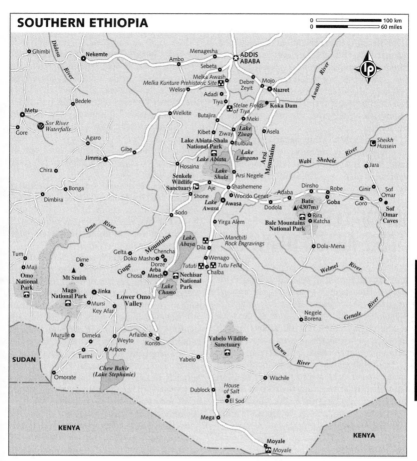

Climate

With elevations varying from 450m in the Lower Omo Valley to 4377m in the Bale Mountains, daytime temperatures in this region range from 10°C to 40°C.

Rain traditionally falls between March and October in the highlands, with July, August and September receiving the most precipitation. April, May and October are the wettest months in the Lower Omo Valley, with sporadic precipitation falling the rest of the year.

Getting There & Away

Ethiopian Airlines (www.flyethiopian.com) connects Addis Ababa and Jimma with Arba Minch.

Overland, the only real options to enter southern Ethiopia are from the north via Addis Ababa and from the south via Kenya at Moyale. Daily buses and minibuses serve both routes. If you have your own vehicle, it's also possible to reach Sodo from Jimma in western Ethiopia. The journey is supposed to take five to six hours in dry season.

Getting Around

Paved roads of variable quality link Addis Ababa with Arba Minch in the southwest and Moyale in the deep south. The remaining roads seem to be in a perpetual state of being resurfaced and range from decent to devastatingly painful.

Daily buses and minibuses cover most routes, with the Lower Omo Valley and remote southeast being the only exceptions. In the past many travellers hopped on the Isuzu trucks that sporadically trundle between villages. Recently the government has regulated against this, and truck drivers caught with foreign passengers are now subject to large fines. The upshot of this is that most drivers will only allow travellers to ride with them for an exorbitant fee. The deeper into the Omo Valley you travel, the more exorbitant the fee.

Most people visiting isolated areas hire 4WDs from tour operators in Addis Ababa (see p270), although a few 4WDs can also be rented in Arba Minch, Jinka and occasionally Konso.

RIFT VALLEY LAKES – ADDIS ABABA TO AWASA

Many travellers motor through this 275km-long corridor without sparing a thought for one of our planet's grandest geographical features – the massive Great Rift Valley. A 4,000km scar that stretches from the Red Sea to Mozambique, the Great Rift Valley is a work in progress and millions of years from now, the rifting process will have split Africa in two.

The most visible manifestation of these subterranean forces is a string of five lakes, all conveniently strung along the road to Awasa. But before reaching them the traveller has two routes to ponder: one via Mojo, the other via Butajira.

South via Mojo

This is the quickest route south and offers more pubic transport, but it's less interesting than travelling via Butajira.

After heading east for 94km, you'll turn south at Mojo. About 20km south from there, you should be able to spot **Koka Dam**. Part of a hydroelectric power station, it supplies most of Addis Ababa with electricity.

Continuing southwards, keep an eye out for the **Oromo tombs** that dot the countryside and the large shadehouses that used to grow flowers for the European market.

South via Butajira

Although public transport is less frequent than that found on the Mojo route, it is still possible to visit the sights outlined below either en route to Butajira or as a two-day return

trip from Addis Ababa. All are within easy walking distance of the road.

Just southwest of Melka Awash village is the **Melka Kunture Prehistoric Site** (admission Birr20; ⊗ 9am-12.30pm & 1.30-5pm), famous for a remarkable prehistoric stone-tool factory discovered in 1963. Extending over 5km on both sides of the Awash River, it encompasses numerous sites dating back 1.7 million years. A series of explanatory panels are posted around the site and a *tukul* (hut) displays some well-captioned finds, including the tools used by the *Homo erectus/Homo sapiens* who once inhabited the area.

The nearest accommodation is in Melka Awash. **Sodo Ber Hotel** (r with shared bathroom Birr20) has small austere rooms with small double beds. The shared bathroom has squat toilets and the shower is nothing more than a pipe sticking out from the wall.

Around 4km south of Melka Kunture, there's a signposted turn-off to Ethiopia's southernmost rock-hewn church, **Adadi Maryam** (admission Birr30). It sits within the village of Adadi, some 12km west of the turn-off. Believed to date from the 12th or 13th century, Adadi Maryam is a semimonolithic church (only three of its four sides are detached from the surrounding strata) and is fairly crude in comparison with its counterparts in Lalibela and Tigray. On Adadi's market days (Thursday and Saturday), public transport runs to and from Melka Awash.

Tiya (admission Birr50, ⊗ 8am-noon & 1-5pm), the most important of several stelae clusters that dot the countryside all the way down to Dila, is found further south, almost 40km from Melka Awash. The site contains around 36 ancient stelae, 32 of which are engraved with enigmatic symbols, notably swords. Almost nothing is known about the monoliths' carvers or their purpose other than they mark mass graves of individuals aged between 18 and 30. The stelae lie 500m from the village of Tiya.

South from Butajira to Sodo

Now that the road has been sealed, an alternative and increasingly popular route is to continue from Butajira directly to **Sodo** via Hosaina. Sodo is a hilly, bustling town at the junction where the Jimma, Arba Minch, Shashemene and Hosaina Roads meet.

There are several hotels in town, of which the **Bekele Mola Hotel** (☎ 0465 512382; camping Birr50, s without bathroom Birr45, s/d with bathroom Birr106/172) is the local favourite. The rooms are nothing special, and you'll need to hold your breath and fortify your courage before entering the shared bathrooms. Look out for the pet dik-dik tiptoeing around the grounds.

Daily buses leave the Sodo station for Arba Minch (Birr17, three hours), Addis Ababa (Birr50, 7½ hours) and Awasa (Birr22, 4½ hours). There are no scheduled services to Jimma.

LAKE ZIWAY ዝዋይ ሐይቅ

Surrounded by blue volcanic hills and covering a massive 425 sq km, Lake Ziway is the largest of the northern group of Rift Valley lakes.

It's an attractive enough place, but it's best known for its birdlife. White pelicans, hammer cops, sacred ibises, African fishing eagles, cormorants, kingfishers and a bird that only a mother could love – the marabou stork – are all easily seen here. One of the best spots to see them is from the earthen 'jetty' in the town of Ziway; you'll find it about 1.5km due east of the Bekele Mola Hotel. The birds are particularly numerous here in the early morning and evening, when they gather to pick at the fishermen's castoffs.

You can pay a local fisherman to take you to the **hippo pods** by motorboat (15 minutes) or rowboat (35 minutes) from the jetty. There is no set price and some hefty negotiation is usually called for. Something like Birr150 for a rowboat and Birr300 for a motorboat would be fair. A boat can take four people.

The lake is also home to five little volcanic islands, of which three once boasted medieval churches. Tullu Gudo, 14km from Ziway and the largest island, is still home to three monasteries, of which **Debre Tsion** is the most famous. According to tradition, it once housed the Ark of the Covenant when priests, fleeing the destruction of the city of Aksum at the hands of Queen Gudit in the 9th century, brought it here. The original church now lies in ruins and a new one has been built. Interestingly, the oldest written documents about Aksum were discovered here.

Currently, rather slow motorboats can be hired from private operators in Ziway. Head for the jetty and inquire there. Starting prices were an absurd Birr800 per person for the return trip to Tullu Gudo. It takes between two and three hours one way. If you're lucky you may be able to hop on an early-morning

boat (around 6am, local price Birr20) that takes locals to the island.

A trip to the nearer islands of Galila and Bird Island cost around Birr300 per boat for both.

Information

There's an internet cafe and Commercial Bank on the Addis–Shashemene Rd in Ziway. The bank exchanges only cash (US dollars and euros).

Sleeping & Eating

Camping is permitted on Ziway's islands. The town of Ziway is a pleasant, laid-back little place, with good, reasonably priced hotels, restaurants and cafes scattered along the Addis–Shashemene road.

Brothers Hotel (☎ 0464 412609; r without bathroom Birr20, d Birr35-45, tw Birr75) Just south of the bus stand, this option is more noteworthy for its local restaurant (mains Birr12 to Birr20). The basic rooms here are good value but ask to see a few first. They get progressively larger and cleaner the more you spend; some even have satellite TV and hot water.

Ziway Tourist Hotel (☎ 0464 413993; r Birr60) Towards the southern end of town. It's worth applying the sniff test if you want to avoid a room that doesn't smell of mildew. The garden restaurant (mains Birr23) has less ambience than its counterpart at the Bekele Mola, but it serves a wider variety of dishes and caters well to Western tastes.

Bekele Mola Hotel (☎ 0464 412077; s/d/tw Birr75/90/90) Behind the Shell station, Bekele Mola's aged but clean rooms surround a pleasant and peaceful courtyard that's full to the brim with birds. The bathrooms are dog-eared and some mattresses are on their last legs, so poke a few before choosing. The shady terrace restaurant (mains Birr35) draws lunchtime crowds on their way to, or back from, the south.

Getting There & Around

Buses leave regularly for Shashemene (Birr15, two hours), Butajira (Birr11, 1½ to two hours) and Addis Ababa (Birr23, three hours). Numerous minibuses also serve Addis Ababa (Birr25). For Debre Zeyit or Nazret, take a minibus to Mojo first (Birr16, 1½ hours).

For Lake Langano, take the Shashemene bus or a minibus to Arsi Negele (Birr10, 45 to 50 minutes); ask to be dropped at the junction for the hotel of your choice.

SOUTHERN ETHIOPIA

Bikes can be hired near the Tele Centre and Brothers Hotel for Birr6 per hour. *Garis* (horse-drawn carts) across town cost Birr1 to Birr2.

LAKE LANGANO ላንጋኖ ሐይቅ

Lake Langano resembles a giant puddle of milky English tea set against the blue curtain of the 4000m Arsi Mountains. The water may be brown and unappealing, but it's one of the few Ethiopian lakes to be declared bilharzia-free and perfectly safe to swim in.

Langano is the obvious base from which to explore Lake Abiata-Shala National Park. Our only advice: avoid the weekends when every man and his ghetto blaster make the 180km trip from Addis Ababa. Weekday rates are also cheaper.

Sleeping & Eating

Accommodation and dining options around Lake Langano are limited to several resorts, two of which are southern Ethiopia's premier ecolodges. The following rates are for week-days (Sunday through Thursday). Add about 50% for weekends.

Karkaro Cottages (Map p173; ☎ 0461 190543; willy warthog@msm.com; camping Birr50) The cottages here may be rented out long term, but you can still pick an acacia tree and camp under the stars if you bring a tent.

Bekele Mola Hotel (Map p173; ☎ 0461191250; camping incl tent Birr100, s/d/q Birr150/312/546) Although the Bekele Mola occupies a pleasant slice of the lake's southwestern shore, the rooms here fall far short of what their price tags warrant. When we visited, the beds were creaky and the sheets worn from years of use. A quick glance through the guest book gave us the impression that most guests found cause for complaint. Many comments were directed at the expensive meals (mains Birr50), which were meant to include a salad bar, but invariably did not.

Wabe Shebele Hotel (Map p173; ☎ 0115 517187; camping with/without own tent Birr63/80 per person, d/tw/q Birr296/296/516) The site is less attractively de-signed and situated than the Bekele Mola, but it's much more peaceful, particularly dur-ing weekends. The cottages here are closely packed and little more than wooden boxes with tin roofs, a table and a bed. Meals cost between Birr20 and Birr40.

Sabana Lodge (Map p173; ☎ 0461 191180; www.sabana langano.com; s/d/tw incl breakfast Birr575/690/690, 🖥) Occupying an elevated position with impres-sive views over the lake, the upmarket Sabana sets the standard for Langano hotels. The modern bathrooms, refined colour scheme, woven ceilings, large comfy beds, landscaped gardens and pavilion-like restaurant make these 25 cottages an obvious choice for those who can afford it.

Bishangari Lodge (☎ 0115 517533, 0911 201317; www.bishangari.com; s/tw without bathroom US$30/54, s/tw with bathroom US$57/101) Hyped as Ethiopia's first ecolodge when it opened in 1997, Bishangari has nine beautiful *godjos* (bungalows) nestled privately along the lake's southeastern shore. Each is decorated with woven ceilings, local artwork and natural woods. There are also 12 traditional and far more down-to-earth *tukuls* (mud huts) with shared facilities. The Tree Bar (mains Birr80) is particularly evocative and is wrapped around a giant fig tree that attracts troops of monkeys. A shuttle runs between the lodge and the Hilton (where their office is located) in Addis Ababa every week-end (Birr1000 shared among the passengers). Room price includes breakfast.

Wenney Eco-Lodge (☎ 0116 185878, 0911 203614; www.wenneyecolodge.com; high season s/tw US$70/90) Wenney offers the same serene surrounds as Bishangari and, like its neighbour, offers guided nature walks, hippo spotting, biking and horse riding. The accommodation is marginally less refined than Bishangari, but the open-air restaurant (three-course meal, Birr95) is beautifully decorated with tradi-tional art and the resident guide is an excep-tional birder. Cars can be rented to visit the national park for Birr950 for four hours.

Getting There & Away

To get to/from Lake Langano, take any bus plying the Addis Ababa–Shashemene Rd, and ask to be dropped off/picked up (just signal) at the turn-off to your hotel.

Wenney and Bishangari Lodges are only 20km off the main drag, but it takes one hour for a 4WD to negotiate the rutted and corru-gated road. Without your own vehicle you will need to arrange transport with the lodges.

LAKE ABIATA-SHALA NATIONAL PARK
አባያታ ሻላ ሐይቅ
ብሔራዊ ፓርክ

West of Lake Langano lie the twin lakes of Abiata and Shala, which form part of the 887-sq-km **Lake Abiata-Shala National Park** (child/adult ad-mission per 48hr Birr25/50, 5-seat vehicle Birr10). Identical

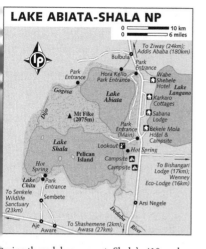

LAKE ABIATA-SHALA NP

twins these lakes are not. Shala's 410-sq-km surface sits within a collapsed volcanic caldera and depths exceed 260m in some areas, while Abiata's highly alkaline waters rest in a shallow pan no more than 14m in depth.

Traditionally, fish thriving in Abiata's waters provided the food for birds that bred in safety on volcanic islands dotting Shala's surface. Pelican Island was one of only seven nesting sites in all of Africa for the great white pelican. We say 'was' because the last decade has seen Lake Abiata suffer greatly at the hands of humans. Illegal settlers have turned the thick woodland into charcoal, and commercial farms and a soda-ash factory have caused pollution and a substantial drop in the water level. The lake's increased salinity has killed the fish population, resulting in the pelicans and other birds deserting their nesting grounds. But flamingos have been lured here by the algae.

There are some nice **lookouts** within walking distance of the main gate, though you'll need to take a guide/scout for directions/security (Birr100 per day). On the northeast shore of Shala, there's a sulphurous **hot spring**, which is often crowded with locals bathing and cooking maize in the thermal waters. At Shala's southwestern shore there's a second hot spring and a stunning, though pint-sized, crater lake. Looking 80m down from the rim to **Lake Chitu** and spotting its semiresident flamingos is a sight worth the effort. The south shore is accessed via Aware or Aje. Note that admission can only be paid at the Hora Kello and main park entrances.

Sleeping & Eating

If the nearby Langano lodges will break the bank, head south to Arsi Negele.

Tsaday Hotel (☎ 0916 824334; Arsi Negele; d/tw Birr25/30) Arsi Negele's best option has cleanish (and we mean that in the broadest sense of the word) rooms with cement floors and passable bathrooms (squat toilets and cold showers). There's no English sign, so look for the battered green gates 50m south of the Commercial Bank.

National Park camping (adult per 48hr Birr20) Camping is permitted anywhere in the park, but two main sites are suggested by officials. Don't leave anything unattended and bring a scout for security.

Getting There & Around

The main park entrance is signposted on the highway. Any bus doing the Addis Ababa–Shashemene run can drop you off.

From the main park entrance to the hot springs is about 8km. If you're driving, road conditions usually make a 4WD essential.

SHASHEMENE ሻሸመኔ
pop 93,200 / elev 1700m

Shashemene is a grubby and raucous town that sits at southern Ethiopia's most important crossroads. It has little to offer besides transportation links, and most travellers prefer to stop in nearby Awasa or Wondo Genet. Shashemene does have one trick up its sleeve, however – it is the unofficial Rastafari capital of Africa.

When Ras Tafari was crowned Emperor Haile Selassie in 1930, he gained subjects far beyond the confines of his own kingdom. In Jamaica, Marcus Garvey's 'return to Africa' movement saw the emperor's coronation as fulfilment of the ancient biblical prophesy that 'Kings will come out of Africa'. Identifying themselves passionately with Ethiopia's monarch, as well as with Ethiopia's status as an independent African state, Garvey's followers created a new religion. In it, the emperor was accorded divinity – the Messiah of African Redemption – and the new faith given his pre-coronation name.

What did the Emperor think of all this? Well, it was said that he was a bit embarrassed by it all. That is until 1963, when he overcame his bashfulness and granted the Rastafarians land in Shashemene. Today the **Rastafarian community** (known locally as

SOUTHERN ETHIOPIA

Jamaica) straddles the main road just north of town. It is readily distinguished by its tri-coloured buildings, dread-locked inhabitants and the beautifully rounded vowels of Caribbean English.

A shared *bajaj* costs Birr2 from town to the now defunct Black Lion Museum. The Rasta boys here are the town's unofficial and, at times, unwelcome guides. They also sell *ganja* (marijuana), which is held sacrosanct in their religion but illegal in Ethiopia.

Five hundred metres down the dirt road opposite the Black Lion is the **Banana Leaf Gallery** (admission Birr15; ☉ hours vary) that houses a small collection of Ethiopian medals and pictures made from dried banana leaves.

Information

There's a post office, Commercial Bank, two options for internet access, BTA Internet Café and Mana Kompiitera Saayibarii (per minute, Birr0.25), and numerous local Ethiopian eateries stretched along the main drag. A new asphalt bypass runs just east of the city centre allowing north/south traffic uninterrupted motoring.

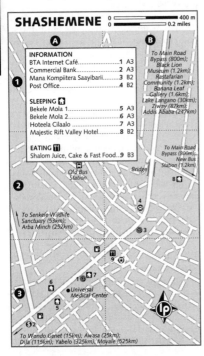

SHASHEMENE　　0 ━━━━ 400 m
　　　　　　　　　　0 ━━━━ 0.2 miles

INFORMATION
BTA Internet Café....................1 A3
Commercial Bank.....................2 A3
Mana Kompiitera Saayibarii........3 B2
Post Office..............................4 B2

SLEEPING 🏠
Bekele Mola 1.........................5 A3
Bekele Mola 2.........................6 A3
Hoteela Cilaalo.......................7 A3
Majestic Rift Valley Hotel..........8 B2

EATING 🍴
Shalom Juice, Cake & Fast Food..9 B3

To Senkele Wildlife
Sanctuary (53km);
Arba Minch (252km)

Old Bus Station

Universal Medical Center

To Main Road Bypass (800m);
Black Lion Museum (1.2km);
Rastafarian Community (1.2km);
Banana Leaf Gallery (1.6km);
Lake Langano (30km);
Ziway (87km);
Addis Ababa (247km)

To Main Road Bypass (800m);
New Bus Station (1.2km)

Bridge

To Wondo Genet (15km); Awasa (25km);
Dila (115km); Yabelo (325km); Moyale (525km)

Sleeping & Eating

Hoteela Cilaalo (☎ 0461 102037; d without bathroom Birr25) The best of the bottom feeders that dot the main street with basic rooms. The bar can get noisy at times.

Bekele Mola 2 (☎ 0461 103348; r Birr65) Although it's less charming than its sister across the street, this modern cement block of a hotel still has clean, if weathered, rooms.

Bekele Mola 1 (☎ 0461 103344; r Birr90) The Bekele Mola 1 may lack atmosphere but the 36 rooms that surround the gravel courtyard are the best deal in town. The bathrooms are well scrubbed with hot water and the bed sheets crisp and white. The restaurant (mains Birr30) is locally regarded as having top-notch Western food.

Majestic Rift Valley Hotel (☎ 0461 105710; maj rifva@ethionet.et; s Birr110, d Birr132-235, tw Birr 242-330; 🖳) Besides the recent addition of 'majestic' to the moniker, little has changed here since the 1970s. The pink 'palace' out back has the best rooms, with balconies, TVs and semi-reliable bathrooms. *Faranji* (foreigners) are charged significantly more than locals, even for the smaller, single rooms in the old building. A multi-level garden with a disused fountain provides a nice spot to relax in, and the friendly staff prepare good local and international fare (mains Birr20 to Birr30).

Shalom Juice, Cake & Fast Food (cake Birr4) Look for the carts piled high with colourful fruit out front and the happy, juice-slurping crowd inside.

Getting There & Away

Shashemene is the principal transport hub of the south and there are two bus stations in the town. The 'new station' is for long-distance transport and is located on the new bypass, northeast of the city centre. Buses you can catch from here include Addis Ababa (Birr33, five hours, four daily), Arba Minch (Birr45, six hours, one daily), Goba (Birr40, six to seven hours, two daily and Moyale (Birr63, 1½ days, one daily) stopping overnight at Yabelo (Birr45, 12 hours).

The 'old bus station' is used by mini buses and serves closer destinations, like Dila (Birr17 to Birr21, three hours), Wond Washa (Birr6, 40 minutes), Ziway (Birr16, two hours) and Awasa (Birr6, 30 minutes, every 15 minutes).

A LOCAL RASTAFARIAN

I first meet Rastafarian Ras Hailu Tefari (Bandi) outside his small gallery on the outskirts of Shashemene where he sells his unique banana leaf 'paintings'. Originally a resident of St Vincent in the Caribbean, he returned to the 'homeland of his heart' in the early 1980s. I asked what prompted him to leave his island paradise for a country that was, at that time, synonymous with famine and starvation.

He told me that life on St Vincent was 'like playing football with no goal to kick to'. Passed over for promotion as a governmental draughtsperson because of a lack of formal training, Ras turned to art. When he heard of the land given by Haile Selassie to the black peoples of the world, he knew that 'only good could follow good'.

Not that life in Ethiopia was initially any easier. 'I had to think how to survive and depend on my skills. I had to learn Amharic. Eventually I got a job as a cartoonist at the *Monitor* [newspaper], which I still have today. I also brought medals and books to sell over.'

Initially many Rastafarians were seen as oddities by the larger communities and accused of spreading drugs and crime. Ras explains how it was for him. 'At first there was some tension. They [Orthodox Ethiopians] were isolated for 1000 years so don't really hug up to anyone and tested us to see if we were lions to live among them. Now they accept us and see we wear the true colours.'

WONDO GENET ወንዶ ገነት

pop 5800 / elev 1723m

Found 15km southeast of Shashemene and surrounded by dense forest, birdsong, a variety of larger wildlife and – in season – fruit and honey, the mountain resort village of Wondo Genet is truly a breath of fresh air.

Although its hot spring-fed pools receive the most accolades from Ethiopians due to their therapeutic powers, we have to say that the surroundings are the true attraction here. A short but interesting walk is to the source of the springs, which is about 10 minutes from the resort hotel. There you'll find cowherds cooking their lunch in the springs: 17 minutes for potatoes, 35 minutes for maize.

The cement **hot springs pools** (admission Birr10.50; 6am-9pm), although soothing to swim in and surrounded by gardens, have more the feel of a water treatment plant than a resort. Local custom is to de-dust yourself under the rudimentary 'showers' before taking a plunge in the pools.

Sleeping & Eating

Abyssinia Hotel (☎ 0461 140203, d Birr60-100, tw Birr120) This hotel, 3km down the hill in Wondo Washa, is far better value than the Wabe Shebele. The cheap doubles in the old block are clean enough, but for a few Birr more you'll get a tile-floored room in the spotless new block and can avail yourself of the hot-water showers. Wondo Washa has a fistful of local eateries serving injera-based dishes.

Wondo Genet Wabe Shebele Hotel (☎ 0461 190705, d/tw incl breakfast Birr261/352) Set amid citrus orchards, flowering gardens and playful colobus and vervet monkeys, this resort sits on a natural balcony overlooking the Rift Valley. With high prices, 1980s decor and run-down bathrooms, you're obviously paying for the location. Guests have free use of the hot springs pools and can eat at the rather incongruous hexagonal restaurant (mains Birr25 to Birr35).

Delicious seasonal fruit can be bought in the area, including papaya, avocado, banana and mango. Try a local favourite: the *kazmir*.

Getting There & Away

From Shashemene, buses and minibuses run regularly (until 5pm) to and from the village of Wondo Washa (Birr6, 40 minutes), which is 3km from the springs. From there, you can walk or take a *gari* (Birr5 per person).

SENKELE WILDLIFE SANCTUARY ሰንከሌ የዱር አራዊት ፓርክ

Originally established to protect the endemic Swayne's hartebeest, the open acacia woodlands of the **Senkele Wildlife Sanctuary** (admission Birr100) also hosts Bohor reedbucks, greater kudus, warthogs, common jackals and oribi antelopes. The globally threatened *Aquila clanga* (greater spotted eagle) is one of 191 bird species documented.

SOUTHERN ETHIOPIA

Thanks to the large numbers of livestock and an influx of illegal settlers, the population of Swayne's hartebeest has been whittled away to a few hundred. Nevertheless this is still the most easily spotted species in this 36-sq-km park.

There's a 65km track around the park, but it's usually only driveable between October and March. From the Borana Hill, around 6km east of the park office, there are good panoramic views. It's also possible to explore on foot.

Sleeping & Eating

As camping is not permitted within the park, the town of Aje provides the closest options.

Zed Hotel (s with shared bathroom Birr10) The best thing we can say about this Aje option is that the sheets are clean. The dimly lit rooms aren't tidy and the shared bathrooms are pretty grim. Cold showers come in buckets. It's not signed, but it's across from the communications tower. You can eat in its restaurant.

Getting There & Away

The park turn-off lies 5km west of Aje. From there, it's at least 10km to the park headquarters. Around 20 minibuses run between Shashemene and Aje daily (Birr5, 30 minutes). In Aje, a contract minibus to the park should cost Birr400 to Birr600 return, including two hours' waiting time.

AWASA አዋሳ

pop 125,315 / elev 1708m

Perfectly poised at Lake Awasa's edge, the capital of the Southern Nations, Nationalities and Peoples' region is both large and attractive. While there are no major sights, the lake and its surrounds offer a relaxing respite from the rigours of travel and makes for a more pleasurable stop than Shashemene, 25km to the north.

Information

The town centre has a telecommunications building, post office and other major services.

Commercial Bank (◷ 8-11am & 1-4pm Mon-Fri, 8-11.30am Sat) Changes travellers cheques, US dollars and euros.

Kibru Medical Center (☎ 0462 210950; ◷ 24hr) Awasa's best medical facility. Includes a pharmacy, clinic and diagnostic laboratory.

M-Link Internet Center (per hr Birr15) Steady connections and CD- and DVD-burning capabilities.

Sights & Activities

The waters of **Lake Awasa**, teeming with tilapia, catfish and barbus, attract good birdlife. Kingfishers, herons, storks, crakes, darters and plovers are among the species commonly seen on the water's edge, while weavers, hornbills and the endemic black-winged lovebird are found in the fig forest and scrub surroundings.

The easiest way to take in the lake and its wildlife is to stroll the footpath at the edge of the lake towards the **fish market** (admission Birr10; ◷ 7am-10am) on the shores of Crow Valley. Wooden boats line the shore, children untangle nets, and massive marabou storks watch with curiosity from nearby treetops. The fishermen are amazingly deft at gutting, scaling, skinning and flicking the eyes out of their catches with their little fingers. One boy's technique also involved ripping the fish's skin off with his teeth!

From the fish market it is also possible to hike up the steep and stubby **Tabour Hill**. Your legs will have long recovered before you forget the view.

To gain a pelican's perspective of Awasa's shimmering waters, clamber into one of the rowboats tied to the pier at the base of the main drag. You may have to haggle hard, but an excursion to **Tikur Wuha** (Black Water) to see the hippos and birds should cost around Birr250 in a motorboat (maximum of five people, one hour return) or Birr200 in a rowboat (three hours' return).

Sleeping

Beshu Hotel (☎ 0462 206957; d with shared bathroom Birr40, d Birr70-80) The rooms here are small and functional. A nice touch is the traditional Sidama hut in the courtyard. Beshu is 100m west of the bus station.

Gebrekiristos Hotel (☎ 046 202780; s/d/tw Birr75/115/115) This oldie-but-goodie is decent value, but it's wise to check a few rooms first as bed size, room size and room amenities (like TVs, fridges and mosquito nets) vary widely.

Atnet Pension (☎ 0462 201686; d Birr100-125, tw Birr225) This would be the pick of the midrange bunch – new rooms, central location, large beds, clean bathrooms, satellite TVs – if i

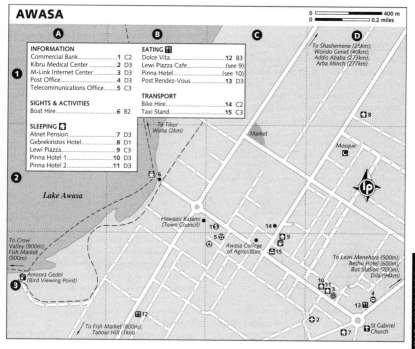

AWASA

INFORMATION	**EATING**
Commercial Bank..............1 C2	Dolce Vita...................12 B3
Kibru Medical Center 2 D3	Lewi Piazza Cafe.............(see 9)
M-Link Internet Center 3 D3	Pinna Hotel..................(see 10)
Post Office.....................4 D3	Post Rendez-Vous 13 D3
Telecommunications Office....5 C3	
	TRANSPORT
SIGHTS & ACTIVITIES	Bike Hire.....................14 C2
Boat Hire.......................6 B2	Taxi Stand....................15 C3
SLEEPING	
Atnet Pension..................7 D3	
Gebrekiristos Hotel............8 D1	
Lewi Piazza.....................9 C3	
Pinna Hotel 1..................10 D3	
Pinna Hotel 2..................11 D3	

To Shashemene (25km);
Wondo Genet (40km);
Addis Ababa (273km);
Arba Minch (277km)

Lake Awasa

To Tikur
Wuha (2km)

Market

Mosque

Hawaasi Katami
(Town Council)

Awasa College
of Agriculture

To Crow
Valley (800m;)
Fish Market
(800m)

Amoora Gedel
(Bird Viewing Point)

To Lewi Menehara (500m);
Beshu Hotel (600m);
Bus Station (700m);
Dila (94km)

To Fish Market (800m;
Tabour Hill (1km)

St Gabriel
Church

weren't for the church next door that occasionally broadcasts prayers at volumes seldom found outside airports. Some mosquito nets would be nice too.

Pinna Hotel 2 (☎ 0462 210336; fax 0462 202343; d Birr290-390, tw/ste 450/990; 🖳) Next door to its older sister (Pinna 1), this place is younger, smarter and brasher. Most rooms have wireless internet and nifty showers that convert into steam baths – just what you need in the Ethiopian heat.

Lewi Piazza (☎ 0462 201654; www.lewihotel.com; incl breakfast Birr300-400, ste incl breakfast Birr1450; 🖳) Opened in 2008, the spotlessly clean rooms here are fairly swish by Ethiopian standards with all the trappings (wireless internet, modern bathrooms, satellite TVs and safes) of a Western chain hotel.

Other decent options include:

Lewi Menehara (☎ 0462 206310; www.lewihotel.com; r Birr150-250;) Rooms range from utterly spartan to incredibly comfy. It's 200m west of the bus station.

Pinna Hotel 1 (☎ 0462 210336; fax 0462 202343; d Birr230-270, ste 320) The showers are cold but rooms include such gadgetry as a satellite TV, a verandah and telephone.

Eating

Post Rendez-Vous (mains Birr20-35) An eclectic outdoor restaurant and popular local hangout, this place is known for its tasty pizza – although these are only available after 6pm when the wood oven is roaring. Insist on seeing the English menu. Some waiters deny having one, preferring to rattle off inflated prices instead.

Pinna Hotel (mains Birr25-45) If the cakes in the ground-floor pastry shop don't sidetrack you, head upstairs to Awasa's most *faranji*-friendly menu. Specialities include ravioli with spinach, roast chicken and veal cordon bleu.

Lewi Piazza Cafe (mains Birr28-50) Although there is great food at both hotel branches of the Lewi chain, the Piazza Cafe is *the* place to bring a date. Coy couples come here to giggle under the patio umbrellas and to share ice-cream sundaes and plates of fries. Those not looking to kiss can opt for the spiced lamb curry or stir-fried chicken with garlic.

our pick **Dolce Vita** (mains Birr30-42) Set amid jacaranda trees this small, family-run restaurant is a bite-sized slice of Italy. Mouth-watering ingredients such as black olives, fresh basil and vine-ripened tomatoes make for some lip-smacking pasta and antipasto dishes.

Getting There & Around

The bus station lies about 1km east from the town centre. Since most southbound services will drive through town before reaching the station, simply ask to hop off in town. Otherwise, shared *bajaj* (short hops cost between Birr1 and Birr3) and taxis are available at the station.

Buses run to Addis Ababa (Birr35, 5½ hours, five daily), Arba Minch (Birr34, 6½ hours, one daily) and Wondo Genet (Birr10, one hour, one daily). Regular minibuses run to Shashemene (Birr6, 30 minutes) and Dila (Birr12, 2½ hours). For Moyale, go to Shashemene or Dila and get a bus from there.

THE SOUTHEAST & BALE MOUNTAINS

SOUTHERN ETHIOPIA

The road that runs east from Shashemene is one of the country's worst. If you sit above the bus's back axle, you'll be bounced off your seat. The locals say the road has been improved, although it is difficult to see how; it's little more than a series of interconnected potholes. It's worth it though. This unique region offers some great trekking amid rare wildlife, a surreally beautiful cave system and a fertile countryside of domed haystacks, humpbacked cattle and fences of living cacti.

DODOLA – HORSE TREKS IN THE BALE MOUNTAINS

Resting between Shashemene and the Bale Mountains National Park, the diminutive town of Dodola has become a base for some unique horse treks. Initially set up by the German aid organisation GTZ, the (newly renamed) Dodola Eco-tourism Tour Guide Association is now self-sufficient and works to conserve the environment by offering local people an alternative income to felling the local forests.

Due to the high altitudes and steep gradients, the association prefers people to trek on horseback but this isn't mandatory, and those with large lungs and legs like llamas can trek on foot.

Planning

The **Dodola Eco-tourism Tour Guide Association** (☎ 0226 660700; www.baletrek.com; dodola_tour@ethionet.et; ☷ 8.30am-5.30pm) is located 50m west of the Bale Mountain Motel, down a dirt road. It's unsignposted but the office is behind the first gate on the right. They organise horses (Birr40 per day), horse handlers (one per two horses, Birr40 per day) and the mandatory guide (Birr120 per day).

Thanks to five simple but self-contained lodges built along the route, it's perfect for those without tents and camping gear. It is, however, best to bring your own sleeping bag – those found within the huts constitute their own ecological niche.

Limited foodstuffs (pasta, rice, lentils, biscuits, cheese, tomato paste etc) can be purchased in Dodola and goats can be bought en route. Stoves, cooking utensils, beer and soft drinks are all found within the lodges. Lodge keepers can provide local meals, but these are an acquired taste – bring supplies! Water is also available but requires treatment before drinking.

Trekking

Treks (trekking fee Birr25 per person) typically start from Dodola and follow a metal road to Changiti (11km, 2½ hours). There is no lodge here, so if you don't wish to stay in one of the permanent tents, it's best to make an early start and continue up the Tikiku Lensho River to the lodge at Wahoro (7km, 2½ hours to 3½ hours). From here it's possible to work your way eastward, spending consecutive nights in a series of 'lodges' (Angafu, Adele, Moldicho and Duro). No hut is more than a five-hour horseback ride from the other, so there is plenty of time to make side trips to waterfalls and the summits of Tute (3705m) and Tullu Hangatu (3546m).

From the last lodge at Duro it takes three hours on horse to descend the 11km to Bucha Raja (2680m), from where you can continue a further 9km (two hours) to the town of Adaba.

To complete the full circuit takes seven days, but since every lodge is within four to five hours of a trailhead, treks of even three days can be catered for. There are plans to develop a trek that will link up to the trails in Bale Mountains National Park further east.

Please review the Safety Guidelines for Trekking (p243) and Responsible Trekking (p244) boxed texts before embarking.

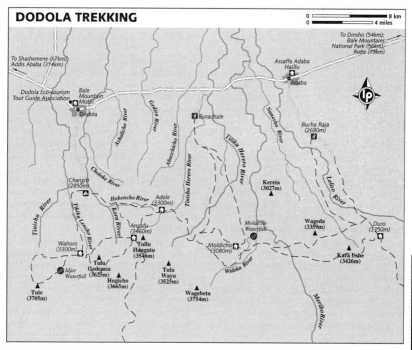

DODOLA TREKKING

Sleeping & Eating

DODOLA

Bale Mountain Motel (☎ 0226 660016; arayasa@ethionet .et; camping Birr30 per person; d without bathroom Birr30, d with bathroom Birr50-60, tw Birr60) Although bare and small, the rooms here are clean and reasonably priced. Check for power before paying extra for the rooms with hot water. Set in a quiet garden, the homely little restaurant can provide meals (Birr18 to Birr24) for those who order in advance.

ADABA

Assaffa Adaba Haillu (☎ 0226 630002; r without bathroom Birr70, r with bathroom Birr120) Imagine concrete block rooms painted blue on the inside, and you'll have a fair idea of what's on offer. Their new four-storey hotel next door was almost finished when we passed. It's just off the main road from where the buses stop for lunch. Bargain hard here as locals pay half the price quoted above.

ON THE MOUNTAINS

Each of the **lodges** (camping Birr30; s without bathroom Birr50) at Wahoro, Angafu, Adele, Moldicho and Duro has eight beds, complete with mattresses and some bedding. The kitchen can be used by campers for a Birr5 fee. Guests and campers must pay Birr5 for a hot shower.

The campsite at Changiti is a little more basic with only **tents** (Birr50 per person) under a permanent shelter.

Getting There & Around

From Dodola, two early-morning buses serve Shashemene (Birr15, three to four hours) along a horrendous section of road. For Dinsho, take the Robe bus (Birr30, 3½ to four hours, four buses daily) and ask to be dropped off. Numerous Isuzu trucks run between Dodola and Adaba (Birr7, 40 minutes).

BALE MOUNTAINS NATIONAL PARK
የባሌ ተራሮች ብሔራዊ ፓርክ

More than any other park in Ethiopia, the Bale Mountains National Park is known for its wildlife. Over 60 mammal species and 260 bird species have been recorded here.

As you approach the park from Dodola, ridges to the east are punctuated with fortress-like escarpments; those to the north are

SOUTHERN ETHIOPIA

gentler, their rounded rock pinnacles dotting the ridges like worn teeth protruding from an old man's gums. Within the park, rivers cut deep gorges; alpine lakes feed streams, and water accepts gravity's fate at several waterfalls. In the lower hills, Highlanders canter along century-old paths on their horses with rich caparisons, and the noise of shepherds cracking their whips echoes around the valley.

Geography & Geology

The park stretches over 2400 sq km and ranges in altitude from 1500m to 4377m.

The Harenna Escarpment splits the park in two, running fracture-like from east to west. To the northeast of the escarpment lies the high-altitude plateau known as the Sanetti Plateau (4000m). The plateau is broken into bits by a series of volcanic plugs and small peaks, including Tullu Deemtu, which at 4377m is the highest point in southern Ethiopia.

To the south, the land gradually falls away from the plateau, and a thick heather belt gives way to heavily forested areas known collectively as the Harenna Forest.

Wildlife

PLANTS

The park can be divided into three main zones. The northern area of the park, around the park headquarters at Dinsho, consists of grassy, riverine plains and bushland of mainly sagebrush and St John's wort. From 2500m to 3300m, woodland of mainly *Hagenia abyssinica* and *Juniperus procera* is found. The abundant wildflowers in the area include geranium, lobelia and alchemilla. Higher up, montane grassland gives way to heather.

The second zone, the Sanetti Plateau, is home to typical Afro-alpine plants, some of which have adapted to the extreme conditions by either remaining very small or becoming very large. The best known is the curious-looking giant lobelia (*Lobelia rhynchopetalum*), which can reach 5m in height. The silver *Helichrysum* or 'everlasting' flowers are the dominant wildflowers. Keep an eye out for the indigenous Abyssinian rose, with its lovely subtle scent.

The third habitat, the moist, tropical Harenna Forest, is home to tree species such as *Hagenia*, *Celtis* and *Podocarpus*.

ANIMALS

The Bale Mountains are a hotspot for endemic wildlife, particularly the Ethiopian wolf and the mountain nyala.

The sighting of an Ethiopian wolf is a highlight of a trip to the Bale Mountains, and is almost guaranteed on the Sanetti Plateau. But there are plenty of other no-less-remarkable endemics to be seen, including Menelik's bushbuck, the giant molerat, grey duikers, Bohor reedbucks, warthogs and the only recently described, bamboo-eating Bale monkey. Serval cats and Anubis baboons are also occasionally seen.

In the Harenna Forest, giant forest hogs, bushpigs, warthogs, colobus monkeys and spotted hyena are found, as well as leopards, lions and African hunting dogs. The last three are rarely seen.

The area around the park headquarters is, ironically, the one place in which many of the larger mammals are easily seen. The animals are less shy here, and the early morning and late afternoon provide great photographic opportunities.

The Bale Mountains are also famous for the incredible number of endemic birds present – there were 16 at the last count. On the plateau, sightings of endemics (the bluewinged goose, wattled ibis, thick-billed raven, Abyssinian longclaw, black-headed siskin, spot-breasted plover and Rouget's rail) are almost guaranteed. The birdlife in the juniper forests around the park headquarters is outstanding too; try to spot the elusive Abyssinian catbirds and yellow-fronted parrots. See p76 for more info on Ethiopia's endemic birdlife.

Planning

All treks begin and end at **park headquarters** (☎ 0221 190758; admission Birr50, vehicles Birr15; 🕑 8.30am-12.30pm & 1.30-5.30pm Mon-Fri, 8am-12.30pm Sat), which sits 2.5km from the village of Dinsho and 160km east of Shashemene. All fees are good for 48 hours and include entry to the small **museum** (🕑 8.30am-6.30pm).

New maps were in the pipeline and should be available from the park headquarters by the time you read this. Bring all your own camping gear or hire it in Addis Ababa – there are slim pickings in Dinsho, although some guides are able to organise camping stoves (Birr35 per day) and tents (Birr50 per day) for their clients.

SOUTHERN ETHIOPIA

THE ETHIOPIAN WOLF

The Ethiopian wolf *(Canis simensis)* is the rarest canid (dog-family member) in the world. Found only in the Ethiopian highlands, it's thought to be on the verge of extinction. Only about 600 wolves are believed to remain in the whole country.

Wolves are found on both sides of the Rift Valley, in the old provinces of Gonder, Wolo, Menz, Arsi and Bale. The Bale Mountains are home to the largest population (approximately 200). In Amharic, the wolf is known as *ky kebero* (red jackal). Though the wolf does look like a jackal, its connection to the wolf family has firmly been established.

Living in family groups of around 13 animals, the wolves are highly territorial and family oriented. When the dominant female in the pack gives birth to her annual litter of between two and six pups, all members chip in, taking turns to feed, look after and play with the young. When it comes to hunting, however, the wolves forage alone, favouring the giant molerats and other rodents.

The main threats to the wolves are rabies and canine distemper caught from the domestic dog population, and crossbreeding (male wolves with female dogs). Locals believe that the antirabies vaccine changes the character of their dogs, or renders them less effective guard dogs. A serious outbreak of rabies in 2008 threatened the Bale Mountain wolves, and a plan was devised in which selected wolf packs were vaccinated to create a 'barrier' and prevent the virus spreading.

WHEN TO GO

The hottest and driest days here fall between December and February, but late September to early December is when the scenery is greenest and the wildflowers are out. Nighttime temperatures between December and January are also the coldest – frost and snow are occasionally seen.

SUPPLIES

There are a few stores in Dinsho selling the barest of basics (pasta and rice). If you're planning more elaborate menus, stock up in Addis Ababa.

Water is available in various places on the mountain, but it should be treated.

GUIDES, HORSES & HANDLERS

Organising the 'team' (guide, horses and horse handler) is done with the representative from the **Nyala Guide Association** (⏰ 8.30am-5pm) at park headquarters and should be arranged the day before you plan to start.

Guides for anything other than a stroll around the headquarters are compulsory and cost Birr120 per day (one to five people), although there is discussion of increasing this to Birr200 per day.

Porters aren't available, but horses (Birr35 per day) and horse handlers (Birr65 per day) can be hired.

Guides and handlers should provide food for themselves. Some bring token offerings or nothing at all and will then look to you for sustenance. Either check they have enough or

bring extra. As if in compensation, guides are usually happy to act as cook, and the handler to collect dead wood.

See the boxed text on p252 for post-trek tipping advice.

Trekking

Most trekking is fairly gentle and undemanding, following good, well-trodden paths or sheep tracks. But don't forget that altitude makes easy-looking terrain quite heavy going.

New campsites and trails were in development at time of research, particularly around the Harenna Escarpment, the bamboo forest near Morobawa and possibly even the seldom-explored Harenna Forest.

Please review the Safety Guidelines for Trekking (p243) and Responsible Trekking (p244) boxed texts before lacing up.

CLASSIC ROUTE

The park's most popular route covers such diverse landscape as the Web Valley moorlands, the Afro-alpine Sanetti Plateau and Keyrensa Valley lava flows. Trekkers have an excellent chance of sighting Ethiopian wolves, klipspringers, colobus monkeys and rock hyrax during this trek.

Day one Walk southwest up the Web Valley following a metal road to the Finch' Abera Waterfall and on to the Sodota campsite (four to five hours).

Day two Continue southwest up the Web Valley to Keyrensa campsite (four to five hours).

Day three Head east to the Rafu campsite, taking in the rock pillars caused by an old lava flow (five to six hours).

Day four Under the shadow of Tullu Deemtu (Bale's highest mountain), head across the Sanetti Plateau to camp by the seasonal Garba Guracha Lake (six hours).

Day five Head north across Shaya Valley to Worgona, from where it is possible to make a side trip to Worgona Mineral Springs (six to seven hours).

Day six Follow the Denka River back to Dinsho (six hours).

MOUNTAINS AND LAKES

A variation on the above allows you to scale the second-highest mountain in Ethiopia (Tullu Deemtu) and take in the seasonal Crane Lakes, which attract thousands of birds from May to October.

Day one Dinsho–Sodota, as described above.

Day two Trek the Wasema Valley to Worgana (six to eight hours).

Day three Bag Mt Batu before walking to the picturesque campsite situated in the Tegona Valley under the sheer cliffs beside the Garba Guracha Lake (six hours).

Day four Trek to the Crane Lakes (six hours) and on to the scree-covered Tullu Deemtu. This area is close to Goba–Dola-Mena Rd, which means it's possible to end your trek here (if you've pre-arranged a 4WD pickup or are prepared to hitch to Goba).

Day five Descend off the Sanetti Plateau to Worgona (six or seven hours).

Day six Worgona to Dinsho via the Denka River.

DAY AND OVERNIGHT EXCURSIONS

If you've limited time you can still see a great deal of wildlife, particularly in the forest around park headquarters where mountain nyala, warthogs and other species reside.

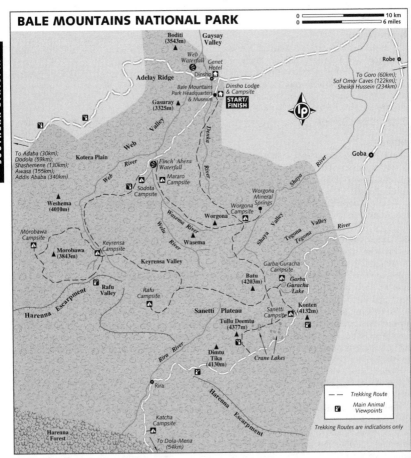

BALE MOUNTAINS NATIONAL PARK

One-day excursions include walks up the Web Valley to Gasuray Peak (3325m) and Adelay Ridge. The Web Gorge takes around 1½ hours to reach and is good for seeing colobus monkeys. For a good chance of seeing the Ethiopian wolf (and the slightest chance of spotting a leopard), continue on to the Finch' Abera Waterfall (two to three hours' walk one way). You could also spend the night at the nearby campsite. Another good overnight excursion is to the Kotera Plain, where Ethiopian wolves are often seen. The walk takes five hours one way.

With your own vehicle, the top of Tullu Deemtu can also be reached by 4WD via Goba and the Sanetti Plateau. If you reach the plateau by 7am, you're almost guaranteed a sighting of the Ethiopian wolf; they spend this time intently searching for food.

Without your own vehicle, catch one of the buses or trucks that ply the Goba–Dola-Mena Rd from Goba. The road takes you right through the park, up over the Sanetti Plateau and down into the Harenna Forest. You can explore the area from the road and then hitch back, which isn't too difficult provided you don't leave it too late in the day.

Fishing

Nine rivers and streams between Adaba and Goba were stocked with trout in the early 1970's. Fishing permits (three days, Birr200) and mandatory fishing guides (Birr200 per day) are available from the park headquarters. There's a short stretch on the Web River with cascading waterfalls and deep still pools that is best for brown trout, while the Shaya River and the narrow and clear Denka River are better for rainbow trout.

Anglers have to provide all their own equipment and there is a limit of five fish per day, all of which must be over 25cm in length.

Sleeping & Eating
DINSHO

Genet Hotel (☎ 0913 434667, r with shared toilets Birr30) This is one of two hotels in town. Both are pretty grim with dank, dark rooms and long-drop toilets. They make the town's best grub (mains Birr13) – they also make the town's only grub.

Dinsho Lodge (☎ 0912 254900; camping per person per 48hr Birr20, dm Birr40, tw/tr without bathroom Birr120/180) Located at park headquarters (park fee applicable) and surrounded by endemic species, a

stay here is a no-brainer. It feels like an abandoned ski chalet, with lots of ageing rustic charm. It's usually pretty cold, but you can buy wood in the village to stock the lodge's fireplace and to heat the sauna. The rooms can accommodate 30 in bunk beds and there's a communal kitchen. Showers are cold – really cold. Scream if you have to.

ON THE MOUNTAINS

Camping (per person per 48hr Birr20) The national park has established various sites for camping. You'll need to be fully independent with tent, sleeping bag and cooking gear.

Getting There & Away

If coming from Addis Ababa, catch an early-morning bus to Robe or Goba and leap off in Dinsho. If the return buses to Addis Ababa are full when passing Dinsho (hail them from in front of the Genet Hotel), head to Shashemene (Birr35, seven hours) and go from there. One daily bus runs to Robe (Birr10, one hour).

ROBE ሮቤ
pop 17,144 / elev 2600m

For most people, their love affair with Robe is brief and unmemorable. Feelings, sparked by an attractive eucalyptus-lined river on the northern edge of town, are typically extinguished seconds later by the sight of Robe itself. At the Thursday market, seek out the delicious local acacia honey, the attractive basketry and the heavy cotton *buluko* (togas).

Sleeping & Eating

Bekele Mola (☎ 0226 650547; d/tw Birr90/150) On the road towards Goba, 350m north of the bus station, Bekele Mola has the town's most comfortable accommodation. Small blocks of rooms are set in a grassy garden with several huge acacia trees. The rooms are clean enough, but the hot water barely trickles from the showerhead. The restaurant (mains Birr30) serves local fare and bland *faranji* food.

Bale Park Hotel (☎ 0226 651197; s without bathroom Birr25, s/d with bathroom Birr50/60) Immediately north of Bekele Mola, just off the main drag, the rooms here are smaller than its counterpart and you have to practically stand on the squat toilet to use the shower.

Mana Nyaata Jeddah (mains Birr15-35) This Muslim restaurant at the north end of town is known for *hanid* (a meal of rice, injera,

French fries and goat meat). It tastes more Middle Eastern than Ethiopian.

There are a couple of cafes serving coffee and cake near the main roundabout – that's the one with the broken fountain.

Getting There & Away

The bus station is at the southern end of town. One bus runs daily to Dinsho (Birr10, one hour), Shashemene (Birr40, eight hours) and Addis Ababa (Birr62, 12 hours). There are regular services to nearby Goba (Birr3, 25 minutes).

GOBA ጎባ

pop 50,650 / elev 2743m

Goba, the old capital of the Bale region, is 14km south of Robe. Goba is in a state of decline and feels like a gold-rush town after the gold has gone. The only reason to visit this ramshackle town is to access the stunning Sanetti Plateau or otherworldly Sof Omar Caves.

Information

There's a bank, several cafes and an internet cafe called Nagi Shope – although you have

better chance of seeing a pack of wolves in town than establishing an internet connection.

Sleeping & Eating

Yilma Amosa Hotel (☎ 0911 238293; d without bathroom Birr40, d with bathroom Birr60) Make this option a last resort as the dirty rooms are often missing door handles and can't be locked.

Batu Terara Hotel (☎ 0226 610712; r Birr60) Set around a courtyard and a public bar, the rooms here are dark and basic but a little cleaner than those at Yilma Amosa.

Goba Wabe Shebele Hotel (☎ 0226 610041; s/d/tw Birr172/230/230, ste Birr383) Even though this is by far the nicest place to stay and Goba's only tourist-grade hotel, you can't help but feel it's slightly overpriced. The large and bland rooms are set in hexagonal configurations around enclosed courtyards. The restaurant, on the other hand, is well regarded and prepares Western dishes, including three-course set meals (Birr71). The staff here can arrange a car for an excursion to the Sof Omar Caves (Birr1500 to Birr2000) or Sanetti Plateau (Birr1200 to Birr1500).

Baltena Hotel (mains Birr10-12; ⊙ noon-midnight) Fronted by a butchery, this local joint serves cheap, mostly meat dishes.

Getting There & Around

Regular minibuses serve Robe (Birr3, 25 minutes), which offers more reliable services to Shashemene and Addis Ababa.

One modified Isuzu truck leaves every morning for Dola-Mena (Birr31, five to six hours) via the Sanetti Plateau from the petrol station on the main road. On Dola-Mena's market days (Wednesday and Saturday), this service is more frequent.

4WDs can usually be rented in Goba; ask around the bus station or at the Goba Wabe Shebele Hotel. Always check on the condition of the road to Dola-Mena as it's occasionally impassable after rains.

SOF OMAR CAVES
የሶፍ አማር ዋሻዎች

If the Web River's water and its suspended sediments weren't the artists and if the sublime carvings weren't welded to the earth's insides, then sections of the Sof Omar Caves would be housed in some of the world's finest galleries.

The labyrinth of caverns stretches some 16km through limestone hills; however,

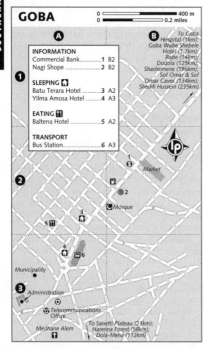

GOBA

0 — 400 m
0 — 0.2 miles

INFORMATION
Commercial Bank.............1 B2
Nagi Shope 2 B2

SLEEPING
Batu Terara Hotel 3 A2
Yilma Amosa Hotel 4 A3

EATING
Baltena Hotel 5 A2

TRANSPORT
Bus Station.....................6 A3

To Goba Hospital (1km);
Goba Wabe Shebele Hotel (1.7km);
Robe (14km);
Dodola (125km);
Shashemene (196km);
Sof Omar & Sof Omar Caves (134km);
Sheikh Hussein (235km)

Market

Mosque

Municipality

Administration

Telecommunications Office

Medhane Alem

To Sanetti Plateau (23km);
Harenna Forest (58km);
Dola-Mena (112km)

SOUTHERN ETHIOPIA

only the first 1.7km can be explored on foot. Luckily, the walkable portion houses the remarkable formations known as the Chamber of Columns, The Dome and The Balcony. With vaulted chambers, flying buttresses, massive pillars and fluted archways, these sections almost resemble an Antonio Gaudí cathedral.

The caves have been an important religious site since ancient times and despite being greatly venerated by Muslims in the area, due to Sheikh Sof Omar reputedly taking refuge here in the early days of Islam, many pagan rites and ceremonies seem to carry on.

Some Sof Omar villagers ask Birr100 for a tour, but Birr50 ought to be adequate. Wear footwear you don't mind getting wet and always bring a torch, though turning it off once in the depths is as eerie as it is extraordinary.

Once in the light of day, twitchers should search for Salvadori's serin, a rare endemic species.

Getting There & Away

From the village of Goro, about 60km east of Robe, infrequent pickups leave for Sof Omar (Birr25, 1½ hours). Sof Omar's market day (Saturday) is the only day there's guaranteed transport. Two daily buses connect Goro to Robe (Birr13, two hours) and Goba (Birr16, 2½ hours).

SHEIKH HUSSEIN ሸ‌ኅ ሁ‌ሴ‌ን

Located north of Sof Omar, Sheikh Hussein is southern Ethiopia's most important centre of Muslim pilgrimage. At least 500 years old, it's dedicated to the 13th-century holy man who was responsible for the conversion of many Bale and Arsi Oromo to Islam. The complex consists of an attractive little mosque, various tombs, and shrines and caves that are found within an hour's walk east.

The most colourful time to visit is during a major pilgrimage, when devotees come here to make wishes and to offer thanks. Feast days are during May and October, with minor ones during February and September; the exact dates depend on the lunar calendar.

Getting There & Away

Unless you time your visit with a pilgrimage, you really need your own vehicle to visit Sheikh Hussein. Daily minibuses from Robe do reach Jara (Birr35, six to seven hours), which is 57km south of Sheikh Hussein, but from there you're on your own.

DOLA-MENA ዶ‌ላ ሜ‌ና
pop 13,062

Although Dola-Mena's intense heat, striking Somali herdsmen and camels are a novelty after the Bale Mountains, the main reason to visit this bleak town is for the captivating 110km journey south from Goba.

After leaving Goba you'll traverse the eastern part of the Bale Mountains National Park, cross the Harenna Escarpment and wind up to the lofty Sanetti Plateau itself. The route is the highest all-weather road in Africa and must rank among the continent's most surreal.

The road takes you through the extraordinary *Podocarpus* woodland known as the **Harenna Forest**. With its twisted trunks draped in 'old man beard' lichens, mosses and ferns, and with cloud swirling around, the forest is straight out of a Grimm brothers fairytale.

After a steady descent you'll eventually find yourself in dusty Dola-Mena. The **Makuriya Mengistu Hotel** (d without bathroom Birr25), centrally placed on the main drag, is the best of the basic options. There are some decent unnamed local restaurants near the mosque.

Getting There & Away

See Goba's Getting There & Away section (opposite) for transport details to Dola-Mena.

If you don't want to backtrack, you'll have to negotiate a passage with one of the hit-and-miss trucks that head the 179km south to Negele Borena. They usually depart every morning if they can round up enough passengers.

NEGELE BORENA ነ‌ገ‌ሌ ቦ‌ረ‌ና
pop 42,958 / elev 1475m

Negele Borena sits at an important crossroads of the remote southeast and serves as a useful transport hub. In itself there are few reasons to visit and fewer to stay, but the town has a dusty charm and the Saturday camel market smacks of the exotic. Fervent birders will undoubtedly pass through here while tracking rare endemic species, like the Sidamo long-clawed lark, Degodi lark, Prince Ruspoli's turaco and Salvadori's seedeater.

The **Green Hotel** (s without bathroom Birr30, s Birr50), southwest of the bus station, is simple and clean. Its restaurant isn't a bad choice for local fare.

COWS & CROWNS

Cattle rearing is the mainstay of the southeast's economy, and cows are greatly prized. Cows supply meat, milk, butter and blood for food, as well as dung for fuel and for building houses. Ownership of cattle confers great social status on Oromo men: traditionally, if a herdsman owns more than 1000, he's entitled to wear a crown.

Getting There & Away

Several trucks per week head south to Mega, departing from the market. From Mega, buses head north to Yabelo and south to Moyale.

SOUTH TO MOYALE

The northern half of this route will take you through verdant *enset* plantations (false banana trees found in much of southern Ethiopia, used to produce a breadlike staple also known as *enset*), past wild coffee and enable you to visit some of southern Ethiopia's most important archaeological sites. Travel the southern half and you may witness singing wells, salt-filled craters and a rare bird or two. Complete the journey and you'll be wiping sweat from your brow and drool from your chin as you stare across the baking plains and desolate glory that is northern Kenya.

DILA ዲላ
pop 61,114 / elev 1570m

From a traveller's perspective the only noteworthy thing about Dila, the administrative capital of Gedea, is that within its sphere of influence lie two of southern Ethiopia's most important stelae fields and some little-known rock carvings. The town of Dila itself is rather unremarkable, but you may want to take the opportunity to check your emails and stock up on amenities before you head south.

Before visiting the stelae sites, you must pay Birr50 at the **Gedeo tourism office** (Gede'iinxxe Zooneke; ☎ 0463 314482; ⏰ 8am-12.30pm & 1.30-5.30pm Mon-Fri) and hire one of their compulsory guides (Birr50 per day). The office is 250m west of the main drag, down the road opposite the Brook Pharmacy.

With over 80 stelae variously carved with facial features, phalluses etc, **Tutu Fella** is the most impressive site. It's accessed from an eastern turn-off, some 3km south of Wenago or 17km south from Dila.

The tapered stones at **Tututi** also mark graves, but are generally larger (up to 7.5m tall) and lack the detailed carving seen at Tutu Fella. The Tututi field rests on a hill 2.3km west of Chalba village, which sits 8.5km south of the Tutu Fella turn-off.

About 10km northwest of Dila are the remote **Manchiti rock engravings**. A vertical rock face hosts an ancient herd of some 50 stylised cows, which were chiselled over 3000 years ago.

Sleeping & Eating

Lalibela Pension (☎ 0463 312300; d without bathroom Birr50, d with bathroom Birr82) Although the 'pretty in pink' paint job may induce convulsions, there is little cause for real alarm here. Bathrooms (shared and private) are sparkling and the Birr82 rooms even have satellite TV. It's signposted off the main street west of Dila Rendez-Vous, a haven of pastries.

Get Smart Hotel (☎ 0463 312955; d without bathroom Birr50, d/tw with bathroom Birr100/150) Generally, the Get Smart Hotel needs to smarten up. The doubles have huge beds, but the rooms themselves have only briefly been introduced to a mop.

Getting There & Away

At 6am a bus (and occasional minibus) departs for Yabelo (Birr35, four hours) and Moyale (Birr50, seven hours). Four or five buses run daily to Shashemene (Birr17 to Birr25, three hours) via Awasa (Birr12 to Birr18, 2½ hours).

YABELO ያቤሎ
pop 18,478 / elev 1857m

Yabelo, 5km west of the Moyale–Shashemene Rd, makes a convenient base for a visit to Yabelo Wildlife Sanctuary. It's also the southern gateway to the Omo Valley via Konso.

Sleeping & Eating

Both of these options are on the Yabelo/Moyale–Shashemene Rd junction. There's also a couple of cheap restaurants and hotels in 'downtown' Yabelo.

Yabelo Motel (☎ 0464 460237; d without bathroom Birr120, d with bathroom Birr200-300) Sitting at the Yabelo junction on the main Moyale–Shashemene Rd, this is the town's only tourist-class hotel. With a tailor-made, *faranji*-friendly menu (mains Birr15 to Birr35) and a flower-filled garden, this is also Yabelo's best restaurant. The rooms are tiled, clean and comfortable and those with an attached bathroom have hot water and satellite TV.

New Green Pension (☎ 0911 765784; d without bathroom Birr50) A short stroll from the Yabelo Motel, this place offers bright and breezy rooms with small verandahs out front. There are no light bulbs in the cramped shower/toilet block but that's OK – there's no generator either.

Getting There & around
Yabelo enjoys its own little micro-economy, where bus fares are typically Birr20 more expensive *from* Yabelo than they are *to* Yabelo.

In town a bus leaves for Konso (Birr25 to Birr45, three hours) at 6am. North/south buses leave from the Total station at the Moyale–Shashemene road junction. If you miss the Shashemene- (Birr65, 12 hours) or Moyale- (Birr35, 3½ hours) bound buses, you may be able to hop a ride on any other bus passing (usually between 9am and 10am).

YABELO WILDLIFE SANCTUARY
ያቤሎ የዱር አራዊት ፓርክ
Covering an area of 2496 sq km, the Yabelo Wildlife Sanctuary was originally created to protect the endemic Swaynes hartebeest. However, it's now better known for two truly unique range-restricted bird species: the Stresemann's bush crow and white-tailed swallow. Why they never stray more than 100km from here is still anyone's guess.

The 25 mammal species inhabiting the acacia woodland and savannah grass include Burchell's zebras, dik-diks, greater and lesser kudus, gerenuks and Grant's gazelles, all quite commonly seen.

Only visitors with a park scout are allowed to enter. Scouts (per day Birr65) are available from the **park office** (☉ 8.30am-12.30pm & 1.30-5.30pm Mon-Fri) in the town of Yabelo.

YABELO TO MEGA
The 100km between Yabelo and Mega offers up an interesting array of cultural and physical phenomena.

Delve into Borena territory near Dublock, about 70km south of Yabelo, where several of the famous *ela* or **'singing wells'** (p188) have been operating for more than a century.

To find them you'll need a guide from Dublock. Borena chieftains now charge entrance fees, which vary widely depending on how many people they bring to work the well. To see the real deal (rather than a performance), come during dry season (January through March) when the cattle come to drink. Getting to some wells involves quite long walks.

The village of **El Sod**, around 20km south of Dublock, lies beside one of Ethiopia's largest salt deposits. Known as the **House of Salt** (admission Birr50 per person, Birr50 per vehicle, compulsory guides Birr100), it's famed for its 100m-deep crater lake, one of four in the region. The lake is about 800m across and is so dark in colour that it looks like an oil slick amid the rose-coloured rocks. Valuable and muddy, black salt has been extracted from the lake for centuries.

From the crater rim it's a half-hour, knee-trembling walk down and an hour, thigh-burning slog back up. It's best to visit during the morning's cooler temperatures when the salt gatherers are actually working. Don't expect to learn much about this fascinating endeavour from the guides – they speak about as much English as their donkeys.

At least nine buses ply the Addis Ababa–Moyale Rd from towns north and south of Dublock and can drop you off at the various turn-offs. From the turn-off for the House of Salt, you will need to hitch the 14km.

MOYALE ሞያለ
pop 25,038 / elev 1090m
There's only one truly compelling reason to visit Moyale: Kenya.

Although a seemingly porous border cuts the one-street town of Moyale in two, the difference in feel between the two sides is immediately palpable. The Kenyan side, with dust-swept dirt streets, expensive petrol being served from barrels and ragtag vehicles trundling in from the punishing northern plains, has a true wild-frontier atmosphere.

Information
Black-market moneychangers hang around the border and change Birr and Kenyan shillings (KSh). Birr1 is about Ksh7.

THE SINGING WELLS OF THE BORENA

The Borena are seminomadic pastoralists who occupy lands that stretch from northern Kenya to the dry, hot plains around Yabelo. Their lives revolve entirely around their cattle and during the long dry season, it's a constant struggle to keep their vast herds alive. To combat the problem, the Borena have developed their own peculiar solution: a series of wells dug deep into the earth. Each Borena family and each clan is assigned its own well.

A series of water troughs are dug close to each well's mouth. Approaching them is a long channel that drops to about 10m below the ground level, which funnels the cattle to the troughs. It's just wide enough to allow two single columns of cattle to pass one another.

When it's time to water the cattle, the men create a human ladder down the well (which can be up to 30m deep), tossing buckets of water between one another from the bottom up to the top, where the troughs are gradually filled. The work is very strenuous, and the men often sing in harmony to encourage one another as well as to reassure the cattle. Several hundred or even thousand cattle come to drink at a time. For travellers, it's certainly a memorable and unique sight.

ETHIOPIA

Commercial Bank (☼ 8am-noon & 1.30-4pm Mon-Fri, 8am-noon Sat) Changes travellers cheques and cash. It doesn't exchange Kenyan shillings or buy back unused Ethiopian birr. It's 2km north of the border.

KENYA

Kenya Commercial Bank (☼ 9am-3pm Mon-Fri, to 11am Sat) Changes cash (US dollars, euros and pound sterling) and travellers cheques. Ethiopian birr are not accepted. There is an ATM.

Post office (☼ 8am-5pm Mon-Fri, to noon Sat) With card phones.

Sleeping & Eating
ETHIOPIA

Fekadu Hotel (☎ 046-4440049; d Birr25) Simple but efficient self-contained rooms set around an excellent courtyard restaurant and a decent bar. The waitresses think foreigners are great.

Tourist Hotel (☎ 046-440513; r without bathroom Birr30) Sheltered behind its cool Rasta-inspired bar, this little sleeping option has colourful rooms that include private showers. The shared toilets are nothing to sing about, but thankfully they're nothing to scream about either.

Hagos Hotel (mains Birr8-12) Have your last Ethiopian meal here. There's a terrace out back and some shady seating below a flowering tree. It's just up from the border.

KENYA

Sherif Guest House (r per person without bathroom KSh150) Sitting above the bank, this guesthouse has reasonably bright and clean rooms. Some of the rooms have mosquito nets, while others have mattresses too soft for their slat bases, so make sure you check out a few before choosing one. The communal toilet is memorable for all the wrong reasons.

Sessi Guesthouse (r per person without bathroom KSh400) It's not much but the Sessi Guesthouse, a short way out of the centre, is far and away the best place to stay in town. It's clean, very quiet and the shared bathrooms come with buckets of piping hot water. The best thing about it is that it's not even a brothel!

Baghdad Hotel II (mains KSh80-150) On the main drag just south of the post office, this is a popular place to eat – sit down, swipe some flies and get stuffed.

Prison Canteen (mains Ksh150-2000) This kitsch place, with its zebra motifs and thatched pavilions, is the canteen for prison workers. It says a lot about the quality of life down here when the best place to eat, drink and party is inside the town jail.

Getting There & Away

Two early-morning buses depart daily for Addis Ababa (Birr95, 1½ days), one overnighting at Dila (Birr50, seven hours), the other at Shashemene (Birr60, 11½ hours). A few minibuses leave daily for Yabelo (Birr35, 3½ hours).

For those driving, fill up on the Ethiopian side – petrol is half the cost and more reliable.

For those heading south into Kenya, get ready for some tooth-rattling rides and see p262 for details.

ARBA MINCH & AROUND

Bordered by verdant mountains and home to Ethiopia's two largest – and arguably most beautiful – Rift Valley lakes, this region is more than a convenient overnight stop on the southern circuit. Arba Minch, southwestern Ethiopia's largest city, is the logical place from which to explore the areas principal attractions – the Nechisar National Park and the highland towns of Dorze and Chencha.

As you approach the area from Shashemene, you'll pass through some of the most fertile land in Ethiopia, where abundant fruit and cotton are grown. Don't miss the opportunity to try the diminutive but incredibly sweet bananas and a local fruit called *gishta,* a kind of custard apple.

ARBA MINCH አርባ ምንጭ
pop 72,507 / elev 1400m to 1600m

Like a rift between two sisters, Arba Minch's dual settlements of Shecha and Sikela are separated by 4km of no-man's land. Rather unfortunately, this split strikes a discord in the personality of both.

If pressed we would say that downtown Sikela is a little more grubby and chaotic than her ever-so-slightly more refined sibling to the south. The eastern fringes of both suburbs have fantastic views over the Rift Valley, its nearby lakes and the lyrically named Bridge of God.

Information

Although there are countless private telecentres, Shecha's telecommunications office is the cheapest, charging standard international rates (see p254). Most banks, including the Dashen Bank, can exchange American Express travellers cheques and cash (euros and US dollars). When their machine is working, it gives cash advances on Visa.

Arba Minch Hospital (☎ 0448 810123; ☼ 24hr) The region's best hospital, just south of Sikela.

ESA Business Center (per hr Birr15) Sikela's best internet connections.

Sol Internet Caffe (per hr Birr15) Shecha's only internet option.

Tourism office (☎ 0468 812046; Shecha; ☼ 8.30am-12.30pm & 1.30-5.30pm Mon-Thu, 8.30am-11.30am & 1.30-5.30pm Fri) See them for trek suggestions for the park, surrounding forests and Guge Mountains. They are also able to help organise 4WDs.

Sights & Activities
LAKES ABAYA & CHAMO

Ringed by savannah plains and divided by the 'Bridge of God', Lakes Abaya and Chamo (Map p192) are truly beautiful. Measuring 1160 sq km, Lake Abaya is the Rift Valley's largest lake. If out on the Abaya's waters, try to spot the Haruras in their high-prowed *wogolo* boats. Made of *isoke* (a very lightweight local wood), the boats are capable of carrying quite heavy loads (including cattle).

Lake Abaya's peculiar red waters are a result of elevated natural concentrations of suspended ferrous hydroxide. While Lake Abaya may look bloody, it is the more conventionally coloured Lake Chamo that you may want to keep your fingers and toes well within the boat. This lake supports large populations of crocodiles (especially around the vicinity of the Crocodile Market, see p192) and hippos, both of which regularly kill unwary fishermen.

ARBA MINCH CROCODILE RANCH

The government **crocodile ranch** (Map p192; admission Birr50; ☼ 8.30am-noon & 1.30-6.30pm) has fallen into serious disrepair over the years and although it's slightly exciting to walk over the cramped, concrete tanks, a visit here is more depressing than inspiring. The crocodiles are hatched from eggs that are collected by scouts or fished directly from the lakes as youngsters and reared on the farm. Most of the hapless crocs are killed at the age of five (when the skin is the best quality), and will end up as handbags or belts in Middle Eastern markets.

The farm is situated off the Addis Ababa road, about 7km from the Sikela. Walk, bike, hitch or arrange a contract taxi at the tourist office or bus station.

Sleeping

Most of Shecha's accommodation and restaurant options outgun Sikela's.

SHECHA

Arba Minch Hotel (☎ 0468 810206; Birr60/80) Simple, Spartan and reasonably clean, this budget hotel is quieter than others and provides mosquito nets.

Bekele Mola Hotel (☎ 0468 810046; camping Birr40, s Birr115-180, d/tw Birr180/180) With views over the Bridge of God and both lakes, it is hard to fault the location or find a better spot for a sun-downer. However, the rooms aren't in the

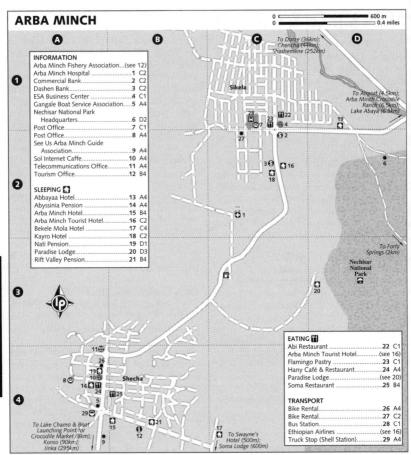

ARBA MINCH

0 — 600 m
0 — 0.4 miles

INFORMATION
Arba Minch Fishery Association...(see 12)
Arba Minch Hospital **1** C2
Commercial Bank...............................**2** C2
Dashen Bank....................................**3** C2
ESA Business Center **4** C1
Gangale Boat Service Association.....**5** A4
Nechisar National Park
　Headquarters...............................**6** D2
Post Office.......................................**7** C1
Post Office.......................................**8** A4
See Us Arba Minch Guide
　Association...................................**9** A4
Sol Internet Caffe...........................**10** A4
Telecommunications Office...........**11** A4
Tourism Office................................**12** B4

SLEEPING 🏠
Abbayaa Hotel................................**13** A4
Abyssinia Pension **14** A4
Arba Minch Hotel...........................**15** B4
Arba Minch Tourist Hotel...............**16** C2
Bekele Mola Hotel **17** C4
Kayro Hotel....................................**18** C2
Nati Pension...................................**19** D1
Paradise Lodge...............................**20** D3
Rift Valley Pension.........................**21** B4

EATING 🍴
Abi Restaurant **22** C1
Arba Minch Tourist Hotel...........(see 16)
Flamingo Pastry **23** C1
Hany Café & Restaurant.................**24** A4
Paradise Lodge...........................(see 20)
Soma Restaurant **25** B4

TRANSPORT
Bike Rental.....................................**26** A4
Bike Rental.....................................**27** C2
Bus Station.....................................**28** C1
Ethiopian Airlines ....(see 16)
Truck Stop (Shell Station)..............**29** A4

Sikela

Shecha

To Dorze (36km);
Chencha (44km);
Shashemene (252km)

To Airport (4.5km);
Arba Minch Crocodile
Ranch (6.5km);
Lake Abaya (6.6km)

To Forty
Springs (2km)

Nechisar
National
Park

To Lake Chamo & Boat
Launching Point for
Crocodile Market (8km);
Konso (90km);
Jinka (295km)

To Swayne's
Hotel (500m);
Soma Lodge (600m)

SOUTHERN ETHIOPIA

---

same league: they're clean but well worn. It's a 10-minute walk to town from here.

Rift Valley Pension (☎ 0468 812531; d/tw Birr130/130) The rooms here are clean, spacious and comfortable with tiled floors, satellite TVs and newish mosquito nets. It isn't the flashest hotel in town but it is the best value.

Soma Lodge (☎ 0488 40396, d Birr300) Like giant, up-turned onions, the beautifully crafted Sidamo huts here each have a small lounge, two bedrooms (with two beds and en suite in each) and fantastic views over Nechisar National Park.

Swayne's Hotel (☎ 0468 811895; www.swayneshotel .com; camping Birr75; s/tw incl breakfast Birr304/386) The hotel's bungalows with their colourful local

artwork, hand-carved wooden furniture and colourful lamps give this place a quirky, yet traditional feel. To make the most of the sensational lake views, request a room numbered between four and 22.

Other options are:

Abbayaa Hotel (☎ 0468 810181; d Birr100) Do the dozen 'Roach Killer' bottles at reception tell you there's a problem, or does it show they care?

Abyssinia Pension (☎ 0468 810381; s/d Birr150/170) Neat and tidy with electric hot-water showers. Slightly overpriced.

SIKELA

Kayro Hotel (☎ 0468 813407; s/d Birr50/70) It may be the best of Sikela's budget choices, but the beds are a squeeze for couples and the bathrooms are a bit grungy. The attached bar can get noisy.

Nati Pension (☎ 0468 813269; d/tw Birr200/260) Painted a startling green and white, you won't miss this quiet place on the way to the airport. Opened in 2009, there is still a whiff of new paint about the large rooms and tiled bathrooms.

Arba Minch Tourist Hotel (☎ 0468 812171; fax 0468 813661; d Birr188-260, tw/q Birr300/350) Since it lacks any views and charges *faranji* double, the Arba Minch Tourist Hotel tries to distract you with reasonably modern rooms boasting satellite TVs, bright windows and quality furnishings. The compound contains coffee and juice bars, a leafy seating area and a restaurant.

Paradise Lodge (☎ 0468 812914; www.lodgeparadise.com; s/d/tw incl breakfast US$36/41/55) This upmarket lodge features quaint, circular, Konso-style huts built from stone and wood. All are well appointed with satellite TVs, writing desks and crisp white linen. Better still, massages and steam baths are available.

Eating

Fish has long been a staple in the diet here, with *asa kutilet* (fish cutlet) being a particular speciality. Sadly, overfishing means it's harder to come by these days.

SHECHA

Hany Café & Restaurant (mains Birr18-30) The English menu only lists the pasta and salad options so if you prefer the spicy national dishes, you'll have to take a stab with the Amharic.

Soma Restaurant (mains Birr25) This unassuming restaurant offers a small variety of mouthwatering fresh fish dishes. During high season the tables are set with tablecloths and there's a generator on standby if needed. The Birr100 *asa filetto* (a grilled *talapia* big enough for two) aside, most dishes are as fairly priced as they are tasty.

Swayne's Hotel (mains Birr30-40) Perched above the national park, this open-air restaurant prepares the best Western fare in town. Pick from the menu or enjoy a set three-course meal for Birr60.

SIKELA

Flamingo Pastry (pastries Birr4) Sikela's best pastries, cakes and fruit juices.

Abi Restaurant (mains Birr10-22) The *asa kutilet* and *asa gulash* are the top picks at this local

eatery. Eat street side or in the courtyard out back.

Arba Minch Tourist Hotel (☎ 0468 812171; mains Birr15-32) Although the service was a tad amateurish, the hotel's leafy compound afforded some relaxing dining with a confusing array of menus to choose between. If fish is not your thing, perhaps the veal shish kebabs might tempt you.

Paradise Lodge (☎ 0468 812914; mains Birr35-40) A grand Konso hut with an intricate spilt bamboo ceiling, a flotilla of elegantly set tables, sensational views anda menu featuring tasty Western and local favourites make this the most impressive of the hotel restaurants.

Getting There & Away

Ethiopian Airlines (☎ 0468 810649) flies between Addis Ababa and Arba Minch on Wednesday and Sunday (US$153, 2½ hours) before continuing on to Jimma (US$116, 50 minutes).

One or two daily buses leave Sikela's bus station for Addis Ababa (Birr67, 12 hours), Awasa (Birr40, 6½ hours), Shashemene (Birr37, six hours), Jinka (Birr40, eight hours), Konso (Birr20, 3½ hours) and Weyto (Birr30, five hours).

Trucks also run south to Konso, Weyto and Jinka. They pick up passengers at Shecha's Shell station, although they are increasingly reluctant to take foreigners.

In theory it is possible to begin a tour to the Omo Valley from Arba Minch. Swayne's Hotel, the Arba Minch Tourist Hotel and Paradise Lodge were renting 4WDs for between US$150 and US$180 per day (including fuel and driver) when we passed. The tourist office also indicated that they could help travellers arrange vehicles, and canny barterers maybe able to negotiate cheaper rates.

Getting Around

Frequent minibuses connect Sikela and Shecha (Birr1.30) from around 6am to 9pm. To reach the airport, grab a contract taxi (Birr50) near Flamingo Pastry in Sikela.

Bikes can be rented near Sikela's post office for Birr25 per hour and opposite the Abbayaa Hotel in Shecha.

NECHISAR NATIONAL PARK
ነጭ ሳር ብሔራዊ ፓርክ

Spanning the narrow, yet mountainous 'Bridge of God' that separates Lakes Chamo and Abaya, Nechisar National Park ranks

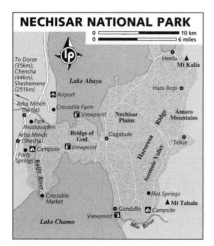

NECHISAR NATIONAL PARK

among the most scenic, yet least visited, national parks in East Africa.

Although only 514 sq km, the park contains diverse habitats ranging from wide-open savannah and acacia woodland to thick bush and sections of riparian forest. The bleached savannah grasses actually spawned the park's name, which means 'white grass' in Amharic.

The diversity of birds and animals is what makes Nechisar special. Ninety-one mammal species are found in the park. In the forest, bushpigs, warthogs, Anubis baboons, thumbless colobus monkeys, genets, bushbucks and vervet monkeys are found. On the savannah plains (where animals are most easily seen), the Burchell's zebra is the most conspicuous, sometimes seen in unusually large herds of 100 animals or more.

Of the antelopes, the most commonly seen is the greater kudu in the cover of the bush, with its beautiful spiralling horns, and the monogamous Guenther's dik-dik, which is often seen in pairs. The Grant's gazelle, with its horns pointing forward, is easy to spot on the plains, as is the endemic Swaynes hartebeest.

Like the mammals, the birds here are equally diverse: 320 species have been counted, including hornbills and bustards. It's also the home of the Nechisar nightjar, Ethiopia's rarest endemic bird (see the sidebar on p75).

Information

Whether entering the **park** (Map p192; admission Birr100 per 48 hr, vehicle Birr30) by land or water, you must first pay park fees at the **park headquarters** (Map p190; ☾ 6am-7.30pm), which is located 1km southeast of Sikela.

As is the trend in the South, guides are now mandatory even though some add little to the experience. Guides can be arranged at the **See Us Arba Minch Guide Association** (Map p190; ☎ 0468 810117; ☾ 8am-noon & 1-4pm) for Birr200 per day or Birr80 per trip to the Crocodile Market. The only exception is the hot springs, where a guide is not required.

Sights
CROCODILE MARKET

Where the Kulfo River empties into Lake Chamo, you'll find oodles of fat and famous crocodiles sunning themselves. The area, simply known as the crocodile market, is truly one of Africa's best crocodile displays.

Since the formation of **Arba Minch Fishery Association** (Map p190; ☎ 0468 810197; ☾ 8am-noon & 1.30-5.30pm) and the **Gangale Boat Service Association** (Map p190; ☎ 0468 814080; ☾ 8am-1pm & 1.30-5.30pm), the only way to visit the crocs is by boat (Birr500 for a group of up to five people – although solo travellers should try to wrangle a discount). It has also become compulsory to hire a local guide (Birr80) from the See Us Guide Association (see above) and to supply or pay for transport for the guide and boat captain to the launching point, 8km southeast of Shecha.

While it's only a 15- to 30-minute boat ride to the croc hotspot, a minimum of 1½ hours should be allowed for the trip. It's best to visit during late afternoon or early morning. Remember to keep your limbs in the boat!

FORTY SPRINGS

Arba Minch, which is Amharic for 'Forty Springs' (Map p192), is named after the innumerable little springs that bubble up in the evergreen forest covering the flats below the town. This scenic spot makes for a nice hike from town and some of the pools are suitable for bathing.

The springs lie just within the park and even though a guide isn't required, park entrance fees are applicable (although it seems common practice to scramble down the track behind the Bekele Mola Hotel and avoid paying the fees altogether). To get here, take the road towards Nechisar National Park; stay right when the road forks. The springs are a further 2.8km.

Sleeping

Most travellers sleep in Arba Minch.

Camping (per tent Birr30) Possible any-where, but there are two official camping grounds: one beside the Kulfo River, south of park headquarters, and the other in the Sermule Valley.

Getting There & Around

Being only a stone's throw from Arba Minch, the park is easily accessible. However, the roads within the park can be treacherous, making a 4WD necessary.

There's a 120km-long complete circuit, as well as a shortened 85km version that covers an excellent variety of landscapes, viewpoints, animals and birds. The short-ened version takes between five and seven hours to complete (including stops). If you're pushed for time, there's a reasonable three-hour circuit.

The tourist office in town (p189) can ar-range 4WDs with local operators for Birr800 to Birr1000 per 8 hours, and contract taxis to the jetty where the boats to the Crocodile Market are moored for Birr160 to Birr200 (including waiting time). Alternatively, catch a public minibus from the roundabout near the See Us Guide Association to the junction where the dirt road runs to the jetty (Birr10 per person). From here it's a 20-minute walk.

DORZE & CHENCHA
ደርዜ ና ጨን ጫ

High up in the **Guge Mountains**, to the north-west of Arba Minch, is the cold and cloudy Dorze territory. The Dorze belong to one of the many Omotic peoples of the southwest, famous for their towering huts, fine cotton *shammas* (cotton togas) and *gabis* (thicker *shammas*). They employ ingenious terracing that allows them to reduce soil erosion on their mountainside farms.

Dorze village (admission per person Birr50; ☑ 9am-5pm) has one of the few Southern Nations' cooperatives that have succeeded in turning the recent influx of tourists into a positive experience for all concerned. The 'tour' usu-ally kicks off with a look through one of the famed Dorze huts (see p194), followed by weaving and spinning demonstrations; in-terestingly, only men weave and women spin in traditional Dorze culture. Photography is permitted throughout the tour.

SOUTHERN ETHIOPIA

ELEPHANTS VERSUS CATTLE

In 1978 there were only an estimated 850 elephants left in Omo and Mago National Parks. By 1994 there were an estimated 657 and by 2006, elephants had only been spotted six times in two years. In Nechisar National Park elephant, black rhinoceros, giraffe, eland, gerenuk, beisa oryx, Grevy's zebra, cheetah and buffalo had all become extinct.

The trend was set to continue until suddenly in 2005 African Parks Network (APN; www .african-parks.org), a nonprofit organisation that had successfully rehabilitated neglected parks elsewhere in Africa, took over the management of both the Omo and Nechisar parks. Besides ensuring their ecological and financial sustainability, they planned on reintroducing some of the recently exterminated animals, building infrastructure and encouraging tourism. It was an ambitious endeavour and one that was to flounder three years later.

The parks are also home to thousands of people and thousands of their cattle. Although the APN claimed it had no intention of resettling the tribes outside the park's boundaries, they refused to put a 'no eviction' clause in its contract and this worried many in the region and some activists abroad.

One particularly vocal opponent of the APN involvement was Native Solutions to Conservation Refugees' (http://conservationrefugees.org) who claimed that even if resettlement did not take place, it was crucial that tribes retain access to vital subsistence resources so that they could continue to obtain a sustainable livelihood.

For the next two years allegations raged. One side claimed that APN effectively made 'Omo people "illegal squatters" on their own land, and the other that sustainable management was incompatible with 'the irresponsible way of living of some of the ethnic groups'.

It all ended in 2008 when, much to the relief of some and the despair of others, APN gave up the management of both parks, citing that to 'continue is simply a waste of scarce resources which can be better applied elsewhere'.

DORZE HUTS

Standing up to 12m high, Dorze huts resemble larger-than-life elephants. Because of their unique construction of vertical hardwood poles, woven bamboo and thatched roofs of *enset* (false-banana tree) leaves, they do not require a central pillar for support.

On the inside a partitioned area is reserved for livestock whose body heat helps heat the huts, while the section that juts out at the entrance serves as a small reception room.

Though fragile-looking, the huts can last up to 60 years until eventually rot and termites get the better of them. The termites eat the homes from the base up, resulting in a progressively shorter and shorter hut with a smaller and smaller door!

Keep an eye out for the piles of white, mushy dough wrapped in green leaves waiting for burial and fermentation. It is the local staple: a kind of unleavened bread made from *enset* (see the boxed text, p67).

For an additional Birr300, the villages will put on a dance demonstration. You will have noticed the children's roadside 'butt-shaker' performances as you travel around the region, but this is your best opportunity to give it a go yourself. Not that we are qualified to comment, but the general idea seems to be to put all your weight on one leg and shake your money-maker for all it's worth.

Colourful **markets** can be found at Dorze on Monday and Thursday; Chencha, which sits 8km northwest of Dorze village, on Tuesday and Saturday; and at Ezo on Thursdays, 10km from Dorze.

The Guge Mountains are also home to Ethiopia's most underrated trekking possibilities. One option would be a five- or six-day cultural journey from Doko Masho to Chosa via Mt Guge (4000m).

Sleeping & Eating

our pick **Mekonen Lodge** (☎ 0913 042381; s/d/tw without bathroom Birr70/140/140) Set in the heart of the Dorze compound described above, these 10 Dorze-style bamboo huts are arranged around a central courtyard that doubles as the restaurant (mains Birr50) and performance arena for the dancing. The huts are a step up from those the locals use and have electricity, bamboo flooring and Western-style beds. The attraction here is the opportunity to immerse yourself in a genuinely friendly community and get an authentic taste of village life without relinquishing all creature comforts.

Getting There & Away

A series of switchbacks afford some spectacular views over Arba Minch and the Rift Valley lakes, although be warned – when it rains, the road is a steep and slippery quagmire.

Four or five Isuzu trucks and minibuses leave Arba Minch's Sikela bus station for Dorze (Birr15, 1½ hours) and Chencha (Birr15, 2 hours) daily. They return when full.

THE LOWER OMO VALLEY

If there's anything in southern Ethiopia that can rival the majesty of the north's historical circuit, it's the people of the Lower Omo Valley. Whether it's wandering through traditional Konso villages, watching Hamer people performing a Jumping of the Bulls ceremony or witnessing the Mursi's mystical stick fights and mind-blowing lip plates, your visit here will stick with you for a lifetime.

The landscape is diverse, ranging from dry, open savannah plains to riverine forests bordering the Omo and Mago Rivers. The vast Omo River meanders for nearly 1000km, from southwest of Addis Ababa all the way to Kenya. There it's the sole feeder of Kenya's massive Jade Sea (Lake Turkana). The river also bisects Ethiopia's largest, wildest and most inaccessible national parks: Omo and Mago.

For a cultural insight into the region, the best time to visit is from June to September, when many celebrations take place, including harvest-home dances, marriage ceremonies, and initiation ceremonies such as the famous bull-jumping rite of passage. The driest period (January and February) increases the odds of animal sightings in the national parks. Avoid coming in October or between mid-March and early June when rains are traditionally the worst. Be aware that just one day of rain can render the roads temporarily impassable, so keep your itinerary flexible.

MARKET DAY IN THE OMO VALLEY

A terrific way to see the Omo's people is at local markets. Since most people have long journeys to and from the towns, markets are best visited between 10.30am and 2pm. The most interesting markets include the following:

Town	Day	Tribe
Arbore	Fri	Arbore & Tsemay
Dimeka	Tue & Sat	Arbore, Hamer & Karo
Jinka	Tue & Sat	Ari, Banna & Mursi
Key Afar	Thu	Banna & Tsemay
Konso	Mon & Thu	Konso
Turmi	Mon	Hamer
Weyto	Sun	Tsemay
Yabelo	Sat	Borena

The markets at Dimeka, Key Afar and Turmi (in that order) are probably the most colourful.

When visiting the villages of the Lower Omo Valley, try and coincide with at least one market day (see above). Otherwise, a good time to visit the villages is between 5pm and 6.30pm, when the workers return from the fields or from market.

A good itinerary that gives you a glimpse of diverse ethnic groups, as well as diverse scenery, begins in Konso and takes you through the little villages of Weyto, Arbore, Turmi, Omorate, Dimeka and Key Afar, before finishing at Jinka.

If you plan on staying in any of these villages, know that accommodation is barebones budget at best and electricity is only at establishments with generators (usually between 6pm and 10pm).

Dangers & Annoyances

Highland! Highland! Highlaaannd! There are only so many times you can be screamed at for your plastic water bottle before your mind coyly flirts with insanity. *Faranji* frenzy (p247) can grip children so strongly in the south that some tourists beat a retreat to their car, wind up the windows, lock the doors and bury their head in their lap, just to gain a little peace.

Photography here can also be rather stressful; see p252 for tips for photographers in Ethiopia. If you don't want to deal with the photography shemozzle, the coffee-table book *Don McCullin in Africa* contains stunning photographs from the Lower Omo Valley.

For many ethnic groups, raiding is a part of life – a means of survival in a very harsh environment. Camps should never be left unattended, and all jewellery, including watches,

is best removed before you mingle with some groups such as the Mursi. Children in the markets, especially at Turmi, often supplement the household income by pickpocketing tourists. Be warned.

Malaria is also prevalent, so precautions are essential (see p371).

KONSO ኮንሶ
pop 4593 / elev 1650m

Konso, despite its lofty ridge-top setting, is little more than a glorified roundabout, surrounded on all sides by ramshackle buildings. But while the town may be unequivocally unattractive, the nearby Konso people (see the boxed text, p196) and their architecturally inspiring villages really take the cake.

If you're interested in visiting some of these villages (p196), you must visit Konso's **tourism office** (☎ 0467 730395; ☯ 8.30am-12.30pm & 1.30-5.30pm Mon-Thu, 8.30-11.30am & 1.30-5.30pm Fri) to pick up visitation forms. They are also able to arrange cars (US$60 per day plus fuel) and a driver (Birr70 per day) if required.

A walk to the **market** (☯ Mon & Thu), which sits 2km west along the ridge, is worthwhile as it proffers grand views over the Rift Valley. Once there, you'll find tea, millet, tobacco, raw cotton, sweet potatoes, butter, incense, cassava and, if you are lucky, old Konso glass beads. By late afternoon many of the men are drunk on *tella* (home-brewed beer), and you will see them staggering home behind their wives who are left to carry heavy bundles unaided.

Around Konso, keep an eye out for the traditional lozenge-shaped beehives placed in the acacias. On the road to Jinka, you'll see young

SOUTHERN ETHIOPIA

boys selling tennis-ball sized clumps of *etan* (incense used in coffee ceremonies).

Sleeping & Eating

Hotels still rely on their generators for power, so don't expect electricity between midnight and 6pm.

our pick **Strawberry Fields Eco Lodge** (☎ 0911 724072; dm/s/d without bathroom, Birr25/50/100) Strung along a ridge with views over the lodge's permaculture garden (sadly there are no strawberries at Strawberry Fields), these Konso-style huts, with their mud and straw walls, grass roofs and compacted earth floors, are the quietest accommodation option in town. As long as you don't expect the Ritz – showers are outside in rudimentary split bamboo stalls, and in some huts the mattresses were placed directly on the floor – most find the serenity more than adequate compensation. It is 1.5km out of town towards Arba Minch.

St Mary Hotel (☎ 0911 547112; s without bathroom Birr30, s/tw Birr50/100) Opposite the Edget Hotel and prone to the same early-morning racket of departing Isuzu trucks, rooms come with temperamental plumbing and hole-free mosquito nets. The food is comparable to that found at the Edget (mains Birr20 to Birr25).

Green Hotel (s/tw Birr60/120) This budget hotel is found on the left, just as you enter town from Arba Minch. The rooms, although slightly cramped, are fairly clean by Omo Valley standards. The showers seldom work but you'll be provided with a bucket.

Edget Hotel (☎ 0467 730300; d/tw Birr60/120) Set on the town's only roundabout, Edget is a popular place to down a cold Coke and a plate of greasy *tibs*. The rooms are worn to the point that showers no longer reliably function (ask for a bucket) and most toilets lack seats.

Getting There & Away

One daily bus from Arba Minch picks up passengers here en route to Jinka (Birr30, 5½ hours, departing between 9am and 10am), via Weyto (Birr7, two hours) and Key Afar (Birr18, four hours). The bus from Jinka does the same while travelling to Arba Minch (Birr20, 3½ hours, departing between 11am and noon).

Minibuses serve Yabelo (Birr20, three hours) and Arba Minch (Birr20, 3½ hours) and early-morning Isuzu trucks depart daily for Key Afar (Birr25), Jinka (Birr30) and Turmi (Birr40).

AROUND KONSO

If you have a vehicle, a great excursion is to the traditional Konso village of **Machekie**. Although it sits atop a rusty bluff and offers astounding views, you'll likely prefer wander-

---

KONSO CULTURE & CONSTRUCTION

Under constant threat from the flanking lowland tribes, the insular Konso have managed to develop a highly specialised agricultural economy and, in the process, one of Africa's most fascinating cultures.

Isolated on hilltop strongholds, traditional Konso villages are defended by sturdy stonewalls encompassing nine separate compounds, one for each of Konso's clans. Each compound can only be accessed on hands and knees, via a wooden tunnel – a compromising position should the visitor turn out to be a foe.

Within each compound there's a *pogala mugla* (representative of the clan chief), a *mora* (thatched two-storey communal house in which adolescent boys spend their nights) and a ceremonial square in which generation poles stand tall (one pole is raised every 18 years).

The squares also contain the famous Konso *wagas,* carved wooden sculptures raised in honour of Konso warriors after their death. Designed according to a strict formula, the 'hero' is usually distinguishable by the phallic ornamental *khalasha* worn on the sculpture's forehead, or by its slightly larger size.

Placed on either side of the hero are between two and four of his wives (identifiable by necklaces and breasts) and the hero's slain enemies (usually smaller and without phallic symbols), or animals (such as leopards) that the hero has killed.

Unfortunately, *waga* erection is dying out. The widespread theft and removal of the statues to Addis Ababa for sale to diplomats and tourists, as well as the work of missionaries who are against ancestor worship, have discouraged the continuance of this ancient tradition.

ing through the narrow maze of stone-walled walkways, *Moringa oleifera* trees and thatch-roofed homes. Despite many thefts, Machekie still has some wonderful *wagas,* some more than 150 years old.

To reach Machekie, head 5km west from Konso towards Jinka, before turning south and following the dirt track another 5km. From there, you'll see the village on the hill 3km to your east. A single track will lead you to the outer rock walls.

Other interesting Konso villages are **Busso** (7km south of Konso) and Gesergio (17km southwest of Konso). **Gesergio** (gas-*ag*-ee-yo), with its bizarre landscape of entrancing sand formations, is the most famous. Thanks to the towering pinnacles resembling skyscrapers, the town is now more commonly known as 'New York'.

While local legend states that the landscape is the result of God's hands digging in search of a chief's stolen sacred drums, science chalks it up to wind and water. To reach Gesergio, follow the directions to Machekie but continue 7km southward instead of turning east along the 3km single track to Machekie.

Before striking out for any of the Konso villages listed above, be sure to visit Konso's Tourism Office (p195) to obtain the required visitation forms (per person Birr50). Be aware that to enter individual compounds you'll likely be charged an additional Birr20 to Birr40 per person, and for every person you photograph an additional Birr1 or Birr2 per picture. Some villages also charge a Birr10 parking fee, although this is not always enforced. Guides can also be hired from the Konso Tourism Office (Birr50 per day) and there is talk of making this compulsory.

At all of the villages described above, '*faranji* frenzy' (p247) occasionally reaches levels bordering on the aggressive. Children can be especially demanding and while giving children gifts may feel good at the time, it often ends up leaving them worse off; see Begging & Giving, p246.

JINKA ጂንካ
pop 22,475 / elev 1490m

Set in the hills above Mago and Omo National Parks, **Jinka** (admission per vehicle Birr50) offers a cool respite from the lowland's steamy confines. Although its services are limited and its central airstrip is now a grazing ground for local cows and sheep, Jinka is often bursting at the

seams with tour groups on their way to see the Mursi in Mago National Park (p198).

Information
Cyber Net (per min Birr1) Slow connections – you may want to download your photos to CD (Birr35) while waiting.

Mursi Indigenous Community Association (MICA ☎ 1916 873012; ☽ 7am-noon & 1-5pm) This association represents the Mursi tribes in the area. Tickets (Birr100 per person) must be purchased here before proceeding to the villages. The office is down a lane northwest of the airstrip.

Pioneers Guiding Association (☎ 0467 751728; andualemgebre@yahoo.com; ☽ 7am-8.30pm) Provides the mandatory guides (Birr150 per day) for trips to the Mursi villages and multiday treks within the Mago National Park. They also rent 4WDs (US$150 per day including driver). The office is next to the airstrip, almost directly opposite the Orit Hotel.

Sights
Jinka's vibrant Saturday **market** sits around 400m northwest of the airstrip and 300m east of the tasty fruit market. It attracts a variety of ethnic groups, among them the Ari, Mursi and Banna (see the boxed text, p200).

The **Ari** are perhaps the most hospitable of the local communities. Their most accessible village is Yetnebarsh, 8km west of town. If you are lucky they may invite you to try *areke* (a local liquor) or some delicious *fruitish* (passion fruit or, as it is locally known, 'fashion fruit').

Perched on a hill northeast of town (look for the green roof halfway up the hill), the **South-Omo Museum & Research Centre** (☎ 0467 750149; admission Birr20; ☽ 9am-noon & 3-5pm Tue-Sat) has an interesting exhibition on the region's cultures. There's even a library with ethnographic DVDs, of which screenings can be requested for Birr10 per person.

Sleeping
Jinka, like most of this region, charges foreigners up to double for everything. Reservations are advised from June to September.

Pioneers Guiding Association (☎ 0467 751728; andualemgebre@yahoo.com; camping Birr25) It is possible to pitch your tent here and use their cold showers.

Rocky Campsite (☎ 0916 855680; camping per person Birr50) About 1.5km east of Jinka's Total station, this campsite is aptly named. Well-defined sites are separated by boulders, hedges and trees. There are cold showers, squat toilets and a couple of thatch-roofed cooking areas (BYO camping stove) on hand.

Goh Hotel (☎ 0467 750033; d without bathroom Birr50, d/tw Birr120/170) Goh's 26 rooms are relatively bright and clean, if slightly aged and worn. With a good selection of rooms across most budgets, Goh tends to attract a wide cross-section of travellers. The doubles' showers are cold water only. Negotiate in low season.

Orit Hotel (☎ 0467 750045; d/tw Birr150/300) Along with its southerly neighbour (Goh hotel), the Orit is a favourite among tour operators. The twin rooms here are quite small but the doubles have sparkling bathrooms, hot water and comfy mattresses. The quality restaurant is also a popular incentive to stay.

Jinka Resort (☎ 0467 750143; camping Birr48 per person, s/d/tw Birr230/460/460) Currently Jinka's most cushy option, the rooms here are large and bright but aren't significantly better than those in the Goh and Orit Hotels. Guests are, however, assured of better water pressure and some peace and quiet among the trees.

Cheap local hotels that will do for a night's kip are:

Mengistu Pension (☎ 0467 750419; d without bathroom Birr50) Often full and usually clean, it's found down a lane north of the airstrip.

Bereka Pension (☎ 0467 750060; d without bathroom Birr60) On the main drag, 200m north of the runway; rooms are frugal with their comforts.

Eating

Tsion Restaurant (juice Birr5, mains Birr15-25) Perfect the art of standing your spoon in your juice at this spot just north of Orit Hotel.

Birtukan (mains Birr8-10) This blue and white resturant, 200m south of the guide association, specialises in cheap, fasting food.

Central Bar & Restaurant (mains Birr9-14) This is the pick of the local eateries. There's an English menu, although only four or five items will be available at any one time. Despite its name, it's not very central: walk 400m out of town on the road to Key Afar.

Orit Hotel (mains Birr12-25) With outdoor dining on an attractively lit terrace, the Orit is often packed during high season. Grab a beer and tuck into Jinka's best pasta.

Goh Hotel (mains Birr20-40) A sound choice with salads, soup, rice and spaghetti, but what is really fun is the menu. Anyone for paper stake or roosted chicken?

Jinka Resort (mains Birr40) If the novelty of injera has worn thin, head to this hotel and satisfy those cheeseburger cravings. We found the service to be pretty slow but then again, some things, including roast lamb, are worth waiting for.

Getting There & Away

Buses depart the bus compound daily for Addis Ababa (Birr100, two days) via Key Afar (Birr13, 1½ hours), Weyto (Birr15, 3½ hours), Konso (Birr30, 5½ hours) and Arba Minch (Birr35, eight hours).

Since local police frown upon tourists riding the local Isuzu trucks, it is best to arrange a seat with the driver and then walk out of town and wait to be collected. The Mobil and Total petrol stations and a spot near the Orit and Omo Hotels are good places to troll for rides. There is no set price and *faranji* tax is in full effect, so negotiate hard.

The **Pioneers Guiding Association** (p197) rents 4WDs with drivers for US$150 per day.

MAGO NATIONAL PARK ማጎ

Although the 2162-sq-km **park** (admission per person Birr100, per vehicle Birr80, mandatory scout Birr65 per day) was originally created to protect lions, leopards, buffalos, elephants and giraffes, widespread poaching means you stand little chance of spotting them. Mammals you can expect to spot are Burchell's zebra, greater and lesser kudu, the defassa waterbuck and the ever so elegant gerenuk. Topis and Lelwel hartebeest are also sometimes seen. Occasionally, large herds of buffalo are reported congregated at sources of water during dry periods. The driest time is January through February.

In order to pay your entrance fee, you will need to travel to the park headquarters that are inconveniently located 30km (a 1½-hour drive) south of the main gate. Scouts, fearful of losing a client, are more organised and wait for 4WDs entering the park from Jinka by the roadside.

Most of the park is below 500m elevation, so temperatures can soar over 40°C; bring plenty of water. Tsetse flies are also problematic – avoid wearing blue or black, which seems to attract them.

Sights
MURSI VILLAGES

The Mursi (p201) is arguably the most anticipated of the South Omo Valley tribes and, o late, they are also the most expensive. Besides the park admission fee (Birr100 per person), park scout fee (Birr65 per group) and park vehicle entrance fee (Birr80), you are required to pay a village entrance fee of Birr100 per person (payable at the Mursi Indigenous Community Association in Jinka, see p197), hire a local guide for another Birr150 (from the Pioneers Guiding Association in Jinka, see p197) and pay individuals for any photos you take. The official current photo rate is adult/child Birr7/5, although Birr1 or Birr2 is also routinely accepted.

These price hikes are largely because all that is 'alien' and 'primitive' have suddenly become commodities and since few cultures on earth epitomise these tribal stereotypes so strongly, the Mursi are finding no shortage of customers.

For many, a trip here represents a unique chance to encounter a culture markedly different from their own. After all, where else can you see half-naked women with massive lip-plates, ritually scarred bodies and such ornate hairstyles?

In reality visiting the Mursi is somewhat of a free-for-all. Every morning convoys of jeeps charge from Jinka to the closest of the Mursi villages. With cameras clicking and Birr flying, the situation soon resembles a human zoo more than a cultural exchange. Tourists line up villagers to 'select' those most worthy of being photographed and the Mursi use various (sometimes aggressive) techniques to extract the most money from them in the process. Care is required if both parties aren't to come away feeling exploited and less than satisfied by the experience.

Sleeping

It's possible to camp (Birr10 per person) within the park, but there are no facilities. Most people return to Jinka.

Getting There & Around

There's no public transport within the park, so you'll have to rent a 4WD from a tour operator in Addis Ababa (see p270) or from the Pioneers Guiding Association (p197) in Jinka.

The roads within the park are the kind that eat 4WDs for brunch, losing themselves in the savannah or petering out to nothing in thick acacia forest. At these times, expect to do as little as 6km/h. Best practice is to travel in convoy and bring extra fuel.

LOWER OMO VALLEY VILLAGES
ዝቅተኛው የኦሞ ሸለቆ መንደሮች

The villages of the Lower Omo Valley are homes to some of Africa's most fascinating and colourful ethnic groups. It's here that ancient customs and traditions have remained almost entirely intact. Animism is still the religion, hostility between neighbouring tribes is still high, internecine warfare is common and some tribes still practise a purely pastoral economy.

Weyto ወይጦ

This little village lies at the junction to Arbore, roughly halfway between Konso and Key Afar. The Tsemay – part farmers, part pastoralists – inhabit the region. There's little reason to stop here, but if you get caught the **Hor Restaurant and Hotel** (☎ 0916 856141; camping Birr30, s/tw Birr60/100) has some stark rooms and the best local food (mains Birr25).

Arba Minch–Jinka buses stop here, but there are rarely any seats. Daily Isuzu trucks serve Konso (Birr50 to Birr100, two hours), Key Afar (Birr40, 1½ hours) and Turmi (Birr50-100, four hours) via Arbore (Birr40, 1½ hours). Locals pay one-fifth the price.

Arbore አሬበራ

Arbore rests 50km south of Weyto on the Turmi road. The Arbore people are a mixed bunch, with ancestry linking back to the Omo Valley and Konso highlands. With their beads and aluminium jewellery, they almost resemble the Borena people. To escape the area's notorious mosquitoes, many Arbore sleep on 5m-high platforms; locals outside the village know it as 'mosquito town'.

South of Arbore, off the main Arbore–Turmi Rd, tracks lead to the strange saline lake of **Chew Bahir** (also known as Lake Stephanie). From Arbore to the junction of the main track is a 35km drive. From the junction to the lake is 60km. Oryx and gazelles are sometimes found near the lake. The ground around the lake is notoriously unstable, so take a police-guide from Arbore. January to December is the best time to visit.

Daily Isuzu trucks ramble past en route to Weyto (Birr40, 1½ hours) and Turmi (Birr50, two hours).

Turmi ቱርሚ

Although tiny, **Turmi** (admission per vehicle Birr50) is indistinguishable from other towns in the region and is surrounded by several traditional

Hamer villages. On Monday, Hamer people descend on Turmi and pack its famed **market**.

Hamer women, with their shimmering coppery-coloured tresses, sell vegetables, spices, butter, milk and traditional items like incised calabashes, head stools, metal arm bracelets and fantastically smelly goatskins decorated with beads and cowrie shells.

The region around Turmi is well known for the famous Hamer and Banna **Jumping of the Bulls ceremony** (see p203). Admission fees of Birr150 per person are asked; the ceremony lasts all day (from 11am to 6pm).

PEOPLES OF THE LOWER OMO VALLEY

The Lower Omo Valley is unique in that it is home to so many peoples in such a small area. Historians believe that the south served for millennia as a kind of cultural crossroads, where Cushitic, Nilotic, Omotic and Semitic peoples met as they migrated from the north, west, south and east.

Described here are some of its most notable peoples. The map on p202 illustrates the geographical distribution of all tribes.

The Ari አሪ

Almost 120,000 Ari inhabit the northern border of Mago National Park. They keep large numbers of livestock and produce large amounts of honey, often used for trade. The women wear skirts made from the *enset* tree.

The Banna በና

Numbering around 45,000, the Banna inhabit the higher ground east of Mago National Park. Most practise agriculture, though their diet is supplemented by hunting. After killing a buffalo, they decorate themselves with clay for a special celebration and feast for the whole village.

The Bumi በ-ሚ

Inhabiting the land south of the Omo National Park are around 8000 Bumi. They occasionally invade the southern plains when fodder or water is scarce.

The Bumi are agropastoralists, growing sorghum by the Omo River as well as fishing and rearing cattle. They also hunt and smoke bees out of their hives for honey. Known as great warmongers, they're regularly doing battle with the Karo, the Hamer and the Surma.

The Bumi use scarification for cosmetic purposes, tribal identification and as indications of prowess in battle. Both men and women use little *pointilles* (dots) to highlight their eyes and cheekbones. The women also scarify their torsos with curvilinear and geometrical designs.

The Hamer ሃመር

The Hamer, who number around 50,000, are subsistence agropastoralists. They cultivate sorghum, vegetables, millet, tobacco and cotton, as well as rear cattle and goats. Wild honey is an important part of their diet.

The people are particularly known for their remarkable hairstyles. The women mix together ochre, water and a binding resin before rubbing it into their hair. They then twist strands again and again to create coppery-coloured tresses known as *goscha*. These are a sign of health and welfare.

If they've recently killed an enemy or dangerous animal, men are permitted to don clay hair buns that sometimes support magnificent ostrich feathers. With the help of special headrests (*borkotos*) for sleeping, the buns last from three to six months, and can be 'redone' for up to one year.

The Hamer are also considered masters of body decoration. Every adornment has an important symbolic significance; earrings, for example, denote the number of wives a man has.

The women wear iron coils around their arms and bead necklaces, and decorate their skin with cowrie shells. The *ensente* (iron torques) worn around the necks of married and engaged women indicate the wealth and prestige of their husband. Unmarried girls wear a metal plate in their hair that looks a bit like a platypus' bill.

The *evangadi* (Hamer night dance) can also be seen or organised. It usually costs around Birr100 per person and lasts three hours. Just don't forget to look up. When you're lucky enough to strike a cloudless night, the twinkling lights in a star-splattered sky seem almost within reach.

SLEEPING & EATING

As Turmi lies at an important crossroads – not only for travellers, but also for locals – a number of hotels have sprouted around the settlement. Most generators start at 6pm.

Green Hotel (camping Birr50, s/d/tw without bathroom Birr50/60/120) This place is essentially the same

---

The iron bracelets and armlets are an indication of the wealth and social standing of the young girl's family. When she gets married, she must remove the jewellery; it's the first gift she makes to her new family.

The Hamer territory stretches east to Chew Bahir, south to the Kenya border and north to Banna territory.

The Karo ካሮ

With a population of about 1500 people, the Karo are thought to be the Omo Valley's most endangered group. Inhabiting the Omo's eastern bank, many of these traditional pastoralists have now turned to agriculture after disease wiped out their cattle.

In appearance, language and tradition, they slightly resemble the Hamer, to whom they're related. The Karo are considered masters of body painting, particularly when preparing for a dance, feast or celebration. Most famously, chalk is used to imitate the spotted plumage of the guinea fowl.

The Karo are also great improvisers: Bic biros, nails, sweet wrappers and cartridges are all incorporated into jewellery and decoration. Yellow mineral rock, black charcoal and pulverised red iron ore are traditionally used.

The Mursi መ-ርሲ

The 8000 or so Mursi are mainly pastoralists who move according to the seasons between the lower Tama Plains and the Mursi Hills in Mago National Park.

Some Mursi practise flood retreat cultivation, particularly where the tsetse fly prohibits cattle rearing. Honey is collected from beehives made with bark and dung. The Mursi language is Nilo-Saharan in origin.

The most famous Mursi traditions include the fierce stick-fighting between the men, and the lip-plates worn by the women. Made of clay and up to 15cm in diameter, the plates are inserted into a slit separating their lower lip and jaw. Due to the obvious discomfort, women only wear the lip-plates occasionally, leaving their distended lips swaying below their jaw. Anthropologists offer several theories to explain the practice: to deter slavers looking for unblemished girls; to prevent evil from entering the body by way of the mouth; or to indicate social status by showing the number of cattle required by the wearer's family for her hand in marriage.

The Surma ሱ-ርማ

Formerly nomadic pastoralists, the Surma now largely depend on the subsistence cultivation of sorghum and maize. The Surma have a fearsome reputation as warriors, in part inspired by their continual search for grazing lands. Fights against the Bumi, their sworn enemies, still occur.

It's believed that the Surma once dominated the area, but their territory has been reduced to the western edges of Omo National Park. The population of 45,000 is split into three subgroups: the Chai, Tirma and Bale. The Surma hunt in the park and make beehive huts. Like the Mursi, the Surma men stick fight and the women don distending lip-plates.

The Surma are also known for their white, almost ghostlike body painting. White chalk is mixed with water to create a kind of wash. The painting is much less ornamental than that found in other tribes and is intended to intimidate enemies in battle. Sometimes snake and wavelike patterns are painted across the torso and thighs.

as its rival, the Tourist Hotel next door. The rooms are a tad shabbier and the prices a tad cheaper. You'll find the squat toilets and drum shower out back; just follow your nose. The restaurant (mains Birr30) has the better coffee of the two.

Tourist Hotel (☎ 0911 190209; d without bathroom Birr70) Each room has a cement floor, a small double bed and a largely futile mosquito net. The squat toilet stall is cleaner than those next door (Green Hotel), although the holey shower shack is less than private. The restaurant (mains Birr20 to Birr30) serves the best food in town, but don't expect anything beyond simple omelettes, pastas and Ethiopian fare.

Kaske Campsite (camping Birr70, camping incl tent rental Birr100, bungalows d/tw Birr350/700) Thanks to a canopy of lush mango trees, there is plenty of shade at this campsite next to the Kaske River. It is one of the prettiest we saw, although it is 3.9km north of Turmi, just off the road to Weyto. Until the restaurant is built, it's a hot and dusty walk to town for meals. The thatched, circular bungalows here are very pleasant and are inspired by traditional Hamer designs.

Evangadi Lodge & Campsite (☎ 0116 632595; www .evangadilodge.com; camping Birr75, camping incl tent rental Birr200, bungalow d Birr500) During high season this acacia-shaded campsite gets as busy as a termite hill after a flood. During such times the price of the spacious bungalows is doubled, the kitchen hut is in hot (no pun intended) demand, and the staff are run off their feet keeping the ablution blocks the cleanest in Turmi. Evangadi is 1km east of town.

GETTING THERE & AWAY

Set at an important crossroads, daily Isuzu trucks leave for Omorate (Birr50, two hours), Arbore (Birr50, two hours), Weyto (Birr100, four hours), Dimeka (Birr50, two hours), Key Afar (Birr100, six hours) and Jinka (Birr150 to Birr200, eight hours). These prices are indicative only. If you get stuck, enlist the help of the manager of the Green Hotel.

Omorate አሞራ·ተ

Omorate is nestled along the baking eastern bank of the **Omo River**, 72km southwest of Turmi. For those without a vehicle, Omorate

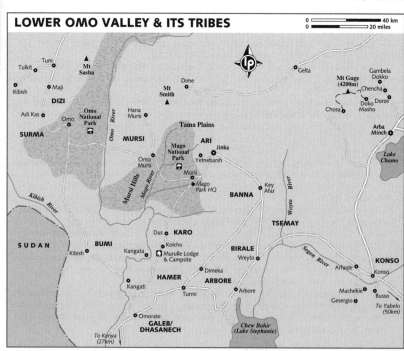

LOWER OMO VALLEY & ITS TRIBES

JUMPING OF THE BULLS CEREMONY

Whipping, teasing, screaming and a whole lot of leaping are part of this infamous ceremony. It's a right of passage into manhood for all young Hamer and Banna boys and is truly a sight to behold. After 15 to 30 bulls have been lined up side by side, each naked boy taking part must leap down the line of bulls, jumping on the beasts from back to back. If they fall, they're whipped and teased by women. If they succeed, they must turn around and complete the task three more times!

During the ceremony young female relatives of the boys beg to be whipped; the deeper their scars, the more love they show for their boy. It's as disturbing as it's intriguing.

Ceremonies typically take part between late February and early April, July through September and the first half of December.

---

is the only place you can actually lay eyes on the mighty river.

As this is a sensitive border area, travellers need to register their passport at the **Main Department for Immigration & Nationality Affairs** (🕐 24 hr) upon arrival.

The town itself is rather unsightly; the real attraction is the traditional **Galeb (Dasanech) villages** (admission per person Birr10) just across the river. To get there you will need to hire a guide (regardless of you actually requiring one) from the newly formed guide association (Birr50) and pay the *faranji* inflated price of Birr40 per person for the return boat trip across the river. Once in the villages, expect to be mobbed by locals fishing for photographs. The going rate is Birr1 or Birr2 per person per photo.

Some canny travellers have opted out of the circus that the situation is fast becoming and visited the more low-key villages on the Omorate side of the river.

There's not much difference between the **Tourist Hotel** (s with shared bathroom Birr40), **Park Hotel** (s with shared bathroom Birr20) and **National Hotel** (s with shared bathroom Birr30). Spread around the police station, they all specialise in grubby, small single cells. Check all three before deciding which currently has the cleanest sheets. We liked the Park Hotel best.

GETTING THERE & AWAY

Omorate is the most difficult to get to of all the southern towns. The police here are particularly vigilant when it comes to fining drivers who pick up *faranji*. Consequently, Isuzu trucks charge exorbitant amounts to travellers. We were told that to catch a lift to Turmi would cost Birr200 (locals pay between Birr20 and Birr30 for the same two-hour ride). Clearly some negotiation would

be in order before coughing out that kind of money!

For details about crossing into Kenya, see p262.

Dimeka ዲሜካ

Like Turmi, which sits 28km to its south, Dimeka is a Hamer village. However, since it borders on Banna territory, its Tuesday and Saturday **markets** (Tuesday is best) attract locals from both tribes.

The **Tourist Hotel** (s with shared bathroom Birr40) is the best of a few weak sleeping options. Its small rooms are old and have holey mosquito nets, squishy foam mattresses and tin ceilings. There are no showers.

Passing Isuzu trucks pick up people heading for Turmi (Birr50, two hours) and Key Afar (Birr50 to Birr60, four hours).

Key Afar ቀይ አፋር

A haven of cool compared to Turmi or Omorate, Key Afar rests on a lush plateau along the Konso–Jinka Rd. Lacking the traditional atmosphere seen in other villages, Key

---

SCAR TISSUE

For most tribes of the Lower Omo Valley, scarification serves as a distinction for brave warriors; the men are not allowed to scarify themselves until they have killed at least one foe. For women, the raised texture of the skin is considered highly desirable, and is said to hold sensual value for men.

Scarification is achieved using a stone, knife, hook or razor blade. Then ash is applied to the wound, creating an infection and promoting scar-tissue growth. As the wound heals, the scar creates the desired knobbly effect on the skin's surface.

SOUTHERN ETHIOPIA

Afar comes alive on Thursday when the local Banna, Hamer and Ari people are in town for the produce **market**, along with every tourist in the vicinity.

The **Nasa Hotel** (☎ 0910 192649; d with/without bathroom Birr70/100) on the road that leads to Weyto is the pick of the local hotels with simple, clean rooms and a low-key restaurant (mains Birr20). There are a couple more hotel options near the junction in the centre of town, but their old sheets and toe-curling tin-shack toilets leave something to be desired.

Arba Minch–Jinka buses can drop you here, but there are rarely empty seats if you want to get on. Daily Isuzu trucks head to Dimeka (Birr50 to Birr60, four hours), Turmi (Birr80, six hours), Weyto (Birr40, 1½ hours) and Jinka (Birr40, two hours).

Kolcho, Kangata & Dus
ኮልቾ፥ ካንጋታ ና ደስ

These three villages all sit between Omorate and Mago National Park. Minuscule Kolcho is arguably the most beautiful, with its lofty views over the Omo River and traditional Karo dwellings. It's also a great place for traditional dancing, though it'll cost you (Birr300 to Birr700 per group depending on size). Dances last around one hour and usually take place at sunset.

Around 1km from Kolcho is **Lake Deepa**, which is a great spot for birdwatching. The Bumi village of Kangata, which lies across the river further south, can also be visited.

It's also possible to arrange traditional dancing at the large village of Dus, north of Kolcho (same prices as Kolcho).

About 6km south of Kolcho is the amazing **Murulle Lodge & Campsite** built by **Ethiopian Rift Valley Safaris** (☎ 0111 552128; www.ethiopianriftvalley safaris.com). To stay at the amazing lodge, you have to be on one of their pricey package tours. However, it's possible to camp here for US$12 per person per night.

The only way to access Kolcho, Kangata, Dus and Murulle is with a private 4WD.

South of Murulle is a beautiful savannah plain where oryx and Grant's gazelles are frequently seen. Oddly there are far more animals reported here than at Mago National Park! There are also 340 bird species in the region. Watch out for the delightful carmine bee-eaters, which fly alongside your vehicle and snap up the insects stirred up by the wheels. The clouds of little quail-like birds that explode like popcorn from the grass as vehicles pass are red-billed queleas.

Omo National Park
ኦሞ ብሔራዊ ፓርክ

If Mago National Park is for the adventurous, **Omo National Park** (admission Birr70, vehicle Birr100) is for the masochists. To state the obvious, travelling in Ethiopia's most remote park is incredibly tough. Because there is virtually no infrastructure within the park, you will need to be totally self-sufficient with your own food, transport and vehicle. The Surma (p200), who live within the park, can only be visited with a 4WD and since the bridge across the Omo River has been washed away, they are only accessible from the west via Tum out of Jimma. They charge Birr200 per group and you also have to take two police escorts (Birr200 each).

Like other parks in Ethiopia, wildlife here has come into conflict with the indigenous tribes who live here and with the recent departure of the African Parks Network (see the boxed text, p193) in 2008, Omo's future, at least as far as the wildlife is concerned, is looking bleaker than ever.

Most who visit here use the services of an Addis Ababa tour operator (see p270).

Eastern Ethiopia

Eastern Ethiopia is a land of desolate beauty. Much of it is characterised by a hauntingly stark landscape of dust-stained acacia scrub and a string of forgettable towns. But concealed beneath this cloak of the commonplace are gems of genuine adventure and priceless moments of shared intimacies.

Undoubtedly, the east's pièce de résistance is the walled city of Harar. There is still a patina of myth about this ancient city, handed down from the days when its markets served as the Horn's commercial hub and attracted powerful merchants, artisans and Islamic scholars.

Today, only time's thinnest veil separates the then from now. When you find yourself pressed up against a Somali camel herder in a narrow lane or share a joke with an Adare merchant, you too will feel that the ghosts of yesteryear still breathe life into Harar.

If the east is the funnel that channels overlanders to Djibouti and Somaliland, then Awash is the neck in the hourglass through which all must pass. By lucky coincidence it's also home to Ethiopia's most accessible national park and offers a rare chance to glimpse the region's disappearing wildlife.

From Awash, a seemingly endless ribbon of asphalt leads north to the desolate southern Danakil. This territory remains virtually unexplored since legendary adventurer Wilfred Thesiger first thrilled the world with tales of the proud Afar and their secret wells.

For those that head east a surprise awaits. The thirsty lowlands give way to the eastern highlands, a land of lush cultivation and stunning views and proof that eastern Ethiopia really is one of those rarest of jewels, a diamond in the rough.

EASTERN ETHIOPIA

HIGHLIGHTS

- Tour **Debre Zeyit's** (p206) crater lakes on a horse-drawn cart in search of birds

- Scramble up **Mt Zuqualla** (p209) and confess your sins at the poignant monastery of Mt Zuqualla Maryam

- Take a photo of the beautiful beisa oryx at **Awash National Park** (p210)

- Bite down on a stick wrapped with meat as hyenas pull it from you mouth in **Harar** (p218)

- Explore the labyrinth of alleyways and shrines in Harar's **old walled city** (p219)

- Share a smile and chew *chat* with Afar camel traders in the shadow of **Asaita** (p213) on the way to Djibouti

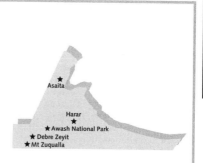

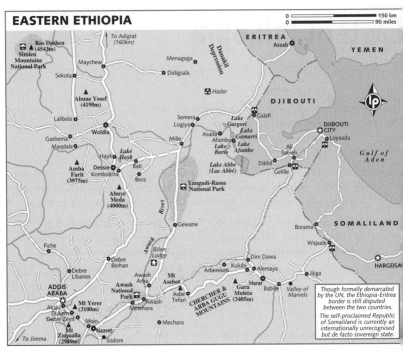

EASTERN ETHIOPIA

Though formally demarcated by the UN, the Ethiopia-Eritrea border is still disputed between the two countries.

The self-proclaimed Republic of Somaliland is currently an internationally unrecognised but de facto sovereign state.

Climate

The lowlands around Asaita and Awash are baking hot (up to 45°C) from May to September and receive little rain. They are also prone to severe droughts. The climate in Debre Zeyit and Nazret is similar to the conditions that prevail in Addis Ababa. The highlands around Dire Dawa, Harar and Jijiga are hot and dry. The main rains fall from July to September.

Getting There & Away

Ethiopian Airlines (www.flyethiopian.com) connects Addis Ababa with Dire Dawa and Jijiga. Most people who enter eastern Ethiopia overland travel by bus or train from Djibouti City and disembark in Dire Dawa. It's also possible to travel from Hargeisa (Somaliland) to Jijiga by bus. For more information see p263.

Getting Around

Good sealed roads connect the main cities, including Asaita to the far northeast. Most cities in this part of Ethiopia are well served by public transport, except for the long stretch from Awash to Asaita, where buses are infrequent.

ADDIS ABABA TO AWASH

The long, well-maintained stretch of roa between Addis Ababa and Awash is a gentl introduction to eastern Ethiopia. Most for eign visitors rush straight through withou stopping, which is a bit of a shame. Althoug there's nothing really jaw-dropping, there ar enough attractions and notable towns to kee you busy for a few days.

DEBRE ZEYIT ደብረ ዘይት

pop 131,200 / elev 1920m

Untidy, scruffy and dusty – first impres sions may leave you wondering why Debr Zeyit, known in the local Oromo language a Bishoftu, is such a favourite playground fo those seeking to escape the capital for a week end. But strung around the town, and not im mediately apparent, is a dishevelled necklac of maars – flat bottomed, roughly circula volcanic crater lakes. While they are a far cr from the Bahamas, they are highly praised b the locals for their beauty and make for a sur prisingly tasty hors d'oeuvre before tacklin the rougher expanses of far eastern Ethiopia

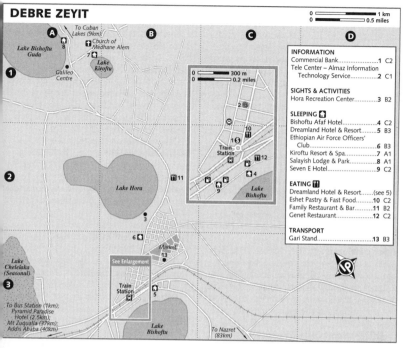

DEBRE ZEYIT

See Enlargement

INFORMATION
Commercial Bank........................1 C2
Tele Center – Almaz Information
  Technology Service..............2 C1

SIGHTS & ACTIVITIES
Hora Recreation Center............3 B2

SLEEPING
Bishoftu Afaf Hotel...................4 C2
Dreamland Hotel & Resort........5 B3
Ethiopian Air Force Officers'
  Club....................................6 B3
Kiroftu Resort & Spa................7 A1
Salayish Lodge & Park..............8 A1
Seven E Hotel..........................9 C2

EATING
Dreamland Hotel & Resort.......(see 5)
Eshet Pastry & Fast Food........10 C2
Family Restaurant & Bar..........11 B2
Genet Restaurant...................12 C2

TRANSPORT
Gari Stand..............................13 B3

Information

Commercial Bank (8-11am & 1-4pm Mon-Fri, 8-11am Sat) Changes cash only (euros and US dollars).

Tele Center – Almaz Information Technology Service (per hr Birr21; 8.30am-8.30pm) Internet. On the road to Lake Hora.

Sights

LAKE BISHOFTU ቢሸፍቱ ሐይቅ

The best way to appreciate the lake is probably from Dreamland Hotel & Resort, drink in hand. The view overlooking the crater rim is breathtaking. To get up close and personal with this body of water, scramble down one of the cattle trails and join the children for a swim. But take care – according to local lore, this, the second-deepest lake in Ethiopia, is home to a sleeping devil. From time to time its evil gases kill the fish and send them bobbing to the surface to be scooped up by delighted waterbirds.

LAKE HORA ሆራ ሐይቅ

Attractively set Lake Hora lays 1.5km north of the town's centre and has some outstanding birdlife. Storks, pelicans, shovellers and grebes, as well as brightly coloured kingfishers, are among the species seen here.

The **Hora Recreation Center** (admission Birr4) can get a bit noisy at weekends, but it's easy enough to escape the crowds: just follow the footpath around the lake as it winds through the forested slopes of the crater. A circumnavigation of the lake takes around 1½ hours. You should go along with another tourist if possible, as hassling (and even theft) has been a problem in the past.

On the first Sunday following Meskel, the Oromo people celebrate Irecha on the shores of Lake Hora. During this time thanks is given to *Waka* (One God) and good fortune sought for the upcoming planting season. Devotees gather around ancient fig trees to smear perfume, butter and *katickala* (a distilled alcohol) on the tree trunks and share ceremonial meals of roasted meat, coffee, *tella* and *araki* (traditional alcoholic drinks).

OTHER LAKES

If you feel lake-addicted after visiting Lake Bishoftu and Lake Hora, follow the road to the north. Walk past the Defence

EASTERN ETHIOPIA

Engineering College and the Agriculture Research Centre until you reach a fork in the road. Go to the right and follow the dirt road until you reach the Galileo Centre. Continue straight on for about 400m, until a dirt road to your left leads down to the shore of the scenic and peaceful **Lake Bishoftu Guda**.

To get to the milky-looking **Lake Kiroftu**, backtrack to the Galileo Centre and take the road on the left leading to the Kiroftu Resort & Spa. Lake Kiroftu is known particularly for its tilapia (freshwater fish) and its varied birdlife.

There are other lakes dotted around Debre Zeyit, including the **Cuban Lakes**, but they lie much further away and are not easily accessible unless you have private transport.

Sleeping

Bishoftu Afaf Hotel (☎ 0114 338299; fax 0114 336220; r Birr85) Although all the rooms are priced the same, not all are capable of delivering hot water or of similar size; ask to see a few. The restaurant overlooking the lime-green waters of Lake Bishoftu is the high point – in more ways than one.

ourpick Salayish Lodge & Park (☎ 0911 996030; www.ethiolodge.net; r Birr200-250) If you're looking for a place to kick back and unwind, then look no further. The quaint, bamboo-thatched rooms are set in gardens filled with rambling bougainvilleas, twittering birds and fruit trees. A two-minute stroll from the atmospheric bamboo-hut restaurant will take you to the crest of a hill that enjoys wide views over Lake Bishoftu Guda. A taxi from town costs Birr30.

Ethiopian Air Force Officers' Club (☎ 0114 338035; s/d/tw Birr250/250/500; ☀) If spending some time with army officials is your idea of a nice retreat, you can bunk down in this 24-room, four-block complex. The general (no pun intended) feel is that some of the shine has been polished off the military brass – the Olympic-sized pool (nonguests Birr20, for example), needs a tad more chlorine.

Dreamland Hotel & Resort (☎ 0114 371520; ethiosoft@yahoo.com; s/tw/ste/q Sun-Thu Birr506/569/822-948/1200; ☐) All rooms in the town's flashiest digs have baths, satellite TV and richly polished furniture. But it's not until sunset, when the low-slung sun gives the balconies a full frontal from the far side of the lake, do the rooms really shine. Friday and Saturday

nights cost around 12% more than the week day rates quoted above.

Kiroftu Resort & Spa (☎ 0911 248213, in Addis Abab 011-6636557; www.kurifturesortspa.com; d incl breakfas US$197-294; ☀ ☐) Popular with Addis Ababa' well-heeled elite, tariffs here include a buffe breakfast for two, a Swedish massage, a pedi cure for one and free use of the pool, movi theatre, kayaks and bikes. The great locatio affords the stone and timber restaurant spec tacular views across Lake Kiroftu.

Other options within town are:

Seven E Hotel (☎ 0114 339888; d Birr60) Although decor is not its strong point, it's good value for those on a budget.

Pyramid Paradise Hotel (☎ 0114 336216; d Birr250-360; ☐) Decent rooms and reliable hot water.

Eating

Eshet Pastry & Fast Food (pastries Birr3-6; ☺ 6am 9.30pm) This lively den's shady terrace is perfect spot to take in the local scene whil sipping a strong *macchiato* (Birr2). If th power is on, so is the TV – loudly.

Genet Restaurant (mains Birr8-20) Just dow the road from the Bishoftu Ataf Hote this modest, family-run eatery serves goo Ethiopian staples at puny prices. The men is not translated into English, but *tibs* (slice lamb, pan-fried in butter, garlic, onion an sometimes tomato) makes for a good standb if communication proves too difficult an starvation looms.

Dreamland Hotel & Resort (☎ 0114 371520; main Birr20-45) With its cliff-top view over Lak Bishoftu's water-filled crater and a reason ably priced menu, Dreamland is arguably th most agreeable place in town to dine.

Pyramid Paradise Hotel (☎ 0114 336216; main Birr22-40) Pull up a plastic chair under one c the tent-like canopies in this popular garde restaurant. The pies and cakes go well with th Sunday-evening coffee ceremony.

Family Restaurant & Bar (☎ 0114 338066; main Birr30-60) Surprise: this place is modelled o an American bar and serves Tex-Mex grub It may push the budget, but where els could you grab invigorating nachos, tacc and guacamole cheeseburgers? Open o weekends only.

Getting There & Around

Buses/minibuses leave every 15 minutes fo Addis Ababa (Birr6/9, one hour) and Nazre (Birr6/10, one hour).

A *gari* (horse-drawn cart) is a great way to visit the lakes. They can be hired at the market, about 800m from the main roundabout. Expect to pay around Birr70/100 per half/full day. Jaunts around town in a local minibus cost Birr1.

MT ZUQUALLA ዝቋላ ተራራ

Debre Zeyit also makes a good base from which to explore the extinct volcanic cone of Mt Zuqualla. Though only rising to just over 600m from the surrounding countryside, the mountain dominates the landscape for miles around. On a clear day, the views from the top are stunning. You can see the Rift Valley to the east and the lakes to the south; Addis Ababa and the Entoto Mountains are just discernible to the northwest.

The crater, measuring 2km across and over 60m deep, contains a holy lake that the local clergy maintain has magical healing properties and is consequently off-limits to swimmers (although pilgrims regularly drink from it). A one-hour return walk through some lovely juniper forest will bring you to a crack between two rocks that only the repentant sinner will be able to squeeze through. We made it.

The **monastery of Mt Zuqualla Maryam** (admission Birr50) is traditionally thought to have been founded by St Gebre Manfus Kiddus (see the boxed text, p57) in the 12th or 13th century, although the site may actually date to the 4th century, when a hermit community may have been established here by St Mercurios.

In March and October, large, colourful festivities are held at the monastery to commemorate St Gebre Manfus Kiddus and draws pilgrims from miles around.

You're welcome to spend the night at the monastery, but don't expect the Ritz. The 'guesthouse' more closely resembles a stable spread with straw. Another possibility is to bring a tent and camp in the church compound. Either way, bring your own food and a sense of adventure.

Getting There & Away

The nearest village to Mt Zuqualla is Maryam Wember, which lies at the foot of the mountain, around 25km southwest of Debre Zeyit.

Usually one or two 4WD vehicles travel daily to Maryam Wember (Birr12 to Birr15, up to two hours) from Debre Zeyit (more on market day on Thursday). From Maryam

Wember, it's a 12km walk (three hours up and 2½ hours down).

If you're not watching the pennies, your best bet is to rent a 4WD in Addis Ababa (see p270).

NAZRET ናዝሬት

pop 228,600 / elev 1712m

Although the man next to us on the bus extolled the virtues of Nazret (its name is derived from Christ's birthplace in Israel), a large, commercial and bustling town just 100km from the capital, they weren't immediately apparent to us – even after some time. Sure, it's a pleasant enough town and it flaunts some good accommodation options, it's just that there is little beyond convenience to make you linger.

Information

Commercial Bank (☎ 0221 111952; ⏰ 8am-noon & 2-5pm Mon-Fri, 8-11am Sat) On the main roundabout.

Z-nice Internet (per min Birr0.20; ⏰ 8am-8pm) Possibly the world's slowest connection. Diagonally opposite the Frank Hotel.

Sleeping & Eating

Hotels are plentiful. Besides those listed here, a short stroll down the main road will bring you to several more reasonably clean options.

Palace Hotel (☎ 0221 113800; r incl breakfast Birr150-230) While the Palace isn't exactly palatial it's brilliant value and opposite the bus station. The well-scrubbed rooms are nothing fancy but are serviceable and come with satellite TV. The large garden is a pleasant spot to unwind in and savour a meal (mains Birr25 to Birr35).

Pan-Afric Hotel (☎ 0221 122720; fax 0221 126888; Addis Ababa Rd; d/tw Birr125/165) This is the closest thing Nazret has to a business hotel, with functional, if threadbare, rooms equipped with satellite TV and prudish bathrooms. The better rooms are the brighter and quieter rooms at the rear. The restaurant (mains Birr20 to Birr35) failed to impress.

Safari Lodge Adama (☎ 0221 122011; leilaworku @hotmail.com; r Mon-Thu Birr380, Fri-Sun Birr400, ste Birr810; 🖪 🖳) Frazzled city slickers from the capital and sun-starved tourists from abroad flock here to sip cocktails in the garden and top up their tans by the pool. This resort has all the perks of a mellow retreat: ideal location, pricey restaurant (mains Birr30 to Birr75), jacuzzi, free wireless internet, a kid-friendly horse and two well-stocked bars. Don't be alarmed by the 1950s UFO hovering above the pool – that's the luxury suite.

Frank Hotel (☎ 0221 112196; Addis Ababa Rd; mains Birr15-35) Elbows out – this is indisputably the most popular eatery in town and it can be a squeeze finding a table come dinnertime. It's a little time-warpish (neon lighting, 1970s reddish tablecloth) but the beer is cold and flows freely. We tried the Western food and while it was fine, it wasn't the culinary delight the crowds promised. Ignore the hotel section – it's shabby.

Getting There & Away

At least 20 buses leave daily for Addis Ababa (Birr12, two hours). One bus and frequent minibuses leave daily for Awash (Birr22, 2½ hours). For Debre Zeyit (Birr8, one hour), Ziway and the Rift Valley lakes it's best to first go to Mojo (Birr5, 15 minutes) as buses leave there every 15 minutes.

When heading south for Bale Mountains National Park, first go to Asela (Birr12, two hours) and change.

AWASH NATIONAL PARK
አዋሽ ብሔራዊ ፓርክ

Easily accessible from Addis Ababa, **Awash National Park** (48-hr admission per child/adult Birr25/50, per vehicle up to 5 seats Birr10, compulsory guide per day Birr50; ☼ 6am-6pm) is one of Ethiopia's most visited parks. However, if you are here for the thrill of staring slack-jawed at lions crunching through bones, you'll be seriously disap-

pointed. This park is much lower-key and recent incursions by neighbouring Kereyu pastoralists (who bring their cattle to graze within the park parameters) have done little to help wildlife numbers. Nevertheless, for those with an interest in birds there is some excellent birdwatching to be had, and an interesting range of volcanic landscapes and dry acacia savannah.

The main gate is 16km before Awash and the park headquarters lies 10km southeast of the main gate inside the park. The park takes its name from the Awash River, the longest river in Ethiopia. The river marks the park's southern boundary, and then veers north before disappearing into the remote and desolate confines of the Danakil region.

Wildlife
BIRDS

The park lies on an important migratory route between the north and the south and is littered with an astonishing amount of birdlife. More than 400 bird species have been recorded in the park, among them six endemics: the banded barbet, golden-backed woodpecker, white-winged cliff chat, white-tailed starling, thick-billed raven and wattled ibis among others.

Two especially good spots to observe birds are around Filwoha Hot Springs and around the camping grounds near Awash River, where doves, barbets and hoopoes are all seen.

Near the river itself, kingfishers and bee-eaters are found. On the plains, bustards are quite easily spotted, and sometimes secretary birds and ostriches. Among the many raptors are tawny and fish eagles, dark chanting goshawks and pygmy and lanner falcons.

MAMMALS

In the south of the park lies the grassy Illala Sala Plains, which attracts most of the larger mammals. The beautiful beisa oryx is easily seen here (in particular, between the park gate and Kereyou Lodge), as are Soemmering's gazelles. Salt's dik-diks prefer the acacia bushes.

In the bushland areas, particularly in the rocky valleys to the north, around the park headquarters and in the area known as Kudu Valley, greater and lesser kudus, defassa waterbucks (though few in numbers now) and warthogs can be seen. Anubis and hamadryas baboons are found in the east side of the park

AWASH NATIONAL PARK

0 —— 10 km
0 —— 6 miles

Kessem River

To Bilen Lodge (30km); Gewane (140km); Mille (290km); Asaita (440km); Galafi (450km)

Awash Arba

Camp Site

Filwoha Hot Springs

To Dire Dawa (310km); Harar (320km)

Kudu Valley

Awash

Lookout

Sabober Plains

Fantale Crater (2007m)

Main Gate

Metehara

Illala Sala Plains

Awash Gorge

Lake Basaka

HQ & Museum

Lookout

Kereyou Lodge

To Nazret (95km); Addis Ababa (210km)

River

Awash

Gotu Camp Sites

Awash Falls

EASTERN ETHIOPIA

as well as around the Filwoha Hot Springs and Fantale Crater.

The colobus monkey is found in the riverine forest. Leopards, lions, black-backed and golden jackals, caracals, servals and wildcats are also found in the park, but thank your lucky stars if you manage to spot one of them – they are rarely seen. Striped and spotted hyenas are often heard at night. The nocturnal aardwolf is also present.

Dangers & Annoyances

Armed guides/scouts are compulsory, even if you plan to stay within your vehicle for the entire day. The official explanation is because of the carnivores but, in reality, robbery from local tribespeople poses the greater risk. The park rangers will invariably insist that you take two guides, for added security, but this isn't really necessary unless you plan to camp overnight.

Tribal conflicts between the Kereyu, Afar and Itu pastoralist tribes are still common and obviously the park is best avoided at these times. Malaria here is a major problem and watch out for both the baboons and the grivet monkeys – they are fast, sneaky and adept camp-pillagers.

Sights

To see the greatest number of animals, come first thing in the morning or late in the afternoon. At noon, many animals retire to the shade of the trees.

In the same complex as the park headquarters is a small **museum** (6am-6pm) filled with the usual stuffed animals, plus some mildly interesting 'interpretative materials' on the area's flora, fauna and people, and some useful animal locator maps. Nearby, there's a viewpoint over the mighty **Awash Falls**, which tumble into the magnificent, 150m deep **Awash Gorge** that forms the park's southern boundary. In the wet season, when there's enough water, you can have a dip in the falls.

FANTALE CRATER ፋንታሌ

Towards the west of the park and 2700m above sea level lies Fantale Crater. With its terrific vistas, total quiet and cool air, this dormant volcano is a great place for a picnic. At the top, the 360-degree view is phenomenal and the elliptical caldera, which measures an enormous 3.5km in diameter, is an eerie sight.

The crater rim lies around 25km (a two-hour drive) from park headquarters.

FILWOHA HOT SPRINGS ፍል ውሃ

Fancy a dip? Head to the Filwoha Hot Springs, in the far north of the park, around 40km from the park headquarters. You can swim in the turquoise-blue pools. They're not as refreshing as they look: temperatures touch 36°C! In the cooler areas of the springs, as well as in the Awash River, crocodiles are found.

Around the springs, look out for the doum palms, much appreciated by the local Afar people who use them to make mats as well as a kind of wine. After 5pm, the area comes alive with birds, and lions can sometimes be heard at night.

Sleeping & Eating

Camping (Birr20) The shady sites along the Awash River in the area known as 'Gotu', 400m south of the park headquarters, are attractive. Of the six spots, the Gumarre (hippo) site is considered the most engaging. At night you can often hear the noises of hippos, hyenas and jackals, which come to the river to drink. Another option is the area around the Filwoha Hot Springs in the northern extreme of the park, with its shady fig trees. Bring everything you need because there are no facilities.

Kereyou Lodge (0912 199685; caravan s/d Birr152/202) This is more a decrepit caravan site than a lodge. The 22 neglected caravans have each been parked under individual tin roofs and are slowly falling into serious disrepair. While the lodge may be overpriced its setting is sublime – it is perched on the edge of a plummeting gorge, and the restaurant (mains Birr30 to Birr40) has a terrace that boasts phenomenal views over the gorge and the Awash River. After some early-morning wildlife viewing, it's a fabulous place for a coffee, a goulash or a surprisingly well-crafted shish kebab while ogling the fabulous chasm below your feet.

Getting There & Around

Walking is not allowed in the park, nor are bikes or motorcycles. Most visitors hire vehicles or come with a tour from Addis Ababa (see p270). In theory it should be possible to hire a contract minibus for around Birr750 in Awash or Metahara. Ask at the bus stations.

A 4WD is necessary for the Fantale Crater and the Filwoha Hot Springs, or during the rainy season (July to September).

AWASH አዋሽ

pop 11,000 / elev 900m

Halfway between Addis Ababa and Dire Dawa, Awash is a good place to get out of the bus and stretch. Awash won't win the Tourist Destination of the Year award but this haphazard town will hold your attention for a short stroll. The derelict railway station – still the town's *raison d'être* – may yet spring to life if the Djibouti–Addis Ababa train is resurrected. Around 600m behind the station lies the giddy-deep Awash Gorge. It is also worth a small peek to soak up the vertigo-inducing views.

On Monday there is a very colourful market that attracts both Kereyu and Afar people. Look out for the Kereyu women in skins and sandals and with braided hair. The men prefer a carefully shaped Afro, often ornamented with combs. Animal fat (a kind of Ethiopian Brylcreem) is used to give it a chic gloss and to keep it in condition.

Sleeping & Eating

Buffet d'Aouache (☎ 0222 240008; d/tw without bathroom Birr52/52, d with bathroom Birr154) Originally built by the French to service the Djibouti railway, these 'no frills, no fuss and no fleas' rooms are excellent value if all you require is a clean bed and a cold shower. Back across the railway tracks, a newer building has hot water, fans, plumper beds and private bathrooms. Decent meals (Birr20 to Birr35) can be had if you order in advance. The downside? Both the nearby Orthodox church and Islamic mosque employ loudspeakers to broadcast their prayers at ungodly hours.

Awash Meridian (☎ 0222 240051; d Birr80-120) The Meridian is expanding, so expect further (and pricier) options in the near future. Built around a dirt courtyard, the hotel is almost a carbon copy of the Genet. The on-site restaurant serves delicious fasting food and the *tegabino* (bean-flour stew). At Birr12 each, it's a steal.

Genet Hotel (☎ 0222 240040; s/d Birr160-170/200-210) At the southwestern end of town, a stone's throw from the bus station, the Genet has a series of clean, functional and unremarkable rooms set around a dusty, and at times muddy, courtyard. There's a decent restaurant here but the menu is only in Amharic. We found the *dorrahih arrusta* (roast chicken) for Birr45 to be good.

Getting There & Away

One bus leaves daily for Gewane (Birr22, two hours), three buses go weekly to Logiya (Monday, Thursday and Saturday, Birr53 to Birr70, eight hours) via Mille (Birr50, seven hours), and two buses leave daily for Nazret (Birr16, three hours).

For Dire Dawa (Birr60 to Birr70, six hours), try to find a seat on one of the 10 buses that pass through Awash from Addis Ababa and Nazret.

AWASH TO ASAITA

The endless road north to Asaita crosses a hauntingly bleak landscape of parched plains, ferocious sun and barren scenery. Besides an aloof Afar tribesman or two picking their way through acacia scrub, their rifles casually slung across their shoulders, and a fistful of unassuming towns, there is little to stop the perpetually curious spiralling into a free-fall of boredom. Be prepared for an almost meditative drive that needs a damn good supply of Amharic pop cassettes.

THE ROAD NORTH TO ASAITA

From the junction with the Addis Ababa–Dire Dawa road, you'll first cross **Awash Arba**, about 14km to the north, and then the featureless town of **Gewane**. Gewane doesn't warrant a lengthy stop, but you'll be overwhelmed by the stark allure of the dramatic volcano that lords over the surrounding plains. After Gewane, the country resembles Djibouti more and more: arid and desolate. The road passes through the **Yangudi-Rassa National Park** but, frankly, don't expect much wildlife; there is probably less here than in any national park in Ethiopia.

Around **Mille**, about 150km north of Gewane, look out for the little domed Afar huts, made from the interwoven leaves of the doum palm, which are light and easy to transport. About 10km south of town lies the junction with the road that heads west to Bati and Dessie.

About 80km northeast of Mille, a track leads to Hadar, the famous archaeological site where the fossilised remains of the hominid Lucy (see p31) was discovered. Today the site remains undeveloped and there is little to see besides a fence.

Continuing north from Mille the road takes you through **Logiya**, a surprisingly bustling town where Ethiopian truck drivers usually overnight. Don't expect airs and graces: it's a rough-and-ready town, with a herd of seedy hotels, brothels and restaurants lining the main drag.

About 8km northeast of Logiya, it's a shock to come suddenly upon **Semera**, the new regional capital of Afar. With its quirky mix of barracks, modern apartment blocks and soulless administrative buildings, it looks like a microscopic version of Brasília emerging incongruously in the middle of the desert. Should you want to explore the lakes around Asaita (see p214), you'll have to stop here to hire a compulsory guide (Birr150 per day) and get a permission paper (Birr100 per person) at the **tourist office** (☎ 0336 660488; 🕑 8-11.30am & 3-5pm Mon-Fri), near the Justice building. For some places, you'll also have to hire an armed policeman (Birr100 per day).

About 10km north of Semera along the main road, an easy-to-miss asphalt road branches off to the right and leads to Asaita.

Sleeping & Eating

If you need to break your journey, the choice of reliable accommodation is very limited. Most hotels are spartan and cater primarily to Ethiopian truck drivers on their way to and from Djibouti port.

Bilen Lodge (in Addis Ababa ☎ 0111 508869; Bilen; tukul s/d incl breakfast US$58/75) This hideaway on the edge of Awash National Park has 16 traditional-style reed huts with concrete floors perched on a mound overlooking the reedy expanse of the Bilen hot springs. The showers are cold and the huts are slightly run-down, making them somewhat overpriced, but birders will love the location and the nearby Afar village makes for an interesting excursion (local guide Birr50, although they'll ask for Birr100). Book through the Village Ethiopia tour agency (p271) in Addis Ababa. Lunch and dinner is an additional US$17 per person per day.

Parki Hotelli (☎ 0332 230113; Mille; s/d Birr60/80, r without bathroom Birr30) A ramshackle building with cell-like, ultrabasic rooms. There's an on-site 'restaurant' serving cheap fare.

Nazret Hotel (☎ 0332 500222; Logiya; r without bathroom Birr30-70) This is usually where UN officials bunk down when in town, which is enough to recommend this place on the main street. Ask for the more recent rooms in the second compound at the back: they come with a fan and a mosquito net. The food is pretty varied (read: pasta, rice and *tibs*) for this part of the country.

Getting There & Away

This is not the road less travelled: countless Ethiopian trucks ply this route to and from Djibouti and, as it is such an important corridor, the road is in excellent condition. Without your own wheels your best bet to get from Awash to Logiya is to hitch a lift with one of these trucks. In the hot season many drivers prefer to travel during the cool of the night (to spare their tyres); however, it's safer for tourists to travel during the day. In Awash, ask around at the petrol stations. The ride should set you back about Birr70.

Bus services are fairly infrequent on this long stretch, although a few do strike northward from Awash (see opposite). From Logiya or Semera to Asaita, services are more frequent; there are several daily departures in the morning (Birr15, about two hours).

From Mille, there's at least one daily bus to Dessie (Birr27, nine to 10 hours). From there you can catch a bus to Addis Ababa (see p165).

There's no public transport to Galafi (the Djibouti border) or to Djibouti City, but it's quite easy to hitch a lift (front seats only) with one of the legions of trucks that overnight in Logiya. The prices we were quoted ranged from Birr200 to Birr300 to Djibouti City (about eight hours).

ASAITA አሳይታ
pop 22,700 / elev 300m

Asaita is a cul-de-sac at the end of the world, about 70km east of Logiya. At first glance, the town is not especially alluring; however, it is the heart of the Afar territory and Asaita prides itself on being the bastion of Afar identity and culture. Tuesday is market day – a must if you're in town.

Asaita is a convenient base from which to explore the 30 salt lakes in the area, the volcanic springs and the Danakil Depression. Just come prepared – the heat is unbearable for nine months of the year.

EASTERN ETHIOPIA

THE AFAR – THE DREADED DANAKILS

The Danakil invariably castrated any man or boy whom they killed or wounded, removing both the penis and the scrotum. An obvious trophy, it afforded irrefutable proof that the victim was male…

Sir Wilfred Thesiger, The Life of My Choice *(1987)*

Fuelled by early accounts from European travellers and explorers, the Afar have gained an almost legendary reputation for ferocity. And, as they are one of the few tribes capable of surviving the harsh conditions of northeastern Ethiopia, perhaps that aura of myth is well deserved.

On your journey north, look out for Afar men striding along in simple cotton *shirits* (sarongs), with their famous *jile* (curved knives) and water-filled gourds hanging at their side or a rifle slung casually across a shoulder. Even today many Afars still lead a nomadic existence and when the herds are moved in search of new pasture, the huts in which the Afars live are simply packed onto the backs of camels and carted away. In the relatively fertile plains around the Awash River, some Afars have turned to cultivation, growing tobacco, cotton, maize and dates. Interclan rivalry is still alive and conflicts occasionally break out.

Information

Commercial Bank (🕑 7-11.30am & 3-5pm Mon-Fri, 7-11.30am Sat) Changes cash (euros and US dollars).

Sights

The little-explored territory and the **salt lakes** scattered around Asaita are something of a holy grail for serious adventurers, but an exploration here shouldn't be undertaken lightly. This area remains one of the most inhospitable corners of the Horn, appearing much the same as when explorer Wilfred Thesiger first laid eyes upon it in the 1920s. The scenery is as stark, desolate and surreally beautiful as it is foreboding.

For those with time (a minimum of three days) and stamina, this remote region can be explored on foot. You'll need to hire an Afar guide and obtain permission from the tourist office in Semera (p213). Several agencies based in Addis Ababa also organise tours in the area (see p270).

Lakes in the region that can usually be visited include **Lake Gamarri** (around 30km from Asaita – known for its hundreds of flamingos); **Lake Afambo** and **Lake Bario** (both near the town of Afambo); and **Lake Abbe**, on the border with Djibouti. Lake Abbe (called Lac Abbé in French-speaking Djibouti) can also be approached from the Djibouti side (see p292).

Sleeping & Eating

Basha Hotel (☎ 0336 550119; d without bathroom Birr40) The best option by far is this hotel, a coin's toss from the Commercial Bank (there's no

sign, so ask around). The hutlike entrance is a bit off-putting, but the swing-a-cat-sized rooms at the rear are set around a pretty courtyard and boast immaculate sheets, surprisingly back-friendly beds, working (though rattling) fans and tolerable shared toilets. At night, you can hear the hyenas, and the camels in the camps of the Afar nomads below. Omelettes, *tibs* and fresh yoghurt are available in the modest restaurant out front.

Lem Hotel (☎ 0336 550050; r without bathroom Birr40) If the Basha is full, this place makes an acceptable plan B, but the bar at the front is noisy.

Getting There & Away

Buses and minibuses leave from the main square. At least five minibuses leave each day for Logiya (Birr15, two hours). There are also regular services to Semera (Birr18, 2½ hours). One bus leaves daily for Dessie (Birr40, ten hours).

For Djibouti, you'll have to take a bus back to Logiya. From there, try to hitch a lift (front seats only) on the steady stream of trucks travelling from Addis Ababa to Djibouti.

At the time of writing there were no 4WDs available for hire in Asaita, and no contract taxis either.

AWASH TO JIJIGA

Motoring east from Awash the landscape seems to get drier and drier, the temperature nudges the mercury incrementally higher, and through dust-smeared windows you can

EASTERN ETHIOPIA

see dust-covered camels softly treading along the verge of the road.

The banality of the landscape is only broken by the people themselves. This is the heart of Oromo country, and on Saturdays many women don their finest beads, most intricate headbands and striking skirts for the weekly markets. The Thursday market at **Asbe Tefari** is the most eye-catching in the region and the women's colourful attire punctuate the otherwise drab landscape like exclamation marks at the end of lifeless sentences.

Around the Chercher Mountains, the first signs of *chat* (p72) cultivation appear; look for the little bushes with shiny, dark-green leaves planted in neat rows. This stimulant is a cherished proclivity of the east and in all likelihood the bus driver will pull over so that he, the conductors and most of the passengers can get to chewing.

As the road climbs from the arid lowlands to the bountiful highlands, the view improves immeasurably and you're taken through some very beautiful scenery with stunning views. The last 120km or so of road before the turn-off to Dire Dawa and Harar (at Alemaya) is one of the prettiest in Ethiopia.

DIRE DAWA ድሬዳዋ
pop 342,800 / elev 1200m

The second-most populous city in Ethiopia, Dire Dawa never fails to elicit strong reactions. Some travellers rave about its remarkably spacious and orderly layout, its tree-lined streets, neat squares and colonial buildings; all a refreshing change from the sweet disorder that so characterises most Ethiopian towns. Others think it's the definition of utilitarian tedium and its gridlike streets an ill-fitting cloak for such a rambunctious country. You decide.

History
The great Addis Ababa–Djibouti railway was supposed to pass through Harar, but with ever-burgeoning costs, the project was falling into difficulties. Then a momentous decision was taken: to bypass the great Chercher Mountains and keep to the lowlands. Instead of passing through the old commercial town of Harar, the railway would pass through a new town, which Menelik chose to call Addis (New) Harar. In 1902 Dire Dawa – as it was known locally – was born.

Since its construction more than a hundred years ago, the railway has deteriorated to the point where derailments are frequent. The worst of these was on 13 January 1985 when a train hurled into a ravine near Awash, killing 428 people. It was the world's 8th-worst rail disaster. Today, although the line is still operational, the poor condition of the tracks means that landlocked Ethiopia relies on convoys of trucks to connect it with Djibouti's port. This however could soon change. Thanks to 50 million euros worth of funding from the European Union, the Ethiopia–Djibouti railway is set to be rehabilitated. In 2007 an Italian Consortium began work consolidating embankments, strengthening bridges and re-laying damaged track. It appears that Ethiopia's iron monster may yet bite back.

Orientation
Despite it being a fairly sprawling town, your chances of getting lost in Dire Dawa are virtually nonexistent. It's simply laid out and is a breeze to navigate. The town is made up of two distinct settlements, divided by the Dechatu wadi (seasonal river). Lying to the north and west of the Dechatu is the 'new town' known as Kezira. On the southern and eastern side of the wadi is the

EASTERN ETHIOPIA

ETHIOPIA'S IRON MONSTER

In the 1890s a man had a dream: to build a railway that would link Ethiopia with French Somaliland (present-day Djibouti) 800km to the east. Carved through some of the most inhospitable terrain in Ethiopia, the railway was planned to forever end the isolation of the Ethiopian highlands.

Each kilometre of line demanded no less than 70 tonnes of rails, sleepers and telegraph poles, as well as massive quantities of cement, sand and water, and food and provisions for an army of workers. To keep the costs down, a narrow gauge of just 1m was used.

To cross the difficult terrain, several viaducts and 22 tunnels (one nearly 100m long) had to be built. In the meantime the local Afars, whose territory the 'iron monster' was penetrating, ran horrific raids on the line at every opportunity, stealing building materials and killing workers. It took no less than 20 years to complete.

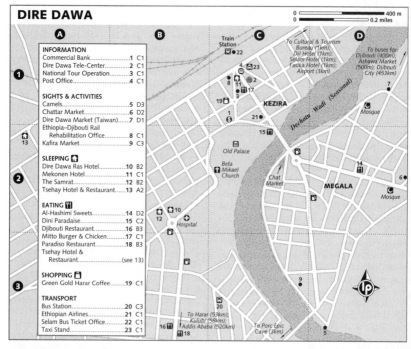

DIRE DAWA

INFORMATION	
Commercial Bank..................1	C1
Dire Dawa Tele-Center..........2	C1
National Tour Operation.........3	C1
Post Office..........................4	C1
SIGHTS & ACTIVITIES	
Camels................................5	D3
Chattar Market.....................6	D2
Dire Dawa Market (Taiwan)....7	D1
Ethiopia–Djibouti Rail	
Rehabilitation Office.........8	C1
Kafira Market.......................9	C3
SLEEPING	
Dire Dawa Ras Hotel............10	B2
Mekonen Hotel....................11	C1
The Samrat.........................12	B2
Tsehay Hotel & Restaurant....13	A2
EATING	
Al-Hashimi Sweets................14	D2
Dini Paradaise.....................15	C2
Djibouti Restaurant..............16	B3
Mitto Burger & Chicken........17	C1
Paradiso Restaurant.............18	B3
Tsehay Hotel &	
Restaurant...................(see 13)	
SHOPPING	
Green Gold Harar Coffee........19	C1
TRANSPORT	
Bus Station.........................20	C3
Ethiopian Airlines................21	C1
Selam Bus Ticket Office.........22	C1
Taxi Stand..........................23	C1

Train Station

To Cultural & Tourism
Bureau (1km);
Dil Hotel (1km);
Selam Hotel (1km);
Fasika Hotel (1km);
Airport (3km)

To buses for
Djibouti (400m);
Ashawa Market
(500m); Djibouti
City (453km)

KEZIRA

Dechatu Wadi (Seasonal)

Mosque

Old Palace

Beta
Mikael
Church

Chat
Market

MEGALA

Mosque

Hospital

To Harar (53km);
Kulubi (58km);
Addis Ababa (520km)

To Porc Epic
Cave (3km)

'old town' known as Megala, which has a distinctly Muslim feel.

Information
Commercial Bank (Kezira; 7.30-11am & 2.30-5.30pm Mon-Fri, 7.30-10.30am Sat) Changes cash and travellers cheques.

Cultural & Tourism Bureau (0251 118712; Dire Dawa Administration Council Bldg, Kezira; 8am-noon, 2-5.30pm) Staff here are unaccustomed to walk-in travellers but may be helpful in a pinch.

Dire Dawa Tele-Center (0251 120908; Kezira; per hr Birr12; 7am-9pm) An Internet cafe that also doubles as a telephone centre.

National Tour Operation (NTO; 0251 111119; Kezira; 8am-noon & 3-5pm Mon-Fri) A government-owned tour company that can sometimes help with tourist info. There's no sign but look for the turquoise building; it's a miracle to find them open.

Post office (Kezira; 8am-noon & 3-6pm Mon-Fri, 8am-noon Sat)

GUIDES
Guides are not really required to explore the markets around town, although one is essential if you wish to visit the prehistoric cave paintings nearby (see p218). **Yigeremu Tadess** (0915 732313; yigeremut@yahoo.com) comes recommended and charges between Birr150 and Birr200 a day. Other reputable guides can be contacted through the Samrat and Selam Hotels.

Sights
Dire Dawa's main highlights are its thriving markets. With its Babel-like ambience, the enormous **Kafira Market**, in Megala, is the most striking. Delving into the organised chaos of its narrow lanes is an assault on the senses. This market attracts people from miles around, including Afar herders, Somali pastoralists and Oromo farmers. Sometimes, around dawn, large camel caravans march in from the Somali desert.

While it is largely produce on display, this is also a thriving contraband market. Merchandise is brought in from Djibouti, either by night caravans across the remote frontiers or carefully concealed in trucks. It also has some distinct 'Moorish-style' architectural features; look out for the striking horseshoe arches that serve as entrances.

EASTERN ETHIOPIA

Ashawa Market, on the outskirts of town, sells everything from beard trimmers to 'designer watches' and baby powder. The nearby **Dire Dawa Market** (also known as Taiwan), as its name suggests, specialises in cheap electronic goods.

To draw knowing smiles from the locals, buy a bag of *chat* (see the boxed text on p72) from one of the small *chat* markets dotted around town. Long-time chewers maintain that the prices at **Chattar Market** are the best.

Foreign influence is still in evidence. Look for Arab, French and Italian styles in some of the architecture and design. Trainspotters can clamber through what remains of the once great Imperial Railway Company of Ethiopia. From the rusty carcasses of disused engines and carriages, a resurrection of sorts is taking place. A polite inquiry at the **Ethiopia-Djibouti Rail Rehabilitation Office** (office three) is usually rewarded with a pass and guided tour (tip expected).

Sleeping

Mekonen Hotel (☎ 0251 113348; Kezira; r without bathroom Birr35) The good news is that this faded glory, housed in an old Italian colonial building, won't hurt the hip pocket, is centrally located and the rooms are large enough to swing several cats in. The bad news? The plumbing seemed on the brink of collapse and the shared bathrooms were a few scrubs shy of being considered clean.

Tsehay Hotel & Restaurant (☎ 0251 110023; Kezira; d/tw shared bathroom Birr35/35, d Birr50) The Tsehay is a bit of a trek from the centre but features cleanish rooms that are frugal with the furniture and dominated by the small double beds. The best asset is the restaurant set in pleasant, hedged gardens.

Fasika Hotel (☎ 0251 111260; Kezira; d Birr120-180, ste Birr250) The cheaper rooms at this midrange place have cramped bathrooms, but you may find them preferable to the windowless mid-quality rooms in the courtyard.

Dire Dawa Ras Hotel (☎ 0251 113225; Kezira; s Birr75, d Birr152-200, tw Birr152-200; 🅿 🖵) The Ras was built in 1964 and nothing seems to have changed since then. A dusty and disused baby grand piano lies neglected under the stairs, and a lobby full of faded and mismatched lounge suites speaks of the hotel's former glory. The double and twin rooms are lighter and brighter than the world-weary singles.

Dil Hotel (☎ 0251 114181; Kezira; d Birr160-240, ste Birr360) Architecturally, this hotel is a sharp-edged, concrete lump of a thing about 1km from the airport, but the bland exterior belies the large and spotlessly clean rooms within. Even the cheapest is large enough for most and the bathrooms are some of the most sparkling in town.

Selam Hotel (☎ 0251 130217; hotelselam200846 @yahoo.com Kezira; d Birr350-500, tw Birr300-500; 🗶 🖵) The blue glass Selam Hotel is the smartest in town with ornately carved and richly polished beds and wardrobes. Hotel staff here can arrange 4WDs and put guests in contact with local guides.

The Samrat (☎ 0251 121400; Kezira; d/tw Birr357/423, ste Birr504-796; 🖳 🖵) The Samrat opened in 2009 and has quickly become the preferred option for high-end Addis Ababa-based tour agencies. The older hotels may be more spacious but the brand new fittings, furnishings and bathrooms can't be beaten. A nightclub is set to open here soon.

Eating & Drinking

Paradiso Restaurant (☎ 0251 113780; Kezira; mains Birr20-50) There's plenty of old-world charm to be had at this 'old time' Italian mansion. The menu roves from palatable Italian dishes to more traditional stomach-stretching portions of *kitfo* and *tibs*.

Tsehay Hotel & Restaurant (Kezira; mains Birr12-27) A prolific bougainvillea and several leafy trees make the alfresco dining here a standout choice. However, something has definitely been lost in the menu's translation and the English manages to make most of the national dishes sound unappealing. Nonetheless, the Ethiopian delicacies, such as the palate-blistering *yequanta firfir* (strips of beef rubbed in chilli, butter, salt and *berbere*), will titillate the taste buds and thrill the gastronomically inquisitive.

Mitto Burger & Chicken (☎ 0251 111206; Kezira; mains Birr10-25) With its trees wrapped in ropes of pulsating lights, tacky upholstery, (loud) satellite TV and a nifty mezzanine for a little flirting, this is the closest thing Dire Dawa has to a snug fast-food joint. If you're pining for Western snacks, including pasta and burgers, this is the place to take your taste buds.

Djibouti Restaurant (☎ 0911 850313; Kezira; mains Birr15-40; 🕑 noon-late) This aptly named and newly opened eatery specialises in what

EASTERN ETHIOPIA

it calls Djiboutian dishes with a Middle Eastern twist. You can dine at the tables inside or order a *shawarma* from the streetside stand.

Al-Hashimi Sweets (Megala; sweets Birr1.50) Battle through the throngs of people to get some lip-smacking baklava. It is so sweet that it frightens dentists.

Dini Paradaise (Kezira; snacks Birr4-13) Set in a large garden near the Old Palace, this is a great place to escape the heat and dust of the town and relax over a cup of coffee, a plate of fruit or delicious cake. Be wary of the tables – the uneven ground meant we wore our *macchiato*.

For a tipple, there are a number of rough-and-ready pub/cafes in the block opposite the train station and fronted by the Mekonen Hotel. From around 6pm the sidewalk tables are packed with men talking politics and sipping coffee and beer.

Shopping

Green Gold Harar Coffee (☎ 0251 101860; Kezira; 🕑 7.30am-noon & 3-5.30pm Mon-Sat) This is the place to stock up on excellent-quality Ethiopian coffee. One kilo of beans/ground beans costs Birr40/33.

Getting There & Away

AIR

Ethiopian Airlines (☎ 0251 113069; www.flyethiopian.com; Kezira; 🕑 7.30-11.45am & 3-5.45pm, Mon-Fri) fly between Dire Dawa and Addis Ababa at least once daily (Birr1684, one hour). It also operates five weekly flights to Jijiga (Birr1178, 20 minutes).

BUS

Four buses run daily to Addis Ababa (Birr66, 11 hours) via Awash (Birr54, six hours), Nazret (Birr54, nine hours) and Debre Zeyit (Birr66, 10 hours). Minibuses run every 15 minutes to Harar (Birr10, one hour).

For Djibouti, a bus departs daily for Djibouti City via Gelille (see p262 for more details).

TRAIN

Trains head east from here for Djibouti City. See p262 for details.

Getting Around

A contract taxi to or from the airport should set you back around Birr40. A short hop in a shared *bajaj* costs Birr1.

AROUND DIRE DAWA

Porc Epic ሐርንዬ ጎደኽርክ ዖኻ

Of the numerous caves within the area that feature prehistoric rock paintings, **Porc Epic** (admission Birr50) is the most accessible. It is 3km south of Dire Dawa and about 140m above a seasonal river. You will need a guide (and possibly a police escort) to find it. The cave isn't spectacular, but excavations have yielded stone-age tools, pottery shards and a mandible from an early *homo sapien*. It is best known for its rock paintings of elephants, lions, hyenas and humans.

Kulubi ቁልቢ

Twice a year, tens of thousands of pilgrims converge on the little town of Kulubi and its slightly ugly, hilltop cathedral, **Kulubi Gabriel**. The church was built by Ras Mekonen to thank St Gabriel for the victory over the Italians at Adwa (see p144). Although very few non-Ethiopians attend, if you're in the area during the biannual festival (at its best on December 28 and July 7), it's well worth a stop.

Vegetarians be warned: some years large quantities of livestock are dispatched with knives by those who have come to express thanks for fulfilment of a wish. Babies, another saintly blessing, also feature prominently and up to 1,000 infants may be christened during celebrations – most of them are named Gabriel.

The pious walk; everyone else catches one of the frequent minibuses from Dire Dawa (Birr15, 1½ to two hours).

HARAR ሐረር

pop 122,000 / elev 1856m

Harar is a place apart. With its 368 alleyways squeezed into just 1 sq km, it's more reminiscent of Fez in Morocco than it is of any other Ethiopian city. Its countless mosques and shrines, coffee-scented streets, animated markets, crumbling walls and charming people will make you feel like you've floated right out of the 21st century and back through time. It is the east's most memorable sight and shouldn't be missed. And, as if that wasn't enough, an otherworldly ritual takes place every night when men feed wild hyenas scraps of meat from their hands.

History

Harar is steeped in history. For centuries, it was a crossroads for every conceivable com-

EASTERN ETHIOPIA

merce and a place where great dynasties of rich and powerful merchants grew and the arts flourished. Harar became the commercial meeting point of Africa, India and the Middle East and right up until 1850, it was home to the Horn's principal market.

In the 17th and 18th centuries, Harar became known as an important centre of Islamic scholarship and spearheaded Islam's penetration into the Horn. In 1854 Richard Burton, the famous British explorer, was the first non-Muslim to penetrate the city disguised as an Arab merchant. Later, the bustling commercial town attracted many foreign merchants from India, Armenia, England and France. The famous French poet Arthur Rimbaud (p221) spent some of his last years here. In 1887 the city surrendered to Emperor Menelik, who sought to expand and unify his highland empire, but the Hararis still retain their own ethnic identity, language and culture to this day.

In 1995, Harar won a kind of independence, with legal recognition as a city-state within the Federal Republic of Ethiopia.

Orientation

Fear not: you can't get lost. Harar's old walled town is so compact that you'll eventually come to a major street or wall that will lead you back to Harar Gate, the main gate. There are six gates in total. Streets lead from each gate and converge in the centre at a bustling square, known as Feres Magala (Horse Market). Radiating out from the square is a maze of little alleyways and passages. The main thoroughfare in the walled city runs from Harar Gate to Feres Megala.

Information

Canal Internet Cafe (new town; per hr Birr21; ☉ 8am-noon & 2-7pm) Look for the sign pointing upstairs.
Commercial Bank (new town; ☉ 8-11.30am & 1.30-4.30pm Mon-Fri, 8-11am Sat) Near Harar Gate. Changes cash (euros and US dollars) and travellers cheques.
Internet Cafe Ras Hotel (new town; per hr Birr21; ☉ 8am-noon & 2-8pm) Internet and CD burning capabilities.
Tourist office (☎ 0256 669300; 1st fl, Ras Makonnen's Palace; ☉ 8-11.30am & 2-5.30pm Mon-Fri) Mildly useful, arranges guides.

Dangers & Annoyances

Water shortages are a major problem in Harar and can affect the city for two or three days

at a time. Power cuts are also a problem; city quarters are supplied by rota and do without for one day a week. Watch your wallet in the market areas, especially around the nimble-fingered and fleet-footed children.

GUIDES

For your first foray into Harar, it's quite a good idea to hire a guide. Guides know the location of less-visited corners and the best Harari houses and arts and crafts shops. Hiring a guide also deters other would-be guides and can help arrange vehicles for out-of-town excursions.

Although there are official guides (ask to see their ID or enquire at the tourist office), there's no official price. Around Birr200 per day is standard. Two guides that come particularly recommended are **Abdul** (☎ 0915 740864) and **Binsam Woldesemayat** (☎ 0913 448811, biniym.weld@yahoo.com).

Sights
INSIDE THE WALLED CITY

Harar's old walled town is a fascinating place that begs exploration. The thick, 5m-high walls around town were erected in the 16th century by an emir in response to the migrations northwards of the Oromo. Within the walls the city is a maze of narrow, twisting alleys and lanes, replete with historic buildings, including 82 small mosques, numerous shrines and tombs, as well as traditional Harari houses.

But what breathes life into these landmarks is the community that still lives within the city walls. Prepare to encounter the magnificent Adare (Harari) women, known for their colourful dresses and orange headscarves, and the sweat-soaked blacksmiths who still labour over forges in much the same way as their forefathers did centuries earlier.

Gates

There are six gates in total; Emperor Menelik added two in 1889 to the four original ones (which date from the 16th century). An exploration of the old walled town (known locally as Jugal) begins at the main, car-friendly gate known as the **Harar Gate** or Duke's Gate, after the first Duke of Harar, Ras Makonnen. The photograph on the gate is Emir Abdullahi, the last of Harar's 72 Emirs and the city's last Muslim leader. The nearby **Shoa Gate** (also known as Asmae Diin Bari in Harari) and the **Buda Gate** are also in good shape.

EASTERN ETHIOPIA

To the north, the **Fallana Gate** is said to be the one Richard Burton entered disguised as an Arab merchant.

Medhane Alem Cathedral

Lying off the main square, the rather un-impressive **Medhane Alem Cathedral** (☉ 6-9am Mon-Tue, Thu, Sat & Sun; 5am-2.30pm Wed & Fri) was originally an Egyptian mosque, but Haile Selassie 'converted' it in the 1940s.

Rimbaud's House የሪምቦ ቤት

Near the middle of the walled city, Rimbaud's House is (yet another) building in which the poet Arthur Rimbaud (see opposite) is said to have lived, although this is not widely believed to be true! It houses a **museum** (admission Birr10;

☉ 8am-noon & 2-5pm Mon-Thu & Sat & Sun, 8am-11am & 2-5pm Fri) dedicated to the poet, with a series of illustrated panels (mainly in French) about his life.

On the 1st floor there is an excellent pho-tographic exhibition of turn-of-the-20th-century Harar, and from the rooftop there's a good view over Harar towards the blue Chercher Mountains.

Ras Tafari's House የራስ ተፈሪ ቤት

Within pouncing distance of Rimbaud's House is the conspicuous Ras Tafari's House. The house was built by an Indian trader and many of its features, such as the Hindu figures on the door, are Eastern in origin. Haile Selassie spent his honeymoon here – hence the house

HARAR

0 ————— 500 m
0 ————— 0.3 miles

INFORMATION
Canal Internet Cafe.....................1 B3
Commercial Bank.........................2 B3
Internet Cafe Ras Hotel..............(see 13)
Tourist Office..............................(see 13)

SIGHTS & ACTIVITIES
Asma'addin Bari Market (New
   Market)..................................3 C4
Emir Nur's Tomb.........................4 C3
Gidir Magala (Main Market)..........5 D3
Handicraft Museum....................(see 13)
Harari National Cultural Centre.....6 D3
Hyena Feeding Site.....................7 C2
Hyena Feeding Site.....................8 D3
Jamia Mosque.............................9 D3
Medhane Alem Cathedral............10 C3
Oromo Market............................11 D3
Ras Makonnen Statue.................12 B3
Ras Makonnen's Palace..............13 D3

Ras Tafari's House.......................14 C3
Recycling Market.........................15 B3
Rimbaud's House & Museum........16 D3
St Mary Catholic Church..............17 D3
Sheikh Abadir's Tomb..................18 D4
Sherif Harar City Museum............(see 14)
Smugglers' Market........................19 B3
Tomb of Said Ali Hamdogn...........20 C3

SLEEPING
Belayneh Hotel.............................21 C4
Heritage Plaza Hotel......................22 B4
Ras Hotel.....................................23 A3
Rewda Guesthouse.......................24 C3
Tewodros Hotel............................25 B3

EATING
Fresh Touch Restaurant................26 A3
Hirut Restaurant...........................27 B3
Ice Cream Mermaid......................28 C3

Kim Café......................................29 B3
Ras Hotel....................................(see 23)
Rewda Café.................................(see 24)

DRINKING
Ali Bal Cafe..................................30 C3
Bar Cottage..................................31 C3
National Hotel...............................32 B3

SHOPPING
Fatuma Safir Ahmed......................33 D3
Nure Roasted Harar Coffee...........34 D3
Zeituna Yusuf Grille's Shop...........35 D3

TRANSPORT
Bus Station...................................36 B3
City Taxi Stand.............................37 C3
Selam Cafe...................................38 C3

EASTERN ETHIOPIA

A B C D

1
2
3
4

27
25
Football
Field
Fallana
Gate
7
Mosque
To Rewda Hotel (300m);
Abadir Guest House (600m);
Tana Hotel (600m);
Dire Dawa (53km)
Ras Makonnen
Sq
Selassie
Church
Feres
Magala
Hospital 9 17 6
Harar
Gate
Erer
Gate
Eper 11
Arch
23
26
12
29
36
19
28
38
30
37
13
33
Sitti Alawiyya Mosque
15
Shoa
Gate
32
Weber
Stationary
Shop
Mekina
Girgir
14
24
20
5
Walled City
(Jugal)
35
8
3
21
Buda Gate
Sanga Gate
Stadium
18
22

To Koremi (19km);
Babille (31km);
Jijiga (102km);
Somaliland (165km)

ARTHUR RIMBAUD – A POET ADRIFT

In 1875 one of France's finest poets turned his back on his poetry, his country, his wild living and his lover to reverse his fortunes and see the world. He was just 21 years old, broke and bitter.

By 1879 Arthur Rimbaud had travelled to Java (with the Dutch Colonial Army from which he later deserted), settled for a time in Cyprus and, in the service of a coffee trader in Aden (Yemen), became the first white man to travel into the Ogaden region of southeastern Ethiopia. He later moved to Ethiopia and lived like a local in a small house in Harar. His interest in culture, languages and people made him popular and his plain speaking and integrity won him the trust of the chiefs and Ras Makonnen, the governor of Harar. His commercial dealings were equally as colourful and included coffee trading and running guns to King Menelik of Shoa.

In 1891 Rimbaud developed a tumour on his right knee. Leaving Harar in early April, he endured the week's journey to the coast on a stretcher. Treatment at Aden was not a success and Rimbaud continued onto Marseilles, where his right leg was amputated. By this time the cancer had spread and he died later that year at the age of 37.

During his self-imposed exile to Ethiopia, Rimbaud's poetry had become increasingly known in France for its daring imagery and beautiful and evocative language. Sadly this belated recognition brought him little satisfaction and he remained indifferent to his fame until his dying day.

I drifted on a river, I could not control
No longer guided by a bargemen's ropes
...
When my bargemen could no longer haul me
I forgot about everything and drifted on.

Extracts from Rimbaud's The Drunken Boat *(1871)*

bears his pre-coronation name. It is now the home of the **Sherif Harar City Museum** (admission Birr20; ◷ 8am-noon & 2-5pm). The museum houses a private collection of weaponry, coins, jewellery, household tools and cultural dresses.

Ras Makonnen's Palace
የራስ መኮነን ቤተ መንግስት
Don't expect a fairy-tale castle! This 'palace' on the main drag is a sharp-edged, charmless, whitish building and now houses a **Handicraft Museum** (admission Birr10; ◷ 8am-noon & 2-5pm Mon-Fri) on the 1st floor. It's nothing flash but it's worth popping your head in. You can also climb to the top floor and soak up the views.

Jamia Mosque ጃሚያ መስጊድ
The Jamia Mosque located just south of the central square is Harar's great mosque. The mosque was built in the 16th century, though according to local tradition, a mosque has stood on the site since the 12th century, long before the foundation of Harar. It is off-limits to non-Muslims.

Gidir Magala ጊደር ማጋላ
Down from Mekina Girgir you'll stumble upon the arcades of the Gidir Magala,

the main market (previously known as the Muslim market) and the city's meat market. It's liveliest on Mondays when Oromo and Somali people come in from the surrounding areas to buy their meat. Watch how the locals hide their purchases from the black kites that swoop down from their high rooftop perches.

St Mary Catholic Church
ቅድስት ማሪያም ካቶሊክ ቤተ ክርስቲያን
Almost opposite Jamia Mosque, St Mary Catholic Church is a haven of peace and a good spot if you need to unwind. It's a Catholic mission dating from the late 19th century. The carved wooden door is particularly attractive.

Mekina Girgir
Leading southeast from Feres Magala, there is a narrow street called Mekina Girgir (Machine Rd). As you amble down this atmosphere-laden lane you'll quickly understand why it was given this name: it's jam-packed with tailors' workshops; hence the name, in reference to the sewing machines. If you were thinking of buying a wedding suit, this is the place!

EASTERN ETHIOPIA

Traditional Adare Houses

Visiting a traditional Adare house is a must (see below), but you'll probably need a guide to find one. The easiest house to find, not far from the Erer Gate (known locally as Argobari), houses the **Harari National Cultural Centre** (admission Birr10; 8am-noon & 2-5pm Mon-Fri). This typical Adare house contains examples of traditional arts and crafts.

Several Adare houses also double as family-run souvenir shops or hotels. If you don't buy anything, it's customary to tip the owner for the tour.

Shrines & Tombs

Shrines devoted to local holy men or religious leaders are even more numerous: over 300 inside and outside the walls – no one has yet managed to count them. Many are very peaceful, beautiful and well-kept places. Admission is occasionally refused to non-Muslims, especially at Sheikh Abadir's Tomb.

Southwest of Gidir Magala is the **Tomb of Said Ali Hamdogn** (admission Birr10), a former religious leader of the town. The tomb looks a little like a miniature mosque without the minaret. Local legend has it that below his tomb lies a well that can sustain the whole city in times of siege.

Another tomb that can be visited is **Sheikh Abadir's Tomb** (admission Birr10), near the southeastern point of the old town. The sheikh was one of the most important preachers of Islam in the region and his tomb still attracts worshippers seeking solutions to daily struggles.

If their prayers are answered, many devotees return to make gifts to the shrine: usually rugs or expensive sandalwood.

Emir Nur's Tomb (admission Birr10), north of central square, is devoted to the ruler who built the city's walls and whose photo adorns Harar Gate. The tomb resembles a spiky, green beehive.

OUTSIDE THE WALLS
Hyena Feeding

As night falls (from around 7pm), two sets of 'hyena men' set themselves up just outside the city walls. One lot near Sanga Gate in the east of the old town, and the other about 200m north of Fallana Gate.

The practice of feeding hyenas is a relatively recent phenomenon (it probably began sometime in the 1950s), although the spectacle is no less interesting for it. Some say it is linked to an older tradition in which hyenas were given porridge to discourage them from attacking townsfolk during times when food was scarce (but this claim has yet to be substantiated).

The ritual starts by calling the hyena by name. The first sight of Africa's second-largest predator is usually of vague shadows and luminous green eyes as they skulk in and out of your torchlight. As the pack grows more confident, they dart forward with their peculiar gait until all reservations are lost and they approach the hyena man to be fed.

Hyenas are far bigger than most people realise and their jaws are some of the strong-

---

ADARE HOUSES

A distinct architectural feature in Harar, the *gegar* (traditional Adare house) is a rectangular, two-storey structure with a flat roof. The house is carefully constructed to remain cool whatever the outside temperature: clay reinforced with wooden beams is whitewashed. Sometimes bright green, blue or ochre murals adorn the facades. A small courtyard conceals the interior of the house from curious passers-by.

The upstairs room used to serve as a storeroom; today it acts as a bedroom. The main living room consists of five raised platforms of different levels, which are covered in well-made rugs, cushions and stools. Guests and members of the household sit on the platform befitting their status.

The walls are usually painted bright red or ochre, said to symbolise the blood that every Harari was prepared to shed during the resistance against Menelik. Hung on the walls are woven cloths or carpets. Eleven niches are carved into the wall. In these, cups, pots and plates made by the Adare women themselves are proudly displayed.

After marriage, newlyweds retire to a tiny, windowless, cell-like room that lies to the side of the living quarters. They remain there for one whole week, during which time they are passed food and water through a hatch by relatives.

A DINNER DATE WITH MULUGATA AND HIS HYENA

Under the watchful gaze of a pack of salivating hyenas, I ask Mulugata Wolde Mariam my most pressing concern – has anyone ever been bitten? He patiently reassures me that within his twenty years of feeding hyenas, no one, not even *faranji*, has ever been bitten. 'Occasionally people are attacked by hyenas but not in town and not by these hyenas. These hyenas know us and we use their names when we call them.'

Mulugata goes on to explain that he first worked as an assistant to another hyena man and now he makes a living from the tourists who come to watch the show. For Mulugata, hyena feeding is all about business. Each morning he collects offcuts of camel and beef from the butchers and cuts them into strips. The strips of meat are easier to handle, he explains. 'You can dangle them (the strips) from up high so the tourists can see their jaws in action or drape them around a stick so that the tourists can feed the hyena themselves. It is particularly good if they bite the stick between their teeth – but not many do this. It is a pity, it's very exciting and makes for good photos; especially if they bring a taxi and use its headlights as floodlights.'

est in the animal kingdom, quite capable of crunching through bones as thick as skulls. Seeing them in action is both enthralling and terrifying. If you are game it is possible to feed the hyenas yourself.

The easiest way to see the show is to let your guide know so that he can forewarn the hyena men. Be sure to establish the fee in advance; in principle, you'll be charged about Birr50 for the 'show', more if you have a video camera (usually Birr100). If you just show up, you'll still be expected to pay.

Other Attractions

No visit to Harar would be complete without wading through the shambolic markets that sprawl outside Harar Gate and Shoa Gate. At first sight this mini-city appears to be an impenetrable latticework of tiny streets and alleys; on closer inspection it reveals a careful organisation with different sections. The **Smugglers' Market** is chock-full of goods from Asia, while the adjoining **Recycling Market** is where men beat metal from spare parts into useful utensils. Elbow your way through the **Asma'addin Bari Market** (New Market; also known as the Christian Market) to find *etan* (incense) from Jijiga; it's sold for the famous coffee ceremonies (see p69). This odoriferous spice market is also filled with bark, roots and twigs used in the preparation of traditional medicine. Make sure you save energy for the no-less-animated **Oromo Market**, off Erer Gate. With its heaps of vegetables, it's exotic and colourful by the bucket load.

After all this sightseeing, you might need a stimulant to keep your spirits high. What

about chewing a leaf (or two) of *chat*? *Chat* markets can be found around most of the city gates, except the Buda Gate, as well as to the south of Feres Magala.

In the centre of Ras Makonnen Sq stands an Italianate equestrian **statue** of the *ras* (duke), cast in bronze by the well-known Amhara artist Afewerk Tekle.

Sleeping

Most of the commendable places are outside the walled town.

Tana Hotel (☎ 0256 668482; new town; r Birr50) This outfit west of the new town is our favourite cheapie. The odd cockroach or two aside, the rooms are essentially clean, the staff friendly and the showers hot. The rooms (which sleep two) come with a tiny TV (local stations only), and there's a bar and restaurant specialising in Ethiopian dishes out front (raw meat, anyone?).

Tewodros Hotel (☎ 0256 660217; new town d Birr60-80, tw without bathroom Birr70) Not many places pride themselves on their view of the local garbage pile, but guests staying in rooms 15, 16, 117 and 18 have the added thrill of watching (or more likely listening to) the hyenas rummaging in the garbage dump during the night. The rooms themselves are in a sad state but will do for a night's kip. There are even cheaper rooms (Birr 40) downstairs, but these were grotty and smelly.

Ras Hotel (☎ 0256 660027; new town; d/tw Birr75/100; 🖳) The government-run Ras, with its bare corridors and cramped rooms, has a boarding-school-cum-psychiatric-institution vibe. The recent price drop, however, means it is fair value.

EASTERN ETHIOPIA

Belayneh Hotel (☎ 0256 662030; fax 0256 666222; new town; s/d/tw/tr Birr130/160/160/230) The big draw-cards here are the outstanding views over the lively Asma'addin Bari Market and the hotel's proximity to the bus station. The rooms themselves are bland, although the bathrooms are roomy with odd, freestanding toilets in their centres.

our pick Rewda Guesthouse (☎ 0256 662211; old town; r with shared bathroom incl breakfast Birr250) From the rolled mat above the door (that indicates an eligible daughter resides within) to the raised seating platforms in the cocoon-like lounge, this Adare house percolates tradition and history into a comfy brew of warm welcome amid exotic decorations. Set in the heart of the old town down a nondescript side street (ask somebody to show you the way at Weber Stationary shop), these five spot-less bedrooms fill quickly in peak season and reservations are advised.

Heritage Plaza Hotel (☎ 0256 6665137; ajaddous @ethionet.et; new town; s/d/tw/ste Birr330/440/495/750; ▯) The 'Plaza' is the newest place to stay in town and is currently popular with tour groups. This three-storey edifice boasts 26 spacious, spotlessly clean, if slightly charac-terless, rooms. The restaurant and bar has passable food.

Eating

Unfortunately Harar's dining options aren't as memorable or as numerous as its historic attractions.

our pick Fresh Touch Restaurant (☎ 0915 740109; new town; mains Birr15-40) Reasonable prices, a tasty selection of national and international dishes, a leafy courtyard and a dedicated pizza oven mean that you will be hard pressed to find bet-ter food in Harar. Two further pluses: the cold drinks are just that – cold – and the bittersweet aroma of roasting coffee wafting from the gar-den stove had us salivating like a hyena.

Hirut Restaurant (☎ 0256 660419; new town; mains Birr15-40; ☺ 11am-9pm) Decorated with tra-ditional woven baskets and specialising in authentic local cuisine, this is the most atmos-pheric place in Harar to sink your teeth into a super-filling *kwanta firfir* (dried strips of beef rubbed in chilli, butter, salt and *berbere*), or swill a glass of Gouder wine. The choice between the cosy lounge and the well-shaded garden is a difficult one.

Ras Hotel (new town; mains Birr12-40) A cold Harar beer and a shish kebab go down a treat on the quiet deck at the back of this hotel restaurant.

Rewda Café (new town; cakes Birr3-6) Drool over the devilish display of cakes and pastries or call in for a decent breakfast at this local fa-vourite. The mauve-suited waiters here are snappy with both their service and their dress sense.

Kim Café (new town; cakes Birr3-5) This cafe is an island surrounded by a sea of cars on all sides. If you don't mind an unhealthy dose of carbon monoxide with your coffee, it's a great place to people-watch.

Ice Cream Mermaid (old town; ice cream Birr8) A peaceful refuge from the crowded strip nearby, this hole-in-the-wall place concocts some flavoursome ice creams, as well as filling cakes and refreshing fruit juices.

Drinking

If you're pining for a beer, there are several local brands to try, including the light Harar beer, Hakim stout and Hakim, a kind of lager. *Sofi* is non-alcoholic, designed for Harar's Muslims. And of course, you'll want to try Harari coffee: it's hailed as one of the best in the world.

Ali Bal Cafe (Feres Magala, old town) Slap bang in the heart of the old town, this is a good place to mull over a coffee or mango juice and watch life go by.

Bar Cottage (old town) This place is a few watts short of being dimly lit and it took a while for our eyes to adjust and appreciate the wood-lined walls and smoke-stained Bob Marley posters. Music kicks off around 7pm – danc-ing follows. It's best at weekends.

National Hotel (new town) Hallelujah! Live music is on from Thursday to Sunday, from around 9.30pm to 2am or 3am. The music is a mixture of Ethiopian/Middle Eastern pop with some traditional tunes thrown in. When not playing, there's football on a big-screen TV – much less exotic.

Shopping

Nure Roasted Harar Coffee (☎ 0256 663136; ☺ Mon-Sat) Just thinking about the scents wafting from this place makes us swoon. One step inside and you're hooked forever. It sells 1kg packets of excellent coffee for Birr50, and there are tours of the roasting and grinding machine out back.

In some of the Adare houses in the old town, the ever-enterprising Adares have set up souvenir shops displaying beautifully made baskets, and silver and amber jewellery. The house of Fatuma Safir Ahmed, just north of the main market, is one. Another is Zeituna Yusuf Grille's shop, south of the market; it's as good as an antique shop, but bring your sharpest bargaining skills! Because these shops are family-run, they may not always be 'open'. Knock on the doors.

Getting There & Around

All transport leaves from the bus station near Harar Gate. Minibuses leave every 15 minutes for Dire Dawa (Birr10, one hour). Around seven buses leave for Jijiga (Birr20, 2½ to three hours) via Babille (Birr10, 45 minutes). Two buses leave daily for Addis Ababa (Birr68, 10 hours). Tickets for the capital should be bought from 10am the proceeding day at the bus station. There are also several minibuses a day to Addis Ababa (early morning departure Birr120, evening departure Birr110, nine hours). They don't leave from the bus station but pick passengers up at their hotel (ask the reception to book for you or buy a ticket at the Selam Cafe in the old town).

Shared/contract taxis cost Birr1/5 for a short hop about town.

AROUND HARAR
Koremi

The tiny, cliff-top village of Koremi, 19km southeast of Harar, is the stronghold of the Argoba, a deeply traditional people whose ancestors arrived in these parts as refugees in the 12th century. Unlike the Adare homes of Harar, the **stone houses** here incorporate neither cement, plaster or lime in their construction. It is said that these unpainted and unplastered homes are what Harar itself must have once looked like before modernisation.

There is no scheduled transport to Koremi, so it's best to hire both a guide and a contract taxi in Harar.

Harar To Jijiga

When visiting Jijiga, getting there is half the fun. The stunning 102km stretch of gravel road is one of the most scenic in eastern Ethiopia, with superb volcanic rock formations, contoured terrain and a strangely seductive, end-of-the-world atmosphere. First you'll pass through the blink-and-you'll-miss-it town of **Babille**, renowned for its **elephant sanctuary**. The elephants are secretive and

scarce but have recently been fitted with radio transmitters for the purposes of ecotourism. Ask at the Ethiopian Wildlife Conservation Department (near Mexico Sq in Addis Ababa) to see how these plans are progressing.

About 4km from Babille, the road passes through the Dakhata Valley, now better known as the **Valley of Marvels**. Here, tall rocks have been sculpted into strange shapes by the elements. Some are topped by precariously balanced boulders, including one that's formed like an arch – a very strange vista indeed.

JIJIGA ጅጅጋ
pop 98,100 / elev 1696m

There is little to see and less to do in Jijiga, but there's a strong whiff of edgy adventure about the place (maybe that's just the camels) and the atmosphere, at this seldom-visited capital of the Somali region, is noticeably different from the rest of the country. Signs are written in Somali, women are veiled and Arab-style mosques dominate the skyline. The large **market** is definitely worth exploring, as are the streets of multihued store fronts where you can sometimes find intricately woven mats, silver jewellery and yellow amber necklaces for sale. Business, including selling contraband smuggled in from Somaliland, is unexpectedly brisk. The **camel and livestock market** is also very interesting.

Information

There's a smattering of internet outlets around town but connections are slow and fleeting. There's also a post office and a telecom office.

Commercial Bank (🕑 8-11am & 2-4.30pm Mon-Fri, 8-11am Sat) Changes euros, US dollars and travellers cheques.

Sleeping & Eating

Despite being an important administrative and commercial centre and surprisingly cosmopolitan, Jijiga is prone to electricity outages. When the power went off while dining in a windowless room, all we could do was sit in the blackness, groping for our Cokes until discovered. Moral of the story? Carry a torch.

Adom Hotel (☎ 0257 753077; r Birr25-80) The range of room sizes is reflected in the range of rates. Aim high for something clean and modest. It lies 100m off the main road; take the first left after the Shell station if coming from Addis Ababa.

Alem Ayu Hotel (☎ 0257 752814; r Birr50) A reliable pick, on the main road, about 500m west from the bus station. The bathrooms are a bit grim but the beds fit the bill for an overnight stop.

Bade Hotel (☎ 0257 752841; fax 0257 752218; s/d/tw Birr100/100/150) The Bade Hotel has the best rooms in town – but not by much. Expect excellent English and slightly saggy beds. Look out for the hotel's neat, bricklike facade on a side street running parallel to the main Harar road.

Djibouti Restaurant (mains Birr10-35) This no-frills eatery tosses up decent local fare and could well be your big chance to tick 'eating *geel* (camel) while watching Al-Jazeera' off that 'must do' list.

London Café (cake Birr5) Cakes, coffee and juices so thick you can stand your spoon in them.

Getting There & Away

AIR

Ethiopian Airlines (☎ 0257 752030) flies every day but Tuesday and Friday to Addis Ababa (Birr2170, 1¾ hours) via Dire Dawa (Birr1178, 20 minutes). The airport is 3km out of town.

BUS

Buses leave throughout the day for Harar (Birr20, 2½ to three hours) but only one leaves for Addis Ababa (Birr125, 1½ days) at around 2pm.

Buses to Wajaale (Birr20, 1½ to 2½ hours) leave at 6.30am. Be sure to arrive early to secure a ticket – our Wajaale bus was so full that the driver had to climb through the window to get to his seat. From Wajaale you can continue on to Somaliland. See p263 for details.

See p263 for details.

EASTERN ETHIOPIA

Western Ethiopia

Undisturbed and seldom visited, Western Ethiopia could be left blank on many travel maps. It boasts neither the historical must-sees of the north, nor the cultural diversity seen in the south. But for some, therein lies its appeal. The few who do come here can rightly call themselves explorers, not travellers. Those people are rewarded with some of Ethiopia's most contrasting scenery.

This region offers an engaging peek into everyday Ethiopian life and is notably the birthplace of coffee. In the lush western highlands the bean still grows wild beneath a canopy of ancient, vine-tangled trees.

Almost 350km due west of Addis Ababa the highland plateau drops dramatically to lowland plains. The remarkable transition sees fields of golden *tef* (an indigenous cereal grain) give way to plantations of verdant banana and mango.

The western lowlands borrows its climate, geography and much of its culture from neighbouring Sudan. Now that tensions on the Ethiopian side of the border have eased, it is once again safe to visit this cul-de-sac of forgotten histories.

One such history is that of Gambela. Until the tide of time passed it by, Gambela was set to become the linchpin in a grand scheme to establish an inland trading route along the Baro River to Egypt. Today it stands as Ethiopia's brave farewell to civilisation before the wilds of Gambela National Park.

The Anuak, one of several interesting cultures in the Gambela region, believe that to continue travelling west is to fall off the edge of the world. The Anuak are wrong on this score. The world doesn't end in Western Ethiopia; it just feels that way.

HIGHLIGHTS

- Wrap your legs around a scrawny horse for a scenic descent into the lake-filled crater of **Mt Wenchi** (p230)

- Search for birds, colobus monkeys and Menelik's bushbuck while meandering on the slopes of Mt Wuchacha in the **Menagesha National Forest** (p229)

- Wipe the sweat from your brow while exploring the village markets of **Gambela** (p237)

- Stare steadily at the striking scenery moving past your window while driving from **Jimma** to **Welkite** (p237) and from **Metu** to **Tepi** (p233), the birthplace of coffee

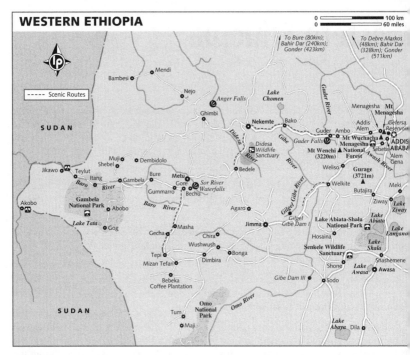

Climate

The western highlands receive almost 1600mm of annual rainfall. Heavy rains fall between April and September, with moderate precipitation in March and October. The highlands never exceed 29°C, or reach frost point.

The western lowlands receive slightly less rain, with most falling between May and October. Unlike the moist highlands, December through February is very dry. Temperatures average 27°C but can reach in excess of 40°C in February and March.

Getting There & Around

Ethiopian Airlines (www.flyethiopian.com) connects Addis Ababa with Gambela via Jimma four times a week. Jimma is also connected twice weekly to Arba Minch.

Most people who enter western Ethiopia overland are travelling by bus from Addis Ababa, which provides access to the southwest via Jimma and to the northwest via Nekemte. The road is sealed from Addis to both Jimma and Nekemte, after which it continues as a metal road of varying quality. Like elsewhere

in Ethiopia, Chinese-led construction crew are in the process of upgrading many road within this area.

If you're travelling with a vehicle it's als technically possible to reach Jimma from Sode in the south and to reach Nekemte from th Addis Ababa–Bahir Dar road in the north.

With the exception of remote lowland areas, most areas are covered by regular bu services. However, during the wet season roads and schedules can run equally amuck

THE WESTERN HIGHLANDS

Carpeted in lush forests, dense patchworks o cultivation, shady coffee plantations and dee river valleys, the western highlands seem lik an Ethiopian Arcadia.

ADDIS ABABA TO AMBO

If you're into birdwatching, a stop at the **Gefersa Reservoir** may be warranted. Wattle ibis, endemic blue-wing geese and, occasion ally, pelicans peruse its sparsely vegetated shores. The reservoir lies 18km west of Addis Ababa and supplies the capital with its water.

Just west of the reservoir is the domed profile of **Mt Menagesha**. According to local tradition, many Ethiopian kings' coronations were held on this forested mountain.

Further west, past the tiny village of Menagesha, turn left at the Tseday Farm Horticulture Development Enterprises sign to access the 18km rough road that leads to the forestry office on the lower slopes of **Mt Wuchacha**. Here you can ditch your vehicle and take to the **Menagesha National Forest** (admission Birr20). Almost a dozen trails (up to 9km in length) meander through the forest, with one even heading above the treeline to Wuchacha's 3380m summit. On the crater's western slopes some of the giant juniper and *wanza* (Podocarpus) trees are said to be over 400 years old.

On foot, the Menagesha forest is more easily accessed from the village of Sebeta on the Addis Ababa–Jimma road. From Sebeta, a solid 3½-hour trek (one way) takes you to the top of Mogli, one of the peaks of Mt Wuchacha.

Addis Alem አዲስ አለም
pop 13,424 / elev 2360m

This unremarkable agricultural town 55km west of Addis Ababa was to be the site of Emperor Menelik II's future capital – Addis Alem literally means 'New World' in Amharic. The emperor had sent engineers and builders to start construction here when Addis Ababa was crippled by late-19th-century firewood shortages. The introduction of eucalyptus trees ended up saving the new flower (Addis Ababa) and killed the new world.

Of the remaining buildings, **St Maryam Church** (admission Birr25) is the most interesting. It stands out for its lavish decoration: the ba-

silica's exterior, as well as the *maqdas* (inner sanctuary), is entirely covered with murals. The adjacent **museum** (admission incl with church; ⓧ 8.30am-3pm Mon-Thu, 9am-4pm Sat & Sun) displays crowns and clothing belonging to Menelik and Haile Selassie, and relics from the Battle of Adwa. The site sits atop a rocky hill 600m south of the main road.

Numerous buses pass heading east to Addis Ababa (Birr10, two hours) and west to Ambo (Birr10, two hours).

AMBO አምቦ
pop 49,500 / elev 2101m

Mineral water is Ambo's claim to fame; it's bottled here and sold throughout Ethiopia. The water is so fizzy that it continues to sparkle even in a glass left overnight! Although you can't visit the factory, you can take a dip in the famous thermal mineral-water **pool** (admission Birr10; ⓧ 6am-8pm Thu-Sun) run by Ambo Ethiopia Hotel. Despite the murky green colour, the pool is cleaned weekly.

The town also offers some fine Italian 1930s architecture and an interesting Saturday market where you can find brightly coloured Ambo baskets.

Almost 2km west of Ambo near Ambo College is **Teltele Park** (admission Birr40), a pint-sized park that encapsulates walking trails and some scenic sections of the Teltele and Huluka Rivers. Nearby are the pretty, 25m-high **Huluka Falls**.

Ambo is the obvious base for an excursion to Mt Wenchi, and former English schoolteacher **Tadessa Hailu** (☎ 0911 894268) charges around Birr100 for his excellent guiding services.

Sleeping & Eating

Jebat Mecha Hotel (☎ 0112 362253; d Birr80) For the price, these are the best-value rooms in town – provided you like green paint and cold showers. The same can be said of its restaurant where Ethiopian dishes cost a reasonable Birr12 to Birr17. It is located on the town's main roundabout.

Ambo Ethiopia Hotel (☎ 0112 362007; amboethhotel@ethionet.et; tw tent Birr100; tw without bathroom Birr47, tw with bathroom Birr85, d with bathroom Birr90-200; ▯) Set around flowering gardens, this old colonial place has bundles of old-world charm at new-world prices. Though it shows its age in places, it's still quite comfortable and some rooms have satellite TV. The classic dining hall (mains Birr30 to Birr45) serves Western and Ethiopian selections. Guests have free use of the town's mineral pool. It is 150m west of the bus station.

Abebech Metaferia Hotel (☎ 0112 362365; tw Birr120-150, d/ste Birr140/250) This modern tower, just east of the bus station, houses Ambo's most comfortable rooms. They are big and bright with tiled bathrooms and nice balconies. The restaurant (mains Birr35 to Birr45) is known locally for quality fare, although we found it to be very average and the marble floors and hard surfaces played havoc with the acoustics.

Getting There & Away

A dozen daily buses serve Addis Ababa (Birr12, three hours), while only one serves Nekemte (Birr30, five hours). For Guder (Birr2, 15 minutes) minibuses run approximately every 30 minutes.

Unofficial, but faster, minibuses leave for Addis Ababa from opposite the Ambo Ethiopia Hotel and cost between Birr15 to Birr20.

MT WENCHI ወንጪ ተራራ

elev 3280m

Resting within the beautiful collapsed caldera of Mt Wenchi, 31km south of Ambo, is **Lake Wenchi**, an island monastery and several hot springs. The scenery, a patchwork of cultivation run through with the occasional stand of natural forest, is a tonic for any city-weary soul.

You must hire a guide (Birr70) from the local guide association office on the road that leads from Wenchi village to the crater rim. You can also hire horses (Birr30 each way) and pay for the boat transfers to the island monastery (Birr20 return) and hot springs (Birr40 return via the monastery) here.

Without a horse, it takes about 45 minutes to walk the 4km down to the lake and just over an hour for the hot slog back up. Horses can do it in half this time. If you have a 4WD it is also possible to drive.

Once at the lake's edge, little wooden boats ferry visitors across to the tiny island monastery of **Cherkos**. Other than a small church, there isn't much here but you can ask to see the large 'Gonder bell', which once belonged (according to tradition) to the Emperor Fasiladas.

From Cherkos the boats continue to the far side of the lake, where you begin a stunning walk through a countryside of grazing horses, babbling brooks (not so good in the wet season) and water-powered mills to the **hot springs**. The springs are said to have magical curative properties and the caves in the surrounding area house pilgrims, here to treat their afflictions.

Besides bringing your own tent and camping near the springs, the only place to stay is at the Mt Wenchi branch of Ambo's **Abebech Metaferia Hotel** (☎ 0113 560122; s/d Birr100/200), which occupies a commanding hilltop position. Rooms are in circular concrete huts with thatched roofs. The attached restaurant serves basic food (mains Birr15 to Birr20) and cold drinks.

Getting There & Away

For those with vehicles, Mt Wenchi makes for a wonderful day trip from Addis Ababa. For everyone else, Mt Wenchi is best visited on Sundays from Ambo when three or four market-bound, Isuzu trucks (one hour, Birr20 to Birr30 each way) leave from a spot 50m south of Jebat Mecha Hotel between 7am and 8.30am. They usually return sometime between 4pm and 5pm.

Private 4WDs with driver can be hired in Ambo. A return trip costs between Birr400 and Birr500. Ask at the bus station or talk to local guide, Tadessa Hailu (see p229).

AMBO TO NEKEMTE

The journey towards Nekemte soon takes you through Guder, 11km west of Ambo. About 1km from Guder, after crossing the river, you'll see a gate for **Guder Falls** (admission Birr5; 7am-6pm). It isn't spectacular but is worth a peek in the wet season. The ubiquitous Ethiopian red wine, Gouder was ostensibly named after the river, and a few vineyards can still be seen covering the surrounding area.

As you climb from Guder the views open up and you'll see endless fields of quilted yellows, reds and greens. Although the views down are great, don't forget to look up too – there are some impressive columnar basalt flows along the road cut above Guder.

About 65km from Ambo, you'll reach an escarpment offering westward vistas over distant volcanic landscapes. Heading further west, things become less cultivated. This area is part of the historical Wolega province and is home to gold reserves and precious frank

WESTERN ETHIOPIA

incense. Both still fetch high prices in Middle Eastern and Egyptian markets.

NEKEMTE ነቀምት
pop 84,500 / elev 2101m

Nekemte, 203km west of Ambo, is the sprawling commercial and administrative centre for the Oromia region's East Wolega zone. Although there's few sights besides a well-put-together museum, Nekemte has decent facilities and makes an obvious spot to break your westward journey.

Information
Besides the services listed below, Nekemte also has a post office, Commercial Bank, a reliable internet cafe and a telecommunications office. All are marked on the map.

Culture & Tourism Office (☎ 0576 611315; ⊗ 8.30am-12.30pm & 1.30-5.30pm Mon-Fri) Friendly although under resourced.

Hiwot Clinic (☎ 0576 612036; ⊗ 7am-12.30pm & 2-5.30pm) A better bet than the local hospital.

Sights
The remains of an Italian military plane shot down by the Black Lion Patriots in 1935 proudly sits in front of the **Wolega Museum** (admission Birr25; ⊗ 8.30am-12.30pm & 2-6pm Tue-Sun). Inside, displays give a good insight into the Wolega Oromo life and culture. It contains traditional musical instruments, as well as displays of the local spinning, carving and basket-weaving industries. Admission includes a guided tour.

Built by the King of Wolega in the 1870s, the **Kumsa Moroda Palace** (admission Birr25; ⊗ 9am-noon & 1.30-5pm Tue-Sun) has only recently been opened to the public after long years of neglect. It sits 1km north of the museum and served as residence to the prominent Worra Bekere family until they were hauled off to Addis Ababa during the Derg. The compound consists of around 10 buildings, and admission includes a guide who can explain what each building was used for (although ours couldn't really speak English but waved his arms with enthusiasm).

Also worth a wander is Nekemte's **market**, which bustles most on Wednesday, Thursday and Saturday. Although the **Church of St Gabriel** casts a nice silhouette from town, it can be classed as good from afar, but far from good.

Sleeping & Eating
Dhalas Cafe & Bed (☎ 0576 611849; d without bathroom Birr50) The austere rooms are large and host beds with comfortable foam mattresses. The shared bathrooms are very clean and boast hot water and toilet seats.

Daniel Hotel (☎ 0576 615999; d Birr60) The receptionist gave us the impression that if she never saw another *faranji* again, it would be too soon. The rooms – when we did see them – aren't that clean and the plumbing was out of order. Its restaurant (mains Birr10 to Birr18), however, was abuzz with more locals than flies and there's a fruit stand next door serving great juice.

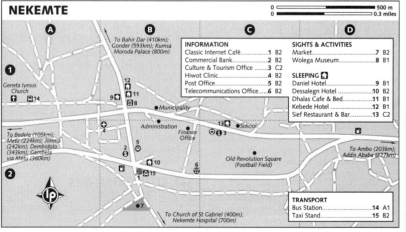

NEKEMTE

0 — 500 m
0 — 0.3 miles

INFORMATION	
Classic Internet Café	1 B2
Commercial Bank	2 B2
Culture & Tourism Office	3 C2
Hiwot Clinic	4 B2
Post Office	5 B2
Telecommunications Office	6 B2

SIGHTS & ACTIVITIES	
Market	7 B2
Wolega Museum	8 B1

SLEEPING	
Daniel Hotel	9 B1
Dessalegn Hotel	10 B2
Dhalas Cafe & Bed	11 B1
Kebede Hotel	12 B1
Sief Restaurant & Bar	13 C2

TRANSPORT	
Bus Station	14 A1
Taxi Stand	15 B2

To Bahir Dar (410km); Gonder (593km); Kumsa Moroda Palace (800km)

Geneta Iyesus Church

Municipality

Administration
Finance Office
School

Old Revolution Square (Football Field)

To Bedele (105km); Metu (224km); Jimma (242km); Dembidolo (343km); Gambela via Metu (360km)

To Ambo (203km); Addis Ababa (327km)

To Church of St Gabriel (400m); Nekemte Hospital (700m)

WESTERN ETHIOPIA

Sief Restaurant & Bar (☎ 0576 612499; d & tw without bathroom Birr60, d with bathroom Birr100) Besides the spotless rooms, clean bathrooms and friendly manager, the big plus here is the huge size of the beds. Rather confusingly (considering this place's name), there is neither a bar nor a restaurant. Apparently they are coming soon.

Kebede Hotel (☎ 0917 811056; d Birr100) This new hotel has yet to erect a sign but you can't miss it – it's the four-storey grey building. The rooms are spotless and light with large windows and clean bathrooms.

Dessalegn Hotel (☎ 0576 616262; d/tw Birr150/200) Although this is Nekemte's top hotel, we recommend it more for its menu (mains Birr20 to Birr30), which includes Western favourites like burgers and pasta. Its rooms are clean, but essentially standard.

Getting There & Away

One daily bus serves Addis Ababa (Birr42, eight hours), though five more pass through each morning and pick up passengers if they have free seats. Other 6am services include Ambo (Birr30, five hours) and Bedele (Birr26, four hours). Both Isuzu trucks and buses run to Dembidolo (Birr47 to Birr69, 12 to 13 hours) and Jimma (Birr36 to Birr57, 10 hours).

NEKEMTE TO BEDELE

The road from Nekemte to Bedele is as smooth as silk – well at least for the first 3km; the other 102km are well-graded gravel. Roughly halfway between Nekemte and Bedele is the 1300-sq-km **Didesa Wildlife Sanctuary**. Although there's currently no access, you'll have a glimpse of its beauty when crossing the Didesa River Bridge. The day we crossed, the bus driver thoughtfully slowed so that everyone could get a glimpse of the hippos below. Unfortunately, one was dead.

BEDELE በደሌ

pop 21,289 / elev 2162m

Bedele lies 105km south of Nekemte and sits at an important crossroads linking Metu, Jimma and Nekemte. Besides a tour of the celebrated **Bedele beer factory** (☎ 0474 450134, ext 21; admission free; ☯ 8am-4pm Mon-Fri), there's little reason to stop.

If you're stuck here, try **Weqinesh Hotel** (☎ 0474 451070; d Birr60). The rooms are small and clean with cold-water showers, small beds

and rock-hard pillows. It's not signposted, but it's above the Oromia International Bank in a pink and green building near the main roundabout.

For eating, head to nearby **Biruk Restaurant** (mains Birr8-12), and sample such delicacies as *kekel* (boiled beef), *dulet* (minced tripe) or *kai wat* (chicken in *berbere* sauce).

Between 6am and noon four buses pass heading for Jimma (Birr35, 3½ hours), while six head to Metu (Birr30, four hours). There's a 6am service to Nekemte (Birr26, 4½ hours) and another to Addis Ababa (Birr65, 12 to 13 hours) via Welkite.

METU መቱ

pop 22,100 / elev 1600m

Spreading over the slope of a small hill 115km west of Bedele is Metu, the capital of the old Ilubador province. For travellers, Metu acts as the primary gateway to the western lowlands, as well as a springboard for trips south through some of the west's most wild and beautiful scenery to Tepi and Mizan Tefari.

Antenna Hotel (☎ 0474 411002; d Birr50-80) sits only 50m from the bus station, making it ideal for an early-morning getaway. Its *faranji*-priced upstairs options are large, clean and bright and have decent bathrooms. The downstairs Birr50 rooms are still clean but lack the finer touches like light bulbs and toilet seats.

The **Sena Hotel** (☎ 0474 414286; d without bathroom Birr30, d with bathroom Birr60) is more noteworthy for its restaurant-cum-bar than for its simple rooms, even though its selection of dishes is limited and vegies are few and far between (mains Birr15). It is near the Commercial Bank, 1.4km east of the bus station.

Buses depart for Gambela (Birr50, six hours, two daily), Bedele (Birr30, four hours, six daily) and Addis Ababa (Birr79, 1½ to two days, 6am) via Jimma (Birr37, nine hours).

To reach Tepi take a minibus to Gore (Birr8, around 35 minutes) and then catch a bus to Masha (Birr20 to Birr27, four hours) and go from there. If you start early enough, you can reach Tepi or Mizan Tefari in a day.

SOR RIVER WATERFALLS ሶር ወንዝ ፏፏት

A worthwhile excursion from Metu is to the Sor River Waterfalls, one of the most beautiful falls in Ethiopia. It lies close to the village of Bechu, 13km southeast of Metu. The last 15 minutes of the one-hour walk (5km) from Bechu takes you through dense forest teeming with birds and monkeys. If it has been raining the mud will be deep enough to suck the sneakers off your feet.

At the falls, Sor River suddenly drops 20m, over the lip of a wide chasm into a fern-lined amphitheatre. Brave souls can take a dip in the pool below.

A daily minibus leaves Metu for Bechu (Birr10, one hour) around 7am. It returns as soon as it's full, which means you may have to walk back to Metu or battle a night of fleas in Bechu. To find the falls, enlist the help of a Bechu villager (tip expected) or ask one of the children who invariably tag along. With a 4WD you could make the return trip from Metu in less than four hours.

METU TO TEPI

Twenty-five kilometres south of Metu is the inconsequential junction town of Gore, from where the road strikes south for Tepi and west to Gambela.

Heading south, the road snakes along a ridge and offers vistas over the western lowlands and flirts with sections of thick forest. Some large trees, shrouded in vegetation, seem to have ecosystems of their own. You may spot a colobus monkey or two peering from vine-draped trees.

North of Masha you'll pass through rolling hills carpeted in tea plantations, before entering thick sections of forest and the occasional stand of bamboo south of town.

After Gecha, the road winds through *enset* (false-banana tree) plantations, traditional villages and lovely areas of forest. As you near Tepi, you'll start to see coffee drying outside homes along the roadside.

In a private vehicle the drive takes between 4½ and seven hours, depending on the season. It's also possible in a day by riding local minibuses, though you'll likely have to change minibuses at Gore and Masha.

TEPI ቴፒ
pop 19,231 / elev 1238m
Tepi is famous for its state-owned coffee plantation. It's Ethiopia's second-largest, and stretches over 6290 hectares. Just over

2000 hectares lies around Tepi while the remainder, including Beshanwaka (a beautiful crater lake), is in the Gambela region about 30km away. The state-run plantation produces about 25,000kg of raw arabica coffee per year.

It used to be possible to prearrange a tour by calling the **Coffee Plantation Development Enterprise** (☎ 0114 168789) in Addis Ababa. It may still be possible to arrange a tour of the plantation through a tour company. Currently your only independent option, and a rather limited one at that, is to wander the trails that radiate from the **plantation headquarters** (☎ 0475 560468). The headquarters are signposted and 400m beyond the main roundabout on the Jimma road. Unfortunately, it's not possible to buy coffee here.

Sleeping and Eating
Tigist Hotel (☎ 0475 5560227; s/d without bathroom Birr20/40, d/tw Birr60/120) Four hundred metres down the road that leads from the bus station and the only multistorey building around, this is somewhat of a mixed bag. The best rooms are on the top floors, far from the pulsating disco. The restaurant here serves *tibs* (pan-fried sliced lamb) and…well actually, just *tibs*.

Coffee Plantation Guesthouse (☎ 0475 560062; d/tw Birr100/160) The semi-detached concrete bungalows vaunt bright-green laminate floors, frilly bedspreads, small verandas and clean washrooms (cold showers). If you order ahead, the 'workhouse club' can prepare meals.

Getting There & Away
Three buses run daily to Masha (Birr21, three hours) and onward transport to Gore and occasionally Gambela. From Gore there are frequent minibuses to Metu (Birr8, 35 minutes). Two buses serve Jimma (Birr60, eight hours). For Mizan Tefari (Birr14, 1½ hours), seven buses run daily.

MIZAN TEFARI ሚዛን ተፈሪ
pop 19,300 / elev 1451m
Mizan Tefari, the old capital of the Bench people, serves as a base for a visit to the 9337-hectare **Bebeka Coffee Plantation** (☎ 0471 118621). The plantation is 28km southwest of Mizan Tefari (an hour's drive) and is Ethiopia's largest and oldest coffee farm.

THE BEAN THAT CONQUERED THE WORLD

At some point between the 5th and 10th centuries, in the Ethiopian kingdom of Kafa, an astute herder named Kaldi noticed that his goats were behaving rather excitedly each time they ate a certain plant's berries. Trying it himself, he discovered that after a few chews and a couple of swallows, he was one hyper herder! When he told the local monastery they reprimanded him for 'partaking in the Devil's fruit' and flung the berries on the fire. They soon changed their minds, however, when they smelt the aroma emanating from the roasting beans.

Soon the monks were drying the berries for transport and shipping them to Ethiopian monasteries far and wide. There, priests would rehydrate them in water, eat the fruit and drink the fluids to keep themselves awake for nocturnal prayers.

Soon Arabs began importing the bean, and in the 15th century the Turks brewed the roasted beans into the drink we know today. From Turkey, coffee spread to Europe via Italy and then to Indonesia and the Americas.

Today an estimated four out of five Americans drink coffee at least once a day, and America (Seattle, to be precise) is the home of Starbucks – a coffee empire that encompass over 16,000 stores in 49 countries.

But the bean didn't stop there. Coffee is now the top agricultural export for 12 countries, with the livelihood of over one hundred million people depending on its production, and has become the world's second most valuable commodity after petroleum!

As with Tepi, there are no longer any official tours, but you may be able to wrangle a letter of introduction by calling the **Coffee Plantation Development Enterprise** (☎ 0114 168789) in Addis Ababa and pleading your case. Armed with such a letter and your own 4WD (the plantation is far too big to take in on foot), the manager will usually provide a guide.

Sleeping & Eating
Aden Hotel (☎ 0473 330542; d without bathroom Birr50, d with bathroom Birr80) is our top choice in Mizan Tefari and sits in a leafy compound west of the main drag at the town's south end. The Birr80 rooms are a decent size. Along with mosquito nets, the rooms sport firm but comfy mattresses, bright windows and clean bathrooms. Its restaurant is good, though prices are quite often susceptible to *faranji* fluctuations.

Bebeka Coffee Plantation Guesthouses (☎ 0471 115744; camping Birr60, dm/d Birr25/90, 2-bedroom cottages Birr200) Set in the thick of the plantation and surrounded by birdlife, the accommodation here is better than its Tepi counterpart. There's a nearby employee lodge with decent meals and satellite TV.

Getting There & Away
Buses run to Tepi (Birr14, 1½ hours, seven daily), Bonga (Birr35, five hours, two daily) and Jimma (Birr33, 7½ hours, one daily).

Since you require your own 4WD for a tour of Bebeka Coffee Plantation, there is little point arriving here on foot.

JIMMA ጂማ
pop 159,000 / elev 1678m
How you interpret western Ethiopia's largest city really depends on which direction you arrive from. Enter from Addis Ababa and it's a smaller and quirkier version of the raucous capital, with wide boulevards, lots of honking horns and a massive coffee pot rising from its main roundabout. Arrive from the wild western lowlands, however, and you'll view Jimma as a place of great sophistication and gentility.

For centuries, a powerful Oromo monarchy ruled the surrounding fertile highlands from its capital at Jiren (now a suburb of present-day Jimma). The region owed its wealth to its situation at the crux of several major trade routes and its abundant crops. At its height, the kingdom stretched over 13,000 sq km. When Menelik came to power in the late 1800s, he required the region to pay high tribute.

When the Italians entered the picture in the 1930s, they had grand plans to create a modern city in the heart of Ethiopia's breadbasket and Jimma was subsequently born from Jiren.

Information
Dr B Cossar Higer Clinic (☎ 0471 112814; ☾ 24hr) Decent facilities and an English-speaking doctor.

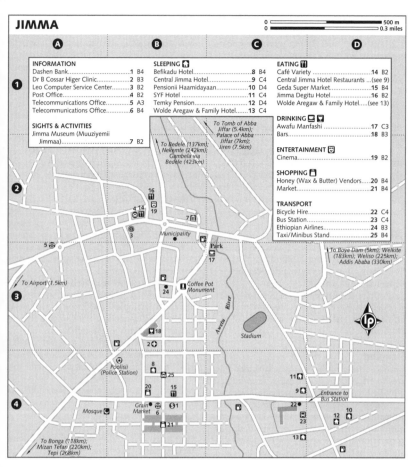

JIMMA

Dashen Bank (8am-noon & 1-5pm Mon-Fri, 8am-noon Sat) The best of the banks, with currency-exchange services and an ATM that accepts Visa.

Leo Computer Service Center (per min Birr0.25) Connections are most reliable on weekdays. CDs can also be burnt here and at the other internet centres nearby.

Post office (8am-6pm Mon-Fri, to noon Sat).

Telecommunications office northside (8am-6pm Mon, Thu & Fri, to 4pm Tue & Wed, to noon Sat); southside (8.30am-5pm) International calls. Standard rates (see p254 for details).

Sights

JIMMA MUSEUM ጂማ ሙዚየም

Admission price to the **Muuziyemii Jimmaa** (admission Birr25; 9am-12.30pm & 2-5.30pm) includes a guided tour in English of the seven small

rooms that make up the museum. We don't want to steal the guide's thunder (such as it is), but our favourite pieces include a ceremonial throne that cost Birr146,000 to build but was only used by Haile Selassie for 20 minutes, and a royal portaloo that looks like a frying pan with a hole in it. Other oddities include a poster with the entire Koran written on it in a script of almost microscopic proportions, and an Italian-made walking stick-cum-gun.

PALACE OF ABBA JIFFAR
የአባ ጇፋር ቤተ መንግስት

Looking more out of America's wild west than the Kafa kingdom, the increasingly fragile **Palace of Abba Jiffar** (admission Birr25; 9am-12.30pm & 2-5.30pm) looks as if a strong wind could blow it away. It sits atop a hill 7km northeast of the town centre, near the village of Jiren.

King Jiffar (1852–1933), who was one of the most important Kafa kingdom rulers, held power at the end of the 19th century. The palace contains a private family mosque (which is still in use) and rooms that used to serve as a library, throne room, reception chamber, king's guard room, sentry tower, courthouse and guesthouse. Almost 1.6km back down the hill lies the tomb of the king.

With the road in its current state, only 4WDs can make it up. Until it's repaired, you'll have to catch one of the town's shared taxis (Birr2) to the Sports Café in front of the university and walk from there or contract a taxi (Birr50, including waiting time).

OTHER SIGHTS

In the vicinity of Jimma, there are various caves, hot springs and a hippo pool (at the Boye Dam, 5km from town) that can be visited; enquire at your hotel.

If you're a connoisseur of Italian Fascist architecture, take a peek at the cinema, post office, municipal buildings and some of the old hotels.

Sleeping

Jimma hotels have openly embraced the *faranji* price scheme – the one where you pay double! Prices listed here are *faranji* rates.

Pensionii Haamidayaan (☎ 0471 116014; s/d without bathroom Birr40/80, s with bathroom Birr45-50) This economical place is decent value, provided your room isn't near the whiffy shared toilets. The attached bathrooms feature squat loos and spray-everywhere showers.

Temky Pension (☎ 0471 112565; s/tw without bathroom Birr40/60, s/tw with bathroom Birr55/70) Although the rooms are similar to those next door, the large lawn, garden tables and cleaner shared toilets make this a better choice. However, the music in the lively garden courtyard can be irritating for those needing an early night.

Wolde Aregaw & Family Hotel (☎ 0471 112731; d without bathroom Birr80, d with bathroom Birr104-150, tw/ste Birr174/222) Opposite the bus station and set in large grounds, you are about 20 years too late to catch this place at its best. The cheaper rooms are better value, although hotel staff only reluctantly rent these to 'rich *faranji*'.

Central Jimma Hotel (☎ 0471 118283; d without bathroom Birr72, d with bathroom Birr84-169, tw Birr121-217, ste Birr217-323; 🖭 🖳) With more room options than

a zebra has stripes, you may want to ask for the 'menu' to help make sense of it all. Although widely regarded as the best hotel in town, the rooms we saw were no better than those at the Wolde Aregaw Hotel. Only some rooms include the use of the pool (which is otherwise Birr14/23 on weekdays/weekends).

Two more options are:

Befikadu Hotel (☎ 0471 111757; d without bathroom Birr60, d with bathroom Birr90) Small and clean, although it's worth keeping your flip-flops handy for the odd roach.

SYF Hotel (☎ 0471 120440; d Birr144-200, tw/ste Birr276/300) This newbie has some clean and tidy options, but some rooms were already musty smelling.

Eating & Drinking

Central Jimma Hotel Restuarants (mains Birr11-48) For a fine view of the bus station, a cold beer and some cheap eats, stick to the roadside cafe. For shish kebab, chicken Maryland and grilled fish, head to the more upmarket poolside Sennait Restaurant.

Jimma Degitu Hotel (mains Birr15-33) The *faranji* food here is quite good (if you remember you're in Ethiopia) and more varied than elsewhere. We happily wolfed down a cheeseburger and some cold French fries.

Wolde Aregaw & Family Hotel (mains Birr15-25) The wood panelling and calf-skin decor give this a lived-in vibe, and if you're at a loose end you can watch the satellite TV in the bar while munching on a steak sandwich. Next door, the restaurant serves meals such as *doro arrosto* (roast chicken) and spaghetti.

Café Variety (light meals Birr17) Its shaded terrace vaunts the best selection of cakes and fruit juices in town. It's popular with students, who flock here for the juice and coffee.

Awafu Manfashi (snacks & drinks Birr1-3) The sound of falling water and the dappled shade of mature trees make this is a great place to unwind and enjoy a quiet drink.

Geda Super Market (⏱ 8am-8pm) The best stocked store in Jimma, though that isn't saying much!

Try tasting the local *besso* drink, made from ground barley. There is a string of swinging bars – or rather dingy dives – marked on the map. They are rough and ready – there's no need to dress up.

Entertainment

Cinema (admission Birr3) Screens Western movies with English subtitles in air-conditioned comfort.

Shopping

Thursday is the main market day; search out Jimma's famous three-legged stools, quality basketware and locally renowned honey.

Getting There & Away

Ethiopian Airlines (☎ 0471 110030; www.flyethiopian. com) flies every day except Monday to Addis Ababa (US$150, one hour to 2½ hours depending on route) and on Wednesday, Friday, Saturday and Sunday to/from Gambela (US$128, one hour). There are also Wednesday and Sunday flights to and from Arba Minch ($US116, 50 minutes).

Two early-morning buses leave daily for Addis Ababa (Birr45, seven hours). The gates to the bus compound usually open around 6am. Get your elbows ready and be prepared for a mad scramble.

Amid the early-morning free-for-all, you'll find a bus for Tepi (Birr41, eight hours), Mizan Tefari (Birr33, 7½ hours), Metu (Birr36, eight hours), Bedele (Birr20, 4½ hours) and Nekemte (Birr37, 9 hours). There are up to six minibuses to Welkite (Birr30, 5½ hours).

Getting Around

Bajajs (auto-rickshaws) cost Birr1 to Birr2 for hops around town depending on distance. No buses or minibuses go to the airport, but locals pay Birr10 for a contract taxi, out-of-towners will be expected to pay more (around Birr50). Men near the bus station gates rent rickety bicycles to *faranji* for around Birr40 per hour. Locals pay Birr10.

JIMMA TO ADDIS ABABA

After Jimma, the road begins to wind back in a northeastern direction towards Addis Ababa. Approximately 57km out of town, the road detours around Gilgel Gibe Dam I. Further south, work on the controversial Gibe III dam is well underway. While it will generate much needed foreign currency by selling its surplus electricity to neighbouring countries, critics fear that it will disrupt the seasonal flooding of the Omo River on which hundreds of thousands of people rely to replenish the soil and rejuvenate the grasses for their cattle.

Much further west you'll see several impressive bulbous rock pinnacles rising from the seemingly subdued plateau in the distance. Once you pass the major outcrop, the road serpentines down into the gaping Gibe River Valley.

If you get stuck at **Welkite**, the **Soressa Hotel** (☎ 0113 300840; d without bathroom Birr45, d with bathroom Birr75-95) has large comfy beds, hot-water showers, satellite TV and clean bathrooms. There are plenty of local restaurants along the main Jimma–Addis Ababa road.

Two buses leave daily for Addis Ababa (Birr23, 2½ hours) and for Jimma (Birr45, five hours). There's one service to Hosaina (Birr30, four hours).

THE WESTERN LOWLANDS

The Gambela federal region is somewhat of an oddity within Ethiopia – its swampy lowlands stand in stark contrast to the lush landscapes seen in the western highlands. Many of its people have stronger cultural ties with neighbouring Sudan than they do with the rest of Ethiopia.

GAMBELA ጋምቤላ

pop 31,282 / elev 526m

Set on the banks of the chocolate-brown Baro River, at a lowly altitude of 526m, Gambela, the capital of the 25,274-sq-km Gambela federal region, is muggy, swampy and sweaty. If you arrive by plane the moist, searing air that slaps your face like a wet towel blowing in the wind comes as quite a shock.

Although the terrible ethnic and political violence that has occurred sporadically over the past decade may seem to say otherwise, the Anuak and Nuer people, although initially appearing reticent and deeply suspicious, are actually incredibly hospitable. Using *daricho,* the Anuak greeting, or *male,* the Nuer greeting, helps break the ice.

History

Thanks to the Baro River being the only truly navigable watercourse in Ethiopia, its strategic and commercial significance has long dictated the fortunes of Gambela's turbulent past.

Prior to the 19th century the Baro River was principally used by raiding slave parties to transport captured men. Later, at the end of the 19th century, Menelik II dreamed of linking Ethiopia with Egypt and Sudan via the White Nile. To help create the great inland shipping service, the emperor agreed to grant the British, who were already in control of Sudan, an enclave on the Baro River. In 1907

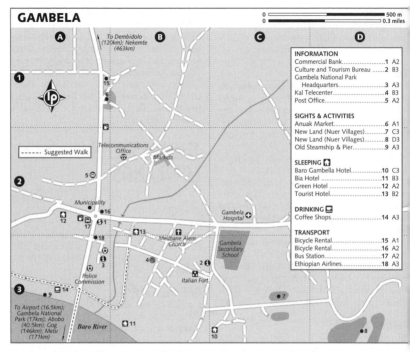

GAMBELA

0   500 m
0   0.3 miles

the site was chosen and Gambela was formally inaugurated as a port and customs station.

Soon steamers were chugging up and down the wide river, laden with valuables ranging from coffee to cotton. Commerce flourished and Gambela boomed.

The Italians briefly captured Gambela in 1936 and vestiges of their fort are still visible. The British won the river port back in 1941 and amazingly made it part of Sudan 10 years later. When Sudan gained its independence in 1956, the protectorate was given back to Ethiopia. It was around this time that the old shipping service formally ceased and Gambela began to sink slowly back into the mud from which it had sprung.

Since 1991 tensions have been running high between the Anuak and the Nuer. In 2006 an armed group of Anuak attacked the Gambela police station and prison and killed several officers, including the state police commissioner, and freed an unknown number of prisoners. This attack was a reprisal against a 2003 massacre in which hundreds of Anuaks were killed (many by Ethiopian government forces) and over 500 homes burnt and looted.

Information

The electricity supply can only be described as erratic, and usually cuts out halfway through composing an email. If you get sick, head to Metu – Gambela's hospital is grim.

Commercial Bank (7.30am-11.30am & 3-5.30pm Mon-Fri, 7.30-11.30am Sat) Exchange US dollars, euros and travellers cheques.

Kal Telecenter (per min Birr0.30) One of many internet cafes.

Culture and Tourism Bureau (0475 511030; 7am-12.30pm & 3-5.30pm Mon-Fri) Thoughtfully tucked away inside the library, where it's unlikely that any traveller would find it.

Gambela National Park Headquarters (0475 510912; omotagwa@yahoo.com; 7am-12.30pm & 3-5.30pm Mon-Fri) Equally as useful as the Culture and Tourism Bureau when it comes to planning trips within the Gambela region.

Dangers & Annoyances

The good news is that the recent tension between the Anuak and the Nuer peoples seems to have dissipated and, at least for the time being, peace prevails. Nonetheless, as a precaution we strongly suggest that you keep your eye on developments around Gambela before visiting the western lowlands.

Security issues aside, your biggest concern should be reserved for some of Gambela's smaller residents – mosquitos. Malaria continues to kill an extraordinarily high percentage of the population here and adequate precautions are essential (see p371). Giardia is also common.

Photographers should know that it is strictly forbidden to take photos of, or from, the bridge. The Anuak and Nuer people are also notoriously camera-shy. Always ask permission before taking photos – if you don't, warm hospitality may turn to aggression.

Sights & Activities

A pleasant walk around Gambela includes the riverside, the old steamship and pier (visible from the riverbank), the bridge and the markets. This walk is marked on the Gambela map.

At sunset, locals gather at the river beneath the bridge to bathe, walk or catch up on gossip. We caused a ripple of disbelief when we stripped down to our shorts and joined them for a swim. Once every few years (usually during the wet season), a villager is taken by a crocodile. Be sure to keep someone tastier between yourself and the open river.

The **Nuer villages** on the outskirts of town, known as 'New Land', can also be visited; a Nuer guide is a good idea and one usually hangs around the Gambela Hotel.

In the north of the town is the **Anuak market**. Vendors sit in the shade of the trees selling cereals, firewood, large Nile perch and tobacco. To pass the time, many indulge in *akowyo* (water pipe) smoking. You can taste the *borde* (traditional 'beer'), served to thirsty market-goers from metal buckets.

Sleeping & Eating

Decent hotels and restaurants are not Gambela's forte.

THE ETHIOPIAN SLAVE TRADE

Ethiopia's slave trade was a lucrative one. From the 16th century right up to the 19th century, the country's main source of foreign revenue was from slaves. At the height of the trade, it's estimated that 25,000 Ethiopian slaves were sold every year to markets around the globe.

Green Hotel (☎ 0475 50426; d without bathroom Birr50) A stone's throw from the bus station, the rooms within the pink blocks are simple, sparse and essentially clean. To shower, ask the manager for a bucket.

Tourist Hotel (☎ 0913 400146; d without bathroom Birr70) This place was undergoing major renovations when we visited. It may end up being the pick of the bunch.

Bia Hotel (☎ 0475 511611; d Birr130) Staff here are lackadaisical to say the least, but the basic rooms have private bathrooms, functional mosquito nets and a pleasant outlook to the river.

Baro Gambella Hotel (☎ 0475 510044; tw Birr200) Sometimes it's worth a few extra birr to be able to sit down on the toilet seat with confidence, but even so the prices here are pretty steep for these dog-eared and dilapidated cottages. Room 11 has the hotel's only air conditioner, although it's hard to know which is worse – putting up the heat or the noise the air-con makes. The restaurant (mains Birr12 to Birr35) is hands down the best in Gambela. It serves local and *faranji* food (such as steak, fish, salad and soup) in large portions.

There is a string of coffee and tea stalls strung along the road following the Baro River. Perched on a log, coffee balanced precariously on one knee and surrounded by Nuer tribesman, this is travel at its rawest.

Getting There & Away

Ethiopian Airlines (☎ 0475 510099; www.flyethiopian .com) flies to and from Addis Ababa (US$192, two hours to four hours depending on the route) and Jimma (US$128, one hour) on Wednesday, Friday, Saturday and Sunday. Flights are frequently cancelled during the rainy season.

Two buses leaves daily for Addis Ababa (Birr105, two days) overnighting at Bedele (Birr70 to Birr80, nine hours) via Gore (Birr40, seven hours) and Metu (Birr50, 6½ hours). An early-morning bus occasionally leaves for Tepi (Birr100, 12½hours), although it may be easier to go to Gore first and change there.

The border to Sudan is once again open, see p263 for details.

Getting Around

A short hop in a shared *bajaj* around town costs Birr1, but they can be contracted for Birr10. The only option besides walking is cycling. Bikes can be rented (Birr6 per hour)

PEOPLES OF THE WESTERN LOWLANDS

The Nuer and the Anuak are the two main ethnic groups within the Gambela region and form the vast majority of the population.

The Nuer

The Nuer people, who are relatively recent arrivals to the region, originated in the Nilotic-speaking regions of Sudan and now form the largest ethnic group in Gambela. They're largely cattle herders and much of Nuer oral literature, including traditional songs and poetry, celebrate their beasts.

Unlike the Anuak, the Nuer like to live together in large villages. Very tall and dark, the Nuer women are fond of ornamentation, including bright bead necklaces, heavy bangles of ivory or bone and, particularly, a spike of brass or ivory that pierces the lower lip and extends over the chin. Cicatrizing (considered sensual) is also widely practised: the skin is raised in patterns and decorate the face, chest and stomach; rows of dots are often traced on the forehead.

The Anuak

The Anuak's language closely resembles that of the Luo tribes in Kenya. Fishing is their main means of survival, though some grow sorghum. Outside Gambela most live in extended family groups, rather than villages, composed of a cluster of huts in a small compound.

Anuak huts are characterised by low doorways and thickly thatched roofs. The eaves, which stretch almost to the ground, keep out both the torrential rain and baking sun.

A common practice among many Nilotic peoples of Ethiopia and Sudan, including the Anuak, is extraction of the front six teeth of the lower jaw at around the age of 12. This is said to have served originally as a precaution against the effects of tetanus or lockjaw.

---

near the municipality building and to the north, just past the Anuak market.

Ethiopian Airlines provides transport to and from the airport (Birr25), which is 16.5km south of town. Passengers meet at the airline office first and, if the flight hasn't been cancelled, proceed to the airport together.

Both the Gambela National Park Headquarters and the Culture and Tourism Bureau claimed they could organise a 4WD (Birr1200 per day including driver and fuel), but when push came to shove, it turned out both cars were inoperable.

GAMBELA NATIONAL PARK
ጋምቤላ ብሔራዊ ፓርክ

Less than 50 years ago, Gambela National Park, spreading over 5061 sq km, was one of Ethiopia's richest places for large mammals. Elephants, lions, leopards, giraffes, buffaloes, topis, tiangs, roan antelopes, hartebeests, Nile lechwe and waterbucks were found here.

However, today's evergrowing need for shelter, firewood, food and land for farming, as well as the influx of Sudanese refugees, has dramatically reduced wildlife and their habitats.

Animals you might realistically hope to see are the common bushbuck, oribi, lesser kudu and the white-eared kob. The best place to spot these animals is 180km or so west of Gambela along the banks of the Baro.

Planning

This is one of the most neglected and threatened parks in Ethiopia and, as there is little to no tourist infrastructure, you have to be totally self-sufficient. The **Gambela National Park Headquarters** (☎ 0475 510912; omotagwa@yahoo.com; admission per 24hr Birr35; ⏱ 7am-12.30pm & 3-5.30pm Mon-Fri) in Gambela organises the compulsory guides (Birr100 per day) and can offer sound advice.

Sleeping & Eating

Camping is really your only option, but thoroughly review the local security situation before considering tenting overnight in the park. If you do deem it safe, you will need to be fully self-sufficient with food and cooking gear. The only other alternative is stay in one of Gog's or Itang's dives.

Getting There & Around

For any trips within the park, you'll really need to come with your own sturdy 4WD.

Occasional public transport runs through the park between Gambela and Gog; enquire at park headquarters.

WESTERN ETHIOPIA

Ethiopia Directory

CONTENTS

ACCOMMODATION

Anyone who visited Ethiopia 10 to 15 years ago will recall joyous nights sleeping in rural hotels that were nothing but stables for animals and urban hotels that were essentially just brothels. No matter where you stayed, fleas were a constant companion. Fortunately, Ethiopian accommodation has come on in leaps and bounds. Fleas, sheep and prostitutes are now the exception rather than the rule.

Camping

Tents are useful in Ethiopia for trekking and the exploration of remote regions. If you're just planning a short trek, tents can be hired from Addis Ababa's tour operators (p270) or from businesses in Lalibela, Gonder and Debark.

Campsites have been set up in some of the national parks and in the Omo Valley, but most lack facilities and consist of little more than a clearing beside a river. It's always essential to treat drinking water at the sites.

There are increasing numbers of upmarket hotels now allowing camping on their grounds, though prices are close to what you'd pay for nice budget accommodation.

All camping fees in this book are per person unless stated otherwise.

Hotels

In Ethiopia, hotels will play home to everyone who's not camping. Even in the capital, there are no hostels, homestays or rental accommodation available to travellers.

Pricing invariably leads to resentment from many travellers as countless hotels (many openly) charge substantially higher rates for *faranjis* (foreigners, especially Western ones). Although you make take offence to a hotel owner calling you a rich *faranji*, remember prices are still dirt-cheap and you'll always be given priority, as well as the best rooms, facilities and service.

Charging same-sex couples more for rooms than mixed couples is also pervasive but less justifiable.

Some hotels (particularly government-owned ones) charge a 10% service charge and 15% tax on top of room prices. We've incorporated these extra charges into the room prices listed.

In Ethiopia, a room with a double bed is confusingly called a 'single', and a room with

---

BOOK YOUR STAY ONLINE

For more accommodation reviews and recommendations by Lonely Planet authors, check out the online booking service at www.lonelyplanet.com/hotels. You'll find the true, insider low-down on the best places to stay. Reviews are thorough and independent. Best of all, you can book online.

PRACTICALITIES

■ The best-known English-language daily newspapers are the government-owned *Ethiopian Herald* and the privately owned *Monitor*. Other weekly private newspapers include the *Fortune*, the *Reporter*, the *Sun, Sub-Saharan Informer* and the *Capital*. Only the *Ethiopian Herald* is available outside Addis Ababa. The weekly *Press Digest* and *Days Update* give useful summaries of the most important stories from the week's Amharic and English press.

■ Radio Ethiopia broadcasts in English from 1.30pm to 2pm and 7pm to 8pm weekdays. The BBC World Service can be received on radios with short-wave reception, though frequencies vary according to the time of day (try 9630, 11940 and 17640 MHz).

■ Ethiopia's ETV1 channel broadcasts in English from 10.30pm to midnight. Many hotels and restaurants have satellite dishes that receive BBC or CNN. Others have South Africa's multichannel DSTV network.

■ Ethiopia's electricity supply is 220V, 50 cycles AC. Sockets vary from the European continental two-pin, earth prong (two round prongs), rated at 600W to the South African/Indian-style plug with two circular metal pins above a large circular grounding pin.

■ Ethiopia uses the metric system for weights and measures.

---

twin beds a 'double'. Single travellers are often forced to pay the same as a couple. In our reviews we've used the Western interpretation of singles, doubles and twins, although singles are listed only where the room price is different from that for a couple.

Reservations are wise in Gonder, Aksum and Lalibela during the major festivals.

While there are no left-luggage facilities in Addis Ababa, most hotels will hold your belongings for no extra charge.

More expensive hotels sometimes quote their rates in US dollars, but all accept payment in Birr. We have quoted prices in the currency the hotel uses.

BUDGET

There are still countless dives, but the number of clean and comfortable budget options continues to rise, especially in the north.

In smaller, out-of-the-way towns, hotels may double as drinking dens and brothels – bring earplugs. Many lack glass windows, only having a shutter to let air and light in.

Maintenance doesn't seem to be a high priority, so the best budget hotels are often those that have just opened. If you hear of a new hotel in town, it may be the best place to head.

MIDRANGE

Although very comfortable compared with Ethiopian budget options, most midrange hotels here would be scraping by as bare-bones budget options in the Western world. They typically include a simple room with private bathroom and satellite TV, as well as an adequate restaurant, secure parking and a garden. Though usually clean and quiet, the majority are looking tired and run-down, and very rarely offer good value for money.

TOP END

There are several top-end options in Addis Ababa, but very little else that really qualifies as true top end elsewhere.

ACTIVITIES

With two amazing 4000m mountain ranges and countless other peaks and valleys hosting unique wildlife, it's little wonder that trekking in Ethiopia has become a major activity. Rock climbing is also possible, but this sport is still in its infancy here. The waterways churning through Ethiopia's topographic delights play home to some fine rafting and fishing. Last but not least, the fact that Ethiopia's skies are blanketed with a plethora of endemic and migratory birds has led to a boom in birdwatching. Grab your binoculars and enjoy!

Birdwatching

The birds of Ethiopia are so numerous, so diverse and so colourful that they attract twitchers from around the globe. To do the birds and the art of birdwatching justice, we've created a special box of key information for birdwatchers on p76. It highlights some o

Ethiopia's most famous birds and gives you the lowdown on where to go to find them and when. The Animals section (p75) of the Environment chapter also delves into some of the species you'll spot while travelling through the country.

Some of Addis Ababa's tour agencies (p270), as well as some excellent agencies abroad, offer great birdwatching tours.

Fishing

Ethiopia's lakes and rivers are home to over 200 species of freshwater fish, including very large catfish (up to 18kg), tilapia, large barbus, tigerfish, the brown and rainbow trout and the famously feisty Nile perch.

Fly-fishing, bait fishing with float and ledger, freelining, threadline spinning and trolling are all permitted fishing practices, but you'll need to be totally self-sufficient as far as equipment is concerned.

Popular fishing spots include Lake Tana in the north and the Rift Valley lakes in the south. Fishing is permitted almost everywhere in Ethiopia.

Rock Climbing

There's untapped potential for rock climbing, particularly around Mekele in the region of Tigray, which offers sandstone climbs in the HVS – E2 (4-5c) range. However, you'll have to come fully equipped and self-sufficient, and prepared to locate your own routes. Contact **Village Ethiopia** (Map pp86-7; ☎ 0115 523497; www .village-ethiopia.net; National Hotel, Menelik II Ave), which has catered to climbers in the past, and hunt down a copy of the beautifully illustrated book

Vertical Ethiopia by Majka Burhardt (it's easy to find in Ethiopia, but difficult elsewhere).

Trekking

Trekking is the highlight of many people's trip to Ethiopia. The whole highland region is littered with tracks and trails that are used by locals to get from field to village and village to market. The adventurous traveller could simply hop off a bus anywhere and start walking. If you prefer your trekking more organised, then hikes lasting from a few days up to two weeks are regularly completed in the striking 4000m surroundings of Simien Mountains National Park (p126), while treks through the rich wildlife of Bale Mountains National Park (p179) typically last four to six days.

Horseback treks in the western range of the Bale Mountains are possible out of Dodola (see p178). Also new on the scene are ecotreks around Lalibela (p163) and fascinating treks run by **Remote River Expeditions** (www.remote rivers.com) through the land of the Surma in the remote southwest. Other areas with serious walking possibilities are around the Tigray rock-hewn churches (p147), the green and lush hills around Korem (p155) and the wonderful escarpments of the Guassa Plateau (p166). A warning: for any of these last three, you would need to be completely self-sufficient.

White-Water Rafting & Kayaking

Rafting began in Ethiopia in the 1970s, when an American team rafted the Omo River in the southwest. Most Addis Ababa tour

---

SAFETY GUIDELINES FOR TREKKING

Before embarking on a trek, consider the following points to ensure a safe and enjoyable experience.

- Pay any fees and obtain any permits required by local authorities.
- Be sure you are healthy and feel comfortable walking for a sustained period.
- Obtain reliable information about physical and environmental conditions along your intended route (eg from park authorities).
- Trek only in regions, and on trails, within your realm of experience.
- Be aware that weather conditions and terrain vary significantly from one region, or even from one trail, to another. Seasonal changes can significantly alter any trail. These differences influence what you should wear and what equipment you carry.
- Ask officials before you set out about the environmental characteristics that can affect your trek and how you should deal with them if they arise.

RESPONSIBLE TREKKING

Trekking in Ethiopia has the potential to put great pressure on the environment. You can help preserve the ecology and beauty of the area by taking note of the following information.

- Carry out all your rubbish. Never ever bury it.

- Minimise the waste you must carry out by taking minimal packaging and taking no more food than you'll need.

- Where there's no toilet, at lower elevations bury your faeces in a 15cm-deep hole (consider carrying a lightweight trowel for this purpose). At higher altitudes soil lacks the organisms needed to digest your faeces, so leave your waste in the open where UV rays will break it down – spreading it facilitates the process. Always carry out your toilet paper (zip-lock bags are best). With either option make sure your faeces is at least 50m from any path, 100m from any watercourse and 200m from any building.

- Don't use detergents or toothpaste within 50m of watercourses, even if they're biodegradable.

- Stick to existing tracks and avoid shortcuts that bypass a switchback. If you blaze a new trail straight down a slope, it will erode the hillside with the next heavy rainfall.

- Avoid removing any plant life as they keep topsoils in place.

- Try to cook on lightweight kerosene, alcohol or Shellite (white gas) stoves instead of burning dead erica wood or eucalyptus. Never burn indigenous trees.

- Be aware of local laws, regulations and etiquette about wildlife and the environment.

- Never feed animals as it messes with their digestive system and leads them to become dependent on hand-outs.

- If camping, try to make camp on existing sites. Where none exist, set up away from streams on rock or bare ground, never over vegetation.

operators (p270) now run trips as do some international operators, such as the incredibly experienced **Remote River Expeditions** (www.remoterivers.com).

The Omo River rafting season is from September to October (after the heavy rains). Tours usually last from one to three weeks. The white water (classed as a comparatively tame three or four on the US scale) is not the main attraction; rather it is the exposure to wildlife (particularly birds) and tribal groups (such as those along the Omo River).

Shorter rafting trips can also be planned on the Blue Nile (a few days) and Awash (one or two days) Rivers. Although two historic expeditions have recently paddled the Blue Nile from Lake Tana to Khartoum and beyond to the Mediterranean, this journey won't be on any travel agency itinerary for a millennium or so.

In theory, excellent kayaking could be had on all the rivers mentioned earlier, but it's not for the inexperienced. Trips need to be well planned, well equipped and well backed up. In the past, some poorly planned trips have gone tragically wrong. Get in touch with th Addis Ababa tour operators, who will pu you in touch with experienced kayaker in Ethiopia.

BOOKS

Aside from the superb books mentione in the the Getting Started chapter (p22 and those listed under sidebars in th History and Culture chapters, further de cent Ethiopian-themed books are provide below.

Graham Hancock, the author of *The Sig and the Seal*, spent 10 years attempting t solve one of the greatest mysteries of all time the bizarre 'disappearance' of the Ark of th Covenant. Though Hancock's research an conclusions raised an eyebrow or two amon historians, this detective story is very read able and gives a good overview of Ethiopia history and culture – however tenuou the facts may be!

Evelyn Waugh's *Remote People*, thoug rather dated now, includes some wry im pressions of Ethiopia in the 1930s. *Waug in Abyssinia* is based on the author's time as a correspondent covering the Italian–Ethiopian conflict in the 1930s. Both books are quite hard to find.

The charming *A Cure for Serpents* by the Duke of Pirajno recounts the duke's time as a doctor in the Horn and is beautifully and engagingly written. Episodes include encounters with famous courtesans, noble chieftains and giant elephants.

The newly reprinted (locally) *Ethiopian Journeys,* by the well-respected American writer Paul Henze, charts travels during the emperor's time.

In Search of King Solomon's Mines entertainingly takes the reader through Debre Damo, Lalibela, Gonder and other exotic Ethiopian locations on author Tahir Shah's quest to find the mythical mines of Solomon. In typical Shah fashion it's full of magic and bizarre encounters.

Thomas Pakenham's fascination with the historical anecdotes revolving around Ethiopia's *ambas* (flat-topped mountains) is the basis of *The Mountains of Rasselas,* an engaging and nicely illustrated coffee-table book on Ethiopia's history.

BUSINESS HOURS

In general, banks, post offices and telecommunications offices are all open the core hours of 8.30am to 11am and 1.30pm to 3.30pm weekdays and from 8.30am to 11am Saturday. However, many open earlier, close later or stay open for lunch.

Most government offices are open from around 8.30am to 12.30pm (to 11.30am Friday) and 1.30pm to 5.30pm Monday to Friday. Private organisations and NGOs open from 8am to 1pm and 2pm to 5pm weekdays. Shops usually operate half an hour later. Outside Addis Ababa, restaurants typically open around 7am or 8am and close around 9.30pm or 10.30pm. The restaurant reviews in this guide don't provide business hours unless they differ from the standards given above.

Cafes are typically open daily from 6am or 7am through to 8pm or 9pm, while *tej beats* (honey-wine bars) usually run daily from 10am to 10pm. Bars open from 6pm to midnight.

Internet cafes are typically open from 8am to 8pm Monday to Saturday. Some have limited hours on Sunday.

CLIMATE CHARTS

Compared with other nations close to the nations, Ethiopia's climate on the whole is very mild. Average daily temperatures on the wide-ranging highlands are below 20°C. It's only the lowland fringes in the east, south and west where daytime temperatures can soar past 30°C.

The majority of rains traditionally fall between mid-March and early October, with the central and western highlands receiving up to 1600mm annually. The far east and northern highlands only receive significant rainfall in July and August (400mm to 1000mm). The far south breaks the trend, receiving most of its rain in April, May and October.

More information on weather patterns can be found in the Climate section of each destination chapter. See also the When to Go section, p18.

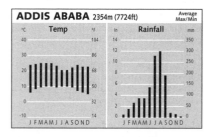

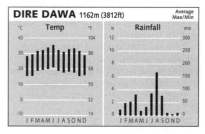

COURSES

Unless you're living in Addis Ababa, there are really no courses of note in Ethiopia. It's likely due to the lack of demand – perhaps most travellers are just too busy trying to absorb the country's history, culture and nature while on the go!

For long stays, the Institute of Language Studies at Addis Ababa University offers four-month language courses (see p96).

ETHIOPIA DIRECTORY

CUSTOMS REGULATIONS

Upon arrival in Ethiopia, visitors must declare foreign currency. There's no limit to the amount of currency that can be brought in, but no more than Birr100 can be exported and imported. You may import 2L of spirits and 200 cigarettes or 100 cigars duty-free.

If you're bringing with you anything of value, such as a video camera or laptop computer, you may be required to register it on your passport as you enter Ethiopia at immigration (to deter black-market trading).

Leaving the country with certain souvenirs can be a problem (see the boxed text, p253).

DANGERS & ANNOYANCES

Compared with many African countries, Ethiopia and its capital, Addis Ababa, are remarkably safe places. Serious or violent crime is rare; against travellers it's extremely rare. Outside the capital, the risk of petty crime drops still further.

A simple traveller's tip? Always look as if you know where you're going. Thieves and con artists get wind of an uncertain newcomer in a minute.

Though the following list may be off-putting and alarming, it's very unlikely you'll encounter any serious difficulties – and even less likely if you're prepared for them.

At the Airport

Commission-seeking taxi touts and guides can be a problem at most airports. Unless you want to take money from your pocket and put it straight into theirs, decide on the hotel you wish to stay at before you step out of the airport and don't let them take you elsewhere. And always negotiate the taxi rate *before* you get in. The majority of Ethiopian taxi drivers are helpful, charming and honest.

Begging & Giving

Many travellers find that the begging they encounter is one of the most distressing aspects of travel in poorer countries.

Ethiopia has more than its fair share of beggars. Some travellers resent being 'targeted' by beggars because they are foreign. However, no matter what you may think, quite rightly you're considered rich and therefore a good bet for a hand-out.

It's difficult to know when to give, to whom and how much. A good rule of thumb is to give

how locals give; small coins dispensed to those who can't make a living, such as the disabled, the ill, the elderly and the blind. Handing out more only increases expectations.

If you don't want to donate money, say instead *igzabier yisteh/yistesh* (m/f; God bless you) with a slight bow of the head. This is a polite and acceptable way of declining to give.

Whether or not to give money, sweets or pens to children is a difficult one. Older Ethiopians are heartbroken seeing younger generations of children, who are no worse off than they were when they were young, begging for money, empty water bottles, food etc. Most children don't beg because they need the items, but because they can get the items. Being rewarded for this behaviour only pulls them from school, robs them of a traditional childhood and makes them believe they need hand-outs from Westerners.

On the other hand, if it's clearly a homeless child then why not try and help, but be wary of giving money as it's sometimes used to buy glue to sniff. Instead buy them a meal or better still, if you're in Addis, get hold of some meal tickets from Hope Enterprises (p89) and hand those out instead.

Civil Disturbances

At the time of writing the Ogaden region, and the areas around Moyale in the south, were experiencing a mix of rebel activity or tribal violence. Though you're highly unlikely to get caught up in it, do keep your ear to the ground for developments.

If you're concerned, check your government's latest security reports on countries (such as those published by the British Foreign Office). Don't let these scare you away as they do tend to err on the side of caution.

Land Mines

Most travellers have nothing to fear from mines, but those trekking in very remote parts of Tigray or driving off-road in the Ogaden region of southeastern Ethiopia or along the Kenyan border should check with local village officials. Keep to well worn routes when possible. A useful phrase might be *Fenjy alle*? (Are there mines here?) Popular trekking areas such as the Simien and Bale Mountains National Parks are perfectly safe.

GUIDELINES FOR GUIDES

Although many official guides exist in Ethiopia today, particularly in the cities along the historical circuit, there are still countless unofficial 'guides' waiting at every corner.

Some of them resort to aggression, hysterics or sulking to extract money from tourists; others resort to hard-luck stories or appeals for 'sponsorship'. Others claim special expertise and that this and other guidebooks are wholly or partly 'wrong'. Some 'guides' in Addis Ababa have even conned apprehensive first-time travellers into taking them along for the entire historical circuit, at a cost of US$20 per day!

Even if the unofficial guide is friendly, they'll know little in comparison to those who've been trained and will likely charge the same fee. Their lack of actual knowledge takes away from your trip and encourages unhealthy migration of potential 'guides' to towns.

Hiring children may seem like a nice way to help, but you're only giving them reason to miss school and, like unofficial guides, they have little knowledge that will benefit your trip.

If you don't want to be one of the many people writing to us with stories of a guide ruining your trip, here are a few tips:

- If possible, hire licensed guides.
- Choose a guide you're comfortable with. Test their knowledge of English and of the sites in advance, perhaps over a coffee.
- Before starting, ensure that your expectations are clearly understood, such as what you want to see and how much time you have.
- Negotiate a fee in advance. Be aware that some may ask initially up to five times the going rate or more. Professional licensed guides' fees are set at Birr150 per day (one to four people) in Gonder and Lalibela. For a knowledgeable guide elsewhere, Birr10 per hour (minimum total fee of Birr20) is very fair. Check this book for quotes.
- If the service has been good, it's fair and polite to tip a bit extra at the end, but don't be pressured into it, particularly if the tour was poor. See the boxed text, p252.

Mobbing & Faranji Frenzy

The infamous '*faranji* frenzy', when shouts of 'You, you, you, you, YOU!' greeted you at every turn is thankfully becoming rarer and rarer – at least in touristy parts of the country. Off the beaten track you can still expect it to be a musical accompaniment to your travels.

If it does start to get to you then just ignoring it or, even better, treating it with humour is probably the best answer in how to deal with it. Anger only provokes children more (there can be few things more tempting than a grumpy *faranji*!). An Amharic *hid!* (clear off!) for a boy, *hiji!* for a girl or *hidu!* for a group is the Ethiopian response and sends children scuttling; however, it can have the reverse effect, and is considered rather harsh from a foreigner.

On a less-friendly note, several travellers have recently complained of kids and beggars in Gonder yelling 'Fuck off' and other such pleasantries to foreigners who won't give them money. Not surprisingly this leaves a very poor impression of the town and hardly incites much sympathy towards the child or beggar's situation.

Scams

Compared with other African countries, Ethiopia has few scams and rip-offs to boast of. Those that do exist, like the siren scam (p89) in Addis Ababa and the notebook scam (where kids beg for notebooks and pens for school, which, if you buy them one, are taken straight back to the shop to exchange for money), are pretty transparent and rather easily avoided.

You'll also hear many 'hard luck' stories, or those soliciting sponsorship for travel or education in Ethiopia or abroad. Although most are not genuine, some stories are sadly true, so don't be rude.

Also look out for fake antiques in shops.

Self-Appointed Guides

High unemployment has spawned many self-appointed and unofficial guides. You will be approached, accompanied for a while, given unasked-for information and then charged. Be wary of anyone who approaches you unasked, particularly at the exit of bus stations etc. Unfortunately, there's almost always an ulterior motive. Be polite but firm and try not to get paranoid!

Shiftas

In some of the more remote areas, such as the southeast's Ogaden Desert, near the Kenyan border, along the Awash–Mille Rd at night and in the far west, *shiftas* (bandits) are sometimes reported. However, most of these places lie far from the main tourist trails. In fact, tourists are very rarely targeted; indeed they are positively avoided for fear of government repercussions.

Theft

Pickpocketing is the biggest concern, but is a problem mainly in Addis Ababa and other large towns, in particular Shashemene, Nazret and Dessie. For tips on thieves' tactics, see Addis Ababa's Dangers & Annoyances section (p90).

Keep an eye on your belongings at bus stations and be wary of people offering to put your bags on the bus roof. Be aware that professional thieves sometimes operate at major festivals and markets, targeting Ethiopians as well as foreigners.

A money belt is best for your passport and cash stash, but not for your daily spending money – keep that separate so you don't have to yank out your money belt each time you spend. It's also a good idea to keep an emergency stash of US$100 hidden somewhere.

EMBASSIES & CONSULATES

The following list isn't exhaustive (almost every African nation has representation in Addis Ababa), but it covers the embassies most of you will likely need.

Australia See Canada.

Belgium (Map p84; ☎ 0116 621291; AddisAbaba@diplobel.org; Fikremaryam Abatechan St)

Canada (Map p84; ☎ 0113 713022; addis@dfait-maeci.gc.ca; Seychelles St) Also represents Australia.

Djibouti (Map pp86-7; ☎ 0116 613200) Off Bole Rd.

Egypt (Map p84; ☎ 0111 550021; egyptian.emb@ethionet.et; Madagascar St)

Eritrea (Map pp86-7; ☎ 0115 512844; Ras Mekonen Ave) Currently closed.

France (Map p84; ☎ 0111 550066; amba.france@telcom.net.et)

Germany (Map p84; ☎ 0111 235139; www.addis-abeba.diplo.de)

Italy (Map p84; ☎ 0111 235717; ambasciata.addisabeba@esteri.it)

Kenya (Map p84; ☎ 0116 610033; kenigad@telecom.net.et; Fikremaryam Abatechan St)

Netherlands (Map p84; ☎ 0113 711100; www.netherlandsembassyethiopia.org) Off Ring Rd.

Somaliland (Map pp86-7; ☎ 0116 635921; between Bole Rd & Cameroon St)

Spain (Map p84; ☎ 0115 550222; embaespet@mail.mae.es; Botswana St)

Sudan (Map pp86-7; ☎ 0115 516477; sudan.embassy@ethionet.et; Ras Lulseged St)

Sweden (Map pp86-7; ☎ 0115 180000; ambassaden.addis-abeba@foreign.ministry.se; Yared St)

Switzerland (Map p84; ☎ 0113 711107; www.eda.adm.ch; Ring Rd)

UK (Map p84; ☎ 0116 612354; http://ukinethiopia.fco.gov.uk; Fikremaryam Abatechan St)

USA (Map p84; ☎ 0115 174000; http://ethiopia.usembassy.gov; Algeria St)

FESTIVALS & EVENTS

Islamic holidays are not particularly conspicuous in Ethiopia, but they are important event for the Muslim population. Festivals includ Ras as-Sana (Muslim New Year), Mawlid an Nabi (Prophet's birthday), Lailat al-Mira' (Prophet's Ascension), Eid al-Fitr (markin Ramadan's end) and Eid al-Adha (Festiva of Sacrifice).

Major Ethiopian Orthodox festivals includ the following:

January

Leddet (also known as Genna or Christmas) 6-7 January. Although less important than Timkat and Meskel, Leddet is still significant. The faithful attend all-night church services, often moving from one church to another. On Christmas day, the traditional games of *genna* (a kind of hockey) and sometimes *gugs* (a kind of polo) are played, along with horse racing. Priests don their full regalia. Lalibela is one of the best places to experience Leddet; Addis Ababa is also good.

Timkat (Epiphany, celebrating Christ's baptism) 19 January. This three-day festival is the most colourful of the year. The church *tabots* (replicas of the Ark of the Covenant) are taken to a nearby body of water on the afternoon of the eve of Timkat. During the night, the priests and faithful participate in a vigil around the *tabots*. The following morning, the crowds gather around the water, which is blessed and then splashed onto them; religious vows are renewed. The *tabot*

MAJOR ISLAMIC HOLIDAYS				
Islamic year	New Year	Prophet's Birthday	End of Ramadan	Festival of Sacrifice
1431	20 Dec 2009	28 Feb 2010	12 Sep 2010	20 Nov 2010
1432	09 Dec 2010	18 Feb 2011	02 Sep 2011	9 Nov 2011
1433	30 Nov 2011	07 Feb 2012	22 Aug 2012	30 Oct 2012

is then paraded back to the church accompanied by much singing and dancing. Gonder is considered the best place to be for Timkat; Addis Ababa is also good.

March–April

Good Friday March/April. From Thursday evening before Good Friday, the faithful fast until the Easter service, which ends at 3am on Easter Sunday.

Fasika (Orthodox Easter) March/April. Fasika marks the end of a vegetarian fast of 55 days, in which no animal product is eaten. Officially, nothing should be consumed until the daily church service finishes at around 3pm. In the past, many of Ethiopia's enemies took advantage of the fasting period to inflict heavy casualties on its weakened armies.

September

Kiddus Yohannes (New Year's Day) 11 September. Ethiopian New Year (also known as Enkutatash) is an important family and social event. Traditionally, new clothes are bought for the occasion, particularly for the children, and relatives and friends are visited. Special feasts are prepared. The traditional game of *gugs* can sometimes be seen.

Meskel (Finding of the True Cross) 27 September. This two-day festival is the most colourful festival after Timkat. Bonfires are built topped by a cross to which flowers are tied, most commonly the Meskel daisy. After the bonfires are blessed, they are lit, and dancing and singing begins around them. Priests don their full regalia. Addis Ababa, Gonder and Aksum are good places to experience Meskel.

Irecha On the first Sunday following Meskel (usually late September or early October), the Oromo people celebrate Irecha on the shores of Lake Hora. During this time thanks is given to Waka (One God) and good fortune sought for the upcoming planting season. Devotees gather around ancient fig trees to smear perfume, butter and katickala (a distilled drink) on the tree trunks and share ceremonial meals of roasted meat, coffee, tella (a traditional beer) and araki (a traditional distilled alcohol).

November

Festival of Maryam Zion 30 November. This is one of Ethiopia's largest festivals, though it's only celebrated in Aksum. See p142 for details.

December

Kulubi Gabriel 28 December. Although not on the official religious holiday list, large numbers of Ethiopians make a pilgrimage to the venerated Kulubi Gabriel church (p218), near Dire Dawa in the east.

FOOD

For information on what you'll find heaped atop your injera or to answer the simple question 'What's injera?', see p66.

Eating out in Ethiopia is ridiculously cheap, with local meals in remote areas costing less than US$1. In large regional cities a local meal will ding you US$1.50, while a Western meal will rob you of US$2 to US$3. If you pull out all the stops and dine on succulent braised lamb with caramelised onions, lentils, lemon and raison orange couscous in Addis Ababa's best restaurant, you'll be out about US$10.

In this book restaurants are listed in price order, with the cheapest first.

If cafes are more known for their pastries and cakes, they'll fall under Eating. Conversely, if it's their coffee or juices that shine, you'll find them under Drinking.

GAY & LESBIAN TRAVELLERS

In Ethiopia and Eritrea, homosexuality is severely condemned – traditionally, religiously and legally – and remains a topic of absolute taboo. Don't underestimate the strength of feeling. Reports of gays being beaten up aren't uncommon and during the course of researching this book, a rumour was circulating that a US diplomat was murdered for being gay. In Amharic, the word *bushti* (homosexual) is a very offensive insult, implying immorality and depravity. One traveller wrote to us to report expulsion from a hotel and serious threats just for coming under suspicion. If a hotel only offers double beds, rather than twins, you and your companion will pay more or may even be refused occupancy.

Women may have an easier time: even the idea of a lesbian relationship is beyond the permitted imaginings of many Ethiopians! Behave discreetly, and you will be assumed to be just friends.

Note that the Ethiopian penal code officially prohibits homosexual acts, with penalties of between 10 days' and 10 years' imprisonment for various 'crimes'. Although gay locals obviously exist, they behave with extreme discretion and caution. Gay travellers are advised to do likewise.

Information on homosexuality in the Horn is hard to come by, even in the well-known gay publications. Try the **International Lesbian & Gay Association** (ILGA; www.ilga.org) for more information.

HOLIDAYS

Ethiopia's public holidays can be divided into three categories: national secular holidays, Christian Orthodox festivals (p248) and Islamic holidays (see the boxed text, p249). During the Christian Orthodox festivals, accommodation is hard to come by in Gonder, Aksum and Lalibela, as are open seats on internal flights. While prices rise for rooms during these times, transportation costs remain the same. It's best to book flights as far in advance as possible to avoid problems. See the relevant towns' sections for more details.

National holidays include the following:

Victory of Adwa Commemoration Day 2 March
International Labour Day 1 May
Ethiopian Patriots' Victory Day (also known as Liberation Day) 5 May
Downfall of the Derg 28 May

INSURANCE

A travel-insurance policy for all medical problems is essential for travel in Ethiopia, while one to cover theft and loss really is helpful but not vital. For information on medical insurance, see p367.

Vehicle insurance is covered on p268.

Worldwide cover to travellers from over 40 countries is available online at www.lonely planet.com/bookings.

INTERNET ACCESS

An internet cafe in Ethiopia is like a pimple on your wedding day – always found where everyone looks and never where nobody can see. In English? Internet cafes are everywhere in Addis Ababa, pretty easy to spot in major towns and nonexistent in places that see few tourists. Most are open 8am to 8pm Monday to Saturday. Many open with limited hours on Sunday.

However, just because internet cafes exist that doesn't mean internet exists and connections in Ethiopia are among the worst on the continent. It can easily take an hour to download one simple, two line e-mail. And that's in Addis! To avoid intense frustration it's better to assume that while in Ethiopia you will not be able to get online. When it does work, costs range from Birr0.20 to Birr0.30 per minute in most places. For those with laptops, a number of upmarket hotels in Addi now supposedly offer wi-fi access. We say 'supposedly' because we never actually managed to get it to work.

See also Internet Resources, p22.

LEGAL MATTERS

Remember that when in Ethiopia, you're subject to Ethiopian laws. If you're arrested, you must (in theory) be brought to court within 48 hours. You have the right to talk to someone from your embassy, as well as a lawyer. For the most part, police in Ethiopia will show you a much respect as you show them. If confronted by the police, always maintain your cool, smile and be polite. Compared with some other African nations, police here rarely, if ever, ask for bribes (we've yet to experience it).

Alcohol

Alcohol cannot be served to anyone under 18 years of age in Ethiopia. Disturbance caused by those under the influence of alcohol is punishable by three months' to one year's imprisonment. Driving while under the influence is also illegal and attracts a fine.

Drugs

Penalties for possession, use or trafficking of illegal drugs (including hashish) are strictly enforced in Ethiopia. Convicted offenders can expect both fines and long jail sentences.

Consumption of the mildly stimulating leaf *chat* (see boxed text p72) is permitted in Ethiopia, but not in Eritrea.

MAPS

For simply travelling around the country on public transport, the maps in this guidebook should suffice. For those of you venturing off into the nether regions with 4WDs, a more detailed map is essential. Since trekking without a guide is illegal in the Simien and Bale Mountains, additional maps aren't necessary, though topographic maps (see the parks' relevant sections for details) can help you plan your routes with more precision.

In Ethiopia, the map produced by the defunct Ethiopian Tourism Commission (1987; 1:2,000,000) isn't bad and can be picked up in some Addis Ababa hotels or in the gift shop next to the Tourist Information Centre in Addis for Birr60.

A more accurate map (although it lacks distance labels between cities) of the same scale is available from the Ethiopia Mapping Authority (p85) in Addis Ababa.

Of the maps currently available outside the country, the best is that produced by International Travel Maps (1998; 1:2,000,000). It's much more up to date than both maps available in Ethiopia.

The Cartographia map of Ethiopia, Eritrea and Djibouti (1996; 1:2,500,000) comes second and isn't a bad choice for the region.

MONEY

Ethiopia's currency is the birr. It's divided into 100 cents in 1, 5, 10, 25 and 50 cent coins, and there are 1, 5, 10, 50 and 100 birr notes. Despite a weekly auction determining exchange rates, the birr is one of Africa's most stable currencies. At least that was still the case at the time of research, but there was much talk of devaluing the birr, which could lead to large fluctuations against hard currencies.

See the inside front cover for exchange rates and p19 for details about the costs of travel.

According to National Bank of Ethiopia regulations, all bills in Ethiopia must be paid in birr. But this isn't enforced and Ethiopian Airlines, most major hotels, most travel agencies and even the Department of Immigration accept (and sometimes demand!) US currency.

One regulation that's strictly enforced is the conversion of birr to US dollars or euros; this transaction can only be done for people holding onward air tickets from Ethiopia. This means people leaving overland must budget accordingly. There are black-market traders around the borders, but rates are poor and it's risky (see right).

ATMs

Bigger branches of the Dashen Bank in Addis Ababa, Bahir Dar, Gonder and Mekele now have ATMs that accept international Visa cards. The service is likely to expand to regional cities and even to other banks quite quickly. Note that MasterCard, Solo, Cirrus or Plus cards do not work in any ATM.

Black Market

Unlike 10 to 15 years ago when almost all currency exchanges were conducted on a fairly open black market that gave significantly higher rates than the banks, things have now tightened up drastically. The black market still exists, and most hotels will exchange US$ cash or Euros for you, but the rates are only about 10% more than that offered by the banks.

The black market is illegal; penalties range from hefty fines to imprisonment. If you do indulge, stick to the shops and be wary of other places, particularly Merkato and the Piazza in Addis Ababa, where there's a good chance of being swindled or robbed.

Cash

As with many African countries the US dollar is the preferred foreign currency in Ethiopia and although the euro is growing in popularity, not all banks will accept it; therefore you should still pack a wedge of greenbacks. You'll have no trouble exchanging US cash wherever there are forex facilities.

While more banks in Ethiopia change cash than travellers cheques, you will usually end up getting slightly worse rates for cash.

Credit Cards

Credit cards (Visa and MasterCard) are increasingly useful in Addis Ababa but remain completely useless (with the exception of some Ethiopian Airlines offices) outside it. The travel agencies, airline offices and major hotels that do accept cards typically ding you 3–5% extra for the privilege of plastic.

Cash advances are possible at a couple of branches of the Dashen Bank in the capital and in larger Historical Circuit cities. Only Addis Ababa's Sheraton can give you US dollars instead of birr.

Tipping

Tips (*gursha* in Amharic) are considered a part of everyday life in Ethiopia, and help supplement often very low wages. The maxim 'little but often' is a good one, and even very small tips are greatly appreciated. It's a great mistake to overtip: it unfairly raises the expectations of locals, undermines the social traditions and may spoil the trips of future travellers. Local guides can start to select only those tourists who look lucrative, and can react very aggressively if their expectations aren't met.

If a professional person helps you (or someone drawing a regular wage), it's probably better to show your appreciation in other ways: shaking hands, exchanging names, or an invitation to have a coffee and pastry are all local ways of expressing gratitude.

Furnishing yourself with a good wad of small notes – Birr1 and Birr5 – is a very good idea. You'll need these for tips, taking photographs etc. You should budget around Birr50 for tips per week.

Travellers Cheques

Travellers cheques remain more useful in Ethiopia than most other countries, and banks in Addis Ababa and the larger towns (but not smaller ones) will exchange them. Like cash, travellers cheques are best carried in US dollars. Note that most banks ask to see your passport and the cheque's proof-of-purchase receipt (which most travellers-cheque companies advise you to leave at home!).

PHOTOGRAPHY & VIDEO

Quite a few internet cafes now offer to burn images to CD through a USB connection. They charge between Birr4 and Birr15 for the service, Birr10 more if you need a CD.

Camera film is increasingly hard to find and expensive and old when you do. Bring supplies from home.

In general most Ethiopians love having their photos taken, though in remote areas people are still suspicious of cameras and many feel seriously threatened or compromised, especially women. Be sensitive. Always ask permission, even if it is only using basic sign language. Best of all, use a local as an interpreter or go-between. Never take a photo if permission is declined.

In other areas, where people are starting to depend on tourists for income, the opposite is true. In the Lower Omo Valley, you'll be chased by people demanding their photo be taken! However, their eagerness has to do with the fee they'll claim for each snap of the shutter (around Birr1 to Birr2 per person per picture). Always agree to an amount first. The whole mercenary and almost voyeuristic affair can be rather off-putting for many travellers.

POST

Ethiopia's postal system is reliable and reasonably efficient. Airmail costs Birr2 for postcards; Birr2 for a letter up to 20g to Africa, Birr2.45 to Europe and the Middle East, and

---

TIPS FOR TIPPING

Tipping can be a constant source of worry, hassle or stress for travellers. This guide has been compiled with the help of Ethiopians.

- In the smaller restaurants in the towns, service is included, and Ethiopians don't tip unless the service has been exceptional (up to 10%).
- In bars and cafes, sometimes loose coins are left. However, in the larger restaurants accustomed to tourists, 10% will be expected.
- In Addis Ababa's midrange and top-end hotels, staff will expect a minimum Birr10 per service.
- Outside Addis Ababa, midrange and top-end hotels' luggage handlers will expect a tip of around Birr2 to Birr5 per bag, and people acting as impromptu guides around Birr10.
- For the assistance of a child, Birr1 or Birr2 is plenty.
- At traditional music and dance shows in bars, restaurants and hotels, an audience shows its appreciation by placing money (around Birr10) on the dancers' foreheads or in their belts.
- Car 'guards' (often self- appointed) expect Birr2 to Birr3.
- Drivers of 4WD rental vehicles make around Birr80 per day in salary, so a tip of Birr40 to Birr60 per day is generous for quality service.
- If the service has been good at the end of the trek, a rule of thumb for tipping guides/scouts/ mule handlers might be an extra day's pay for every three days' work.
- Professional English-/German-/Italian-speaking guides hired from Addis Ababa travel agencies for multiday 4WD tours make around Birr250 per day, so a nice tip would be Birr50 to Birr80 per day.

IN SEARCH OF SOUVENIRS

During the last several hundred years, thousands of manuscripts and other national treasures, including gold and silver crosses and even a giant stele (!), have left Ethiopia as 'souvenirs'. Most will probably never be recovered.

Today, tourists, antique dealers, professional thieves and even diplomats are responsible for the disappearance of works of art. In 1996 a German tourist removed several items from the National Museum at Aksum, and in March 1997 a Belgian tourist almost succeeded in removing Lalibela's famous 7kg gold cross. Things became so critical that the World Bank recently funded a four-year project to try and create a nationwide, computerised inventory of Ethiopia's treasures.

At the current rate of 'souvenir' removal, it's thought that Ethiopia will be bereft of most of her treasures by 2020. If you don't want to risk wasting money on a souvenir that can't leave the country, have a look at the following list of banned souvenirs.

List of Banned Souvenirs

The following list is adapted from the official catalogue of objects that are now denied export permits. Be warned that much parchment is currently being denied permission.

- Animal and plant fossils and any prehistoric items such as stone tools, bones or pottery
- Anything of outstanding anthropological or ethnographical interest
- Anything with an ancient inscription on it
- Old processional or hand crosses that bear the names of kings or religious leaders; or any currently in use at churches or monasteries
- Any items (including manuscripts, books, documents or religious objects such as chalices, crosses and incense burners) currently serving in churches
- Any old wooden items
- Coins and paper money not currently in circulation
- Any endangered species or their products, such as ivory, tortoiseshell or leopard skins
- Any items of exceptional artistic interest, whether old or modern
- Art with outstanding historical value, such as engravings with historical figures
- Any items formerly belonging to the emperor, his family or to Ethiopian nobles

Exportation Permits

Although you may have been told that you'll need an exportation permit from the Department of Inventory and Inspection at the National Museum if you plan to leave Ethiopia with anything that looks antique, this is no longer the case.

As of late 2005 customs officials at Bole International Airport and Addis Ababa's main post office, now trained in the art of antiquities, will make the determination as to whether your souvenir can leave Ethiopia. If you haven't declared questionable souvenirs and they're discovered by officials, you'll likely have the item confiscated and have a lot of explaining to do.

Birr3.45 to the Americas, Australia and Asia. Letters should take between five and eight days to arrive in Europe; eight to 15 days for the USA or Australia.

International parcels can only be sent from the main post office in Addis Ababa (Map pp86–7). Posting a small parcel of between 1kg and 2kg costs Birr13.90 worldwide.

Prices of airmail parcels are different for each country, with a 1kg parcel to Australia/Canada/UK/Italy costing Birr228.40/256.05/242.60/

182.10. For each extra 500g to the same countries, you'll pay approximately Birr57/62/41/29. All parcels are subject to a customs inspection, so leave them open until you've had their contents inspected at the counter.

There's a free poste restante service in Addis Ababa (address mail to 'Poste Restante, Addis Ababa, Ethiopia') and in many of the larger towns. When you collect it, it will likely be under your first name instead of your surname.

SHOPPING

Ethiopia has rich history of arts and crafts. To get an idea of what will be sold throughout the country, see p64. To see the top end of quality and artistry, visit the Ethnological Museum in Addis Ababa (p90) before hitting the markets and shops.

Good souvenir shops are found in the capital, as well as major towns on the historical circuit. Quality and creativity ranges from poor to very high, so it's worth comparing shops and wares. Prices always depend on your negotiation skills. Don't forget the export regulations (see the boxed text, p253). While not illegal, you should try and avoid buying crafts made from indigenous woods.

The *gabi* (white cotton toga worn by the highlanders) makes a great (albeit bulky) travelling companion. It serves as a blanket, pillow, mattress, cushion (on long bus journeys) and wrap against the cold.

Bargaining

Prices are usually fixed. Haggling over prices can sometimes greatly offend Ethiopians. All the usual discounts apply for long stays in hotels, low season, extended car hire etc, and you shouldn't hesitate to ask for them in these instances.

The few exceptions, where haggling is almost expected, are at the local markets and with the local taxi and *gari* (horse-drawn cart) drivers. Don't forget that haggling is meant to be an enjoyable experience. Just remember the aim is not to get the lowest possible price, but one that's acceptable to both you and the seller. If you're light-hearted and polite about it, you'll end up with a much better price!

SOLO TRAVELLERS

Travelling solo in Ethiopia can be incredibly rewarding, but it can also be more expensive. There are no cheap organised tours for solo travellers to just sign up for in Ethiopia. If you have a group, you can do a trip together and share costs. If you're alone, you'll have to find people to share with or cover all the costs yourself. The biggest cost issue is transport. If you have limited time and still want to explore areas such as the Lower Omo Valley and remote rock-hewn churches of Tigray, you'll have to shoulder the cost of an expensive 4WD hire.

Similar problems arise for boat trips onto Lake Tana and the Rift Valley lakes, as well as with treks into the Simien and Bale Mountains, where things including transport, guide fees and tent rental must be borne individually. However, in the cases of Lake Tana and the Simien Mountains, you'll usually have an easy time locating people to share costs in Bahir Dar and Gonder respectively. You could also try to meet up with other travellers through the forum on the Lonely Planet website, lonelyplanet.com/thorntree.

Few hotels offer single occupancy rates, so you'll be paying double what you'd be paying if you were sharing.

Although travelling alone puts you at greater risk for petty theft (which still isn't high), it also increases the number of Ethiopians who'll be looking out for your welfare. For specific details about travelling alone as a female, see p257.

The biggest benefit of travelling solo is that you'll unintentionally be more open to conversing with locals. A distant second-place finisher would have to be all the times you manage to get the last seat on the last bus heading somewhere special.

TELEPHONE

Ethiopia's telecommunications industry is entirely government-run – and it shows. The industry is in desperate need of privatisation as currently making a phone call is certain to turn you grey and, just like with the internet (run by the same company), it's best to assume that you won't be calling home very much.

Countless shops operate as 'telecentres' and can normally/sometimes/once in a while connect you to the big wide world for Birr15 to Birr25 per minute. Some hotels offer phone services, but they are usually at least 20% more expensive.

When calling abroad from Ethiopia, use ☎ 00 followed by the appropriate country code. Collect calls are only available at the telecommunications offices and can be made to the UK, USA and Canada only (Australia, Germany and France should be possible in the near future); you still have to pay a 'report charge' of Birr5 to Birr8, plus a Birr10 (refundable) deposit.

Cheap local calls can also be made from telecommunications offices, telecentres and public phone boxes. Most boxes take both coins and cards (sold at the telecommunications offices in denominations of Birr25, Birr50 and Birr100).

OH, TO BE YOUNG AGAIN

Another great Ethiopian time-keeping idiosyncrasy that confounds many a traveller is the calendar. It's based on the old Coptic calendar, which has its roots in ancient Egypt. Although it has 12 months of 30 days each and a 13th month of five or six days, like the ancient Coptic calendar, it follows the Julian system of adding a leap day every four years without exception.

What makes the Ethiopian calendar even more unique is that it wasn't tweaked by numerous popes to align with their versions of Christianity, like the Gregorian calendar (introduced by Pope Gregory XIII in 1582) that we Westerners have grown up on.

What does this all mean? It means the Ethiopian calendar is 7½ years 'behind' the Gregorian calendar, the Millennium has only just past and you're seven years younger and have seven years fewer wrinkles and bulges, as well as a bit more hair of a far nicer colour!

Note: all Ethiopian numbers were changed in 2005 to have 10 digits. The old six-digit numbers now trail a new four-digit area code that must always precede the old number, no matter where you're calling from.

Important telephone numbers and Ethiopia's country code are inside this book's front cover.

Mobile Phones

The speed with which Ethiopia's mobile phone network has expanded would make Starbucks blush. However, like all other aspects of Ethiopian telecommunications, the service can hardly be described as reliable. Whether you're using your home phone on a roaming plan or a locally bought phone and SIM card, expect days to go by when, despite having a reception, it's impossible to actually make a call – and as for sending a text message…

TIME

Ethiopia is three hours ahead of GMT/UTC.

Time is expressed so sanely in Ethiopia that it blows most travellers' minds! At sunrise it's 12 o'clock (6am our time) and after one hour of sunshine it's 1 o'clock. After two hours of sunshine? Yes, 2 o'clock. The sun sets at 12 o'clock (6pm our time) and after one hour of darkness it's…1 o'clock! Instead of using 'am' or 'pm', Ethiopians use 'in the morning', 'in the evening' and 'at night' to indicate the period of day.

The system is used widely, though the 24-hour clock is used occasionally in business. Be careful to ask if a time quoted is according to the Ethiopian or 'European' clock (*Be habesha/faranji akotater no?* – Is that Ethiopian/foreigner's time?). For the purposes of this book, all times quoted are by the European clock.

TOILETS

Both sit-down and squat toilets are found in Ethiopia, reflecting European and Arab influences respectively. You'll usually only find squat jobs in the bottom end of the budget-hotel bracket.

Public toilets are found in almost all hotels and restaurants, but may not form your fondest memories of Ethiopia. In small towns and rural areas, the most common arrangement is a smelly old shack, with two planks, a hole in the ground and all the flies you can fit in between. You may suddenly find that you can survive the next 1000km after all.

Toilet paper is very rare in any toilet; you're best advised to carry your own.

TOURIST INFORMATION
Local Tourist Offices

In 2005 the Ethiopian government unceremoniously sacked the heads of the Ethiopian Tourism Commission (ETC) and created the new Ministry of Culture and Tourism. Thankfully, this ministry kept open the ETC's ever-helpful Tourist Information Centre in Addis Ababa's Meskal Sq (see p89).

The offices of the Tigrai Tourism Commission in Aksum, Mekele and Wukro have to be the most helpful and prepared. Other tourist offices exist elsewhere, but few are worth the effort of visiting (Konso's and Arba Minch's being the exceptions).

While in Addis Ababa, the most accurate information on travel outside the capital region is available through tour operators (see p270), though naturally they will expect to sell you something. Outside Addis Ababa, hotel managers and the traveller grapevine are your best sources for up-to-date information.

Tourist Offices Abroad

No national tourist office exists abroad. The Ethiopian embassies and consulates try to fill the gap, but they generally just hand out the usual tourist brochures.

An active, non-political organisation in the UK is the **Anglo-Ethiopian Society** (www.anglo-ethiopian.org), which aims 'to foster a knowledge and understanding of Ethiopia and its people'. Membership costs from £15 annually. The society holds regular gatherings, including talks on Ethiopia. A well-stocked library on Ethiopia and Eritrea is open to members. There's a tri-annual Newsfile.

TRAVELLERS WITH DISABILITIES

There's no reason why intrepid disabled travellers shouldn't visit Ethiopia. The recent civil war left many soldiers disabled, so you should expect to find at least some degree of empathy and understanding.

For those with restricted mobility, all the sites on the historical route are easily reached by internal flights. Passengers in wheelchairs can be accommodated. Car rental with a driver is easily organised (though expensive). Some rough roads can be hard on the back.

Taxis are widely available in the large towns and are good for getting around. None have wheelchair access. In Addis Ababa a few hotels have lifts; at least two (the Sheraton and Hilton hotels) have facilities for wheelchair-users. Kerb ramps on streets are nonexistent, and potholes and uneven streets are a hazard.

Outside the capital, facilities are lacking, but many hotels are bungalow affairs, so at least steps or climbs are avoided.

For those restricted in other ways, such as visually or aurally, you'll get plenty of offers of help. Unlike in many Western countries, Ethiopians are not shy about coming forward to offer assistance.

A valuable source of general information is the **Access-Able Travel Source** (www.access-able.com). This site has useful links.

Before leaving home, visitors can get in touch with their national support organisation. Ask for the 'travel officer', who may have a list of travel agents that specialise in tours for the disabled.

VISAS & DOCUMENTS

Be aware that visa regulations can change. The Ethiopian embassy in your home country is the best source of up-to-date information.

Currently, all visitors except Kenyan and Djiboutian nationals need visas to visit Ethiopia.

Nationals of most Western countries can obtain tourist visas on arrival at Bole International Airport. Aside from some queuing, the process upon arrival is painless and the one-month tourist visa costs only US$20, substantially less than that charged at some Ethiopian embassies abroad. Some people arriving without US dollars have managed to pay the visa in euros. Immigration officials in Addis Ababa told us that they don't require onward air tickets, though some people have been asked for them.

Ethiopian embassies abroad may require some or all of the following to accompany visa applications: an onward air ticket (or airline itinerary), a visa for the next country you're planning to visit, a yellow fever vaccination certificate and proof of sufficient funds (officially a minimum of US$50 per day). Ethiopian embassies in Africa are usually less strict.

Presently, the only multiple-entry visas issued are business visas (except for US citizens who can get two-year multiple entry tourist visas for US$70). To acquire a one- to three-month business visa at an embassy, you'll need a letter from your employer in addition to the items mentioned earlier. One-month business visas (US$20) are available upon arrival at the airport, but only if your company has made arrangements (in person) with the Department of Immigration in Addis Ababa prior to your arrival.

If your citizenship isn't one that can acquire a visa at Bole and there's also no Ethiopian diplomatic representation in your country, you may be able to ask Ethiopian Airlines or a tour operator to order you a visa before your arrival. Visas cannot be obtained on arrival without prior arrangement at immigration.

Travellers of all nationalities can obtain transit visas on arrival or at the embassies abroad; these are valid for up to seven days.

The **Department of Immigration** (Map pp86-7; ☎ 0111 553899; ☯ 8.30am-12.30pm & 1.30-5.30pm Mon-Fri) issues single-/multiple-entry visa extensions for US$20/30. Multiple-entry extensions are for those on business or for travellers with exceptional circumstances (ie making a return air trip to Tanzania where there is no Ethiopian diplomatic representation). The process takes 24 hours. The office is off Zambia St.

Other Documents

In theory a yellow-fever vaccination certificate is mandatory, as is a vaccination against cholera if you've transited through a cholera-infected area within six days prior to your arrival in Ethiopia. These are rarely checked, but you probably wouldn't want to risk it.

Documentation needed to bring a vehicle into Ethiopia is covered on p267.

All important documents (passport data page and visa page, credit cards, travel insurance policy, air/bus/train tickets, driving licence etc) should be photocopied. Leave one copy with someone at home and keep another with you, separate from the originals.

Visas for Onward Travel

DJIBOUTI

Bring US$30 and one passport photo to the **Djibouti Embassy** (Map pp86-7; ☎ 0116 613200; ⏰ 9am-11am & 2.30-4.30pm Mon-Fri) early in the morning and you'll usually have your visa the same day. It's off Bole Rd.

KENYA

The **Kenyan embassy** (Map p84; ☎ 0116 610033; kenigad@ethionet.et; Fikremaryam Abatechan St; ⏰ 9am-1pm & 2-5pm Mon-Fri) charges US$20 or Birr249 for three-month tourist visas. One passport photo is required. Applications are taken in the morning only, with visas being ready the following afternoon. Visas are also easily obtained at the Moyale border (p262) and at Jomo Kenyatta International Airport in Nairobi.

SOMALILAND

The **Somaliland office** (Map pp86-7; ☎ 0116 635921; between Bole Rd & Cameroon St; ⏰ 8.30am-12.30pm & 2-3.30pm Mon-Fri) produces one-month tourist visas for US$40 or three-month visas for US$60. They require one passport photo and it's issued while you wait. Hanging on the office wall is a poster advertising the tourist attractions of Somaliland; the biggest picture is of blown-up buildings in Hargeisa.

SUDAN

Unless you're using the services of a registered Sudanese tour company, then obtaining a tourist visa at the **Sudan embassy** (Map pp86-7; ☎ 0115 516477; Ras Lulseged St; ⏰ 8.30am-12.30pm Mon, Wed & Fri for visa service only) is a mission impossible if ever there was one. Prepare for a lot of sweat, tears, headaches and then a big, fat 'No'. All applica-

> **FEMALE PHOBIA**
>
> In some of the monasteries and holy sites of Ethiopia and Eritrea, an ancient prohibition forbids women from setting foot in the holy confines. But the holy fathers go strictly by the book: the prohibition extends not just to women but to all female creatures, even she donkeys, hens and nanny goats.

tions are sent to Khartoum for approval, so the process of being told you can't have one can take over a month to complete. However, don't go changing those plans just yet as there is one way in. Transit visas, allowing up to a fortnight in Sudan, are issued fairly easily. For this you require a letter of introduction from your own embassy, an onward visa for Egypt, a couple of photos and, for most nationalities, US$100 cash. Americans, you get to pay US$200. It normally takes two days to issue.

WOMEN TRAVELLERS

Compared with many African countries, Ethiopia is pretty easy-going for women travellers. The risk of rape or other serious offences is likely lower than travelling in many Western countries. The best advice is to simply be aware of the signals your clothing or behaviour may be giving off and remember these unspoken codes of etiquette.

Drinking alcohol, smoking, and wearing excessive make-up and revealing clothes are indications to the male population of 'availability', as this is also the way local prostitutes behave. Apart from the young of the wealthier classes in Addis Ababa, no 'proper' woman would be seen in a bar.

Many cheap hotels in Ethiopia double as brothels. Ethiopian men may naturally wonder about your motives for staying here, particularly if you're alone. While there's no cause for alarm, it's best to keep a low profile and behave very conservatively – keep out of the hotel bar, for example, and try and hook up with other travellers if you want to go out.

Also be aware that accepting an invitation to an unmarried man's house, under any pretext, is considered a latent acceptance of things to come. Dinner invitations often amount to 'foreplay' before you're expected to head off to some seedy hotel. Even a seemingly innocent invitation to the cinema can turn out to be little more than an invitation to a good snog in the back row!

Be aware that 'respectable' Ethiopian women (even when they're willing) are expected to put up a show of coyness and modesty. Traditionally, this formed part of the wedding night ritual of every Amhara bride: a fierce struggle with the groom was expected of them. Consequently, some Ethiopian men may mistake your rebuttals for encouragement. The concept even has a name in Amharic: *maqderder* (and applies equally to feigned reluctance for other things such as food). If you mean no, make it very clear from the start.

If there aren't any other travellers around, here's a quick trick: pick a male Ethiopian companion, bemoan the problems you've been having with his compatriots and appeal to his sense of pride, patriotism and gallantry. Usually any ulterior plans he might have been harbouring himself are soon converted into sympathy or shame and a personal crusade to protect you!

Adultery is quite common among many of Ethiopia's urban population, for men as well as women. For this reason, a wedding ring on a woman traveller (bogus or not) has absolutely no deterrent value. In fact, quite the reverse!

The one advantage of Ethiopia being a relatively permissive society is that Western women (in particular, white women) aren't necessarily seen as easier than local women, something that's common in many developing countries due to Hollywood cinematic 'glamour'.

With all this talk of keeping Ethiopian men's potential advances at bay, it's odd that the biggest actual hindrance to women travellers is priests! See the boxed text, p257.

Ethiopia Transport

CONTENTS

GETTING THERE & AWAY

Flights, tours and rail tickets can be booked online at www.lonelyplanet.com/bookings.

ENTERING ETHIOPIA

Entering Ethiopia by air is painless, even if you have to pick up your visa upon arrival at Bole International Airport. Important visa and document information is found on p256.

Ethiopian border officials at land crossings are more strict but equally fair. You *must* have a valid visa to enter overland as none are available at borders. Those entering with vehicles should have all the necessary paperwork (p264) and expect a lengthier process.

For visa and other document information, see p256.

THINGS CHANGE...

The information in this chapter is particularly vulnerable to change. Check directly with the airline or a travel agent to make sure you understand how a fare (and ticket you may buy) works and be aware of the security requirements for international travel. Shop carefully. The details given in this chapter should be regarded as pointers and are not a substitute for your own careful, up-to-date research.

AIR
Airports & Airlines

Addis Ababa's **Bole International Airport** (Map p84) is the only international airport in Ethiopia. Although modern, upon arrival there's little more than a 24-hour bank, a restaurant and a few cafes; baggage carts are free. When departing, there's an internet lounge, a bar and duty-free shops.

Ethiopia's only international and national carrier, **Ethiopian Airlines** (airline code ET; www.flyethiopian.com), is rated as one of the best airlines in Africa and has a good safety record. Ethiopian Airlines is also one of the largest African carriers, with a modern fleet of 737s, 757s, 767s and ten 787 Dreamliners. There are 50 or so offices worldwide, which sell both international and domestic tickets directly. Alternatively the website is safe and reliable for online bookings. Ethiopian Airlines isn't usually the cheapest option with which to fly into Ethiopia, but it does offer some good perks: a generous baggage allowance, the option of changing your return date as many times as you wish at no extra charge, and if there are two or more of you, 50% off domestic flights (see p264).

If you want to fly with a European airline such as BMI, Luthansa or KLM, double-check that you will actually be on one of their planes and not on an Ethiopian Airlines plane. They route share with Ethiopian and commonly bundle their passengers onto Ethiopian Airlines and then kindly charge you more than you'd have paid if you'd bought directly with Ethiopian!

AIRLINES FLYING TO/FROM ETHIOPIA

BMI (Map pp86-7; airline code BD; ☎ 0116 620815; www.flybmi.com; TK International Building, Bole Rd, Addis Ababa)

EgyptAir (Map pp86-7; airline code MS; ☎ 0111 564493; www.egyptair.com; Churchill Ave, Addis Ababa)

Emirates (Map pp86-7; airline code EK; ☎ 0115 181818; www.emirates.com; Dembel City Centre, Addis Ababa)

KLM (Map pp86-7; airline code KL; ☎ 0115 525495; www.klm.com; Hilton Hotel, Menelik II Ave, Addis Ababa)

Kenya Airways (Map pp86-7; airline code KQ; ☎ 0115 525548; www.kenya-airways.com; Hilton Hotel, Menelik II Ave, Addis Ababa)

CLIMATE CHANGE & TRAVEL

Climate change is a serious threat to the ecosystems that humans rely upon, and air travel is the fastest-growing contributor to the problem. Lonely Planet regards travel, overall, as a global benefit, but believes we all have a responsibility to limit our personal impact on global warming.

Flying & Climate Change

Pretty much every form of motor travel generates CO_2 (the main cause of human-induced climate change) but planes are far and away the worst offenders, not just because of the sheer distances they allow us to travel, but because they release greenhouse gases high into the atmosphere. The statistics are frightening: two people taking a return flight between Europe and the US will contribute as much to climate change as an average household's gas and electricity consumption over a whole year.

Carbon Offset Schemes

Climatecare.org and other websites use 'carbon calculators' that allow jetsetters to offset the greenhouse gases they are responsible for with contributions to energy-saving projects and other climate-friendly initiatives in the developing world – including projects in India, Honduras, Kazakhstan and Uganda.

Lonely Planet, together with Rough Guides and other concerned partners in the travel industry, supports the carbon offset scheme run by climatecare.org. Lonely Planet offsets all of its staff and author travel.

For more information check out our website: lonelyplanet.com.

Lufthansa (Map pp86-7; airline code LH; ☎ 0111 551666; www.lufthansa.com; Cameroon St, Addis Ababa)
Saudi Arabian Airlines (Map pp86-7; airline code SV; ☎ 0115 512637; www.saudiairlines.com; Ras Desta Damtew St, Addis Ababa)
Sudan Airways (Map pp86-7; airline code SD; ☎ 0115 504724; www.sudanair.com; Ras Desta Damtew St, Addis Ababa)
Yemenia (Map pp86-7; airline code IY; ☎ 0115 526440; www.yemenia.com; Ras Desta Damtew St, Addis Ababa)

Tickets

For Ethiopia, flights during the month of August, over Easter, Christmas and New Year should be booked well in advance. Ethiopians living abroad tend to visit their families during this time, and tour groups often try to coincide with the major festivals. Ticket prices are highest during this period.

Numerous travel agencies and online ticket sources are mentioned in the following sections under the region or country they each are located in. One truly international website that can't be categorised is www.flights.com.

INTERCONTINENTAL (RTW) TICKETS

It's possible to include Addis Ababa as part of a round-the-world (RTW) ticket. Check with one of the major airlines that form the

Star Alliance (www.staralliance.com) or **One World** (www.oneworldalliance.com).

Africa

Ethiopian Airlines has one of the widest networks in Africa and flies to numerous African destinations, including all neighbouring nations except Eritrea. Fares on Ethiopian Airlines and other African couriers vary drastically throughout the year, depending on the high seasons of each individual country.

Rennies Travel (www.renniestravel.com) and **STA Travel** (www.statravel.co.za) have offices throughout Southern Africa. Check their websites for branch locations. In Nairobi, **Let's Go Travel** (☎ 020-444 7151; www.lets-go-travel.net) is reliable.

Australia

There are no direct flights from Australia to Ethiopia. **Qantas** (www.qantas.com) and its code-sharing partner **South African Airways** (www.flysaa.com) fly to Johannesburg, from where you can connect to Nairobi. You'll have to book the Nairobi–Addis Ababa flight separately. This is typically cheaper than buying separate Australia–Johannesburg and Johannesburg–Addis Ababa tickets.

Via the Middle East is usually slightly cheaper; try Emirates via Dubai to Addis. Other routes include via Mumbai on Qantas,

or via Mauritius on **Air Mauritius** (www.air
mauritius.com). Note, these last two only get you
to Nairobi.

STA Travel (☎ 1300 733 035; www.statravel.com.au)
and **Flight Centre** (☎ 133 133; www.flightcentre.com.au)
have numerous offices throughout Australia
and are worth checking out.

Canada
There are no direct flights between Canada
and Ethiopia. Currently BMI, KLM
and Lufthansa offer the easiest connections, through London, Amsterdam and
Frankfurt respectively.

Canadian discount air ticket agencies tend
to have fares around 10% higher than those
sold in the USA. **Flight Centre** (☎ 877-967 5302;
www.flightcentre.ca) is usually reliable and has
1500 Canadian outlets. **Travel Cuts** (☎ 800-667
2887; www.travelcuts.com) is Canada's national
student travel agency. For online bookings
try www.expedia.ca.

Continental Europe
Numerous weekly Ethiopian Airlines flights
serve Brussels, Stockholm, Paris, Frankfurt
and Rome. KLM and Lufthansa have daily
flights to Addis Ababa.

FRANCE
Recommended agencies are:
Anyway (☎ 08 92 30 23 01; www.anyway.fr)
Lastminute (☎ 04 66 92 30 29; www.lastminute.fr)
Nouvelles Frontières (☎ 01 49 20 65 87; www.nou
velles-frontieres.fr)

GERMANY
Recommended agencies are:
Expedia (www.expedia.de)
Lastminute (☎ 01805 284 366; www.lastminute.de)
STA Travel (☎ 069 743 032 92; www.statravel.de) For
travellers under the age of 26.

ITALY
One recommended agent is **CTS Viaggi** (☎ 06
441 1166; www.cts.it), specialising in student and
youth travel.

THE NETHERLANDS
One recommended agency is **Airfair** (☎ 0900
771 7717; www.airfair.nl).

SPAIN
A recommended agency is **Barcelo Viajes** (☎ 902
200 400; www.barceloviajes.com).

Middle East
EgyptAir, Emirates, Saudi Arabian Airlines
and Yemenia serve the Middle East and com-
bine to link Ethiopia with Lebanon, Israel,
Saudi Arabia (Jeddah and Riyadh), the United
Arab Emirates and Yemen.

In Dubai, **Al-Rais Travels** (www.alrais.com) is a
good travel agent, while the **Israel Student Travel
Association** (ISTA; ☎ 03-7777111) is helpful.

New Zealand
The story for New Zealand is much the same
as that for Australia, with code-sharing partners Qantas and SAA only getting you as far
as Nairobi. However, if you go through agents
(in person or online), they should be able to
combine airlines to get you straight to Addis
Ababa via Bangkok or Dubai.

Both **Flight Centre** (☎ 0800 243 544; www
.flightcentre.co.nz) and **STA Travel** (☎ 0870 160 0599;
www.statravel.co.nz) have branches throughout
the country.

UK & Ireland
BMI and Ethiopian Airlines both have daily
flights between London and Addis Ababa.

Discount air travel is big business in
London. Recommended travel agencies are:
Flight Centre (☎ 0870 499 0040; www.flightcentre.co
.uk)
Flightbookers (☎ 020 3320 3320; www.ebookers.com)
North-South Travel (☎ 01245 608 291; www.north
southtravel.co.uk) Donates part of its profit to projects in
the developing world.
STA Travel (☎ 0871 230 0040; www.statravel.co.uk)
Travel Bag (☎ 0871 703 4700; www.travelbag.co.uk)

USA
Ethiopian Airlines only serves Washington
DC, so you'll likely have to fly through
Europe on BMI, KLM or Lufthansa (or their
American code-sharing partners).

Discount travel agents in the USA are
known as consolidators. San Francisco is the
ticket consolidator capital of America, although some good deals can be found in Los
Angeles, New York and other big cities.

Peruse the following websites for the cheap-
est flight options:
CheapTickets (www.cheaptickets.com)
Expedia.com (www.expedia.com)
Orbitz (www.orbitz.com)
STA Travel (www.statravel.com)
travelocity (www.travelocity.com)

ETHIOPIA TRANSPORT

LAND

Travelling to Ethiopia by land is an adventure you'll never forget, no matter where you come from or how you do it.

Djibouti

Border formalities are usually pretty painless crossing between Djibouti and Ethiopia, but you *must* have your visa prior to arriving as none are issued at the border (see Visas for Onward Travel on p257).

ROAD

There are two current road routes linking Djibouti and Ethiopia: one via Dire Dawa and Gelille, and one via Awash and Galafi.

The Gelille route is best for those without vehicles as daily buses link Djibouti City and Dire Dawa. The journey takes 10 to 12 hours, though it involves changing buses at the border. In Djibouti City, **SPB** (Map p289; ☎ 812445) buses depart at dawn from Ave Gamel Abdel Nasser; tickets cost DFr2500 (make sure you purchase yours at least a day before your trip to ensure a seat).

In Dire Dawa, the tongue-twisting **Shirkada Gaadidka Dadweynaha Ee Yaryar Dhexe Iyo Xamuulkaa** (Map p216; ☎ 0253 878434) runs daily buses to Djibouti from its office northeast of the 'old town' of Megala. Buses depart around 3am and tickets cost Birr130. **Selam Buses** (Map p216; ☎ 0251 117938) operate a similar service from their office in the yellow shipping container next to the train station. Buses depart at 2am and tickets also cost Birr130. In both cases, tickets should be bought the day before.

Although longer, the Galafi route accessed from Awash is best for those driving as it's sealed the entire way. Even locals with 4WDs prefer this route over the Gelille route, which is only sealed on the Djibouti side. For those coming from northern Ethiopia, this route can be accessed via a shortcut at Dessie.

Those without vehicles can also travel via Galafi. A sporadic evening bus (DFr2000) from Djibouti City reaches Galafi (5km from the border) in the morning after overnighting in Yoboki. From Galafi, you must rely on hitching a lift with one of the many trucks heading into Ethiopia. The first town with regular buses to Awash or Dessie is Mille (p212). Those using this route to leave Ethiopia can hitch a lift with trucks over-nighting in Logiya (p213) right to Djibouti City (Birr150 to Birr200, eight hours).

TRAIN

A dilapidated, hot and painfully slow train also covers the Djibouti City–Dire Dawa route. From Dire Dawa the train is scheduled to leave on Tuesday, Thursday and Saturday mornings at 7am, arriving 308km later at 5pm – although delays are not just common, they're a given.

From Djibouti the train leaves Wednesdays, Fridays and Sundays.

First-class tickets cost Birr93 in Dire Dawa and DFr4200 in Djibouti City, and 2nd class costs Birr76/DFr2500. First class is by no means comfortable, but it's a world above 2nd class. Tickets should be bought the day before travel from the station.

In theory the train is supposed to run all the way to Addis Ababa, but this leg is currently out of commission.

Eritrea

There are three traditional entry points from Eritrea into Ethiopia: Asmara to Adwa and Aksum via Adi Quala; Asmara to Adigrat via Senafe; and Assab to Addis Ababa via Serdo and Dessie. However, all these border crossings have been indefinitely closed since the 1998 war.

With relations on their current path, it seems sadly unfeasible that the borders will be reopened during the lifetime of this book.

Currently, the only feasible way of crossing from Ethiopia to Eritrea is by plane travelling via a third country. Travelling via San'a in Yemen is the most obvious and cheapest way. A much more roundabout route is via Cairo in Egypt.

Kenya

There are usually few problems crossing between Ethiopia and Kenya. The only feasible crossing is at Moyale, 772km south of Addis Ababa by road. Moyale has two incarnations, one on either side of the border.

The northern, Ethiopian, version of Moyale is well connected to the north and Addis Ababa by bus, along a pretty good, but often potholed section of sealed road (transport details are found on p188). Though security is normally not a problem along the main north–south route and in and around Moyale there had, at the time of writing, been some serious tribal fighting in the area and tensions were running high.

The southern, Kenyan, side of Moyale is truly in the middle of nowhere, some 600km north of the nearest sealed road and around 800km north of Nairobi. That said, a daily bus connects Moyale with Marsabit (KSh600, 8½ hours) and Isiolo (KSh1500, 17 hours). Trucks servicing the same destinations pick up passengers near the main intersection. From Isiolo there's regular transport to Nairobi (KSh500, 4½ hours).

For those of you in your own vehicles, the road between Moyale and Marsabit is long and hard (on you and your 4WD – bring at least two spare tyres). Thankfully the banditry problems of the past seem to be largely under control, although outbreaks of tribal fighting and banditry do still occur. While this normally takes place well away from the main Marsabit–Moyale Rd, in early 2009 serious tribal fighting occurred almost to the gates of Moyale. Armed convoys are no longer used along this route. The Wajir route south is still not considered safe. Either way, be sure to check the security section before setting out from Moyale. Also make sure you fill up before leaving Ethiopia as the petrol is half the price.

The Ethiopian and Kenyan borders at Moyale are open daily. Kenyan three-month visas are painlessly produced at **Kenyan immigration** (6.30am-6pm) for the grand sum of US$50. It's payable in US dollars (some have managed to pay in euros), but not Ethiopian birr. Transit visas cost US$20 (valid for seven days). **Ethiopian immigration** (8am-noon & 2-6pm Mon-Fri, 9am-11am & 3-5pm Sat & Sun) cannot issue Ethiopian visas; these must be obtained at an Ethiopian embassy prior to arrival at the border.

If you're heading south and have a serious 4WD, there's a more adventurous crossing well west of Moyale near Omorate in the Lower Omo Valley. Although there's now an **Ethiopian immigration post** (7.30am-5pm) in Omorate that can stamp you out, there's still no Kenyan post to issue you a visa, so you must obtain one from the Kenyan embassy in Addis Ababa beforehand (see Visas for Onward Travel on p257). Once you reach Nairobi you'll have to get it stamped; immigration officials are used to this.

The remote and sandy track to Kenya is accessed along the road to Turmi, 13km north of Omorate. A long day of driving should get you to Sibiloi National Park and the Koobi Fora research base. From there, it's a tricky seven-hour drive south to Loyangalani. This route will reward you with one of East Africa's greatest sights, Lake Turkana, but it's only for the truly well prepared. It should never be attempted in wet season, and a guide is a must.

This route isn't technically possible heading north because Ethiopia requires a Kenyan exit stamp in your passport. If you don't mind being turned back, you could always try your luck – bring lots of fuel.

Somaliland

Ready for adventure? Daily buses run along the dusty desert track (though the current road works might be about to make dust and bumps a fond memory) between Jijiga and the border town of Wajaale (Birr20, 1½ to two hours; 6.30am). Get stamped out at Ethiopian immigration (look for the MAO building on the main street) before walking to the gate, where customs will perform their perfunctory search. From there, cross no-man's-land (about 200m) to Somaliland's immigration shack, where they'll stamp your passport and check your visa. The visa must have been acquired in advance as none are issued at the border (see Visas for Onward travel on p257 for details).

The Commercial Bank at Wajaale can change American Express travellers cheques, US dollars and euros.

Minibuses (Birr70) and taxis (US$50) run from the border to Hargeisa, Somaliland's capital, which is about 90km to the southeast.

Sudan

The main border-crossing point with Sudan is the Metema crossing, 180km west of Gonder. It's imperative that you've obtained your Sudan visa in Addis Ababa (not an easy task; see p257) before heading this way.

From Gonder one bus leaves daily for Metema (Birr31, six or seven hours). Buy the ticket early in the morning (around 7am) of the previous day as the route is popular. Several travellers have written about being harassed and robbed in Metema, so keep your guard up.

After reaching Metema the next morning, you can walk across the border into the Sudanese town of Gallabat. From Gallabat,

---

ENTERING ETHIOPIA OVERLAND

The overland route from South Africa through southern Africa and East Africa to Ethiopia is quite well trodden, and should present few problems, though the last section through northern Kenya is the toughest and still suffers from sporadic banditry. If you're heading on to Cairo and the end of Africa things start to get more complicated after Ethiopia – the main complication goes by the name of Sudan. Visas are notoriously hard to obtain (though Addis Ababa is one of the easier places in which to get one, see p257) and the road from Gonder to Sudan can best be described as an 'adventure', but then adventure is why you're doing this, right?

Border officials can be lax or stringent, but they're usually not unfair. If you're travelling with a vehicle, make sure you have a valid international driving license, a *carnet de passage* (a guarantee issued by your own national motoring association that you won't sell your vehicle in the country you are travelling), the vehicle's registration papers and proof of third-party insurance that covers Ethiopia (see the Car & Motorcycle section on p267 for details about driving licences, road rules, road conditions in Ethiopia etc).

For important visa and documentation information see p256.

---

you can catch a truck to the nearest large town of Gedaref (eight to 10 hours).

Be prepared for some mega-bumpy roads around the border. In wet season even trucks get stuck between Gallabat and Gedaref.

If you're coming from Sudan, stay overnight in Gedaref (better than Gallabat), then catch a dawn truck straight though to Shihedi via Gallabat. The bus from Shihedi to Gonder departs at around 7am.

After years of war and instability, the borders between Southern Sudan and southwestern Ethiopia are once again open, although it is a matter of speculation if this extends to non-Ethiopian/Sudanese travellers. In Gambela we were advised that it was possible to catch the daily bus to Jikawo (Birr22, five hours) and from there, a shared taxi to Adora (Sudan). Another option would be to hang around the river in Gambela in the hope of securing passage on one of the small boats that occasionally travel to Akobe via the Baro River. While both these routes may be possible in theory, very few travellers have actually done it and, as this portion of the Sudanese border still experiences intermittent violence, we do not recommend it.

GETTING AROUND

AIR
Airlines in Ethiopia
The national carrier, **Ethiopian Airlines** (www .flyethiopian.com), uses Fokker 50s and DHC Twin Otters to provide the only regular domestic air service. As mentioned earlier in this chapter, they have a solid safety record.

It's well worth considering a domestic fligh or two, even if you're travelling on a budget While prices cannot be described as cheap (Addis to Bahir Dar is around US$140 one way) it does eliminate long, bumpy bus rides With the lower-altitude flying of the domestic planes and the usually clear Ethiopian skies you'll still see some stunning landscapes, too If you want a window seat, check in early.

Standard security procedures apply at al airports, though there'll be more polite grop ing than screening at the remote ones. The baggage limit is 20kg on domestic flights Don't bring bulky hand luggage as the inte riors are quite small.

Most flights leave from Addis Ababa, but they are rarely nonstop, which means you can also jump from one town to another For instance, the daily Addis Ababa–Aksum flight stops at Bahir Dar, Gonder and Lalibela en route.

If there's two or more of you, and if you fly into Ethiopia from outside Africa on Ethiopian Airlines, Ethiopian Airlines offers you 50% of the standard domestic rates. These flights must be booked at the same time as your international ones, but you can change the exact date later without penalty. Domestic flights can be booked online from abroad. For domestic schedules and the standard fares, see the pertinent city's Getting There & Away section.

If buying tickets in Ethiopia, standard rates always apply, whether buying the ticket a month or three hours in advance. However booking early to ensure a seat is particularly important on the historical circuit and during major festivals.

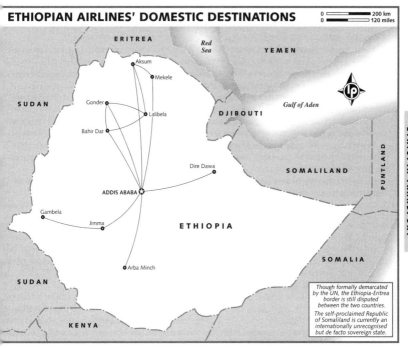

ETHIOPIAN AIRLINES' DOMESTIC DESTINATIONS

Though formally demarcated by the UN, the Ethiopia-Eritrea border is still disputed between the two countries.

The self-proclaimed Republic of Somaliland is currently an internationally unrecognised but de facto sovereign state.

It's *essential* to reconfirm all flights. Officially, this should be done 72 hours in advance. In practice, you can normally get away with 48 hours in advance, but never leave it less than 24 hours. If you're visiting the historical route and are not spending more than 72 hours in any one place, you don't need to reconfirm each leg.

Beware that schedules are occasionally forced to change due to weather or mechanical difficulties, so try not to plan an itinerary that's so tight that it doesn't make allowances for these changes.

BICYCLE

Bicycling in Ethiopia offers a smooth way to navigate sprawling towns, and a painfully rewarding way to explore the country. If you're only interested in the first option, you'll find reasonable bikes for hire in most large Ethiopian towns (Birr5 to Birr10 per hour). If want to cycle across the country, come well prepared with a sturdy bike, plenty of spare parts, a good repair kit and the capacity to carry sufficient amounts of water. Cycles new and second-hand can be bought in Addis

Ababa, but they are not generally the type of bike you'd wish to conquer the historical circuit with!

In the past, irregular terrain and brutal roads have scared off most adventure addicts and their bicycles, but with today's greatly improving road network it may just be the right time for you to give it a try. For general road conditions, see p268.

Cyclists should show the usual caution when travelling around the country: never travel after dark, be wary of thieves and keep the bicycle well maintained. Brakes need to be in good working order for the mountainous highland roads.

Be particularly wary of dogs (and the risk of rabies); sometimes it's best to dismount and walk slowly away. Cycling in the rainy season can be very hard going.

Punctures are easily repaired: just head for any *gommista* (tyre repairer) or garage. Many mechanics are also more than happy to help with cycle problems, and often turn out to be ingenious improvisers.

Note the customs regulation regarding the importation of a bicycle. A deposit must

---

THE JOYS OF BUS TRAVEL

Riding the buses around Ethiopia can provide some real highs and some real lows.

There are astounding cliff-top views. There are butt-clenching moments when you think you and your bus are about to be quickly introduced to that cliff's bottom.

There's the joy and honour of holding an Ethiopian's baby in your arms. There's the pleasure of cleaning that baby's bodily fluids off your only pair of trousers.

There's the common decency of everyone keeping their windows closed on a cold morning. There's the moment when it reaches 40°C inside and you realise that wasn't common decency, but rather an innate fear of deadly moving air that keeps those windows shut. You decide to open the window before you pass out with heatstroke and the entire bus erupts into shouts of horror.

There's the smell of fresh oranges permeating through the bus after a quick stop at streetside sellers. There's the moment when you plug your nose and officially bestow upon the bus the title of Vomit Comet.

To enjoy your memorable bus jaunts, bring a sense of humour, a lot of patience and a little understanding. Oh, and if you're fond of kids, don't forget some wet wipes!

---

usually be left (amounting to the cycle's worth) at customs at the port of entry on arrival. When you leave, this will be returned. This is to deter black-market trading.

Cycles are accepted aboard Ethiopian Airlines international flights. On domestic flights you'll need to check first in advance as it depends on what type of plane is covering the route on that given day.

Finally, a few tips from a seasoned African cyclist: check and tighten screws and nuts regularly, take a spare chain, take a front as well as rear pannier rack, and pack a water filter in case you get stuck somewhere remote.

BUS

A good network of long-distance buses connects most major towns of Ethiopia. One government bus association and around a dozen private ones operate in Ethiopia, though you'll rarely be able to tell the difference between any of them. The biggest differentiating trait between government and private buses is the pre-departure rituals.

Government buses sell seat-specific tickets in advance and passengers must wait in line while the bus is loaded. After that's completed, the queue is paraded around the bus before tickets are checked and the boarding barrage occurs. Private buses simply open the doors and start selling tickets to the flood of passengers as they cram in. Needless to say, private buses are usually the first to leave. They also tend to be slightly more comfortable than government ones. Recently a new breed of bus has taken to the roads of Ethiopia and these ones actually are pretty plush (air-con,

reclining seats, on-board toilets, TVs an even free snacks). The biggest company Selam Buses, but there are a number of oth ers, some of which have even better buse These bus services are mentioned under th relevant towns.

In most cases when you arrive at the bu station there'll only be one bus heading i your direction, so any thoughts about it bein private or government are a waste of time get on and get going!

Once on the road, you'll realise that a buses are slow. On sealed roads you can expec to cover around 50km/h, but on dirt road 30km/h or less. In the rainy season, journey can be severely disrupted. Thankfully, ne roads are spreading rapidly across the lan and turning many troublesome dirt section into slick sections of sealed road. The on drawback so far has been the increase in roa accidents due to speed (though the rate is sti low by African standards).

Unlike most African countries, standin in the aisles of long-distance buses is illeg in Ethiopia, making them more comfortabl (note that we've said more comfortable, whic is a far cry from saying comfortable!) an safer. On the longer journeys, there are usuall scheduled 20-minute stops for meals.

The major drawback with bus travel is th size of the country. For the historical circu alone, you'll spend a total of at least 10 day sitting on a bus to cover the 2500km.

Although most long-distance buses ar scheduled to 'leave' at 6am or earlier, the don't typically set out before 7am as most ar demand-driven and won't leave until full. T e safe you should make an appearance at the prescribed departure time. Remember that the Ethiopian clock is used locally (see p255), though Western time is used when quoting bus times in this book.

In remote areas long waits for buses to fill is normal – some may not leave at all. In general, the earlier you get to the bus station, the better chance you have of catching the first bus out of town.

On those journeys quoted in this book with durations longer than one day, there are overnight stops en route (Ethiopian law stipulates that all long-distances buses must be off the road by 6pm). In many cases you won't be allowed to remove luggage from the roof, so you should pack toiletries and other overnight items to take with you in a small bag on the bus.

Smaller and more remote towns are usually served by minibuses or Isuzu trucks (see p270).

Costs
Buses are very cheap in Ethiopia. Both government-run and private buses work out at around US$1.50 per 100km.

Reservations
Tickets for most long-distance journeys (over 250km) can usually be bought in advance. If you can, do: it guarantees a seat (though not a specific seat number on private buses) and cuts out the touts who sometimes snap up the remaining tickets to resell for double the price to latecomers. Most government ticket offices are open daily from 5.30am to 5.30pm. For short distances (less than 250km), tickets can usually only be bought on the day.

If you would like a whiff of fresh air on your journey, get a seat behind the driver as he tends to buck the trend and keep his window cracked open. Though on the flip side, if there's an accident these are often the worst seats to be in!

CAR & MOTORCYCLE
Bring Your Own Vehicle
If you're bringing your own 4WD or motorcycle, you'll need a *carnet de passage* (a guarantee issued by your own national motoring association that you won't sell your vehicle in the country you are travelling), the vehicle's registration papers and proof of third-party insurance that covers Ethiopia.

Driving Licence
Although Ethiopian law recognises international driving licences, it fails to do so for longer than seven days. Officially, once you reach Addis Ababa you're supposed to acquire an Ethiopian-endorsed licence.

This is rarely enforced and most overlanders we met hadn't bothered with this convoluted process and had yet to encounter any problems – roll the dice if you so please.

Fuel & Spare Parts
Fuel (both petrol and diesel) is quite widely available, apart from the more remote regions such as the southwest. Unleaded petrol is not available. Diesel costs from around Birr7.50 per litre, while petrol (called Benzene in Ethiopia) costs around Birr8.95 per litre. Note that your vehicle's fuel consumption will be 25% higher in Ethiopia than at sea level because of the increased altitudes.

While there are helpful garages throughout the country (ask your hotel to recommend one), spare parts are not abundant outside Addis Ababa. It's wise to take stock while in Addis and acquire all that you may need for the journey ahead, whether it be Sudan or Kenya. Thanks to Toyota Land Cruisers being the choice of most tour operators, their parts are more plentiful and less expensive than those for Landrovers.

Hire
Even with the recent road improvements, you still really need a 4WD to explore the country. Despite competition between the numerous tour agents in Addis Ababa (see p270) that hire 4WDs, prices are steep and range from US$120 per day for older vehicles to US$180 for luxurious newer models. Most companies include unlimited kilometres, a driver, driver allowance (for their food and accommodation), fuel, third-party insurance, a collision damage waiver and government taxes in their rates; check all these details, and ask if service charges will be added afterwards and if there are set driver's hours.

Know that prices are always negotiable and vary greatly depending on the period of rental and the season. Despite the hassle, you'll always pay much less organising things yourself in Ethiopia rather than hiring an agency at home to arrange it.

ETHIOPIA TRANSPORT

ETHIOPIA TRANSPORT

TRAVELLERS' LORE

Once there was a dog, a goat and a donkey. They wanted to go on a journey together, and
decided to take a taxi. The donkey paid and got out, the dog paid, got out but never got his
change, and the goat got out but never paid.

To this day, and whenever a vehicle passes, the dog still chases his change, the goat still
scatters at the first approach, and the donkey just plods tranquilly on.

Ethiopian folk tale

Though expensive, the chief advantage of
4WD hire over bus travel is the time that can
be saved. Trip durations are at least halved
and there's no waiting around in remote regions for infrequent and erratic buses. Note
also that some national parks can only be
entered with a 4WD.

The mandatory drivers (currently no agency
offers self-drive 4WD) can be very useful as
guides-cum-interpreters-cum-mechanics.
Although tips are expected afterwards (see
the boxed text, p252), a nice gesture during
the trip is to share food together (which costs
very little).

Some Addis Ababa-based agencies have
branch offices in towns on the historical route
and can rent 4WDs, but only by prearrange-
ment. Increasingly, private individuals rent
to tourists. Be aware of the risks, particularly
regarding insurance and the condition of
the car.

Self-drive cars are only hired for use in
and around Addis. If you're still interested
in hiring one to toot around the capital, you
must have a valid international driver's licence and be between 25 and 70 years old.
Vehicles cost between US$35 and US$50
per day with 50km to 70km free kilometres.
They usually require a deposit of Birr1000
to Birr2000.

Motorcycles are not currently rented.

Insurance

Third-party vehicle insurance is required by
law. Thankfully, unlike some other African
countries, which demand that vehicles are
covered by an insurance company based in
that country, Ethiopia only requires your insurance from elsewhere is valid in Ethiopia.
Although not mandatory, we'd also recommend comprehensive coverage.

If you don't have either, the numerous
offices of **Ethiopian Insurance Corporation** (www
.eic.com.et) sell third-party/comprehensive
insurance.

Road Conditions

Ethiopian roads continue to improve bu
even so, the vast majority remain unpave
We hope you like dust and potholes!

From Moyale on the Kenyan borde
north to Awasa and from Arba Minch t
Shashemene, the roads are sealed but rathe
potholed, while the stretch from Awasa t
Addis Ababa is much better. The unsurface
roads connecting Jinka and the Lower Om
Valley to Arba Minch and Yabelo rang
from bad to tolerable. During the wet sea
son Omo can be almost impossible to reac
The same can be said for the roads headin
east from Shashemene to Bale Mountair
National Park.

Sealed roads head west from Addis Abab
reaching Nekemte and Jimma. The lowlan
roads can be diabolical in the rains.

Decent sealed roads all but link Addi
Ababa to Gonder. New sealed sections hav
also all but linked Woldia, Mekele and Adigra
on the historical circuit. The sealed sectio
connecting Woldia to Addis Ababa is cur
rently being upgraded. The rest of the north
ern historical circuit ranges from finely grade
gravels to course corrugations.

Harar and Dire Dawa, both 525km east o
Addis Ababa, are connected to the capital wit
good sealed roads.

Road Hazards

On the outskirts of the towns or villages, loo
out for people, particularly children playin
on the road or kerbside. Night driving is nc
recommended. *Shiftas* (bandits) still operat
in the more remote areas. Additionally, som
trucks park overnight in the middle of th
road – without lights.

In the country, livestock is the main hazar
camels wandering onto the road can caus
major accidents in the lowlands. Many ani
mals, including donkeys, are unaccustome
to vehicles and are very car-shy, so alway
approach slowly and with caution.

Land mines still pose a threat throughout the country; drivers should always stay on sealed roads or existing dirt tracks. During the rainy season, some roads, particularly in the west and southwest, become impassable. Check road conditions with the local authorities before setting out.

Road Rules
Driving is on the right-hand side of the road. The speed limit for cars and motorcycles is 60km/h in the towns and villages and 100km/h outside the towns. The standard of driving is generally not high; devices such as mirrors or indicators are more decorative than functional. On highland roads, drive defensively and beware of trucks coming fast the other way. Also keep a sharp eye out for a row of stones or pebbles across the road: it marks roadworks or an accident. Most vehicles don't have seatbelts.

HITCHING
In the past, if someone asked for a ride in Ethiopia, it was usually assumed that it was because they couldn't afford a bus fare and little sympathy was spared for them. Many Ethiopians also suspected hitchers of hidden motives such as robbery.

However, for some towns not readily served by buses or light vehicles, hitching is now quite normal, and you will be expected to pay a 'fare'. Negotiate this in advance. The best place to look for lifts is at the hotels, bars and cafes in the centre of town.

Be aware that the density of vehicles on many roads is still very low in Ethiopia; on the remote roads, you'll be lucky to see any. nongovernmental organisation (NGO) vehicles sometimes oblige, but you'll be expected to contribute towards fuel.

HITCHING

Hitching is never entirely safe, and it's not recommended. Travellers who decide to hitch should understand that they are taking a small but potentially serious risk. Hitching is safer in pairs. Additionally, try and let someone know where you're planning to go. Women should never hitch alone.

LOCAL TRANSPORT
In many of the larger towns, a minibus service provides a quick, convenient and cheap way of hopping about town (from around Birr0.75 for short journeys). 'Conductors' generally shout out the destination of the bus; if in doubt, ask.

Taxis operate in many of the larger towns, including Addis Ababa. Prices are reasonable, but foreigners as well as well-heeled Ethiopians are always charged more for 'contract services' (see the boxed text, below). Ask your hotel for a fare estimate.

Garis (horse-drawn carts) are a popular local means of getting about town. They're cheap (usually no more than Birr1 to Birr2) and are useful to travellers in two ways particularly: as cheap transport to hotels from bus stations and for city tours. Be aware that in many towns now they are banned from operating on the principal roads and must stick to the back ones. Most drivers speak little or no English; you may have to enlist a local to act as interpreter.

Bajas (motorised rickshaws) are common in many towns and a seat in a shared *baja* across town shouldn't cost more than Birr1. Hiring the vehicle for you alone will cost about Birr5 for the same trip.

ETHIOPIA TRANSPORT

TAXI TERMINOLOGY

In the towns, villages and countryside of Ethiopia and Eritrea, taxis offer two kinds of service: 'contract taxis' and 'share-taxis'. Share-taxis ply fixed routes, stop and pick people up when hailed and generally operate like little buses. They become 'contract taxis' when they are flagged down (or 'contracted') by an individual or a group for a private journey. The fare is then split between all the passengers in the taxi.

Though not really 'taxis' at all, minibuses, trucks, 4WDs and various other kinds of cars can all be contracted in the same way as contract taxis. Contracting a large minibus for yourself is seen as perfectly normal if you should want to. Before hiring a contract taxi, always negotiate the fare before you get in, or you may be asked to pay far above the going rate at the end of the journey.

THE EMPEROR'S NEW SHOES

Building a railway across the Horn of Africa was never going to be easy. So when two European engineers arrived in Addis Ababa in 1894 to propose such a scheme to Emperor Menelik II, they would have been prepared for the challenges of hacking a rail line through the mountains, but they probably never expected that their first challenge would involve shoes. Menelik was intrigued by the idea of a railway line, but he wanted proof that these two men knew their stuff. In order to test them, Menelik placed the men in a room under armed guard, gave them a length of twine and a sheet of leather, and ordered them to make him some shoes by dawn. Unstitching their own shoes, the engineers used these as patterns and by first light the Emperor had a fine pair of new shoes – and some years later a railway line!

Minibuses & Isuzu Trucks

Minibuses are now commonly used between towns connected by sealed roads or to cover short distances. They cost slightly more than buses, but they leave more often and cover the distances more quickly. You'll usually find them at bus stations.

In more remote regions where the roads aren't conducive to buses, like the Lower Omo Valley, Isuzu flatbed trucks carrying goods between villages are often the best way to get around. A seat in the cabin usually costs twice as much as riding in the back. Prices are always negotiable. Petrol stations or market areas are commonly the collection points.

TOURS

For the independent traveller, incorporating an organised tour into your travels in Ethiopia is useful for four things: specialised activities such as white-water rafting, access to remote regions with limited public transport such as the Lower Omo Valley or the Danakil Depression, 'themed trips' (such as birdwatching) with expert guides, and to help those with limited time who are keen to see as much as possible.

If you're interested in taking a tour, contact the agencies in advance and compare itineraries and prices.

To reduce the cost of tours (few are cheap), hook up with a group of other travellers, or contact the agency far in advance to see if there are pre-arranged tours that you can tag onto. You'll need to be flexible with your dates. The forum on the Lonely Planet website www.lonelyplanet.com is an ideal place to hook up with other travellers.

NTO, the government-owned travel agency, once had a monopoly. Today service leaves something to be desired compared with the numerous private operators base in Addis Ababa.

Agencies offer all or some of the following: guides, 4WD hire, camping-equipment hire, historical route tours, birdwatching an wildlife viewing, white-water rafting, fishing Omo Valley tours, photo safaris, Simien an Bale Mountain trekking, Rift Valley lake trip and Danakil and Afar excursions. Some hav branches in towns outside Addis Ababa, fror where (if prebooked) you can hire a 4WD o guide or take a tour.

Though prices are officially fixed, most ar very open to negotiation, particularly durin the low season. Many agencies now accep credit cards.

All 4WD hire prices listed here includ mandatory driver, driver allowance and in surance. Most charge extra for guides an camping equipment, and some tack on extr fees for mileage and fuel. It's always wort negotiating, especially in the off season.

The following list is far from exhaustiv but it includes those recommended by trave lers and Ethiopians in the tourism industry

Abeba Tours Ethiopia (Map pp86-7; ☎ 0115 159530; www.abebatoursethiopia.com; Ras Hotel, Gambia St) Friendly and very professional, this operator seems to go th extra mile for their customers. They specialise in the Danak but can arrange tours throughout the country. Jeep hire is US$135 per day, including fuel, drivers allowance and all taxes. The drivers they use are about the best in the busines

Four Seasons Travel & Tours (Map pp86-7; ☎ 0116 613121; fsta@ethionet.et; Bole Rd) A reasonable outfit charging US$105 per day for a 4WD. Prices include mileage, but fuel is extra.

Galaxy Express Services (Map pp86-7; ☎ 0115 510355; www.galaxyexpressethiopia.com; Gambia St) This long-established agency offers various Ethiopia tour packages. Travel is in new Land Cruisers, which cost at least US$170 per day, including unlimited mileage, driver and insurance. On-the-road service is good, but the office staff could learn to be more polite! It's also an Avis agent and rents self-drive cars for use in and around Addis Ababa.

Green Land Tours & Travels (Map pp86-7; ☎ 0116 299252; www.greenlandethiopia.com; Cameroon St) Green Land is one of the biggest agencies, with various hotels and camps set up throughout Ethiopia. Prices for 4WD, guide, fuel and mileage start at US$120 per day excluding fuel.

Red Jackal Tour Operator (Map p91; ☎ 0111 559915; www.redjackal.net; Itegue Taitu Hotel, Piazza) Prices for tours to Ethiopia's south and north range from US$125 to US$145 per vehicle per day. These include fuel and mileage.

Travel Ethiopia (www.travelethiopia.com) Ghion Hotel (Map pp86-7; ☎ 0115 525479); National Hotel (Map pp86-7; ☎ 0115 525478; Menelik II Ave) A self-professed 'ecominded' tour company with multilingual guides (English, French, Italian and German) and quality 4WD vehicles for US$190 per day. The Ghion Hotel is off Ras Desta Damtew St.

T-Tam Travel & Tour (Map pp86-7; ☎ 0115 514055; www.ttamtour.com; Bole Rd) This established agency charges US$138 per day for 4WDs, but fuel is not included. It's also an IATA ticketing agent.

Village Ethiopia (Map pp86-7; ☎ 0115 523497; www .village-ethiopia.net; National Hotel, Menelik II Ave) This agency offers everything from birdwatching and ethnic tours in the south, to rock climbing in Tigray. It also specialises in the Danakil Depression and has a lodge near its toasty confines. Rental of a 4WD will set you back from US$150 per day, including fuel, drivers allowance etc.

TRAIN

The Addis Ababa–Dire Dawa train is indefinitely out of action, though the Dire Dawa–Djibouti City section is still chugging along (see p262).

ETHIOPIA TRANSPORT

Somaliland

Somaliland

Yes, you can! For seasoned (and well-prepared) travellers in search of a totally unusual trav experience, Somaliland, one of the most bizarre political entities in the world, is a goldmin Las Geel shelters some of the best preserved rock paintings in the world; the port town Berbera boasts too-perfect-to-be-real beaches on its doorstep; Hargeisa, the capital, has fascinating camel market; there's a profusion of volunteer opportunities for those who wa to get involved; and there's also the chance to – wait for it – go diving. Travel logistics a easy to handle – access from Djibouti and Ethiopia is a doddle.

Opening the door to a country that doesn't officially exist adds to the thrill. The sel proclaimed Republic of Somaliland was formed in 1991 after the collapse of unitary Somali While the rest of Somalia has been a no-go zone for travellers for two decades, Somaliland h restored law and order within its boundaries. It has a representative government, a capital, flag, a currency, an army, free press and an administration, but it hasn't gained internation recognition yet and remains in limbo, despite the diplomatic efforts of its leaders.

If you're worried about security issues, rest easy: the safety of Westerners is taken ve seriously and foreigners are welcome, provided they behave sensibly. That said, Somalilar is *not* a regular holiday destination. It's economically crippled, tourism infrastructure is lim ited and it desperately lacks foreign investment to rebuild the economy. And despite wh officials claim, there's still an element of uncertainty regarding the security situation. G an update before setting off. One thing is sure: you'll feel like you're on another planet. L the adventure begin!

SOMALILAND

HIGHLIGHTS

- Nurse a soft drink, feast on fresh fish and relax on porcelain-sand beaches in **Berbera** (p280)

- Impress your friends back home: 'What did you do in Somaliland?' 'I dived the **Bay of Berbera**!' (p280)

- Dream of purchasing your own ship of the desert at **Hargeisa's camel and goat market** (p276)

- Visit one of the world's finest open-air galleries of prehistoric rock art at **Las Geel** (p278)

- Immerse yourself in the laid-back, provin-cial towns of **Sheekh** (p281) or **Burcao** (p281)

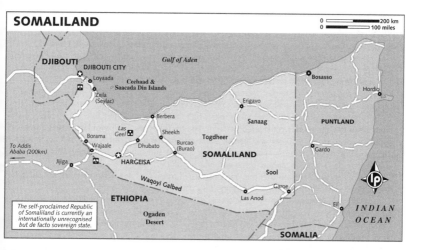

SOMALILAND

HARGEISA

Pop 1.2 million

You'll never forget your first impression of Hargeisa. We're not talking about roadblocks and militiamen wielding machine guns (you're not in Mogadishu); instead we're referring to a hassle-free, intriguing and energising city. The streets are alive, the roads are busy and the air thick with a very bearable cacophony of mobile phones, vehicle horns and calls to prayer. Sure, the capital of Somaliland still bears the scars of the civil war that destroyed the country in the past decades, but it's a city in transition. It's so astonishing to see that Hargeisa has all the conveniences a traveller could hope for: good-value hotels with English-speaking staff, a couple of tasty restaurants, internet cafes, electronics stores, tea shops, markets, bus stations, taxis…but no alcohol (it would be too good to be true!). It's a free-market economy, and it shows.

Hargeisa lacks standout sights but if you like your markets colourful, clamorous and spilling into the surrounding streets, appreciate raw magnetism and enjoy the feeling of being the only tourist wandering its streets, Hargeisa might just get under your skin.

ORIENTATION

No city map is available, barring the one in this book, but you can't really get lost in Hargeisa. Most places of interest to travellers, including shops, businesses and hotels, are on or around the main thoroughfare, Independence Rd. Most streets don't have names; use the MiG jet, the Oriental Hotel and mosques as landmarks. The airport is about 5km from the centre.

INFORMATION

INTERNET ACCESS

There's a profusion of internet cafes in the centre (access is around US$1 per hour).

MEDICAL SERVICES

For medical treatment, **Edna Adan Hospital** (☎ 4426922; www.ednahospital.org) offers excellent facilities. It's staffed by qualified, English-speaking doctors (mostly volunteers).

MONEY

Most transactions can be conducted using US dollars, but if you want to change money, head to one of the **Dahabshiil** (www.dahabshiil .com; Independence Rd; ⏰ 7am-noon & 1-5.30pm Sat-Thu) branches. You can also find **moneychangers** near the Oriental Hotel. Most hotels also change money and don't take commission. Somaliland is a strictly cash economy – forget about travellers cheques, credit cards and ATMs. Money transfers from a number of countries (see p282) are possible.

POST & TELEPHONE

There's no post office in Hargeisa. You'll have to use courier services, such as DHL (hotel staff can assist with this).

Making phone calls is easy and cheap. You can also bring your mobile phone and buy a

READ THIS FIRST

Somaliland was safe at the time of writing, and our on-the-ground research included Hargeisa, Las Geel, Berbera, Sheekh and Burcao. That said, foreigners must be accompanied by an armed soldier outside Hargeisa. If you don't have a soldier with you, you'll be turned back at checkpoints.

Since the murder of three aid workers by Somali terrorists from Mogadishu in 2003, local authorities have taken the safety of Westerners very seriously, to the point of being overprotective, and no wonder. If other foreigners were to encounter a 'problem', the diplomatic efforts of the country to gain international recognition would be ruined. This restrictive rule will be lifted, it is said, when the situation is considered perfectly safe for foreigners. The problem is that another group of terrorists from Mogadishu illegally entered Somaliland in October 2008 and committed suicide bombings in Hargeisa in an attempt to destabilise the country. The targets included the presidency, the Ethiopian Liaison Office and one UN office.

There are so few travellers that can't really be targets for this kind of terrorist, but should the number of foreigners grow significantly, they could well be.

Your first impressions are likely to be a kind of euphoria ('oh, I feel safe here, and it's great to have the country to myself'), but beware this false sense of security; keep in mind that Somaliland is still not a conventional country, and that its borders are not terrorist-proof. The Somalilanders have established law and order in their separatist territory, but as long as their unruly brothers from Puntland and Southern Somalia don't settle for peace, there will be an element of risk.

It's our duty to tell you.

Keep your ears to the ground and seek local advice before setting off.

Organising a police escort

All hotels can arrange a police escort. It costs about US$15 to US$20 per day for a soldier (one is enough), plus food (but he'll provide his daily dose of *chat*!). Having a soldier can even be fun! By 2pm, your guardian angel will have started chewing *chat*, and will be completely stoned until 7pm at least. Soldiers can also act as interpreters and de facto guides.

There is a way to escape this rule. The people at the Oriental Hotel (ask for Said or Abdi Abdi, and leave them a tip for the service) will tell you how to get a special permit that allows you to travel to Berbera without the mandatory escort; they have good relations with a chief police officer, who will issue a kind of 'laissez pass' with your name on it. This should be enough to let you through, but it's a good idea to buy a few bunches of *chat* to facilitate things at the various checkpoints between Hargeisa and Berbera.

local SIM card from **Telesom** (Independence Rd) or any other mobile phone company.

TOURIST INFORMATION

Hotel owners (especially at the Ambassador and the Oriental Hotel, among others) are the best sources for travel information and can also help with visa matters, escort and car rentals. You can also contact the Director of Tourism at the **Ministry of Tourism** (☎ 4424561; shabeelle7@yahoo.com; ☻ 8am-1pm Sat-Thu).

DANGERS & ANNOYANCES

Relax. Law and order reign in Hargeisa. You can explore the city on your own; an escort is not mandatory in the capital. That said, the usual precautions apply. Avoid walking alone at night, don't be ostentatious with valuables, and beware of pickpockets in crowded areas.

Always ask permission before taking photographs, especially when you're in a market.

SIGHTS

Let's be frank: it's the ambience and the sense of exploration that are the pull here. Visually Hargeisa is fairly underwhelming, with nothing much of interest except perhaps the city war memorial – a Somali Air Force **MiG jet** and the imposing **Jama Mosque**.

An essential part of the Hargeisa experience is the **camel and goat market**, which lies on the outskirts of town. It's a fascinating place to wander. Always ask permission before taking photographs.

The **gold market**, a short stagger from the Oriental Hotel, is another wonderful place. There's a cluster of **goldsmiths** on the main street, too.

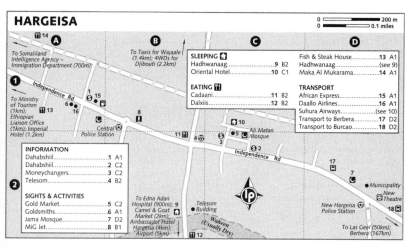

HARGEISA

0 — 200 m
0 — 0.1 miles

SLEEPING
Hadhwanaag..........................9 B2
Oriental Hotel.....................10 C1

EATING
Cadaani...............................11 B2
Dalxiis................................12 B2

Fish & Steak House.............13 A1
Hadhwanaag......................(see 9)
Maka Al Mukarama..............14 A1

TRANSPORT
African Express....................15 A1
Daallo Airlines.....................16 A1
Suhura Airways...................(see 10)
Transport to Berbera............17 D2
Transport to Burcao.............18 D2

To Somaliland
Intelligence Agency –
Immigration Department (700m)

To Taxis for Wajaale
(1.4km); 4WDs for
Djibouti (2.2km)

Independence Rd

To Ministry
of Tourism
(1km); Imperial
Hotel (1.2km)

Ethiopian
Liaison Office
(1km); Imperial
Hotel (1.2km)

Central
Police Station

Ali Matan
Mosque

Independence Rd

INFORMATION
Dahabshiil.............................1 A1
Dahabshiil.............................2 C2
Moneychangers.....................3 C2
Telesom................................4 B2

SIGHTS & ACTIVITIES
Gold Market..........................5 C2
Goldsmiths............................6 A1
Jama Mosque........................7 D2
MiG Jet.................................8 B1

To Edna Adan
Hospital (900m); 9
Camel & Goat
Market (2km);
Ambassador Hotel
Hargeisa (4km);
Airport (5km)

Telesom
Building

Waheen
(Usually Dry)

New Hargeisa
Police Station

Municipality
New
Theatre

To Las Geel (50km);
Berbera (167km)

SLEEPING

Hargeisa has a surprisingly high number of good-value options to suit all budgets. The following options come recommended as they're used to dealing with foreigners. As there are no street signs, most hotels do not have street addresses. Prices include breakfast.

Hadhwanaag (☎ 521820, 300851; hhbulbul@hotmail .com; s US$8-10, d US$12-15) As far as Hargeisa prices go, the Hadhwanaag is good value. The low-slung building occupies a leafy compound and is a five-minute walk away from the main drag. The staff's attention to detail could be sharper (you'll have to ask for a fan), but the rooms are well kept and worth every shilling.

FAST FACTS: SOMALILAND

- **Area** 637,657 sq km
- **ATMs** none
- **Borders** Ethiopia and Djibouti (both are open to travellers)
- **Capital** Hargeisa
- **Languages** Somali
- **Money** Somaliland shilling US$1 = SlSh 6500 approx
- **Population** 3.5 million
- **Seasons** wet (Mar-Jun & Sep-Dec), dry (Jul-Aug & Jan-Feb)
- **Telephone** country code ☎ 252-2
- **Time** GMT/UTC + 3

Oh, and you can eat well here at the restaurant (p278). Hassan, the English-speaking owner, is very cluey and can help you with logistics. Free wi-fi.

our pick Oriental Hotel (☎ 514999; www.oriental hotelhargeisa.com; s/d US$15/30; 🖥) The closest Hargeisa comes to a travellers' hang-out, the Oriental can't be beaten for convenience. Its ultra-central location is ideal if you want to immerse yourself in Hargeisa; from your room you can feel the heartbeat of the city. It's nicely laid out, with the reception area opening onto the pleasant sun-filled patio. Rooms are medium-sized and functional. Ask for Said or Abdi Abdi; both are well-travelled, speak excellent English and will go the extra mile to help you with logistics. There's an on-site restaurant, but the food is only so-so.

Imperial Hotel (☎ 515000, 520524; imperialhotel101 @hotmail.com; Independence Rd; s/d US$20/30; 🖥) A good, quality choice, the modernish Imperial Hotel is in a calm neighbourhood, but within walking distance of the centre. Expect well-appointed rooms, good bedding, working fans, salubrious bathrooms and a good restaurant in a courtyard at the back. Rooms upstairs get more natural light. Wi-fi is available.

Ambassador Hotel Hargeisa (☎ 526666; www .ambassadorhotelhargeisa.com; Airport Rd; s/d US$45/80; 🍽 🖥) Drop anchor here for a night or two if you need to reassure your family at home that you're looking after yourself. With its efficient, English-speaking reception staff, prolific facilities and surgical cleanliness, the Ambassador exudes an international confidence. The squeaky-clean rooms are equipped with everything to ensure a comfortable stay, including satellite TV, glittering bathrooms, wi-fi, a restaurant and a bar (not licensed). Staff do an excellent job with car rental, tour guides, police escort and visa matters. Its single drawback is its location away from the central buzz – it feels like an isolated fortress, about 4km from the centre, near the airport. Not very Hargeisa, but it's quiet. And when you phone home and describe your lodgings, your mum will feel better. Priceless!

EATING & DRINKING

Hargeisa features a string of decent eateries. All the places listed open for breakfast, lunch and dinner. No alcohol is served, but you'll enjoy superb Somali tea and fresh fruit juices.

Maka Al Mukarama (fruit juices US$2.50; 🕑 7am-8pm) Put some bounce in your step with a glass of mango juice at this juice haven. Cakes are also available.

Cadaani (Independence Rd; mains US$1-3) You can't miss this bustling cafeteria – look for the red-and-white building near Telesom. It rustles up simple dishes such as spaghetti and sandwiches. The outdoor terrace is ideal for honing your people-watching skills.

Hadhwanaag (mains US$2-5) Near the Dalxiis, and located at the hotel of the same name, Hadhwanaag is another wonderful place to sample Somali specialities like *loxox* (injera-like bread with butter, eggs and honey; we can't get enough of pronouncing it: *lo-cho-ch*), fish dishes (especially the tuna), mutton ('divine', according to our Somali friends), chicken and roast beef. Enjoy your plunder under a gazebo in the plant-filled garden, but leave room for the Yemeni desserts – the *fata mus* (a concoction with banana) and the *fata timir* (a concoction with dates) will satisfy everyone except your personal trainer.

Fish & Steak House (Independence Rd; mains US$2-5) This peaceful oasis, set back from the main drag, promises a haven from the clamour outside. The cooks here have worked in Djibouti, and the menu is more eclectic than anywhere else in Hargeisa. From lasagne and shrimps to chicken curry and beef with pepper sauce, everything that emerges from the kitchen is produced with plenty of savoir faire.

ourpick Dalxiis Restaurant (mains US$3-5) The Dalxiis is an enticing 'park restaurant', with a garden-like setting. Get your fingers dirty experimenting with the wide range of Somali dishes, including *geel hanid* (roast camel), basmati rice, mutton and grilled fish. Order *ber geel* (camel's liver) at breakfast. Feeling conservative? Stick to *loxox* (if you can pronounce it).

GETTING THERE & AWAY
Air
See p282 for details on flights to/from Somaliland.

The **airport** (Airport Rd) is about 5km north of the centre.

Land
Regular shared taxis travel between Hargeisa, Berbera, Sheekh, Burcao, and Wajaale at the Ethiopian border. They leave from various departure points (north of town for Wajaale and Djibouti; two blocks east from the Oriental Hotel for Berbera; and beside the Municipality building for Sheekh and Burcao). They cost from US$5 to US$12 depending on the destination. There are also daily services to Djibouti (see p283).

GETTING AROUND
A taxi ride in the centre should cost no more than US$3, and about US$10 to the airport.

AROUND SOMALILAND

LAS GEEL
Las Geel is indisputably Somaliland's pièce de résistance. Were it not in Somaliland, this fantastic **archaeological site** (entrance fee US$20) would immediately be declared a World Heritage Site. Sadly (well, not quite – it's great that the place isn't crowded with tourists), as long as Somaliland is not recognised by the international community, it will remain a hidden gem.

Hundreds of magnificent neolithic rock art paintings in perfect condition, representing humans and animals, adorn the walls of several interconnected caves and shelters. Some paintings exceed one metre in length and their state of preservation is exceptional – nothing can convey the sort of response you're likely to have the minute you see them. There are even some very risqué scenes. This archaeological wonder was only brought to light in 2003, following

GET ENGAGED – VOLUNTEER OPPORTUNITIES IN SOMALILAND

One of the best ways to have a truly unique experience in Somaliland is to spend some time in a rewarding volunteer position. While researching this book, we've unearthed a number of locally run programs. We met all the people in charge of placements and we visited all places listed to assess their suitability. There's no language barrier – English is the lingua franca. Male and female volunteers are welcome.

All the people we met told us they could ensure the safety of volunteers, but it's wise to review the local security situation before settling in. See the boxed text, p276.

Note that board and lodging are provided, but you'll have to pay for your international airfares.

Edna Adan Hospital (Hargeisa)

The best-resourced hospital in the country welcomes health professionals, including general practitioners, gynaecologists, paediatric surgeons, midwives, pharmacists, radiologists and microbiologists. Students are accepted if they've completed at least four years of study.

Contact Edna Adan, Director (☎ 4426922; www.ednahospital.org) for more information.

University of Hargeisa

With 2200 students in 2009, the University of Hargeisa is quickly expanding. Foreign lecturers in law (with a specialisation in constitution law, judiciary reform, civil law systems and civil procedures) are in hot demand. One semester minimum.

Contact Mohamoud Hussein Farah, Dean, Faculty of Law (☎ 4423533; salin100@yahoo.com).

Havoyoco (Hargeisa)

The Horn of Africa Voluntary Youth Committee (Havoyoco) is an NGO that was founded in 1992 in Hargeisa. Its objectives include raising awareness on social issues (such as HIV or family life education, through an itinerant circus in remote settlements), capacity building and youth training (especially street children who were members of militia). Volunteers who can train youth in masonry, carpentry, cooking, sewing and mechanics are welcome. Minimum three months.

Contact Ahmed Muhamad, Executive Director (☎ 4428854; havoyoco@hotmail.com) or Ifrah Rashid Mohamed, Human Resources Assistant (☎ 4418288; ifrahrashid@yahoo.com).

Sheekh Secondary School

The small town of Sheekh is a major educational centre, and a welcoming place where you'll quickly be made to feel at home. There's a shortage of teachers in the following subject matters: English, biology, chemistry, history and geography. Pupils are from 10 to 22 years old.

Contact Mohamed Ibrahim Abdilahi, District Education Officer (☎ 730148; sheekhdeo @yahoo.com).

Sheekh Technical Veterinary School

Somaliland is heavily reliant on livestock farming for its foreign exchange earnings and needs more professionals to sustain livestock export and meet the demands of the livestock industry, especially livestock product inspection and animal health. Supported by Terra Nuova (www .terranuova.org), the state-of-the-art Sheekh Technical Veterinary School seeks volunteers in the following fields: veterinary epidemiology, quality management, food safety and standards and library management. Minimum one semester.

Contact: Cyprien Biaou, Project Manager (☎ 4447746; biaou2001@yahoo.fr)

University of Burcao

This low-key university (1200 students) on the outskirts of town needs teachers in the following fields: English (from secondary to university level), health and business administration. No minimum stay is required.

Contact Abdisalam Yassin Mohamed, Vice Chancellor (☎ 4436481; universityburao@hotmail .com, univburao@gmail.com).

THE JOYS OF (PIONEER) DIVING IN SOMALILAND

'I saw a TV program on the BBC about Somaliland, and this sparked my curiosity,' says Steve Atkinson, the British dive instructor who runs Somaliland's sole diving centre, at the Maan-Soor Hotel in Berbera. 'After meeting the owner of the Maan-Soor Hotel, we decided to set up a diving base in 2008.' How is the diving near Berbera? 'To be honest, the shores near Berbera are sandy, the visibility is usually low and there are no healthy coral reefs, but at least it offers something to do for travellers and expats. I'd call it "weekend diving". And there's the novelty factor!'. Are there other areas that are worth diving? 'The islands off Zeila are fantastic. We're still in the exploratory phase, but we plan to organise dive expeditions out there, with camp sites on the beach. The waters are clear and there's fish in abundance. Plus you really feel you've reached the end of the earth; it's like Southern Egypt 20 years ago,' says Atkinson.

Are the islands off Zeila (Ceebaad and Saacada Din) really the ultimate? In Djibouti City, we met Bruno Pardigon, who runs Dolphin Excursion (p292), and who has also done reconaissance dives off Zeila. 'There's potential, but it cannot compare with, say, the Sept Frères Archipelago off the Djiboutian coast. I didn't find the corals very exciting, and the fish species are the same as anywhere else in the Red Sea. The seascape is fairly dull because there aren't any drop-offs.'

You be the judge!

---

research conducted by a team of French archaeologists. There's a small museum at the entrance of the site with panels in English.

It's about 50km from Hargeisa, along the road to Berbera (the turn-off is at Dhubato village and Las Geel is about 6km down the road). You'll need a guide and a private vehicle to get there, both easily arranged in Hargeisa. Hotels charge from US$60 to US$100 per vehicle.

BERBERA
pop 35,000

The name alone sounds impossibly exotic, conjuring images of tropical ports, spices and palm oil. If the reality is a little more prosaic, it's a great place to chill a while nonetheless. It's hard to believe when you see it, but Berbera was once a busy town. Today this shady town consists mostly of crumbling buildings and mud-and-thatch houses.

Berbera's potential is immense, though. It's a nice little earner for Somaliland thanks to land-locked Ethiopia's need for a cheap, friendly port.

In the centre, there's an **old mosque** that's worth a peek. You can also delve into the small **market** area and soak up the atmosphere. Not far from Al Xayaat Restaurant, the tiny **fishing harbour** deserves a few photo snaps (but ask permission first).

Berbera is also bound by blissful beaches, about 4km from the centre, including **Baathela Beach**, just in front of Maan-Soor

Hotel. At dawn, dolphins can be seen frolicking in the bay – memorable.

Let's see; have we missed anything? Oh right. Diving is available in Berbera! There's a small, English-run **diving centre** (☎ 4138607 steve_atk@hotmail.co.uk) based at the Maan-Soor Hotel. A single dive costs US$40 (equipment included). See the boxed text above for more information.

Sleeping & Eating

Al Madiina Hotel (☎ 740254; r without bathroom US$3, with bathroom US$5-30; 🍴) Right in the centre, this venture doesn't feel the need for fancy touches and what you see is what you get, which in this case is a bed plonked in a threadbare room. The shared bathrooms are OK.

Esco Hotel (☎ 740767; r without bathroom & with fan US$6, r with bathroom & air-con US$25; 🍴) A coin's toss from Al Xayaat Restaurant, the Esco has a mixed bag of rooms to suit all budgets. The better rooms have air-con. Plumbing could do with a bit of maintenance, but mattresses will keep the chiropractor away, the sheets get a regular spin in the washing machine and the fans are working.

Maan-Soor Hotel (☎ 4244240; http://maan-soor .com; s/d US$40/60; 🍴) When we walked into the Maan-Soor we rubbed our eyes. A resort-style hotel in such a remote place? Was that the effect of *chat* on our weak brains? No. The owner, Abdulkader, is a consummate businessman who's eager to promote Berbera as a beach holiday destination, and this hotel is a first step. It consists of 16 clean-as-a-pin 'cottages' scattered around a large property just spitting distance from Baathela beach. Amenities include an attached restaurant, satellite TV and a dive centre. The only downside to the hotel that we could come up with is that the rooms don't face the sea. It's about 2.5km away from the centre.

Al Xayaat Restaurant & Fish House (☎ 740224; mains US$3; ☾ lunch & dinner) Lap up a reviving fruit juice and scoff a grilled fish at this colourful eatery overlooking the bay, and you'll leave with a smile on your face. While eating you'll be surrounded by a menagerie of cats, crows and seagulls expecting a titbit. Ali, the amiable owner, speaks good English.

Getting There & Away
Regular shared taxis travel between Hargeisa and Berbera (US$5; 150km).

SHEEKH
pop 15,000
From Berbera and the coastal plain, you can make a beautiful journey along the switchback ascent to the central plateau on the Berbera–Burcao road and stop at the hill town of Sheekh, which is a welcome refuge from the heat of the lowland areas. This is one of the main educational centres in the country, with a well-established veterinary school and various colleges, which give the town a surprisingly dynamic feel.

Sheekh boasts a small **necropolis**, called Ferdusa, which dates from the 13th century. There's not much to be seen, as the site has not been excavated yet.

Sheekh is approximately halfway between Berbera and Burcao. You can break up your Somaliland odyssey at **Mashaallah Hotel** (☎ 730167; r incl breakfast US$7-12), which has ordinary rooms set around a courtyard.

BURCAO (BURAO)
pop 185,000
The capital of Todgheer province and the second-largest city in the country, Burcao feels a bit rougher around the edges than Berbera or Hargeisa, but that's part of the adventure. There's nothing of tangible interest here, but you can soak up the atmosphere at the livestock market and enjoy being the focus of attention – as a tourist, you'll be something of a novelty here!

You'll find a few internet and telephone outlets, as well as bureaux de change in the centre.

Sleeping & Eating
Barwaaqo Hotel & Restaurant (☎ 715800; barwaaqo hotelburco@hotmail.com; s/d US$10/15) This modernish pile gets an A+ for its spotless rooms, ultra-central location, good beds and hygienic bathrooms. Another bonus is the rooftop restaurant, which trots out excellent fish and meat dishes with the added treat of splendid views over Burcao. We saw a number of (veiled) female guests too, so it's a sensible choice for women travellers.

Shamaxle Restaurant (mains US$4-7; ☾ lunch & dinner) By far our favourite eatery in town. The location, in a leafy compound right by the Todgheer River, at the foot of a bridge (ask for directions), is top-notch. And the juicy *hanid* (roast lamb) will have your tastebuds leaping around for joy. For breakfast, try *suqaar* (minced goat meat with potato, onions and garlic). Ask for Zahra, the female owner, who has lived in the USA and speaks very good English.

Getting There & Away
Shared taxis leave for Hargeisa (US$5 to US$10) via Berbera.

SOMALILAND DIRECTORY
ACCOMMODATION
Surprise: the overall quality of the lodgings we visited was much higher than in Eritrea or in Ethiopia, and much better value than in neighbouring Djibouti. There's a fairly good range of options, at very affordable prices (a cheapie doesn't cost more than US$5). What's more, staff usually speak very good English.

BUSINESS HOURS
All shops, offices and businesses are closed on Friday, but most restaurants are open every day.

DANGERS & ANNOYANCES
Follow what hotel staff will tell you – an armed soldier (at your own expense) and a tour guide might be compulsory outside Hargeisa. Check the situation while in Hargeisa. All travel in the Sool region is currently unsafe due to conflict in Puntland, which claims this province.

SOMALILAND

EMBASSIES & CONSULATES

The only official foreign representation in Somaliland is the **Ethiopian Liaison Office** (Map p277; 8.30am-noon Sat-Thu), which acts as a de facto embassy.

Somaliland Liaison Offices abroad include:

USA (202 4670602; 3705 South George Mansion, Falls Church, VA 22041)

Ethiopia (Map pp86-7; 11 635921; fax 11 627847; Bole Rd District, Addis Ababa)

France (0950815094, 0617677075; wakiil_sl_fr@hotmail.fr; 19 rue Augustin Thierry, 75019 Paris)

UK (020 79619098; 102 Cavel Street; London E1 2JA)

MONEY

There are no ATMs anywhere in Somaliland, so carry considerable amounts of US dollars (vastly preferable to euros) that can be exchanged for shillings in hotels, shops and bureaux de change. Most hotels and shops also accept payment in US dollars. There's no chance of changing your travellers cheques. If you need to wire money, **Dahabshiil** (www .dahabshiil.com) transfers can be made at the various Dahabshiil offices in Hargeisa. Dahabshiil has offices in Australia, Canada, Holland, Ireland, New Zealand, the UK and the USA, among others.

TELEPHONE

There are several private telephone companies including Telesom and Telecom in Somaliland. International telephone calls made from Somaliland are the cheapest in Africa (less than US$0.30 per minute).

VISAS

You will need a visa to enter Somaliland. Visas are *not* issued at the airport. The most convenient place to get a visa is Addis Ababa. They are issued while you wait through the Somaliland Liaison Office (see above) and cost US$40 for a one-month visa.

In the UK, the USA and France, you can contact the Somaliland Liaison Office. Another option is to go through a local sponsor, such as the Oriental Hotel (p277), the Ambassador (p277) or the Director of Tourism (see p275). Email them the (scanned) ID pages of your passport and give them at least three days to organise the visa. They will email a visa certificate back to you as an attached document. Print it and present it upon arrival at the airport (or at any land border).

> **DEPARTURE AND ARRIVAL TAX**
>
> International departure tax is US$32, payable in cash. Arrival tax is US$22. You'll also have to change US$50 at the airport.

Note that this is a certificate; the original visa should have been deposited at the immigration office at the airport (or at the border post, if you arrive by land) by your sponsor. In many cases your sponsor will be waiting for you at the airport with the original visa. If you plan to enter Somaliland at Wajaale (from Ethiopia), ask your sponsor to send the original visa to the Somaliland border post (your sponsor will put it in an envelope and give it to a reputable taxi driver heading to Wajaale). Hotels charge US$20-50 for the service, and expect that you spend a couple of nights with them.

Visas for Onward Travel

Ethiopia The Ethiopian Liaison Office (see left) can issue Ethiopian visas. You'll need two photos, US$20 and a letter from the Somaliland Intelligence Agency – Immigration Department (Map p277). The whole process should take less than a day.

SOMALILAND TRANSPORT

GETTING THERE & AWAY
Entering Somaliland

Entering Somaliland, whether by air, land or sea, is a surprisingly painless process, provided you have your visa ready and your passport at hand. You'll be asked to pay an immigration tax (US$20) and an airport tax (US$2), and you'll have to change US$50 at a ludicrously unfavourable exchange rate (half the normal exchange rate).

If you arrive by land, you'll be exempt from paying taxes.

Passport

To enter Somaliland you must have a valid passport and a visa.

Air
AIRPORTS & AIRLINES

Somaliland has two international gateways for arrival by air: Hargeisa and Berbera. Hargeisa is the busiest. Daallo Airlines, the national carrier, as well as Ethiopian Airlines and Suhura Airways, use Hargeisa, while African Express uses Berbera.

Airlines with offices in Hargeisa include the following:

African Express (Map p277; ☎ 523646; www.africanexpress.co.ke; Independence Rd)

Daallo Airlines (Map p277; ☎ 523003; www.daallo.com; Independence Rd)

Suhura Airways (Map p277; ☎ 524411) In the same building as Oriental Hotel.

The Ethiopian Airlines office was closed at the time of writing but should have reopened by the time you read this – most probably somewhere on Independence Rd.

TICKETS

The most common routes are from Djibouti or Addis Ababa. From Europe (London and Paris), Daallo Airlines operates weekly services to Djibouti, from where there are connections to Hargeisa. Prices start at €750 (return).

From Djibouti, Daallo Airlines has four weekly flights to Hargeisa (US$120, 40 minutes). For Addis Ababa (Ethiopia), Daallo Airlines flies from Hargeisa twice a week (one way/return US$200/325), while Suhura Airways has a weekly flight (one way/return US$200/230). Ethiopian Airlines had suspended its flights to Hargeisa at the time of writing but should have resumed them by the time you read this.

Other destinations served by Daallo Airlines include Bosasso (Puntland), Mogadishu (southern Somalia) and Nairobi (Kenya; via Mogadishu).

From Berbera, African Express operates flights to Dubai (UAE; US$330/430 one way/return; twice weekly), Nairobi (Kenya; US$420/770; twice weekly) and Aden (Yemen; US$210/280; once weekly).

If you're coming from Australasia, your best bet is to fly to Dubai and find an onward connection to Djibouti (and on to Hargeisa or Berbera).

Land

DJIBOUTI

The land border between Somaliland and Djibouti is open. Shared taxis (usually 4WDs) ply the route on a daily basis from Hargeisa to Djibouti City – a strenuous 20-hour journey on a gravel road (about US$30). Taxis usually leave Hargeisa around 4pm so as to travel by night and avoid the scorching heat. They drive in convoy – a matter of survival in case of a breakdown in this desolate area. Bring food and plenty of water, as none will be available during the trip. The border crossing is at Loyaada.

ETHIOPIA

From Jijiga in eastern Ethiopia there's regular bus traffic to the border town of Wajaale (see p263 and p225). In Wajaale, take a contract taxi (about US$50) or a minibus (about US$5) to Hargeisa, about 90km to the southeast. Ask to be dropped in front of your hotel. Expect a couple of checkpoints, but no hassle.

Sea

It's possible to cross the Red Sea to either Aden or Mokha (Yemen)! Yemeni boats carrying livestock leave from Berbera but there's no fixed schedule – they usually run on a twice-weekly basis. It costs about US$30 to US$50 and the crossing takes about 30 hours. Contact one of the shipping agencies in Berbera, such as Tawfiq Shipping Trading & Fishing Company or Al Salam Shipping Agency. They'll handle immigration formalities for you. You'll have to pay 'passport fees' (US$30).

GETTING AROUND

Somaliland has a few sealed roads (like from Hargeisa to Berbera and from Berbera to Burcao). Medium-sized buses and crowded 4WDs service routes between major Somaliland settlements.

You can also hire a taxi for about US$70 per day (fuel and escort are extra) or a 4WD with driver for about US$140.

SOMALILAND

Djibouti

Djibouti

Never heard of Djibouti? Don't feel bad. Despite being well linked to Ethiopia and Somaliland, it's more famous for its military bases and busy port than for its tourist attractions. Which is a shame, because this tiny speck of a country packs a big bunch. What it lacks in size, it more than makes up for in beauty, especially if you're a fan of geological oddities. Tramping on the salt crust of Lac Assal (the third-lowest point on earth), and wandering amid hundreds of spikelike limestone chimneys belching out puffs of steam around Lac Abbé are just a few of the many revelatory experiences on offer.

Of all East African countries, Djibouti is the most outdoor-friendly, with an excellent mix of land and water activities (bliss if you've come from landlocked Ethiopia!). Diving fiends rave about the Gulf of Tadjoura and Les Sept Frères Archipelago, while kitesurfers are thrilled by the optimal year-round conditions in the Gulf of Tadjoura. When it comes to snorkelling alongside whale sharks, the Bay of Ghoubbet is unsurpassable. For those who prefer to keep their feet dry, hiking opportunities abound, from guided walks in the Forêt du Day to memorable multiday treks led by Afar nomads along ancient salt routes.

Barring Djibouti City, the country is refreshingly void of large-scale development. It's all about ecotravel, with a smattering of sustainable *campements touristiques* (traditional huts with shared showers and toilets) in the hinterland – the perfect way to immerse yourself in local culture.

Sure, Djibouti is pricey, but it's worth the splurge. And while much of the Horn is embroiled in disputes, Djibouti stands out as a haven of stability. Priceless!

HIGHLIGHTS

- Soak up the atmosphere of the chaotic **Marché Central** (p288) in Djibouti City

- Get wet! Take a **kitesurfing course** (p292), dive the wreck of **Le Faon** (p292) in the Gulf of Tadjoura or snorkel alongside **whale sharks** (p292) in the Bay of Ghoubbet

- Take a tour to **Lac Assal** (p291), the lowest point on the African continent

- Recharge on a porcelain-white beach on **Moucha Island** (p291)

- Immerse yourself in the Martian landscape of **Lac Abbé** (p292)

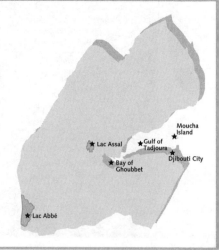

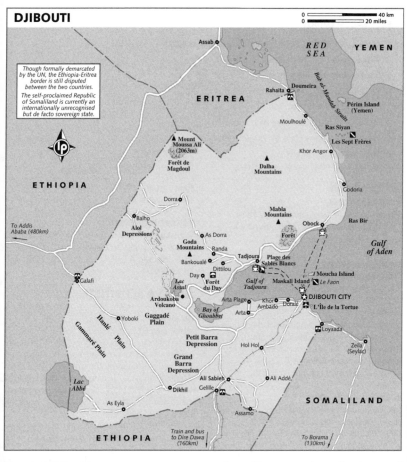

DJIBOUTI

Though formally demarcated by the UN, the Ethiopia-Eritrea border is still disputed between the two countries.

The self-proclaimed Republic of Somaliland is currently an internationally unrecognised but de facto sovereign state.

DJIBOUTI

DJIBOUTI CITY

pop 600,000

'*Bonjour chef* – after a long-haul or regional flight, what a surprise to be greeted in French. Then dine on *steak de boeuf sauce Roquefort* and *baguettes*. Due to its colonial past, and the current heavy French military presence, Djibouti City is like a Gallic outpost in the Horn. Truth is, Djibouti is a strange African anomaly, with jarring cultural and social combinations and surprisingly cosmopolitan vibes. Traditionally robed Afar tribesmen, stalwart French legionnaires (and the odd GI), sensuous Somali ladies and frazzled businessmen with the latest mobile phones stuck to their ear all jostle side by side.

Around 1pm, a cacophony of car horns and shouting breaks out, heralding the marvellous news: *chat*, the nation's daily addiction, has arrived, fresh from Ethiopia. Then a heavy torpor descends on the town, and all activity ceases until 4pm.

Djibouti City boasts good infrastructure, including hotels, bars (a note for those who've just come from Somaliland: yes, they're licensed), clubs and restaurants, but it doesn't come cheap. If you've arrived from a neighbouring country, be prepared for a financial shock.

Djibouti City is mostly an air hub (mainly for military purposes) and a busy port. Sights are scarce, but it's the obvious place to organise forays into the fantastic hinterland or boat excursions.

FAST FACTS: DJIBOUTI

■ **ATMs** a few in Djibouti City (but only one ATM accepts MasterCard)

■ **Best season** October to March

■ **Borders** Ethiopia and Somaliland open

■ **Capital** Djibouti City

■ **Languages** Arabic, French, Afar, Somali

■ **Money** Djibouti Franc (DFr); US$1 = DFr177

■ **Telephone** country code ☎ 253; international access code ☎ 00

■ **Time** GMT/UTC + three hours

INFORMATION
Internet Access
There's a slew of internet outlets in the centre. They all offer fast connections. Expect to pay around DFr400 per hour.

Medical Services
Pôle Médical (☎ 352724; ☽ 8am-noon & 4-7pm Sat-Thu) A well-equipped clinic. It's off Pl du 27 Juin 1977.

Money
There are banks and two bureaux de change in the centre, as well as a few Visa-friendly ATMs (but only one ATM accepts MasterCard).
Banque Indosuez Mer Rouge (Pl Lagarde; ☽ 7.30am-noon & 4-7pm) Changes cash and has two ATMs.
BCIMR Pl Lagarde (☽ 7.30-11.45am Sun-Thu); Plateau du Serpent (Ave F d'Esperey; ☽ 7.45-noon & 4-5.15pm Sun-Thu) The branch on Place Lagarde has two ATMs, but only one was functioning at the time of writing.
Dilip Corporation (Pl du 27 Juin 1977; ☽ 8am-noon & 4-7.30pm Sat-Thu) Authorised bureau de change. Changes cash (no commission) and does cash advances on Visa and MasterCard. It also accepts travellers cheques.
Mehta (☎ 353719; Pl du 27 Juin 1977; ☽ 7.30am-noon & 4-7.30pm Sun-Thu) Authorised bureau de change. Next door to Dilip, Mehta also changes cash (no commission) and usually accepts travellers cheques but charges a 2% commission.
Saba Islamic Bank (off Pl du 27 Juin 1977) Has one ATM, which accepts both Visa and MasterCard.

There's also a small bureau de change in the departure hall at the airport, but it closes around 6pm.

Post & Telephone
The most convenient places to make an international or a local call are the various telephone outlets scattered around the city centre.

Main post office (Blvd de la République; ☽ 7am-1pm Sat-Thu) North of the centre.

Tourist Information
Tourist office (☎ 352800; www.office-tourisme.dj; Rue de Foucauld; ☽ 7am-1pm Sat-Thu, 4-6pm Sat, Mon & Wed) Mildly helpful. To the southeastern side of Place du 27 Juin 1977.

SIGHTS & ACTIVITIES
Djibouti City is big in atmosphere but short on sights. The European Quarter, with its whitewashed houses and Moorish arcades, is a strange mix of the Arab and the European. To the south lies the shambolic Pl Mahmoud Harbi, dominated by the minaret of the great **Hamoudi mosque**. Nearby, the chaotic **Marché Central** (Central Market), is a must. It's a criss-cross of alleyways where stalls and shops are lined cheek by jowl.

The only decent beach is at the Kempinski hotel (p290), but there's an entrance fee of DFr3000.

Diving, kitesurfing, whale-shark spotting and hiking can all be organised from Djibouti City (see the boxed text p292).

SLEEPING
The choice of budget accommodation is limited, and most hotels tend to be dull multi-storey blocks with only slightly more character than a wet rag.

Budget
Hotel Horseed (☎ 352316; Blvd du Général de Gaulle; s/d without bathroom DFr5000/7500; ✖) Despite being raggedy, the Horseed is worthwhile if you're strapped for cash. Rooms are presentable, though cleanliness is only just OK in the shared bathrooms – wear flip-flops and pray you're not the last in line to shower.

DJIBOUTI CITY

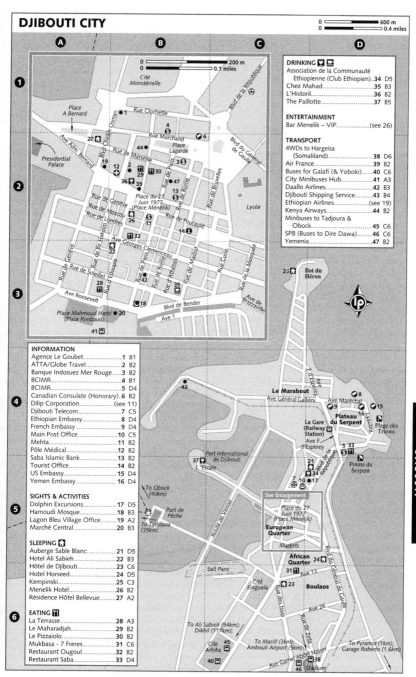

DRINKING 🍷 🍴
Association de la Communauté
  Ethiopienne (Club Ethiopien)....**34** D5
Chez Mahad.............................**35** B3
L'Historil................................**36** B2
The Paillotte...........................**37** B5

ENTERTAINMENT
Bar Menelik – VIP...............(see 26)

TRANSPORT
4WDs to Hargeisa
  (Somaliland).......................**38** D6
Air France...............................**39** B2
Buses for Galafi (& Yoboki)...**40** C6
City Minibuses Hub................**41** A3
Daallo Airlines.......................**42** B3
Djibouti Shipping Service.......**43** B4
Ethiopian Airlines..............(see 19)
Kenya Airways.......................**44** B2
Minibuses to Tadjoura &
  Obock...............................**45** C6
SPB (Buses to Dire Dawa).....**46** C6
Yemenia..................................**47** B2

INFORMATION
Agence Le Goubet.....................**1** B1
ATTA/Globe Travel...................**2** B2
Banque Indosuez Mer Rouge....**3** B2
BCIMR.......................................**4** B1
BCIMR.......................................**5** D4
Canadian Consulate (Honorary)..**6** B2
Dilip Corporation...............(see 11)
Djibouti Telecom.......................**7** C5
Ethiopian Embassy.....................**8** D4
French Embassy..........................**9** D4
Main Post Office.......................**10** C5
Mehta.......................................**11** B2
Pôle Médical............................**12** B2
Saba Islamic Bank.....................**13** B2
Tourist Office...........................**14** B2
US Embassy..............................**15** D4
Yemen Embassy........................**16** D4

SIGHTS & ACTIVITIES
Dolphin Excursions..................**17** D5
Hamoudi Mosque......................**18** B3
Lagon Bleu Village Office.........**19** A2
Marché Central.........................**20** B3

SLEEPING 🛏
Auberge Sable Blanc.................**21** D5
Hotel Ali Sabieh.......................**22** B3
Hôtel de Djibouti......................**23** C6
Hotel Horseed..........................**24** D5
Kempinski................................**25** C3
Menelik Hotel..........................**26** B2
Résidence Hôtel Bellevue.........**27** A2

EATING 🍴
La Terrasse..............................**28** A3
Le Maharadjah.........................**29** B2
Le Pizzaiolo.............................**30** B2
Mukbasa - 7 Freres...................**31** C6
Restaurant Ougoul...................**32** B2
Restaurant Saba.......................**33** D4

DJIBOUTI

Hôtel de Djibouti (☎ 356415; Ave 13; s/d DFr6300/8600; 🔀) Located in the heart of the African Quarter and appropriately colourful. Try and fight tooth and nail to get a room at the back of the hotel; if you don't the crazy road noise will be make the idea of sleep a wishful dream. Keep your expectations in check, especially regarding the quality of the plumbing.

Auberge Sable Blanc (☎ 351163; d with/without bathroom DFr7700/6700; 🔀) A short stagger from Blvd de la République, this little modern construction is a discreet place (sometimes used by adulterous couples, we were told!) with clean if rather unloved rooms and salubrious bathrooms.

Midrange

Hotel Ali Sabieh (☎ 353264; alsabhot@intnet.dj; Ave Georges Clemenceau; s DFr10,400-11,500, d DFr14,200; 🔀) While most rooms are petite and charmless, the attentive staff, well-sprung mattresses and rooms that are scrubbed by a team of cleaning addicts make this a sure-fire bet. It's ideally positioned, right in the thick of things.

Menelik Hotel (☎ 351177; menelikhotel@intnet.dj; Pl du 27 Juin 1977; s/d with breakfast DFr15,500/20,200; 🔀 🖳) It's hard to top the Menelik's location, smackdab in the centre. Service is excellent and the modernish rooms provide excellent levels of comfort and hygiene but, to be honest, you pay for the location. Credit cards (Visa only) are accepted but you'll pay a painful 5% commission. Free wi-fi.

Residence Hôtel Bellevue (☎ 358088; bellevue @intnet.dj; Blvd Cheikh Osman; s DFr17,000-19,000, d DFr19,000-21,000; 🔀) The Bellevue gets by on its handy location, a waddle away from restaurants, bars and clubs. The well-equipped rooms are decent enough but they lack any real sparkle. Angle for a room with a sea view.

Top End

Kempinski (☎ 325555; www.kempinski.com; Ilot du Héron; s DFr82,000-88,000, d DFr88,000-94,000; 🔀 🖳 🐕) Well-heeled Arabian businessmen, high-ranking European military officers, folks from various Western intelligence agencies and African bigwigs – they all end up here. It's all very 'Bond, James Bond'. Away from 007 fantasies, you know exactly what you'll be getting at the swanky Kempinski: shiny-clean rooms and a host of top-notch facilities. What you won't be getting is any kind of indication that you are in Djibouti but, as you flake out on the beach or do laps in the gleaming pool, you probably won't be that bothered.

EATING

If you've just come from Ethiopia (and you're weary of injera) or Somaliland (and you've had your fill of goat meat), now's your chance to broaden your culinary experiences. The city is endowed with a smattering of restaurants that will please most palates – a testimony to the French presence. If you're on a budget, you'll also find inexpensive snack stands in the centre of town.

our pick **La Terrasse** (☎ 350227; Rue d'Ethiopie; mains DFr400-700) Bargain! This place has plenty of character and serves up 'good Ethiopian food at good prices in a good atmosphere', as one regular patron put it. It occupies a rooftop, with a moodily lit dining area and an open kitchen – not to mention the heady scents of incense. If only it were licensed. It's open for dinner only.

Restaurant Saba (☎ 354244; Ave Maréchal Lyautey; mains DFr1200-2500; 🕑 lunch Sat-Thu, dinner daily) Close to the railway station, this unpretentious joint serves well-prepared fish and meat dishes without fuss. Some reliable choices are skewered fish, fillet of barracuda, *pavé de boeuf* (beef steak) and *poisson yemenite* (oven-baked fish). There are some good pastas and salads (from DFr700), which will gladden vegetarian hearts, as well as superb fruit juices.

Le Pizzaiolo (☎ 354439; Rue d'Ethiopie; mains DFr1300-3000) Perfect crusts and well-chosen ingredients are two of the components that make Le Pizzaiolo the best pizza place in town. Pasta and meat dishes are also available.

Restaurant Ougoul (☎ 353652; Ave Georges Clemenceau; mains DFr1600-4400) *The* place towards which all heads turn when it comes to tasting a range of bounteous marine offerings. Push the boat out with, say, lobster (grilled, stuffed, flambéed or thermidor), prawns, crab, barracuda, wahoo or grouper. Deadly.

Mukbasa – 7 Freres (☎ 351188; Ave 13; fish dishes DFr2000) This straightforward eatery specialises in *poisson yemenite* (oven-baked fish). It's served with a chapatti-like bread and a devilish *mokbasa* (purée of honey and either dates or banana). It's so finger-licking good that you'll quickly forget about the dull decor.

Le Maharadjah (☎ 356616; Rue d'Ethiopie; mains DFr2600-3700) Elegant Maharadjah takes its inspiration from the Middle East, with an ample selection of tastebud-titillating specialities. Among the many winners are *shish tawooq* (chicken grilled on skewers), *kofta* (meatballs) and *shanklish* (goats' cheese served with onions, oil and tomatoes). Open for dinner only.

DRINKING

If you've come to Djibouti from dry Somaliland, rejoice! There's no shortage of watering holes in Djibouti City, especially around Pl du 27 Juin 1977.

Popularly considered to be Djibouti City's most esteemed bar, **L'Historil** (Pl du 27 Juin 1977) has an appealing terrace that offers excellent people-watching opportunities. Other G-spots of the city's bar scene include the **Paillotte** (Port de Pêche), easily the hippest place when we visited, and the down-to-earth **Association de la Communauté Ethiopienne de Djibouti** (west of Blvd de la République), also known as 'Club Ethiopien', where a bottle of St George costs only DFr400. Club Ethiopien also serves good Ethiopian fare at puny prices.

Our favourite juice bar is **Chez Mahad** (off Rue de Madrid; juices DFr200-400; 7.30am-noon & 4-8.30pm Sat-Thu, 4-9pm Fri), which has a dizzying array of fruity concoctions.

Plenty of teahouses are scattered around the centre.

ENTERTAINMENT

Most clubs are on or around Rue d'Ethiopie, in the European Quarter. They are at their liveliest on Thursday and Friday nights. Entrance is free, but a beer costs upwards of DFr1000. **Bar Menelik – VIP** (Pl du 27 Juin 1977), in the basement of Menelik Hotel, was the 'most happening' (meaning 'least sleazy') place at the time of research.

GETTING THERE & AWAY

Air

For details of international flights to and from Djibouti City, see p296.

Boat

There are talks of opening a ferry route between Djibouti City, Tadjoura and Obock. Check while in Djibouti City. Meanwhile, you can rely on the speedboats that carry the precious *chat* to Tadjoura and Obock.

Car

For 4WD rental (from DFr25,000 per day, with driver), contact the following outfits:
Garage Roberto (352029; Route de Boulaos)

Marill (327433; Route de l'Aéroport)
Pyramid (358203; Route de Boulaos)

Local Transport

Minibuses leave from various departure points south of town. They connect Djibouti City to Ali Sabieh, Tadjoura, Galafi (at the Ethiopian border), and Obock. Most minibuses leave early in the morning and only when they are full. Most journeys cost from DFr500 to DFr2000, depending on distance.

Train

See p262 for more information on the Djibouti City–Ethiopia train.

GETTING AROUND

The central hub for city minibuses (all tickets DFr50) is on Pl Mahmoud Harbi. A taxi ride within the centre costs about DFr500 (DFr1000 to/from the airport).

AROUND DJIBOUTI

MOUCHA ISLAND

It ain't the Bahamas, but this island, easily accessible from Djibouti City, is a welcome respite from the hustle and bustle of the capital, with uncrowded beaches and warm waters. The **Lagon Bleu Village** (250296, 847247; http://bluelagon.net; Moucha Island; s incl full board from DFr16,000;) is a good place to take up a Robinson Crusoe lifestyle without sacrificing comfort, with 19 well-equipped bungalows, a good restaurant and a **diving** centre (see p292). As an indication of prices, a two-day/one-night full-board package, including transfers to/from Djibouti City, costs from DFr18,000/9500 per adult/child. Day trips are also possible (from DFr8000/5000, including lunch). For bookings, contact ATTA/Globe Travel (see p297).

LAC ASSAL

Just over 100km west of the capital lies one of the most spectacular natural phenomena in Africa: Lac Assal. Situated 150m below sea level, this crater lake is encircled by dark, dormant volcanoes. It represents the lowest point on the African continent. The aquamarine water is ringed by a huge salt field, 60m in depth. The salt field has been mined by the Afar nomads for centuries, and they

DJIBOUTI

can still be seen loading up their camels for the long trek south to Ethiopia.

There's no public transport to Lac Assal. Most visitors come with tours (see p297) or hire their own vehicles from the capital. A tour should set you back about DFr15,000.

LAC ABBÉ

You'll never forget your first glimpse of Lac Abbé. The scenery is sensational: the plain is dotted with hundreds of limestone chimneys, some standing as high as 50m, belching out puffs of steam. Located 140km southwest of

---

GET ACTIVE IN DJIBOUTI!

When it comes to outdoor activities, Djibouti delivers.

Diving

Djibouti is a great destination for divers. Most diving takes place off the islands of Maskali and Moucha in the Gulf of Tadjoura, where you'll find a variety of dive sites for all levels. A hot favourite is the wreck of *Le Faon*, a huge cargo ship that lies in 27m of water on a sandy floor. The weak point is the low visibility, which seldom exceeds 10 to 15 m.

If you want to see a dazzling aggregation of pelagics, Les Sept Frères Archipelago can't be beaten. However, this is not for the faint-hearted because of the rough seas and strong currents. Trips to Les Sept Frères Archipelago are expensive due to the distance and are usually organised in the way of live-aboards.

You'll find two professional dive centres staffed with qualified instructors who speak English.
Dolphin Excursions (☎ 350313, 812300; www.dolphin-excursions.com; Blvd de la République)
Lagon Bleu (☎ 825733; http://bluelagon.net; Moucha Island; Djibouti City office ☎ 250296; off Pl du 27 Juin)

Whale-shark spotting

Fabulous! The Bay of Ghoubbet is one of the best places in the world to snorkel near a massive whale shark. During the peak season (October to January), the question isn't whether you will see a shark, but how many you will see. 'It's amazing to see how closely you can approach these graceful giants,' one tourist told us.

This activity has exploded in recent years. However, the way it is conducted leaves something to be desired. Dolphin Excursions and Lagon Bleu (see above) are two of the more ecologically sensitive companies.

Hiking & Trekking

Hiking is popular in the Goda Mountains. From canyons and valleys to waterfalls and peaks, the mountainscape is fantastic and you'll be rewarded with lovely vistas. Most *campements touristiques* can organise guided nature walks, from one-hour jaunts to more challenging day hikes.

Various treks led by Afar nomads can also be arranged along ancient salt routes in western Djibouti. It's the best way to immerse yourself in traditional nomadic culture. Duration varies from two-day hikes near Lac Assal to 10-day expeditions as far as Ethiopia.

The following operators have good credentials:
Dolphin Excursions (☎ 350313, 812300; www.dolphin-excursions.com; blvd de la République) Ask for Nicolas or Bruno.
Ermano (☎ 830804; ermanofr@yahoo.fr) Ask for Ermano.
La Caravane de Sel (☎ 810488; caravanedusel@hotmail.com) Ask for Said Baragoita.

Kitesurfing

The combination of constant, strong breezes, protected areas with calm water conditions and the lack of obstacles make Djibouti a world-class destination for kitesurfers. In the Bay of Ghoubbet, winds can reach 35 knots and blow about 300 days a year. For beginners, Île de la Tortue, near the international airport, is a hot favourite, with shallow waters and more manageable breezes (about 15 knots). 'And there's the added thrill of fantastic mountainous backdrops,' says Dante Kourallos, who runs **Djibouti Kitesurf** (☎ 828614, 357233; www.djiboutikitesurf.com). Tuition and courses for all levels can be arranged, as well as a half-day 'discovery' session (€70).

DJIBOUTI

Djibouti City, it is often described as 'a slice of moon on the crust of earth'. *Planet of the Apes* was filmed here, and it's no wonder.

Though desolate, it is not uninhabited. Numerous mineral-rich hot springs feed the farms of local nomads who graze their camels and goats here. The banks of the lake are also where flamingos gather at dawn.

There are three *campements touristiques* (traditional huts with shared showers and toilets) near Lac Abbé. The best organised is **Campement Touristique d'Asbole** (☎ 822291; full board DFr8000), which lies on a plateau that proffers stupendous views of the big chimneys. As in all *campements,* accommodation is rudimentary, but who cares? You'll be hypnotised by the scenery anyway. Prices include a guided walk to the chimneys.

To get there, you'll need to rent a 4WD with driver or take a tour from the capital (see p297). The *campement touristique* can organise transfers if you can find a group of people.

GODA MOUNTAINS

If you want to get away from it all, look no further. Northwest of the Gulf of Tadjoura, the Goda Mountains rise to a height of 1750m and are a spectacular natural oddity. This area shelters one of the rare speckles of green on Djibouti's parched map, like a giant oasis – a real relief after the scorched desert landscapes. It can also be a shock for visitors, some of whom find it inconceivable that the tiny settlements of **Dittilou**, **Bankoualé** or **Randa** belong to the same country as the one they left on the burning plain just one hour before.

The Goda Mountains shelter Djibouti's only national park, **Forêt du Day National Park**.

This area offers ample **hiking** opportunities. Owners of *campements touristiques* will be happy to suggest guided walks suited to your level of ability.

Sleeping & Eating

The Goda Mountains are favoured by expats in search of cool air, and there's a smattering of traditional, ecofriendly *campements touristiques*. Showers and toilets are communal. The prices quoted include guided walks.

ourpick Campement Touristique de la Forêt du Day (☎ 354520; Day; full board DFr8000) If you like peace, quiet and sigh-inducing views, you'll have few quibbles with this atmospheric *campement* in the Forêt du Day National Park,

at an altitude of 1400m. The traditional huts are welcoming, the toilet block is in good nick, and electricity is solar-generated. Other draws include the host of walking options available, and the healthy food.

Campement Touristique de Dittilou (☎ 810488; Dittilou; full board DFr8000) The *das* (traditional huts) are set against a lush and totally peaceful landscape, at the edge of the national park. It's a good base for hiking – don't miss the waterfall of Toha (a three-to-four-hour return visit).

Campement Touristique de Bankoualé (☎ 814115; Bankoualé; full board DFr8000) Another ecofriendly camp (electricity is solar powered) in a scenic location – it overlooks a lush valley and there's an Afar village nearby, where you can stock up on local handicrafts. Huts 5 and 6 boast the best views. The toilet block is well scrubbed, and the food gets good reports. Houmed, the owner, is a beekeeper, and the homemade honey is delicious. There are excellent hiking possibilities, too.

Getting There & Away

The most convenient way to visit the area is on a tour (see p297) or with a rental 4WD. Transport can also be organised by the *campements* if there's a group (usually a minimum of four people).

TADJOURA
pop 25,000

Originally a small Afar village trading in slaves, this whitewashed town is now a quiet backwater. Poor and run down, its setting is nevertheless attractive, nestled in the shadow of the green Goda Mountains with the bright blue sea lapping at its doorstep.

If you're after sustainably produced local handicrafts, the women's run **Association des Femmes de Tadjoura** (Tadjoura; ☒ 7.30am-12.30pm & 4-6pm Sat-Thu) sells colourful Afar basketware.

Plage des Sables Blancs, 7km east of Tadjoura, is tranquillity incarnate and a lovely place to sun yourself, with a good string of white sand.

Sleeping & Eating

Hôtel-Restaurant Le Golfe (☎ 424091, 424153; hot _rest_legolfe@hotmail.com; bungalows DFr10,000; ☒ ☒) Under French-Ethiopian management, this low-key but well-kept resort popular with French soldiers and their families is situated in a relaxing waterfront setting, about 1.5km from the town centre. The 14 units are not

DJIBOUTI

fancy but functional, and there's a good onsite restaurant (seafood!) with a terrace facing the sea. There's no beach to speak of but the owners can organise transfers to Plage des Sables Blancs.

Plage des Sables Blancs Campement (☎ 354520; Plage des Sables Blancs; full board DFr13,000) Right on the beach, this is a good place to chill out for a couple of days. Accommodation is simple (beds and mattresses only). Transfers can be organised from Djibouti City at weekends (DFr17,000 flat rate, including full board). Contact Agence Le Goubet (see p297).

There's a smattering of cheap and cheerful eateries right by the seafront.

Getting There & Away
There is a good sealed road from the capital. Regular morning buses ply the route between Djibouti City and Tadjoura (about DFr1500, three hours).

You can also take one of the *chat*-laden dhows or speedboats that leave every day sometime between noon and 2pm from Port de Pêche in Djibouti City (DFr600 to DFr1000 one way).

There are plans to launch a twice-weekly passenger ferry service between Djibouti City and Tadjoura; check while in Djibouti City.

OBOCK & LES SEPT FRÈRES ARCHIPELAGO
The last significant town before the border with Eritrea, Obock exudes a kind of 'last frontier' feel, light years away from the hullabaloo of Djibouti City. With the completion of the sealed road from Tadjoura in 2008, tourism is slowly, slowly taking off in this area.

It has a couple of sights, including **Ras Bir lighthouse**, about 6km east of the centre, and the eerily quiet **Cimetière Marin** (Marine Cemetery), on the western outskirts of town.

You can lay your head at the welcoming **Village Mer Rouge** (☎ 810799, 862812, 357444; d DFr8000-10,000; 🖭), about 2km west of the centre. Choose between the six rustically cosy bungalows on the beach, the 'hill bungalows' (with air-con, but no views) or the stylish 'luxury bungalows' with all mod cons, everything sparkly clean and splendid sea views. Expect some water shortages, though. Staff are young locals that were trained in Djibouti City – a nice initiative. The on-site restaurant serves up toothsome local dishes,

including fresh seafood. Various tours in the area can be organised.

Just off the coast, at **Les Sept Frères Archipelago**, the Bab al-Mandab Strait separates two worlds, the Red Sea and the Gulf of Aden. The archipelago offers fantastic **diving** (see p292).

Getting There & Away
The road is entirely sealed from the capital. A regular morning minibus service operates between Djibouti City and Obock (about DFr2000, about 4½ hours).

You can also take one of the *chat*-laden speedboats that leave every day sometime between noon and 2pm from Port de Pêche in Djibouti City (around DFr1500 one way, about 1½ hours).

There are plans to launch a twice-weekly passenger ferry service between Djibouti City and Obock; check while in Djibouti City.

DJIBOUTI DIRECTORY

ACCOMMODATION
Djibouti's accommodation is limited. Most hotels are in the capital, with few options outside. Hotel categories are limited in range; most of them fit into the upper echelon and are expensive.

A rather popular option that is developing around the major attractions in the hinterland is the *campements touristiques*. These are traditional huts with shared showers and toilets. These low-key establishments are great places to meet locals and get an authentic cultural experience. They're family-run, which ensures your money goes straight into local pockets. They're also a good budget option, although there's no public transport to get to them.

BUSINESS HOURS
Most government offices, shops and institutions are open 7.30am to 1.30pm Sunday to Thursday. Private businesses re-open from 4pm to 6pm. Friday is the weekly day off for offices and most shops, and Saturday and Sunday are normal working days.

DANGERS & ANNOYANCES
Djibouti is a relatively safe country, and serious crime or hostility aimed specifically at travellers is very rare. However, the usual big-city precautions apply.

Djibouti's security services are known for being sensitive and active. There is no reason why travellers should attract the attention of the police, but if it happens, remain polite and calm, the enquiry is usually harmless.

EMBASSIES & CONSULATES

Djiboutian diplomatic representation abroad is scarce, but there are embassies in Ethiopia and Eritrea (see p248 and p357), as well as in France, Egypt, the USA and Yemen. In countries without representation, travellers should head for the French embassy, which acts for Djibouti in the issuing of visas.

The following is a list of nations with diplomatic representation in Djibouti City. All embassies are are closed on Fridays.

Canada (☎ /fax 355950; Pl Lagarde)

Ethiopia (☎ 350718; fax 354803; Ave F d'Esperey)

France (☎ 350963; www.ambafrance-dj.org; Ave F d'Esperey)

USA (☎ 353995; www.djibouti.usembassy.gov; Plateau du Serpent)

Yemen (☎ 352975; Plateau du Serpent)

Note that Somaliland had no representative office in Djibouti at the time of writing, but there were talks of opening one. Due to the border dispute between Eritrea and Djibouti, the Eritrean embassy was closed at the time of writing.

For details on getting visas for neighbouring countries, see p296.

HOLIDAYS

As well as major Islamic holidays listed in the Ethiopia Directory (p249), these are the principal public holidays in Djibouti:

New Year's Day 1 January

Labour Day 1 May

Independence Day 27 June

Christmas Day 25 December

MAPS

The best map is the 1:200,000 map published in 1992 by the French Institut Géographique National (IGN).

MONEY

There are several banks and a couple of authorised bureaux de change in the capital. Outside the capital, banking facilities are almost nonexistent. The euro and the US dollar are the favoured hard currencies.

> **PRACTICALITIES**
>
> ■ Djibouti uses the metric system.
>
> ■ Djibouti uses the 220V system, with two-round-pin plugs.
>
> ■ The most widely read newspaper is *La Nation* (www.lanation.dj), published weekly in French.

Djibouti City has a few Visa-friendly ATMs. At the time of research, only one ATM accepted MasterCard (see p288).

TELEPHONE

There are no area codes in Djibouti. International and local calls are best made from the post office or from one of the numerous phone shops (look for the *cabine telephonique* signs). Mobile phones are also widespread. Depending on which mobile network you use at home, your phone may or may not work while in Djibouti – ask your mobile network provider. You can also bring your phone and buy a local SIM card from **Djibouti Telecom** (off Blvd de la République, Djibouti City; ☉ 7.30am-noon Sat-Thu).

TOURIST INFORMATION

The only tourist office in the country is to be found in Djibouti City (see p288). Travel agencies are also reliable sources of travel information (see Tours p297).

Information for travellers is hard to come by outside the country. In Europe, the most knowledgeable organisation is the **Association Djibouti Espace Nomade** (ADEN; ☎ 01 48 51 71 56; aden@club-internet.fr; 64 rue des Meuniers, 93100 Montreuil-sous-Bois).

VISAS

All visitors, including French nationals, need visas. Tourist visas cost from US$30 to US$60 depending on where you apply, and are valid for one month. Visas can be obtained at the nearest Djibouti embassy (including Addis Ababa and Asmara if you're in the Horn) or, where there is none, from the French embassy. Note that travellers from most Western countries can also obtain a tourist visa on arrival at the airport; it's issued on the spot. It costs DFr5000 for three days and DFr10,000 for one month. Payment can also be made in US dollars or in euros.

DJIBOUTI

Visas for Onward Travel

For information on embassies and consulates, see p295.

Ethiopia A one-month single-entry visa cost DFr3600 (DFr12,600 for US nationals). You need to supply two photos. It takes 24 hours to process. Visas are also easily obtained at Bole International Airport in Addis Ababa. Open 8am to 1pm Sunday to Thursday and 9am to 1pm Saturday.

Yemen Visas are valid for one month and cost DFr7000. You need one photo and a copy of your passport. It takes 24 hours to process. Visas are also easily obtained at San'a international airport.

DJIBOUTI TRANSPORT

GETTING THERE & AWAY
Entering Djibouti

Djibouti has one international gateway for arrival by air, **Ambouli Airport** (☎ 341646), about 5km south of Djibouti City. There are also several land borders with neighbouring Ethiopia and Somaliland. The border with Eritrea was indefinitely closed at the time of writing.

Disembarkation at the airport is usually simple. You might be asked for an address or contact in the country; in this case, mention a hotel in Djibouti City. Crossing at land borders is relatively easy too, but be sure to have your passport stamped with an entry/exit stamp if you enter/leave the country.

PASSPORT

To enter Djibouti you must have a valid passport and a visa.

Air
AIRPORTS & AIRLINES

The only airport handling international traffic is Ambouli Airport. All airlines flying to/from Djibouti have an office or a representative in Djibouti City. They are closed on Friday.

Air France (☎ 351010; www.airfrance.com; Pl du 27 Juin 1977)

Daallo Airlines (☎ 353401; www.daallo.com; Rue de Paris)

Ethiopian Airlines (☎ 351007; www.ethiopianairlines .com) It's off Blvd Cheikh Osman.

Kenya Airways (☎ 353036; Pl Lagarde) Will probably be moving to the ATTA/Globe Travel office at some stage in the future.

Yemenia (☎ 355427; www.yemenia.com; Rue de Paris)

TICKETS
Africa & the Middle East

There are no longer any direct flights between Djibouti and Eritrea. You'll have to travel via San'a (Yemen). Yemenia has five weekly flights to San'a (from DFr30,000 one way).

Ethiopian Airlines has daily flights between Djibouti and Addis Ababa (from DFr60,000 return).

Kenya Airways operates three weekly flights between Djibouti and Nairobi (DFr80,000 return).

Daallo Airlines has four weekly flights from Djibouti to Hargeisa (Somaliland; DFr32,000 return), with connections to other cities in Somalia, as well as twice weekly flights to Dubai.

Australasia

Your best bet is to fly to Addis Ababa (Ethiopia), San'a (Yemen), Dubai (UAE), or Nairobi (Kenya), and then continue to Djibouti with Ethiopian Airlines, Yemenia, Daallo or Kenya Airways, respectively.

UK & Europe

Daallo Airlines has one to two weekly flights from London and Paris to Djibouti. Prices start at €850 return. Air France has a weekly flight from Paris (from €1200). Yemenia has two to three weekly flights from major European capitals to Djibouti via San'a (from €800).

Land
ERITREA

Travel overland to Eritrea is no longer possible. When the border was open, shared taxis (usually 4WDs) travelled from Obock to Moulhoulé (with no fixed schedule), the last town before the border. Then other taxis plied the route from Moulhoulé to Assab in Eritrea.

ETHIOPIA
Bus

There is a daily service between Djibouti City and Dire Dawa – a strenuous 10- to 12-hour ride on a gravel road. Take your first bus to the border town of Gelille, then another bus to Djibouti City; see p262.

From Djibouti City, buses leave at dawn from Ave Gamel Abdel Nasser. The company is called **SPB** (☎ 812445). Buy your ticket

(DFr2500) at least a day in advance to be sure of getting a seat.

Hitching

Hitching is never entirely safe in any country, and we don't recommend it. Still, if you want to enter Djibouti from Ethiopia via the border town of Galafi, you can hitch a lift (front seats only) with one of the legions of trucks that ply the route between Addis Ababa and Djibouti City via Awash, Gewane, Logiya and Dikhil. This option is best avoided by women.

Train

Passengers can take the old Djibouti City–Addis Ababa train as far as Dire Dawa in Ethiopia. The train leaves three times a week. From Djibouti City to Dire Dawa (via Ali Sabieh), it'll cost you DFr4200 in 1st class, minimum duration 13 hours. You're well advised to buy your ticket one day in advance at the **railway station** (Ave F d'Esperey; 7am-noon Tue, Thu & Sat).

See p262 for more information.

SOMALILAND

4WDs depart daily to Hargeisa from Ave Gamel Abdel Nasser. They usually leave around 3pm (it's wise to buy your ticket in the morning). The border crossing is at Loyaada. It costs DFr5000. Be warned: it's a taxing journey. Bring plenty of water.

Sea

It's possible to board a freight boat to Aden or Mukha (Yemen) from Djibouti port. It costs DFr8000. Inquire at **Djibouti Shipping Service** (870274; 7.30am-noon Sat-Thu) at the entrance of the port, just before the gate, to the left. Ask for 'Okar Transit'.

GETTING AROUND

The road network links all major villages in the country with the capital. The Route de l'Unité, a good sealed road, covers the 240km from the capital around the Gulf de Tadjoura, as far as Obock.

Public transport is available between Djibouti City and major towns.

Tours

Because of the lack of public transport, Djibouti is not properly geared up for DIY tourism. The only way of getting to some of the country's principal attractions is by joining an excursion. They're expensive (from DFr15,000 per person), but the price includes food and accommodation. Try to be part of an existing group – the more people, the less you pay. Your chances of joining an existing tour group are decidedly greater at weekends.

Agence Le Goubet (354520; valerie@riesgroup.dj; Blvd Cheikh Osman) Can organise trips to Plage des Sables Blancs and make bookings in the *campements touristiques*. Also sells flight tickets. Ask for Valerie, who can get by in English.

ATTA/Globe Travel (353036, 250297; atta@intnet. dj; off Pl du 27 Juin 1977) A long-standing operator, with good credentials. Can organise tours. Also sells flight tickets.

Dolphin Excursions (350313, 812300; www.dolphin -excursions.com; Blvd de la République) Run by Bruno Pardigon, this well-established operator can organise all kinds of tours throughout the country, on land and at sea, including multi-day guided treks, excursions to Lac Abbé and Lac Assal, as well as live-aboard dive boats to Les Sept Frères Archipelago. Bruno speaks good English.

Ermano (830804; ermanofr@yahoo.fr) Friendly Ermano is a university teacher and tour guide who knows everything about the Afar culture. He can organise all kinds of cultural and hiking trips.

DJIBOUTI

Eritrea

PATRICK SYDER

Eritrea

Let's start with the bad news. In just 10 years, Eritrea has gone from being a success story and a model state for the whole of Africa – egalitarian, well governed, promising, optimistic – to being one of the most isolated nations in the world. The once progressive government has slipped to become a repressive regime. The economy is in a shambles and Eritreans are doing it tough.

Now let's move onto the brighter side. Being locked in a time capsule and almost completely unexploited by commercial tourism, Eritrea offers excitement and challenges for travellers who have a hankering for secretive places. Though some parts of the country are out of bounds (especially Dankalia and Western Eritrea), the sense of discovery is overwhelming. Southern Eritrea combines quintessentially Abyssinian landscapes – escarpments, plateaus and soaring peaks – with an array of archaeological sites. Heading north, the market town of Keren offers a fascinating glimpse into Eritrea's diverse cultural fabric. On the Red Sea coast, Massawa, a Zanzibar-esque town redolent with Islamic influence, is the starting point for trips to the Dahlak Islands, a bijou archipelago with peroxide-blonde beaches and thriving reefs that offer pristine diving conditions.

The cherry on top is Asmara, Eritrea's utterly adorable capital and a whimsical art deco city. Who knows it boasts the most dazzling collection of colonial architectural wonders in Africa? And the frothiest *macchiatos* this side of the Colosseum?

Here's the paradox: despite the tough political and economic landscape and the odd travel restriction, Eritrea remains one of the most inspiring destinations in the Horn, with a unique blend of Abyssinian, Arabic and Mediterranean influences – which makes it all the more tempting to peek into.

HIGHLIGHTS

- Discover **Asmara**'s (p320) fantastic Italian colonial architecture and its lively cafe culture

- Soak up the languid atmosphere of multi-ethnic **Keren** (p333), Eritrea's beguiling second city

- Hike up to the church of **Tsada Amba** (p336) and confess your sins while gazing in awe at the fabulous panorama

- Dream of a vanished civilisation at **Qohaito** (p337), whose ruins include an Egyptian tomb and beautifully preserved rock paintings

- Meander among **Massawa**'s (p345) crumbling old houses and cap off the day with grilled fish at **Sallam Restaurant** (p347)

- Sunbathe on the sparkling beaches of **Madote Island** (p349), camp on **Dissei Island** (p349) and dive at the Camels in the **Dahlak Archipelago** (p349)

- Hop on Africa's most atmospheric **train** (p331), and be ready for the most scenic ride of your life.

ERITREA

SNAPSHOT ERITREA

Today Eritrea is not exactly a wonderland. While foreigners can expect to enjoy themselves in Eritrea, the picture is much less rosy for Eritreans. The state has taken control of all private companies, and the country has one of the most restrictive economies on the planet. Food shortages, skyrocketing prices and rationing of staples are the order of the day. In 2003, 1kg of meat cost Nfa20, 1kg of sugar was Nfa5, and they were readily available. Today they cost Nfa120 and Nfa150 (a quarter of the average monthly salary!) respectively and Eritreans have to wait in queues at state-run stores to get their monthly rations or buy them on the black market.

Freedom of speech is a thing of the past. According to the US-based Committee to Protect Journalists, Eritrea is one of the world's leading jailers of journalists. In the name of 'protecting national security', a number of journalists and domestic dissenters have 'disappeared' or are kept incommunicando. What's more, the government is turning its country into a 'giant prison', according to a report released by Human Rights Watch. Men under 52 years of age and women under 47 are not allowed to travel out of the country. In theory, anyone under 50 has to serve 18 months national service. In practice, most young Eritreans have been serving for years, with no hope of ever getting out. Incidentally, the army is also used as cheap labour for construction works. 'I'm proud of being Eritrean, and I'm ready to fight for my country', says an Eritrean woman in Asmara, 'but this government is stealing my youth, I don't see an end to my national service; I have no hope, no future, no job. I love my country but I want to go abroad because of the blocked situation', she deplores. For young Eritreans, the only way to escape indefinite military conscription is to attempt to flee the country, either via Djibouti, Ethiopia or more commonly Sudan, and then to try to get to Europe – a very risky journey.

Today, reaching a final peace agreement with Ethiopia is a pressing issue but both President Isaias Afewerki and his Ethiopian counterpart Meles Zenawi are unable (or unwilling) to seal an agreement, which partly explains the persistence of the senseless border conflict. Eritreans want peace and are weary of this never-ending feud with Ethiopia (not to mention the more recent border dispute with Djibouti) but, according to Human Rights Watch, the government uses the unresolved border dispute to keep the country on permanent war-footing.

A compounding issue is the attitude of the regime towards foreign institutions. Every outside influence is viewed with growing suspicion. Most western NGOs have had to leave the country over the last few years. No wonder that the sense of isolation is mounting.

The end result? Eritrea has won the less-than-enviable sobriquet of 'the North Korea of Africa'.

Despite these harsh realities and the clampdown on civil liberties, Eritreans show an exceptional resilience and have not entirely lost hope in the future of their country. They wait for better times and an unexpected change at the head of the state.

HISTORY

In the Beginning

Eritrea's earliest inhabitants are thought to have been related to the Pygmies of Central Africa. Later, they intermingled with Nilotic, Hamitic and finally Semitic peoples migrating from across Africa and Arabia. By around 2000 BC, close contacts had been established with the people of the Nubian lowlands to the west and those from the Tihama coast of southern Arabia to the east. Some ruins in Eritrea are thought to date from the pre-Aksumite Civilisation.

Aksumite Civilisation

Around the 4th century BC, the powerful kingdom of Aksum began to develop. Situated in Tigray, in the north of modern Ethiopia (around 50km from present-day Eritrea), Aksum lay just 170km from the Red Sea. Much foreign trade – on which Aksum's prosperity depended – was seaborne, and came to be handled by the ancient port of Adulis in Eritrea.

On the way to Adulis (a 12- to 15-day journey from Aksum) many exports, including rhinoceros horn, gold, hippopotamus hide, slaves, apes and particularly ivory, passed through Eritrean towns, including Koloe (thought to be present-day Qohaito in the south). Some of the goods exported were Eritrean in origin, including obsidian, a black volcanic rock.

ERITREA

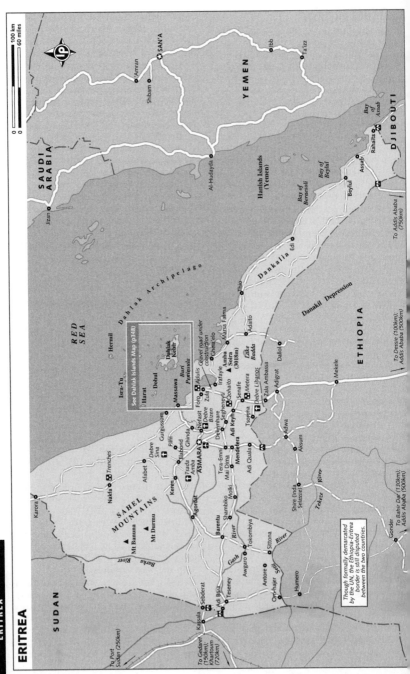

ERITREA

Arrival of Christianity

According to the Byzantine ecclesiastical historian Rufinus, Christianity was brought to the region by accident when Christian Syrian merchants travelling home from India were shipwrecked on the Red Sea coast. Whatever its origin, by the 4th century AD, Christianity had become the Aksumite state religion. The new religion had a profound impact on Eritrea's culture, influencing much of the country's art and literature.

The Rise of Islam & the Decline of Aksum

Islam, the arrival of which coincided with Christian Aksum's decline in the 7th century, was the other great influence on the region. Though not directly responsible for the empire's collapse, the expansion of the religion was concomitant with the increasing power of the Arabs, who fast became the new masters of the Red Sea. Aksum's commercial domination of the region was over.

Islam made the greatest inroads in the Dahlak Islands. Muslims traders also settled in nearby Massawa on the mainland.

Aksumite authority had long been challenged by other forces too, with incursions, attacks, rebellions and even mass migration by neighbouring tribes, particularly the Beja tribe, a Cushitic people originating from present-day Sudan.

After the settlement of the Beja in the interior of the country, and the Arabs on the coast, the Ethiopians were unable to recover the influence the Aksumites had held over the region for another thousand years.

The Turkish & Egyptian Imprints

The Turks first arrived in the Red Sea at the beginning of the 16th century. For the next 300 years (with a few short-lived intervals) the coast, including the port of Massawa, belonged to the Ottomans.

By the middle of the 19th century, new powers were casting covetous eyes over the region. The Egyptians, under Ali Pasha (Mohammed Ali), invaded modern-day Sudan and occupied parts of Ethiopia. Soon after, the western lowlands of modern-day Eritrea were also taken, including the port of Massawa.

Under threat, the Ethiopian emperor, Yohannes, eventually forced a battle. In 1875 at Ghundet, near Adi Quala in modern-day southern Eritrea, and later at Gura, near Dekemhare, Yohannes inflicted resounding defeats on the Egyptian armies.

The power vacuum left by the departing Egyptians was soon to be filled by yet another meddling foreign power – Italy.

The Italians Step In

During the partition of the continent by the competing European powers in the second half of the 19th century, France grabbed Djibouti (which then became known as French Somaliland) and Britain snatched Aden in Yemen, as well as a stretch of Somali coastline. Italy wasn't going to miss out on a piece of the pie. Italian colonisation started in 1869 near Assab. In 1885 the Italians occupied Massawa.

Alarmed by further expansion and the threat it posed to his kingdom, Yohannes challenged the Italians, but was killed in battle with the Mahadists (Sudanese) in 1889.

FAST FACTS

- **Population** 5.7 million (estimated)
- **Area** 124,320 sq km
- **GDP per capita** US$240
- **Average life expectancy** 51 years (men), 55 years (women)
- **Number of Eritreans in refugee camps in Sudan** 200,000 (estimated)
- **Number of Eritreans in uniform** (male and female) 300,000
- **Fine if you're caught changing money on the black market** Nfa2,000,000
- **Number of journalists detained without charge** 18
- **Average monthly income of a hotel receptionist** US$40-50
- **Number of newspapers** 1

ERITREA

As the struggle against the Mahadists pre-occupied the Ethiopians, the Italians were left to get on with the realisation of their military ambitions.

Relations were at first good with the new Ethiopian emperor, Menelik, and in 1889 the Treaty of Wechale was signed. In exchange for granting Italy the region that was to later become Eritrea, the Italians recognised Menelik's sovereignty and gave him the right to import arms freely though Ethiopia. However, relations began to sour a few years later.

Towards the end of 1889 the Italians turned their attention to the south. In 1890, they took Adwa and Mekele in Ethiopian territory, as well as Aksum and Adigrat a few years later.

Following the Battle of Adwa in 1896, when the Ethiopians resoundingly defeated the Italian armies (for more details, see p144), new international boundaries were drawn up: Ethiopia remained independent and Eritrea became, for the first time, a separate territory – and an Italian colony.

Italian Rule

Of all Italy's colonies (Eritrea, Libya and Italian Somaliland), Eritrea was considered the jewel in the crown. Apart from providing a strategic base for imperial ambitions (particularly against Ethiopia), it boasted vital access to the Red Sea, as well as potential for mineral and agricultural exploitation. For this reason, much effort was put into industrialising the little country, and major schemes began to be developed, including the building of the great railway between Massawa and Asmara in 1909 (which was later extended to Keren) and the construction of a national network of roads.

By the end of the 1930s, Eritrea was one of the most highly industrialised colonies in Africa. By 1930 Massawa had become the largest port on the East African coast.

The Italians initially governed Eritrea indirectly through local chieftains. Later, a series of provinces was created, administered by a large body of Italian civil servants, headed by a governor.

British Takeover

In May 1936 Italy avenged itself for the defeat at Adwa and triumphed over the Ethiopians. In 1940, with the outbreak of WWII, Italy declared war on Britain, and soon became embroiled in conflicts in what was then Anglo-Egyptian Sudan. Though initially successful, Italian campaigns in this area were soon repulsed by reinforced British armies.

Soon British forces were giving chase to the Italians, pursuing them into Eritrea, and capturing Agordat. The year 1941 marked a turning point: the British took the strategically important town of Keren before defeating the Italians in Asmara. The colony became an administration of the British.

The British attempted to maintain the status quo in the territory largely due to practical constraints. They left in place the old Italian administration, but the colony inevitably sank into a state of demoralisation and decline. When the course of WWII changed, the territory lost its strategic importance and in 1945 the British began a slow withdrawal.

By 1946 the country was in trouble. The economy was floundering, unemployment was soaring, and unrest was brewing.

Arranged Marriage with Ethiopia

In 1948 Eritrea's fate was pondered by a commission consisting of the UK, the USA, France and the Soviet Union. Unable to reach a decision, the commission passed the issue on to the UN's General Assembly.

ITALIAN APARTHEID

From 1922 to 1941 a system of discrimination existed in Eritrea and Ethiopia that was remarkably similar to the apartheid system of South Africa.

Local and Italian children were educated at different schools; non-Italian adults were prevented from learning basic skills or professions; on buses and in cinemas, Italian passengers sat in the front, whereas locals were obliged to sit at the back; marriage between Italians and locals was forbidden by law, with a punishment of up to five years in prison for offenders.

Thousands of locals were evicted from their houses and resettled in reservations far from where the Italians lived. The best agricultural land was seized, rent for town houses was often not paid and there were continual abuses of law.

In 1947 a commission of inquiry found the population divided into three main factions: pro-Ethiopian Unionists (mainly Christian), anti-Unionists (mainly Muslims in favour of a Muslim League) and members of a Pro-Italia party (many of them Italian pensioners). The commissioners, whose findings reflected the political interests of their respective governments, produced totally different conclusions and recommendations.

In 1950 the very contentious Resolution 390 A (V) was passed. Eritrea became Ethiopia's 14th province and disappeared from the map of Africa.

Unmatched Couple

This 'shotgun wedding', as it has been described, between Eritrea and Ethiopia was never a happy one. Little by little, Ethiopia began to exert an ever-tighter hold over Eritrea, as both industry and political control were shifted to Ethiopia's capital, Addis Ababa. The Eritrean economy stagnated and the province's autonomy dwindled. Eritrean politicians and leaders were soon ousted, Ethiopian Amharic replaced Tigrinya as the official language in schools, and protests against the regime were suppressed with brutality.

The repeated appeals by the Eritrean people to the UN fell on deaf ears. With the start of the Cold War in the 1950s, the Americans had set their sights on establishing a communications centre in Asmara. When, in the early 1960s, Ethiopia formally annexed Eritrea in violation of international law, Cold War politics ensured that both the USA and the UN kept silent.

With no recourse to the international community, the frustration of the Eritrean people grew. In 1961, in the little town of Amba Adal in the western lowlands, a small group of men led by Hamid Idriss Awate assailed one of the much-resented Ethiopian police stations and stole some pistols. The fight for independence had begun.

Time for Divorce

The first resistance movements on the scene included the ELM (Eritrean Liberation Movement), the (Christian) People's Liberation Front (PLF), and the (Muslim) Eritrean Liberation Front (ELF). From the latter two, a splinter group emerged, the Eritrean People's Liberation Front (EPLF),

which called for social revolution as well as national independence. It was only after periods of bloody civil war and the defeat of the ELF in 1981, that the EPLF emerged as the leader of unified forces.

Nevertheless, the resistance continued to make progress, and in 1978 the Eritreans were on the brink of winning back their country. However, just on the point of victory, yet another foreign power decided to intervene.

In 1974 Colonel Mengistu Haile Mariam, a communist ruler, had come to power in Ethiopia. Three years later the Soviet Union began to arm his troops. In the face of massive aerial bombardment and an army bristling with modern weaponry, the EPLF was obliged to retreat. The famous Strategic Withdrawal, as it is known, later proved to be crucial to the movement's survival.

Eight major offensives were carried out against the Eritrean fighters from 1978 to 1986, all of which were repulsed. From 1988 the EPLF began to inflict major losses on the Ethiopian army, capturing first its northern headquarters in Afabet, then the large highland town of Keren. In 1990, amid some of the fiercest fighting of the war, the EPLF took the strategically important port of Massawa.

By this time, however, Mengistu's regime was threatened from within, and civil war had broken out in Ethiopia. In 1991 Mengistu was overthrown and fled to Zimbabwe. His 140,000 Ethiopian troops laid down their weapons and ran. The EPLF walked into Asmara without having to fire a single bullet.

Freedom, at Last!

In April 1993 the Provisional Government of Eritrea held a referendum on Eritrean independence. More than 99.81% of voters opted for full Eritrean sovereignty, and on 24 May 1993 independence was declared. Eritrea was back on the African map.

In early 1994 the EPLF dissolved itself and re-formed as the People's Front for Democracy and Justice (PFDJ) under the chairmanship of the head of state, President Isaias Afewerki. Some members of the old ELF were also invited to join the team.

After the war, the little nation worked hard to rebuild its infrastructure, repair the economy and improve conditions for its people. Wide-ranging laws, policies and constitutional rights were drawn up, from protection of the environment and positive discrimination

ERITREA

MAIMING MINES

During the Struggle, two million land mines were laid, which works out at almost one for every Eritrean inhabitant. However, the guerrillas quickly learnt to turn the deadly weapons against those who had laid them. Replanted up to 10 or 12 times, the mines accounted for 30% of all Eritrean People's Liberation Front (EPLF) victories.

Since independence, the government has tried hard to rid the land of mines, but thousands still remain.

towards people with disabilities at work, to the rights of women and the fight against AIDS. Eritrea was also at pains to establish good international relations with, among others, Ethiopia, the Gulf States, Asia, the USA and Europe.

However, this progress was seriously undermined in 1998, when war broke out with Ethiopia (see p47 for details).

Eritrea Today

The current situation can be summed up as 'neither peace nor war' or 'a country frozen in time'. The psychological war between Eritrea and its arch enemy Ethiopia is ongoing, and the border dispute rumbles on. Late in 2005, the two countries were on the brink of war – again. Early in 2008, the UN began pulling its peacekeeping force (UNMEE) out of the country due to lack of fuel supplies, following restrictions imposed by the Eritrean government. In May 2008, the UN peacekeeping mission had withdrawn completely from Eritrea (some observers say the Eritrean authorities forced it to leave), and there was no solution in sight to reach terms on the border issue. Ethiopian troops still occupy the border town of Badme, which was 'awarded' to Eritrea by the UN Boundary Commission.

As if this wasn't enough, Eritrea clashed with Djibouti, its southern neighbour, in June 2008. The case in point? Another border dispute. Fighting broke out between Djiboutian and Eritrean troops in the Ras Doumeira border area. Who started hostilities? Both countries reject charges of having instigated the aggression, but there are strong suspicions that the Eritreans launched the attack first. Several Djiboutian soldiers were killed. The UN Security Council passed a resolution in January 2009 urging the two countries to step back from an escalation of conflict and re-establish dialogue.

Moreover, Eritrea is also accused of aiding the Islamic Court forces that took power in Somalia in 2009 after defeating the Ethiopian-backed Somalia Transitional Federal Government.

Eritrea's mounting isolation is increasingly problematic. While the intransigent Eritrean government has lost the support of the international community, it is growing

A LONG, LONG WAR

The Struggle, as resistance to Ethiopian rule became popularly known, was a major event in the history of the Horn. Lasting for 30 years, it shaped – physically and psychologically – the Eritrean nation and its people. For the first time, a real sense of national identity was forged.

But the price of Eritrea's freedom was high. The war wrecked the country's infrastructure and economy, cost 65,000 lives and drove at least a third of the population into exile. It was not a story of vast armies, brilliant leadership and sweeping conquests. For three decades, a tiny guerrilla force (which numbered at most 40,000 during its last days) was able to thwart the might of a country 10 times its size, which was backed by two superpowers and had all the modern weaponry of the 20th century.

Initially a ragbag bandit force, the resistance fighters operated in tightly organised cells, taught their soldiers history, philosophy, political economy and to read and write, as well as guerrilla tactics. Equality of all people was advocated; soldiers had to respect the gender (many soldiers were women), ethnic group, religion and race of their fellow fighters.

In response to the devastating blanket bombing inflicted by the Ethiopians, whole villages were constructed underground, with schools, hospitals, factories, printing presses, mills, pharmacies, workshops and entertainment halls. The remains of these 'towns' can be seen today in the village of Nakfa (p335) in the north of Eritrea.

ERITREA

FIGHTER'S SALUTE

Shoulder contact is used for greeting in Eritrea. When two male friends meet, they clasp hands, then lean towards one another and hit each other's right shoulders, usually three times. This sign of great comradeship is called the 'fighter's salute'. As a foreigner, you're not supposed to try this type of greeting – it's pretty hard to imitate, and you would probably look awkward!

---

notoriously dictatorial under the rule of its president Isaias Afewerki. Civil liberties have been curbed, freedom of press and speech is nonexistent and any foreigner suspected of criticising the regime runs the risk of being expelled.

The economy is in tatters, with food and oil shortages, and many young Eritreans try to flee abroad. Mass conscription has deprived many industries of manpower and there is no longer a private sector. Foreign investments are almost nonexistent. Remittances from diaspora Eritreans are virtually the only source of income.

THE CULTURE
The National Psyche
Eritreans remains something of an enigma to most Westerners. All things considered, the lack of tangible international image and stereotypes about Eritrea and its people is a chance rather than a drawback.

Eritreans are different in temperament from their neighbours (which partly explains the bitter relations between the two countries). 'Rather die than surrender', could be their motto. Years of invasion have created a siege mentality and a sense of isolation. A deep-seated desire to protect the integrity of their nation, founded understandably by historic circumstances, has led to an attitude of self-preservation and, one would say, mulishness. Eritreans have a fierce pride in their own history, and their decades of struggle against the Ethiopians. Though impoverished, the nation has from the outset shown self-reliance, vigour and independence. Eritreans are not about to become anyone's vassal and this stoic attitude has elicited both passionate admiration and furious exasperation from visitors, aid workers and international organisations alike. Their ability to endure hardships without moaning is notorious. Tradition and a deep-rooted attachment to the land play an integral part in the national psyche too.

You'll soon realise that Eritreans are a withdrawn people who have to be coaxed into friendship, but if you succeed you'll discover a steely strength hidden beneath their stoic facade. Initially indifferent to strangers (at least by comparison with other African nations), Eritreans may appear somewhat taciturn at first meeting, but once the ice has broken you will find intense friendships. This guarded nature is hardly surprising, however, considering the country's history of oppression. This does not mean that they are standoffish or cold. Towards the traveller, Eritreans show exceptional politeness and hospitality.

Lifestyle
The contrast in lifestyle between Asmara and elsewhere is stark. Asmara is a city with allure, where people take the art of living seriously no matter the state of the economy. Asmarans are notorious *bon vivants* and take the dolce vita very seriously – a legacy of the Italian era. Nobody would miss the daily ritual of a cup of *macchiato* at a pavement terrace during the evening *passeggiata*. Then there is the rest of Eritrea: a monochrome mix of provincial town and rural landscape, where poverty is about the only prevalent excess.

Sadly, both the economic turmoil and the hard line followed by the Eritrean government have severely impacted lifestyles and standards of living. Scratch the surface and you'll soon realise how hard Eritreans are hit by the economic crisis and lack of freedom. Life's a struggle for many households, with the cost of commodities having skyrocketed over the last few years. Eating out and holidays have been curtailed radically, and waiting queues in front of state-controlled stores are now a common sight in Asmara. Food rationing has become a fact of life. A certain weariness can be felt. Diaspora Eritreans who returned to the country and have invested in the country are in a bit less of a predicament – they understandably enjoy a better quality of life.

In a country where most people have lost faith in their government, the family remains one pillar of society on which Eritreans continue to depend. Family ties remain fiercely strong. Religious occasions and public holidays are vigorously celebrated, as are more personal, family events, such as weddings.

Population

The Eritrean people are a highlight of the country. The population is estimated to be 5.7 million. Eritrea might be a tiddler of a country by Africa's standards, but it hosts a kaleidoscopic range of tribes. Cultural diversity forms an integral part of the social fabric. There are nine ethnic groups, each with their own language and customs, as well as a handful of Italians who live in Asmara.

Approximately 35% of the population are nomadic or seminomadic. About one million Eritreans live abroad, mostly in Europe and the USA.

TIGRINYA ትግርኛ

The Tigrinya make up approximately 50% of the Eritrean population and inhabit the densely populated central highlands, extending over the provinces of Dubub, Central and the area of Adi Keyh. They are largely Orthodox Christian, with just a small minority of Muslims who are known as Jiberti. The very distinct plaited hairstyle of the women has for centuries been depicted in local art.

Their language, Tigrinya, is one of the country's official languages.

TIGRÉ ትግርኛ

The Tigré make up about 30% of the population, and inhabit the northern lowlands, from the Sudanese frontier to the western limits of the Danakil.

A heterogeneous people, the Tigré are divided into groups and clans. Most Tigreans are Muslim, and they are both sedentary and nomadic.

Tigrean society is traditionally hierarchical, with a small aristocracy known as *shemagille* ruling the masses. When the village leader dies, his power passes to his offspring.

Tigrean oral literature is rich. Fables, riddles, poetry, funeral dirges, war cries and supernatural stories colour the different elements of Tigrean life. The Tigré are also known for their love of singing and dancing, usually to the accompaniment of a drum and a guitar.

SAHO ሳሆ

The Saho make up 5% of the population. They inhabit the coast and the hinterland south of Asmara and Massawa. Towards the end of April, when the rains stop in the lowlands, many Saho leave the coastal area and trek with their livestock up to the highlands near Adi Keyh. When the rains stop in September, they return for the wet season on the coastal lowlands.

The Saho people are predominantly Muslim, and feelings of ethnic identity are less strong among them than other groups. Known as great pastoralists, they fought for centuries with the highlanders over the pastures of the mountains. Today they often tend other people's cattle, including those of the Tigrinya, in exchange for grain. Many Saho children (up to the age of 16) wear little leather pouches around their neck, which are full of herbs and spices to ward off evil spirits.

Some Saho are farmers who have settled in the highlands south of the country. Honey is an important part of the Saho diet and they are known as good beekeepers. In the past they were also reputed warriors, and were often enlisted to escort trade caravans between central Ethiopia and the port of Massawa.

AFAR አፋር

The Eritrean Afars, also known as the Danakils, make up 5% of the population and inhabit the long coastal strip stretching from the Gulf of Zula into Djibouti. Predominantly nomadic pastoralists, the Afar people are Muslim, though elements of ancient ancestor-worship still persist.

Since early times the Afar territory has been divided into kingdoms and ruled by individual sultans who have always remained fiercely independent of any foreign power.

The sole inhabitants of one of the most inhospitable regions on Earth, the Afars have acquired a fearsome reputation among Western travellers and explorers during the last 100 years.

The men still carry the famous *jile* (curved knife), and some file their teeth to points. Afar oral literature reveals a high esteem for military prowess, with a whole repertoire of war chants. See also the boxed text, p214.

HEDAREB ሃዳረብ

The Hedareb, along with their 'brother' tribes the Beni Amer and Beja, make up 2.5% of the population, and inhabit the northwestern valleys of Eritrea, straddling the border with Sudan.

ERITREA

Most Hedarebs are nomadic and travel great distances in search of pasture. They are Cushitic in origin (probably directly descended from the ancient Beja tribe) and speak mainly Tigré and an ancient Beja language (though this is in decline, as it is replaced by more dominant languages).

The Beni Amer are a strongly patriarchal, socially stratified, almost feudal people. Their skills as camel drivers and rearers are legendary. Many of the men scarify their cheeks with three short, vertical strokes – the Italians called them the '111 tribe'.

BILEN ብሌን

The Bilen inhabit the environs of Keren and make up approximately 2% of the population. Cushitic in origin, the Bilen are either settled Christian farmers or Muslim cattle rearers.

Bilen traditional society is organised into kinship groups. The women are known for their brightly coloured clothes and their gold, silver or copper nose rings which indicate their means and social status. Like the Beja language, Bilen is slowly being replaced by Tigré, Tigrinya and Arabic, due to intermarriage, economic interactions and because Arabic is taught in local schools. Henna tattoos that mimic diamond necklaces or little freckles are fashionable among the women.

KUNAMA ኩናማ

The Kunama inhabit the Gash Barka province in the southwestern corner of Eritrea, close to the Ethiopian and Sudanese border, and make up 2% of the population. Barentu is their 'capital'. The Kunama are Nilotic in origin, and very dark skinned. They are the original inhabitants of the region.

A few Kunama are Muslim, some are Christian, but the great majority are animist. According to their beliefs, the higher divinity, Anna, created the sky and the earth but is largely indifferent to human fate. The spirits, by contrast, must be placated before every event, even ploughing a field.

The Kunanma only recognise the authority of the elders and the village assemblies. The community is closely knit, and many educated Kunama abandon the city to return to their traditional home.

The Kunama are known for their dances, and have developed more than 25 dance forms, often re-enacting great historical events or victories.

NARA ናራ

The Nara, also known as the Baria, make up about 1.5% of the population and inhabit the Barka Valley near the Sudanese border. Along with the Kunama, they are the only Nilotic Eritrean tribe, and are mainly Muslim. They have three characteristic vertical scarifications on the cheeks, similar to those of the Hedareb.

The Nara practice mixed farming and share many customs with their neighbours, the Kunama.

RASHAIDA ራሻኢዳ

The Rashaida are the only true Eritrean nomads. Making up just 0.5% of the population, they roam the northern coasts of Eritrea and Sudan, as well as the southern reaches of the Nubian desert. Like their neighbours, the Beja (related to the Hedareb), they live by raising cattle and are Muslim.

The Rashaida were the last of the Semitic people to arrive in Eritrea in the middle of the 19th century. Their language is Arabic.

The magnificent Rashaida women are famous for their black-and-red geometrically patterned dresses, and their *burkas* (long, heavy veils) elaborately embroidered with silver thread, beads and sometimes seed pearls.

The Rashaida are known for their great pride; marriage is only permitted within their own clan. They are expert goat and cattle rearers, as well as merchants and traders along the Red Sea coasts.

Sport

Cycle races take place in many of the larger towns. Streets are cordoned off, and everyone comes to watch. The most popular cycling event is the annual Giro d'Eritrea, a 10-day race across the country. It is held in February or March.

By far the most popular spectator sport in Eritrea is football (soccer). Local TV even broadcasts Champions' League games. Basketball and volleyball are also followed with some reverence.

Multiculturalism

With nine ethnic groups and languages as well as several religions, Eritrea is a model of cultural diversity. Since the beginning of time,

Eritrea has attracted migrants, merchants and meddlesome foreign powers. Today these influences are reflected in the country's diverse ethnic population. During the war, religious, ethnic and gender differences were set aside in favour of unity against the Ethiopians. In Asmara, the Great Mosque, the Orthodox church, the Catholic cathedral and the synagogue stand placidly in the same precinct. Intermarriage is common and there's no racial ghetto. The government ensures that each ethnic group has a voice in the decision-making process. There's no immigration as such but diaspora Eritreans bring a refreshing influx of outside influence.

Media

Eritrea has a disastrous record regarding freedom of press; since 2008, it has ranked bottom in the Worldwide Press Freedom Index, replacing North Korea – this says it all. All privately owned news sources were abolished in 2001 and the government has been battling the press for years, jailing free-speaking journalists without charge, on the grounds that they 'harm national security'. More than 18 independent journalists have 'disappeared' these last years, and at least four have died in jail. The state-run *Haddas Eritrea* is the only newspaper in the country, often featuring headlines bellowing how the country is following the right path and how perverse the Ethiopian leaders are.

Surprisingly, there's no ban on satellite TV. The few Eritreans who can afford a satellite dish can tune in to the BBC, CNN or Euronews to get a different view of news and reality.

WILES & WAYS

For weddings, religious festivals and special occasions, Tigré and Tigrinya women love to get their hair done. The mass of tiny plaits go right up to the scalp, and can take a whole morning to prepare.

Married women can additionally have the palms of their hands and their feet tattooed with curvilinear patterns of henna. Fashionable teenagers prefer to have their gums tattooed. Pricked until they bleed, the gums are rubbed with charcoal. The resulting blue colour sets off a dazzling set of teeth, and is considered a mark of great beauty.

Religion

The population of Eritrea is almost equally divided between Christians and Muslims. Christians are primarily Orthodox; the Eritrean Orthodox church has its roots in the Ethiopian one (see p55). There are also small numbers of Roman Catholics and Protestants, as a result of missionary activity. The Muslims are primarily Sunnis, with a Sufi minority.

Roughly speaking, the agriculturalist Orthodox Christians inhabit the highland region and the Muslims are concentrated in the lowlands, the coastal areas and towards the Sudanese border. Some animists inhabit the southwestern lowlands.

There are at least 18 monasteries in Eritrea. Following the raids of the famous 16th-century Muslim leader, Ahmed Gragn the Left-Handed, almost all of them were safely tucked away in very remote and inaccessible places. Three of the oldest and most important are Debre Bizen (near Nefasit), Debre Libanos (near Senafe) and Debre Sina (near Keren).

Women in Eritrea

It is true that many Eritrean women enjoy a greater degree of equality in Eritrea than women in most other African countries. This refreshingly liberal attitude has been won by Eritrea's women themselves, who themselves contributed more than one-third of troops in both the recent wars against Ethiopia. In Asmara, they can be seen wearing the latest fashion clothes. However, Eritrea remains a deeply conservative country and the 'double liberation' (for their country and for their gender) expected after independence has not been as forthcoming as some had hoped. In rural areas, prejudices remain deeply rooted.

In the towns, several active, well-organised women's groups have sprung up in the last few years.

The status of women is something to behold. Eritrean women have guaranteed representation in parliament. They enjoy their own national holiday, equal property rights and the right to divorce, and also have equal rights to the custody of their children in any settlement. Eritrean women have attitude. In Asmara, women who were soldiers during the war can be seen wearing old jeans and T-shirts.

ERITREA

ASMARA'S EMERGING CONTEMPORARY ART SCENE

In a country so cut off from the outside world, it's refreshing to see that there's a growing artistic consciousness in Eritrea, and that Asmara has a small but dynamic contemporary plastic arts scene. Some talented painters and plastic artists include Abraham Hailemichael, Binyam Tekle and Mibrak Ghirmatsion. From the figurative to the symbolic, their respective styles, techniques and palettes differ, despite the lack of a Fine Arts school in Asmara and the absence of outside influences. It should be noted, however, that no political innuendo against the regime is to be found in their work.

The Alliance Française in Asmara (p318) sponsors some painters and promotes their work. In 2005, it published *Ten Contemporary Eritrean Artists* (you may get hold of a copy at the Alliance Française), a catalogue that presents the works of the most representative Eritrean artists.

Their canvasses are sometimes exhibited in the Alliance Française, Casa degli Italiani and various hotels in the capital, as well as in the **Gallery** (Map p317; ☎ 07199670; Sematat Ave; ⏰ 10am-12.30pm & 3-8pm Mon-Sat), Asmara's sole gallery, which has a good assortment of paintings (and a few carvings) on sale – the best place for an original souvenir.

Arts

DANCE

Dance plays a very important social role in Eritrea. It marks the major events of life, such as births and marriages, and is used in celebrating special occasions and religious festivals. Dances traditionally permitted young girls and boys to meet, and warriors to show off their prowess.

The dances of the Kunama and Hedareb are particularly exuberant.

MUSIC

Traditional musical instruments of Eritrea have their roots in Ethiopia. They include the *krar* and *wata*, both string instruments; the *shambko*, a type of flute; and the *embilta*, a wind instrument.

Though sharing some similarities, each of the nine ethnic groups has its own distinct melodies and rhythms.

Atewebrhan Segid is considered one of the leading traditional musicians and singers in Eritrea today. The famous Eritrean singer Yemane Gebremichael, known as the 'father of the poor', died in 1997.

Unfortunately, venues offering live music with both traditional troupes and modern ensembles are sorely lacking. To hear traditional music, your best bet is to attend one of the many traditional festivals and ceremonies across the country.

Established local stars include Faytinga, Helen Meles, Samuel Berhane, Vittorio Bossi, Tesfay Mehari and Abraham Afewerki. Faytinga is the most famous singer internationally.

LITERATURE

The Italians imposed their own language and literature (and Latin alphabet) on the country, as did the British and Ethiopians.

During the Struggle for Independence from Ethiopia, writing in the vernacular was encouraged through such publications as the fighters' magazine *Mahta* (Spark) and *Fitewrari* (Avant Garde).

Today Eritrean writers are publishing and producing increasing amounts of poetry, fiction and drama (mainly in Tigrinya and Arabic). Famous novelists include Alemseged Tesfai, Solomon Drar and Bruk Habtemikael.

In recent times, the nine languages of the nine ethnic groups have adopted written scripts: six have adopted the Latin alphabet and one Arabic. The other two, Tigrinya and Tigré, have always used the Ge'ez-derived script of ancient Aksum.

ARCHITECTURE

Eritrean vernacular architecture depends on both its ethnic and geographical origin. In the cool highlands, the traditional house is the *hidmo*. Built on a rectangular plan, the house is constructed with dry-stone walls topped with a thick, earthen roof, supported both inside and out with strong wooden pillars.

In the lowlands, where warmth is less of a concern, people traditionally live in huts. Depending on the ethnic group, the hut walls are made of adobe (sun-dried brick), wood or stone, and have thatched roofs.

In Asmara and many of the larger towns, such as Keren, Massawa and Dekemhare, the

ERITREA

colonial heritage can be seen in the Italian-style buildings (see the boxed text, p323). Many of them, in Asmara and Massawa in particular, are remarkable historical and artistic pieces, but most of them are in urgent need of restoration.

PAINTING

The country's ancient Orthodox church has long provided an outlet for painting. Most church walls are painted with colourful and dramatic murals. Canvas and parchment manuscripts, some several hundred years old, are illustrated with delightful and sometimes very beautiful biblical scenes.

FOOD & DRINK

Eritrea is not exactly the gastronomic capital of Africa but it's certainly better and more varied than you would expect, especially in Asmara, with a good choice of Italian and traditional Eritrean dishes. And nothing can beat a strong *macchiato* and a melt-in-your-mouth pastry at an outdoor table early morning or late afternoon.

Most types of food are reasonably priced, the only exception being imported food. A dinner for two comes to around Nfa250. People eat early in Eritrea (usually between 6.30pm and 8pm).

Staples & Specialities
ITALIAN

Along with their roads, towns and bridges, the Italians left another legacy: *macchiato*, pizza and spaghetti. Italian dishes are available in all restaurants throughout Eritrea. Outside the capital, these may be limited to just one dish: lasagne or spaghetti bolognese.

In the capital, the choice is much more extensive, with both *primi piatti* (first courses, usually pasta dishes, especially *penne, fusili,* tagliatelle) and *secondi piatti* (main dishes, usually fish or meat) on offer.

TRADITIONAL

Shiro, kitfo, zilzil, kwanta, fir fir, berbere…If you have visited Ethiopia, you'll soon realise that traditional Eritrean cuisine is almost the same as in Ethiopia; see p66 for a complete rundown of typical local dishes, ingredients and food etiquette, and a glossary of food terms. Most of the terms used are the same as in Ethiopia, except for *wat,* the fiery and ubiquitous sauce, which is known as *tsebhi*

in Tigrinya; injera (large Ethiopian version of a pancake/plate), which is sometimes called *taita* in Tigrinya; *tibs* (sliced lamb, pan fried in butter, garlic, onion and sometimes tomato), known as *tibsi* in Tigrinya; and *kai wat* (lamb, goat or beef cooked in a hot *berbere* sauce), known as *zigni* in Tigrinya.

Eritrean food can sit heavily in the stomach but is no less mouthwatering for it. If you like hot food, try the delicious *silsi,* a peppery fried tomato and onion sauce served for breakfast. Another popular breakfast dish is *ful* (based on chickpea purée), with *frittata,* omelette or scrambled egg with a bit of pepper.

Capretto often features on menus. It's roast goat, sometimes served like a rack of lamb. Another succulent choice is *gored gored* (chunks of fresh beef cooked with seasoned butter and *berbere*).

Desserts aren't a traditional part of the diet and usually consist of fruit salad or synthetic crème caramel, but you could head for a pastry shop any time of day and gobble a croissant or a piece of cake. Eritrean yogurt (served in a glass) is a much better bet. It's sometimes served with exquisite local honey.

In the western lowlands, look out for boys selling *legamat,* a deep-fried dough sold hot in newspaper cones in the early morning; it's delicious for an early breakfast.

In the far west, food is heavily influenced by the proximity of Sudan. One popular and very tasty dish is *sheia,* lamb drizzled with oil and herbs then barbecued on very hot stones until it sizzles. It's delicious. It's usually served with *ades,* a lentil dish, and a stocklike soup known as *merek.*

In Massawa, the Arabic influence is evident. Kebabs and Yemeni-style charcoal-baked fish are both widely available.

Drinks
ALCOHOLIC DRINKS

In the capital and towns, all the usual favourites are available, including whisky, gin, vodka and beer. As many are imported, they tend to be expensive.

Local varieties include Asmara gin, which is a bit rough around the edges (as you will be the morning after drinking it), but it is soon knocked back. A shot of gin (about Nfa13) is only slightly more expensive than mineral water (Nfa10).

The local beer, called Asmara Beer, is popular among both Eritreans and foreigners who are happy to guzzle it down with a pizza or a plate of tagliatelle. It's manufactured in Asmara, has a mild, quite smooth flavour and is very drinkable. It's also cheap at about Nfa15, but it's not always available. Imported beers can be found but they cost from Nfa90.

As for the red Asmara or Keren wine – it is no huge cause for celebration. Local wines are very reasonably priced in restaurants, usually between Nfa60 and Nfa90 per bottle. Imported wine starts at about Nfa200.

If you're not catching an early bus out of town the next morning, try the local *araki*, a distilled aniseed drink, a little like the Greek ouzo. *Mies* is a delicious local wine made from honey, and comes in varying degrees of sweetness (the drier it is, the more alcoholic). Don't miss it. In Dankalia, try the delicious – but very powerful – *doma* palm wine.

NONALCOHOLIC DRINKS

In Asmara and, to a lesser degree, the larger towns, innumerable little cafes and bars dot the centre. In true Italian style, frothy *macchiato*, espresso and fragrant cappuccino topped with delicate layers of foam are all served, along with a selection of pastries and cakes.

The Eritreans seem to get a fix from large amounts of sugar, which is copiously applied to all hot drinks and even fresh fruit juices. If you don't want sugar, you'll have to make that clear when you order. Ask for *beze sukkar*.

Outside the capital and in the country, sweet black tea is the most common drink. Following Islamic traditions, it is often offered as a gesture of welcome to guests. In the lowlands, cloves are often added. In the west, near the Sudanese border, coffee is sometimes spiced with ginger. If you don't want it, ask for *beze gingebel*.

The water in Asmara is considered safe to drink but, as in many places, new arrivals may experience problems with it. Various makes of bottled water (known in Tigrinya as *mai gas*) can be bought in all the towns and some villages. Local brands include Dongollo and Sabarguma (which has a lighter fizz).

Fresh fruit juices (most commonly mango, papaya, guava and banana) are sold in Asmara and some of the larger towns – they're truly delicious.

A few fizzy soft drinks, including Coke, are available, but they're expensive.

Glass bottles are recycled; save them and you can exchange them for full ones.

Where to Eat & Drink

The capital is well endowed with restaurants, bars, cafes, fast-food and pastry shops. Unlike other African countries, there are no street eats. You will also find several supermarkets, some stocked with Dubai imports. Outside the towns, local shops have a very limited selection of food products for sale and the choice of dishes on offer in the restaurants is pretty limited. In Asmara, most restaurants have their menu translated into English.

Sadly, there were some food shortages throughout the country at the time of writing, and some staples were in short supply.

Vegetarians & Vegans

Vegetarians are relatively well catered for, at least by African standards. Most restaurants have several vegetarian options, especially on Wednesday and Friday, the traditional fasting days. If you're after vegetarian food, ask for *nai tsom*, a selection of vegetable dishes similar to the Ethiopian *beyainatu*. And of course, you can always order a plate of spaghetti.

Habits & Customs

As important as the style or quality of the food is the ceremony. You won't forget your first meal, shared from a large plate with fellow diners and accompanied by injera. Tear off a piece of injera with your right hand and wrap it around the food served with it. Your host might even feed the tastiest morsel directly into your mouth – don't cringe, this is a mark of great friendship.

If you enjoyed your meal, express your satisfaction with a useful Tigrinya word that will please your host: *te-oom* (delicious).

ENVIRONMENT
The Land

With a land area of 124,320 sq km, Eritrea is about the size of England or the state of Pennsylvania in the USA. The coastline measures around 1000km and off it there are more than 350 islands.

Eritrea has three main geographical zones: the eastern escarpment and coastal plains, the central highland region, and the western lowlands.

The eastern zone consists of desert or semi-desert, with little arable land. The people inhabiting the region are generally nomadic pastoralists or fishing communities.

ERITREA

The northern end of the East African Rift Valley opens into the infamous Dankalia region in the east, one of the hottest places on Earth. This semidesert lies in a depression up to 120m below sea level, and is home to several salt lakes.

The central highland region is more fertile, and it is intensively cultivated by farming communities.

The western lowlands, lying between Keren and the Sudanese border, are watered by the Gash and Barka Rivers. Farming is practised, but less intensively than in the highlands.

Wildlife

In the past, Eritrea was home to a large range of animals, including buffaloes, cheetahs, elephants, giraffes and lions. With the loss of the forests and the decades of civil war, many of these animals have disappeared.

BIRDS

Eritrea's range of habitats is surprisingly diverse, and its birdlife is correspondingly rich. About 560 species of birds have been recorded, including the rare blue sawwing.

The isolated and uninhabited Dahlak Islands, and the rich feeding grounds that surround them, attract large numbers of nesting sea birds from all over the Red Sea (and from the Mediterranean and the Gulf). Some 109 species have been recorded on the islands, including the Arabian bustard and osprey.

Eritrea also lies within a popular migratory fly way. Hundreds of species of wintering and migratory coastal and sea birds can be seen crossing between the continents of Africa and Arabia.

On the Buri Peninsula, the ostrich and Arabian bustard are commonly seen. Sea birds include gulls, terns, boobies and, on the coastline and islands, many species of wader.

In the lush, evergreen, tropical forests in the Semenawi Bahri area northeast of Asmara, birdlife is particularly abundant. Species include the near-endemic white-cheeked turaco and the Narina trogon.

See also p76 for more information.

MAMMALS & REPTILES

Mammals commonly seen today include Abyssinian hares, African wildcats, black-backed jackals, common jackals, genets, ground squirrels, pale foxes, Soemmering's gazelles and warthogs. Primates include vervet monkeys and hamadryas baboons.

Lions, greater kudus and Tora hartebeests are said to inhabit the mountains of Gash-Barka province, north of Barentu. On the Buri Peninsula, dik-diks and dorcas gazelles can be seen. In the area between Omhajer and Antore, in the country's southwest, Eritrea's last population of elephants is said to roam around – buy a lottery ticket if you happen to spot one!

MARINE LIFE

Major Eritrean marine ecosystems include the coral reefs, sea-grass beds and mangrove forests.

In the Red Sea at least 350 species of coral are known to exist. Eritrea's coral is mainly found as 'patch reef' extending from the surface to a depth of around 15m to 18m; below this, coral development tends to be limited.

Eritrea is home to at least three species of mangrove, despite its location on the northerly limits of the mangrove ranges. They are found along the coast and on the Dahlak Islands.

Five species of marine turtle have been recorded. Most common are the green and hawksbill turtles. The green turtle is quite often spotted around the Dahlak Islands, as are dolphins and sharks.

The Eritrean and Sudanese coastlines are thought to be home to at least half of the 4000 to 5000 endangered dugongs (sea cows) estimated to inhabit the Red Sea.

Collecting coral, shells or plant life from the beaches and waters is forbidden in the Dahlak Islands.

ENDANGERED SPECIES

The greatest threat to wildlife in Eritrea is the degradation of habitat. Almost all of

---

THE RED, RED SEA

Eritrea is said to derive its name from the Greek word erythrea, meaning 'red'. It was coined from the famous Periplus of the Erythrean Sea, a trade or shipping manual written by a Greek-speaking Egyptian sailor or merchant around the 1st century AD. The erythrea (or 'red of the sea') is so named because the water turns a vermilion shade as a result of newly spored algae during certain periods.

BIRDS GALORE

Birdwatching in Eritrea is a treat, and twitchers are sure to get a buzz – there are many desirable new ticks for their list! We met Solomon Abraha, who is a regular contributor to the African Bird Image Database (his images can be seen on www.birdquest.net/afbid/and http://members.tripod. com/kilnsey/birdwatching_in_eritrea/index.htm) and a member of the International Ecotourism Society (www.ecotourism.org). He's keen to promote birdwatching in Eritrea and plans to run dedicated birding excursions:

How would you characterise birdlife in Eritrea? There are 2600 species of birds in Africa, including 560 to 660 species in our tiny country – you get the picture. Sixteen Important Bird Areas (IBA) have been identified in Eritrea so far, and I reckon we have between 13 and 18 endemic species. We're also lucky that industrial pollution is virtually nonexistent here, which creates favourable habitats for birds.

What makes birdwatching in Eritrea different from Ethiopia? Sure, Eritrea is much smaller than Ethiopia, which means we have fewer spots; on the plus side, they are within easy reach of Asmara. And for seabirds, Eritrea is unbeatable; we have an immense coastline as well as the Dahlak Islands.

What are your favourite birdwatching spots? My favourite area extends from Adi Keyh to Senafe, with Qohaito in between. Here you're guaranteed to spot endemic species; plus I can enjoy the fantastic scenery and the archaeological sites. I also love Filfil, because of the greenery and the diverse wildlife. My third-best site would be the Keren area. It has lots of vegetation and water resources, which attracts lots of birds. The good thing with birdwatching in Eritrea is that our birding sites are truly peaceful – you can easily commune with nature.

What's your favourite species? I love the white-cheeked turaco – it's so colourful. It can be seen relatively easily in the Filfil area. My second favourite is the blue-breasted bee-eater – it's incredibly photogenic.

What's the best season for birding? The best season runs from September to the end of April, when the migratory birds are here. But whatever the season, it's always a success because birdlife is so rich here.

Why is Eritrea not yet on birdwatching tours in East Africa? We have the potential to be a great birdwatching destination in Africa. We have the spots, the scenery, the logistics – hotels, cars, drivers and guides – and good resources, including specialised books in English and websites, but a few things need to be ironed out; for instance, it's still forbidden to import binoculars into Eritrea. But I have hope that this ban will be lifted any time soon for birders.

Eritrea's animals (with the exception of the baboon, ostrich and gazelle) are considered endangered within the country's perimeters. Internationally, the Nubian ibex (which has probably disappeared from Eritrea) is considered dangerously threatened. Concerns have also been expressed for Eritrea's elephant populations. A century ago, significant numbers inhabited Gash-Barka province. Now it is thought that less than 100 elephants exist in the country.

Plants

The landscape of eastern Eritrea is characterised by acacia woodland (several species), brushland and thicket, semidesert vegetation, riverine vegetation and mangrove swamp.

The highland region is dominated by an indigenous species of juniper (*Juniperus procera*) and wild olive (*Olea africana*).

Various species of acacia are also found. In degraded areas, various eucalyptus plantations have been established.

The Semenawi Bahri (Green Belt area) is in the northeast of Asmara, around the village and valleys of Filfil. It contains the last remnant of mixed, evergreen, tropical woodland in Eritrea. At an elevation of between 900m and 2400m, it stretches north to south for about 20km.

The landscape to the west is made up mainly of woodland savanna, brushland, thicket and grasslands (*Aristida*). Around 50% of the firewood needed for the population of Asmara is collected from this area, resulting in serious deforestation. Species include the doum palm (*Hyphaenea thebaica*), found particularly along the Barka River, eucalypts and various acacias. Other species include baobab (*Adansonia digitata*),

ERITREA

toothbrush tree (Salvadora persica) and tamarisk (Tamarix aphylla).

Endangered species of flora include the eucalypt (Boswellia papyrifera), the baobab and the tamarind tree (Tamarindus indica).

National Parks

There are no formal national reserves or parks in Eritrea, although their establishment is expected sooner or later.

There are no marine parks either, but several islands in the Dahlak group have been proposed, and research has been conducted to study the fragile ecosystem of these islands in greater detail.

Environmental Issues

Eritrea's environment has been greatly impacted by war, famine and demographic pressure. Much of Eritrea's farming is still subsistence or semisubsistence, so land productivity is vital to the population's survival.

Today population growth is the biggest problem, placing increased demands on the land and leading to overgrazing and overcropping. Adding to woes is the practice of 'shifting cultivation' in the southwestern lowlands (in which whole areas of vegetation are burnt before planting), which is also seriously detrimental to the region's flora.

Deforestation poses a great threat to the country. Less than 1% of the country is covered by woodland, as compared with 30% a century ago – this says it all. During the war with Ethiopia, troops on both sides cleared forests for the construction of shelters, trenches and other fortifications. The traditional hidmo also requires large quantities of wood. In times of famine, trees provide emergency rations for the people and their livestock. Above all, the trees prevent soil erosion. Eritrea's current water shortages and low-yielding land are directly linked to the destruction of the forests. Measures to combat deforestation include a nationwide program of tree planting and the establishment of nearly 100 nurseries nationwide, but nothing has been implemented yet.

ASMARA አስመራ

pop 1,062,000 / elev 2347m

Africa is famous for many things, but pleasant cities – especially capitals – are not one of them. Then Asmara comes along.

Scene: elderly gentlemen wearing double-breasted suits and dapper Fedora hats chatter over strong macchiatos extracted from a vintage espresso machine while a group of statuesque beauties wearing the latest European fashions struts by. A set for a Fellini movie? No. It's actually a bustling pavement terrace on Harnet Avenue, the palm-studded main thoroughfare, at 6pm – passeggiata time. This sheer incongruity is a legacy of the Italian era, when Eritrea was the pride of the colonial empire and Asmara its diamond tiara. Today it remains an architectural marvel, with a stunning mix of rationalist, Art Deco, cubist, expressionist, futurist and neoclassical styles.

Asmara is blessed with the most agreeable climate. Set on the East African escarpment, it boasts balmy temperatures and cloudless blue skies eight months a year. Its relaxed pace of life is infectious. In many ways you'll feel like you've been teleported to a southern Italian town, with tempting pastry shops, ice-cream parlours and pizzerias.

The city also exudes an undeniably African and Arab atmosphere. In the morning you'll hear the sound of the cathedral bells and the footsteps of the Orthodox monks on their way to Mass, as well as the Muslim call to prayer.

Sadly, Asmara's ability to dazzle has been marred over recent years by the battered economy and the clampdown on civil liberties. Gone is the dolce vita – belt-tightening is now the order of the day. Queuing in front of food stores and petrol stations is now a daily chore. During the day, business is slack. At night, streets are dark and deserted. The city that was once buzzing has vanished. Asmarans stoically suffer in silence. One day, they say, their once-flamboyant city will shine again. Meanwhile, they remain incorrigible bon vivants; even when there is so little money. Nothing can detract them from the daily ritual of a caffeine fix.

One thing is sure: the day you leave the city, you'll bid it 'Ciao, bella'.

HISTORY

The town was settled in the 12th century by shepherds from the Akele Guzay region, in the southeast of the country. Encouraged by the plentiful supplies of water, they founded four villages on the hill that is now the site of the Orthodox church of Enda Mariam. The site became known as Arbate Asmere (Four Villages), from which the name Asmara is

ASMARA

500 m
0.3 miles

Irga Building	17	A4
Italian Cemetery	18	A3
Mai Jah Jah Fountain	19	D3
Medebar Market	20	E1
National Museum	21	B3
Selam Hotel	22	B2
Tobacco Factory	23	D3
Villa Roma	24	C3

SLEEPING

Africa Pension	25	C3
Embasoira Hotel	26	C3
Midian Hotel	27	B4
Sunshine Hotel	28	C4

EATING

Al Khaima Restaurant	29	C3
Al Sicomoro Bar & Restaurant	30	A4
Blue Bird Bar & Restaurant	31	B3
Da Fortuna Gelato Italiano	32	D3
Golden Fork Fast Food	33	A4
Massawa Fast Food	34	B4
Milano Restaurant	35	D3

DRINKING

Bar Aquila	36	B4
Bar Zilli	37	B4
Cinema Roma	(see 12)	
Crispi Bar	38	B2
Zara	39	B3

ENTERTAINMENT

Cinema Roma	(see 12)	

SHOPPING

African Curio Shop	40	B3
Gallery	41	A4

TRANSPORT

EgyptAir	42	E2
Leo Car Rental	43	A4
Main Bus Terminal	44	C1
Nasair	45	C1
Second Bus Terminal	46	C1
Third Bus Terminal	47	C1

INFORMATION

Alliance Française	1	A2
Awghet Bookshop	2	E2
Department of Immigration	3	B2
Djiboutian Embassy	4	C4
Himbol	5	E2
Italian Embassy	6	B3
National Museum Office	(see 21)	
UK Embassy	7	B2
US Embassy	8	C4
Yemen Embassy	9	B2

SIGHTS & ACTIVITIES

Africa Pension	(see 25)	
Asmara Piscina	10	B3
Capitol Cinema	11	B2
Cinema Roma	12	B3
Enda Mariam Orthodox Cathedral	13	E2
Fiat Tagliero Building	14	A4
Former Governor's Palace	15	B3
Former Sandals Monument (War Memorial)	16	B3

Hadish Adi Quarter

Gezzabanda

City Park

Asmara University

Orotta Hospital

Saba Stadium

See Central Asmara Map (p320)

To Asmara War Cemetery (1.5km); Nefasit (25km); Debre Bizen Monastery (28km); The Red Sea Coast

To Train Station (200m)

To Sudan Embassy (400m)

To Chidel; Eritrean Cultural Centre (200m)

To Dameca Tours (400m); Ghezabanda Airport (1km); Lufthansa (600m); Orthodox Tewahdo Church Headquarters (700m); Hidmona (1km); Shamrock (1km); Kanae Palace (2km); Massa (2km); Asmara Airport (4km)

ERITREA

derived. Soon it developed into a small but bustling trading centre.

At the end of the 19th century, Ras Alula, the dashing Tigrinya *negus* (prince) made it his capital and the centre of a flourishing caravan trade.

The town then caught the eye of Baldissera, the Italian general, and in 1889 he took it over. Italian architects and engineers got to work and had soon laid the foundations of the new town: Piccola Roma, as it was dubbed, was born.

In 1897 the first governor of Eritrea, Governor Martini, chose Asmara (in preference to Massawa) as the future capital of the Italian East African empire. Amid dreams of great military conquests in Abyssinia during the Mussolini era, the town was greatly enlarged.

During the Struggle, Asmara was the last town held by the occupying Ethiopian army and, from 1990, it was besieged by the EPLF. By a fortuitous turn of events, the Ethiopian dictator Mengistu was overthrown in 1991, his troops fled Eritrea and a final confrontation in the capital was avoided. Asmara was left intact. It was one of the very few Eritrean towns to survive the war undamaged.

ORIENTATION

Like most colonial towns, Asmara was built according to a strict urban plan. It's clearly laid out and is a breeze to navigate.

The centre encompasses the area on and just north of Harnet Ave (the main artery), marked by Bahti Meskerem Sq at the eastern end of Harnet Ave and the former Governor's Palace in the west. To the south of Harnet Ave was once the Italian residential quarter. The areas to the northeast and well outside the confines of the town centre are the residential quarters of the local population.

To the southwest, Sematat Ave leads to the Tiravolo District, where several midrange hotels and nightclubs are clustered. Further to the southwest you'll reach the airport, about 6km from the centre. The train station is about 1.5km east of the centre.

Maps

The Municipality of Asmara produces an excellent town map (Nfa20), *Asmara City Map & Historic Perimeter,* which covers the city in detail and pinpoints historic buildings. It's available in some bookshops.

INFORMATION
Bookshops

Awghet Bookshop (Map p317; Bahti Meskerem Sq; 8am-7pm Mon-Sat) Has a mediocre selection of books on Eritrea but you may find the very useful *Asmara City Map & Historic Perimeter.*

Cultural Centres

Alliance Française (Map p317; ☎ 115270; www .afasmara.org.er; Ararb St; 9-11.30am & 2-6pm Mon-Fri) Has a library and a program of exhibitions.

British Council (Map p320; ☎ 123415; 175-11 St; 8.30am-12.30pm & 2.30-6pm Mon-Fri) Has a respectable library as well as a reading room stocked with British newspapers and magazines.

Emergency

Ambulance (☎ 122244)
Police (☎ 207799)

Internet Access

Internet services have sprung up all over town in recent years, so it is not hard for webheads to get their regular hit. Be warned that connection can be exasperatingly slow; try early morning or late evening. It costs about Nfa10 per hour.

Medical Services

There's a profusion of pharmacies around town.

Cathedral Pharmacy (Map p320; Harnet Ave) Opposite the Catholic cathedral.

Sembel Hospital (off Map p317; ☎ 150175; HDAY St) The most reputable hospital in town, on the road to the airport. The standard fee is US$30 per consultation. Also has dental services.

Money

Changing money won't cause any headaches: rates are fixed daily by the government and are the same everywhere in the country, whether for cash or travellers cheques, and there's only one government-run exchange bureau (Himbol). All transactions must be registered on your currency declaration form. There's a black market, but it's illegal and the penalties incurred are huge (see p359).

There are currently no ATMs in Asmara.

Commercial Bank of Eritrea (Map p320; ☎ 122425; Harnet Ave; 8-11am & 2-4pm Mon-Fri, 8-11am Sat) Changes cash and travellers cheques. Also acts as an agent for Western Union.

Himbol Bahti Meskerem Sq (Map p317; ☎ 120735; Bahti Meskerem Sq; 8am-8pm); Harnet Ave (Map p320;

☎ 115962; Harnet Ave; ◷ 8am-8pm Mon-Fri, 8am-noon & 2-7pm Sat & Sun) Changes cash and travellers cheques, and can do cash advances on your credit card for a commission of 7%. Also acts as an agent for Western Union.

There's a Himbol booth at the airport; it's open to meet all arriving flights and changes cash only.

Post
Main post office (Map p320; ◷ 8am-noon & 2-6pm Mon-Fri, 8am-12.30pm Sat) Just north of the western end of Harnet Ave.

Telephone & Fax
Eritel (Map p320; Harnet Ave; ◷ 8am-8pm) At the western end of the street. You can make international calls in the special cabins, or local calls. Phonecards are available. There's also a fax counter.

Tourist Information
In addition to the tourist office, the most reliable sources of information are the travel agencies.
Tourist Information Centre (Map p320; ☎ 124871; Harnet Ave; ◷ 7am-noon & 2-6pm Mon-Fri, 7am-noon Sat) Next to Sweet Asmara Caffe. Has some brochures and issues the compulsory travel permit.

Travel Agencies
The three main travel agencies in Asmara are listed here. For details of the sort of tours they

offer, see p366. Flights can be booked through these agencies or through the various airline offices in Asmara.
Damera Tours (off Map p317; ☎ 181907, 181027; www.dameratours.com; Warsai Ave; ◷ 8am-noon & 2.30-6pm Mon-Sat) In the same building as Lufthansa.
Erinine (☎ 127300, 122271; www.erinine.com; Asmara)
Explore Eritrea Travel & Tours (Map p320; ☎ 125555, 120259; explore@tse.com.er; Adi Hawesha St; ◷ 8.30am-noon & 2-6pm Mon-Sat) English-speaking staff offer a range of travel services throughout the country.
Travel House International (Map p320; ☎ 201881/2; www.travelhouseeritrea.com; 175-15 St; ◷ 8am-noon & 2-6pm Mon-Fri, 8.30am-noon & 3.30-6pm Sat) A well-regarded travel agency, opposite the Casa degli Italiani restaurant. Ask for Tedros, who knows the country very well and speaks good English. All kinds of tours can be organised, including birdwatching trips. Villa rentals can also be arranged.

Travel Permits
To travel outside Asmara you'll need a travel permit, obtainable at the Tourist Information Centre. Keep it with you when you travel outside Asmara as you'll have to present it at checkpoints. Provided you're a tourist (and not a journalist or an NGO worker), it's a pretty straightforward affair, just a mere form to fill in and sign, listing all your intended destinations in Eritrea. If you rent a car or a 4WD, you'll have to mention the registration number and the make. The permit is usually issued the same day, provided

---

ASMARA IN...

Two Days

Kick off the day with a *macchiato* at **Casa degli Italiani** (p327). Then make sure to get your bearings over the urban sprawl you're going to embrace by climbing up the **bell tower** (p321) of the Catholic cathedral. Next, wind your way to the nearby **Great Mosque** (p322) and delve into the jumble of streets of the **central market** (p322) area to soak up the atmosphere. By this time you'll be in need of a rest, so enjoy a delectable lunch at **Massawa Fast Food** (p327). Mission accomplished, continue to **Medebar Market** (p322) for a salutary lesson in waste management. Need to sate a sweet tooth? Make your way to **Da Fortuna Gelato Italiano** (p328) for a flaky croissant. Suitably re-energised, you can prepare yourself for the evening *passeggiata*. Stroll down Harnet Ave and watch the world go by at the snazzy **Moderna** (p329). Is it dinner-time yet? Take your weary bones to the **Blue Bird Restaurant** (p328) and treat yourself to a proper feed in traditional surrounds. Next door, hip **Zara** (p329) is a good spot to loosen up over well-shaken cocktails.

Start off day two with a hearty *ful* at the **Al Khaima Restaurant** (p327) – you'll need the calories to complete our **city walking tour** (p324). Now, pause at the **Al Sicomoro Bar & Restaurant** (p327) for the best tortellini in town. Head to the **National Museum** (p323) for some cultural sustenance followed by a bout of entertainment at the **bowling alley** (p322). Be sure to be on Harnet Ave by 6pm for your daily dose of *passeggiata*. Return to your hotel to put on your glad rags, grab a cab and head to **Hidmona** (p330) or **Warsa** (p330) where you'll wind 'n' grind the night away in good company.

ERITREA

you come early in the morning. Don't forget your passport.

A permit is also necessary to visit the monasteries, but it was not issued to foreigners at the time of writing. For more details on permits, see p362.

DANGERS & ANNOYANCES

Asmara is fundamentally a very safe city, especially compared with other African cities. It's generally safe to stroll around day or night in the centre. However, women should use their common sense and avoid walking alone in deserted and dark streets.

Very few streets are lit at night. It's a bit intimidating but there's no particular risk of getting mugged.

Begging is actively 'discouraged' by the government and it's still rare to see beggars in central Asmara.

Do *not* take photographs of public buildings and institutions, such as ministries and banks, or of potential contentious subjects, such as people waiting in queues. We've heard that some travellers who took such pictures have been arrested.

SIGHTS

Asmara's greatest attraction is undoubtedly its gobsmacking collection of buildings revealing its colonial past (see the boxed text, p323). As you walk around the town, you will see splendid examples of the Art Deco, international, cubist, expressionist, functionalist, futurist, rationalist and neoclassical architectural styles, that will enthral even the least culturally inclined travellers. How the buildings have managed to step viably into the 21st century without a complete restoration is a mystery. To top it off, viewing much of it doesn't cost a cent.

Most of Asmara's major sights are clustered in the centre or within easy distance from it.

Harnet Ave

The best place to start exploring is the **former Governor's Palace** (Map p317), which stands majestically at the western end of Harnet Ave. With its pediment supported by Corinthian columns, this architectural wonder is thought to be one of the finest neoclassical buildings in Africa. Unfortunately, it is not currently possible to visit it because it's an official building. So frustrating!

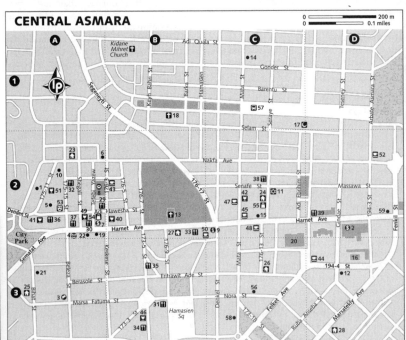

CENTRAL ASMARA

Within staggering distance of the Governor's Palace, the **Opera House** (Map p320) is one of Asmara's most elegant early-20th-century buildings. Completed around 1920, this eclectic building combines a Renaissance scallop-shell fountain, a Romanesque portico supported by classical columns and inside, above multitiered balconies, a spectacular Art Nouveau ceiling.

By contrast, the adjacent **Ministry of Education** (Map p320) looks strikingly austere. Typically Fascist, indeed. Built during the 1930s as the Casa del Fascio (the Fascist Party headquarters), it mixes the classical (the right-hand section) with the monumental and Fascist. Its soaring tower has strong vertical elements, including three gun-slit windows. The steps, string courses (projecting bands of bricks) and mouldings give the building harmony.

Ambling down Harnet Ave you'll soon come across Asmara's most iconic monument, the elaborate, brick-walled **Catholic cathedral** (Map p320). Consecrated in 1923, it is thought to be one of the finest Lombard-Romanesque-style churches outside Italy – this says it all. The cathedral's lofty interior is an absorbing sight: the altar is made of Carrara marble and the baptistry, confessionals and pulpit are carved from Italian walnut. Masses are celebrated every Sunday at 6.30am (in Tigrinya), 9.30am (in Italian) and 11am (in English) in the cathedral. The tallest structure in Asmara, the narrow, Gothic **bell tower** (☉ 8-11am & 2-5pm) makes a useful landmark and offers smashing views over the town. Ask at the 'Ufficio Parrocchiale' for the key. A donation is expected.

Another eye-catching building, the nearby **Cinema Impero** (Map p320) is part of a grand rationalist terrace built in 1938. The imposing cinema is made up of three massive windows that combine strong vertical and horizontal elements with 45 porthole lamps (which look like huge wireless buttons). In the lobby, all the marble, chrome and glass features are original. The cavernous auditorium seats 1800 people and is decorated with motifs such as lions, nyalas and palm trees depicted in Art Deco style. Next door, the **Bar Impero** (Map p320), where cinemagoers traditionally enjoyed an apéritif before the film, is also original. Look out for the bevelled-glass cake-and-fruit cabinet, the 'zinc' bar, the dark wood panels and the old cash machine.

Further east, it's impossible to miss the imposing **Municipality building** (Map p320). Though built in the 1950s, this monolith is firmly rationalist. The two geometric wings are 'stripped Palladian' in style, and are dominated by a soaring central tower. The windows are beautifully detailed. Look out for the 'crazy majolica' façade in green and beige.

South of Harnet Ave

A block southeast of the Municipality building, the **bowling alley** (Map p320; 194-4 St; ☺ 8am-8pm) is one of the few genuine 1950s alleys left in the world. It was probably built for US servicemen when they were manning military bases in the region. The reloading system is still manual. Look out also for the bowling motifs on the balustrades, the blue and white lockers and the carved wooden benches. The colourful early 'pop art' window is spectacular at sunset. Across the road from the bowling alley is a **garage** (Map p320; 194-4 St), possibly built in the 1950s. The roof of the building features zigzags.

Further south, you'll stumble across one of the most elegant pieces of architecture in Asmara, the **Mai Jah Jah fountain** (Map p317; Marsatekly Ave). It cascades down the hillside in a series of rectangular steps. Sadly, it was out of service at the time of research. Above the fountain is the attractive suburb of Gezzabanda, which is full of impressive villas.

Tucked away in a residential district further west, the **Africa Pension** (Map p317; Keskese St) is a gem of place. This huge cubist villa was built in the 1920s by an Italian magnate. It is characterised by its elegant marble staircase and the ring of 40 marble urns. Today a solemn and slightly ludicrous bronze bust of Augustus Caesar stands guard in the once-formal garden. The villa is now a very affordable hotel (see p325). You like it? Book a room!

Opposite the Africa Pension, you can't but be dazzled by the gleaming **Villa Roma** (Map p317; 173-3 St). Built in 1919, it epitomises the Roman style. The marble staircases, louvred shutters, curving balustrades, shady portico, fountain, and loggia with cascading purple bougainvillea are typical features of the ideal Roman villa. Today it is the residence of the Italian ambassador.

Just off Harnet Ave, near the Eritel building, the quirky **Odeon Cinema** (Map p320; Bihat St), with its authentic Art Deco interior, is attractive. The box office, bar, bevelled mirrors, black terrazzo and Art Deco strip lights are a good introduction to the large auditorium.

Heading downhill on Felket Ave, south of the centre, past a row of old shops and 1950s Formica bars with fly-bead doors, you'll see several attractive villas and buildings, including the **tobacco factory** (Map p317; Felket Ave). It is regarded as the most adventurous Art Deco building in Asmara.

North of Harnet Ave

The sprawling **central market** (Map p320; ☺ morning Mon-Sat), just north of Eritrea Sq, is one of Asmara's major attractions. The best time to visit is early on Saturday (from 7am), when people come in from all over the country. However, it was pretty tame when we visited because of the economic downturn in the country. Highlights include the spice market, filled with colourful women from different ethnic groups. The souvenir market is a great place to browse too, and is more interesting than the shops in the town. You can find, among other things, local basketwork, wooden masks, musical instruments, decorated gourds, warrior knives and skin paintings.

Duck up northeast to soak up the atmosphere of the **Medebar Market** (Map p317; Qelhamet St). No doubt you'll be awestruck the minute you enter this mind-boggling place. It is like an open-air workshop where absolutely everything is recycled. Moseying around the alleys of this market is a uniquely unforgettable experience. The air is filled with hammering, sawing and cutting; old tyres are made into sandals, corrugated iron is flattened and made into metal buckets, and olive tins from Italy are made into coffee pots and tiny scoopers.

Thread your way back to the south until you reach the **Great Mosque** (Kulafah Al Rashidin; Map p320; Selam St). Completed in 1938 by Guido Ferrazza, this grand complex combines rationalist, classical and Islamic styles. The symmetry of the mosque is enhanced by the minaret, which rises on one side like a fluted Roman column above Islamic domes and arches. The *mihrab* (niche indicating the direction of Mecca) inside consists of mosaics and columns made from Carrara marble. Ferrazza's style is also seen in the great square and market complex surrounding the mosque.

Another outstanding monument, the **Enda Mariam Orthodox Cathedral** (Map p317; Arbate Asmara St), to the east, was built in 1938 and is a curious blend of Italian and Eritrean architecture. Its central block is flanked by large square towers. Rather garish mosaics of stylised Christian figures are framed vertically above the entrance. Traditional elements of Aksumite architecture can be seen, such as the massive horizontal stone beams. The four objects that look like broken elephant tusks suspended on the northern side of the compound are century-old 'bells'. These make a surprisingly musical sound when 'rung' (beaten with a stick).

Asmara's synagogue (Map p320; Seraye St) is also worth a peek. Its pediment, Doric columns and pilasters make it very neoclassical. As is usual in Asmara, the wrought-iron gates are handcrafted.

If you haven't run out of stamina, head west of the central market to the **Greek Orthodox Church** (Map p320; Selam St). The church has frescoes, carved wood and candles.

West of Harnet Ave

If you need to recharge the batteries before tackling the western outskirts of the centre, the **city park** (Map p317; Sematat Ave; 6.30am-10.30pm) makes a perfect transition point in which to unwind and to relish a well-deserved fruit juice. Come here late afternoon, when it's full of life and chatter.

Then you can make your way to the **Capitol Cinema** (Map p317; Denden St). It was built in 1937. The massive horizontal elements and sweeping curves are typical of the expressionist movement. Unfortunately the building looks rather scruffy and is in urgent need of a face-lift.

A five-minute walk from Capitol Cinema, the **Selam Hotel** (Map p317; Mariam GMBI St) was undergoing a major renovation at the time of writing. Built in the 1930s, it was one of a chain constructed by an Italian company. Interesting interior details include the arts and crafts serving cabinets and the 'disc'-type lamps in the dining room, the old murals and the purple 'beehive' lamps in the rear courtyard.

Asmara's strong point is its buildings, rather than its museums, but if you have an hour to spare it's also worth popping your head into the **National Museum** (Map p317; Mariam GMBI St; admission free; 9-11am & 3-5pm Thu-Tue), west of the Governor's Palace. It contains exhibits on the ethnic groups of Eritrea, giving a basic introduction to traditional life in the countryside, as well as various artefacts found in the country's main archaeological sites.

The 1930s **Asmara Piscina** (swimming pool; Map p317; Kohayto St; admission Nfa40; 9am-8pm) is housed in a yellow building, off Sematat Ave. If it's open, take a peek inside this modernist structure. Interior details include the Leonardo sporting figures on the walls and a rather refreshing bluish colour scheme.

Back to the main thoroughfare, you can't miss the **Cinema Roma** (Map p317; Sematat Ave), across the avenue. It's another fine example of Italian architecture. The appealing exterior features four entrances with double doors and a magnificent marble-coated

---

ART (DECO) ATTACK

Another litter-strewn African capital disfigured with concrete eyesores? Not here. Asmara is one of the most entrancing cities in Africa. It usually comes as a surprise to many travellers to discover a slick city crammed with architectural gems harking back to the city's heyday as the Piccolo Roma (small Rome). Isolated for nearly 30 years during its war with Ethiopia, Asmara escaped both the trend to build postcolonial piles and the push towards developing-world urbanisation. Thus, it has kept its heritage buildings almost intact. Wander the streets in the centre and you'll gaze upon a showcase of the Art Deco, international, cubist, expressionist, functionalist, futurist, rationalist and neoclassical architectural styles.

When Mussolini came to power in Italy in 1922, he nursed two ambitions relating to Italy's role in the Horn: to avenge Italy's defeat at Adwa (see p144) and to create a new Roman Empire in Africa. To realise these dreams he needed a strong industrial base. Labour, resources and lire were thus poured into the new colony and, by the 1930s, it was booming. By 1940 Eritrea had become the second-most industrialised country in sub-Saharan Africa. At the same time – and encouraged by il Duce – a new and daring architectural movement called rationalism was springing up in Italy. Eritrea, in common with many colonies, became an experimental architectural laboratory in which new and exciting ideas could be tested. Asmara, or Piccola Roma, soon came to epitomise the new philosophy: it was not just beautiful, but was well planned, well built and, above all, functional. Today Asmara remains a model Art Deco town, although a number of buildings are decaying for lack of funds.

The best way to see Asmara's built heritage is to walk around town (see p324). *Asmara – Africa's Secret Modernist City*, by Edward Denison, is the most comprehensive book on the subject.

façade sporting the letters ROMA below four square windows.

Ambling down Sematat Ave, you'll reach a roundabout which used to be home to a quirky war memorial: a pair of giant sandals made of sheet metal. This sculpture was meant to commemorate the victory of the Eritrean fighters in the Struggle. Note that Eritrean soldiers are equipped with plastic sandals, not combat boots. At the time of writing the monument had just been dismantled for unknown reasons. Whether it will be re-erected is anybody's guess.

Don't even think of leaving town until you've seen the **Fiat Tagliero Building** (Map p317; Sematat Ave), at the southern end of Sematat Ave. Perhaps the most outstanding in Asmara, this quirky monument is another superb example of a futuristic building. Built in 1938, it is designed to look like a plane (or a spaceship, or a bat). The central tower with its glass 'cockpit' is similar to many structures in Miami, USA. A sandal's throw from the Fiat Tagliero Building, the harmonious **Irga Building** (Map p317; Sematat Ave) is both neoclassical in its proportions and very modern.

With its well-tended graveyards, the old **Italian Cemetery** (Map p317) is well worth a small detour.

East of Harnet Ave

On the road to Massawa on the periphery of Asmara (2km from the centre), is the beautifully tended **Asmara War Cemetery**, dating from 1941. Interred here are 280 men killed during the Ethiopian campaign. There is also a Hindu burial ground for the Indian soldiers who fought alongside the British.

WALKING TOUR

With its ideal weather, profusion of historic buildings, lack of hassle and unhurried pace of life, it's hard to imagine a better place than Asmara for a walking tour. This saunter covers the main sights in the centre.

Start at the magnificent **Opera House** (**1**; p320) and **Ministry of Education** (**2**; p321) at the western end of Harnet Ave. Keep striding east down the main artery, where you'll pass the well-proportioned building of the former **Bank of Eritrea** (**3**) on your right. Asmara's most obvious landmark, the lofty **Catholic cathedral** (**4**; p321) soon comes into view. The stunning façade of the **Cinema Impero** (**5**; p320) is 150m to the east. Next door, **Bar Impero** (**6**; p321) is an ideal pit stop for a caffeine fix. Turn left into Seraye St and walk along until you reach the main junction with Nakfa Ave.

Turn right into Nakfa Ave then left into Adi Ebrihim St and you'll soon see the **Great Mosque** (**7**; p322) standing majestically. Follow Selam St for about 100m to the west, then

---

WALK FACTS

Start Opera House
Finish Albergo Italia
Distance About 4km
Duration Half a day

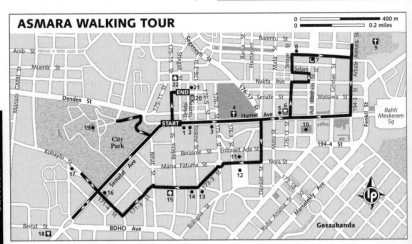

ASMARA WALKING TOUR

take the first street on the right (Seraye St). You'll enter the **market area (8)**. Explore it at leisure before heading to **Enda Mariam Orthodox Cathedral (9**; p322) that looms to the east. Walk down Arbate Asmera St until you emerge on Harnet Ave. Travel two blocks down Harnet Ave past the monumental **Municipality building (10**; p321). Continue west and turn left into Denkel St. Walk two blocks and turn right into Nora St.

The **Hamasien Square (11)**, which was once the heart of the Greek community, is a good place to unwind. On the corner on the east side you'll spy an old school that resembles a Greek temple. To the south, you can't miss the ochre building of the **Eritrean Election Commission (12)**.

From the piazza, head west through the next square (which has a palm tree in the middle) and up the hill (173-3 St). Near the top of the hill you'll stumble across the **Africa Pension (13**; right) and the lovely **Villa Roma (14**; p322). About 100m to the west, the conical roof of the quirky **Hamasien Hotel (15)** beckons. On the northern side of the hotel, descend 171-10 St. The steps lead you down to Bihat St. Take 171-3 St, which begins between the Dutch embassy and the Crystal Hotel, then turn right into 171-4 St, which will bring you to Sematat Ave. On the corner have a look at **Cinema Roma (16**; p323). Cross Sematat Ave and walk down Kohayto St until you reach the **Asmara Piscina (17**; p323).

If you haven't run out of stamina, backtrack to Sematat Ave and mosey south along the avenue until the next roundabout, which once hosted the Sandals war monument. After a tipple at historic **Bar Zilli (18**; p329), proceed back to Harnet Ave. Have a peek at the **Governor's Palace (19**; p320) that sprawls on your left (it's impossible to go near). Then head back to Harnet Ave and turn left into 175-15 St, which starts opposite the Eritel building. Walk two blocks and you'll see a cluster of historic buildings, including the **main post office (20**; p319), the former building of the **Commercial Bank of Eritrea (21)** and the glamorous **Albergo Italia (22**; p326). Book a room here if you can afford it – you've really earned it!

FESTIVALS & EVENTS

Asmara hosts many religious and secular festivals throughout the year. For more information, see p358.

SLEEPING

Asmara boasts a cluster of accommodation options, from very affordable guesthouses and good-value midrange options to one boutique hotel. Most places rate zero on the charm scale but are usually well equipped and fairly comfortable.

Most of Asmara's accommodation is concentrated in and around the centre, but there are also several good midrange places further afield on the road to the airport in the Tiravolo district.

Some hotels quote their prices in US dollars or in euros but accept local currency, provided you have your currency declaration form. If you pay in hard currency, the transaction must be registered on your form.

Budget

Pensione Pisa (Map p320; ☎ 124491; Harnet Ave; d without bathroom Nfa100-120) You're not going to be overwhelmed by this modest pension housed in an apartment but at these prices you didn't expect the red carpet, right? The rooms are basic but clean and spacious (bar the one single), and the poky shared bathrooms won't make you squirm. Its main selling point is its peerless location, just opposite the cathedral.

ourpick Africa Pension (Map p317; ☎ 121436; Keskese St; d without bathroom Nfa180-230) Asmara's budget golden child, this pension is for shoestringers who want to surround themselves with character. Housed in a cubist villa dating from the 1920s, it still carries whispers of that bygone era with its marble staircase, generoussized rooms with tiled floors and a serene garden. Although the rooms show their age a bit and the furnishings are dated, Africa Pension has that comfiness of favourite old clothes you never throw away. Location is ace – you're in a placid neighbourhood, a jaunt from Harnet Ave. Sweet staff, too.

Khartoum Hotel (Map p320; ☎ 128008; 176-13 St; s without bathroom Nfa200-250, d without bathroom Nfa250-300, s/d Nfa300/380) The super-central Khartoum is kept spotless, prices are good and if you want a comfy sleep without blowing big bucks, you can't go wrong here. If there's one thing to moan about, it's the teensy singles, such as room 5; a bit more dosh simply gets you a more spacious 'suite' (especially rooms 14 and 19). There's a bar-restaurant downstairs and a pastry shop just around the corner.

Midrange & Top End

Top Five Hotel (Map p320; ☎ 124922/19; fax 124931; Marsatekly Ave; s/d Nfa210/370) A good lair in this price bracket, with uncluttered rooms that are kept in good nick. It's in a convenient location and it has courteous staff. The big boon here is the lively restaurant, which has an excellent reputation and an attractive setting.

Concord Pension (Map p320; ☎ 110073; fax 110186; Seraye St; s/d Nfa300/400) Tucked back slightly from the road, Concord has the feel of a friendly B&B, features an agreeable plant-filled courtyard and is ultracentral – that's the good news. The bad news is that the rooms are on the cramped side – be prepared to trip over your backpack when going to the bathroom.

our pick Midian Hotel (Map p317; ☎ 126232; www .midianhotel.com; 172-4 St; d with breakfast US$50; 🖳) This is possibly the best deal in this price bracket. Cool, crisp bed linen, sterile bathrooms, bright rooms, modern furnishings and competent staff make for an excellent stay, and there's a restaurant with a comprehensive menu. It's located in a peaceful area and sensibly set a little way back from the main avenue but is close enough to the centre to be worthwhile. Netheads will also appreciate the free wi-fi.

Crystal Hotel (Map p320; ☎ 120944; www.crystal hoteleritrea.com; Bihat St; s incl breakfast US$45-58; d incl breakfast US$58-77) You can't go wrong at this tightly managed outfit in a quiet street near Harnet Ave. It boasts clean-smelling, appealing rooms with modern furnishings, spanking clean bathrooms, satellite TV, colourful bedspreads, decent breakfast, obliging staff and free wi-fi. An added bonus is the restaurant (mains from Nfa50), featuring excellent local and Italian specialities. Payment with credit cards incurs 5% commission.

Sunshine Hotel (Map p317; ☎ 127882; reservations @sunshineasmara.com; BDHO Ave; s/d incl breakfast US$40/50, ste US$47/65; 🖳) The Sunshine is a solid middle-of-the-road option with its efficient yet down-to-earth staff and no-nonsense rooms. One grumble: the standard rooms are a bit on the small side. The garden at the back looks like a mini oasis. Add an extra 10% to the quoted prices if you pay with credit card.

Embasoira Hotel (Map p317; ☎ 123222; www .embasoirahotel.com; Beleza St; s incl breakfast US$40-48, d incl breakfast US$57-68) A favoured haunt of European tour groups, the Embasoira exudes an international confidence. Rooms are practical with no flouncy embellishments – just good lighting, not-too-saggy mattresses and salubriou bathrooms. The real steal is the lovely gar dens at the back, which are overflowing with blossoming tropical plants. There's a bar and restaurant, and it's in a refreshingly quiet and peaceful area. Credit cards are accepted, but with 8% commission. Wi-fi is available.

Albergo Italia (Map p320; ☎ 120740; www.albergo italiaasmara.com; Nakfa Ave; s incl breakfast US$90-135, d incl breakfast US$135-165, ste s/d US$165/190) The most styl ish accommodation in Asmara, the Albergo Italia is more like a rich relative's mansio than a hotel. Ideally positioned near the French embassy, it features well-appointed rooms decorated with period furniture and communal areas awash with heritage aes thetics. However, we've heard reports tha housekeeping can be a little slack here, and at the time of writing no wi-fi was available nor were credit cards accepted. There's also a cafeteria and restaurant.

When we passed by, there were rumours that the massive **Asmara Palace Hotel** (☎ 153700 www.asmarapalace.com; Airport Rd; s/d from US$140/180 🅿 🛇 🖳 🕏), on the road to the airport, was going to close.

EATING

Asmara will seem like a gourmet haven if you're returning to the city after time spent elsewhere in Eritrea. Most places serve both Eritrean and Italian dishes. Many Asmara restaurants – particularly the more upmarket ones – add a tax o up to 15% to bills. Unless otherwise specified most places are open every day for lunch and dinner. Note that most of the larger restaurants close around 10pm. Given the food shortages not everything was available when we visited.

Some of the smarter hotels have their own restaurants and serve average to excellen local and international food, though at more expensive prices than elsewhere.

Budget

Cathedral (Map p320; Harnet Ave; mains Nfa20-50) Just opposite the Catholic cathedral, this ambient spot dishes up good fare at wallet-friendly prices.

American Bar (Map p320; Harnet Ave; mains Nfa40-60) This fast-food joint serves up decent burgers and explosively fruity cocktails. The street side terrace allows for a dash of people-watching – unless you prefer to ponder over the harmonious proportions of the Ministry of Education building, just opposite.

Pizza Napoli (Map p320; ☎ 123784; Adi Hawesha St; pizzas Nfa50-90) In this unpretentious, yet authentic, joint you'll find 26 varieties of crispy pizzas. The quality isn't exactly earth shattering, but neither is the bill, and they're served on a wooden plate – a nice touch.

Golden Fork Fast Food (Map p317; ☎ 202477; Warsay St; mains Nfa40-110) If you need to quieten a growling stomach, or are just looking for a tasty pastry or a thick sandwich, this snazzy cafeteria will fit the bill. In warm weather, the voluminous interior spills out onto the terrace.

Midrange

Alba Bistro (Map p320; ☎ 202421; Adi Hawesha St; mains Nfa45-100) Brimming with good cheer, this place is an ideal refuelling stop after a walking tour in the area. Its energetic staff serve up pasta, meat and fish dishes, as well as tempting ice creams. The menu is full of pictures of what your meal should, but probably won't, end up looking like. It's also a good place to start the day: tuck into a scrumptious brekky and you'll leave with a smile on your face.

our pick **Massawa Fast Food** (Map p317; ☎ 114503; Geregr Sudan St; mains Nfa45-110) This attractive restaurant is the perfect place for your first taste of Eritrea. It has received high marks from expats (and our own stamp of approval) for its quality fare – try *shiro* (chickpea puree), *kitfo* (spiced raw beef) and *tibsi* (beef), all served with style by diligent waitresses. The lovely outdoor dining area is ideal for an alfresco meal. Salads, pastas and pizzas also feature on the menu. And the yogurt with honey is Nfa30 worth of true love.

New Fork Restaurant (Map p320; ☎ 116571; 173-5 St; mains Nfa45-110) New Fork was the flavour of the month when we visited. It buzzes all day long with folks munching on hearty salads, zesty pastas and savoury meat and fish dishes. The eclectic menu also includes Eritrean classics – think *kitfo* (spiced raw beef) and *tibsi*.

Milano Restaurant (Map p317; ☎ 120422; Felket Ave; mains Nfa50-90) Push the entrance door and you'll probably find yourself saying 'this place is drab'. However, if you venture into the dining room at the back, you'll find a lovingly exotic corner, with low wooden tables and plenty of knick-knacks. These intimate surrounds are perfect for your first awkward attempts at injera. If you want to stick to Western-style food, there is also a good selection of Italian dishes.

> ### EATING OUT IN ASMARA
>
> The impact of the economic crisis in Eritrea can be measured in the restaurants, among other places. Asmara has good dining options but life has become so hard for cash-hungry Eritreans that they can't really afford a full meal in these venues. Don't be surprised if you are the only customer who actually eats – most patrons just sit and ask for a *mai gas* (bottle of water), an Asmara gin or a cup of coffee.

Casa degli Italiani (Map p320; ☎ 120791; 175-15 St; mains Nfa50-140; ☒ closed dinner Sun) Recipe for a perfect morning: grab an outdoor table at this courtyard restaurant and order up a frittata. Italian ingredients pervade the lunch and dinner menu; try the well-presented *piatto del giorno* (dish of the day: osso bucco, lasagne, cannelloni…).

Sun Pizza & Fast Food (Map p320; Seraye St; mains Nfa50-150) If pasta offerings or pizzas make your stomach quiver with excitement, slide into this Italian restaurant. We devoured the Asmarina pizza, laden with cheese and *zigni* (just don't blame us if it sets your tastebuds on fire). The decor is rustically cosy, with sturdy wooden tables.

our pick **Al Khaima Restaurant** (Map p317; ☎ 116469; 173-1 St; mains Nfa50-165) *The* spot for a restorative morning fry-up. We're talking about *ful* (based on chickpea purée) and omelettes (or liver, if you want to impress your friends), all served with a *chapatti*-like bread. Lunch (and dinner) moves into Yemeni-influenced dishes, such as *mendi* fish (oven-baked). Enjoy your meal in the shady courtyard (yeah!). No alcohol is served (boo!).

Spaghetti & Pizza House (Map p320; ☎ 122112; Harnet Ave; mains Nfa50-180; ☒ Tue-Sun) This trattoria-like venue has a loyal cult following among Italian expats, and it's no surprise – it cooks up scrumptious Italian fare. Our friends at the Italian school swear it makes Asmara's best pizza, and we won't argue. Fish dishes also grace the menu.

Al Sicomoro Bar & Restaurant (Map p317; ☎ 202826; 189-6 St; mains Nfa70-140) A favourite haunt of expats and well-heeled locals, Al Sicomoro is famous for its flavoursome pasta (our friends can't get enough of the homemade tortellini). If tortellini, penne or spaghetti aren't doing it for you, delve into salads, fish and meat

ERITREA

dishes, or hoe into lip-smacking Eritrean staples. And don't skip dessert (hmm, the unctuous tiramisu!). Pity about the off-putting location, though; it's on the 2nd floor of a boring high-rise.

Blue Bird Bar & Restaurant (Map p317; ☎ 117965; Sematat Ave; mains Nfa80-150) You wouldn't know it from the street, but the Blue Bird is one of the most atmospheric places in town for great Eritrean food. *Zilzil tibs* (strips of beef, fried and served slightly crunchy with *awazi* sauce) comes to mind, as does *kwanta fir fir* (strips of beef rubbed in chilli, butter, salt and *berbere* then usually hung up and dried; served with torn-up injera). Western dishes are also available.

Hidmona (off Map p317; ☎ 182979; Expo Park; mains Nfa85-130) Hidmona is an eclectic mix of restaurant, cafe, bar and disco. Bookmark it if you're after a traditional experience: traditional food in traditional surroundings with traditional music in the evening. Oh, and the waiters are in traditional costume too. Everything is tasty, but we recommend the *zilzil tibs* and the *gored gored*. Eat confidently with your fingers if you want to look local.

Quick Eats

Da Fortuna Gelato Italiano (Map p317; 173-18 St; ⏱ 8.30am-10pm) Make this ice-cream parlour the last place you visit in Asmara, lest you find yourself returning compulsively for a *cono* (scoop; Nfa15) or a *coppetta* (cup; Nfa25 to Nfa45). A few examples of available flavours, just to make your mouth water: tiramisu, *fiordilatte* ('milk' ice cream), *nutellone* (ice cream with Nutella)…

Helbana (Map p320; 173-5 St; ⏱ 7am-9pm) It's more or less the same story in this kooky ice-cream parlour, with a tempting selection of flavours, including guava, chocolate and vanilla.

Self-catering

ourpick Barka Dairy Farm Products (Map p320; Marsa Fatuma St; ⏱ 8.30am-1pm & 4.30-8.30pm Mon-Sat, 8.30am-1pm Sun) Delicious Italian cheese in Asmara? Yes, it's possible. This treasure-trove offers fantastic smoked cheese (Nfa250 per kilogram), provolone, spongy mozzarella, tangy parmesan, ultra fresh milk, rich cream and pasta… It's gonna be a *g-o-o-d* picnic on the Dahlak Islands!

Wikianos supermarket (Map p320; ☎ 200789; Harnet Ave; ⏱ 8am-1pm & 3.30-9pm Mon-Fri, 8am-1pm Sat) Opposite the Municipality building. It has the best selection of products. Most food is imported, so prices are much higher than in local supermarkets.

DRINKING

Asmara prides itself on its atmosphere-laden cafes. Most of the time they are packed with Asmarans sipping the ubiquitous *macchiato*. Sometimes it's hard to distinguish between a cafe and a bar as you can drink just about anywhere and any time.

Cafes & Pastry Shops

See the boxed text on opposite for a list of our 10 favourite places. The following ones are also good places to get your fill.

Most places listed in this section serve pastries (usually made on the premises), fruit juices and beers, and are also great for breakfast. Most are open by 7am, some earlier, and close around 9pm.

Rosina (Map p320; Harnet Ave) A great early morning stop for pastries and coffee. There are even pizza slices kicking around behind the glass cases.

Sesen Pasticceria (Map p320; Adi Hawesha St) This low-key pastry shop is laden with atmosphere. It sells good cakes and acceptable cappuccinos.

Sweet Asmara Caffe (Map p320; Harnet Ave) Expanding waistlines for decades, this sleek pastry shop almost directly opposite the Catholic cathedral entices with croissants, buns, cakes and pizza slices. And, of course, coffee.

ourpick City Center Pastry (Map p320; 176-3 St) With an appetising selection of croissants and other delicacies, this pastry shop should be the carb-lovers' first port of call on this side of Harnet Ave. It is usually packed to the rafters with young Eritreans in the late afternoon.

Modka Caffe & Pastry (Map p320; ☎ 118382; 173-3 St) A little corner of tranquillity, a block south from the grinding pace of Harnet Ave, this is a great spot to refuel over teas, coffee and pastries.

Mona Lisa Snack Bar & Pastry (Map p320; Mata St) Ignore the two tacky pillars at the entrance and grab a chair in the vast, vivacious room inside. Tempting pastries and good brews.

ourpick Capri (Map p320; Mata St; juices Nfa10-20) Ah, Capri and its oh-so-smooth, oh-so-thick fruit juices! See the heap of bananas on the counter and the rows of papaya, mango and

ERITREA

ASMARA BAR & CAFE CRAWL

Asmara is packed with cafes oozing soul and character, some of which are housed in heritage buildings. Note that the distinction between cafe and bar is a bit blurred; they all serve coffee, beer and local gin. They are open every day from around 7am to 9pm or later. Here are a few favourites.

Old Asmarinos recommend the delightfully old-fashioned, hanky-sized **Tre Stelle Bar** (Map p320; Nakfa Ave) at the eastern end of Nakfa Ave. Look at the vintage Gaggia coffee machine and at the vintage pool table in the room at the back. So Asmarino!

With its vintage *billiardo* (pool table), faded football posters plastered on the walls, chequered floor, Art Deco bar and its old Campari advertisements, **Bar Aquila** (Map p317; Fred Hollows St) looks like it's come straight out of a Fellini film.

The **Odeon Cinema** (Map p320; Bihat St) is a very inspiring place. The Art Deco bar on the south side of the lobby features on the cover of the *Asmara – Africa's Secret Modernist City* book, and no wonder: it is one of Asmara's finest historic interiors, with a melange of vertical and horizontal lines, and two spherical ceiling lights made of glass 'petals'.

For a bout of entertainment, expats recommend the bowling alley complex (see p322) of the **Multi Sport Bowling** (Map p320; 194-4 St). You can while away the hours trying your hand at skittles in the company of Eritrean families, and sip a cuppa in between.

The cafeteria in the lobby area of **Cinema Roma** (Map p317; Sematat Ave) is a killer. It's high on personality, with dark wood fixtures and an impressive old projection camera. The retro feel is offset by the loud TV.

Boasting one of the most intact modernist interiors of the city, **Crispi Bar** (Map p317; Denden St) has got soul to boot. Revive your spirits with a *macchiato* or an Asmara gin if you dare, and marvel at the soothing, earth-toned '30s decor. The rounded chrome bar is a stunner, and the stools would not look out of place in a design museum.

Wax nostalgic in the heritage-style **Bar Zilli** (Map p317; Sematat Ave), with its curved walls and porthole windows.

Almost next door to Cinema Impero, **Bar Impero** (Map p320; Harnet Ave) is another endearing cafe with a more traditional feel. Enjoy a treat or sip a *macchiato* while watching the sophisticated swagger of beautiful young things passing by at *passeggiata*.

With its wonderfully laid-back palm-shaded courtyard, **Casa degli Italiani** (Map p320; Harnet Ave) is the perfect salve after (or before) a day spent exploring the city. It's also popular at lunchtime (see p327).

Mmm! We can still smell the scent of freshly baked cakes and the aroma of coffee wafting from the door of **Bar Vittoria** (Map p320; Adi Hawesha St).

guava on the shelves? They are just waiting to be squeezed and blended with milk or ice cream – mmm! Pity about the large, neon-lit interior – it's about as charming as a hospital waiting room.

Moderna (Map p320; Harnet Ave) This buzzing venue on the main drag concocts melt-in-the-mouth croissants and cakes – it's the perfect spot to start the day. It has a pavement terrace that is packed elbow-to-elbow during *passeggiata*.

Janti (Map p320; 194-4 St) Come early evening, Janti is packed to the gills with young Eritreans.

Albergo Italia (Map p320; Nakfa Ave) The most sophisticated place in town for a cuppa, with prices to match.

Bars

See the boxed text, above for a rundown of the not-to-be-missed places. The following places are also worth considering, and usually stay open longer: until 10pm or 11pm during the week, and until at least 1am at the weekend.

Zara (Map p317; Sematat Ave) This snazzy lounge bar is a popular hang-out for well-heeled diaspora Eritreans on holiday and foreigners alike. Snuggle up in an armchair and get all indecisive over the dozens of gut-filling cocktails on offer (from Nfa100). It's a good place to warm up before hitting the clubs.

Bar Royal (Map p320; Harnet Ave) Towards the western end of Harnet Ave. It's congenial and buzzing in the late afternoon.

ERITREA

PASSEGGIATA

Times are hard in Eritrea, but good-natured hedonism has not vanished in Asmara, as testified by the *passeggiata*. Don't miss this daily ritual. As in Italy, join the evening event (between 5pm and 6.30pm), when the whole town promenades up and down Harnet Ave and the adjacent streets to see what's new, catch up with friends, hear the latest gossip, flirt, window-shop, and generally take things easy. All terraces and cafes fill up with chattering locals sampling a cappuccino. You can feel the communal spirit, going back to the days of the Struggle. Grab a seat at a well-positioned cafe and watch the world strut by. You're not in Africa, but in a Fellini film!

Tavern (Map p320; 175-11 St) The closest thing Asmara has to a pub, it certainly has novelty value. Guinness? Dream on!

The bars of the larger hotels are also worth a try (see p326).

ENTERTAINMENT

Most of the country's facilities for leisure and entertainment are in Asmara. Here you'll find cinemas showing films in English (and sometimes Italian) and nightclubs.

There's good potential for partying in the capital but it was very quiet when we visited. The economy was in such a shambles that few Asmarans could afford to go out. The ones who do are mostly moneyed diaspora Eritreans who have returned to the country to live or who are on holiday.

Nightclubs

Locals love to dance, but Asmara was not particularly on its feet when we visited – the economic crisis also reflects on the nightlife. Still, you'll find a couple of places for whooping, whistling, sweating and jigging. Places are scattered around various parts of the city and are fairly safe for single women travellers (at least in comparison with other African cities), but expect to be the focus of attention. Men should be aware that most of the women in the smaller bars and nightclubs are prostitutes.

Iskista (traditional dancing) features a lot of shaking of body parts (some of which is hard to imagine, until you see it). It's certainly unique in style. If you can give it a go, you'll win a lot of friends, however inept and awkward you may feel.

Most clubs open only on Friday and Saturday (from around midnight to 5am). Entrance costs about Nfa100, depending on the venue and on the day, and local beer (when available) costs between Nfa30 and Nfa50. Transport is not a problem; taxis usually line up outside the nightclubs.

Mocambo (Map p320; Adi Hawesha St) One of the most hip nightclubs, Mocambo doesn't pick up until after midnight, but once it does, it rocks – girls shake it with a hustle Beyonce would approve of.

Hidmona (off Map p317; Expo Park, Warsay St) The most authentic place in town. It gets frantic at weekends, with a live band knocking out Eritrean tunes and plenty of drinks flowing. Here you won't see expats swooning with local girls but only Eritreans indulging in *iskista*. It's also a bar-restaurant (see p327) where you can rest your danced-out bones.

Warsa (off Map p317; Tiravolo District) Everybody seems to have a good time at this Asmara institution. It's very much a local nightclub, but it's fine for adventurous foreigners too. If you want to rub shoulders (and other parts of the anatomy) with locals dancing to Eritrean beats, this is the place! It also features groups playing traditional music.

Shamrock (off Map p317; Expo Park, Warsay St) Opposite Hidmona, Shamrock has a broader repertoire. The atmosphere is festive at weekends (but fairly tame the rest of the week) and the music is always danceable.

Cinemas

The historic decor is as much fun as the flicks. It costs about Nfa10.

Cinema Impero (Map p320; Harnet Ave) One of the best places in town. It shows action-packed American and Indian films (in the original language).

Cinema Roma (Map p317; Sematat Ave) Another well-known cinema, with a superb auditorium.

SHOPPING

The number of souvenir shops in Asmara is limited. For variety and colour, your best bet is to head to Medebar market (p322).

Roasted Coffee (Map p320; Seraye St; ☺ 8am-12.30pm & 3-6pm Mon-Sat) Caffeine addicts, steer clear of this venture or you'll be hooked forever. It sells 1kg packets of excellent Eritrean (we say Eritrean, not Ethiopian!) coffee for Nfa160 – the best souvenir! Have a look at the old roasting and grinding machines at the back.

Jolly Shop (Map p320; ☎ 121062; Adi Hawesha St) One block north of Harnet Ave. Items range from traditional paintings to carved figures, jewellery and pottery.

African Curio Shop (Map p317; ☎ 121109; Sematat Ave) Just off the roundabout. A good place to stock up on *mesob* (hourglass-shaped woven tables), pottery, woodcarvings and traditional clothing.

Ghidei – Eritrean Cultural Centre (☎ 124950; Rahayta St) An authentic place cheerfully decorated with Eritrean artefacts that are sometimes on sale. It's southwest of the centre.

There are goldsmiths and leather shops in the street running parallel to Harnet Ave, a block north.

GETTING THERE & AWAY
Bus
The **city bus terminal** (Map p320; Eritrea Sq) lies next to the central market.

The long-distance bus station is about 10 minutes' walk due north of Harnet Ave, and is split into three different terminals. The ticket office at the main bus terminal is open from 5am to 6pm daily.

Buses to Nefasit or Ghinda (Nfa12, one hour), Massawa (Nfa30, 3½ hours), Assab (Nfa201, two days), Agordat (Nfa45, five hours), Barentu (Nfa62, six hours) and Teseney (Nfa91, one day) leave from the **main bus terminal** (Map p317; off Afabet St). There are numerous buses to Massawa until late in the afternoon. For the other destinations, buses leave early in the morning. Tickets to Barentu, Teseney and Assab should be bought one day in advance. For Assab, there are two buses per week.

Buses to Keren (Nfa33, three hours) leave every half hour from the **second bus terminal** (Map p317; Falket Sayb St). If you want to continue to Nakfa, you must change at Keren.

Southbound buses to Dekemhare (Nfa12, one hour), Mendefera (Nfa16, two hours), Adi Quala (Nfa25, three hours), Adi Keyh (Nfa32, four hours) and Senafe (Nfa35, six hours) leave from the **third bus terminal** (Map p317; Fengaga St). There is no fixed schedule for these buses. Most buses leave early in the morning and when they are full. Tickets are sold on the bus.

Train
An old train trundles along a remarkable railway line constructed during the Italian era (see the boxed text below). The line runs between Asmara and Nefasit. Using this train is way more than a means of getting from Asmara to Nefasit – it's a thrilling experience. It leaves every Sunday from the **train station** (☎ 123365) at 8am and arrives in Nefasit at 9.45am, before returning to Asmara at 10am (arrival time: noon). It costs US$50 or Nfa750. Seats must be booked in advance, as a minimum of 10 passengers is needed.

For groups, it's possible to charter the train down to Massawa.

GETTING AROUND
Central Asmara is so small that almost all places can be reached within 20 minutes on foot.

To/From the Airport
A taxi to/from the airport should cost around Nfa150 (Nfa300 at night).

Bicycle
It's not a bad idea to navigate around the city by bicycle. Traffic is limited and the roads are in good shape. Riding a bike is forbidden on Harnet Ave, Nakfa Ave and Sematat Ave. The **Travel House International** (Map p320; ☎ 201881/2; www.travelhouseeritrea.com; 175-15 St; ⏰ 8am-noon & 2-6pm Mon-Fri, 8.30am-noon & 3.30-6pm Sat) can organise bike rental for about Nfa100 per day.

THE REBIRTH OF THE OLD RAILWAY

The old Italian railway, which climbed from Massawa 2128m up the escarpment to Asmara, passing through three climate zones, 30 tunnels and 65 bridges, is a masterpiece of civil engineering. At independence, Eritrea appealed for help to rehabilitate the old line. 'Impossible,' said most. 'Too expensive,' said some; 'It depends,' said others. Undeterred, the Eritreans pulled the old railway workers, metal forgers and blacksmiths out of retirement, called for volunteers and set to work. The great line reopened in 2003 and ranks among the world's great scenic railways. Each year it attracts a fair share of train buffs from all over the world.

ERITREA

Bus

Red Mercedes buses serve all parts of the town, as do smaller white buses (Coaster). It costs Nfa1 for journeys within town with the big bus and Nfa1.50 by minibus. Buses 0 and 1, which run along Harnet Ave and out to Tiravolo District, are probably the most useful for travellers.

Car & Motorcycle

Asmara is the obvious base from which to rent a car. See p365 for details on the most reliable car-hire companies.

Taxi

If you hire the taxi for yourself, or take it off the main routes, it will cost about Nfa60. There are no meters, so you should always agree on a fare in advance. At night, fares usually double. On Harnet Ave, taxis can be found 24 hours a day.

AROUND ASMARA

Asmara is a good base to explore the country, and there are some excellent places within a day's trip, such as Filfil, renowned for its superb landscape and wildlife, and Debre Bizen monastery, which gives an enlightening glimpse of the religious heritage of the country.

FILFIL ፍልፍል

Forests, vegetation, greenery…hallelujah! Arriving in Filfil is like entering another world. Amid the arid starkness of the surrounding landscape, Filfil rises up oasislike before you, cool, lush and verdant – a magical sight. In an instant, sterility gives way to greenery and ochre browns are replaced by disco green.

It's home to Eritrea's last remnant of tropical forest. There are also plantations of coffee and fruit trees. The forest is evergreen,

so it's good to visit any time of year, but it's particularly lush from October to February, after the heavy rains.

Filfil is one of the best places in Eritrea to see birds and mammals. Vervet monkeys and hamadryas baboons are easily seen, and gazelles, duikers, bushbucks, klipspringers and even leopards have been reported.

Getting There & Away

Filfil lies about 75km north of Asmara and is accessible by a sealed road. There's no public transport so you'll have to hire a car (ideally with a driver to guide you). The journey should take around two hours (one way) from Asmara, and makes a great half-day trip. There are exceptional views along the way.

DEBRE BIZEN MONASTERY ደብረ ቢዜን ገዳም

If you're searching for a place to find your inner peace, there's no better site than the monastery of Debre Bizen, which lies 2400m above sea level, near Nefasit (east of Asmara). It was founded in 1368 by Abuna Philippos. The library at the monastery contains more than 1000 manuscripts as well as various church relics, including crowns, robes and incense burners. On a clear day, the view from the monastery is breathtaking: you can see the Dahlak Islands in the Red Sea. The birdlife is good in the woodlands around the monastery.

As with many Orthodox monasteries, Debre Bizen is not open to women (or any female creatures, including hens and female donkeys!). But even if you can't enter the monastery, the journey still makes a great hike.

From Nefasit, it's a 1½- to two-hour steep walk. A local will show you the start of the path up to the monastery.

Men need to obtain a permit (see p362) to visit the monastery. At the time of writing,

---

THE MOST SCENIC ROAD IN ERITREA

Here's a tip: from Asmara, consider following the sealed road to Filfil (take the road to Keren; after 21km, you'll reach the turn-off to Filfil, which lies 55km to the northeast), and then south (another 40km) all the way down to the coastal plain (instead of backtracking directly to Asmara), where it joins the road from Massawa to Asmara. It's certainly the most scenic loop in Eritrea, with innumerable hairpin bends (hair-raising, *really*!), jaw-dropping vistas, cool air and sometimes a veil of mist which adds a touch of the bizarre. The whole circuit takes makes a great day excursion.

permits were not issued to foreigners, but we met some travellers who hiked up to the monastery without the permit and were made welcome by the monks nonetheless (but there's no guarantee).

Bring lots of water (only rainwater is available). You will be welcomed with *sewa* (home-brewed beer) and bread when you arrive.

Men are welcome to stay at the simple monastery guesthouse (with just a bed or goatskin) for a couple of days. There's no charge but it's normal to make a contribution to the upkeep of the monastery. Simple gifts are a good idea too (sugar, coffee, candles etc).

Getting There & Away

To get to Debre Bizen, take any bus heading to Massawa and get off at Nefasit (about 45 minutes). Getting back to Asmara is problematic, as most buses proceeding from Massawa are full when they pass through Nefasit. It's easier to hire a taxi for the day from Asmara (around Nfa1500).

ASMARA TO MASSAWA

Be prepared for a dizzying downhill trip. The journey from Asmara to Massawa is one of the most dramatic in Eritrea. In just 115km, the road descends nearly 2500m, plummeting through mountains often clad in mist, around hairpin bends and over old Italian bridges. Built by the Italians in 1935–36, the road was the most important in the country, linking the capital with the coast. You'll find several good viewpoints along the way. Don't forget your camera!

Around 25km east of Asmara lies the little town of **Nefasit**, the starting point for trips to the Debre Bizen Monastery (opposite). The monastery, perched high above the town, is just visible from the road.

Ghinda is 47km from Asmara and halfway to Massawa. It lies in a little valley that traps the warm, moist air from the coast. Rainfall is much higher than normal here and its green, terraced hillsides supply the fruit and vegetable markets of Asmara and Massawa. The Jiberti (Tigrinya Muslims) inhabit the area. Prohibited in the past from owning and cultivating land, they became instead great craftspeople, artists and scholars.

Nearby, across the River Dongollo, is the triple-arched **Italian bridge** with the inscription in Italian Piedmontese *Ca Custa Lon Ca Custa* (Whatever It Costs), said to be a reference to the Italian purchase of the Bay of Assab in the late 1860s.

Getting There & Away

Take any bus or minibus plying the route from Asmara to Massawa and ask to be dropped at the town of your choice.

There's also a weekly train service from Asmara to Nefasit (see p331).

NORTHERN ERITREA

Though Northern Eritrea represents a big chunk of the country, you won't be spending too much time out there because much of the region, including the highly symbolic town of Nakfa, is closed to foreigners. Be positive; at least the enjoyable market town of Keren, easily accessible from Asmara, is open to travellers. And there are the mountains of Tsada Amba, which will leave you breathless (literally!).

KEREN ከረን
pop 75,000 / elev 1392m

Set on a small plateau and surrounded by mountains, Keren effortlessly assumes the mantle of the country's second most attractive town (after Asmara, of course) and offers a fascinating glimpse into provincial Eritrea. It's an active market town with an agreeable multiethnic buzz – the Tigré, the Tigrinya and the Bilen have all made Keren home.

Keren also boasts an enticing mishmash of architectural styles – mosques, churches and colonial buildings from the Italian era. Though austere and arid, the surrounding landscape has a peculiar appeal. Ancient baobab and acacia trees dot the plains, and at dusk, the ruggedly good-looking mountains turn a shade of blue. Around Keren the beautiful Bilen women, adorned with large gold rings in their noses and henna tattoos on their necks and faces, can be seen squatting in the shade of acacia trees.

Trade blossomed once Keren was connected to Asmara by the old Italian railway, and the little town grew rapidly. Today it is the third-largest town in the country and is still an important centre of commerce.

ERITREA

MADONNA OF THE BAOBAB

Close to Keren's market area is an ancient and gnarled baobab tree. Long venerated by the locals, it is believed to mark the spot from which fertility springs.

In the late 19th century, the Sisters of Charity built a small chapel in the tree, in the place where the city's orphans played, and it became known as St Maryam Dearit – the Madonna of the Baobab.

In 1941 some Italian soldiers took refuge in the tree from British planes. Though the tree was hit, it, the Italians and the shrine survived.

Today, according to Tigrinya tradition, if a woman desires a husband or a child, she must prepare coffee in the shade of the tree. If a traveller passes by and accepts a cup, her wish will be granted.

Try to time your trip around Keren's camel market, on Mondays – very atmospheric.

Orientation & Information

The centre of Keren is marked by the Giro Fiori (Circle of Flowers) roundabout.

Commercial Bank (8am-noon & 2-4.30pm Mon-Fri, 8-11am Sat) Changes cash and travellers cheques.

Eritel (8am-8pm Mon-Sat) Telecommunications, next door to the post office.

Post office (8am-noon & 2-6pm Mon-Fri, 8am-noon Sat) About 100m off the Giro Fiori.

Sarina Hotel (Asmara Rd; per hr Nfa20; 8am-9pm) Has internet access.

Sights & Activities

Keren's markets are some of the most interesting in the country and are great for an afternoon's exploration. The **covered market** immediately behind Keren Hotel sells fruit, vegetables, baskets and other household objects. Branching off the covered market are narrow alleyways, columns and low porticoes filled with the whirring machines of tailors and cloth merchants. Beyond, descending towards the well-tended **Italian cemetery**, lies the **grain market**. In another quarter of the covered market, the workshops and boutiques of the **silversmiths** can be found. Keren is traditionally the place to buy silver. Although it's a little cheaper than in Asmara (Nfa60 to Nfa100 per gram), the choice may not be as good.

If you're in town on a Monday between 9am and 2pm, don't miss the clamour of the picturesque **camel market**, 2km out of town on the road to Nakfa. It's a fascinating place to wander, with dozens of camels and busy traders.

Because of its strategic position, Keren was the scene of bitter fighting between the Italians and the British during WWII. This past is conjured up at the **British War Cemetery**, off the Agordat road, about 2.5km northwest of the centre. In it, 440 Commonwealth troops lie buried, including the Hindu soldier Subadar Richpal Ram of the Sixth Rajputana Rifles, who was posthumously awarded the Victoria Cross, Britain's highest military decoration for bravery.

Just past the cemetery, a small **statue of the Madonna** watches over the road from Agordat in the west.

If you continue on foot a further 30 minutes, you come to the shrine of **St Maryam Dearit** (see the boxed text, above), 2.5km out of town. On 29 May every year, there's a pilgrimage to the site, and hundreds of people congregate to dance and sing; if you're in the region at this time, don't miss it.

The old Italian **railway station** (now a bus station) and the old **residential area** testify to Keren's Italian heritage. As in Asmara, some of the architecture is exceptional for the period. Several Italian Roman Catholic churches dot the town, including **St Antonio** and **St Michael**.

Overlooking the town to the northeast is the **Tigu**, the Egyptian fort at 1460m, dating from the 19th century. At its foot lay the ruins of the old Imperial Palace, which was destroyed during the Struggle in 1977. There are good views from the top of the fort.

Sleeping & Eating

Keren has a couple of bland places for budget and midrange travellers, but no upscale options.

Albergo Sicilia (401059; Agordat Rd; r without bathroom Nfa75-90, r Nfa135) The rooms are rough and ready and the bathrooms may raise a few eyebrows but fear not, this is a bearable budget hang-out. It occupies a time-warped colonial house with a flowery courtyard and is close to everything. Keep your expectations in check and you won't be disappointed.

Yohannes Hotel (☎ 401422; Agordat Rd; s without bathroom Nfa77, d without bathroom Nfa88-132, s/d Nfa165/200) A coin's toss from Albergo Sicilia, the Yohannes is not a bad option for an overnight stay, even if the basic bed frames appear to have been filched from an orphanage. Upstairs, the more expensive ones (especially rooms 21 and 32) have bouncier mattresses and get more brightness than the usual Hannibal Lecter lighting scheme.

Sarina Hotel (☎ 400230; fax 402685; Asmara Rd; s incl breakfast Nfa225-390, d incl breakfast Nfa340-520; 🖳) This is usually where tour groups bunk down when in town, which is enough to recommend this well-organised venture about 2km from the centre, on the road to Asmara. This is no beauty queen, architecturally speaking, but it sports spruce rooms and prim bathrooms and there's a good on-site restaurant (mains from Nfa50).

Restaurant Ficki & Selam (Giro Fiori; mains Nfa50-80) There's a good reason that the 'love and peace' restaurant gets favourable reviews from locals and tourists alike – its *capretto* (Nfa75) is expertly cooked. The small terrace overlooking Giro Fiori works a treat on a balmy evening.

Senhit Hotel – Aregay Restaurant (☎ 401042; mains Nfa50-80) Ignore the hotel section – the pongy communal toilets will make you squirm. The real steal is the restaurant – local gourmands swear it prepares the best *capretto al forno* (wood-fired goat) in town. So, Ficki & Selam or Aregay? You be the judge. It's near Giro Fiori.

Heran Pastry (cakes Nfa5; 🕑 7am-8pm) Fresh yogurt – say no more! Off Giro Fiori, this is our favourite refuelling stop for stodgy pastries accompanied by a fresh yogurt.

Drinking

The veranda of the Estif Memorial Cafe & Restaurant (near the post office) is a good place for a sundowner while watching the world go by. The terrace at the Keren Hotel (near the post office) is also an ideal place to sip a beer or an *ariki*. The interior is so frumpy that it's almost charming. Overlooking Giro Fiori, the Red Sea Hotel is a popular watering hole with a shady outdoor area.

Getting There & Away

Keren lies 91km northwest of Asmara. The road is in good condition.

To Asmara, nearly 30 buses depart daily (Nfa33, three hours). For Barentu, around three buses leave each morning (Nfa31, four hours). For Teseney, one bus departs each morning (Nfa70, eight hours); for Agordat there are three daily buses (Nfa20, three hours). For Nakfa, there are three weekly buses (Nfa52, eight to nine hours). For Massawa, change at Asmara.

For the Debre Sina monastery, take a minibus to Elaborid (Nfa10), from where you can charter a 4WD taxi.

AROUND KEREN

There are a couple of monasteries around Keren, including the **Debre Sina monastery**, thought to date from the 6th century. The older, inner part of the church (which unlike many monasteries in Eritrea is open to both men and women) is hewn into the rock and, according to local tradition, is 2100 years old. The troglodyte dwellings of the 60 nuns and priests who live there can also be visited.

The monastery is around 35km east of Keren. From Keren, you can take a bus to Elaborid, where you can arrange a 4WD taxi (Nfa800 to Nfa1000, depending on your bargaining skills). Then it's a 15-minute walk to the monastery.

NAKFA ናቅፋ

elev 1780m

Mention Nakfa to any Eritrean, and they will immediately refer to the Eritrean Resistance. This tiny, remote village lying some 221km from Asmara in the remote and wild province of Sahel has achieved cult status among the whole population, and no wonder. In 1978, after the famous Strategic Withdrawal, Nakfa became the EPLF's centre of resistance. Located on a strategic supply route to Sudan, it received some of the most intense and continuous assaults of the entire war. Nakfa has become the symbol of the Eritrean independence, and it's like a site of pilgrimage for many Eritreans. It even gave its name to the country's new currency.

Nakfa is a poignant place, even for those who are not normally military-minded. You'll see underground towns as well as the Tsa'abraha Underground Hospital. Unfortunately, the town has been off limits to travellers for about 10 years, for obscure reasons – 'because of road works' is one of many official explanations.

ERITREA

HIKING UP TSADA AMBA

One word: awesome. South of Keren, the hike up to the church of Tsada Amba, perched at an altitude of 2100m on the eponymous mountain, is a thrilling experience. It requires a bit of gumption (and money), but it's worth every bead of sweat (and nakfa), and you'll be rewarded with truly exceptional vistas. This hike can be covered in one day, but we suggest that you allow two days (from Asmara). In theory, you need a permit from the Orthodox Headquarters in Asmara (p362); in practice, the risk of being turned back by the monks is low.

From Keren, drive about 18km to the west (on the Agordat road), until you come to a junction. Turn left and follow the dirt track. A 4WD is essential. You'll skirt a bulky mountain to your left – this is Tsada Amba. After 30km, you'll reach a dead end in a river bed, at the base of the mountain (about 1050m).

Hire a local guide at the nearby village, then start the ascent. The path climbs fairly steeply up the western flank of the valley, amid rocky boulders. After 1½ hours you come to a place called Gimja Worq, which is a 'base camp' for the monks, at 1530m. You'll be welcomed by the monks, who will provide bread and tea and may treat you to a foot massage – a nice touch! You can overnight on the terrace of a concrete building. Mats are provided, as well as Vivienne Westwood silk sheets...kidding. Just mats. Donations are welcome.

The next morning, tackle the ascent to the top of Tsada Amba, along a mule path. Allow 1¾ hours for the rocky slog up to the church, which sits atop a ridge, at 2100m. The ample reward for all this effort is the sensational view, embracing Tsada Amba, the central mountains and the flat expanses of the Western Lowlands dotted with cute villages.

Do not attempt to go to the monastery itself, which sits at the tip of the ridge. Your guide might tell you that 'some tourists did it', but we strongly advise against attempting the perilous crossing to get there. It would involve crawling along a razor's edge, with sheer vertical drops either side. The monks cross this narrow strip of rock totally unperturbed, but don't try to emulate them!

The walk downhill to Gimja Worq takes about 1½ hours. From there, instead of backtracking down to the riverbed, ask your guide to take the path that leads to the village of Belo (1815m), reached after two hours, where your driver can pick you up. From Belo, it's a 22km ride on a dirt road to reach the main Keren–Asmara road.

Try to make this excursion coincide with Keren's Monday camel market. Start early from Asmara on Monday; visit the camel market in Keren in the morning; then ask your driver to drop you (and your guide) at the beginning of the trail (don't start the ascent later than 3pm). Spend the night in Gimja Worq, with the monks. The next morning, climb up to Tsada Amba. You should be down at Belo village early in the afternoon (where your driver will pick you up), to be back in Asmara in time for *passeggiata*.

Check the situation with the tourist office in Asmara.

Getting There & Away

There are three weekly buses from Keren to Nakfa (Nfa52, eight to nine hours). Although it's just about 110km from Keren, the ride is nonetheless tiring. The road after Afabet is very rough in parts and winds through the mountains.

SOUTHERN ERITREA

Good news: Eritrea's south remains open to travellers (with the notable exception of Debre Libanos). All the better, because this is the most scenic part of the country, with a gorgeous mix of jagged peaks, bulky rocky outcrops, vast plateaus, vertigo-inducing gorges, awesome escarpments and a smattering of intriguing towns and villages in between – this is the Abyssinia you've been dreaming about.

For history buffs, southern Eritrea offers an unparalleled opportunity to step back in time. It's like an open-air archaeological site, with monasteries cut into cliffs and modest yet enigmatic ruins that testify to former flourishing civilisations. And there's Dekemhare, complete with heritage buildings from the Italian era.

Overall this is the easiest part of the country in which to travel. Don't miss it.

DEKEMHARE ደቀምሓረ

pop 26,000 / elev 2060m

If you're serious about Art Deco, don't miss Dekemhare. This laid-back town has a handful of well-preserved colonial buildings. The Italians had planned to make it the industrial capital of Eritrea, and Dekemhare became an important industrial centre where offices, warehouses and factories were concentrated. During the war of independence, however, the town suffered much damage, and today just two of the old factories still operate. Other remains of colonial days include the old market with its iron roof to protect the fruit, vegetables and grain.

Information

Commercial Bank of Eritrea (8-11.30am & 2-5pm Mon-Fri, 8-11.30am Sat) Cannot change travellers cheques, but does change cash.

Eritel (8am-noon & 2-7pm)

Post office (8am-noon & 2-5.30pm Mon-Fri, 8am-noon Sat)

Sleeping & Eating

Dahlak Hotel (641840; off Mendefera Rd; s/d Nfa70/120) An Eritrean friend sagely informs us, 'This is an excellent deal here'. 'Excellent' is a relative term, but it's cheap, secure and reasonably clean – a holy trinity for tired travellers. The on-site restaurant has an eclectic menu that runs the gamut from *capretto* (roast goat) to pasta. Bonus: you're just spitting distance from two lovely Art Deco buildings.

Park Hotel (641304; fax 641959; Mendefera Rd; s Nfa110-220, d Nfa220-330) A nice surprise. On the outside it looks like a Brutalist monolith, but on the inside the Park is easier on the eyes, with clean tiles, kitschy bedcovers (some sport lovely brocaded hearts – nice try) and spick and span bathrooms. The restaurant (mains from Nfa50) has a varied menu with good Eritrean and Italian fare.

Castello Pastry Shop (7am-8pm) If you want to treat yourself, this place in the centre, opposite the cinema, has tempting pastries – provided flour is available. There's an adjacent bar.

Getting There & Away

Dekemhare is 37km from Asmara. For Asmara there are about 30 buses a day (Nfa12, one hour); Adi Keyh has about three buses daily (Nfa18, two hours); for Senafe, you'll need to change at Adi Keyh.

There's a rough road that winds from Dekemhare to just north of Mendefera. Two morning buses travel to Mendefera daily (Nfa15, around two hours).

AROUND DEKEMHARE

At the exit from a gorge, at the approach to some experimental agricultural nurseries, is the village of **Segheneyti**, about 20km from Dekemhare. It is dominated by the huge Catholic Church of St Michael and two forts from which there are good views.

If you're after sustainably produced local textiles, make a beeline for the **Saganeiti Women Training Centre Workshop** (Segheneyti; 8am-noon & 2-5pm Mon-Sat). This workshop run by Capucin Sisters employs local women, and you can see them at work. There's a small shop where you can buy *netsela* (white cotton cloth) and more colourful ceremonial dresses (from Nfa200).

Continuing south of Segheneyti, the road traverses the plain of Deghera, known popularly as the **Valley of the Sycamores** for the magnificent sycamore figs that march across the plain. At dusk, the trees make one of the most beautiful natural sights in all of Eritrea. Many are at least 300 years old. Village assemblies, community debates and advisory sessions from the elders still take place under their branches.

ADI KEYH ዓዲ ቀይሕ

pop 23,000 / elev 2390m

The dust-swirling city of Adi Keyh, 104km from Asmara, boasts one green mosque, a nice Catholic church and an afternoon market that should be chaotic if the economy was not in the doldrums. It's a staging post for visiting the archaeological ruins of Qohaito.

You can bunk down at the **Central Hotel** (650632; s Nfa130-150, d Nfa130-250), which sports tiled bathrooms, tidy rooms and firm mattresses. There's also a restaurant (mains from Nfa50).

Around one to three buses leave daily for Senafe (Nfa10, 45 minutes), and only one to two buses were running daily to Asmara (Nfa32, four hours) at the time of writing.

QOHAITO ቐሓይቶ

Shrouded in peaceful solitude amid a vast, barren plateau, the archaeological site of Qohaito is a must-see for anyone with an interest in Eritrea's ancient past. Don't expect colossal monuments, though – the scant finds of this site are not exactly gripping. Instead, come here to ponder over its former grandeur and you'll leave happy.

To top it off, the scenery is captivating on a clear day: the air is pure, the surrounding mountains make a perfect backdrop and there's a special kind of beauty in the barrenness of the plateau.

History

According to some specialists, the ancient town of Qohaito flourished at the time of the great Aksumite kingdom and provided a staging post between the ancient port of Adulis in the north and the capital of the kingdom, Aksum, in the south. Even if it was not the case (some modern scholars favour Metera), Qohaito's importance in the ancient world during this time is obvious.

Very little is known about the exact history of the settlement. A few ancient chronicles record that Qohaito was still flourishing in the 6th century AD. However, like Adulis and Metera, it then vanished very suddenly in the next 100 or 200 years.

At an altitude of 2700m, Qohaito lies high above the port of Adulis and the baking lowlands, and may also once have served as a summer retreat for the Aksumite merchants. The traces of cultivated areas found between the buildings have led to the belief that Qohaito was once a garden city.

Orientation & Information

Situated 121km south of Asmara, Qohaito's impressive ruins are spread over a large area measuring 2.5km wide by 15km long. As much as 90% of the ruins remain unexcavated, and information – even the age of the sites – remains scarce. Admission is free but you will need to get a permit from the National Museum office in Asmara (see p323).

If you want to visit the rock art sites or the great canyon, you should ask at the village of Qohaito for a guide. One guide who speaks passable English is Ibrahim. He'll check your permit and will expect a small tip (Nfa50 should be okay).

Sights

GREAT CANYON

Wow! A short walk from Qohaito takes you to the edge of a vast canyon that plummets dramatically. Come here on a clear day (get there early in the morning, as it tends to cloud

over later) and you'll be rewarded by truly orgasmic views.

A word of warning: don't stand too close to the edge of the canyon – it's easy to feel dizzy, and there's no fence.

TEMPLE OF MARIAM WAKIRO
ማርያም ዋቒሮ ቤተ - መቅደስ

Although it does not play in the same league as Macchu Picchu, the Temple of Mariam Wakiro ranks among Qohaito's most important ruins. Four columns rise out of a mass of stones and fallen pillars. One of the columns is topped by an unusual four-sided capital. The temple was built on a rectangular plan on a solid platform, and may have been the site of a very early Christian church or even a pre-Christian temple. Nearby, other pilasters and platforms attest to the existence of at least half a dozen other temples.

EGYPTIAN TOMB
ሓወልቲ መቓብር ግብጻውያን

To the north, a little less than 1km from the ruins of Mariam Wakiro, lies an ancient underground tomb dug out of sandstone. Discovered in 1894, the tomb faces east, overlooking the Hedamo River. Rectangular and built with large blocks of stones, its most distinctive features are the two quatrefoil (flower-shaped) crosses carved on the inside walls; go inside otherwise you won't see them.

SAPHIRA DAM ሳፊራ ግድብ

This structure, situated beyond the new village mosque, measures 67m long and 16m deep and is constructed of large rectangular blocks of stone. For around 1000 years, it has served the local Saho people as the main source of water. It's supposedly Qohaito's greatest claim to fame, although it's pretty boring from a visual point of view – it's just a pool, after all.

A team of German archaeologists has suggested – amid hot controversy – that the structure may actually be a water cistern dating to the Aksumite period, and not a dam dating to the pre-Aksumite period as had previously been thought.

ADI ALAUTI CAVE & GORGE

There are several rock art sites scattered in the area. The most easily accessible and the best-preserved one is the cave of Adi Alauti. Getting there is half the fun. It involves a beautiful 30-minute walk along a mule path down the edge of a vertiginous gorge. The views of the surrounding mountains, including Mt Ambasoira (3013m) to the south (the highest peak in Eritrea), are stunning. Far below, you can make out the terraced fields and tiny *tukuls* (thatched conical huts) of a seemingly inaccessible Saho settlement. In the cave, a close inspection reveals a large number of animals, including camels, giraffes, hyenas and gazelles, depicted in ochre and white.

It's definitely worth the sweat, if only for the jaw-dropping vistas.

Getting There & Away

From Adi Keyh, it's an 11km drive south until you reach the left-hand turn-off from the main road, marked by a signpost; then it's a further 10km along a dirt road to the village of Qohaito. A 4WD is essential to cover the latter stretch. Public transport being almost nonexistent, your best bet is to book a tour with one of the travel agencies in Asmara or to rent a 4WD with driver. You could also charter a minibus from Adi Keyh.

SENAFE ሰንዓፈ

pop 15,000

The fate of Senafe is closely linked to geopolitics. The last Eritrean town of any size before the Ethiopian border, 139km from Asmara, Senafe feels like a depressed outpost, due to the tension between the two countries. While the surrounding craggy mountainscape is sensational, Senafe still bears the scars of its extreme battering during the conflict with Ethiopia – think gutted buildings, heavy military presence and disorganised infrastructure. This shouldn't stop you visiting, though. Senafe has a few good surprises up its sleeves. The not-to-be-missed ancient city of Metera is just 2km south of town, and the dramatic rocky outcrop of Amba Metera will tempt the hiker in you.

Information

There are few facilities in Senafe. The town has no bank and the telecom office was not in operation at the time of writing.

Military – immigration office (off the main street) Opposite the temporary hospital, about 100m past the bus station. It's housed in a crumbling, concrete building, behind a ruined house, and it's staffed by the military. If you have your travel permit delivered by the Tourist Information Centre in Asmara, and provided things are quiet at the border, it will issue the permit to visit Metera on the spot.

Post office (☺ 8am-noon & 2-6pm Mon-Fri)

Sights & Activities

Apart from the archaeological site of Metera, Senafe is known for the huge rocky outcrops that dominate the plain. You can hike to the top of **Amba Metera**, one of the outcrops, in about an hour. Local boys soon appear and will guide you for a tip (about Nfa50). The most popular route takes 45 to 60 minutes; the last section involves a scramble over boulders; in one place, a fixed rope helps you up a short section in which grooves are chiselled into the rock. If you're not confident enough, don't attempt it – you don't really need to go to the top to savour the dizzying view that recalls Senafe's name, which is supposedly derived from the Arabic: 'Can you see San'a?'

Make sure you go early in the morning, as it gets very hazy later on.

On the way to Amba Metera, you can't miss the venerable **Kidane Mehret Church**, which was extensively restored in 2007 with the support of Alliance Française in Asmara. Its originality comes from the construction method (called 'monkey head') and the materials that were used to build it. The supporting walls incorporate wooden beams that protrude from the exterior of the walls; they look like rows of monkey scalps.

The **grain and vegetable market**, located just over 1km outside town, is worth a peek, particularly on Saturday, the major market day.

Sleeping & Eating

Senafe Hotel (main street; r without bathroom Nfa45) A tolerable option, with spartan, hanky-sized rooms and saggy mattresses. It's near the main intersection.

Star Hotel (main street; r Nfa80) This is good value if you're just looking for somewhere to hang your hat before taking off to Metera or Amba Metera the next morning. Rooms come with private bathroom and are arranged around a flowery courtyard. They are scrubbed, if a little musty. Try not to wrinkle your nose too much and enjoy a stiff drink and a well-prepared roast goat at the attached restaurant. It's at the southern fringe of town, just past the temporary hospital.

Momona Hotel (main street; mains Nfa35-50) Was the only decent hotel before the war but was destroyed by the Ethiopians. The restaurant at the back of the compound is open, though. It serves *capretto*, pasta and *zigni* (meat cooked in a hot sauce) at puny prices, but the service is painfully slow.

ERITREA

Getting There & Away

Buses from Senafe go to Adi Keyh at least every hour (Nfa9, 45 minutes). To Asmara (Nfa35, four hours), three to four buses were plying the route every morning at the time of writing. They leave around 7am.

AROUND SENAFE
Monastery of Debre Libanos

Aaargh! The monastery of Debre Libanos (also known as Debre Hawariyat) could well be one of the highlights of any trip to Eritrea but – you've got used to it by now – it's strictly off-limits to foreigners due to its proximity to the ultra-sensitive Ethiopian border. Let's make a wish: the border dispute with Ethiopia is settled once and for all by the time you read this, and the monastery is again accessible. If it comes true, the walk to the monastery makes for an exhilarating excursion.

Debre Libanos is the oldest monastery in Eritrea. Embedded into a steep cliff, it's thought to date from the 6th century. It is open only to men (a rule that is strictly enforced) but other parts on the other side of the valley can be visited by women, including a collection of 60 mummified bodies (supposed to date from the 4th century).

Debre Libanos is accessible from the very remote village of Hamm, perched dramatically on a high plateau, with sweeping views all around. Hamm can be reached in less than two hours by foot from the village of Haaz, about 25km southwest of Senafe (a 4WD is essential). The walk from Haaz is worthwhile for its scenery of dramatic peaks and valleys and vertiginous views south into Ethiopia. From Hamm, a steep and fairly difficult descent takes you down to the monastery (around 50 minutes down). From the monastery, it's a one-hour walk across the valley to reach the site of the mummified bodies. From there your guide should be able to show you a quicker way back to Hamm (about one hour), but expect a steep ascent. Altogether, expect a six-hour loop (minimum) from Haaz.

There is a guesthouse some 10 minutes from the monastery where guests can stay for free (on a goat skin on the floor); a contribution for the monastery is expected.

A fun alternative is to approach Debre Libanos from Tsorena, about 30km to the northwest.

To get there, a 4WD with driver is needed.

Remember that, even if the monastery is again accessible to visitors, you'll need a permit obtainable at the Orthodox Tewahdo Church Headquarters in Asmara (see p362). At the time of writing, the Orthodox Tewahdo Church did not issue permits to foreigners – allegedly for security reasons.

METERA መተራ

The site of Metera is a must-see if you're serious about history or archaeology. However, if you're coming to Metera expecting to find archaeological sites to rival Greece or Italy, you're are going to be sorely disappointed, as remains are visually underwhelming. This doesn't mean a visit here isn't worthwhile, far from it. Metera is an Eritrean highlight – it's just that around these parts it's more about atmosphere, and that's something Metera has in abundance, especially if you happen to be here late afternoon on a clear day; the truly magical light adds a touch of poignancy and eeriness to the site.

History

Like Qohaito, Metera flourished around the time of the ancient civilisation of Aksum. The scattered ruins testify to the existence of a once large and prosperous town.

Metera is important for three main reasons: for its age – some of it, from about the 5th century BC, actually pre-dates Aksum; for its huge size – it spreads over at least 20 hectares, making it the largest Aksumite site after Aksum itself and Aksum's port, Adulis; and for its unusual character – it is the only place in the Aksumite civilisation where a large bourgeois community is known to have thrived.

If you've visited Aksum in Ethiopia, you'll soon recognise the typical Aksumite architectural features present at Metera, such as construction in tiers. There are also big differences from Aksum, such as the plan and layout of the buildings. Nevertheless, it is clear that there were very strong cultural ties between Aksum, Adulis and Metera, not just during the Aksumite period, but earlier too.

Orientation & Information

The site lies about 2km south of Senafe. Admission is free but you'll need a permit from the National Museum office in Asmara (see p323). In Senafe, you'll also need to obtain a permit from the military (see p339) which is issued on the spot.

If you want to do full justice to this site, your best bet is to visit it with a knowledgeable guide. Contact one of the travel agencies in Asmara (see p319).

Sights

THE STELE ሓወልቲ - ሕልፊ እምነ መቻብር

One of Metera's most important objects is its enigmatic stele. Unique in Eritrea, the stele is known for its pagan, pre-Christian symbol of the sun over the crescent moon, engraved on the top of the eastern face. Like the famous Aksum stelae, it faces eastward.

Standing about 5m tall, the stele has an inscription near the middle in Ge'ez. An unknown king dedicates the stele to his ancestors who had subjugated the 'mighty people of Awanjalon, Tsebelan'.

Inexplicably, the stele was uprooted from its original position on the hill, and was at one time broken into two pieces. Today it is at the foot of the hill Amba Saim, in front of the open plain.

EXCAVATIONS

Metera was 'discovered' in 1868, when Frenchman Denis de Rivoire reported its existence. In 1959 the Ethiopian Institute of Archaeology began major excavations under the French archaeologist Francis Anfray. From 1959 to 1965 Anfray excavated various sites. A large mound 100m northwest of the stele revealed a large central building – perhaps a **royal palace** or a villa – attached to an annexe of living quarters. A huge wall surrounds the whole complex. Excavations revealed several burial chambers in the larger building; in one of them, the skeleton of a chained prisoner was discovered.

Between 1961 and 1962, two additional mounds were investigated. Excavations exposed a large, square, multiroomed complex, built on a sturdy podium. A **tomb chamber** was also unearthed – but, curiously, it was empty.

In the middle of the ruins, one of the building structures, made from finely chiselled, large blocks of limestone, contains a stairway that descends into a corridor. Though collapsed, the remains of what seems to be an **underground tunnel** are visible. According to local legend, this tunnel dates from the time of King Kaleb, and leads all the way to Aksum, hundreds of kilometres to the south. Curiously, a similar entrance

is said to exist in Aksum, but it is blocked by a large boulder. A more modern hypothesis – and almost as exciting – is that the 'tunnel' is a deep burial chamber containing great sarcophagi.

Objects unearthed at Metera in the last 50 years include some beautiful and amazingly well-preserved gold objects – two crosses, two chains, a brooch, necklaces and 14 Roman coins dating from between the 2nd and 3rd centuries AD – found in a bronze vase. Bronze coins minted by the great Aksumite kings have also been found, as have many 'household' items.

Only a tiny part of Metera has been excavated. Big mounds lie tantalisingly untouched all around. The ancient people's tombs – hidden somewhere among the rocks – still await exploration, and may yield remarkable finds.

Getting There & Around

Metera is just 2km from Senafe, so is easily reached on foot or by 4WD.

MENDEFERA መንደፈራ

pop 65,000 / elev 1980m

Glamorous it may not be, but Mendefera has managed to retain a lively ambience despite Eritrea's economic woes. The capital of Dubub province, it's refreshingly active.

Reflecting an old rivalry, the town is dominated by two churches: the Orthodox San Giorgio and the Catholic church school, situated on opposite hills.

The town's name refers to the hill around which the town grew up. Mendefera (literally meaning 'No One Dared') is a reference to the fierce resistance put up by the local people against Italian colonisation. The hill was never taken.

Information

Commercial Bank (8am-noon & 2-5pm Mon-Fri, 8-11am Sat) Can change cash (euros and US dollars) and travellers cheques.

Eritel (8am-8pm) At the main roundabout.

Post office (8am-noon & 2-6pm Mon-Fri, 8am-noon Sat) At the main roundabout.

Sleeping & Eating

Mendefera has several places to stay. Most hotels are scattered along the road to Adi Quala, on the southern outskirts of town. Most places have their own restaurant and welcome nonguests.

ERITREA

Mereb Hotel (☎ 611443, 611636; Adi Quala Rd; r Nfa200-280) The Mereb is a sure-fire bet, with well-maintained rooms, English-speaking staff (ask for Saba, the lady who runs the place), hot showers, bladder-friendly toilets and the odd chance of scoring a room with garden views at the back. Throw in a good restaurant (mains Nfa40 to Nfa80) and you're laughing. It's about 800m from the post office, on the road to Adi Quala.

HG Family Hotel & Recreation Centre (☎ 07114479, 07136652; Adi Quala Rd; r without bathroom Nfa200, r Nfa300) The bad news: the incongruous location, about 5km south of town on the road to Adi Quala. Now let's move onto the good news. Hush and seclusion reign supreme here, and the front garden overflowing with colourful plants works a treat. The restaurant is excellent and feels like a mini-museum, complete with the mandatory goatskins, wooden chairs and artefacts. The 15 rooms don't live up to the surroundings but are well equipped. Your hosts, Alem and Haile, are friendly to boot, speak good English and can pick you up at the bus station.

Green Belt Bar & Restaurant (Asmara Rd; mains Nfa25-60) Almost opposite St George Bar & Restaurant, this modernish venture is like a German car: reassuring and well organised. The menu includes sandwiches, *capretto* and *tibsi*.

St George Bar & Restaurant (Asmara Rd; mains Nfa40-70) It doesn't look much from the outside (and it's hard to read the faded sign), but this eatery comes recommended by locals. It does all the staples with the expertise of a grandmother. Do the litmus test here: the lack of decor inversely matches the quality of the food.

Kangaroo Pastry (Asmara Rd) This unfussy cake shop serves a variety of delectable sweets, including spongy cakes, but not kangaroo.

Getting There & Away

Mendefera's bus station is a 20-minute walk from the town centre, off the road to Asmara. To Asmara, around 30 buses depart daily (Nfa16, two hours). To Adi Quala, around 10 buses go daily (Nfa8). To Dekemhare, two buses leave in the morning (Nfa15, three hours).

ADI QUALA ዓዲ ቋላ
elev 2054m

Adi Quala functions as a frontier town (it's the last town of any size before the Ethiopian border). The status of frontier town can be either a blessing or a damnation. In the case of Adi Quala, it's more a damnation. With the border with Ethiopia being indefinitely closed, this town is another casualty of war – it has lost much of its vitality and *raison d'être*, and it was out of bounds for foreigners at the time of writing.

Adi Quala features an attractive **tukul church** on the southern edge of the city. The church has some interesting frescoes, including a depiction of the battle of Adwa. It's a good place to see traditional Eritrean religious painting if you haven't already.

Getting There & Away

To Asmara, about 10 buses run daily (Nfa25, 4½ hours). When the border with Ethiopia reopens, there will be regular services to Adwa.

THE RED SEA COAST

What a change. A mere three-hour bus or car ride from Asmara (and a whopping loss of 2500m in altitude) will transport you to yet another world. It's immediately noticeable that the coastal town of Massawa looks not west towards the Abyssinian highlands but east across the water towards Arabia. With its distinct atmosphere and refreshingly humble scale, it's a great place to kick back for a few days. Be warned, though: from April to October, it's scorching hot.

Luckily, the Eritrean coast has remained wild, pristine and untouched, and tourist infrastructure is scarce. If your idea of the perfect holiday is drinking cocktails in a skimpy bikini at a swanky resort, change your plans.

Then there are the mysterious, outrageous and strangely seductive Dahlak Islands, which are haphazardly scattered off the coast. This archipelago is the kind of place you go to just drop off the planet for a while. A couple of days sailing around them or camping on their beaches makes for a memorable experience. It requires a bit of gumption (and luck) to get there, but this adds savour and spice to the adventure.

MASSAWA ባጽዕ
pop 35,000

Though only about 100km to the east of Asmara, Massawa could not be more different from the capital. The history, climate, architecture and atmosphere of the town seem to come from another world. Massawa has a more Arab feel to it, reflecting its centuries-old connection with Arabia on the other side of the Red Sea. Entering Massawa Island, you could be forgiven for thinking you're in Zanzibar or Yemen, and it's pure joy to explore the alleyways and streets flanked by low, whitewashed buildings, porticoes and arcades.

The sad thing is that these fragile architectural beauties are gradually disintegrating due to a lack of funds. Most visitors are shocked by the derelict state of a number of historic buildings. Various restoration schemes were under investigation a few years ago, but nothing has been done yet.

Like Asmara, Massawa has been severely hit by the battered economy. During the day, business is slack, and you won't see more than a couple of cargo ships in the international harbour. Nightlife? Dream on. Lots of bars and clubs have closed down due to the economic downturn. The city that was once buzzing has vanished.

Massawa is still a fascinating place to explore because of its exotic (and melancholic) character. It's also hassle-free and pretty safe – no mean feat for a port. Plus, the seafood is fresh, and when it's paired with a cold beer (when available) and a starry sky, with the smell of frankincense wafting from the doors of private homes...well, you get the picture.

One major drawback is the heat. With the high coastal humidity, the town can seem like a sauna, and there's marginal variation between day- and night-time temperatures. The best time to visit Massawa is from October to April.

Massawa is also the obvious launching pad for exploring the Dahlak Islands.

History

Massawa's natural deep harbour and its position close to the mouth of the Red Sea and the Indian Ocean have long made it the target of foreign powers. It was occupied by the Portuguese, Arabs, Turks and Egyptians; finally, the British held it for a time before they all but handed it over to the Italians in 1885. Trade in Massawa flourished throughout these occupations; everything – slaves, pearls, giraffes, incense, ostriches and myrrh – passed through the port.

Massawa's buildings reflect its history of occupation. The Ottoman Turks, who occupied the city for nearly 300 years, had the biggest influence on the architecture. Their successors, the Egyptians, also left a legacy of buildings and public works, including the elevated causeways, an aqueduct and the governor's palace. In 1885 the Italians occupied Massawa, and the town became their capital until it was superseded by Asmara in 1897. During this time, many of the fabulous villas were built.

Once one of the most beautiful cities on the Red Sea, Massawa was all but flattened during the Struggle for Independence. Around 90% of the town was blitzed by Ethiopian blanket bombing, and great scars are still visible.

Orientation

The town of Massawa consists of two islands, Taulud and Massawa, and a mainland area. The mainland area, called Massawa, is largely residential, and a long causeway connects it to Taulud Island. Taulud is home to some old Italian villas, the administrative buildings, and a few of the town's smarter hotels.

A shorter causeway connects Taulud to the second island, known simply as Batsi (or Massawa Island). This is the oldest part of town and in many ways its heart. The port is here, along with most of the restaurants and bars.

Information

Note that business hours in Massawa differ from those in the rest of the country. Government offices open from 6am to 2.30pm Monday to Friday from June to September and from 8am to noon and 4pm to 6.30pm Monday to Friday from October to May. Private businesses open from 6am to noon and 3pm to 6pm Monday to Friday the whole year.

BIT Internet Training Software (Massawa Is; per hr Nfa10; 7am-10pm) Under the arcades on the seafront. Very slow connections.

Commercial Bank of Eritrea (Massawa Is; 7-11.30am & 4-5pm Mon-Fri, 7-10.30am Sat) Changes cash and travellers cheques (US dollars and euros).

Eritel (Massawa Is; 7am-10pm) Telecommunications office. In the same building as the post office.

Post office (Massawa Is, 7am-noon & 4-6pm Mon-Fri, 7am-noon Sat)

ERITREA

ERITREA

MASSAWA

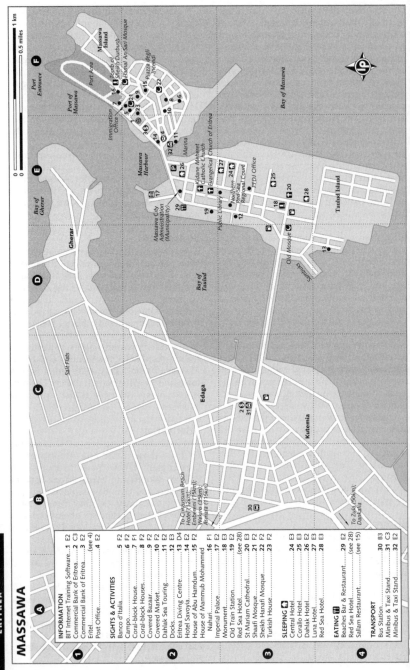

Sights

MASSAWA ISLAND ባጽዕ ደሴት

Even if many buildings are in a very bad shape, they boast a dilapidated charm that is uniquely unforgettable. Start your exploration with a cup of coffee and delve into the maze of little streets. Fear not, you're never lost for long.

As you come over the causeway from Taulud Island, a broad sweep of white, arcaded *palazzi* (palaces) stretches out before you. On the corner, opposite the transport office, you'll see the **Hotel Savoiya** (no sign) with its long gallery.

Near the port entrance there is a good example of a 17th-century **coral-block house**. For centuries, coral was the local building stone. Heading back towards the causeway, you'll pass the **Banco d'Italia**, an exact copy of its 1920s original and a mishmash of styles, including Gothic windows and towers. Unfortunately, the building is dilapidated and awaits restoration. In a square beyond the Banco is a rare example of a **Turkish house** with a domed roof, now partially restored. Turn back towards the port entrance, passing by the **Shaafi Mosque**. Founded in the 11th century but rebuilt several times since, it's worth a quick look.

As you keep heading towards the port, you'll come across the ancient **house of Mammub Mohammed Nahari** with soaring Ottoman-style windows on every side. Unfortunately, they are particularly decrepit. Around this area are some large and ornate 18th-century Armenian and Jewish **merchant houses**.

About 100m from Sallam Restaurant is the **house of Abu Hamdum**. It used to have a *mashrabiyya* (trellised) balcony, which allowed cool breezes to enter and the air inside to circulate. It's a remarkable example of Turkish Ottoman architecture, but it needs urgent restoration. Continue on until you get to the Piazza degli Incendi (meaning 'Square of the Fire', after it was the scene of a great fire in 1885), in the centre of which is the **Sheikh Hanafi Mosque**. At over 500 years old, this mosque is one of the oldest surviving structures in the city. Sheikh Hanafi was a great teacher, who funded his students' studies in Egypt. The walls of the courtyard are decorated with stuccowork and inside hangs a remarkable chandelier from the glassworks of Murano near Venice in Italy.

Passing through the piazza, notice the small group of **coral-block houses** with finely detailed façades on your right. Then turn left into the Campo, a huge square lined on all sides by houses with trellised balconies, finely carved wooden doors and shutters of Turkish or Egyptian origin.

To the north of the Campo is the **covered market**. Behind and to the north of the market lies the Massawa Hotel, bringing you into the main commercial artery of the town. Turn right towards the heart of the old town then take the first left. This area was the old **covered bazaar**. Its ancient roof – in the Turkish style – was beamed like an upturned boat; at the time of writing, there was only a very small section remaining.

TAULUD ISLAND

Just north of the gates of the Dahlak Hotel is the **Imperial Palace**, overlooking the harbour. The palace was badly damaged during the Struggle for Independence. In its present state, it gives a very vivid idea of how all Massawa looked shortly after the war. The original palace was built by the Turkish Osdemir Pasha in the 16th century. The present building dates from 1872, when it was built for the Swiss adventurer Werner Munzinger. During the federation with Ethiopia, it was used as a winter palace by Emperor Haile Selassie, whose heraldic lions still decorate the gates. It's usually possible to wander around the grounds.

Back on the causeway road, you'll see to your right the restored municipal buildings. Head south down the tree-lined road, past the Dahlak Hotel. Hotels and villas line the eastern shore. Some of the villas are exceptionally beautiful, combining elements of Art Deco style with traditional Moorish arcades and huge *mashrabiyya* balconies. After about 500m you'll find yourself at the Orthodox **St Mariam Cathedral**, which is at the end of the causeway from the mainland. Opposite the cathedral is the massive **monument** to the Eritrean Struggle for Independence. Three huge tanks are preserved where they stopped in the final assault on the town in 1990, and now stand on a black marble base which is lovingly cleaned each morning.

South of the cathedral is the famous **Red Sea Hotel**, scene of many glamorous balls in the 1960s and 1970s. Devastated in the war, it has been rebuilt and is now a reputable hotel.

Take the road on the western side of Taulud and head north, passing by the causeway leading to the mainland. Look out for birds in

ERITREA

the mud flats around the causeway. Pelicans are quite common visitors. Continuing north, you'll pass the **old train station**, built during the Italian occupation, with its columns and elegant facade. There is access to the *sambuk* (dhow) **docks** just south of the train station, and it's worth taking a look at these traditional boats. Then you can recharge the batteries at the Beaches Bar & Restaurant (see opposite), housed in the rather ugly 'Twin Towers' (no joke) building!

Activities

DIVING

Massawa is the starting point for trips to the Dahlak Islands, Eritrea's main diving destination (see p349). Trips to the islands and equipment hire can be organised in Massawa through the **Eritrea Diving Center** (☎ 552688, 552198; fax 551287; Taulud Is). For details, see p350.

FISHING

If you want to go fishing, you can hire a boat and a captain and set off. A half-day's rental of a small boat in the Bay of Massawa costs about Nfa3000 for one to three people, including the boat captain. Contact **Dahlak Sea Touring** (☎ 07123126; Massawa Is).

SNORKELLING

Green Island (also known as Sheikh Saïd Island) is 10 to 20 minutes from Massawa and is the most accessible place for decent snorkelling and tolerable beaches. To be frank, it ain't Bora Bora, but it can make an excellent retreat if you need some hush and a place to rest your sightseeing-abused feet. Contact Dahlak Sea Touring or the Eritrea Diving Center (see p350 for contact details and prices).

SWIMMING

Don't expect porcelain sand and translucent waters lapping your toes – beaches are *not* Massawa's forté. If you really fancy a dip, try the stretch of sand at the Gurgussum Beach Hotel (opposite) on the mainland. It's OK, though it suffers a bit from litter and algae due to tidal fluctuations. You could also head to Green Island (see above).

Sleeping & Eating

It's best to avoid the hotels on Massawa Island, as they're noisy and decrepit. Though less central, Taulud is much quieter and offers better standards in more polished surroundings, but prices are fairly high for Eritrea. A brief reminder: though most hotels are close to the shore, there's no beach where you can cool off.

Most hotels have on-site restaurants and welcome nonguests.

TAULUD ISLAND

Corallo Hotel (☎ 07113852; r Nfa160-270; 🛞) It's good budget-hotel fodder here. Let your hair down in the light and breezy rooms that occupy a renovated colonial building that exudes crusty charm. The more expensive ones have (noisy) air-con, high ceilings, tiled floors and balconies with sweet vistas. Baths get all the proper scrubbing. The restaurant is an added bonus.

Luna Hotel (☎ 552272; d Nfa160-280; 🛞) Another good-value venture, the Luna has pleasantly simple rooms but bathrooms are microscopic and there are no views to speak of despite its proximity to the sea. The more expensive rooms have air-con. The real steal is the restaurant, with a good choice of pasta, salads and Eritrean specialities (mains from Nfa60). If you want a recommendation, go for the macaroni or the fried shrimps.

Central Hotel (☎ 552002; s/d Nfa275/410, ste Nfa495; 🛞) Boasting an enviable location by the shore, the well-managed Central Hotel won't get you writing home but the rooms are neat and serviceable. The weak point? Most rooms overlook the car park at the back. Tip: angle for rooms 202, 203, 204 and 205, which have (oblique) sea views. The restaurant gets an A+ for its eclectic menu and savoury dishes (mains from Nfa60). The fried shrimps are truly delicious. You can eat alfresco, right by the seashore.

Red Sea Hotel (☎ 552839; fax 552544; s/d Nfa450/550; 🛞) This Italian-designed hotel is still regarded as one of the best options in Massawa but the decor is beginning to age, the '80s-style furnishings are rickety and the carpets are permanently stained from goodness knows what. However it's well equipped and has 50 tidy rooms with air-con, satellite TV, springy beds, balcony, large bathrooms and partial sea views. Facilities include a restaurant and gardens at the back. If you can forgive the dull dining room, the food is generally good quality (mains from Nfa70).

Dahlak Hotel (☎ 552818; fax 551282) The massive Dahlak defies financial viability: it has been undergoing a major extension (and renovation) for, say, almost seven years, and it still wasn't open when we passed through! One day, *insh allah*, it should feature excellent facilities, including a swimming pool and a marina. The owner has also embarked on the construction of a new hotel on Dissei Island (see p349).

Beaches Bar & Restaurant (mains Nfa60-110) Beaches? What beaches? Found at the back of the rather incongruous 'Twin Towers' building, this is the only independent restaurant on Taulud Island. Nosh on tasty Eritrean staples or tuck into a plate of spaghetti.

MASSAWA ISLAND
You'll find a handful of cheap eateries on and around the main street, as well as a smattering of well-stocked supermarkets.

Sallam Restaurant (fish dishes from Nfa150; ☺ dinner) This fish restaurant doesn't look like much from the outside (plastic chairs and dim lighting) but it's a Massawa institution. Everything is so fresh it's almost writhing. There are no menus; just choose your glistening beastie in the fridge and it's barbecued *a la Yemeni*: the whole thing is sliced in half, smacked against the walls of a fire pit and baked to a black crisp. It's sprinkled with hot pepper and served with a *chapatti* flat bread – a delight. While eating you'll be surrounded by plenty of cats expecting a titbit – hey, stop mewing when I'm eating! No alcohol, but the traditional coffee served by a friendly lady across the street is a great way to end the meal.

There are no places more atmospheric to partake in a restorative breakfast than the little cafeterias dotted along the arcades, on the western side of Massawa Island. Yasmin Cafeteria is a hot favourite.

MAINLAND
Gurgussum Beach Hotel (☎ 547002; fax 547008; r Nfa330-950; ⚒) On the mainland, 12km from Massawa on a moderate stretch of beach. This sprawling venue is the closest thing Massawa has to a resort, though 'resort' is an optimistic description. At least there's an acceptable beach. The rooms vary in size, shape and plumbing quality, but overall it's clean. There's a decent restaurant and an open-air bar on the premises. It's popular with Eritrean families at the weekend. During the week, you'll have the whole place for yourself. To get there from

Massawa Island, hire a taxi (Nfa150) or take a minibus on Saturday or Sunday (Nfa10).

Drinking
There's a slew of modest bars and cafeterias on Massawa Island. Don't expect elaborate cocktails and nifty decor: they're rather down-at-heel affairs serving only beer, Eritrean gin (good luck!), sodas and coffee. Single male travellers will soon find they have plenty of local female company. Most bars have large terraces on which to idle away the late evening hours. Just follow your nose.

Getting There & Away
BUS
There are frequent buses leaving from the bus station on the mainland for Asmara (Nfa30, 3½ to four hours). The last bus departs at about 5pm. For Assab, you will have to go to Asmara and catch the bus there, as the buses pass through Massawa but don't take passengers as they are usually full. For Foro (to visit Adulis) in the south, one bus leaves daily, at noon (Nfa20, two to 2½ hours).

CAR
The road to Massawa is sealed and in good condition. A 2WD car can make the journey from Asmara in less than three hours.

Getting Around
MINIBUS
The town minibuses (with 'Taxi' written on the front) are plentiful, fast and efficient. They can be flagged down anywhere, and are great for hopping between the islands and getting to Gurgussum Beach Hotel (Nfa15) at weekends. Short journeys around town cost Nfa3.

TAXI
A taxi ride costs about Nfa60. To the Gurgussum Beach Hotel a taxi costs Nfa150. An unofficial taxi stand can be found at the entrance of Massawa Island.

AROUND MASSAWA
North of Massawa, stretching along the sandy coast into Sudan, lies the traditional territory of the enigmatic Rashaida people (see p309). Around 4km out of Gurgussum, a track branches right off the Massawa road. A few Rashaida camps are visible between the villages of **Emberemi** and **Wekiro**. A peek into their world is as fascinating as ever, but

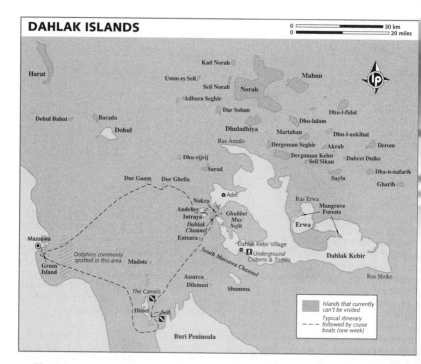

DAHLAK ISLANDS

Islands that currently can't be visited

Typical itinerary followed by cruise boats (one week)

you'll need a 4WD and a local guide who speaks Arabic. It's essential to show respect towards the people and not attempt to take any photos until you have clear permission. It's a good idea to bring some simple gifts, such as tea and sugar. You may well be expected to buy something, such as the traditional silver jewellery, and it's normal to haggle over the prices.

DAHLAK ISLANDS ዳህላክ ደሴት

Some 350 islands lie off the Eritrean coast, the majority (209) of which make up the Dahlak Archipelago. The ultimate pristine getaway, the Dahlak Islands are not for everyone. This isn't some glammed-up, theme-park holiday spot – the only superlatives that spring to mind are 'austere', 'raw', and 'desolate', so come prepared. Largely arid, barren and flat, the islands have a maximum altitude of 15m. Fresh water is very scarce, and very few of the islands are inhabited (only three within the archipelago).

Totally removed from the clutter that comes with conventional paradises – fully-fledged resorts, crowded beaches, dishevelled

nightlife – the Dahlak Islands are almost a void on the tourist radar. There are reasons for that: tourist infrastructure is almost nonexistent, and its treasures yield themselves only to those who make the effort. It's worth it, though. Nature lovers looking to explore these austere islands or snorkel amid the colourful coral reefs, splashing about in sparkling sapphire waters, will love it here. Seekers of peace and solitude will find nirvana, where the environment is both harsh and unique. Divers will be delighted, too, with a slew of absolutely untouched dive sites. It's also great for birding, and beach bums revel the solitude on forgotten beaches.

Try to join a group and camp overnight on one of the islands – this will be the highlight of your trip.

Information

You need a permit to visit any of the Dahlak Islands, except Green Island. The permit costs US$20 (or Nfa320) per person for the first three days, then US$10 for each day after that. If you're joining a tour or hiring a boat, the permit should be organised for you. Don't forget your passport.

Independent travel is not possible, and there aren't any regular boat services to the islands. You'll have to go through a boat rental operation or a travel agent in Asmara.

There aren't any facilities on the islands, but a hotel was being constructed on Dissei Island at the time of writing – check out while in Massawa.

Sights

DAHLAK KEBIR ዳህላክ ከቢር

This is the largest island (more than 650 sq km) in the archipelago, with nine villages and a population of 2300. The island has been inhabited for at least 2000 years and is known for its archaeological ruins. The islanders speak their own dialect, Dahalik, guard their own customs and traditions, and seem to use the same centuries-old building techniques as their ancestors. Most islanders make a living from the sea, either fishing in village coopera- tives or collecting sea cucumbers and shark fins for the Middle East, India, the Philippines and China.

On the southern coast of the island, 300m southeast of the village of Dahlak Kebir, lie some of Eritrea's most ancient relics, includ- ing 360 or so **underground cisterns**, cut from the madreporic (coral) limestone. The cisterns catch rainwater and are the main source of water for the islanders, though the water from some is not drinkable now.

Around 50m southwest of the cisterns lies a huge and ancient necropolis, with literally thousands of **tombs** marked by small, up- right basalt stones, beautifully inscribed with Kufic (ancient Arabic) script. The tombs are thought to date from at least AD 912 to the 15th century.

DISSEI

A hot favourite with Italian expats, Dissei is one of the most easily accessed islands (about 45 minutes by boat from Massawa). It's very scenic, with a series of hills, rocky headlands, lovely coves and a smatter- ing of alluring beaches lapped by fantastic swimming opportunities, in turquoise clear waters. Camping on one of the beaches certainly makes for a memorable Robinson Crusoe experience.

There's a small settlement on this island, the destiny of which should change quite

rapidly in the coming years. The owner of the Dahlak Hotel in Massawa has launched the construction of a luxurious resort, with a dozen bungalows. It should be completed, er, heaven knows when.

MADOTE

Gorgeous! North of Dissei, Madote is a low, flat island that plays in the same league as any idyllic island in the Bahamas, the Seychelles or the Maldives. This unspoilt delight is made for those who love nothing better than splashing in tranquil lapis lazuli waters or working their suntan on powder- soft beaches that are so perfect you'll think they're a mirage. Thrillingly, there'll be no one else around to pinch you and tell you you're dreaming.

There's excellent snorkelling offshore, too.

Camping on the beach is possible, but there's not a single tree from where to sling your hammock.

DUR GHELLA & DUR GAAM

These two islands lying northeast of Massawa are also easily accessible (about 50 minutes by boat) and offer some vegetation, mangroves and excellent beaches. They're also popular with the expat community, and snorkelling is reputedly very good.

Activities

DIVING & SNORKELLING

You're going to love this: diving and snor- kelling in the Dahlak Archipelago are totally unhyped, and you'll feel like Cousteau ex- ploring unchartered territory – memorable. Sure, the diving industry is still embryonic and the Dahlak Islands are far less charismatic than, say, Egypt, but this is a very good thing. There's a wide choice of untouched reef dives suitable for all levels, as well as a handful of wrecks thrown in for good measure. How many dive boats? Only one: yours. A treat if you've been fighting for space in more popu- lar dive destinations.

The reefs are also spared pollution from industry and marine traffic. As a result, the fish population has grown to a dense level and the reefs may well be home to one of the last pristine subaquatic coral environments in the Red Sea. Snapper, jackfish, barra- cuda, parrotfish, sweetlips, unicorn fish and fusiliers all form enormous schools. Giant

ERITREA

specimens of groper are frequently seen, and large Napoleons, bumphead parrotfish and lyretail cod are common sightings.

And sharks? Well, the southern Red Sea was once famous for its shark population but shark life is not as abundant as it once was due to commercial fishing. However, reef and nurse sharks, turtles, stingrays and dolphins are all common. Manta rays and dugongs are occasionally seen.

To really appreciate the reefs, you need to bear a few things in mind. Because the reefs lie on a shallow continental shelf, there are no vertical drop-offs or 'deep blues' around the Dahlak Islands, and the coral growth is not as profuse here as in the northern Red Sea. During the summer, the water temperatures on the plateau rise to the upper limit of coral tolerance. Dense algae, plankton spore and sediment are also thought to inhibit growth. Most coral is found as fringing 'patch' reefs, ranging from the surface to a depth of around 15m to 18m.

The biggest cause of disappointment is visibility, which frequently drops to between 10m and 15m, or even less. The best time for water visibility seems to be during the summer months (end of June to end of August), when temperatures outside touch 45°C. At this time, the sea can seem like a bath: surface temperatures of up to 36°C have been reported. Average water temperatures range from 27°C to 29°C, so a 3mm tropical wetsuit offers more than adequate protection.

A few signature dives include **Seil**, a craggy islet that lies a short boat ride from Dissei, and **Camelli** ('the camels'), which refer to two interconnected rocky islets, also in the vicinity of Dissei. Both sites feature prolific marine life and healthy corals of the hard and soft varieties. If you have a hankering for wrecks, the **Urania**, off Dahlak Kebir, will keep you entertained. 'The good news is that you don't need to be a strong diver to enjoy the Dahlak Islands, because the average depth doesn't exceed 25m', notes one Italian teacher based in Asmara. An insider's tip? 'Combine a diving trip with a picnic (and camping) on either Dissei or Madote, and you'll be in seventh heaven' – we confirm.

Snorkelling also features high on the list, with the best snorkelling off Dissei, Madote, Seil and Camelli.

Diving Services

At the time of writing, the **Eritrea Diving Center** (☎ 552688, 552198; fax 551287; Taulud Is, Massawa) was the only diving operation organising diving trips to the islands. At the time of writing, this structure was professionally run, gear was in good shape and divemasters followed the standard safety procedures. Staff are competent and speak English. Including all gear, the cost of a single dive is Nfa600. Courses are also available. Snorkelling gear is also available for rent (about Nfa150 for mask, fins and snorkel).

All divers must be certified (you will be asked for evidence), and each dive must be accompanied by a local dive master.

Tours

Cruises around the islands, usually lasting anything from two days to a week, can be organised through the best travel agencies in Asmara (see p319). Boats range from beautiful Turkish *caiques* with private cabins and bathrooms to converted *sambuks*. Chefs, dive masters and crew are provided, as are air cylinders (boats have their own compressors). Some have diving and fishing equipment for hire. Prices depend on the type of boat and the number of persons. The bigger the group, the cheaper it is. Be prepared to spend at least US$150 per day per person.

Sleeping

It's possible to camp on some of the islands, including Dissei, Madote and Dur Gaam. Some boat operators hire out full camping equipment; fresh water for showering is included in the price. Some Italian expats swear by Dissei (the east or north of the island); others rave about Madote. We're still undecided; both are top-notch.

Bring plenty of mosquito repellent.

Getting There & Away

You'll need to hire a boat. The journey from Massawa to most of the islands takes between 45 minutes and two hours by motorboat.

Boats can be hired for picnic excursions, fishing, snorkelling or diving trips to the islands. Boat operators advise making reservations one week to 10 days in advance. However, if you do just turn up, something can almost always be organised within 24 hours. If a boat is available, it takes about an hour to get it ready. The services of a boat captain are always included in the price. Check that the boats look reasonably seaworthy and are carrying sufficient life jackets and supplies of water.

None of the boats are currently fitted with compressors. A maximum of 10 air cylinders can be carried at one time.

Now let's come to the tricky subject: the price. Rates are roughly Nfa240 per nautical mile, which makes about Nfa10,000 for Dissei, Madote or Dur Gaam, Nfa10,500 for Dur Ghella and Nfa15,500 for Dahlak Kebir. There's an overnight charge of Nfa4000.

Still ready to go? Contact the following operators:

Eritrea Diving Centre (☎ 552688; fax 551287; Taulud Is) Good, fast boats.

Dahlak Sea Touring (☎ 07123126; Massawa Is) Run by Btzuamlak Gebre Selassie who is better known as Maik. Has reliable boats.

Erinine (☎ 127300, 122271; www.erinine.com; Asmara) Has regular two-day cruises aboard a dhow (two to four times a month, at weekends). From Nfa2300 per person.

Small boats can take up to eight passengers. If you're travelling solo, your best bet is to team up with a group. You stand the best chances at weekends, when expats from Asmara rent a boat to relax on the islands. If there's space available, they'll be happy to have you on board, provided you share the expenses. Contact the abovementioned operators or the travel agencies in Asmara (p319) – they'll let you know when there's a group departing.

ADULIS አዱሊስ

To be frank, we're at a loss as to why this site has such a name. Lying 59km to the south of Massawa, near the village of **Foro**, the ancient Aksumite ruins of Adulis have a high historical significance but visually it's not particularly exciting. Adulis' present condition belies its former grandeur, and many travellers are disappointed. It remains around 98% unexcavated; almost everything is still underground. If you're not an archaeology fiend, it's probably not worth the hassle to go there.

History

Once numbering among the greatest ports of the ancient world, Adulis was the site of large and elegant buildings and a bustling international port. Inhabited since at least the 6th century BC, the site is the oldest in Eritrea.

Like modern-day Massawa, Adulis' importance lay in its port, and by the 3rd century AD the port had grown to become one of the most important on the Red Sea. Trade at this time flourished from the Mediterranean all the way to India.

Adulis' fortunes waxed and waned with the ancient kingdom of Aksum. Like Aksum, its heyday came during the 3rd and 4th centuries AD. It then went into decline, before a brief revival in the 7th century. The town supplied all sorts of foreign goods, including gold, myrrh and frankincense, to all the major Aksumite towns of the interior: Aksum, Qohaito, Metera and Keskese.

Orientation & Information

To visit Adulis, it's best to pick up a guide at Foro. Try asking for Salhé, who has long accompanied the archaeologists working on the site. He speaks quite good Italian and Arabic, and passable English. From Foro it's around 7km to Adulis, in the direction of Zula.

Don't forget that you need a permit from the National Museum Office in Asmara to visit the site (see p362).

Getting There & Away

The road from Massawa as far as Adulis is sealed. If you're driving, you can usually find a guide at Foro.

From Massawa, one bus leaves daily for Foro around noon (Nfa25, two hours). To return to Massawa, there's a bus from Foro at 6am. Chartered bush taxis can also make the journey (Nfa100). Ask around at Foro.

DANKALIA ዳንከሊያ

So frustrating! Most of Dankalia is now out of bounds (foreigners are allowed to go as far as Buri Peninsula, but no further south). Sighhh... Imagine a narrow strip of land about 50km wide that stretches south of Massawa down to Djibouti (about 600km), along the coastline. You can't miss it on the map: it looks like a long peninsula protruding from the south of the country. It's a volcanic desert blessed with otherworldly, lunar landscapes, with a strong appeal. This secretive world is known as one of the hottest and most inhospitable places on Earth: there's little to see, nothing to do, and no

ERITREA

great destination awaiting you at the other end. The journey is hot, tiring and demanding. But the sense of exploration is real.

As if that was not enough, Dankalia is the territory of the legendary Afar people, described as one of the fiercest tribes on Earth (see p53). A journey into Dankalia gives a fascinating glimpse into their way of life.

If, by chance, Dankalia is again open to travellers during the lifetime of this book, don't miss the opportunity to get there – it's bound to be one of the highlights of your trip.

The best time to go is from November to December or from March to April. At the height of summer, the heat is unbearable; in winter, the sparse rain can quickly turn the tracks and wadis (valleys) into a quagmire.

SOUTH TO ASSAB

Most villages on the Danakil coast survive from a mixed economy of fishing, salt mining and animal husbandry. The millennia-old trading contact with the Arabian peninsula still thrives; in some places smuggling with Yemeni merchants has proved a more lucrative means of income.

Irafayle

The little fishing village of Irafayle (meaning Place of Elephants – slim chance now) lies 87km from Massawa and marks the boundary between the provinces of Akele Guzay and Dankalia. Here, Afar territory and its desolate landscape begins. The village offers simple refreshments and accommodation.

The bay around the **Gulf of Zula** has good sandy beaches and snorkelling, and birdlife is plentiful along the shore. The British General Sir Robert Napier landed here in 1868 to rescue the hostages held by the Emperor Tewodros.

The **Buri Peninsula** is probably one of the best places in Eritrea for wildlife. Ostriches, hamadryas baboons and gazelles (Soemmering's and Dorca) are all quite frequently seen. The wild ass is also reported, though it's now very rare. Mangroves, good beaches and huge salt flats also characterise the area. If you have the time, a detour into the peninsula is worthwhile. Ask for a guide at Ghela'elo, some 70km from Zula.

Marsa Fatma ማርሳ ፋጡማ

Marsa Fatma, 158km from Massawa, is the starting point for a visit to the crater lake known as **Lake Badda**, around two hours

(43km) west of the village of **Adaito**. Lying below sea level, seasonal water from the Tigré Mountains collects here, feeding the agricultural plantations.

South of Marsa Fatma, the fishing village of **Thio** (245km from Massawa) offers food and accommodation. The village, with its brightly painted wooden huts, is worth a stroll.

Edi ዕዲ

Edi, 130km from Thio, is another Afar fishing village and also offers food and accommodation. Some 70km south of Edi, the **Bay of Beraesoli** features a stunning lunar landscape. There are several islands off the coast.

Some 60km further south, you'll reach the village of **Beylul** (515km from Massawa), surrounded by palms. You'll be offered the *doma*, a local palm wine. From Beylul, it is another 61km until Assab.

ASSAB ዓሰብ
pop 75,000

Poor Assab. Once upon a time it was a thriving port town. Today it's almost completely cut off from the outside world and feels like a ghost town. Situated less than 100km from Ethiopia, at the southern extremity of the desolate and inaccessible Dankalia region, it has always been a bit of an outpost. For centuries, and up until recently, it was Ethiopia's principal port of access to the Red Sea. However, the dispute with Eritrea in 1998 ended that. The diversion of all Ethiopian commerce via Djibouti has made Assab even more of a backwater, and the recent closure of the border with Djibouti has made matters worse. A feeling of dereliction emanates from the town.

The few optimistic people we met in Eritrea think that Assab could be resurrected when the conflict with Ethiopia is settled and the border with Djibouti reopens.

Assab's average annual temperature is 29.5°C, though it can reach 46.5°C. Annual rainfall is just 58mm. The coolest time is between November and February.

Getting There & Away
BUS

Incredibly, a bus service connects Assab to Massawa (and on to Asmara). The track between the two cities has been improved and the service is now relatively reliable, though still tiring and uncomfortable. After heavy rain, when the track becomes too muddy, services might be cancelled.

Two buses a week ply the route between Asmara and Assab; the journey takes approximately two days. Tickets should be bought one day in advance. Bring all the food and water you can carry.

The border between Eritrea and Djibouti was indefinitely closed at the time of writing, due to the tension between the two countries. Before this, it was possible to find shared taxis to Rahaita (around 112km from Assab) in the south or even to Moulhoulé in Djibouti; from there, it was relatively easy to continue your journey to Obock with Djiboutian bush taxis.

WESTERN ERITREA

So sad that this region is now closed to foreigners, because it has a truly peculiar appeal. Time seems to have stood still in these often forgotten lowlands, which lack the development and bustle of the densely populated south or east. A bit like the Australian outback, western Eritrea seduces with wild expanses and empty spaces – not to mention its fascinating inhabitants. Take the Kunama for example, who rank among the more enigmatic in Eritrea. In climate, geography, religion, industry, people and way of life, Eritrea's Muslim lowlands could not be more different from the Christian highlands. The more you forge west, the more you feel a Sudanese flavour.

During the Struggle, many towns in the west witnessed bloody fighting. The relics of war are visible everywhere: tank carcasses, blown-up bridges, rubble and bullet holes – poignant remnants of a not-so-distant past.

This area is also famed for its birdlife, and with lots of endemic species it has the potential to attract twitchers from around the globe.

The road is entirely sealed between Asmara and Teseney.

AGORDAT አቄርደት
pop 25,000 / elev 615m

Situated 160km west of Asmara, Agordat is not particularly engaging. The town seems to have been severely hit by the transfer of the administration of the Gash Barka province to Barentu. The sickly state of the economy does not help and business is slack.

There's a post office, a telecom office, a branch of the Commercial Bank and a couple of ultrabasic hotels.

Like most towns in the west, Agordat has an overwhelmingly Arab feel to it – even the colonial governor's **palace** is Moorish-inspired. Other major Muslim landmarks include the **mosque** – the second-largest in Eritrea – and the **marketplace**, one of the most important in the lowlands.

You'll find several cheap eateries around the market and the bus station. Most places have a small terrace where you can unwind and have a drink in the evening.

Buses leave from the main square, close to the ticket office. One to three buses depart early each morning for Asmara (Nfa17, five hours); about four buses travel daily to Keren between 6am and 4pm (three hours); one minibus goes to Barentu. For Teseney, you should go to Barentu and change buses there.

BARENTU ባረንቱ
pop 16,200 / elev 980m

In the heart of western Eritrea, and the seat of the regional Gash Barka administration, Barentu does not have the forlorn atmosphere that can be felt in Agordat. Heading west, it's a relaxed place to hang out and a convenient spot to break a journey to Teseney or Sudan. There's not much to see or do here, but the town exudes a congenial ambience without being overwhelming. In the evening, the main street fills up with college students in blue shirts – a superb sight in its own right.

Barentu is also the heartland of the Kunama people, one of the most fascinating of Eritrea's ethnic groups (see p309). Barentu's Thursday or Saturday market ranks as one of the most colourful in the country.

Barentu has a post office, an Eritel office, a branch of the Commercial Bank of Eritrea as well as a few very simple hotels, such as Unite Family Hotel or Merhaba Hotel.

The bus station is on the outskirts of the town, on the road to Teseney. For Asmara, several buses leave daily. Four buses go daily to Keren. To Teseney, five buses leave daily. For Agordat, there are regular minibus services.

TESENEY ተሰነይ

pop 15,000 / elev 585m

This large frontier town is just 45km from the Sudanese border. The status of border town usually does not bode well but Teseney is unexpectedly vibrant and thrives on trade and smuggling with neighbouring Sudan.

At first sight the town seems like a large, sprawling, rubble-strewn conglomeration, devoid of trees, beautiful architecture or anything of interest. But Teseney has an intriguing atmosphere and is unlike any other town in Eritrea.

The town has long been a meeting place for various ethnic groups from both countries. You can visit the various Rashaida markets on the outskirts of the town, where the Rashaida people sell virtually everything from petrol to satellite dishes.

Teseney hosts a branch of the Commercial Bank, a post office and an Eritel centre.

There are a few of cheap hotels in Teseney; try the Luna Hotel and the Khartoum Hotel.

For cheap and tasty fare in the evening, nothing beats the souq area, known locally as Shuk al Shab (Market of the Masses in Arabic). It is straight out of Sudan. It's home to a huge open-air restaurant; you just join the rabble (most of them truck drivers from Sudan) at the long wooden tables and wait to be served. It's lively and fun and the evening air fills with the smoking and sizzling of the *sheia*. Beer is not available, but you can swallow delicious yogurts or guzzle exquisite orange juices.

From June to August, watermelons are sold by the roads around the town.

Teseney's bus station lies about 500m east of Shuk al Shab. There are regular buses to Barentu (119km, Nfa35, three hours) and Asmara (Nfa91, one day).

Teseney is a jumping-off point to Sudan but the border was not open to foreigners at the time of writing. Should it reopen, you'll find a handful of minibuses and shared taxis that leave every morning to Adi Bara, at the border (one hour), from where you can find transportation to Kassala, the nearest Sudanese town of substance.

ERITREA DIRECTORY

ACCOMMODATION

Tourism is still in its infancy in Eritrea, and accommodation is limited. Asmara naturally has the widest choice of available options, along with Massawa.

Prices for budget accommodation average US$8 to US$12 for singles and US$10 to US$15 for doubles. For midrange hotels, you'll pay about US$15 to US$30 for singles and US$20 to US$60 for doubles. A top-end venture will set you back up to US$200. These prices apply to hotels in the capital. In the rest of the country, rates are usually cheaper. Most midrange and top-end hotels have restaurants. Unless otherwise stated, all rooms have private bathrooms.

In Eritrea, a room with a double bed is usually called a 'single', and a room with twin beds a 'double'. In our reviews we've used the Western interpretation of singles, doubles and twins. In many places you'll just be quoted a flat rate for the room irrespective of occupancy.

Camping

Alas, there are no official camping facilities in Eritrea, but camping on the beach in the Dahlak Archipelago is popular among expats, and one of the highlights of the country.

Pensione & Hotels

There's a stark contrast between Asmara and the rest of the country. The capital boasts hotels of all categories that will suit all wallets. The real shame though is the lack of imaginative and different places to stay. Most places, including top-drawer options, rate zero in the charm department. Elsewhere the hotel scene is much more modest, except maybe in Massawa, and accommodation is quite humdrum and no cause for great excitement. Lack of investment is the main explanation. In Asmara, you should find someone who can speak English at the reception.

Pensione usually refers to a small hotel, with only a few rooms. Many budget hotels also have cold water only (not a worry in the lowlands). Though breakfast is provided by some, you will usually be charged extra for it. Towels and soap are usually not provided in budget hotels. Power cuts are common in rural areas.

All the small towns have hotels. They're often spartan affairs. Many lack running water (you get a bucket shower instead) and cleanliness of bathrooms leaves something to be desired.

In the torrid lowlands, including Massawa, many people sleep on beds in the courtyards and on the verandas or rooftops. The cheap hotels, which do not have any air-conditioning or ceiling fans, usually have similar arrangements.

In the rural areas, accommodation is sometimes little more than a bed in a hut, without running water, electricity or even washing facilities.

Few hotels accept credit cards. The ones that do charge a hefty commission (up to 10%!). In Asmara, some midrange and top-end hotels quote their prices in US dollars and in euros. If you pay in hard currency, don't forget to have the transaction registered on your currency declaration form. Payment can also be made in local currency (at the official rate), and you may be asked to show your currency declaration form.

ACTIVITIES

Eritrea has great potential for outdoor pursuits but there are no proper facilities. Because of the war and the lack of funds, nothing has been really developed yet.

Birdwatching

Eritrea is heaven for birdwatchers (see p315). The best birdwatching opportunities can be found around the Semenawi Bahri area (Filfil), around Massawa and in the Gash Barka area. Sadly, there's no infrastructure yet. There's potential but it's still embryonic and much has to be done to promote this activity. The owner of Travel House International in Asmara (see p319) is passionate about birdwatching and may organise tailor-made birdwatching trips on request.

ERITREA

Diving & Snorkelling

Eritrea's best-known activity is diving in the Red Sea. The Dahlak Islands off the coast near Massawa are currently the only place where organised diving and snorkelling takes place. A word of warning, though: it has nothing to do with the northern Red Sea. Diving in Eritrea is still on a very low-key scale (but that's part of the appeal). At the time of writing, there was only one operator based in Massawa.

Again, keep your expectations in check. Visibility is far from exceptional and most sites require a tedious (and expensive) boat ride from Massawa. Though the islands are opening up, access is still limited, monopolised by a few boat companies charging very high prices. At the moment, most destinations are out of the reach of budget travellers. To make it worthwhile and affordable, a minimum of eight divers is usually required – a condition which, in practice, is not easy to meet.

But if you can afford a trip – even just snorkelling – the opportunity is not to be missed. The sites are absolutely pristine and there are no crowds – you'll feel like a pioneer.

For more information, see p349.

Hiking & Camel Trekking

In theory hiking is possible in the various hills and mountain ranges in the east of the country, but unfortunately there are no signposted paths and you should consider hiring a local guide because some areas are still not cleared of land mines. Suggested hikes include Amba Metera (p339), near Senafe, and the fantastic climb to the church of Tsada Amba (p336), near Keren.

Some travel agencies in the capital can organise treks into the hinterland by camel (for contact details see p319).

BUSINESS HOURS

Private businesses, shops and post offices keep various hours. In general, most open from 8am to noon and 2pm to 6pm Monday to Friday, and on Saturday morning. Many shops in the capital stay open until 7.30pm.

Most banks open from 8am to 11am and from 2pm to 4pm Monday to Friday, and from 8am to 11.30am on Saturday.

In Massawa and Assab, government offices open from 6am to 2.30pm Monday to Friday during the hot season (June to September) and from 8am to noon and 4pm to 6.30pm Monday to Friday the rest of the year. Private businesses open from 6am to noon and 3pm to 6pm Monday to Friday the whole year.

In Muslim areas, business hours are shorter during Ramadan, and cafes and restaurants may be closed during the day.

Normal opening hours for restaurants are 7.30am to 10pm, cafes 7.30am to 8pm and bars 8am till late.

Reviews won't list business hours unless they differ from the standards given here.

CLIMATE

Eritrea's climate corresponds to its geography. The low, eastern zone is by far the hottest area. Temperatures range from a torrid 30°C to 39°C during the hot season (June to September) and from 25°C to 32°C during the cooler season (October to May). During the rains from July to September, the roads north can become impassable.

Rainfall on the coast is less than 200mm per year, and occurs mostly from December to February. The high humidity in the coastal region makes temperatures seem much higher than those further inland.

In the Dankalia region, temperatures can reach 50°C in the shade! Rainfall is practically zero.

In the highland zone, the average annual temperature is 18°C (17°C in Asmara). May

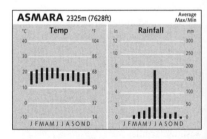

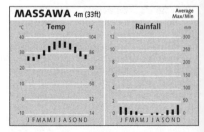

is the hottest month, when daily temperatures can reach around 30°C. The coldest months are from December to February, when lows can approach freezing point. Temperatures can vary by up to 20°C between day and night. Light rains fall from March to April, with heavy rains from the end of June to the beginning of September.

In the western zone, temperatures range from 30°C to 41°C in the hot season (April to June). December is the coolest month (13°C to 25°C). Rainfall mirrors that in the highland zone.

See also p19.

CUSTOMS REGULATIONS

On arrival at the airport, any major electronic items (such as expensive cameras, laptops, video cameras) must be registered at customs. This is to deter black-market business. On departure the items will be signed off. If anything is stolen during your stay in Eritrea, make sure you immediately obtain a police statement registering the loss.

Duty-free allowances include 1L of alcohol and 200 cigarettes.

Since January 2005 any person entering the country must fill in a foreign currency declaration form. The declaration form is mandatory for changing money so don't lose it. You'll have to hand it in upon departure and an official will check your statement.

It is strictly forbidden in theory to export any nakfa from Eritrea. In practice, an allowance of up to Nfa50 is permitted to allow for any problems or needs.

DANGERS & ANNOYANCES
Checkpoints

There are army checkpoints at the entrance and exit of each major town. They are pretty straightforward and foreigners never get hassled or asked for bribes; just show your passport and your travel permit (see p362) and you'll be OK.

Crime

Eritrea is a very safe country in which to travel. Muggings are unheard of, pickpocketings rare, corruption not visible and everyone lets everyone else get on with their business.

Asmara is an extremely peaceful city and the crime rate is incredibly low, but minor incidents of street crime are occasionally reported. With the economy squeezed ever

tighter by the war with Ethiopia, such incidents will inevitably become more common. Markets all over the world attract pickpockets, and no less so in Asmara, so take some basic precautions. Outside the capital, the crime rate is even lower.

In the far western and northern areas bordering Sudan, a few incidents of bandit and terrorist attacks against Eritrean civilians are reported from time to time, but foreigners are not allowed to travel to these areas. It's still wise to keep your ear to the ground.

Land Mines

After several decades of war, the biggest threat outside the capital is the risk of land mines and unexploded munitions. Despite the government's best efforts, thousands still litter the countryside; they continue to sporadically kill and maim the population.

Most mines are confined to the sites of major battle fronts but there is some element of risk anywhere fighting has occurred. Areas north and west of Keren and around Ghinda are still thought to be heavily mined.

Check with local government and local village officials before travelling in less-frequented areas. Never stray off the road.

EMBASSIES & CONSULATES
Embassies & Consulates in Eritrea

All embassies and consulates are based in Asmara. They are open from Monday to Friday and keep regular business hours. Visa applications are usually received in the morning.

Djibouti (Map p317; ☎ 125990; Saro St)
Egypt (Map p320; ☎ 120056; Marsa Fatuma St)
France (Map p320; ☎ 126599; Nakfa Ave)
Germany (off Map p317; ☎ 186670; Saba Bldg, Warsay St)
Italy (Map p317; ☎ 120160; 171-1 St)
Sudan (off Map p317; ☎ 115546; Gezzabanda District)
UK (Map p317; ☎ 120145; Mariam GMBI St)
USA (Map p317; ☎ 120004; http://eritrea.usembassy.org; 173-1 St)
Yemen (Map p317; ☎ 123910; off Denden St)

FESTIVALS & EVENTS

The best festivals and celebrations in Eritrea are linked to religious and secular holidays. See above.

FOOD

For a rundown of the culinary delights in Eritrea, see the Food & Drink section (p312).

ERITREA

The restaurant scene is fairly low-key except in Asmara, and prices won't make you cringe. Given the state of the economy, there are severe food shortages in the country, even in Asmara, and not everything is available on the menus.

GAY & LESBIAN TRAVELLERS

Homosexuality is severely condemned by traditional and religious cultures and is a topic of absolute taboo. Eritrea's penal code concerning homosexuality is currently still based on Ethiopian law (see p249). Although homosexuality obviously exists in Eritrea, local gays behave with extreme discretion and caution. Gay and lesbian travellers are advised to do likewise.

HOLIDAYS
Public Holidays

Eritrea's public holidays can be divided into three categories: national (secular) holidays, Christian Orthodox holidays and Islamic holidays.

The country follows the Gregorian (European) calendar, with 12 months to the year. However, the Eritrean Orthodox church (derived from the Ethiopian Orthodox church), follows the Julian calendar, which has 13 months. Some events, therefore, trail those of the Gregorian calendar by around one week. Muslim holidays are based on the Hejira calendar, which is 10 or 11 days shorter than the Gregorian calendar, so these holidays fall 10 or 11 days earlier each year. The precise dates of these holidays are determined by the moon.

National holidays include the following:

New Year's Day 1 January
International Women's Day 8 March
Workers' Day 1 May
Liberation Day 24 May
Martyrs' Day 20 June
Start of the Armed Struggle 1 September

The main Christian Orthodox holidays:

Leddet (Christmas) 7 January
Timkat (Epiphany) 19 January
Tensae (Easter) March/April (variable)
Kiddus Yohannes (Orthodox New Year) 11 September
Meskel (Finding of the True Cross) 27 September

Islamic holidays include Lailat al-Miraji, Eid al-Fitr, Eid al-Adha Arafa (the Muslim New Year), Al-Ashura, and Eid Mawlid al-Nabi (the Prophet's birthday).

For more information on the religious holidays listed in this section, see p248.

INSURANCE

A travel insurance policy covering all medical problems (including emergency evacuation cover) is essential for travel in Eritrea, while one to cover theft and loss really is helpful but not vital. For information on medical insurance, see p367.

INTERNET ACCESS

In Asmara, you'll never be far from an internet cafe. Webcams, CD burning and USB connections for uploading digital photos are increasingly standard, but connections were frustratingly slow at the time of writing. Fees are usually around Nfa10 per hour. All internet cafes have English keyboards. Outside the capital, internet access is harder to find. There are a few outlets with internet access in Massawa and Mendefera.

If you're bringing a laptop, a handful of upmarket hotels in Asmara provide wi-fi access.

The 🖳 symbol in this book indicates that a hotel has an internet-enabled computer for guests to use.

LEGAL MATTERS

Foreign visitors are subject to the laws of the country in which they are travelling. Penalties for possession, use or trafficking of illegal drugs are strictly enforced in Eritrea. Convicted offenders can expect long jail sentences, fines and possible confiscation of personal property.

Note that consumption of the mildly intoxicating leaf *chat* isn't permitted in Eritrea.

Exchanging money at the black market (outside the banks) is strictly illegal. If you do indulge, be aware that you're taking a big risk: a two-year imprisonment sentence and a fine of up to Nfa2 million.

MAPS

A country map is useful, but not vital, given that most travellers rent a car with driver.

The best map currently available is the one produced by ITMB Publishing in Canada (1:9,000,000). Most map suppliers should stock it, including **Stanfords** (☎ 020-7836 1321; www.stanfords.co.uk), in London. For those planning a longer trip in the Horn, Reise Know-How Verlag's 1:8,000,000 (*Ethiopia, Eritrea,*

Somalia, Djibouti) and Michelin's 1:4,000,000 map 11745 *(Africa North and East – Arabia)* are very useful.

At the time of writing, no maps of the country were available in Eritrea. Your best bet is to get one before leaving home.

MONEY

The unit of currency is the nakfa (Nfa). It was introduced in November 1997 to replace the old Ethiopian birr. It is divided into 100 cents, and is available in 5, 10, 25, 50 and 100 cent pieces, and in 1, 5, 10, 20, 50 and 100 nakfa notes.

For exchange rates, see the table on the inside front cover of this guide. For information on costs, see p19.

ATMs

There are currently no ATMs in Eritrea.

Black Market

Oops, this is a very touchy issue in Eritrea since the government has taken drastic measures to eradicate the black market. Changing money on the black market still exists but is no longer widespread due to the heavy penalties incurred. However, it's tempting to change money on the black market because official rates massively overvalue the nakfa (up to double at the time of writing!). But if you do indulge, you're taking a very big risk. People who do take the risk always conduct their transaction very discreetly, with somebody they know. US dollars and euros are the hot favourites.

The government introduced a currency declaration form in 2005, which makes changing money on the black market more complicated to handle – it would involve not declaring all one's funds when filling in the currency declaration form at the airport. Again, one is taking a big risk.

Cash

While most major currencies are accepted in Asmara, US dollars (cash or travellers cheques) and euros are the best currencies to carry. Not only are US dollars and euros easier to exchange outside the capital, but you have to pay for certain things in US dollars or euros, including some air tickets and the departure tax.

Credit Cards

The larger hotels in the capital, some airlines and, increasingly, some travel agents accept credit cards but they usually charge an additional 5% to 10% commission; check in advance.

Himbol in Asmara can do cash advances on your credit card but the commission exacted is a ludicrous 7%.

Moneychangers

You can change cash with a minimum of hassle at the Commercial Bank of Eritrea in all major towns and cities. Himbol exchange offices in Asmara also change money. Each transaction must be registered on your currency declaration form. Don't lose time shopping around and comparing rates; they are fixed nationwide by the government and there is no commission.

Travellers cheques can also be changed without fuss in Asmara, as well as in the bigger branches of the Commercial Bank of Eritrea outside the capital.

INTERNATIONAL TRANSFERS

If you need to wire money, **Western Union** (www.westernunion.com) transfers can be made at the Commercial Bank of Eritrea and at the Himbol exchange office in Asmara. Using the service of this global money-transfer company is a handy way of receiving money in Eritrea.

Tipping

The practice of tipping is expected in the towns only. In the rural areas, you may even have your tip returned to you.

In the smaller restaurants in the towns, service is included, and Eritreans don't tip unless the service has been exceptional (in this case, Nfa2 to Nfa5 would be an appropriate amount to leave). In bars and cafes, loose coins are sometimes left. However, in the larger restaurants accustomed to tourists, at least 10% will be expected, and in the larger hotels, staff will expect a bare minimum of Nfa10.

Travellers Cheques

It's not a bad idea to carry travellers cheques in Eritrea since the exchange rates are the same as cash and no commission is applied. Moreover, the process is pretty straightforward.

Travellers cheques are best carried in US dollars or euros, although most major currencies can be exchanged in the banks in the capital and some banks in the bigger towns.

Don't forget to list your travellers cheques on your currency declaration form upon

ERITREA

arrival, otherwise you won't be able to cash them.

PHOTOGRAPHY & VIDEO

Print film and film developers are easy to find in the capital. Outside Asmara, it's difficult to find film except in the larger towns, and it may not always be within its use-by date. Most internet cafes in Asmara allow you to upload photos and burn CDs, and some digital supplies can be found in Asmara.

Photographing People

In some areas, people such as the colourful Rashaida and the enigmatic Afars are more accustomed to photographers, and understandably want to benefit from it too. They may ask for money. The fee should always be agreed in advance. In some places, you may be charged a fee for taking videos, though this does seem to be randomly applied.

It's a bad idea to snap an Orthodox monk without obtaining permission first.

Restrictions

Certain subjects in Eritrea are considered 'sensitive'. Do not take photographs of military or police installations or their personnel, or even airports and bridges. Civil engineering and government buildings are off limits too.

Outside the capital, it's fine to take pictures of war relics.

POST

The Eritrean postal service is considered quite reliable, albeit not the speediest. Postage for the first 20g is Nfa7 worldwide, except for neighbouring countries, which are cheaper. Postcards cost Nfa6 worldwide. Courier services are available in Asmara.

SHOPPING

Eritrea's tourism industry is not yet greatly developed, and you won't find many shops catering to tourists. Most curios are imported from other countries (such as the wooden carvings and sculptures from Kenya).

Shops sell intricate silver and gold jewellery (priced by weight), fabrics, ceramics and basketware. Quality (and some might say taste) is variable, so it's worth taking a good look around before you buy.

More unusual and interesting souvenirs include little pewter crosses, which are often crudely fashioned.

Gabi, the equivalent of a toga worn by the local men, are also available. They are quite bulky, but can be turned to a multitude of uses – blankets, ground sheets, pillows and wraps – while you're travelling.

In some of the shops along Harnet Ave, ivory carvings and turtle shells are still available. Apart from the environmental arguments against buying these, it is also illegal to import them into most Western countries.

You can buy the works of Eritrean artists at The Gallery (p311) in Asmara.

Outside the capital, simple pottery, basketware and combs can be found in local markets.

Bargaining

Unlike in other places in Africa, corruption is not the norm in Eritrea. Overcharging of tourists is very rare in the country, and prices are usually firmly fixed; haggling can offend Eritreans. However, all the usual discounts apply, and it's always worth asking for them for long stays in hotels, extended car hire and the like.

The one exception where haggling is almost expected is in the local shops and markets; there are no fixed prices. In shops, prices are rarely displayed.

SOLO TRAVELLERS

As the level of day-to-day harassment is negligible, solo travellers will find travelling alone a breeze. You may be a minor curiosity in rural areas, but that's part of the fun, after all. However, it is an advantage to join a group (if any) if you want to hire a car so you can share costs.

TELEPHONE & FAX

To call Eritrea from abroad, dial your international access code, then ☎ 291 (the country code for Eritrea), then 1 (the area code) and the local number. International calls can be made from the telecommunications office (called Eritel) found in all the main towns. International rates are the same all day, and costs are calculated per minute: about Nfa15 for North America and Nfa20 for Europe, the Middle East and Australasia. National calls cost between Nfa2 and Nfa9 (Nfa0.60 within Asmara). Telephone cards are available in denominations of Nfa14, Nfa27, Nfa34, Nfa62 and Nfa121 and can be used at any Eritel office. International calls can't be made from phone boxes; you'll have to go to an Eritel office.

Mobile phones are widespread. The expanding network covers major towns throughout the country. Mobile phone numbers use eight digits: a two-digit number starting with 0, followed by six-digits. To reach a mobile phone from outside Eritrea, dial the country code, then the mobile number without the initial 0. At the time of writing, foreign mobile phones were not functioning in Eritrea for lack of roaming agreements with foreign countries, and tourists were not allowed to buy local SIM cards.

Faxes can be sent and received from some of the telecommunications offices. It is also possible to make calls and send or receive faxes from the larger hotels, but rates are much more expensive than from telecommunications offices.

TIME

Eritrea is three hours ahead of GMT/UTC. There is no daylight saving time.

TOILETS

Both the sit-down and squat types of toilet are found in Eritrea, reflecting Italian and Arab influences respectively.

In the highlands, the sit-down type tends to prevail. In the Muslim lowlands such as in Massawa, the squat style is more commonly found (but only in the cheaper hotels). Toilet paper is very rare in either, so carry your own.

TOURIST INFORMATION

Eritrea's tourist facilities are fairly woeful, with little literature and only one tourist office, in Asmara. On the bright side, it's usually staffed by English-speaking students as part of their military service, but don't expect esoteric tips. However, it's a mandatory stop because it issues travel permits for foreign visitors.

There's one good, unofficial source of information on Eritrea: the local travel agents in Asmara (p319), who generously offer information without always expecting you to engage their services in return. They're knowledgeable and resourceful.

Outside Eritrea, the Eritrean embassy or consulate in your home country (the few that exist) is your best bet, but tourist literature is generally limited.

TRAVELLERS WITH DISABILITIES

The good news is that disabled visitors can expect to find a sympathetic and accommodating attitude from Eritreans, who are quick to offer assistance. The bad news is that travelling in Eritrea can be challenging for the disabled. The country lacks the convenient infrastructure and services that make getting around easier for those with disabilities. Very rarely will you find wheelchair-accessible toilets or wheelchair ramps, and very few hotels are equipped with (working) lifts or facilities for travellers with wheelchairs.

Car hire with a driver is easy to organise, if expensive.

VISAS & DOCUMENTS

All foreign nationals require visas for entry to Eritrea. Visas should be obtained from the Eritrean embassy or consulate before you leave your home country. If there isn't any diplomatic representation in your home country, obtain a visa from the nearest one.

Due to the bitter relations Eritrea has with its neighbours, note that it's not possible to get a visa in Ethiopia or in Djibouti. Yemen is the only option.

For visa applications, you'll need your passport (valid for at least three months) and two passport photos. Some embassies also require you to show proof of an onward ticket as well as a reference letter from your employee before they'll issue a visa. Most embassies require you to possess a certificate as evidence of yellow-fever vaccination if you will be arriving in Eritrea within six days of visiting an infected area.

The visa application form may require an address in Eritrea and a 'reference'. If you don't have any, find a hotel and tour operator in this chapter, and use these names. Applications can be made by post, and normally take 48 hours to process.

You usually have to travel within three months of the date of issue of the visa.

Tourist visas are for single entry only, and are valid for 30 days from the date of arrival in Eritrea. They cost between US$50 and US$60.

ERITREA

TRAVEL RESTRICTIONS

At the time of writing, most of Dankalia (south of Ghela'elo), Nakfa, Adi Quala and Western Eritrea were off-limits to travellers. Only Asmara, Filfil, Massawa, the Dahlak Islands, Keren, Dekemhare, Mendefera, Adi Keyh, Qohaito, Senafe and Metera were accessible to foreigners. A travel permit is needed for all these places bar Asmara.

Let's see; have we missed anything? Oh right. At the time of research, the Orthodox Tewahdo Church, which controls access to all monasteries throughout Eritrea, did not issue permits to foreigners – allegedly for 'rehabilitation works'. In practice, tourists have continued to go to the monasteries despite the ban and without permits; the probability that you are turned back by the monks is fairly low, but there's no guarantee, especially if you come across an overzealous monk. The situation is variable so check when you're in Asmara.

Travel Permits

Due to the ongoing tension with Ethiopia (and, to a lesser extent, Djibouti), travelling in Eritrea has become pretty bureaucratic and there are increasing travel restrictions (see the boxed text above).

Head first to the Tourist Information Centre (p319) in Asmara, where you'll fill in a form and list all the places you intend to visit in the country (be extensive). If you rent a car or a 4WD, you'll have to mention the model of the car and the registration number. The permit is usually processed the same day.

Then you'll be asked to make a few copies. Keep this travel permit (as well as the copies) at all times when outside Asmara, as you'll be asked to show it at checkpoints, along with your passport.

Eritrea's 'national treasures' are protected by paperwork. To visit any of the archaeological sites of Eritrea, you'll need to get a special permit from the **National Museum office** (Map p317; ☎ 122389; Mariam GMBI St, Asmara; ⏲ 8.30-11.30am & 2.30-5.30pm Mon-Fri), on the 1st floor of the National Museum building. You'll need your passport and Nfa150 per site (or US$10). The paper can be issued immediately; the staff are helpful and efficient. If you're taking a tour, your agency should do this for you. Bring your passport.

You'll also need a permit to visit the Dahlak Islands, but this should be handled by the travel agency or the owner of the boat that takes you there. It costs US$20.

To visit the monasteries obtain a permit from the **Orthodox Tewahdo Church Headquarters** (off Map p317; ☎ 182098; Warsay St; ⏲ 8am-noon & 2-4.30pm Mon-Fri) in Asmara (ask for the 'monastery tour application'). It's about 300m past the Lufthansa office, across the street. It costs Nfa150 or US$10 per monastery. At the time

of writing such permits were no longer issued to foreigners (see the boxed text above).

Visa Extensions

In Asmara, the **Department of Immigration** (Map p317; ☎ 200033, ext 204; Denden St; ⏲ 8am-noon & 2-5pm Mon-Fri) will extend your visa twice for a further 30 days. This costs Nfa600 and you will need one photo, photocopies of your passport details and visa page, and a Nfa1 stamp. Payment must be made in cash and with exact change. It usually takes 24 hours to process. Applications must be made before the old visa expires.

Visas for Onward Travel

For contact details of embassies and consulates in Eritrea, see p357.

Djibouti One-month entry visas cost US$30, require two photos and an exit visa from the Eritrean authorities (issued by the Department of Immigration). They are issued within 24 hours. Visas are also available at Ambouli Airport in Djibouti City.

Sudan Obtaining a visa at the Sudan embassy is not an easy task. You'll need two photos, a letter of invitation from a sponsor in Sudan and a copy of your passport pages. Then the application is sent to Khartoum (Sudan). If the answer is favourable, you'll pay US$50 (US$150 for US citizens) and you'll have to take a medical examination at Sembel Hospital. Expect a long processing time (up to three weeks).

Yemen One-month entry visas cost US$55 (US$130 for American citizens), require two photos, a valid return air ticket and a medical examination at Sembel Hospital (go figure!). They are processed within 24 hours. It's much easier to get your visa on arrival at San'a international airport.

WOMEN TRAVELLERS

With a very low national crime rate and an unusually liberal policy towards women, Eritrea must be one of the safest and least restrictive countries on the continent for women travellers. Use your common sense, though; all the usual precautions apply, such as safety in numbers.

ERITREA TRANSPORT

GETTING THERE & AWAY

Eritrea's isolation has been growing over the last few years. Flying is the only way to enter the country; it's no longer possible to travel overland. There are only a few airlines that serve the country.

Entering Eritrea

As long as you have a visa (p361), entering Eritrea should be no sweat. You will be asked to fill out a currency declaration form (see p357).

PASSPORT

Other than needing a visa, there are no entry restrictions for any nationalities bar Ethiopians.

Air

Travel during the months of May, July and August, and over Easter, Christmas and New Year should be booked well in advance. Eritreans living abroad tend to visit their families during this time and most flights are more expensive.

See p259 for general travel information.

AIRPORTS & AIRLINES

Eritrea's one international airport is 6km from the capital. The privately-run Nasair is the national carrier.

The following airlines fly to and from Eritrea and have offices in Asmara:

EgyptAir (airline code MS; Map p317; ☎ 127034; www .egyptair.com.eg; Bahti Meskerem Sq)

Lufthansa (airline code LH; off Map p317; ☎ 186904; www.lufthansa.com; Warsay St)

Nasair (airline code UE; Map p317; ☎ 200700; www .nasair.aero; off Adal St)

Yemenia (airline code IY; Map p320; ☎ 121035; www .yemenia.com; Harnet Ave)

AFRICA & MIDDLE EAST

EgyptAir has three flights a week between Asmara and Cairo for US$450/650 one way/return.

Yemenia has two flights weekly between Asmara and San'a (US$177/285).

Nasair operates twice weekly between Asmara and Dubai (US$640 return). It also operates weekly flights to Nairobi (US$840 return) via Khartoum (US$440).

ASIA

The best connections from Asia are via Dubai (United Arab Emirates), from where there are connections to Asmara with Nasair.

AUSTRALIA & NEW ZEALAND

There are no direct flights from Australia and New Zealand to Eritrea. The best routing is through Cairo (via Singapore) or via San'a (Yemen). You can also fly to Dubai (United Arab Emirates), and then continue to Eritrea with Nasair. Plan on from about A$2500 return.

UK & CONTINENTAL EUROPE

Lufthansa flies three times a week from Frankfurt to Asmara for around €920 return. EgyptAir flies to Asmara (via Cairo) from London or Paris twice a week for around €800. Yemenia has flights from Paris, London, Frankfurt and Rome to Asmara (via San'a) starting from €800.

At the time of writing, Nasair was going to launch weekly flights between Asmara and Milan (via Rome), and between Asmara and London.

USA

United Airlines and Lufthansa fly on a code-share basis three times a week from various US cities to Asmara (via Frankfurt), and a return trip will set you back anything from US$2000 to US$2300.

Land

BUS

There are no bus services between the neighbouring countries and Eritrea.

DJIBOUTI

There's only one border crossing, at Rahaita/Moulhoulé, about 110km south of Assab, but

---

DEPARTURE TAX

Eritrea levies a US$20 or €20 for outbound passengers on international flights. It's paid in cash after check-in.

ERITREA

it's not open because of the tension between Eritrea and Djibouti.

When the border was open, shared taxis (usually 4WDs) travelled from Assab to the border (with no fixed schedule), from where it was possible to find onward transport to Obock.

For more information on this border crossing, see p296.

ETHIOPIA

As long as the conflict with Ethiopia remains unresolved, the borders between the two countries will remain closed. The most convenient way to get to Ethiopia is to go through San'a (Yemen) or Cairo (Egypt).

When the situation between the two countries improves, you'll be able to use one of the three sealed roads connecting Eritrea with Ethiopia: the first goes from Asmara via Mendefera and Adi Quala to Aksum in Ethiopia; the second route goes from Asmara via Dekemhare and Adi Keyh in Eritrea to Adigrat in Ethiopia; and the third route connects Assab in the south with Addis Ababa.

SUDAN

At the time of writing, it was not possible to cross the border from Eritrea to Sudan. Check the current situation when you get there.

The road is sealed from Asmara to Teseney, near the border.

Sea

Eritrea has two ports, Massawa and Assab, but there's no scheduled passenger services and you won't be allowed to embark anyway.

GETTING AROUND

While the conflict with Ethiopia remains unresolved, travel around Eritrea may be slightly restricted. A travel permit (see p362) is necessary to travel outside Asmara, and a number of areas are off-limits to foreigners (p362). However, this might change, so check the situation when you get to Asmara.

Bicycle

If you're ready to sweat it out, it's not a bad idea to get around by bicycle. Given the outrageous price of petrol, traffic is minimal. The only real problem is the steep roads, except in the western lowlands where there is flat terrain. Oh, and there's the heat too. After a couple of weeks, you'll be ready for the Tour de France!

Asmara is also a great city in which to cycle. It's possible to hire bikes in one place only, see p331.

Boat

At the time of writing there were no regular boat services between Massawa and Assab on the Red Sea.

Bus

The bus service in Eritrea is reasonably efficient and extensive, but few would call it comfortable – expect something resembling a battered school bus. Coverage of Keren, Massawa, Mendefera and Dekemhare is excellent. Services thin out the further away from the capital you get. There are usually at least 10 buses a day between the larger towns (Asmara, Massawa and Keren), and in principle one bus a day between the smaller ones.

Fares used to be very cheap, but with the soaring fuel prices and shortages it's become a bit less economical. However, the bus still remains the best mode of transport for budgeteers. Services run between 6am and 4.30pm or 6pm but it's wise to start your journey early in the morning. For long-distance journeys (those taking three hours or longer), buses usually leave between 5.30am and 6.30am.

The major drawback of bus travel is that it's time-consuming. Progress on the road is often slow. Additionally, buses don't adhere to fixed timetables; they depart when they're full. For long-distance journeys, you need to be at the bus station by 6am to buy a ticket and be guaranteed a seat. It's not usually possible to buy tickets in advance, except for the journey between Asmara and Teseney and between Asmara and Assab.

Car & Motorcycle

Over long distances in Eritrea, cars can be twice as quick as buses. It gives you freedom of movement and it's a great way to visit the country at your own pace.

> **FUEL CRISIS**
>
> See these long queues in front of the petrol stations? Petrol is in short supply in Eritrea, as a result of the country's lack of hard currency to purchase it. This might affect bus schedules and vehicle hire.

ERITREA

CYCLING IN ERITREA *Tom Hall*

Eritreans love their cycling. At weekends races are cheered by enthusiastic, ululating crowds and the annual Giro d'Eritrea in February is the country's biggest sporting event. If this gets your legs twitching, here are a few pointers on two-wheeled travel in Eritrea.

Bike hire isn't common in Asmara. Your hotel can probably arrange a mountain bike for a morning, but they won't know what to charge you so be ready to negotiate. For anything more serious consider bringing your own wheels. Workshops in the market area of Asmara can fix most problems but lack sophisticated spare parts. If you think you might need a titanium screw or a specialised pedal clip, bring one with you.

Lots of the day excursions from Asmara in this book could be done by bicycle, at least one way. If your brakes are in good order the ride from Asmara to Nefasit, complete with hairpin bends and baboons for company, is thrilling. At the bottom, simply flag down a passing bus and ask them to put your bike on the roof for the ride back up. One bus I travelled on had two live goats on the roof for most of the journey, so a bike won't pose a problem! The area around Massawa is flat, hot and windy so cycling is best limited to local exploring. Always take as much water as you're likely to need and keep protected from the sun. Seek local advice before setting out.

If you do any cycling, remember to keep your passport and travel permit with you for going through checkpoints when leaving and entering towns. Cycling isn't allowed on the main streets of downtown Asmara – a hangover from pre-independence days when cyclists played a prominent role in agitating against Ethiopian targets.

DRIVING LICENCE

To hire a car, you must have a valid international driving licence and be over 25 years old.

FUEL & SPARE PARTS

At the time of research, petrol was in short supply in Eritrea and prices were exorbitant. In Asmara petrol was Nfa38 per litre and diesel Nfa17 (more realistically Nfa35 at the black market). Fortunately, distances between most destinations are quite short.

HIRE

Vehicle hire is expensive in Eritrea. If you're just planning on travelling on the main routes between towns, a 2WD vehicle is sufficient. But some sights, including Qohaito, are only accessible by 4WD. There are roadblocks on the outskirts of town, but it's usually hassle-free provided you have your travel permit with you.

Fortunately, the country is small and, with your own wheels, most of its attractions can be seen in quite a short period. If you're travelling solo, or as a couple, you can reduce the cost by joining up with other travellers to hire a car plus a driver/guide. Most vehicles accommodate around five passengers.

A deposit of around Nfa2000 is required to rent a 4WD; for a car it's around Nfa1000.

A driver is usually provided for your 4WD, which is a great help. Having someone who speaks Tigrinya and knows the roads is absolutely priceless. Sometimes there's an additional charge if you want the driver to work more than eight hours in a day; check in advance. Note that the car make and model and its registration number must be registered on your travel permit, otherwise soldiers won't let you through at roadblocks.

Cars cost Nfa400 to Nfa700 per day, and 4WDs cost Nfa1700 to Nfa2000 per day, including third-party insurance. The first 50km to 90km driven are free, and each additional kilometre costs between Nfa2 and Nfa3. For Assab, there's usually a surcharge of Nfa500 per day. If you want to hire a car with a driver, add Nfa100 to Nfa150 per day to the daily charge. Note that payment is by cash only.

Cars can be rented from the following agencies in Asmara:

Africa Rent Car (Map p320; ☎ 121755; afrecar@yahoo .com; Nora St)

Fontana Rent a Car (Map p320; ☎ 120052; fax 127905; Mata St)

Leo Car Rental (Map p317; ☎ 125859, 202306; Sematat Ave)

ERITREA

ROAD CONDITIONS
There's a small but surprisingly good network of sealed roads connecting Asmara to the north (until Keren), south (until the Ethiopian border), east (until Massawa) and west (until Barentu). The dirt road between Massawa and Assab has been much improved; it's now sealed from Massawa to Foro (59km).

ROAD HAZARDS
The road hazards that exist in Ethiopia also apply in Eritrea: precipitous roads, curfews, children playing, livestock wandering, land mines and roads that are impassable in the rainy season.

ROAD RULES
Driving is on the right-hand side of the road.

Hitching
Hitching is never entirely safe in any country, and we don't recommend it. Given the scarcity of traffic, hitching is not really an option in Eritrea anyway.

Local Transport
Taxis are plentiful in Asmara and can also be easily found in Massawa, Keren and Mendefera.

Tours
In Asmara there's a handful of reputable travel agencies that organise tours around the country. Tours can be tailored to your time, means and interests; from one-day birdwatching excursions around Asmara or weekend trips to the beach in Massawa, to boat trips to the Dahlak Islands or, possibly, expeditions in Dankalia (note that Dankalia was off-limits to travellers at the time of writing). Travel agencies also offer hotel and flight reservations and car hire. The following agencies get good reports from travellers and have plenty of experience in guiding foreigners:

Explore Eritrea Travel & Tours (Map p320; ☎ 125555, 120259; explore@tse.com.er; Adi Hawesha St)

Travel House International (Map p320; ☎ 201881/2; www.travelhouseeritrea.com; 175-15 St)

Train
The old Italian railway that stretched between Massawa, Asmara, Keren and Agordat was another casualty of war. Many of its tracks were pulled up to reinforce trenches. See also p331.

However, a section of the tracks has been repaired and there's now a regular train service on Sunday mornings between Asmara and Nefasit (US$50 or Nfa750 return, one hour), provided there's a minimum of 10 people aboard. The train leaves Asmara at 8am and is back around noon. The train can also be chartered to go as far as Massawa. Contact the **train station** (☎ 123365) in Asmara for more details.

Health

CONTENTS

One who hides his illness has no medicine; one who hides his problem has no remedy.

Ethiopian proverb

As long as you stay up to date with your vaccinations and take some basic preventive measures, you'd have to be pretty unlucky to succumb to most of the health hazards covered in this chapter. Africa certainly has an impressive selection of tropical diseases on offer, but you're much more likely to get a bout of diarrhoea (in fact, you should bank on it), a cold or an infected mosquito bite than an exotic disease such as sleeping sickness.

BEFORE YOU GO

A little planning before departure, particularly for vaccinations or if you have a pre-existing illness, will save you a lot of trouble later. Before a long trip get a checkup from your dentist, and from your doctor if you have any regular medication or chronic illness, eg high blood pressure or asthma. You should also organise spare contact lenses and glasses (and take your optical prescription with you); get a first-aid and medical kit together; and arrange necessary vaccinations.

It's tempting to leave it all to the last minute – don't! Many vaccines take several doses over a period of up to six weeks, so you must visit a doctor six to eight weeks before departure. Ask your doctor for an International Certificate of Vaccination (otherwise known as the yellow booklet), which will list all the vaccinations you've received. This is necessary, as proof of yellow fever (and possibly cholera) vaccination is mandatory in Ethiopia.

Travellers can register with the **International Association for Medical Advice to Travellers** (IMAT; www.iamat.org). Its website can help travellers to find a doctor who has recognised training. Those heading off to very remote areas might like to do a first-aid course (contact the Red Cross or St John's Ambulance) or attend a remote medicine first-aid course, such as that offered by the **Royal Geographical Society** (www.wildernessmedicaltraining.co.uk).

If you're bringing medications with you, carry them in their original containers, clearly labelled. A signed and dated letter from your physician describing all medical conditions and medications, including generic names, is also a good idea. If you're carrying syringes or needles be sure to have a physician's letter documenting their medical necessity.

How do you go about getting the best possible medical help? It's difficult to say; it really depends on the severity of your illness or injury and the availability of local help. If malaria is suspected, seek medical help as soon as possible or begin self-medicating if you're off the beaten track (see p371).

INSURANCE

Medical insurance is crucial, but many policies differ. Check that the policy includes all the activities you want to do. Some specifically exclude 'dangerous activities' such as white-water rafting, rock climbing and motorcycling. Sometimes even trekking is excluded. Also find out whether your insurance will make payments directly to providers or will reimburse you later for overseas health expenditures (in Ethiopia and Eritrea many doctors expect payment in cash). Ensure that your travel insurance will cover the emergency transport required to get you to a hospital in a major city, to better medical facilities elsewhere in Africa, or all the way home, by

HEALTH

air and with a medical attendant if necessary. If you need medical help, your insurance company might be able to help locate the nearest hospital or clinic, or you can ask at your hotel. In an emergency, contact your embassy or consulate.

Membership of the **African Medical & Research Foundation** (Amref; www.amref.org) provides an air evacuation service in medical emergencies in many African countries, including Ethiopia, Eritrea and Djibouti. It also provides air ambulance transfers between medical facilities. Money paid by members for this service goes into providing grassroots medical assistance for local people.

RECOMMENDED VACCINATIONS

The **World Health Organization** (www.who.int) recommends that all travellers be covered for diphtheria, tetanus, measles, mumps, rubella and polio, as well as for hepatitis B, regardless of their destination. The consequences of these diseases can be severe, and outbreaks of them do occur.

According to the **Centers for Disease Control & Prevention** (www.cdc.gov), the following vaccinations are recommended for all parts of Africa: hepatitis A, hepatitis B, meningococcal meningitis, rabies and typhoid, and boosters for tetanus, diphtheria and measles. Proof of yellow-fever vaccination is mandatory for travel to Ethiopia and Eritrea. Depending on where you've travelled from, cholera vaccination may also be required.

MEDICAL CHECKLIST

It's a very good idea to carry a medical and first-aid kit with you, to help yourself in the case of minor illness or injury. Following is a list of items you should consider packing.

- Acetaminophen (paracetamol) or aspirin
- Acetazolamide (Diamox) for altitude sickness (prescription only)
- Adhesive or paper tape
- Antibacterial ointment (eg Bactroban) for cuts and abrasions (prescription only)
- Antibiotics (see your medical health professional for the most useful ones to bring)
- Antidiarrhoeal drugs (eg loperamide)
- Antihistamines (for hayfever and allergic reactions)
- Anti-inflammatory drugs (eg ibuprofen)
- Antimalaria pills
- Bandages, gauze, gauze rolls

- DEET-containing insect repellent for the skin
- Iodine tablets (for water purification)
- Oral rehydration salts
- Permethrin-containing insect spray for clothing, tents, and bed nets
- Pocket knife
- Scissors, safety pins, tweezers
- Sterile needles, syringes and fluids if travelling to remote areas
- Steroid cream or hydrocortisone cream (for allergic rashes)
- Sunblock
- Syringes and sterile needles
- Thermometer

Since falciparum malaria predominates in Ethiopia, consider taking a self-diagnostic kit that can identify malaria in the blood from a finger prick.

INTERNET RESOURCES

There's a wealth of travel health advice on the internet. For further information lonelyplanet.com is a good place to start. The World Health Organization publishes a superb book called *International Travel and Health,* which is revised annually and is available online at no cost at www.who .int/ith. Other websites of general interest are **MD Travel Health** (www.mdtravelhealth.com), which provides complete travel health recommendations for every country, updated daily, also at no cost; the **Centers for Disease Control and Prevention** (www.cdc.gov); and **Fit for Travel** (www.fitfortravel.scot.nhs.uk), which has up-to-date information about outbreaks and is very user-friendly for travellers on the road.

It's also a good idea to consult your government's travel health website before departure, if one is available.

Australia (www.dfat.gov.au/travel)
Canada (www.hc-sc.gc.ca/english/index.html)
UK (www.doh.gov.uk/traveladvice/index.htm)
USA (www.cdc.gov/travel)

FURTHER READING

- *A Comprehensive Guide to Wilderness and Travel Medicine* by Eric A Weiss (1998)
- *Healthy Travel* by Jane Wilson-Howarth (1999)
- *Healthy Travel Africa* by Isabelle Young (2000)

- *How to Stay Healthy Abroad* by Richard Dawood (2002)
- *Travel in Health* by Graham Fry (1994)
- *Travel with Children* by Cathy Lanigan (2004)

IN TRANSIT

DEEP VEIN THROMBOSIS (DVT)

Blood clots can form in the legs during flights, chiefly because of prolonged immobility. This formation of clots is known as deep vein thrombosis (DVT), and the longer the flight, the greater the risk. Although most blood clots are reabsorbed uneventfully, some might break off and travel through the blood vessels to the lungs, where they could cause life-threatening complications.

The chief symptom of DVT is swelling or pain of the foot, ankle or calf, usually but not always on just one side. When a blood clot travels to the lungs, it could cause chest pain and breathing difficulty. Travellers with any of these symptoms should immediately seek medical attention.

To prevent the development of DVT on long flights you should walk about the cabin, perform isometric compressions of the leg muscles (ie contract the leg muscles while sitting), drink plenty of fluids, and avoid alcohol.

IN ETHIOPIA & ERITREA

AVAILABILITY & COST OF HEALTH CARE

Health care in Ethiopia and Eritrea is varied: Addis Ababa and Asmara have good facilities with well-trained doctors and nurses, but outside the capitals health care is patchy at best. Medicine and even sterile dressings and intravenous fluids might need to be purchased from a local pharmacy by patients or their relatives. The standard of dental care is equally variable, and there's an increased risk of hepatitis B and HIV transmission via poorly sterilised equipment. By and large, public hospitals in the region offer the cheapest service, but will have the least up-to-date equipment and medications; mission hospitals (where donations are the usual form of payment) often have more reasonable facilities; and private hospitals and clinics are more expensive but tend to have more advanced drugs and equipment and better trained medical staff.

Most drugs can be purchased over the counter in the region, without a prescription. Try to visit a pharmacy rather than a 'drug shop' or 'rural drug vendor', as they're the only ones with trained pharmacists who can offer educated advice. Many drugs for sale in Africa might be ineffective: they might be counterfeit or might not have been stored under the right conditions. The most common examples of counterfeit drugs are malaria tablets and expensive antibiotics, such as ciprofloxacin. Most drugs are available in larger towns, but remote villages will be lucky to have a couple of paracetamol tablets. It's strongly recommended that all drugs for chronic diseases be brought from home. Although condoms are readily available (sometimes boxes – yes boxes! – are in hotel rooms), their efficacy cannot be relied upon, so bring all the contraception you'll need. Condoms bought in Africa might not be of the same quality as in Europe or Australia, and they might have been incorrectly stored.

There's a high risk of contracting HIV from infected blood if you receive a blood transfusion in the region. The **BloodCare Foundation** (www.bloodcare.org.uk) is a useful source of safe, screened blood, which can be transported to any part of the world within 24 hours.

INFECTIOUS DISEASES

It's a formidable list but, as we say, a few precautions go a long way…

Cholera

Cholera is usually only a problem during natural or artificial disasters, eg war, floods or earthquakes, although small outbreaks can also occur at other times. Travellers are rarely affected. It's caused by a bacteria and spread via contaminated drinking water. The main symptom is profuse watery diarrhoea, which causes debilitation if fluids are not replaced quickly. An oral cholera vaccine is available in the USA, but it's not particularly effective. Most cases of cholera could be avoided by close attention to good drinking water and by avoiding potentially contaminated food. Treatment is by fluid replacement (orally or via a drip), but sometimes antibiotics are needed. Self-treatment isn't advised.

HEALTH

Dengue Fever (Break-bone Fever)

Spread through the bite of the mosquito, dengue fever causes a feverish illness with headache and muscle pains similar to those experienced with a bad, prolonged attack of influenza. There might be a rash. Mosquito bites should be avoided whenever possible. Self-treatment: paracetamol and rest. Aspirin should be avoided.

Diphtheria

Found in all of Africa, diphtheria is spread through close respiratory contact. It usually causes a temperature and a severe sore throat. Sometimes a membrane forms across the throat, and a tracheostomy is needed to prevent suffocation. Vaccination is recommended for those likely to be in close contact with the local population in infected areas. More important for long stays than for short-term trips. The vaccine is given as an injection alone or with tetanus, and lasts 10 years.

Filariasis

Tiny worms migrating in the lymphatic system cause filariasis. The bite from an infected mosquito spreads the infection. Symptoms include localised itching and swelling of the legs and/or genitalia. Treatment is available.

Hepatitis A

Hepatitis A is spread through contaminated food (particularly shellfish) and water. It causes jaundice and, although it's rarely fatal, it can cause prolonged lethargy and delayed recovery. If you've had hepatitis A, you shouldn't drink alcohol for up to six months afterwards, but once you've recovered, there won't be any long-term problems. The first symptoms include dark urine and a yellow colour to the whites of the eyes. Sometimes a fever and abdominal pain might be present. Hepatitis A vaccine (Avaxim, VAQTA, Havrix) is given as an injection: a single dose will give protection for up to a year, and a booster after a year gives 10-year protection. Hepatitis A and typhoid vaccines can also be given as a single dose vaccine, hepatyrix or viatim.

Hepatitis B

Hepatitis B is spread through infected blood, contaminated needles and sexual intercourse. It can also be spread from an infected mother to the baby during childbirth. It affects the liver, causing jaundice and occasionally live failure. Most people recover completely, bu some people might be chronic carriers of th virus, which could lead eventually to cirrhosi or liver cancer. Those visiting high-risk area for long periods or those with increased socia or occupational risk should be immunise Many countries now give hepatitis B as pa of the routine childhood vaccinations. It given singly or can be given at the same tim as hepatitis A (hepatyrix).

A course will give protection for at leas five years. It can be given over four weeks c six months.

HIV

HIV, the virus that causes AIDS, is a enormous problem throughout Ethiop and Eritrea. The virus is spread throug infected blood and blood products, b sexual intercourse with an infected part ner and from an infected mother to he baby during childbirth and breastfeeding It can be spread through 'blood to bloo contacts, such as with contaminated instru ments during medical, dental, acupunctu and other body-piercing procedures, an through sharing used intravenous needle At present there's no cure; medication tha might keep the disease under control i available, but these drugs are too expensiv for the overwhelming majority of African and are not readily available for travelle either. If you think you might have bee infected with HIV, a blood test is neces sary; a three-month gap after exposure an before testing is required to allow antibodie to appear in the blood.

Leishmaniasis

This is spread through the bite of an infecte sandfly. It can cause a slowly growing ski lump or ulcer (the cutaneous form) and som times a life-threatening fever with anaem and weight loss. Dogs can also be carriers the infection. Sandfly bites should be avoide whenever possible.

Leptospirosis

It's spread through the excreta of infecte rodents, especially rats. It can cause hepatit and renal failure, which might be fatal. It unusual for travellers to be affected unle living in poor sanitary conditions. It causes fever and sometimes jaundice.

Malaria

Malaria is a serious problem in Ethiopia and Eritrea, with one to two million new cases reported each year. Though malaria is generally absent at altitudes above 1800m, epidemics have occurred in areas above 2000m in Ethiopia. The central plateau, Addis Ababa, the Bale and Simien Mountains, and most of the northern historical circuit are usually considered safe areas, but they're not risk-free.

For short-term visitors, it's probably wise to err on the side of caution. If you're thinking of travelling outside these areas, you shouldn't think twice – take prophylactics.

The disease is caused by a parasite in the bloodstream spread via the bite of the female Anopheles mosquito. There are several types of malaria – falciparum malaria is the most dangerous type and makes up 70% of the cases in Ethiopia and Eritrea. Infection rates vary with season and climate, so check out the situation before departure. Unlike most other diseases regularly encountered by travellers, there's no vaccination against malaria (yet). However, several different drugs are used to prevent malaria, and new ones are in the pipeline. Up-to-date advice from a travel health clinic is essential as some medication is more suitable for some travellers than others. The pattern of drug-resistant malaria is changing rapidly, so what was advised several years ago might no longer be the case.

Malaria can present in several ways. The early stages include headaches, fevers, generalised aches and pains, and malaise, which could be mistaken for flu. Other symptoms can include abdominal pain, diarrhoea and a cough. Anyone who develops a fever in a malarial area should assume they have a malarial infection until a blood test proves negative, even if they have been taking antimalarial medication. If not treated, the next stage could develop within 24 hours, particularly if falciparum malaria is the parasite: jaundice, then reduced consciousness and coma (also known as cerebral malaria) followed by death. Treatment in hospital is essential, and the death rate might still be as high as 10%, even in the best intensive-care facilities in the country.

Many travellers are under the impression that malaria is a mild illness, that treatment is always easy and successful, and that taking antimalarial drugs causes more illness through side effects than actually getting malaria. In Africa, this is unfortunately not true. Side effects of the medication depend on the drug being taken. Doxycycline can cause heartburn, indigestion and increased sensitivity to sunlight; mefloquine (Larium) can cause anxiety attacks, insomnia and nightmares, and (rarely) severe psychiatric disorders; chloroquine can cause nausea and hair loss; and atovaquone and proguanil hydrochloride (malarone) can cause diarrhoea, abdominal pain and mouth ulcers.

These side effects are not universal, and can be minimised by taking medication correctly, eg with food. Also, some people should not take a particular antimalarial drug, eg people with epilepsy should avoid mefloquine, and doxycycline should not be taken by pregnant women or children younger than 12.

If you decide that you really do not wish to take antimalarial drugs, you must understand the risks, and be obsessive about avoiding mosquito bites. Use nets and insect repellent, and report any fever or flulike symptoms to a doctor as soon as possible. Some people advocate homeopathic preparations against malaria, such as Demal200, but as yet there's no conclusive evidence that this is effective, and many homeopaths don't recommend their use.

People of all ages can contract malaria, and falciparum causes the most severe illness. Repeated infections might result eventually in less serious illness. Malaria in pregnancy frequently results in miscarriage or premature labour. Adults who have survived childhood malaria have developed immunity and usually only develop mild cases of malaria; most Western travellers have no immunity at all. Immunity wanes after 18 months of nonexposure, so even if you have had malaria in the past and used to live in a malaria-prone area, you might no longer be immune.

If you're planning a journey through a malarial area, particularly where falciparum malaria predominates, consider taking stand-by treatment. Emergency stand-by treatment should be seen as emergency treatment aimed at saving the patient's life and not as routine self-medication. It should be used only if you'll be far from medical facilities and have been advised about the symptoms of malaria and how to use the medication. Medical advice should be sought as soon as possible to confirm whether the treatment has been successful. The type of stand-by treatment used will depend on local conditions, such as drug resistance, and on what antimalarial drugs were being used before stand-by treatment. This is worthwhile because you want to avoid contracting a particularly serious form such as cerebral malaria, which affects the brain and central nervous system and can be fatal in 24 hours. As mentioned earlier, self-diagnostic kits, which can identify malaria in the blood from a finger prick, are also available in the West.

The risks from malaria to both mother and foetus during pregnancy are considerable. Unless good medical care can be guaranteed, travel throughout Africa when pregnant – particularly to malarial areas – should be discouraged unless essential. Self-treatment: see stand-by treatment (earlier) if you're more than 24 hours away from medical help.

Meningococcal Meningitis

Meningococcal infection is spread through close respiratory contact and is more likely in crowded situations, such as buses. Infection is uncommon in travellers. Vaccination is recommended for long stays and is especially important towards the end of the dry season. Symptoms include a fever, severe headache, neck stiffness and a red rash. Immediate medical treatment is necessary.

The ACWY vaccine is recommended for all travellers in sub-Saharan Africa. This vaccine is different from the meningococcal meningitis C vaccine given to children and adolescents in some countries; it's safe to be given both types of vaccine.

Onchocerciasis (River Blindness)

This is caused by the larvae of a tiny worm which is spread by the bite of a small fly. Th earliest sign of infection is intensely itch red, sore eyes. Travellers are rarely severel affected. Treatment in a specialised clini is curative.

Poliomyelitis

Generally spread through contaminate food and water. It's one of the vaccine given in childhood and should be booste every 10 years, either orally (a drop o the tongue) or as an injection. Polio ca be carried asymptomatically (ie showin no symptoms) and could cause a transie fever. In rare cases it causes weakness or pa ralysis of one or more muscles, which migl be permanent.

Rabies

Rabies is spread by receiving the bites o licks of an infected animal on broken skin It's always fatal once the clinical symptom start (which might be up to several month after an infected bite), so postbite vaccina tion should be given as soon as possibl Postbite vaccination (whether or not you'v been vaccinated before the bite) prevent the virus from spreading to the centra nervous system. Animal handlers shoul be vaccinated, as should those travelling t remote areas where a reliable source of post bite vaccine isn't available within 24 hour Three preventive injections are needed ove a month. If you have not been vaccinate

---

THE ANTIMALARIAL A TO D

- A – Awareness of the risk. No medication is totally effective, but protection of up to 95% is achievable with most drugs, as long as other measures have been taken.

- B – Bites – avoid at all costs. Sleep in a screened room, use a mosquito spray or coils, sleep under a permethrin-impregnated net at night. Cover up at night with long trousers and long sleeves, preferably with permethrin-treated clothing. Apply appropriate repellent to all areas of exposed skin in the evenings.

- C – Chemical prevention (ie antimalarial drugs) is usually needed in malarial areas. Expert advice is needed as resistance patterns can change, and new drugs are in development. Not all antimalarial drugs are suitable for everyone. Most antimalarial drugs need to be started at least a week in advance and continued for four weeks after the last possible exposure to malaria.

- D – Diagnosis. If you have a fever or flulike illness within a year of travel to a malarial area, malaria is a possibility, and immediate medical attention is necessary.

you'll need a course of five injections start-ing 24 hours or as soon as possible after the injury. If you have been vaccinated, you'll need fewer postbite injections, and have more time to seek medical help.

Schistosomiasis (Bilharzia)

This disease is spread by flukes (minute worms) that are carried by a species of fresh-water snail. The flukes are carried inside the snail, which then sheds them into slow-moving or still water. The parasites penetrate human skin during paddling or swimming and then migrate to the bladder or bowel. They're passed out via stool or urine and could contaminate fresh water, where the cycle starts again. Paddling or swimming in suspect freshwater lakes or slow-running riv-ers should be avoided. There might be no symptoms. There might be a transient fever and rash, and advanced cases might have blood in the stool or in the urine. A blood test can detect antibodies if you might have been exposed, and treatment is then possible in specialist travel or infectious disease clinics. If not treated the infection can cause kidney failure or permanent bowel damage. It's not possible for you to infect others.

Tuberculosis (TB)

TB is spread through close respiratory contact and occasionally through infected milk or milk products. BCG vaccination is recom-mended for those likely to be mixing closely with the local population, although it gives only moderate protection against TB. It's more important for long stays than for short-term stays. Inoculation with the BCG vaccine isn't available in all countries. It's given routinely to many children in developing countries. The vaccination causes a small permanent scar at the site of injection, and is usually given in a specialised chest clinic. It's a live vaccine and should not be given to pregnant women or immunocompromised individuals.

TB can be asymptomatic, only being picked up on a routine chest X-ray. Alternatively, it can cause a cough, weight loss or fever, sometimes months or even years after exposure.

Trypanosomiasis (Sleeping Sickness)

Spread via the bite of the tsetse fly. It causes a headache, fever and eventually coma. There's an effective treatment.

TAPE WORMS

These parasites are relatively common in Ethiopia and the Horn. Eating Ethiopian traditional food like *kitfo* and *tere sega* (raw meat dishes) in rural areas is usually the cause. Consider having your stool tested when you get home to avoid future health problems.

Typhoid

This is spread through food or water con-taminated by infected human faeces. The first symptom is usually a fever or a pink rash on the abdomen. Sometimes septicaemia (blood poisoning) can occur. A typhoid vaccine (ty-phim Vi, typherix) will give protection for three years. In some countries, the oral vac-cine Vivotif is also available. Antibiotics are usually given as treatment, and death is rare unless septicaemia occurs.

Yellow Fever

Yellow fever is spread by infected mosqui-toes. Symptoms range from a flu-like illness to severe hepatitis (liver inflammation) jaun-dice and death. The yellow-fever vaccination must be given at a designated clinic and is valid for 10 years. It's a live vaccine and must not be given to immunocompromised or pregnant travellers.

Travellers must carry a certificate as evidence of vaccination to obtain a visa for Ethiopia and Eritrea, though Eritrea only requires one if you're arriving within six days of visiting an infected area. You may also have to present it at immigration upon arrival. There's always the possibility that a traveller without a legally required, up-to-date certificate will be vaccinated and detained in isolation at the port of arrival for up to 10 days or possibly repatriated.

TRAVELLERS' DIARRHOEA

Although it's not inevitable that you'll get diarrhoea while travelling in Ethiopia and Eritrea, it's certainly very likely. Diarrhoea is the most common travel-related illness: fig-ures suggest that at least half of all travellers will get diarrhoea at some stage. Sometimes dietary changes, such as increased spices or oils, are the cause. To help prevent diarrhoea, avoid tap water (see p375). You should also only eat fresh fruits or vegetables if cooked

HEALTH

or peeled, and be wary of dairy products that might contain unpasteurised milk. Although freshly cooked food can often be a safe option, plates or serving utensils might be dirty, so you should be highly selective when eating food from street vendors (make sure that cooked food is piping hot all the way through). If you develop diarrhoea, be sure to drink plenty of fluids, preferably an oral rehydration solution containing water (lots), and some salt and sugar. A few loose stools don't require treatment but, if you start having more than four or five stools a day, you should start taking an antibiotic (usually a quinoline drug, such as ciprofloxacin or norfloxacin) and an antidiarrhoeal agent (such as loperamide) if you're not within easy reach of a toilet. If diarrhoea is bloody, persists for more than 72 hours or is accompanied by fever, shaking chills or severe abdominal pain, seek medical attention.

Amoebic Dysentery

Contracted by eating contaminated food and water, amoebic dysentery causes blood and mucus in the faeces. It can be relatively mild and tends to come on gradually, but seek medical advice if you think you have the illness as it won't clear up without treatment (which is with specific antibiotics).

Giardiasis

This, like amoebic dysentery, is also caused by ingesting contaminated food or water. The illness usually appears a week or more after you have been exposed to the offending parasite. Giardiasis might cause only a short-lived bout of typical travellers' diarrhoea, but it can also cause persistent diarrhoea. Ideally, seek medical advice if you suspect you have giardiasis.

ENVIRONMENTAL HAZARDS
Heat Exhaustion

This condition occurs following heavy sweating and excessive fluid loss with inadequate replacement of fluids and salt, and is particularly common in hot climates when taking unaccustomed exercise before full acclimatisation. Symptoms include headache, dizziness and tiredness. Dehydration is already happening by the time you feel thirsty; aim to drink sufficient water to produce pale, diluted urine. Self-treatment: fluid replacement with water and/or fruit juice, and cooling by cold water and fans. The treatment of the salt-loss component consists of consuming salty fluids

as in soup, and adding a little more table salt to foods than usual.

Heatstroke

Heat exhaustion is a precursor to the much more serious condition of heatstroke. In this case there's damage to the sweating mechanism, with an excessive rise in body temperature; irrational and hyperactive behaviour and eventually loss of consciousness and death. Rapid cooling by spraying the body with water and fanning is ideal. Emergency fluid and electrolyte replacement is usually also required by intravenous drip.

Insect Bites & Stings

Mosquitoes might not always carry malaria or dengue fever, but they (and other insects) can cause irritation and infected bites. To avoid these, take the same precautions as you would for avoiding malaria (see p371). Use DEET-based insect repellents. Excellent clothing treatments are also available; mosquitoes that land on treated clothing will die.

Bee and wasp stings cause real problems only to those who have a severe allergy to the stings (anaphylaxis). If you're one of these people, carry an 'epipen': an adrenaline (epinephrine) injection, which you can give yourself. This could save your life.

Scorpions are frequently found in arid or dry climates. They can cause a painful bite that is sometimes life-threatening. If bitten by a scorpion, take a painkiller. Medical treatment should be sought if collapse occurs.

Fleas and bed bugs are often found in cheap hotels. Fleas are also common on local and long-distance buses and in the rugs of some remote churches. They lead to very itchy, lumpy bites. Spraying the mattress with crawling insect killer after removing bedding will get rid of them.

Scabies is also frequently found in cheap accommodation. These tiny mites live in the skin, particularly between the fingers. They cause an intensely itchy rash. The itch is easily treated with malathion and permethrin lotion from a pharmacy; other members of the household also need treating to avoid spreading scabies, even if they do not show any symptoms.

Snake Bites

Basically, do all you can to avoid getting bitten! Do not walk barefoot, or stick your hand into holes or cracks. However, 50% of people bitten by venomous snakes are not actually injected with poison (envenomed). If you are bitten by a snake, do not panic. Immobilise the bitten limb with a splint (such as a stick) and apply a bandage over the site, with firm pressure, similar to bandaging a sprain. Do not apply a tourniquet, or try to cut or suck the bite. Get medical help as soon as possible so you can get treated with an antivenene if necessary.

Water

Never drink tap water unless it has been boiled, filtered or chemically disinfected (such as with iodine tablets). Never drink from streams, rivers and lakes. It's also best to avoid drinking from pumps and wells: some do bring pure water to the surface, but the presence of animals can still contaminate supplies.

Bottled water is available everywhere, though it's better for the environment if you treat/filter local water.

Language

CONTENTS

THE ETHIOPIC SYLLABARY

The unique Ethiopic script is the basis for the alphabets of Amharic, Tigrinya and Tigré. The basic Ethiopic syllabary has 26 characters; Amharic includes another seven, and Tigrinya another five characters to cover sounds that are specific to those languages.

The alphabet is made up of root characters representing consonants. By adding lines or circles (representing the vowel sounds) to these characters, seven different syllables can be generated for each consonant (eg **ha**, **he**, **hë**, **heu**, **hi**, **ho**, **hu**). As with Roman script, the characters are written from left to right on a page.

ETHIOPIAN AMHARIC

Amharic is Ethiopia's national language. It belongs to the Afro-Asiatic language family, in the Semitic language sub-group, which includes Arabic, Hebrew and Assyrian.

While regional languages such as Oromo, Somali and Tigrinya are also important, Amharic is the most widely used and understood language throughout the country. It is the mother tongue of the 12 million or so Amhara people in the country's central and northwestern regions, and a second language for about one third of the total population.

Amharic word endings vary according to the gender and number of people you're speaking to. Gender is indicated in this guide by the abbreviations 'm' (to a male), 'f' (to a female) and 'pl' (to more than one person, regardless of gender). There are also general modes of address that can be either informal or polite, indicated by the abbreviations 'inf' and 'pol' respectively.

For a more comprehensive guide to the language, get a copy of Lonely Planet's *Ethiopian Amharic Phrasebook*. It has useful introductory sections on pronunciation and grammar, and includes Amharic script throughout.

PRONUNCIATION

While many of the sounds of Amharic will be familiar to you, there are some sounds for which there are no English equivalents. Keep your ears tuned to the way Ethiopians pronounce their language – this will be a good start in mastering pronunciation.

In general, stress falls equally on each syllable. Like English, a raised tone at the end of a sentence signifies a question.

Vowels

a	as in 'mamma'
e	as in 'let'
ə	as the 'a' in 'ago'; shorter and flatter than **eu** below
eu	as the 'e' in 'her', with no 'r' sound
i	as in 'bit'
o	as in 'hot'
ō	a cross between the 'oa' in 'coat' and the 'au' in 'haul'

u		as in 'flute' but shorter
ay		as the 'ai' in 'bait'
ai		as in 'aisle'

Consonants

ch	as in 'church'
g	as in 'get'
gw	as in 'Gwen'
h	as in 'hit'; at the end of a sentence it's like a short puff of breath
kw	as the 'q' in 'queen'
j	as in 'jump'
s	as in 'plus' (never a 'z' sound)
sh	as in 'shirt'
z	as in 'zoo'
ny	as the 'ni' in 'onion'
r	a rolled 'r'
'	a glottal stop, ie a momentary closing of the throat, like the 'tt' in the Cockney pronunciation of 'bottle'

You should also be aware of the Amharic consonant sounds that have no English equivalents – 'glottalic' or 'explosive' variants of some consonants, made by tightening and releasing the vocal chords. To explain these sounds in any depth goes beyond the aim of this guide. Instead, their nearest English equivalents have been used.

ACCOMMODATION

Where is a ...?	... የት ነው-?	... yeut nō?
bed	አልጋ	alga
cheap hotel	ርካሽ ሆቴል	rakash hotel
good hotel	ጥሩ ሆቴል	taru hotel
hotel	ሆቴል	hotel
room	ክፍል	kafal

Do you have ...?	... አለ	... alleu?
Is there ...?		
a room/bed	አልጋ	alga
a single room	አንድ አልጋ	and alga
a double room	ሁለት አልጋ	huleutt alga
a quiet room	ፀጥ ያለ ክፍል	seut yaleu kafal
hot water	ሙቅ ውሃ	muk wuha
showers	ሻወር	shaweur
water for	መታጠቢያ	meutateubiya
bathing	ውሃ	wuha

How much is the room/bed for ...?
አልጋ ለ ... ስንት ነው-? *alga leu ... sant nō?*

one night		
አንድ ማታ		and mata
one week		
አንድ ሳምንት		and samant

Does it include breakfast?
ቁርስንም ይጨምራል?
kursanam yicheumaral?

I'd like to see the room.
ክፍሉ-ን ማየት እፈልጋለሁ-
kaflun mayeut afeullagallō

Can I see a different room?
ሌላ ክፍል ማየት እችላለሁ-?
layla kafal mayeut achalallō?

I leave tomorrow.
ነገ እሄዳለሁ-
neugeu ahedallō

CONVERSATION & ESSENTIALS

Hello/Greetings.		
ጤና ይስጥልኝ		tenastallan (lit: 'may you be given health')
Hello.		
ሰላም		seulam (lit: 'peace be with you')
Hello.		
ታዲያስ		tadiyass (inf)
How are you?		
ደህና ነህ?		deuna neuh? (m)
ደህና ነሽ?		deuna neush? (f)
ደህና ነዎት?		deuna not? (pl)
እንደሙን ነህ?		andeuman neuh? (m) (pol)
እንደምን ነሽ?		andeuman neush? (f) (pol)
I'm fine.		
ደህና ነኝ		deuna neuny
Good night.		
ደህና ደር		deuna deur (m)
ደህና ደሪ		deuna deuri (f)
ደህና ይደሩ		deuna yideuru (pol)
Goodbye.		
ደህና ሰንብት		deuna seunbat (m)
ደህና ሰንብች		deuna seunbach (f)
ደህና ሰንብቱ		deuna seunbatu (pl)
Goodbye/See you.		
ቻው-!		chow (inf, as in Italian ciao)
Good luck!		
መልካም እድል!		meulkam adal!
Yes.		
አዎ		ow
OK.		
እሺ		ashi
No. (not the case/not so)		
አይ		ai (pronounced 'eye')
No. (not there/not available)		
የለም		yeulleum
Maybe.		
ምናልባት		manalbut
Please.		
እባክህ		abakah (m)
እባክሽ		abakash (f)
እባክዎን		abakon (pol)
እባካቹ-		abakachu (pl)

LANGUAGE

LANGUAGE

Thank you.
አመሰግናለሁ *ameuseuganallō*
Thank you very much.
በጣም አመሰግናለሁ *beutam ameuseuganallō*
Don't mention it.
ምንም አይደለም *mənəm aideuleum*
Excuse me.
ይቅርታ *yikərta*
Sorry.
አዝናለሁ *aznallō*
What's your name?
ስምህ ማነው? *səməh man nō?* (m)
ስምሽ ማነው? *səməsh man nō?* (f)
ስምዎት ማነው? *səməwot man nō?* (pol)
My name is ...
ስሜ ... ነው *səme ... nō*
What country are you from?
ከየት አገር ነህ? *keu yeut ageur neuh?* (m)
ከየት አገር ነሽ? *keu yeut ageur neush?* (f)
ከየት አገር ነዎት? *keu yeut ageur not?* (pol)
I'm from ...
ከ ... ነኝ *keu ... neuny*
Are you married?
አግብተሃል? *ageubtəhal?* (m)
አግብተሻል? *ageubtəshal?* (f)
I'm married.
አግብቻለሁ *agəbəchallō*
I'm not married.
አላገባሁም *alageubahum*
May I take a photograph?
ፎቶ ማንሳት ይቻላል? *foto mansat yichalal?*

DIRECTIONS
Where is ...?
... የት ነው? *... yeut nō?*
I want to go to ...
ወደ ... መሄድ እፈልጋለሁ *weudeu ... meuhed əfeullagallō*
How do I get to ...?
ወደ ... እንዴት አደዳለሁ? *weudeu ... əndet əhedallō?*
Is it near/far?
ቅርብ/ሩቅ ነው? *karb/ruk nō?*
Can I walk there?
በግር ያስኬዳል? *beugar yaskedal?*
Can you show me on the map?
ካርታው ላይ ያሳየኛል? *kartow lai yasayunyal?* (pol)
Turn left.
ወደ ግራ ታጠፍ/ታጠፊ *weudeu gra tateuf/tateufi* (m/f)

Turn right.
ወደ ቀኝ ታጠፍ/ታጠፊ *weudeu keuny tateuf/tateufi* (m/f)
Go straight ahead.
በቀጥታ ሂድ/ሂጅ *beukeutata hid/hij* (m/f)
on the (left/right)
በ (ግራ/ቀኝ) በኩል *beu (gra/keuny) beukul*
at the next corner
የሚቀጥለው መታጠፊያ *yeumikeutallō meutateufiya*

to the north	ወደ ሰሜን	*weudeu seumen*
to the south	ወደ ደቡብ	*weudeu deubub*
to the east	ወደ ምስራቅ	*weudeu məsrak*
to the west	ወደ ምዕራብ	*weudeu maʿarab*
in front of	ፊት ለፊት	*fit leu fit*
behind	በስተጀርባ	*beusteujeurba*
highway	አውራ ጎዳና	*owra godana*
main road	ዋና መንገድ	*wanna meungeud*
street	መንገድ	*meungeud*
village	መንደር	*meundeur*

HEALTH
I'm sick.
አሞኛል *amonyal*
I need a doctor.
ሐኪም እፈልጋለሁ *hakim əfeullagallō*
doctor
ሐኪም *hakim*
hospital
ሆስፒታል *hospital*
medical centre
የህክምና ጣቢያ *yeu həkəməna tabiya*

I'm allergic to ...
... አይስማማኝም *... aismamanyəm*
antibiotics
አንቲ ባዮቲክ *antibiyotik*
penicillin
ፔኒሲሊን *penisilin*

I have ...

... አለብኝ	... alleubəny	
diabetes		
ስኳር በሽታ	səkwar beushata	
nausea/vomiting		
ያስመልሰኛል	yasmeuləseunyal	
stomachache		
ሆዴን ያመኛል	hoden yameunyal	

EMERGENCIES – AMHARIC

Help!
እርዱኝ!   ərduny!

It's an emergency!
አስቸኳይ ነው-!   ascheukwai nō!

There's been an accident!
አደጋ ነበር   adeuga neubbeur!

Thief!
ሌባ!   leba!

Go away!/Leave me alone!
ተመለስ!   teumeulleuss!

I'm lost.
መንገድ ጠፍቶብኛል   meungeud teuftobanyal

Where is the toilet?
ሽንት ቤቱ የት ነው-?   shant betu yeut nō?

Call ...!
... ጥራ/ጥሪ   ... təra/təri! (m/f)
   the police
   ፖሊስ   polis
   an ambulance
   አምቡላንስ   ambulans

LANGUAGE DIFFICULTIES

Do you speak ...?
... ትችላለህ?   ... təchəlalleuh? (m)
... ትችያለሽ?   ... təchəyalleush? (f)
   English
   እንግሊዝኛ   ənglizənya
   Amharic
   አማርኛ   amarənya

Yes, I speak (English).
አዎ (እንግሊዝኛ) እችላለሁ-
ow, (ənglizənya) achəlallō

I don't speak (Amharic).
(አማርኛ) አልችልም
(amarənya) alchəlləm

Does anyone here speak English?
እንግሊዝኛ የሚችል አለ?
ənglizənya yeumichal alleu?

Do you understand?
ገባህ?   geubbah? (m)
ገባሽ?   geubbash? (f)

I don't understand.
አልገባኝም   algeubanyam

I understand.
ገብቶኛል   geubtonyal

Is there a translator?
አስተርጓሚ አለ?   asteurgwami alleu?

Please speak slowly.
እባክህ ቀስ ብለህ ተናገር
əbakəh keuss bəleuh teunageur (m)
እባክሽ ቀስ ብለሽ ተናገሪ
əbakash keuss bəleush teunageuri (f)

Please write it in Roman script.
እባክዎን በእንግሊዝኛ ይፃፉልኝ
əbakon beu anglizənya yisafuliny

NUMBERS

Although there are Amharic script numerals, Arabic numerals (ie those used in English) are now commonly used throughout Ethiopia. Amharic is used when referring to numbers in speech.

½	ግማሽ	gəmash
1	አንድ	and
2	ሁለት	huleutt
3	ሶስት	sost
4	አራት	arat
5	አምስት	aməst
6	ስድስት	sədast
7	ሰባት	seubat
8	ስምንት	səmant
9	ዘጠኝ	zeuteuny
10	አስር	assər
11	አስራ አንድ	assra and
12	አስራ ሁለት	assra huleutt
13	አስራ ሶስት	assra sost
14	አስራ አራት	assra arat
15	አስራ አምስት	assra aməst
16	አስራ ስድስት	assra sədast
17	አስራ ሰባት	assra seubat
18	አስራ ስምንት	assra səmant
19	አስራ ዘጠኝ	assra zeuteuny
20	ሃያ	haya
21	ሃያ አንድ	haya and
30	ሰላሳ	seulassa
40	አርባ	arba
50	አምሳ	hamsa
60	ስልሳ	salsa
70	ሰባ	seuba
80	ሰማንያ	seumanya
90	ዘጠና	zeuteuna
100	መቶ	meuto
1000	አንድ ሺ	and shi
2000	ሁለት ሺ	huleutt shi
100,000	መቶ ሺ	meuto shi

LANGUAGE

SHOPPING & SERVICES
Where is a/the ...?
... የት ነው-?   *... yeut nō?*
  bank
  ባንክ   *bank*
  church
  ቤተ ክርስቲያን   *beteu kərastiyan*
  city centre
  መሃል ከተማ   *meuhal keuteuma*
  ... embassy
  የ ... ኤምባሲ.   *yeu ... embassi*
  market
  ገቢያ   *geubiya*
  mosque
  መስጊድ   *meusgid*
  pharmacy
  ፋርማሲ/   *farmasi/*
    መድሃኒት ቤት   *meudhanit bet*
  police station
  ፖሊስ ጣቢያ   *polis tabiya*
  post office
  ፖስታ ቤት   *posta bet*
  public toilet
  ሽንት ቤት   *shənt bet*
  restaurant
  ምግብ ቤት   *məgəb bet*
  tourist office
  የቱሪስት ቢሮ   *yeu turist biro*
  university
  ዩኒቨርስተ   *yuniveursiti*

What time does it open/close?
በስንት ሰዓት ይከፈታል/ይዘጋል?
beu sant seu'at yikeufeutal/yizzeugal?
I want to change money/travellers cheques.
ገንዘብ/ትራቭለርስቼክስ መቀየር እፈልጋለሁ-
geunzeub/travleur chek meukeuyeur afeullagallō
I want to make a (local/international) call.
(አገር ውስጥ/ውጭ አገር) ስልክ መደወል እፈልጋለሁ-
(ageur wəst/wəch ageur) səlk meudeuweul afeullagallō

Where is a/an ...?
... የት ነው-?   *... yeut nō?*
  bakery
  ዳቦ ቤት   *dabbo bet*
  bookshop
  መጽሐፍ ቤት   *meusəhaf bet*
  clothes shop
  የልብስ ሱቅ   *yeu ləbs suk*
  general store
  ሸቀጣ ሸቀጥ መደብር   *sheukeuta sheukeut meudeubar*
  market
  ገቢያ   *geubiya*
  shop
  ሱቅ   *suk*

Where can I buy ...?
  ... የት ይገኛል?   *... yeut yigeunyal?*
I'm just looking.
  እያየሁ- ነው-   *əyayō nō*
I want a (larger/smaller) ...
  (ተለቅ ያለ/አነስ ያለ) ...   *(tallək yaleu/anneus yaleu) ...*
  እፈልጋለሁ-   *afeullagallō*
How much is it?
  ስንት ነው-?   *sənt nō?*
That's (very) expensive.
  (በጣም) ው-ድ ነው-   *(beutam) wədd nō*
Do you have anything cheaper?
  ርካሽ አለ?   *rakash alleu?*

TIME & DAYS
What time is it?
  ስንት ሰዓት ነው-?
  sant seu'at nō?
It's (one) o'clock.
  (አንድ) ሰዓት ነው-
  (and) seu'at nō
It's a quarter past (one).
  (አንድ) ሰዓት ከሩብ ነው-
  (and) seu'at keurub nō
It's half past (one).
  (አንድ) ሰዓት ተኩል ነው-
  (and) seu'at teukul nō

When?	መቼ	meuche?
in the morning	ከጠዋቱ	keu teuwatu
in the evening	ከምሽቱ	keu məshatu
at night	ከሌሊ.ተ	keu lelitu
now	አሁን	ahun
today	ዛሬ	zaray
tonight	ዛሬ ማታ	zaray mata
tomorrow	ነገ	neugeu
yesterday	ትናንትና	tanantana
Monday	ሰኞ	seunyo
Tuesday	ማክሰኞ	makseunyo
Wednesday	ሮብ	rob
Thursday	ሃሙስ	hamus
Friday	አርብ	arb
Saturday	ቅዳሜ	kadame
Sunday	እሁ-ድ	ahud

TRANSPORT
Where is the ...?
  ... የት ነው-?   *... yeut nō?*
  airport
  አይሮፕላን ማረፊ.ያ   *airoplan mareufiyaw*
  bus station
  አው-ቶብስ ጣቢ.ያ   *owtobəs tabiya*
  bus stop
  አው-ቶብስ ማቆሚ.ያ   *owtobəs makomiya*

taxi stand
ታክሲ ማቆሚያ   *taksi makomiya*
ticket office
ትኬት መሸጫ   *tiket biro*
train station
ባቡር ጣቢያ   *babur tabiya*

What time does the ... arrive/leave?
... መቼ ይደርሳል/ይነሳል?
... *meuche yideursal/yineusal?*

boat	ጀልባ	*jeulba*
bus	አውቶብስ	*owtobəs*
car	መኪና	*meukina*
minibus	ውይይት	*wəyayət*
plane	አይሮፕላን	*airoplan*
train	ባቡር	*babur*
truck	የጭነት መኪና	*yeu chaneut meukina*

How much is it to ...?
ወደ ... ስንት ነው-?   *weudeu ... sənt nō?*
I'd like to reserve a ticket to ...
ወደ ... ትኬት በቅድሚያ መግዛት እፈልጋለሁ-
weudeu ... tiket beukəd miya meugzat əfeulləgallō
I'd like a one way ticket to ...
ወደ ... መሄጃ ብቻ ትኬት እፈልጋለሁ-
weudeu ... meuheja bəcha tiket əfeulləgallō
I'd like a return ticket to ...
ወደ ... ደርሶ መልስ ትኬት እፈልጋለሁ-
weudeu ... deurso meuls tiket əfeulləgallō
Which bus goes to ...?
የትኛው አውቶብስ ወደ ... ይሄዳል?
yeutənyow owtobəs weudeu ... yihedal?
Does it go to ...?
ወደ ... ይሄዳል?
weudeu ... yihedal?
Can you please tell me when we get to ...?
እባክህ ... ስንደርስ ንገረኝ?
ə-ba-keuh ... sə-nə-deurss nə-geu-reuny? (m)
እባክሽ ... ስንደርስ ንገሪኝ?
ə-ba-keush ... sə-nə-deurss nə-geu-riny? (f)
This is my stop/destination.
ወራጅ አለ
worajal-leu
next
የሚቀጥለው-
yeumikeutəllō

I want to rent a ...
... መከራየት እፈልጋለሁ- ... *meukeurayeut əfeulləgallō*
bicycle
ቢስክሌት   *bəsklet*
car
መኪና   *meukina*

TIGRINYA

Tigrinya is the principal language of Eritrea and is also widely spoken in Tigray province in Ethiopia. It belongs to the Ethiopic branch of the Semitic language family. Like Amharic, it uses the syllabic alphabet of classical Ethiopic or Ge'ez (see The Ethiopic Syllabary on p376).

Tigrinya word endings vary according to the gender of the person you are speaking to; this is indicated in this guide where relevant by the abbreviations 'm' (to a male) and 'f' (to a female).

PRONUNCIATION
Vowels

a	as in 'mamma'
e	as in 'men'
ee	as in 'heed'
i	as in 'bit'
o	as in 'or', with no 'r' sound
oo	as in 'cool'
u	as in 'put'
ay	as in 'bait'
ai	as in 'aisle'
ō	a cross between the 'oa' in 'coat' and the 'au' in 'haul'

Consonants

Most consonants sound similar to their English counterparts but, like Amharic, there are some consonant sounds not found in English. The transliterations in this guide are designed for ease of use and are not meant as a detailed phonetic representation of all the consonant sounds of Tigrinya. By pronouncing the words and phrases clearly you should be able to make yourself understood. Listening to the everyday speech of the people is the best way to master some of the more complex sounds of the language.

ch	as in 'church'
g	as in 'get'
h	as in 'him'
j	as in 'jump'
ny	as the 'ni' in 'onion'
q	like a 'k' from far back in the throat
r	as in 'run'
s	as in 'plus' (never a 'z' sound)
sh	as in 'shirt'
ts	as the 'ts' in 'its'
z	as in 'zoo'

LANGUAGE

LANGUAGE

ACCOMMODATION

camping ground	metkel dinquan/teinda bota
guesthouse	maeref agaysh/albeirgo
hotel	hotel
youth hostel	nay mena-esey hostel

Do you have any rooms available?	medekesi kiflee alekado?
How much is it per night/person?	neha-de leiti/seb kenday yikifel?
Is breakfast included?	kursi mesoo hisub d'yu?

single bed	kelete arat
double bed	hadde arat
for one/two people	neha-de/kelete seb
for one/two nights	neha-de/kelete leiti

CONVERSATION & ESSENTIALS

Hello.	selam
Welcome.	merhaba
Good morning.	dehaando hadirka/ hadirkee (m/f)
Good afternoon.	dehaando weelka/ weelkee (m/f)
Good evening.	dehaando amsika/ amsikee (m/f)
Good night.	dehaan hideru
Goodbye.	dehaan kun (also Italian ciao)
Yes.	u-we
No.	aykonen
Please.	bejaka/bejakee (m/f)
Thank you.	yekanyeley/yemesgin
That's fine, you're welcome.	genzebka/genzebkee (m/f)
Excuse me.	yikrai-ta
I'm sorry.	aytehazeley
How are you?	kemay aleka/alekee? (m/f)
I'm fine, thanks.	tsebuk, yekeniyeley
Pleased to meet you.	tsebuk afleto/leila yigberelna
What's your name?	men semka/semkee? (m/f)
My name is ...	shemey ... iyu
Where are you from?	kabey metsika/metsikee? (m/f)
I'm from ...	a-nne kab ... iye
Are you married?	temereka dikha? (m) temerekee dikhee? (f)
How many children do you have?	kenday kolu-oot (deki) alowuka/ alowukee? (m/f)
I don't have any children.	deki yebeleyn.
I have a son.	wedi aloni
I have a daughter.	gual alatni
May I take your photograph?	kese-alekado?

DIRECTIONS

Where is ...?	abey alo ...?
I want to go to ...	nab ... kikeid delye
How do I get to ...?	kemey geire naboo ... yikeid?
Is it far/near?	rehooq/kereba diyu?
Can I walk there?	baegrey kikedo yikealdo?
Can you show me the direction?	ket-hebreni tikealdo?
Go straight ahead.	ket elka kid
Turn left/right.	netsegam/neyeman tetewe

HEALTH

I need a doctor.	a-nne hakim/doctor yedliyeni a-lo
Where is the hospital?	hospital/beit hikimina abey alo?
I have a stomachache.	a-nne kirtset aloni
I'm diabetic.	a-nne shikor/shikoria himam aloni
I'm allergic to penicillin.	a-nne nay pencillin kute-at aloni
diarrhoea	witse-at
medicine	medhanit/fewsi
nausea	egirgir/segedged

EMERGENCIES – TIGRINYA

Help!	hagez/redi-at!
Leave me alone/ Go away!	hidegeni!/kid bejakha!
I'm lost.	a-nne tefi-a aloku
Call ...!	... tsewe-a!
a doctor	hakim/doctor
the police	police

LANGUAGE DIFFICULTIES

Do you speak (English)?	(engiliznya) tezarebdo/ tezarebido? (m/f)
I don't speak Tigrinya.	a-nne tigrinya ayzareben
I understand.	yirede-anee iyu/teredioonee
I don't understand.	ayeterede-anen

NUMBERS

1	hadde
2	kelete
3	seleste
4	arba-ate
5	hamushte
6	shedushte
7	shewate
8	shemonte
9	tesh-ate
10	aserte
20	isra
30	selasa

40	arba-a
50	hamsa
60	susa
70	sebe-a
80	semanya
90	tese-a
100	mi-eetee
1000	sheh

SHOPPING & SERVICES

I'm looking for ...	ne ... yenadi alekoo
a bank	bank
the hospital	hospital/ beit hikmena
the market	idaga/shooq
a pharmacy	farmacha/beit medhanit
the post office	beit busta
a public telephone	nay hizbi telefon
the tourist office	nay turist haberaita beit tsihfet

What time does it open?	saat kenday yikifet?
What time does it close?	saat kenday yi-etso?
Do you have ...?	... alekado?
How many/much?	kenday?
this/that	eizee/etee
How much is it?	kenday iyu waga-oo?
I'm just looking.	nikeree tirah iye
That's too expensive.	aziyu kebiruni
bookshop	mesheta metsahifti
clothes shop	mesheta kidawenti
market	idaga/shouq
local products	nay kebabi etot/firyat

TIME & DAYS

What time is it?	saat kenday koynoo?
today	lomee/lomee me-altee
tomorrow	tsebah
yesterday	timalee
morning	niguho
afternoon	dehri ketri
night	leytee

Monday	senui
Tuesday	selus
Wednesday	reboo
Thursday	hamus
Friday	arbi
Saturday	kedam
Sunday	senbet

TRANSPORT

Where is the ...?	abey alo ...?
airport	aryaporto/maerefi nefarit
bus station	maerefi autobus
bus stop	autobus tetew tiblelu

When does the next ... leave/arrive?	tikitsil ... saat kenday tinekel/te-atu?
boat	jelba
bus (city)	autobus (ketema)
plane	auroplan/nefarit
taxi	taksi
train	babur

LANGUAGE

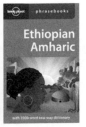

Also available from
Lonely Planet:
*Ethiopian Amharic
Phrasebook &
Africa Phrasebook*

Glossary

Ethiopian and Eritrean culinary terms are found under Eat Your Words on p72. For information on the languages of Ethiopia and Eritrea see p376.

abba – a prefix used by a priest before his name; means 'father'

abuna – archbishop of the Ethiopian and Eritrean Orthodox church, from the *Ge'ez* word meaning 'our father'

agelgil – round, leather-bound lunch boxes carried by locals

amba (also *emba*) – flat-topped mountain

Ato – literally 'sir'; equivalent of 'Mr'

azmari – itinerant minstrel (Ethiopia)

beat – Amharic word meaning 'place' that is attached to the end of other words, eg *buna beat, shint beat* (Ethiopia)

buluko – heaviest type of *shamma*, used in cold areas such as the Bale Mountains (Ethiopia)

buna – coffee (Ethiopia)

chat – mildly intoxicating leaf that's consumed primarily in eastern Ethiopia and Djibouti; it's illegal in Eritrea

contract taxi – private, or nonshared, taxi

Derg – Socialist military junta that governed Ethiopia from 1974 to 1991; derived from the *Ge'ez* word for 'committee'

dhow – see *sambuk*

dula – wooden staff carried by many Ethiopian highlanders

emba – see *amba*

enset – false-banana tree found in much of southern Ethiopia, used to produce a breadlike staple also known as *enset*

EPLF – Eritrean People's Liberation Front; victorious guerrilla army in the 'Struggle for Independence'

Falasha – Ethiopian Jew

faranji – foreigner, especially Western ones (Ethiopia)

gabeta – ancient board game

gabi – slightly thicker version of the *shamma*, worn by men

gada – age system of male hierarchy among the Oromo

gari – horse-drawn cart used for transporting passengers and goods in the towns

Ge'ez – a forerunner of modern Amharic

gegar – a rectangular, two-storey structure with a flat roof

gommista – tyre repair shop (Italian)

injera – an Ethiopian pancake upon which sits anything from spicy meat stews to colourful dollops of boiled veg and cubes of raw beef

jellabia – hooded cloak with wide sleeves (Eritrea)

jile – the curved knife that is carried by Afar nomads

kemis – white cotton dress worn by Ethiopian highland women

Kiddus – Saint, eg Kiddus Mikael translates to St Michael

maqdas – inner sanctuary of a church (Holy of Holies)

mesob – hourglass-shaped woven table from which traditional food is served (Ethiopia)

mies – see *tej*

natala – women's equivalent of a *shamma*, but with a decorated border *(tibeb)*

negus – prince (Ethiopia)

ras – title (usually of nobility but given to any outstanding male) similar to duke or prince

sambuk – traditional Arab vessel (or *dhow*) rigged with a lateen (triangular) sail, plying the Red Sea and Indian Ocean (Eritrea)

sewa – see *tella*

shamma – a white, light cotton toga; see also *gabi*, *natala* and *buluko*

shifta – traditionally a rebel or outlaw; today a bandit or roadside robber

shint beat – toilet (Ethiopia)

tabot – replica of the Ark of the Covenant, kept in the *maqdas* of every Orthodox church

tankwa – traditional papyrus boat used on Lake Tana and elsewhere (Ethiopia)

tef – an indigenous grass cultivated as a cereal grain; the key ingredient of injera

tej – wine made from honey, popular in Ethiopia; known in Eritrea as *mies*

tella – home-brewed beer made from finger millet, maize or barley, popular in Ethiopia; known in Eritrea as *sewa*

tibeb – the decorative border of a woman's shawl (Ethiopia)

tukul – traditional cone-shaped hut with thatched roof; like South Africa's rondavel

wadi – a river that is usually dry except in the rainy season

Weizerit – equivalent of 'Miss' (Ethiopia)

Weizero – literally 'lady', now equivalent of 'Mrs' (Ethiopia)

The Authors

JEAN-BERNARD CARILLET
Coordinating Author, Somaliland, Djibouti, Eritrea

A Paris-based journalist and photographer, Jean-Bernard is a die-hard Africa lover and diving instructor. He has travelled the length and breadth of the African continent for nearly 20 years now. After four trips in the Horn, he thinks that Asmara is the best place on earth to sip a frothy *macchiato*, Djibouti is Africa's best-kept secret (ah, Lac Abbé!) and Somaliland, er, the most bizarre country he has ever visited. He's eager to discover the rest of Somalia – when it becomes more traveller-friendly. Jean-Bernard has also coauthored Lonely Planet's *West Africa* and writes for various travel magazines.

STUART BUTLER
Addis Ababa, Northern Ethiopia

English-born Stuart first visited Ethiopia in the early '90s, shortly after the fall of the Derg. He was utterly infatuated with what he saw and has returned a number of times since: each time the country has woven its spell on him a little more. Stuart still finds Ethiopia a truly unique country and one that, even with a lifetime of study, would still surprise. Stuart's travels, both for Lonely Planet and various surf magazines, have taken him beyond Ethiopia, as far as the coastal deserts of Pakistan and the jungle of Colombia. He now lives in southwest France.

DEAN STARNES
Southern Ethiopia, Eastern Ethiopia, Western Ethiopia

Ethiopia has long topped Dean's wish-list of places to visit, but until relatively recently it had managed to sidestep all of his African itineraries. When he did finally visit, he was amazed he hadn't made the trip sooner and is now busy plotting his return.

Until that time, he's happy to spend his days in Auckland, New Zealand, where he alternates between writing for Lonely Planet, freelancing as a graphic designer and shirking responsibilities. His book, *Roam: the Art of Travel*, and website, www.deanstarnes.com, feature photography from Ethiopia and stories about his wayfaring ways.

THE AUTHORS

LONELY PLANET AUTHORS

Why is our travel information the best in the world? It's simple: our authors are passionate, dedicated travellers. They don't take freebies in exchange for positive coverage so you can be sure the advice you're given is impartial. They travel widely to all the popular spots, and off the beaten track. They don't research using just the internet or phone. They discover new places not included in any other guidebook. They personally visit thousands of hotels, restaurants, palaces, trails, galleries, temples and more. They speak with dozens of locals every day to make sure you get the kind of insider knowledge only a local could tell you. They take pride in getting all the details right, and in telling it how it is. Think you can do it? Find out how at **lonelyplanet.com**.

Behind the Scenes

THIS BOOK

This edition of *Ethiopia & Eritrea* was written by Jean-Bernard Carillet, Stuart Butler and Dean Starnes. The Environment chapter was written by naturalist David Lukas. Previous editions were authored by Frances Linzee Gordon, Matt Phillips and Jean-Bernard Carillet. This guidebook was commissioned in Lonely Planet's Melbourne office, and produced by the following:

Commissioning Editors Holly Alexander, Stefanie Di Trocchio
Coordinating Editor Jessica Crouch
Coordinating Cartographer David Kemp
Coordinating Layout Designer Jim Hsu
Managing Editor Imogen Bannister
Managing Cartographers David Connolly, Amanda Sierp
Managing Layout Designer Sally Darmody
Assisting Editors Lindsay Brown, Justin Flynn, Jocelyn Hargrave, Rowan McKinnon
Assisting Cartographers Anita Banh, Andras Bogdanovits, Ross Butler
Cover Image research provided by lonelyplanetimages .com
Project Managers Eoin Dunlevy, Sarah Sloane

Thanks to Lucy Birchley, Jessica Boland, Helen Christinis, Rebecca Davey, Brigitte Ellemor, Lisa Knights, Evan Jones, Katie Lynch, John Mazzocchi, Lucy Monie, Adrian Persoglia, Averil Robertson, Juan Winata

THANKS
JEAN-BERNARD CARILLET

A huge thanks to everyone who helped out and made this trip an enlightenment, including Solomon, Tedros, Mehret, Alain, Thomas, Adriano, Fabrizio, Dottore Marco, Lia, Said, Shabeelle, David, Nico, Bruno, Vicente, Dominique, Abdurazak, Ermano and all the people I met on the road – you're all so charming.

At LP I'm grateful to Holly Alexander and Stefanie Di Trocchio for their trust and constant support. The carto and design teams also deserve huge thanks for their input.

It has been a huge pleasure to work with Stuart, Dean and David, my three high-calibre coauthors, who share the same passion for the Horn, as well as Simon, who has an eye on everything. Congrats, guys!

At home, a phenomenal *gros bisou* to my daugher Eva, who gives a direction to my otherwise roving life.

STUART BUTLER

Firstly, and most importantly, I must thank Heather for once again putting up with me vanishing into

---

THE LONELY PLANET STORY

Fresh from an epic journey across Europe, Asia and Australia in 1972, Tony and Maureen Wheeler sat at their kitchen table stapling together notes. The first Lonely Planet guidebook, *Across Asia on the Cheap*, was born.

Travellers snapped up the guides. Inspired by their success, the Wheelers began publishing books to Southeast Asia, India and beyond. Demand was prodigious, and the Wheelers expanded the business rapidly to keep up. Over the years, Lonely Planet extended its coverage to every country and into the virtual world via lonelyplanet.com and the Thorn Tree message board.

As Lonely Planet became a globally loved brand, Tony and Maureen received several offers for the company. But it wasn't until 2007 that they found a partner whom they trusted to remain true to the company's principles of travelling widely, treading lightly and giving sustainably. In October of that year, BBC Worldwide acquired a 75% share in the company, pledging to uphold Lonely Planet's commitment to independent travel, trustworthy advice and editorial independence.

Today, Lonely Planet has offices in Melbourne, London and Oakland, with over 500 staff members and 300 authors. Tony and Maureen are still actively involved with Lonely Planet. They're travelling more often than ever, and they're devoting their spare time to charitable projects. And the company is still driven by the philosophy of *Across Asia on the Cheap*: 'All you've got to do is decide to go and the hardest part is over. So go!'

the Ethiopian wilds for such a long time and for keeping everything running smoothly once deadline approached. Thanks also to Toby Adamson, Gillian and Dan for company on the road, Abraham for his superb driving skills, Tania and Cheru for answering endless questions, several shared meals and helping organise everything. Thanks also to Dawoud Sulayman in Gonder and Simien and all the hundreds of Ethiopians who helped out in their own way.

DEAN STARNES

It would be wrong not to acknowledge the legacy of work from previous editions and help and assistance from authors extraordinaire Jean-Bernard Carillet and Stuart Butler. I'm deeply indebted to the team at Lonely Planet including Stefanie Di Trocchio, Holly Alexander (for giving me the gig in the first place), Adrian Persoglia and Brigitte Ellemor.

On the road the long drives were greatly enhanced by the witticism of Petra Yssennagger, Willem Bekkema, Paula Johnson, Laura Pena, Emily Kirby and Jen Eggener and the expertise offered by Nibret Adem, Binsam Woldesemayat, Ras Hailu Tefari and Tadessa Hailu. I'm particularly grateful to Tania O'Connor and Cheru Alemu and their guides Wondimu Kedru and Abraham Abera Addisu.

At home my love and thanks go to my wife, Debbie and my mum and dad for all their support in ways too numerous to list.

CONTRIBUTING AUTHOR
DAVID LUKAS

David Lukas wrote the Environment chapter. A professional naturalist who lives on the edge of Yosemite National Park, David leads natural-history tours around the state and writes about the environment for a wide variety of publications, including over 20 Lonely Planet guides.

OUR READERS

Many thanks to the travellers who used the last edition and wrote to us with helpful hints, useful advice and interesting anecdotes:

Ciaran Aiken, Adam Alagiah, Debbie Amos, Tim Bayne, Ulrich Becker, Joachim G Behrmann, Kendra Bischoff, Liz Bissett, Mike Bissett, Scott Anthony Blackburn, Guillaume Blanc, Lister Bolton, Avi Bram, Robin Bronen, Suvi Brown, Andrew Buck, Eva Burnham, Linda Cassidy, Hanne Kingo Christensen, Matthew Cooper, Laure Curt, Dieter Cverhoff, Shane Dallas, Ben De Castelet, Jeremy Ell, Peter D Ellis, Tobias Elwert, Georgina Fenton, Jessica Freeman, Erik Futtrup, Tone Marie Galteland, Eddie Game, Elizabeth Game, Richard Green, Yvette Haakmeester, Mary Hardy, Chris Haywood, Andy Heald, Mark Hodgson, Antoinette Kavanagh, Erika Keane, Amrach Kinfe, Zoltan Konder, Ulrich Kroll,

SEND US YOUR FEEDBACK

We love to hear from travellers – your comments keep us on our toes and help make our books better. Our well-travelled team reads every word on what you loved or loathed about this book. Although we cannot reply individually to postal submissions, we always guarantee that your feedback goes straight to the appropriate authors, in time for the next edition. Each person who sends us information is thanked in the next edition – and the most useful submissions are rewarded with a free book.

To send us your updates – and find out about Lonely Planet events, newsletters and travel news – visit our award-winning website: **lonelyplanet.com/contact**.

Note: we may edit, reproduce and incorporate your comments in Lonely Planet products such as guidebooks, websites and digital products, so let us know if you don't want your comments reproduced or your name acknowledged. For a copy of our privacy policy visit lonelyplanet.com/privacy.

Julie Lawson, David Lee, Jessica Lobbett, Louise Logan, Geoffroy Magnan, Lionel Mann, Ryan Meck, Peter Mellert, Elizabeth Muldrow, Catherine Phillips, Peter Pindak, Nikolaj Rasmussen, Izhar A Razack, Lynette Reid, James Rollin, Michael Schagerl, Valeska Schaudy, Anya Schiffrin, Brigitte Schumann, Getinet Seyoum, Adebayo Shinkaiye, Matthew Shorter, Matthias Siebeck, Paul Simon, Ayalew Sisay, Dawit Tesfay, Marco Todte, Maarten Van Delft, Michou Van Den Bossche, Dirk Van Der Auwera, Remco Van Der Kort, Sonja Van Der Sar, Rob Van Elburg, Stefan Weninger, Paul Woods, Sebastian Zahn, Lillian Zaremba, Rachel Zuback.

ACKNOWLEDGMENTS
Many thanks to the following for the use of their content:

Globe on title page ©Mountain High Maps 1993 Digital Wisdom, Inc.

Internal photographs p8 by MARKA/Alamy. All other photographs by Lonely Planet Images, and by Patrick Syder p5; David Else p6; Frances Linzee Gordon p7 (#5); Ariadne Van Zandbergen p7 (#1); Leonard Zell p9; Andrew Burke p10; Frances Linzee Gordon p11 (#1); Jane Sweeney p11 (#3); Frances Linzee Gordon p12.

All images are the copyright of the photographers unless otherwise indicated. Many of the images in this guide are available for licensing from Lonely Planet Images: www.lonelyplanetimages.com.

Index

000 Map pages
000 Photograph pages

000 Map pages
000 Photograph pages

GREENDEX

The following attractions, accommodation options, restaurants and charities have been selected by Lonely Planet authors because they demonstrate a commitment to sustainability. For more tips about travelling sustainably in the Horn, turn to the Getting Started chapter (p18). We want to keep developing our sustainable-travel content. If you think we've omitted someone who should be listed here, email us at lonelyplanet.com/contact. For more information about sustainable tourism and Lonely Planet, see lonelyplanet.com/responsibletravel.

MAP LEGEND
ROUTES

Primary	Pedestrian Overpass
Secondary	Walking Tour
Tertiary	Walking Tour Detour
Lane	Walking Trail
Unsealed Road	Walking Path
Mall/Steps	Track

TRANSPORT
- Ferry — Rail
- Bus Route

HYDROGRAPHY
- River, Creek — Water
- Swamp — Lake (Dry)
- Mangrove — Lake (Salt)

BOUNDARIES
- International — Regional, Suburb
- State, Provincial — Ancient Wall
- Disputed — Cliff

AREA FEATURES
- Airport — Forest
- Area of Interest — Land
- Beach, Desert — Market
- Building — Park
- Campus — Rocks
- Cemetery, Christian — Sports
- Cemetery, Other — Urban

POPULATION
- ○ CAPITAL (NATIONAL) ◉ CAPITAL (STATE)
- ● Large City ○ Medium City
- ○ Small City ○ Town, Village

SYMBOLS

Sights/Activities: Beach, Castle/Fortress, Christian, Diving/Snorkelling, Islamic, Jewish, Monument, Museum/Gallery, Point of Interest, Ruin, Trail Head, Zoo/Bird Sanctuary

Eating: Eating

Drinking: Drinking, Cafe

Entertainment: Entertainment

Shopping: Shopping

Sleeping: Sleeping, Camping

Transport: Airport/Airfield, Border Crossing, Bus Station, Cycling/Bicycle Path, General Transport, Parking Area, Petrol Station, Taxi Rank

Information: Bank/ATM, Embassy/Consulate, Hospital/Medical, Information, Internet Facilities, Police Station, Post Office/GPO, Telephone

Geographic: Lighthouse, Lookout, Mountain/Volcano, National Park, Pass/Canyon, Shelter/Hut, Waterfall

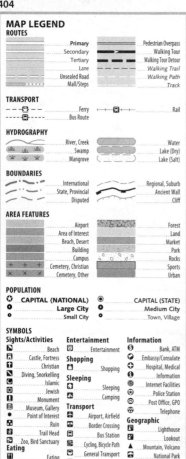

Hope this book will help you find your "ways". Have a fun and safe journey baby... I will be waiting... 林莉芬 Len

Happy Valentines! 2011

LONELY PLANET OFFICES

Australia
Head Office
Locked Bag 1, Footscray, Victoria 3011
☎ 03 8379 8000, fax 03 8379 8111
talk2us@lonelyplanet.com.au

USA
150 Linden St, Oakland, CA 94607
☎ 510 250 6400, toll free 800 275 8555
fax 510 893 8572
info@lonelyplanet.com

UK
2nd fl, 186 City Rd,
London EC1V 2NT
☎ 020 7106 2100, fax 020 7106 2101
go@lonelyplanet.co.uk

Published by Lonely Planet Publications Pty Ltd
ABN 36 005 607 983

© Lonely Planet 2009

© photographers as indicated 2009

Cover photograph: Four people standing on top of a cliff overlooking the southern Rift Valley, Eritrea, Africa/Franz Aberham. Many of the images in this guide are available for licensing from Lonely Planet Images: www.lonelyplanetimages.com.

Printed by Fabulous Printers Pte Ltd
Printed in Singapore.